WITHDRAWN

CHALLENGES OF SOCIAL STUDIES INSTRUCTION IN MIDDLE AND HIGH SCHOOLS

DEVELOPING ENLIGHTENED CITIZENS

Margaret A. Laughlin
University of Wisconsin–Green Bay

H. Michael Hartoonian
University of Wisconsin–Madison

CHALLENGES OF SOCIAL STUDIES INSTRUCTION IN MIDDLE AND HIGH SCHOOLS

DEVELOPING ENLIGHTENED CITIZENS

Harcourt Brace College Publishers

Fort Worth Philadelphia San Diego New York Orlando Austin San Antonio
Toronto Montreal London Sydney Tokyo

Text Design: Suzanne Montazer, Bookman Productions
Cover Art: Kevin Tolman

Publisher: Ted Buchholz
Senior Acquisitions Editor: Jo-Anne Weaver
Developmental Editor: Tracy Napper
Project Editors: Jeff Beckham, Sandy Walton, Juliet George
Production Managers: Erin Gregg, Tom Urquhart, Serena B. Manning
Senior Art Director: Diana Jean Parks
Art Director: Garry Harman
Picture Development Editor: Lili Weiner

Copyright © 1995 by Harcourt Brace & Company

All rights reserved. No part of this publication may be reproduced or transmitted in any form or by any means, electronic or mechanical, including photocopy, recording, or any information storage and retrieval system, without permission in writing from the publisher.

Requests for permission to make copies of any part of the work should be mailed to: Permissions Department, Harcourt Brace & Company, 6277 Sea Harbor Drive, Orlando, FL 32887-6777.

Address for Editorial Correspondence: Harcourt Brace College Publishers, 301 Commerce Street, Suite 3700, Fort Worth, TX 76102.

Address for Orders: Harcourt Brace & Company, 6277 Sea Harbor Drive, Orlando, FL 32887. 1-800-782-4479, or 1-800-433-0001 (in Florida).

(Copyright acknowledgments precede the index and constitute a continuation of this copyright page.)

PRINTED IN THE UNITED STATES OF AMERICA

ISBN:0-15-500098-5

Library of Congress Catalog Card Number: 94-75933

4 5 6 7 8 9 0 1 2 3   039   10 9 8 7 6 5 4 3 2 1

PREFACE

WE ARE LIVING during a period in the history of education characterized by unparalled public dissatisfaction, enormous legislative reform efforts, and significant attempts to redefine the nature of such traditional content areas as mathematics, science, and social studies. In this context, social studies teachers need a more complete understanding of their area of specialty. They need to articulate, support, construct, deliver, and evaluate social studies learning experiences for students who would be enlightened citizens of the republic. This is the purpose of this text.

Schools exist, in part at least, to pass on the common cultural heritage from one generation to the next. The role of schools is to create a climate where a sense of social, civic, and economic unity can emerge from individuals with diverse cultural backgrounds. Schools must help students learn and apply such civic values as respect for individuals, the law, the common good, the rights of others, the freedom of beliefs, and, finally, for life itself. At times these values will conflict with one another, but the enlightened citizen/student will develop the willingness and ability to resolve these differences with civility and discipline.

In order to become enlightened citizens, students of all backgrounds should understand their common cultural heritage. This heritage is found in the study of the humanities, mathematics, sciences, languages, and, most importantly, in social studies. Knowledge gained through the integrated study of anthropology, economics, geography, history, philosophy, political science, psychology, and sociology can give students the courage to see with sensitive eyes the fullness of what it means to be human. This knowledge can provide citizens with the wisdom and the will to construct private and public policies that will extend what is good in our culture into the future. Students need to become more than just passive learners; they need to become the active link between the past and the future.

This textbook is based on the philosophical foundations sketched above. It assumes that everyone can learn and that learning is most likely when educators create safe and meaningful environments and hold high expectations for student achievement and purpose. Because we believe that clarity and structure are also important to learning, we have organized this textbook around four fundamental questions: What? Why? How? and How Do You Know?

Part One: Why Teach Social Studies? discusses the purposes and essential elements of social studies education. The most important intellectual work of a teacher is to know and be able to articulate a rationale for what he or she is teaching. Students should come away from their teacher preparation programs with a rationale for teaching social studies even though it is likely to change as they gain experience and grow professionally.

Part Two: What Social Studies Content Is Worth Knowing? discusses the social studies content areas, curriculum patterns, the inquiry processes, and values education. There is so much content from which to choose. Chapters 3, 4, 5, and 6 answer the following questions: Should instruction be organized around major themes? Should lessons be presented in a chronological order? Should all of the social studies disciplines be addressed? What world regions should students study? Finally, in order to become a truly effective teacher your students will have to know how social studies courses fit into the total academic program.

Part Three: How Is Social Studies Instruction Implemented? addresses how to implement social studies instruction. Chapters 7, 8, 9, 10, and 11 provide information on planning for instruction, creating effective learning environments, promoting active learning, and helping students become strategic learners. Two factors will always determine how a person teaches: (1) *what he or she knows* about learning theory, course content, the students being taught, the local community, and the world; and (2) *who he or she is,* as a human being. Teachers should base their methods and strategies on research and practice, but teaching at its best will always transcend technique and embrace artistry. Knowledge of how to teach will be something to work on every day and think about always.

Part Four: How Are Students and Programs Evaluated? addresses the evaluation of social studies programs and students. Chapter 12 discusses this important issue thoroughly, because finding out if what we do as educators really makes a difference is a constant concern for teachers. Students, parents, and the general public are interested in student achievement and how well their school compares with other schools. What kind of assessment is appropriate for each instructional program? Should the same standards be applied to all students? What right does the public have to know the achievement levels of students? How should teachers be evaluated? By whom? It should be clear that if teachers do not address the topic of evaluation adequately someone else will do it for them.

Part Five: What Challenges and Opportunities Lie Ahead? includes the important topics of technology, professional responsibilities, and curriculum trends. New forces will always influence the scope of social studies and the work of the social studies teacher. The Epilogue addresses issues that will carry social studies into the 21st century. New challenges are suggested that demand of teachers a commitment to continue their professional growth.

A Challenge

The major features of this textbook include: (1) a strong philosophical base that will allow students to develop critical perspectives on social studies education; (2) a series of focus activities for students that address the fundamental topics that social studies teachers need to consider; (3) a clear set of questions and activities dealing with how to include both theory and practice in the act and art of teaching; (4) an extension of the ideas in each chapter through suggested resources, research, and learning activities; (5) a set of suggestions and strategies for teaching in a diverse, multicultural, and interdependent world; and (6) methods for designing, implementing, and evaluating quality social studies lessons and programs. Welcome to the challenge!

Acknowledgements

We would like to thank the following reviewers for taking time to respond to the developing manuscript: Beverly Armento, Georgia State University; Ambrose Clegg, Kent State University; Catherine Cornbleth, SUNY Buffalo; Fred Drake, Illinois State University; Terrie Epstein, University of Michigan; Ron Pahl, California State University, Fullerton; Jeff Passe, University of North Carolina, Charlotte; Paul Robinson, University of Arizona; Thomas Russell, University of South Alabama; Sam Davis and Mary Ann Davis for their help in editing and designing the text; and for their ideas and suggestions, James Leming, University of Southern Illinois–Carbondale; Fred Newmann, University of Wisconsin–Madison; and Donald Bragaw, East Carolina University; and Norris Sanders, University of Wisconsin–Green Bay. Jeanne Sullivan spent hours on the computer and assisted with checking references for the bibliography.

We also thank our students and other colleagues who have influenced our thinking by challenging our ideas. Kathryn A. Koch has contributed to this textbook by writing Chapter 11 "Helping Students Become Strategic Learners." Her efforts are appreciated.

We dedicate this book to our families and friends, especially Ann, Cricket, George, Linc, Mary, and Patty

CONTENTS

PREFACE

PART I
Why Teach Social Studies?

CHAPTER 1   The Purposes of Social Studies Education   5
- Why Teach Social Studies?   6
- History of Social Studies   8
- Social Studies Curriculum Patterns   15
- Definitions of Social Studies   16

CHAPTER 2   The Essentials of Social Studies   25
- Essentials of Social Studies Education   28
- Key Themes of Social Studies Education   33
- The Use of Themes in Instruction   38
- Developing Your Own Rationale Statement   40

PART II
What Social Studies Content Is Worth Knowing?

CHAPTER 3   Knowledge in Social Studies   49
- The Nature of Social Knowledge   50
- Social Studies Disciplines   56
- Social Scientists and the Social Sciences   70
- Social Studies and Other Content Areas   72

CHAPTER 4   Characteristics and Organizational Patterns of Social Studies   79
- The Major Characteristics of Social Studies   80
- Organizing Social Studies Programs   81
- Curriculum Patterns   84
- Organizing Social Studies Content   88
- Influence of Newer Content Areas on the Social Studies Curriculum Patterns   92

CHAPTER 5

Inquiry in Social Studies   101
- Creating and Using Social Knowledge   102
- The Universal Nature of Social Knowledge   115
- Using Social Studies to Understand Human Problems and Institutions   116
- Content and Social Inquiry (Reasoning) Skills   117
- Conceptual Model   122
- Classrooms Conducive to Social Inquiry   124

CHAPTER 6

Values Education   129
- What Is Values Education?   133
- History and the Social Sciences   137
- Approaches to Values Education   139

PART III
How Is Social Studies Instruction Implemented?

CHAPTER 7

Learning Theory, Social Studies Curriculum, and Instructional Practices   165
- Learners' Responsibilities   166
- Teacher "Folk Wisdom"   167
- How Have Research Findings Influenced Social Studies Instruction?   169
- Developmental and Learning Theories   169
- How Are Students Motivated?   185
- What Are Some Guidelines Concerning Classroom Discipline?   189

CHAPTER 8

Characteristics of Successful Curriculum and Instructional Plans   197
- Planning for Curriculum and Instruction   198
- Long-Range Planning   200
- Unit Planning   202
- Daily Lesson Planning   207
- Social Studies and the World of Work   229
- Social Studies for Community Service (Volunteerism)   231

CHAPTER 9

Effective Learning Environments for Students   239
- Organizing Students and Classrooms for Effective Learning   240
- Gifted and Talented Students   246
- Special Needs Students   248

"At Risk" Students   250
Students from Various Ethnic and Cultural Backgrounds   251
Protecting Academic Freedom   252

CHAPTER 10   Promoting Active Social Studies Learning   259
Learning Activities that Motivate Students   260
Selecting Instructional Materials   283
Going Beyond the Textbook   286
Cocurricular Activities Related to Social Studies Content   291

CHAPTER 11   Helping Students Become Strategic Learners by Katheryn A. Koch   305
Definitions of Intelligence, Thinking, Reading, Listening, and Studying   306
Toward More Effective Learning   308
Asking Questions   313
Learning Strategies   318
Teaching Guidelines   333

PART IV
How Are Students and Programs Evaluated?

CHAPTER 12   Evaluation in Social Studies   349
Goals of Evaluation   350
Types of Evaluation   352
Issues in Testing   360
Measuring Student Learning—Illustrative Examples   363
Evaluating Social Studies Programs   380

PART V
What Challenges and Opportunities Lie Ahead?

CHAPTER 13   The Information Age and Technology   395
Influences of New Technologies   396
Computers in the Schools   398
Computer Programs for Social Studies   403
Instructional Techniques Used in Computer Programs   406
Evaluating Computer Software   412
Databases   416

Additional Educational Technologies 418
Ongoing Issues 424
Abuses of Technology 429
Future Uses of Computers in Social Studies 431

CHAPTER 14 Professional Social Studies Teachers 439
Opportunities for Professional Growth 440
Professional Expectations of Teachers 445
Career Opportunities 453
Causes of Job-Related Stress for Teachers 456

EPILOGUE How Might the 21st Century Shape Social Studies Education? 465
What Might the World Look Like in the 21st Century? 466
What New Responsibilities Will Citizens Face in the 21st Century? 471
How Might Social Studies Education Change in the Future? 472
What Role Should Social Studies Educators Have or Take in Shaping the Future of Education? 475

> I go on this great republican principle, that the people will have the virtue and intelligence to elect [people] of virtue and wisdom.
>
> *James Madison*

PART I

Why Teach Social Studies?

THE INSTITUTION OF education addresses society's need to pass on the cultural heritage (major ideas and values of a people) from one generation to the next. In the United States this means that while individuals have diverse cultural backgrounds, the role of the school is to create a climate where a sense of social, civic, and economic unity can emerge from this diversity. Education must enrich cultural and individual diversity while at the same time provide for common knowledge and values that will help us understand who we are as a people. Schools must help students learn and apply civic values such as respect for each individual, the law, the common good, the rights of others, the freedom of beliefs, and life. At times these values will conflict with one another, but the enlightened citizen/student will develop a willingness and ability to resolve these differences with civility and discipline.

Education is central in a republic like the United States where self-government and civic responsibility are necessary, since the foundation of society is the "enlightened citizen." In a sense, the business of the United States citizen is part personal and part public. Pericles, Athens' first citizen, articulated the dual role of the individual in 431 B.C.:

> Here each individual is interested not only in his own affairs, but in the affairs of state as well. Even those who are most occupied with their own businesses are

extremely well informed on general politics. . . . We do not say that a man who takes no interest in politics is a man who minds his own business; we say that he has no business here at all.

Enlightened citizens of a democracy understand their duty to self *and* community. These individuals possess a working knowledge of the economic, political, and social factors that make up the human environment in which we all must function. They understand the rule of law, legal limits to freedom, and majority rule with minority rights. They appreciate fair play and cooperation, and they demand high standards in the character and work of themselves and others. These individuals are in touch with the cultural heritage of their society. Without a conscious effort to teach and learn these things, a free republic will not long endure. Thus, our first priority as a society, our first public policy goal, is to ensure our survival as a free nation through the development of enlightened citizens.

Within this context the school has two purposes that seem to conflict with one another: 1) to develop enlightened citizens and 2) to preserve the best of the cultural heritage. These purposes establish the social studies as the most fundamental program within the general school curriculum. The major responsibility for developing enlightened citizens belongs in the social studies rather than in other curricular areas because the social studies teachers are most qualified by their training and the social studies curriculum most appropriate by its subject matter to assume this task. It is with this responsibility in mind that we investigate the nature of education and the purposes of social studies.

The following focus questions will help us to develop a rationale and define issues in social studies:

1. What are the essentials of social studies?
2. What are the purposes of social studies education?
3. What is the current status of social studies curriculum patterns?
4. How has the definition of social studies changed over the years?

FOCUS ACTIVITY

Citizenship and Social Studies

Ideally, rationales for education tell us that students go to school to develop themselves to the limits of their abilities; to acquire the skills and attitudes necessary for employment; to achieve personal happiness; and to become responsible citizens of their society. While social studies must address all four goals, its major focus is on citizenship. Throughout this textbook we will encourage you to test and expand your concept of social studies, citizenship, and citizenship education.

To begin this task, form several groups of three to five individuals and try to arrive at a consensus of agreement or disagreement for each of the statements that appear below. You should also resolve through group consensus any disagreements on the meaning of words. Once you have reached consensus on all statements, each group should defend its decisions by writing two short essays: one defining citizenship and the other suggesting how you should teach responsible citizenship.

1. There is no difference between the concepts of the "good person" and the "good citizen."

   _____ agree   _____ disagree

2. Citizenship is another term for good human relations.

   _____ agree   _____ disagree

3. There are no differences between obligations to society and to fellow citizens.

   _____ agree   _____ disagree

4. Providing for the public good is the major responsibility of the citizen.

   _____ agree   _____ disagree

5. The best way for students to learn citizenship skills is through their involvement in activities that closely simulate the behavior of the good citizen.

   _____ agree   _____ disagree

6. An individual can behave justly if, and only if, he or she believes that society itself is just.

   _____ agree   _____ disagree

In Chapter 1 you will find several quotations that state the role or purpose of social studies. Each group should choose the quotations that best fit its understanding of social studies and suggest reasons for these choices.

> When we are planning for posterity, we ought to
> remember that virtue is not hereditary.
>
> *Thomas Paine*

CHAPTER 1

The Purposes of Social Studies Education

FOCUS QUESTIONS

- How is social studies defined?
- How have social studies been viewed over the years?
- What is the current status of social studies curriculum patterns?
- Why teach social studies?

OVERVIEW

Middle and high school students are wonderful at asking *why*. Why do we have to study history or economics or civics?

Developing responses to these questions may be the most important task of the social studies educator. Education, or any endeavor for that matter, becomes mindless if it has no purpose. In education, we must answer the *why* question before we can determine *what* to teach, *how* to teach it, and *how we know* that we are making any difference. In other words, rationale or purpose gives us the criteria for making choices about what to teach. Without rationale, teaching one thing would be just as valid as teaching something else. Developing an ever-evolving rationale is a continuing activity for the professional educator. Teachers will find their rationales becoming more sophisticated and complex as their experience and knowledge increase.

Why Teach Social Studies?

In a general sense, the answer to the question "Why teach social studies?" is similar to the answer given for any academic area. We educate for self-development, employment, personal happiness, and citizenship. All school programs address these general purposes. However, social studies takes a greater responsibility for the citizenship goal. Social studies also contributes significantly to the goals of self-development, employment, and personal happiness, but we must view all four goals within an inclusive set, with each goal drawing meaning from the others. For example, it is difficult, if not impossible, to tell where education for employment ends and education for citizenship begins.

Goals of Education

Most educators believe that education should have both extrinsic and intrinsic goals. Some would say that education needs no specific goal, because it is an end in itself. Consider your own attitudes about the purposes of social studies education and then study the following statements made by a variety of individuals and organizations over the last 200 years. What do these statements have in common? To what extent have the purposes of education changed over time?

> The people are the ultimate guardians of their own liberty. For this purpose the . . . first stage, where *they* will receive their whole education is proposed, . . . to be *chiefly historical. History,* by apprising them of the past will enable them to judge the future; it will avail them of the experience of other times and other nations; it will qualify them as judges of the actions and designs of men; it will enable them to know ambition under every disguise it may assume; and knowing it, to defeat its views. . . . Every government degenerates when trusted to the rulers of the people alone. The people themselves therefore are its only safe depositories. And to render even them safe their minds must be improved to a certain degree. This indeed is not all that is necessary, though it be essentially necessary. . . . The influence over government must be shared among all the people. (italics added)
>
> *Thomas Jefferson, Reasons for Establishing the Public Schools in Virginia, 1779.*

... [T]he Constitution of the United States and of our own State, should be made a study in our Public Schools. ... [A]nd, especially, the duty of every citizen, in a government of laws, to appeal to the court for redress, in all cases of alleged wrong, instead of undertaking to vindicate his own rights by his own arm, and, in a government where the people are the acknowledged sources of power, the duty of changing laws and rulers by an appeal to the ballot, and not by rebellion, should be taught to all the children until they are fully understood.

Horace Mann, On the Defense of Free Men, 1849.

Good citizenship should be the aim of social studies in the high school. While the administration and instruction throughout the school should contribute to the social welfare of the community, it is maintained that social studies have direct responsibility in this field. Facts, conditions, theories, and activities that do not contribute rather directly to the appreciation of methods of human betterment have no claim. Under this test the old civics, almost exclusively a study of Government machinery, must give way to the new civics, a study of all manner of social efforts to improve humankind. It is not so important that the pupil know how the President is elected as that he shall understand the duties of the health officer in his community. The time formerly spent in the effort to understand the process of passing a law over the president's veto is now to be more profitably used in the observation of the vocational resources of the community. In line with this emphasis the committee recommends that social studies in the high school shall include topics as the following: Community health, housing and homes, public recreation, good roads, community education, poverty and the care of the poor, crime and reform, family income, savings banks and life insurance, human rights versus property rights, impulsive action of mobs, the selfish conservatism of tradition, and public utilities.

National Education Association (NEA) Commission on the Reorganization of Secondary Education—Preliminary Statement on the Social Studies, 1913.

... [T]he prime purpose of the public school is to serve the general welfare of a democratic society, by assuring that the knowledge and understanding necessary to exercise the responsibilities of citizenship are not only made available but actively inculcated.

... [S]chools have a commitment to elevate the civic goal of unity above the particularist goals of special and self-serving interests in the society. This is one of the most sensitive and complicated of all the tasks of public education, for it is extremely difficult to draw the line between the values of diversity (which a democratic society prizes) and of divisiveness (which may threaten the very society itself). Most modern school systems in the world are torn by two conflicting drives. On the one hand, to help build national unity out of diverse racial, cultural, ethnic, religious, and linguistic groups, and, on the other, to honor the drive of particularist groups that demand their own schools for the teaching of different languages, religious beliefs, ethnic customs, or regional aspirations....

R. Freeman Butts, "The Public School: Assaults on a Great Idea," The Nation, *April 30, 1973, pp. 553–560.*

These quotations support the idea that the major goal of the public schools in general and the social studies in particular should be citizenship education. These expressions span 200 years, yet remain remarkably similar in their commitment to citizenship education. Let us now consider a brief history of social studies and see how the ideals and principles suggested above have or have not been implemented in the social studies curriculum.

History of Social Studies

One of the most important perspectives that social studies educators should keep in mind is that, even though the field of social studies is relatively young, it is based on the historical ideas stated above. Writing in 1977, Barr, Barth, and Shermis stated:

The ambiguity and confusion in the field of social studies can be explained in two ways. First, it is a field that is clearly in the process of emerging. Having been organized for only 60 years or so, the social studies is a new professional field. It did not spring to life fully formed. It has slowly and often painfully evolved as a field, and it is most certainly still evolving. Not until the last two decades has a body of research begun to be developed, and even more recently have scholars attempted to develop conceptual schemes to explain the diversity in the field. (p. 15)

Thoughtful social studies teachers also need to understand that this young content area already has developed several "traditions" and a rather stormy history.

Background History for the Social Studies

Social studies as a separate educational domain was not born until the 20th century (NEA, 1916 and Murra, 1970). Before the early part of this century, the social sciences, if taught at all, were included within the content of history classes. (See reports or statements of the NEA Committee of 10, 1893, and the

American Historical Association [AHA], Committee of Seven, 1899). Many leaders in the social science disciplines wanted separate courses in the public schools. This was obviously difficult because high school for most students was only four years (grades 9–12), while there were at least eight distinct social science disciplines.

During the early 20th century, many people questioned the viability of the history and social studies curriculum. These questions seemed appropriate amid the rapid social changes caused by immigration, the World War, new technologies, and so forth, taking place at that time. At the same time history and social science discipline organizations such as the American Historical Association and the American Political Science Association failed to define and defend their subject area's unique relevance to the primary purpose of precollegiate education. There was also a great deal of political maneuvering as each organization tried to gain acceptance with the public. This caused several leading educators to break with tradition and to incorporate these social science disciplines into a new field called social studies. They identified this new field as that area of the curriculum devoted to the "cultivation of good citizenship" (NEA, 1916). The major intellectual leaders in this group included John Dewey, George Counts, Harold and Earle Rugg, and Edgar Wesley.

In response to these changes the NEA established the Commission on the Reorganization of Secondary Education in 1913. This Commission created a subgroup, called the Committee on Social Studies, to examine the content and focus of history and the social sciences in precollegiate education. The recommendations that emerged in the report from this committee in 1916 offered the schools a new way to organize the content (scope and sequence) of social studies courses for young Americans. It involved two three-year cycles for the period of secondary education that included:

Junior cycle
Grade 7. Geography/European history
Grade 8. American history
Grade 9. Civics

Senior cycle
Grade 10. European history
Grade 11. American history
Grade 12. Problems of democracy—social, economic, and political[1]

---

[1] "Report of the Committee on the Social Studies of the Commission on the Reorganization of Secondary Education of the NEA—The Social Studies in Secondary Education: A Six Year Program adopted Both to the 6-3-3 and the 8-4 Plan of Organization," Arthur William Dunn, Secretary (Washington, DC, Government Printing Office, 1916) p. 12.

This sequence gained widespread support and over the years began to challenge the curriculum pattern espoused in 1896 by the American Historical Association (AHA), which had emphasized history.

In reflecting on this modest yet revolutionary document, historians have come to realize that it was a benchmark in American social studies education. This is the case not only because the report gave respectability to the term "social studies," a curriculum term that was less than five years old, but also, society was changing so rapidly that it seemed to beg schools for better ways of understanding the world. The two fundamental curriculum changes suggested in the report were the introduction of the new ninth grade "Civics" and 12th grade "Problems of Democracy" courses. This report also introduced the concept of one-year courses in European and American history. It bestowed a significant degree of prestige on social studies matters in the NEA and alerted curriculum developers to the personal and social needs of students. With these reports and through the power of the NEA, colleges lost some of their former control over the school curriculum. The report supported the idea of localizing curriculum development and opened the doors of the secondary school to all of the social science disciplines. It suggested that social studies education should gain direction from the needs of society rather than solely from the dictates of scholarly disciplines. The cultivation of good citizenship became the dominant purpose of social studies. The training of the individual as an efficient member of society in the nation and in the world community became the major goal. In 1921, the National Council for the Social Studies (NCSS), the professional organization for social studies educators, was founded in part to serve as an umbrella organization for history and the social sciences for K–12 school programs.

Social Studies in a Time of Depression and War

It is difficult to find a single unifying thrust for the period of social studies curriculum development from 1916 to 1950. For some educators and school systems it was a time of tradition, but for most it was a period of experimentation. It was also a period of philosophical controversy. For example, there was great debate over the goals of education and methods of teaching. There was discussion on the nature of the child, and just how much responsibility educators should give students for their own learning. Although individual educators might have resolved these controversies to their own satisfaction, there was no national consensus.

Perhaps it was the tenor of the times because, while Americans were still trying to adjust to the societal changes that had taken place prior to 1900, they faced in rapid succession a new series of tangible world-changing events. These included World War I, the battle over the League of Nations, "subversive threats," the Great Depression, World War II, and the period of post-war readjustment.

At the same time, the invisible fabric of American society, from its folkways and mores to the basic political and economic institutions, was undergoing a number of great changes. The schools, sensitive barometers of American society, reflected the turmoil and frustration as well as the optimism and exhilaration of the times. In this era new and often controversial ideas and forces engulfed American schools. These included immigration, the threat of communism, the fear of nuclear war, and civil rights. These forces influenced all grade levels and areas of study. In this climate it is not surprising that social studies educators could not reach agreement on matters of purpose and content (Rumpf, 1976; Wronski and Bragaw, 1986).

Social Studies and the Social Sciences

The years following World War II and the Korean War were a time for special social studies "projects." Focal points included an attempt to further international understanding by the North Central Association's Foreign Relations Project; the furtherance of economic understanding through the activities of the Joint Council on Economic Education (now the National Council on Economic Education); special efforts to enhance human relations by the Anti-Defamation League (ADL), the National Conference on Christians and Jews (NCCJ), and the Southern Regional Council; and one more attempt to improve instruction related to participatory democracy through the operation of the Citizenship Education Project (Teachers College, Columbia University) and similar programs.

In the post-Sputnik era of the late 1950s and 1960s the public endorsed curriculum reform primarily in science, mathematics, and foreign languages. This endorsement grew out of a realization that, while some schools had developed sound instructional programs on the basis of local curriculum planning, other schools had made only makeshift adaptations. It also grew out of a recognition that in a majority of the nation's schools a heavy proportion of their content and materials were outdated. The social studies did not escape this criticism.

In 1958 the NEA appointed a National Commission on the Social Studies, which reviewed basic changes and movements in American society and called for a full-scale reappraisal of the social studies curriculum. It pointed out that much of the social studies content being taught was outmoded, either in terms of societal needs or because it had been superseded by recent research in the social sciences and in education. It urged closer cooperation between social studies specialists and social scientists. It pointed out the need for a national study that would give definite guidance to local school systems without prescribing a single set program.

Although some leaders of social studies education in the United States continued to call for clarification on the scope, sequence, and other curriculum issues described above, their concerns went unheeded. Instead, the activities of private foundations and the United States Department of Health, Education, and Welfare and its "Project Social Studies" generated competition among the several social studies disciplines. By the mid-1960s the National Science Foundation (NSF) joined the "funding scene" and initiated projects in some of the social science disciplines. The National Defense Education Act (NDEA) also provided the opportunity for teachers to study history and the social sciences during summers and the academic year. Many teachers earned advanced degrees in these programs. By the early 1970s, the list of federally funded social studies projects had grown to more than ninety.

New Problems and the New Social Studies

The implementation of the "new social studies" in the late 1960s and 1970s brought renewed intellectual vigor to this area of the curriculum, but it also created new problems. For example, middle and high school teachers began to use pedagogical methods such as small group work and individual projects, which elementary teachers had used for many years. The cognitive (inquiry) skills were identified by Bloom and colleagues in *Taxonomy of Educational Objectives: The Classification of Educational Goals: Handbook I: The Cognitive Domain* (1956) and affective skills were identified in *Taxonomy of Educational Objectives: The Classification of Educational Goals: Handbook II: Affective Domain* by Krathwohl, Bloom, and Masia (1964). These books influenced the goals, instructional materials, and teaching styles of teachers who had thought of themselves as "subject matter specialists," for example, history teachers.

Several concomitant problems developed in both elementary and secondary schools. For example, some educators rejected a balanced approach to social studies by overemphasizing one content area like sociology while ignoring other important areas like geography. Another problem emerged when some teachers led students down a bewildering trail of inquiry exercises that sharpened the data-gathering and processing skills, but had no substantive destination or content focus. Still other difficulties developed as teachers encouraged their students to tell their peers "how they felt" about issues and assigned equal validity to all such feelings. Such learning activities of the schools sometimes made a mockery of rational decision making. While most of these programs incorporated new ideas into the social studies curriculum, little attention was given to their relationship to the overall purposes of social studies education. For this reason many of these "approaches" seemed mindless or without direction.

The social science disciplines had now improved their status and their acceptability as discrete courses in American middle and high schools. This occurred mainly because more social scientists became involved with curriculum, and social science organizations became more active in curriculum decision making at the national level. Anthropology, psychology, political science, economics, and sociology became common course offerings in addition to history and geography. This expansion of subject matter was undoubtedly healthy, but here too, there were problems. For example, the proliferation of new courses caused a lack of program coherence at the secondary level. Concerned educators began asking questions such as the following: What students are taking all of these courses? How can we ensure that the electives chosen by an individual learner provide him or her with a tentative, yet comprehensive frame of reference? How can we provide meaningful orchestration to these somewhat disparate courses?

Further complicating the picture were developments in the general area of the curriculum. For example, nonsexist, multiethnic texts that more accurately portrayed the status of minorities and addressed gender issues began to be used. Publishers and teachers developed better ways to utilize media and role-playing activities in social studies classrooms. There was also pressure to develop and use "teacher-proof" materials. It was believed that these materials would more or less "teach themselves" to students, leaving teachers with a do-nothing role. These conflicts and ideas of the past still constitute some of the major challenges confronting today's social studies teachers and students, and, in a sense, make up part of our traditions.

Looking at recent professional journals in social studies such as *Social Education,* some things seem clear. There seems to be more agreement that the major goal of social studies is citizenship education and that social studies is a basic element of any general program of studies in the elementary, middle, and high schools. Also, teachers are integrating social studies with other curriculum areas in the elementary and middle schools more than before. However, educators disagree on whether to teach the single disciplines, such as economics, geography, and so forth, at the high school level. Concurrently there is rising interest in interdisciplinary content such as environmental studies, law-related education, global studies, and multicultural education. This conflict is also reflected in recent disagreements about national social studies standards and whether these standards should be integrated or stand alone in single disciplines.

It is safe to assume that these areas of attention and conflict will be with us for some time and that they have significant impact upon our profession. You may want to survey other social studies teachers to see what they think are the major issues today.

The short history of social studies is often confusing and contradictory. However, the social studies does have its traditions, and one interesting question to ask is whether the traditions are moving away from each other or coming together.

Traditions Within the Field of Social Studies

The social studies community has identified at least three, and possibly as many as six, different traditions or orientations that are used today (Barr, Barth, and Shermis, 1977). A tradition is a set of beliefs, customs, or world views that develops over time and is handed down from one generation or from one colleague to the next. Knowledge of tradition helps answer the following questions: In what do we believe? What can we expect of each other?

"Traditions" in social studies help form the foundation for the rationale teachers use to direct their instructional programs. This simply means that different teachers have different reasons for teaching social studies such as:

Social science/history knowledge
Reflective thinking
Policy making
Critical inquiry
Personal/social development
Citizenship

While the most common goal for social studies is citizenship, one or more of the above rationales are often used to reach that common goal.

For example, teachers who are directed by the social science and history tradition believe that the best way to teach citizenship is through the mastery of history and social science concepts, methods, and problems. Teachers who use critical inquiry as a rationale base think that they can best promote citizenship by developing the students' ability to critique social institutions and human behavior using criteria such as justice, human rights, and citizen responsibilities. In addition to these two traditions, some teachers believe that students should develop the skills for private and public policy making. Others believe that attending to the social/physiological/moral development of students is the best road to enlightened citizenship. A preference for reflective thinking would emphasize the use of knowledge to solve problems, and there are teachers who would say that citizenship is best promoted by inculcating democratic values.

What is important for you to remember is that these traditions can expand your perspective of social studies. In addition, they can serve as criteria to construct and evaluate your rationale. They can also help with decisions about content, materials, and methods. For example, if you construct your rationale upon the belief that citizenship is best developed through history and social science you will, no doubt, use different content and materials than you would if you built your rationale on personal/physiological/moral development.

As you move through your career you will think about your reasons for teaching social studies, and while you may share a common rationale with other educators, in the end, you will develop a personal rationale.

Social Studies Curriculum Patterns

In describing the status of almost anything, it is important to use the perspective of history. The present situation is only temporary; therefore, it is important to reconsider the curricular patterns developed by those committees and commissions described previously. If we return to the 1916 recommendations of the NEA, we find that the curriculum patterns across the nation still seem to adhere to this design (see National Survey: Social Studies Education K–12, by the Council of State Social Studies Specialists, 1993).

Since 1988, there have been changes in high school graduation requirements and course offerings, but these changes have been marginal. For example, more states are recommending that students take classes in economics and geography. Courses in history are increasing with the current media interest in what our students do not know about the past. As of 1992 the United States Department of Education has also received attention because of its emphasis on history and upon national testing in the social studies curriculum. The following chart compares the social studies curriculum patterns of 1960, 1990, and the present. You might want to think about your own "ideal" sequence for the middle school and secondary social studies curriculum and complete the following chart. How does the present day curriculum compare with the past?

Grade Level	1960*	1990*	Present
6	Western Culture	World Culture	Interview teachers in a nearby school to determine a present-day curriculum pattern.
7	European History	World Geography/History	
8	United States History	United States History	
9	Civics	Civics/World History	
10	World History	World History	
11	United States History	United States History	
12	American Problems	American Government/Economics	

SOURCE: *Project SPAN, as reported in *Social Education,* May 1980, by Superka, Hawke, and Morrissett. Council of State Social Studies Specialists Survey, 1993. Des Moines: Iowa State Department of Education.

Definitions of Social Studies

What is the unique contribution of social studies to the education of the individual? What special role does social studies play in the achievement of personal and social goals?

If we consider the three major goals of education, which are citizenship, self-development, and employment, we see that the most important focus of the social studies is citizenship. In a sense, social studies attempts to develop a balance between the private and public person. Writers such as Sennett (*The Fall of Public Man,* 1977) and Bellah et al. (*Habits of the Heart,* 1985) have warned against the tendency to overemphasize our private economic world and to undervalue our responsibility to the public good. This emphasis on private concerns tends to undermine the meaning that the founders had for the republic (see, for example, *The Federalist,* number 10). In 1788, James Madison, speaking in defense of the new Constitution, said:

I go on this great republican principle, that the people will have virtue and intelligence to select men of virtue and wisdom. Is there no virtue among us? To suppose that any form of government will secure liberty or happiness without any virtue in the people is an absurd idea.

Following are definition statements made by a former president of the National Council for the Social Studies, by the National Council for the Social Studies, by a high school teacher, and by a middle school teacher. We have included these to give you a "personal" view of what some practitioners think about the scope and purpose of social studies. They provide a rationale for social studies and the current status of curriculum. The Board of Directors of the NCSS adopted a definition of social studies in 1992 as well as a set of standards for social studies.

A Definition of the Social Studies

There is little use in defining the social studies as a content field without clearly stating how that content helps prepare citizens. History, for instance, may be little more than propaganda intended to close the minds of citizens, to silence their questions, and to impose uniformity on a society; or we may use history as it should be in a democracy, to open the minds of citizens, to increase their capacity to ask critical questions and to make reasoned decisions. To say that we should teach more or less history is a meaningless assertion unless we know how we are going to teach history and toward what end.

As to goals, the social studies in a democracy must serve two somewhat opposing purposes. It must socialize youth, that is, make youth fit into the ways of society; at the same time, it must counter-socialize youth. It must develop their capacity to engage in critical thinking, to ask important questions, to solve problems, to make intelligent decisions and to act independently from the crowd. These attributes are more important to democracy than blind loyalty to poorly understood principles.

We should broadly conceive the content as including not only history, which we may consider the core because of its all-inclusive nature, but the social sciences, literature, journalism, the arts and above all, ethics. Social problems are never merely factual problems; they are basically problems of what is right and good behavior. With respect to such questions, the humanities have quite as much to say as do the social sciences.

The content listed above becomes meaningful only when we apply it to solving social problems. Social studies is not just information for us to memorize; it is the knowledge about human affairs which we acquire from the study of society. It turns out, therefore, that the questions and problems that we choose to pursue are the real content of the social studies. If we ask only trivial questions that we may answer from memory it is unlikely that the content will serve the purposes of democratic citizenship education. For democracy to be well served we should frame the content by asking questions that require thinking, study in depth and decision making. These are the kinds of questions that scholars and citizens consider in resolving the problems of society.

Shirley H. Engle, former NCSS president, 1989.

Social studies is the integrated study of the social sciences and humanities to promote civic competence. Within the school program, social studies provides coordinated, systematic study drawing upon such disciplines as anthropology, archaeology, economics, geography, history, law, philosophy, political science, psychology, religion, and sociology, as well as appropriate content from the humanities, mathematics, and natural sciences. The primary purpose of social studies is to help young people develop the ability to make informed and reasoned decisions for the public good as citizens of a culturally diverse, democratic society in an interdependent world.

National Council for the Social Studies, 1992.

Social studies is the study of all aspects of a society. This includes belief structures, the various ways of group living, division of labor, technical and intellectual skills, and geographic influences. Social studies also focuses on civic responsibility and social awareness and includes fact-based knowledge so that we, as a society, can have an informed and socially conscious electorate. Social studies also needs to promote understanding of this knowledge and information. As world economies change it is also imperative that an awareness of the global marketplace and the changing face of capitalism be addressed.

Within social studies education issues of the self, the group, the political unit, and the world help to shape students. Social studies should promote an awareness of the decision-making process. Social studies should help students and ultimately the society to seek and carefully analyze information, to look for and determine costs when making decisions and to make rational, informed decisions.

America faces new challenges as we go into the 21st century. Changing and evolving conditions throughout the world means we need to continue to promote the thinking skills, decision-making skills, and communication skills that social studies hold at its heart.

Social studies subjects and curriculum give our students, and ultimately, our society, a soul, a vision, and an understanding that the true costs of decisions lie in the future. We who teach social studies have this responsibility for promoting a vision and an understanding of the past, the present, and the future.

Pamela Engel, Pulaski Community Schools, Wisconsin, 1992.

All learners need the ability to respond to a myriad of data and be able to make choices based on what information is at hand. Most learners tend to be historical isolates—cut off from the idea of an historical continuum; and it is extremely important that the social sciences guide students through the thinking processes and literally plug them into the idea they are part of a whole.

Students today come into any learning environment equipped with many positive skills and attitudes, along with some really tremendous handicaps; i.e., divorced parents, drug babies, drug environment, poverty, etc. They need to be given a sense of self-worth and instilled with the idea that they can make a difference.

Based on these concepts, I feel that the social studies is the one discipline area that can be flexible enough to teach children the thinking skills, communication skills, and the human skills necessary to carry them into the 21st century. Through social studies all the other "academics" can be taught, and it is probably the *most prepared* academic area, both with its instruction and with its research, to succeed.

Lawrence Brown, Rocklin Unified School District, California, 1992.

What do these statements have in common? Is there a difference of emphasis among the statements? To what extent do the two classroom teachers have a different view of social studies than the former NCSS president? The NCSS statement?

The fundamental premise of our republic is the belief that virtue and education work together. Individuals will be virtuous if, and only if, they are educated in justice, temperance, and courage, and have opportunities to share their wisdom with others in the improvement of society. For example, there is a need for environmental law that maintains a balance between a concern for all people and nature and for the impact of such laws on individuals or institutions. This is a never-ending process of negotiation between the public good and private or institutional interests. Therefore, the first goal of education in this nation must be to develop individual dignity *and* the public good, together.

The focus of social studies is both the public good and individual dignity. These items may seem contradictory, but they are, in fact, complementary. The public good, the good of the community, is meaningful only when every individual is treated with dignity and respect simply because he or she is human and endowed with inalienable rights. Further, the celebration of individual diversity is what defines unity—from many, one.

SUMMARY

The development of a rationale for *why* we teach social studies is, perhaps, the most important responsibility of a teacher. Without a rationale we run the risk of becoming mindless in our instructional programs. Rationales, of course, have their roots in the traditions of the academic areas we teach and in the perceived needs of society and students. Thus, a knowledge of students, society, and the content area is a necessary condition for developing a rationale.

An operational definition of social studies is also necessary to answer the question, Why should we teach social studies? You have had an opportunity to look at the history, traditions, definitions, and representative rationales of the content area of social studies. You have now started the process of constructing your own rationale of social studies education. As you develop practical applications in your teaching of social studies it is important to keep your rationale in mind.

Discussion Questions

1. Why do you want to teach social studies?
2. What does it mean to be an "educated person"?
3. Consider the statements in Chapter 1 about the purpose of education in our republic.
    a. How would you describe the major categories or focus points in the statements?
    b. What central points or goals do you think you should add to the statements?
    c. Why do you think the construction of a rationale is so complex?
4. Which traditions of the social studies seem most compatible to your visions of the future? Why?
5. What content base do you think is necessary for the middle and secondary school social studies program? Why?
6. Do you think social studies education would benefit if someone could develop a common definition for this field of study? Explain and defend your answer.
7. Do you think that the definition of social studies should be the same for both middle school and high school programs? Why?
8. Do the definitions of social studies that appear in Chapter 1 suggest to you an integrated content, a single discipline content, or a combination of both? Explain your answer.

Student Learning Activities

1. In a group of three to five students write a definition of social studies. Once you have defined social studies, prepare a survey questionnaire asking several people to respond to your questions regarding the nature of social studies. A cover letter explaining the purpose of your survey should be attached to the survey. You should survey at least five different categories of people, such as middle school and/or high school students, business persons, high school or middle school teachers not in social studies, university professors, government leaders, parents, and retired citizens. You may want to include in your survey some of the following questions:
   a. Is the definition of social studies sufficiently clear to be useful in determining the goals of the social studies program in the middle and high school curriculum?
   b. Is the definition of social studies sufficiently clear to be useful in identifying those content areas that should be included in the social studies curriculum in middle and high schools?
   c. What content should be included in social studies instruction in both middle and high school?
   d. To what extent should some topics receive greater attention than others? What topics should be emphasized?

You may want to construct other questions to be included in your survey.

2. After you and your group have analyzed the survey results you should respond to the following questions:
   a. Is your definition of social studies sufficiently clear to be useful in communicating with peers and colleagues? That is, can you explain social studies to other people in a more concise and meaningful way?
   b. Do the people you have surveyed agree with your definition? If not, how can these differences be resolved?

In light of your survey, you may want to rewrite your definition and share your revised definitions with classmates for further discussion.

References

American Historical Association. Committee of Seven. 1899. *The Study of History in the Schools.* New York: Macmillan.

Barr, R. D., Barth, J. L., and Shermis, S. S. 1977. *Defining the Social Studies.* Bulletin No. 51. Arlington, VA: National Council for the Social Studies.

Bellah, R. N., Madsen, R., Sullivan, W. M., Swidler, A., and Tipton, S. M. 1985. *Habits of the Heart: Individualism and Commitment in American Life.* Berkeley: University of California Press.

Bloom, B. S., Englehart, M. D., Furst, E. J., Hill, W. N., and Krathwohl, D. R. 1956. *Taxonomy of Educational Objectives: The Classification of Educational Goals: Handbook I: The Cognitive Domain.* New York: David McKay.

Brown, L. 1993. Personal correspondence with the authors.

Butts, R. F. 1973. "The Public School: Assaults on a Great Idea." *The Nation,* Vol. 216, No. 18, April 30. 553–560.

Council of State Social Studies Specialists. 1993. *National Survey: Social Studies Education K–12.* Des Moines: Iowa Department of Education.

Engel, P. 1993. Personal correspondence with the authors.

Engle, S. H. 1989. Personal correspondence with the authors.

Jefferson, T. 1779. "Reasons for Establishing Public Schools of Virginia." In *Notes on the State of Virginia* (2nd American ed.). Philadelphia, 1794.

Jones, T. J. 1913. "Statement of the Chairman of the Committee on Social Studies." In C. Kingsley (Ed.), *Preliminary Statements by the Chairman of the Committee of the Commission of National Education Association on Reorganization of Secondary Education.* United States Bureau of Education, Bulletin 1913, No. 41. Washington, DC: Government Printing Office, 1913.

Krathwohl, D. R., Bloom, B. S., and Masia, B. B. 1964. *Taxonomy of Educational Objectives: The Classification of Educational Goals. Handbook II: The Affective Domain.* New York: David McKay.

Madison, J. 1788. "Federalist Paper Number 10." In *Federalist Papers,* various editions.

Mann, H. 1849. "In Defense of Free Men." In L. A. Cremin (Ed.), *The Republic and the School: Horace Mann on the Education of Free Men,* 1957. New York: Bureau of Publications, Teachers College, Columbia University.

Murra, R. 1970. "The Birth of NCSS—As Remembered by Earle U. Rugg." *Social Education,* Vol. 34, No. 8, November. 728–729.

National Council for the Social Studies. 1992. *Definition of Social Studies.* Washington, DC: National Council for the Social Studies. (Available from NCSS).

National Education Association. 1893. *Report of the Committee of Ten on Secondary School Subjects. Committee on History, Civil Government and Political Economy.* Washington, DC: Government Printing Office.

National Education Association. 1916. *The Social Studies in Secondary Education: A Six Year Program Adopted Both to the 6-3-3 and the 6-4 Plan of Organization:* a Report of the Committee on Social Studies Commission of the Reorganization of Secondary Education of the NEA, A. W. Dunn, Secretary. Bulletin 28. Washington, DC: Government Printing Office.

Pericles. ND. In *Plutarch's Lives.* 1977. J. Dryden (Trans.) New York: Random.

Rumpf, A. H. 1976. "Historical Review." In *Program Improvement for Social Studies Education in Wisconsin.* Bulletin No. 7250. Madison, WI: Wisconsin Department of Public Instruction.

Sennet, R. A. 1977. *The Fall of Public Man.* New York: Knopf.

Superka, D. P. and Hawke, S. 1982. *Social Roles: A Focus for Social Studies in the 1980s.* Boulder, CO: Social Science Education Consortium, Inc.

Superka, D. P., Hawke, S., and Morrissett, I. 1980. "The Current and Future Status of Social Studies." *Social Education,* Vol. 44, No. 5, December. 362–369.

Wronski, S. P. and Bragaw, D. H. (Eds.). 1986. *Social Studies and Social Sciences: A Fifty-Year Perspective.* Bulletin No. 78. Washington, DC: National Council for the Social Studies.

Additional Readings

Bradley Commission of History in Schools. 1988. *Building a History Curriculum: Guidelines for Teaching History in Schools.* Washington, DC: Educational Excellence Network.

Brandt, R. (Ed.). 1988. *Content of the Curriculum.* ASCD Yearbook. Alexandria, VA: Association for Supervision and Curriculum Development.

Butts, R. F. 1960. "Search for Freedom: The Story of American Education." *NEA Journal,* Vol. 49, No. 3, March. 33–48.

Engle, S. H. and Ochoa, A. S. 1988. *Education for Democratic Citizenship: Decision Making in the Social Studies.* New York: Teachers College Press, Columbia University.

Hertzberg, H. W. 1971. *Historical Parallels for the Sixties and Seventies: Primary Sources and Core Curriculum Revisited.* Publication No. 135. Boulder, CO: Social Science Education Consortium.

Hertzberg, H. W. 1981. *Social Studies Reform, 1880–1980: SPAN Report.* Boulder, CO: Social Science Education Consortium.

Jarolimek, J. 1981. "The Social Studies: An Overview." In H. D. Mehlinger and O. L. Davis, Jr. (Eds.), *The Social Studies.* Eightieth Yearbook of the National Society for the Study of Education. Part II. Chicago: University of Chicago Press.

Lybarger, M. B. 1991. "The Historiography of Social Studies: Retrospect, Circumspect, and Prospect." In J. P. Shaver (Ed.), *Handbook of Research on Social Studies Teaching and Learning.* New York: Macmillan. (Readers are encouraged to examine other chapters included in this publication.)

Social Education. 1986. Vol. 50, No. 7, November/December. 484–542. Special issue discussing "Scope and Sequence Alternatives for Social Studies."

Social Education. 1989. Vol. 53, No. 6, October. 375–403. Special issue discussion of "Alternative Scopes and Sequences" options in social studies.

Note: Readers may be interested in the work of the following organization in understanding additional background issues in social studies.

National Center for History in the Schools, University of California at Los Angeles, 405 Hilgard Avenue, Los Angeles, CA 90024-1521.

National Council for History Education, 26915 Westwood Road, Suite A-2, Westlake, OH, 44145.

> We are of course a nation of differences. Those differences don't make us weak. They're the source of our strength.
>
> *Jimmy Carter*

CHAPTER 2

The Essentials of Social Studies

FOCUS QUESTIONS

- What are the essentials of a content area and how are they related to the development of an instructional program?
- How do changing content themes help define social studies?
- What is the proper focus of social studies?
- What is the relationship of social studies to the civic health of the republic?
- What is your rationale for teaching social studies?

OVERVIEW Historical and cultural contexts determine what is essential to an individual or institution. Therefore, any definition of essentials must consider the heritage (history) as well as the social, economic, religious, and political institutions of contemporary society. What is essential to social studies, then, is that which is essential to the republic: enlightened citizens who understand the proper balance between public and private life. Understanding and developing this balance is what makes the social studies unique. Social studies has the responsibility to instill in students the knowledge, skills, attitudes, and desire to participate in the public life of the republic.

A statement of "essentials" forms the core of a field of study. The following excerpts from the National Council for the Social Studies' *Characteristics of an Excellent Social Studies Program*, written in 1993 as part of the publication on national social studies standards, presents the essence of social studies.

Characteristics of an Excellent Social Studies Program

The major goal of this document is to establish curriculum standards in social studies. Excellent social studies programs exhibit a number of interrelated characteristics that address the goals of society and the needs and interests of learners as they draw upon a variety of academic fields. They are characterized by qualities such as those listed below.

Necessary conditions for learning	Teachers and learners need adequate time, space, and high quality resources and materials in order for students to engage in meaningful learning experiences. A variety of methods of learning and ways of demonstrating achievement must respect differences in students' modes of thinking. Continuous assessment occurs and learners are able to demonstrate achievement through a variety of forms of evaluation.
Developmentally appropriate skills, knowledge, and attitudes for all learners	Social studies stimulates high levels of thinking about content that challenges all learners from the earliest grades and throughout life. Students at every level should participate in a learning community in which social studies topics and processes are experienced as part of a regular program and are experienced in ways that actively engage them as is appropriate to their development and maturity.
Integration of knowledge from a variety of fields	Social studies integrates content, processes, and perspectives derived from a variety of related disciplines (e.g., history, geography, political science, sociology, psychology, economics, anthropology, archaeology, as well as law, religion, and philosophy). Social studies also contributes to interdisciplinary efforts which draw from such areas as science, mathematics, and the humanities, especially when areas are linked by a powerful theme or issue.

Thoughtful social and civic participation requires learners to acquire and use knowledge drawn from a range of disciplines, to examine multiple perspectives, and to make reasoned decisions as they formulate plans to address problems and persisting issues.

A combination of breadth and depth	Social studies demands attention to both breadth and depth. In-depth study helps learners construct thorough understandings of highly important topics. Breadth of study helps learners establish connections across a range of social studies topics. Over the years, breadth of coverage has too often reduced the opportunity of in-depth study. An effective balance of depth and breadth provides students with greater expertise in a few highly significant topics while developing the learners' capacities to construct meaningful context that explains relationships among the in-depth topics.
Effective application of knowledge	Social studies presents concepts and generalizations in historic, present, and future contexts, while learners construct meaning from making connections within and across disciplines. Powerful themes often serve as organizers to help learners recognize connections. Learners are able to collect data from print and data-gathering technologies, and to organize, analyze, interpret, evaluate, and put information to use in addressing problems and issues.
The inclusion of valuing	Values are inherent in the study of human and social phenomena. Systematic acknowledgment and investigation of values enables students to recognize the power of values as the prime motivator for thought and action. Social studies focuses on processes that assist students to develop civic and humanitarian values.
The incorporation of persistent issues and current dilemmas	Recurring issues and dilemmas characterize the social world. Social studies incorporates and addresses those significant issues of the past, issues of more recent origin and those that will challenge us in the future. Citizens have been and remain challenged by issues which call for examining such issues as the relationship of "individual welfare" and the "common good" or "unity" and "diversity." These and other issues serve as important areas of focus for social studies.

An inquiry emphasis in the learning process	Social studies programs enable students to use and apply strategies for investigating social phenomena. Students should engage in active learning that embodies the methods, materials, and attitudes of scholars from the social sciences, humanities, natural sciences, and other fields as they construct meaning about social and civic life.
Emphasis on decision-framing, decision-making, and problem-solving processes	Frequent examination of past and current decisions and consequences assist learners to practice decision-making and problem-solving processes. Learners are able to formulate, investigate, and consider important decisions and problems as well as value an informed approach to dealing with issues from the past, present, or those related to the future.
Active participation in social and civic life	Informed, thoughtful involvement in the processes and practices of democratic institutions and civic life requires the application of social studies knowledge as citizens regularly address issues affecting the definition and realization of the public good

These characteristics have been dealt with in greater detail in various NCSS publications and policy statements including *A Vision of Powerful Teaching and Learning in the Social Studies: Building Social Understanding and Civic Efficiency* (1993); *Social Studies in the Middle School* (1991); *Social Studies for Early Childhood and Elementary School Children: Preparing for the Twenty-First Century* (1988); *Social Studies Curriculum Planning Resources* (1990). The latter includes three scope and sequence models, various position statements, and sets of guidelines including "Essential Characteristics of Citizenship Education Program"; "Essential Characteristics of a Citizenship Program: Criteria Checklist"; "Global Education"; "Study About Religions in the Social Studies Curriculum"; and "Thinking About Science, Technology and Society in Social Studies: Education for Citizenship in the 21st Century" (National Council for the Social Studies, 1990). Copies of these policy statements are available from the NCSS, 3501 Newark St. N. W., Washington, DC, 20016.

We also encourage you to study the *Statement of Ethical Principles* found in the appendix at the end of this chapter. It is also available from NCSS.

Essentials of Social Studies Education

In 1979 the National Council for the Social Studies and eleven other professional associations reaffirmed the value of a balanced education for all students. Such "programs contribute not only to the development of students' capacity to read and compute, but also link knowledge and skills with an understanding and commitment to democratic principles and their application." The NCSS statement includes the following "essentials" for the social studies (National Council for the Social Studies, 1981).

Citizen participation in public life is essential to the health of our democratic system. Effective social studies programs help prepare young people who can identify, understand, and work to solve the problems that face our increasingly diverse nation and interdependent world. Organized according to a professionally designed scope and sequence, such programs should meet the following goals:

1. Begin in preschool and continue throughout formal education and include a range of related electives at the secondary level
2. Foster individual and cultural identity
3. Include observation of and participation in the school and community as part of the curriculum
4. Deal with critical issues and the world as it really is
5. Prepare students to make decisions based on American principles
6. Demand high standards of performance and measure student success by means that require more than the memorization of information
7. Depend on innovative teachers, broadly prepared in history, the humanities, the social sciences, and educational theory and practice
8. Involve community members as resources for program development and student involvement
9. Lead to citizenship participation in public affairs

Knowledge

Students need knowledge of the world at large and the world at hand, the world of individuals and the world of institutions, the world of past, present, and future. An exemplary social studies curriculum links information presented in the classroom with experiences gained by students through social and civic observation, analysis, and participation.

Classroom instruction that relates content to information drawn from the media and from experience focuses on the following areas of knowledge:

- History and culture of our nation and the world
- Geography—physical, political, cultural, and economic
- Government—theories, systems, structures, and processes
- Social institutions—the individual, the group, the community, and the society
- Economic institutions
- Intergroup and interpersonal relationships
- Worldwide relationships of all sorts among nations, races, cultures, and institutions

From this knowledge base, exemplary programs teach beliefs, skills, concepts, and generalizations that can help students understand the sweep of human affairs and ways of managing conflict consistent with democratic procedures.

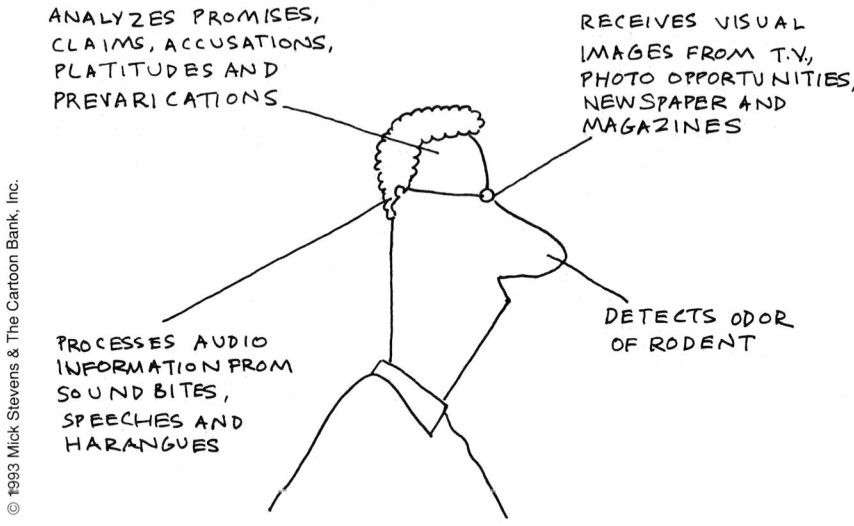

Democratic Beliefs

Fundamental beliefs drawn from the Declaration of Independence and the United States Constitution with its Bill of Rights form the basic principles of our democratic constitutional order. Exemplary school programs do not indoctrinate students to accept these ideas blindly, but instead present knowledge about their historical derivation and contemporary application essential to understanding our society and its institutions. Not only should teachers and students discuss such ideas as they relate to the curriculum and to current affairs, teachers should also mirror these ideas in their classrooms and schools should embody them in their daily operations.

These democratic beliefs depend upon such practices as due process, equal protection, and civic participation and are rooted in the following concepts:

- Justice
- Equality
- Responsibility
- Freedom
- Diversity
- Privacy

Due process, equal protection, and privacy can be taught through an examination of Supreme Court cases and incidents that occur within the school such as locker searches, dress codes, and censorship of school newspapers. Concepts of justice, equality, and freedom can be addressed in history courses dealing with civil rights issues. Responsibility for actions and civic participation opportunities are inherent in student government activities. This content can be taught through the use of media, role playing, and other learning activities.

Thinking Skills

It is important that students connect knowledge with beliefs and action. To do that, students should develop their thinking skills through regular systematic practice throughout the years of formal schooling. Fundamental to the goals of social studies education are those skills that help assure rational behavior in social settings.

In addition to strengthening reading and computation, there is a wide variety of thinking skills essential to the social studies that can be grouped into four major categories:

- *Data-Gathering Skills*. Learning to:
  Acquire information by observation,
  Locate information from a variety of sources,
  Compile, organize, and evaluate information,
  Extract and interpret information,
  Communicate orally and in writing.

- *Intellectual Skills*. Learning to:
  Compare things, ideas, events, and situations on the basis of similarities and differences,
  Classify or group items in categories,
  Ask appropriate and searching questions,
  Draw conclusions or inferences from evidence,
  Arrive at general ideas,
  Make sensible predictions from generalizations.

- *Decision-Making Skills*. Learning to:
  Consider alternative solutions,
  Consider the consequences of each solution,
  Make decisions and justify them in relationship to democratic principles,
  Take action, based on those decisions.

- *Interpersonal Skills*. Learning to:
  See things from the point of view of others,
  Understand one's own beliefs, feelings, abilities, and shortcomings and how they affect relations with others,

Use group generalizations without stereotyping and arbitrarily classifying individuals,
Recognize value in individuals different from one's self and groups different from one's own,
Work effectively with others as a group member,
Give and receive constructive criticism,
Accept responsibility and respect the rights and property of others.

Participation Skills

As a civic participant, the individual uses the knowledge, beliefs, and skills he or she has learned in the school, the social studies classroom, the community, and the family as the basis for action.

Connecting the classroom with the community provides many opportunities for students to learn the basic skills of participation, from observation to advocacy. For example, high school students might acquire an empty city lot, clean it up, and make a playground for younger children. To do this the students would have to be advocates for the project, find ways to acquire the lot, see if the neighborhood would like a playground or park, raise money, work with city officials, plan and do the construction work, and so forth. To teach participation, social studies programs need to emphasize the following kinds of skills:

Work effectively in groups—organizing, planning, making decisions, taking action
Form coalitions of interest with other groups
Persuade, compromise, bargain
Practice patience and perseverance in working for one's goal
Develop experience in cross-cultural situations

Civic Action

Social studies programs that provide practice in social participation represent an ideal professional standard because they combine acquiring knowledge and skills with applying democratic beliefs to life. Working to achieve that ideal is vital to the future of our society. However, even if excellent programs of social studies education were in place, there would often remain a missing element—the will to take part in public affairs. Formal education led by creative and humane teachers can provide the knowledge, the tools, and the commitment for a thoughtful consideration of issues and can even stimulate the desire to be active. But to achieve full participation in our diverse society adult citizens must value and model involvement to emphasize for young people the merit of taking part in public life. For example, young people can work with the community to improve the quality of life by helping prepare policies on such community activities as building bike paths or introducing better recycling programs. Students who are 18 years old should be encouraged to register and vote in local, state, and national elections. The voting registration process is easier now that the Motor Voter Bill (1993) has been signed into law by President Clinton. One can register to vote when registering a car or obtaining a drivers license. Since the right to vote was given to 18-year-olds, voters in the 18 to 24 age range have an overall poor voting record.

Key Themes of Social Studies Education

Powerful ideas form the organizational framework of every discipline. These ideas or themes define a subject field and show relationships between that field of study and more general knowledge. Themes help teachers bridge the gap between what to teach and how to teach it.

Any list of major social studies themes is arbitrary and subject to change. In this textbook we will consider the following ten fundamental ideas:

- Citizenship
- Culture
- Global perspectives
- Tradition and change
- Human rights
- Social contract
- Freedom and justice
- Scarcity and choice
- Causality
- Spatial relationships

These themes can be useful to teachers as they organize lessons, units, and even the total curriculum. Each lesson that teachers develop will address one or more of these themes. For example, in a unit on urban life in third-world nations, the teacher might organize activities, materials, and even field trips around themes like human rights or scarcity and choice.

1. Citizenship

Citizenship, that is, membership in a civic society like the United States republic, involves both obligations and privileges. Students need to understand how government and politics actually work. They need to understand the underlying purposes and values of government in a free society. In social studies classes students need opportunities to learn and practice their roles, rights, and responsibilities as effective citizens of a democracy. Social studies teachers should design their classes to help develop informed, analytical, and committed citizens. This is done best through modeling behavior of the teacher and through establishing the value of respect in the classroom.

2. Culture

Each human society (and groups within larger modern societies) has particular patterns of behavior that make up its culture. A culture consists of language, tools, customs, social institutions, beliefs, rituals, games, attitudes, clothing, music, works of art, and more. Within social groups, individuals learn accepted ways of meeting needs and coping with problems of living in that society. These ways of perceiving, thinking, and behaving are a part of their culture. To know one's cultural heritage is first of all to know one's history.

However, culture is constantly changing and at an accelerating rate caused by innovation and intercultural borrowing. Change in one facet of a culture may bring about changes in other aspects.

Cultural pluralism, people from different backgrounds living side by side, is a reality in our own country and the world. Each culture contributes its perspectives, beliefs, and traditions to the whole. A social studies program that explores the uniqueness of different groups of people actually enriches students' understanding of the world by transmitting varying viewpoints. Correspondingly, omitting such study and experiences would mean leaving out most of the people who populate the United States and the world.

We need to communicate with one another as local, national, and global neighbors, and therefore, we must learn to listen to the perspectives of other people. Furthermore, because some groups of people face cultural assimilation and even extinction, it is important to build in young citizens a sense of responsibility for preserving cultural pluralism by allowing students the opportunity to understand how they are part of a global system made up of many different cultures.

3. Global Perspectives

The problems of global interdependence have become operational facts of life for all Americans. We must develop an expanded literacy on global interdependence, a basic understanding of the forces at play in the world which now affect our lives so directly in order to help Americans cope more effectively with the problems of interdependence. By helping correct cultural myopia and astigmatism, global education reduces ethnocentrism and thus better prepares students to cope with the complex realities of nationalism and cultural differences on an international scale, and learning to see that the national interest in a world perspective and the world interest in a national perspective are two sides of the current coin. . . . Global education is a challenge that has the potential to reinvigorate American education with a sense of mission. (Council of Chief State School Officers, *Report on Global Studies*, 1976, used in American Forum Conference, Indianapolis, June 1993.)

Global studies is not an ideology, a discipline, or a definitive field of knowledge. It is the integration of many subject areas to give students a global perspective. Educators have become aware of the compelling need to prepare students for life in a world of rapidly expanding demands and shared horizons. Whether or not global studies ever becomes a discipline, its implications for all of education are profound. Thus, many states and local schools have developed programs in such areas as global geography, global history, and international economics.

4. Tradition and Change

People, events, and ideas change. History records the struggles between those who favor and those who oppose change. Change is continuous and the rate of change, although uneven in different cultures and societies, is accelerating.

Accelerating rates of change place greater importance on anticipating the future. Clearly, we cannot predict the future with accuracy, but we can envision various scenarios and be ready for more than one possibility. You might want to research some of the methods futurists have developed for dealing with the future. These include scenario writing, such as projecting values, dreams, and problems into the future through written narratives; trend extrapolation, such as taking demographic and climatic data and projecting the direction of social and natural systems; technological assessment, such as evaluating the impact of technology on social institutions; and brainstorming, such as listing many potential solutions to a problem spontaneously.

Important as change is in our lives, we must recognize that human experiences are continuous and interrelated. Continuity is a fact of life. All persons, events, actions, and change are the outcome of things that have gone before. We are inevitably a product of our past and in some ways restricted by it. Students should learn how change and continuity constantly influence their lives. Change, or turning points in history, become a part of every lesson as social studies programs deal with trends, revolutions, and social evolution.

5. Human Rights

Human rights have individual, group, and societal dimensions. Assertion of one's own rights implies a recognition of others' rights. Individuals and societies have the right to be free from hunger and the right to speak and write freely. People have a right to be free from the fear of torture.

Individuals within societies have the right to participate freely in choosing their form of government. Finally, cultures have the right to exist and to be free from the fear of extinction.

Human rights are also a standard for the social studies classroom. All students must be respected as individuals with the capability of contributing to the class. The classroom is a place where students must feel and be safe to practice such freedoms as reflective inquiry. That is, the right of free speech is diminished when students have little knowledge to discuss.

6. Social Contract

We establish governments to provide protection and essential public services. Government authority is that legitimate power that is recognized and sanctioned by custom, institutions, laws, constitutions, or morality. In a democracy, a form of government in which political decision making rests with citizens and their representatives, authority is sanctioned by the consent of the governed. Social justice should guide the exercise of democratic political authority, which should strive to ensure the greatest amount of individual freedom under law and seek a fair distribution of privileges and resources to all citizens. This is the social contract we "sign" as citizens of the republic, and as members of a social studies class, a school, and the larger community. Above all, this means shared responsibility to one another.

7. Freedom and Justice

United States citizens enjoy the protection of several basic social guarantees that assure their freedom to believe, think, and act as individuals. Social studies should help students understand and value freedom of assembly, speech, the press, religion, inquiry, and criticism, and the right to a public education. These social studies classes should also help students learn how to maintain our basic freedoms and rights.

In our society we place great value on fairness. We insist on "equal justice under law" for all citizens including the weak and powerless. Students should study issues regarding the fair distribution of benefits and burdens, fair procedures for making decisions, and fair means for correcting wrongs or injuries.

8. Scarcity and Choice

A fundamental conflict exists between unlimited economic demands and limited natural and human resources. This conflict creates the basic economic problem of scarcity that confronts all societies. Individuals and societies must continuously make choices about how to use the scarce resources available to them.

Every society faces four fundamental choices:

- What and how many goods and services should the economy produce?
- How many natural resources, human resources, and capital tools should the economy use for production? How should the economy use these resources and tools?
- Should the economy use goods and services for immediate consumption or further production?
- How should a society divide its economic output among its members?

A less frequently noted principle in economics is the belief that scarcity creates scarcity. The concept is a self-fulfilling prophecy. This is the "Tragedy of the Commons" described by Garrett Hardin in his book by that name. With everyone lining up to "top off" their gasoline tanks in 1973, there was not enough to go around. As states cut back on funding for university programs there are fewer classes offered in the social studies education sequence. This will cause more students to sign up as early as possible, creating even greater scarcity. We must balance the concepts of scarcity and choice with concepts of sufficiency and sharing. A more economically advanced society should address both sides of this equation rather than just one.

9. Causality

All acts and events have causes and consequences, but social acts and events often have causes and consequences that are unexpected. Therefore, we must include methods of determining cause and effect from many sources such as linguistics, the humanities, and social statistics as well as from history and the social sciences.

Language complicates cause-and-effect reasoning by offering many words and phrases that suggest cause but allow laxity in logic. For example, take a bold statement such as "Slavery caused the Civil War." This invites criticism but it also sharpens our focus and is preferable to the following statements, which are less provocative and yet insidious: "We can explain the Civil War in terms of plantation slavery," or "Slavery led to the Civil War." Therefore, it is important to give greater attention to semantic distinctions.

Causes of an event are rarely simple, and consequences may lead to unexpected developments or side effects. We need to become more sophisticated in our reasoning and more humble about deciding what we can and cannot do with current knowledge.

10. Spatial Relationships

History helps us place ourselves in time, while geography helps us locate ourselves in space. Spatial relationships explain where people, events, and things are located and why.

Our well-being is dependent upon our understanding of the interactions between people and the environment. A sense of place, location, and region is essential to making decisions about where and how we live. People adapt to or modify natural settings based upon their values. People also use maps and other tools to understand their physical environments. Students need to be aware that the planetary ecosystem is a comprehensive and integrated network of places and functions all in spatial relationships to one another.

The Use of Themes in Instruction

Although grounded in our history and culture, any list of themes such as those described above will slowly change. For example, today we perceive cause and effect with greater complexity than we did just a few years ago. Freedom in an industrialized, interdependent world has many more limitations than in a world of open, natural frontiers. In defining justice or fairness we have alternated between "equality of opportunity" and "equality of results" and currently we are somewhere in between. By teaching the themes, we are not passing along eternal truths; rather, we are asking young people to examine these major ideas of society and see how they apply to their own lives.

For us as teachers, however, themes also play several important roles. They help us organize our instructional patterns and go beyond the specific discipline we are teaching. Themes also help us organize our own thinking about a particular unit and generate different perspectives. Furthermore, themes can serve a research purpose by forming focus areas that students can investigate from different perspectives. Finally, themes can serve as a communication link among teachers as they discuss important ideas across the school curriculum.

A theme also provides a focus for the curriculum and for student activities which could extend beyond the textbook. We can see the relationship between themes and activities in the following example.

Theme

Citizenship

Unit

Local Government

Activity

A major issue facing the local community is a new landfill. Therefore, the class is assigned to interview members of the city council about their stand on the issue of a new landfill for the community.

Skills	Attitudes	Concepts/Content
Interviewing	Willingness to ask questions	Citizenship
Formulating questions		Structure of city government
Listening	Willingness to work on the project in the evening	Public opinion
Gathering data		Environment
Drawing conclusions	Willingness to be open to different views	Scarcity

Outcome

The students will take an informed position on the issue of a new landfill. They may then decide to circulate a petition, write letters to the editor or to members of the city council.

Teachers should build activities using skills, attitudes, concepts, and content. They should also relate these activities to a major social studies theme. Within a 6–12 curriculum, a theme could provide a communication link among teachers at different grade levels. For example, teachers might decide to place different emphasis on the theme of "Citizenship" at each grade level. Students at the middle school level might grapple with a problem such as hunger at both the local, national, or international level. As students research the topic and gather information from a range of resources, the teacher would ask them to prepare statements indicating how the problem may be alleviated through individual behaviors or some action on the part of government or private enterprise.

At the high school level students might practice citizenship by constructing a public policy on the military involvement of U.S. forces in a regional conflict somewhere in the world. The conflict should be a *real* conflict in the world at the present time. What principles are involved in the conflict? Does the United States have any self-interest in keeping peace in that part of the world? How would the process unfold if the United States were to get involved? What timeline would we follow? Students could consider these and other questions, formulate a policy of action (or no action), and submit it to their congressional delegation.

Teachers will develop classroom activities to teach various concepts, skills, content, and attitudes, but the sophistication of these activities will vary depending upon the maturity of their students. By dealing with a common theme, teachers at various grade levels will have ample opportunities to discuss the nature of their common curriculum.

Themes can help answer a number of important questions in the social studies curriculum:

1. What content is most important?
2. How should we address this content at different grade levels?
3. What content should we use to construct tests or evaluation programs?
4. Do the learning activities relate to major content areas in a direct way?

Now that you have considered the essentials and themes of social studies you should take the time to develop your own rationale statement concerning social studies. That is, what is the main purpose of social studies?

Developing Your Own Rationale Statement: An Exercise

Developing a rationale or statement of purpose is critical in planning a reasonable and coherent social studies program. Most often rationale statements have several underlying assumptions. These include the nature of the discipline, our world, society, students, and the teaching/learning processes. When teachers develop formal rationale statements they also reflect on the place of the social studies curriculum within the overall philosophy, goals, and programs of the school district. A rationale statement provides a needed opportunity to communicate the importance of social studies education to the students, their parents, and the larger community.

In the following pages we present several perspectives concerning the nature and purpose of the social studies. Over the years and in various settings other perspectives have arisen. Your task is to examine thoughtfully each of these statements and decide what you believe to be the purposes of social studies at this time. When you complete this course, you may want to review your initial thinking about social studies and decide if you still hold these views.

Directions and Procedures

a. Read each of the following statements carefully and decide which statement best represents your own position. For each statement mark the appropriate symbol.

SA = Strong Agreement
A = Agreement
D = Disagreement
SD = Strong Disagreement

b. If none of the statements adequately reflects your own beliefs, either revise one of the existing statements or write your own original statement.
c. Rank each statement from 1 to 6 (or 7 if you wrote your own statement) in the order of your preference. The number 1 should indicate your first choice, and the number 6 (or 7) should indicate your last preference.
d. After you have completed this task as an individual, form a small group with three to five fellow students. Try to determine if there is agreement on the purposes of the social studies program. In discussing these statements, you may want to consider why there is agreement related to some of the statements. It is also useful to discuss the disagreements as well. The small groups may share their ideas concerning areas of agreement and disagreement with each other. To what extent is it possible to reach a consensus on the purposes of social studies?
e. Based on your discussions, as a group you are to develop a rationale statement for your social studies program. Compare your rationale statement with those prepared by other groups. Is there a consensus of the purpose of social studies? How can you reconcile differences?

Perceptions About the Purposes of Social Studies Education

Directions: Listed below are several statements that reflect purposes of social studies programs. Read the statements carefully and decide your responses to each statement.

Rank Order

1. _____ The main purpose of teaching social studies in our schools is to ensure that students *learn social studies information* as one of the basic subjects and disciplines in our schools. The emphasis ought to be placed on developing literacy and acquiring discipline-based knowledge and skills. Social studies instruction should stress a mastery of the content. Students need to learn history in order to pass on our cultural heritage to the next generation. They should learn geography to understand location and so forth.

2. _____ The main purpose for teaching social studies in our schools is to *understand people as social beings* and as a part of a larger social context. In our democratic society it is necessary for students to learn the skills and values that can help them participate in our society. Students learn to analyze and evaluate information, distinguish fact from opinion, and make intelligent public and personal policy decisions. The overall goal is to help develop a just and humane society.

3. _____ The main purpose for teaching social studies in our schools is to give students all-inclusive views of themselves. Social studies should deal with the physical, emotional, intellectual, aesthetic, moral, and spiritual dimensions of the student. Social studies teachers should plan their instruction to *integrate analytic and intuitive thinking with other creative curriculum areas* such as the arts and humanities. Students should become aware of their inner selves in order to develop well-integrated personalities, and to be relatively free of unnecessary personal problems and anxieties.

4. _____ The main purpose for teaching social studies in our schools is to develop the students' *intellectual and problem-solving abilities* by using the cognitive skills of analysis, synthesis, and evaluation. The curriculum should include a variety of learning activities in which teachers help students by stimulating the development of independent thinking. The teacher often probes the student's thinking and reasoning to encourage further reflection and consideration in the study of human activities.

5. _____ The main purpose for teaching the social studies in our schools is to help *build a better society.* Such a program would deal with social justice, pluralism, social issues, and skills of participation.

6. _____ The main purpose for teaching social studies in our schools is to emphasize the development of a *positive self-concept* and skills in communicating with others. The basic emphasis is on personal growth and interaction. Teachers use various interpersonal learning activities such as role playing, class meetings, and human relations communication skills. These activities will develop a sense of well-being so students will become conscientious producers-consumers and effective participants in citizenship activities.

7. _____ Write your own statement.

SUMMARY

In this chapter we have presented essential program components and important content themes fundamental to your perception of social studies. This perception will continue to change and increase in sophistication as you grow in your profession. At the present time you must begin to understand your reasons for teaching social studies (earning a living, getting into the middle class, passing on the cultural heritage, helping to create a better world, etc.). It is necessary, both for yourself and for the larger professional community of social studies educators, that you develop a clear and powerful rationale for teaching social studies. It is important to communicate this rationale to students, parents, other educators and the general public.

Discussion Questions

1. Do you think lists such as the *Statement of Ethical Principles,* the *Essentials of the Social Studies,* and the major themes give direction for teaching social studies in today's world? Why or why not?
2. How would you compare and contrast the purposes of social studies with other academic areas in the middle and high school curriculum?
3. How would you go about constructing a rationale for a social studies curriculum? How would you go about constructing a rationale for a separate social studies course that you are teaching?
4. If you make a commitment to building the public good and individual dignity, what rewards will you earn and what sacrifices must you make?
5. The ten themes suggested in this chapter can serve a number of classroom purposes from lesson organizers to criteria for material selection. The themes are also interdependent in the sense that teaching and learning one theme will lead to another. Discuss how you would use one (or more) theme to teach another. How, for example, would you use the theme of tradition and change to teach about culture? Do the same with all ten themes.

Student Learning Activities

1. Contact at least three social studies teachers and ask if they would share their personal statements of philosophy (rationale) or the philosophy (rationale) of their social studies program with you. Compare these statements.
2. Rationale is "an explanation of controlling principles of opinion, belief, practice, or phenomena" (Webster's Seventh *New Collegiate*

Dictionary). Rationale deals with the *why* of curriculum and instruction. Interview a teacher (or preservice student) who is teaching some area of the curriculum other than social studies. Ask why we should include (*their subject*) in the curriculum. Compare your rationale statement of social studies with the rationale statement made for another subject by the person you interviewed.
3. Survey a group of middle or high school students to find out what they view as essential about social studies. What questions will you ask these students?

APPENDIX A

Statement of Ethical Principles

Ethical principles suggest rightful behaviors and responsibilities of educators, and they relate content, student, and culture to one another.

Principle One. It is the ethical responsibility of social studies professionals to set forth, maintain, model, and safeguard standards of instructional competence suited to the achievement of the broad goals of the social studies.

Principle Two. It is the ethical responsibility of social studies professionals to provide to every student, insofar as possible, the knowledge, skills, and attitudes necessary to function as an effective citizen.

Principle Three. It is the ethical responsibility of social studies professionals to foster the understanding and exercise of the rights guaranteed to all citizens under the Constitution of the United States and of the responsibilities implicit in those rights.

Principle Four. It is the ethical responsibility of social studies professionals to cultivate and maintain an instructional environment in which the free contest of ideas is prized.

Principle Five. It is the ethical responsibility of social studies professionals to adhere to the highest standards of scholarship in the development, production, distribution, or use of social studies materials.

Principle Six. It is the ethical responsibility of social studies professionals to concern themselves with the conditions of the school and community with which they are associated.

APPENDIX B

During 1993 and 1994 the National Council for the Social Studies was in the process of developing curriculum standards for the social studies. NCSS has identified ten thematic interrelated curriculum strands that represent a holistic scope of the content that students should experience throughout every grade level from elementary through high school. The ten thematic strands are as follows.

	Culture	Social studies programs should include experiences which provide for the study of *culture and cultural diversity*.
	Time, Continuity, and Change	Social studies programs should include experiences that provide for the study of *ways human beings view themselves in and over time*.
	People, Places, and Environments	Social studies programs should include experiences that provide for the study of *people, places, and environments*.
	Individual Development and Identity	Social studies programs should include experiences that provide for the study of *individual development and identity*.
	Individuals, Groups, and Institutions	Social studies programs should include experiences that provide for the study of *interaction among individuals, groups, and institutions*.
	Power, Authority, and Governance	Social studies programs should include experiences that provide for the study of *how people create and change structures of power, authority, and governance*.
	Production, Distribution, and Consumption	Social studies programs should include experiences that provide for the study of *how people organize for the production, distribution, and consumption of goods and services*.
	Science, Technology, and Society	Social studies programs should include experiences that provide for the study of *relationships among science, technology, and society*.
	Global Connections	Social studies programs should include experiences that provide for the *study of global connections and interdependence*.
	Civic Ideals and Practices	Social studies should include experiences that provide for the study of the *ideals, principles, and practices of citizenship in a democratic republic*.

SOURCE: Taken from the NCSS Curriculum Standards, 1994.

References

Council of Chief School Officers. 1976. *Report on Global Studies.* Washington, DC: Council of Chief State School Officers.

Hardin, G. 1971. *The Tragedy of the Commons.* New York: Phoenix/BFA Films & Video.

National Council for the Social Studies. 1980. *Statement of Ethical Principles.* Washington, DC: National Council for the Social Studies. (Copies are included in the NCSS *Social Studies Tool Kit,* ND, and are available from NCSS.)

National Council for the Social Studies. 1981. "Essentials of Social Studies." *Social Education,* Vol. 45, No. 3, March. 162–164.

National Council for the Social Studies. 1990. *Social Studies Curriculum Planning Resources.* Dubuque, IA: Kendall/Hunt.

National Council for the Social Studies. 1993. *Characteristics of an Excellent Social Studies Program.* Washington, DC: National Council for the Social Studies. (Copies are available from NCSS.)

National Council for the Social Studies. 1994. *NCSS Curriculum Standard.* Washington, DC: National Council for the Social Studies. (Copies are available from NCSS.)

Additional Readings

Bellah, R. N., Madsen, R., Sullivan, W. M., Swidler, A., and Tipton, S. M. 1985. *Habits of the Heart: Individualism and Commitment in American Life.* Berkeley: University of California Press.

Butts, R. F. 1980. *The Revival of Civic Learning: A Rationale for Citizenship Education in American Schools.* Bloomington, IN: Phi Delta Kappa.

Dewey, J. 1916. *Democracy and Education: An Introduction to the Philosophy of Education.* New York: Free Press.

Hartoonian, H. M. 1991. "The Philosophical Perspective." In R. E. Gross and T. Dynneson (Eds.), *Social Science Perspectives on Citizenship.* New York: Teachers College Press, Columbia University.

Hook, S. 1962. *The Paradoxes of Freedom.* Berkeley, CA: University of California Press.

Shaver, J. P. 1967. "Social Studies: The Need for Redefinition." *Social Education,* Vol. 31, No. 7, November. 588–592, 596.

Shaver, J. P., Davis, O. L., and Helburn, S. W. 1979. "The Status of Social Studies Education: Impressions from Three NSF Studies." *Social Education,* Vol. 43, No. 2, February. 150–153.

> Education is the leading of human souls to what is best, and making what is best out of them; and these two objects are always attainable together, and by the same means. The training which makes [people] happiest in themselves also makes them most serviceable to others.
>
> *John Ruskin*

PART II

What Social Studies Content Is Worth Knowing?

In Part I we considered why we teach social studies. In Part II we will discuss what to teach.

The knowledge of most worth to citizens of our republic is knowledge that they can use to decide personal and social issues ethically and effectively. This knowledge provides the basis for rational decision making and for thoughtful policy making in our economic, political, and social behaviors. The amount of information is so vast that scholars divide our knowledge into subject areas or disciplines in order to make the knowledge more accessible.

Social studies educators must continually deal with three attributes of knowledge: knowledge as content, knowledge as methodology, and knowledge as shared experiences. These attributes relate directly to the conception of knowledge held within academic disciplines. A field of knowledge includes a specific *content* base made up of facts, concepts, generalizations, and theories. It also includes *methods* used by scholars and students to acquire and apply this knowledge. Finally, knowledge is also the *shared experiences* of the community of scholars, students, and citizens interested in the field and its relationship to everyday life.

The community of scholars helps define the values that direct study and criticism. It provides a frame of reference that helps students develop questions about what methods and content to use in finding out about the world.

FOCUS QUESTIONS

- What knowledge is of most worth?
- What is the meaning of the phrase "Knowledge is a social creation"?
- Why is the decision of what to teach in social studies such a complex issue?

FOCUS ACTIVITY

Survey several middle and high school teachers and students you know on the following questions:

- What should we teach in middle and high school social studies programs?
- Which social studies disciplines does the public seem to perceive as most important? What disciplines do educators think are most important? What disciplines do students say are most important?
- Are teachers more concerned with the coverage of information or with student-developed projects? Why?

From your survey data, what tentative conclusions would you reach about what to teach in social studies?

Organize a panel of university faculty and students to discuss the question, "What social studies content is worth knowing?" Compare the data from middle school and high school teachers and students with the responses from university faculty and students.

All things are connected like the blood which unites a family. All things are connected.
Chief Seattle

CHAPTER 3

Knowledge in Social Studies

> **FOCUS QUESTIONS**
> - What is the nature of social knowledge?
> - How do the disciplines of the social studies complement each other?
> - How do the disciplines of the social studies help us deal with personal and social issues?
> - What relationships exist between the social studies and other areas of the curriculum?

OVERVIEW One of the most important things that teachers do is encourage students to learn about their social world, who they are, and the interaction between human systems and the environment through the disciplines we call academic subjects. Social studies programs provide students with knowledge of anthropology, economics, geography, history, philosophy, political science, psychology, religion, and sociology. Developing a content base is a necessary prerequisite in social studies instruction. Social studies also helps learners build a bridge to other academic areas such as science, literature, the arts, and mathematics. Social studies provides a social context where students can apply this knowledge and these skills to help make social and personal policies.

To all of us who work in the social studies field, decisions about what to teach are always difficult and often challenging. There is always so much to do and so little time to accomplish our goals. In order to make better decisions about what to teach we need to understand the nature of knowledge in the social studies and our role in helping students grapple with content issues. Three of the most important issues to keep in mind are *knowledge versus information, broad perspective versus narrow concentration,* and *content versus method*. The social studies teacher must develop a functional definition of knowledge. How is knowledge different from information? What should we teach? Information? Knowledge? Both? What perspectives do we provide students if we teach only history or only economics? Is it possible to teach one social studies discipline without using others? What is the difference, if any, between content and method? Social studies teachers should be clear about such issues simply because they must make decisions every day about what is the most valuable content for their students.

The Nature of Social Knowledge

Almost everything about the social world is more complex than we lead students to believe. Most people think that information that comes from the teacher, textbook, or other instructional materials is knowledge. However, this is an incorrect assumption. Collections of data that come from textbooks and teachers remain information, not knowledge. Knowledge is something individuals or groups create for themselves through interactions with other people, with the instructional materials, and with the setting (context).

Suppose that we would like our students to understand the generalization that while all people have similar basic needs, people express these needs differently in different cultures. The question for the teacher is "How can I help the student create his or her own generalization about the functional relationship between needs and culture and prove the validity of the student's own generalization?"

This might be accomplished by providing the students with information about foods, family relationships, religious practices, and the like, among several cultural groups. From observations and study the student would create and test his or her own generalization. The creation would have many of the attributes of the teacher's generalization but would be uniquely the student's because the student had created, tested, and used it. For example, a student might create the statement "While all people need to eat, what and how they eat is a function of geographic location, religious traditions, wealth of the region, and health practices." Another student might conclude that "Different cultural groups even within the same society will eat different kinds of food for reasons of location, tradition, wealth, and health."

The challenge for the teacher is to help students use the information they receive to create knowledge for themselves. For this creative process to work teachers must use powerful content-based concepts. (See definitions and examples at the end of the chapter.) Principles such as justice, equality, freedom, and diversity become powerful when students see the relationships among these concepts within a subject area. For example, in the study of economics, students could use these concepts as criteria for examining information about public tax policy. How just is our tax system? What impact does tax policy have on equality and freedom? How should diversity of income and age affect tax policy?

An historian could apply these same concepts to information about the civil rights movement of the 1950s and 1960s. The words used by an historian or economist to label the principles are the same, but they are used differently because in one case they are part of an economic structure of knowledge and in the other case they are used within an historical context. Students use these concepts to create meaning. Creating knowledge is the process of making meaning out of information.

Concepts such as culture, scarcity, environment, power, and status become powerful when teachers relate them to the basic content areas of social studies. It is also becoming clear that teachers should integrate concepts from the arts, literature, mathematics, and science into social studies programs. For example, in the study of an environmental issue like the location of a landfill for solid waste, the teacher will have to use information from science to allow students to understand how the water cycle affects the ground water under the site, mathematics to understand the probability of toxic leakage, and design to deal with the aesthetic quality of the landscape.

The dividing lines between disciplines are disappearing. From psychohistory to bioethics, the academic areas now reflect the realities of contemporary life and research, which no longer have such neat divisions. Computers have made the most noticeable recent impact by making it easier to apply statistics and probability to the social science disciplines. These developments make it more interesting, but also more difficult for educators to decide what to teach.

Five Knowledge-Related Activities

In order to implement this type of creative, meaning-making instructional program with its emphasis on major ideas, teachers will need to place a high priority on developing specific abilities within their students. Students will need the following abilities in order to relate disciplined study to personal meaning and real-life policy making (Bragaw and Hartoonian, 1988). Students should practice all of them in a sequence that seems right for the task at hand.

1. Students will have to develop an information base and make connections between previously learned and new information. The most important attribute of this ability is the idea of "connections." A sound factual base is a necessary condition for making information connections that move one toward knowledge. However, the teacher must help students extend this information to areas that are new to the learners. In order to probe the nature of societies, teachers must encourage their students to see the connections between human needs and the institutions people build to meet those needs. For example, students come into class knowing that all people have basic needs. The teacher extends this knowledge by having students explore the relationships between needs and institutions. That is, the need for social order and security led to the development of different institutions of government. These different forms of the institution come about because of different cultural beliefs and practices. With this "connection" in mind, the study of any society becomes more meaningful.

It may well be as Hunt and Metcalf observed in 1955, "There is only one role which facts can play in meaningful learning—to function as data in conceptualization. If they do not, they may, perhaps, be memorized and retained for awhile, but their meaning and future usefulness will be slight" (Hunt and Metcalf, p. 41). This ability to conceptualize is knowing how to use data to form stories, descriptions, and mental images to understand the universe of information available to us. This means that facts and knowledge are parts of the same whole. One does not come before the other; facts are necessary to create knowledge, and knowledge is necessary to structure facts. They must work together.

■■■■■■■ People live at the intersection of environment and culture. This interaction defines needs (climate, economic development, etc.) and institutions are constructed to meet these needs.

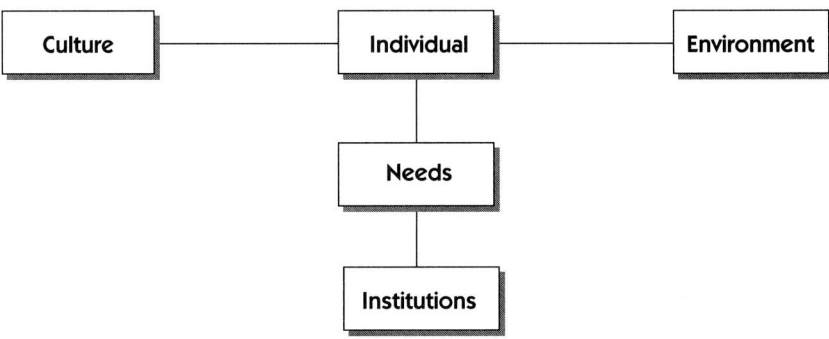

2. Students will need to use different perspectives and patterns of logic in considering themselves and others. Students must think about how different people explain their world, what evidence these people use to support their explanations, and what biases they have in their views of the world. Thinking about human interactions and institutions demands the abilities to conceptualize, reason, and evaluate. For example, we know that even with the same basic facts, two different people (or cultures) can come to different perspectives and policies. When environmentalists want to clean up a river while businesses and labor unions want to protect jobs, we can see how different logics and perspectives can lead to different policies, even using the same data. Similarly, the people who make their homes in the rain forest of the Amazon basin will see the world in quite a different way from the ranchers and timber cutters who are changing the Amazon environment.

We can more easily see why people act and live the way they do if we understand patterns and perspectives. This means the teacher should plan activities that allow the students to see patterns in thinking and actions.

3. Students will need to create knowledge. A student creates knowledge when he or she turns public information into private meaning. The student can do this by developing new stories, explanations, models, pictures, dramas, music, or other modes of communication that extend previously learned knowledge into new settings, times, questions, and issues. For example, the teacher may ask the students to design new model communities, write dramas about social institutions in different cultures, or prepare position papers on changes in fiscal policy that could make the country more prosperous. In all cases students will use these new conceptions to build upon or replace their previous notions about the world.

4. Students will need to communicate and negotiate with others. Communication abilities such as reading, writing, listening, and speaking are all necessary skills of the enlightened citizen. In addition, citizens need skills of negotiation. These skills include the abilities to defend a position on a controversial issue, analyze and communicate value positions, use bargaining strategies, understand possible consequences of alternative decisions, and work for compromise within group standards.

5. Students will need to make thoughtful personal and public policy decisions. Making personal and public policy decisions means that students must be able to conceptualize a problem or issue. Then they must create a plausible sequence of relationships between events and consequences, suggest alternative sequences, and evaluate these alternatives. Finally, students must learn to implement a decision, and, where necessary, make revisions based on new evidence or personal experience.

Therefore, teaching students to acquire knowledge that is the most beneficial (the contents of most worth) incorporates the key ideas from the social studies disciplines and allows the teacher to develop the five abilities discussed above. The underlying assumption is that these abilities can empower students creatively to confront and work to resolve the major issues of their lives and times. Let us look at the five abilities again as criteria for selecting the content of most worth.

- *Teachers should build into each social studies program and lesson an initial and dynamic factual base.* However, those facts that are of most worth deal with connections rather than isolated information. For example, knowing the number of farmers in the United States is not important by itself. Information that deals with the percentage of farmers in the economy and their contribution to the gross domestic product (GDP) is much more meaningful. We should know the magnitude of the national debt compared to national worth, or the relationship between the resources spent on the nation's defense industry and the total income of the people of the nation. Educators need to include facts that enable students to make historical and geographic connections. For example: How have income levels changed over the last 75 years in the United States? Where is the population center of the United States today? Where was it 75 years ago? How has the employment landscape changed in that time?

- *Perspectives and patterns of time and space* are basic to content selection. History and geography are parts of the same whole. What does a map of the world look like with China at its center? What was going on in China or Alexandria (in North Africa) as compared to activities in Western Europe in 800 A.D.? The answers to these questions suggest that time and place orientations provide patterns for thinking about institutions, issues, problems, and possibilities. These ideas of time–space perspective provide important criteria for content selection. They give rise to the following questions: Does this content allow students to "travel" to different times and places, thus enabling them to see connections and meanings? Does this content allow students to analyze institutions in particular times and places as a way to gain insights into how their own world functions?

- In using *communication/negotiation* as a criterion for content selection we must take into account two notions of human interaction. One obvious idea is that communication/negotiation is a matter of skill development in reading, writing, listening, and speaking. These skills are important to all school subjects. Therefore, the teacher must give students enough time in class to write, for example. The teacher must guide students in their communication skill-development process. The less obvious notion related to communication and content selection is the need to go beyond personal experiences and to sample those ideas from past and contemporary societies. For example, students might study United States presidents from the past and construct a set of criteria by which to judge the best of them. They could then use these criteria to justify voting for a candidate in a contemporary election. These ideas help us carry on enlightened discussion and bring meaning to persistent questions like, "Is there too much violence in the media?" "Is it possible for an individual to be just in an unjust society?" "To what extent should the sale of handguns be controlled?" "How should minority rights be protected?" "What responsibility does the United States have for helping economically poor nations?" and "What is happiness?"

As important as it is to sample ideas that connect certain themes across the ages, students must also know how to deal with the mass of information available today, in other words, how to discriminate and discern what is important versus what is not. Thus, methodology is a most important criterion for content selection. How do historians and social scientists collect, organize, interpret, and communicate information?

We should also be able to use these communication abilities in negotiating personal and social policies. Teachers need to construct lessons that will help students learn about the give and take in human relationships by developing skills in consensus building, bargaining, and debating. For example, students can learn conflict skills by studying the local school budget and deciding what programs to cut and what programs to retain. They can then present their recommendations to the local school officials.

- In order to *create knowledge* students will need content that allows them to complement ideas they gain from the text and classroom discussion. Teachers should give special attention to art, music, and literature as well as science and mathematics. Teachers need to encourage students to develop their own ideas about an issue and to construct generalizations or theories about the topic they are studying. If we were introducing a unit on the Middle Ages, for example, and would like our students to understand better the relationship between art (including architecture) and history, we might show slides of Romanesque and Gothic architecture, paintings of peasant life and religious subjects, listen to church and folk music, and then have students construct a set of generalizations about life in the Middle Ages. By using content and perspectives from several disciplines students will feel more free to experiment with their own explanations of social and personal issues. The students then feel ownership in the ideas they create and are willing to share them if the teacher creates a climate of mutual respect.

- Students who successfully learn these abilities can *make enlightened policy decisions* at both personal and societal levels. Consider, for example, the issue of whether a state should build a new maximum security prison. The teacher should first of all develop factual background on the issue, including alternative positions, and stress those data among which connections can be drawn. For example, what is the relationship between incarceration and state crime rates? How much will a new prison cost? How will the money for the prison be raised? What economic trade-offs will be necessary in the state budget? What are some political considerations to take into account? Can the students conceptualize the issues from the given data? Second, students can present different perceptions of the issue based upon different political orientations. They could role play the different positions through a series of "public hearings." Within those hearings students can practice communication and negotiation skills. They could formulate public policy based on their research and discussions.

We might apply the same strategies when studying the New Deal, the TVA, the New Frontier, welfare programs, and the like. That is, how is policy made? By whom? For whom? How is it evaluated? Therefore, we should select the content that enables students to engage in formulating policy.

The content of most worth, therefore, is that which allows students to develop the five abilities discussed above. These skills are fundamental to enlightened citizenship.

Social Studies Disciplines

Within the middle and secondary school social studies curriculum, there is room for discrete social studies disciplines such as history or economics as well as integrated courses. Examples of these integrated courses include civics (combining disciplines such as political science, economics, history, and psychology) and global studies (combining disciplines such as anthropology, geography, history, political science, economics, and sociology). A sound content base is necessary to imaginative and comprehensive teaching. The teacher's ability and willingness to use questions, ideas, and methods from the various social studies disciplines will enhance his or her instructional effectiveness.

For the social studies teacher, perhaps the most important consideration is to think of the content areas as wonderful sources of questions. Content questions actually shed light in two different directions. On one hand, they help us understand the nature of the disciplines we want to study. On the other hand, these questions help us define and understand issues of personal and social interest.

As previously discussed, the contemporary list of social studies disciplines commonly includes anthropology, economics, geography, history, philosophy, political science, psychology, religion, and sociology, and teachers can also use other disciplines such as the sciences, mathematics, and the humanities. Educators generally agree, however, that the central focus is on history and the social sciences. We do not intend the following descriptions to teach you about the disciplines, but to offer you a glimpse of them. We encourage you to pursue additional study in the disciplines that interest you.

Anthropology

Many scholars suggest that, because the Greek word "anthropos" means *people* and "logos" means *the study of,* every social studies teacher is, in a sense, teaching anthropology. Anthropology is the study of people in the broadest sense. Using mostly methods of observation and narrative, anthropologists study the fundamental institutions of human society and the cultures in which they exist. In essence, anthropologists study the cultural practices and values of human beings. Modern anthropology offers a framework for social studies that teaches the common problems facing all human beings.

Economics, history, geography, philosophy, political science, psychology, and sociology all treat material that is incorporated into the all-encompassing perspective of anthropology. For this reason, social studies teachers can use anthropology to enrich their own understanding of the curriculum or to stimulate students to a fuller comprehension of these fields. We should view anthropology as a way to study human life and as an analytical tool that one can pick up for brief use or hold for more constant study. Anthropology can also be a valuable testing ground for generalizations drawn by other disciplines.

In the past, anthropology tended to be an esoteric study concerned with racial classifications and the descriptions of exotic peoples. During the past half-century, however, anthropology has moved toward the analysis of cultural practices and values. Anthropology emphasizes cross-cultural comparisons.

These comparisons and generalizations can help us become more objective toward groups in our own society as well as those of differing cultural backgrounds.

Malcolm Collier, who first made the connection between social studies and anthropology in 1971 in *Social Sciences in the Schools: A Search for Rationale,* makes the following statement on anthropology and teaching:

> The social studies program in the secondary school frequently incorporates a selection of the data and concepts fundamental to anthropology, but only recently have formal courses in anthropology been offered in our nation's high schools. But how much can we give the children, in view of the realities of the classroom and of the social studies curriculum? The menu for the whole banquet could be rich to the point of indigestibility.
>
> . . .The data of anthropology have this crucial potential: they come from the period of human history before national history, before even ethnic history, and can serve the purpose of establishing a common background of the species. (Collier, 1971)

Basic Concepts and Questions from Anthropology

Human   Humans are a species of gregarious mammals sharing most physical and behavioral characteristics with other mammals but differing from all other animals.

Over thousands of years, human societies have incorporated these features into rich and varied sociocultural systems.

Needs   Like all animals, humans need air, food, warmth, sleep, exercise, and mates. Humans meet these needs within social groups.

Culture   Culture is a set of patterned behaviors learned by individuals within a social group. Cultures usually persist through generations and define the basic needs and secondary wants and how people can satisfy them.

Cultural Universals   Cultural universals are behaviors that meet basic needs and that are present in every human society. These include the following:

   a. *Language*
   b. *Formal relationships*
   c. *Economic structure based on exchange*
   d. *Social norms*
   e. *Rituals*
   f. *Technologies*
   g. *Arts*
   h. *Methods of handling illness*
   i. *Worldviews*

Cultural Ecology This involves interdependence and interaction of a human society with its habitat.

Cultural Change Because neither the habitat nor the social, political, or economic condition of a society is ever completely stable, societies must innovate or eliminate behaviors to maintain a successful adaptation to their environments.

Before leaving anthropology, it might be interesting to apply some of the concepts, questions, and methods to some institutions that are familiar to us. Perhaps we can obtain greater insight into these institutions by applying anthropological content. Look at families, school, work, play, and so on. You can continue the list until you come across something that interests you. Using a comparison among people in two or more different cultures, such as Japan, United States, or Mexico, try to develop generalizations from questions such as the following:

- What are the needs of the society and how are they met through institutions?
- What are the norms of these societies?
- What rituals do these societies practice?
- How are these societies changing?
- What special language do these societies use?
- How do these societies use technologies?
- What commonalties and differences do these societies have with each other?

Economics

Economics is a policy science. It is the disciplined inquiry of making rational choices about limited resources and unlimited wants. It is the study of how society chooses to produce and distribute goods and services in a world of scarce resources. Economics helps us understand these choices and the trade-offs or opportunity costs that are part of every decision. There are two classic types of economic systems. A market economy is where decisions about production and distribution are made in decentralized markets by more or less independent actors. A command economy is where these kinds of decisions are made by central planners.

Economists view the world from two vantage points: micro-economics and macro-economics. Micro-economics addresses decisions made by individuals and firms: How much should our company produce? How many employees should we hire? What percentage of my income should I save this year? Macro-economics addresses broad national and international issues: What are the causes of inflation? How much will the economy grow this year? What can we expect with regard to unemployment rates?

Basic Concepts and Questions from Economics

The Basic Economic Problem   The basic economic problem of any society deals with the questions and trade-offs of what to produce, how to produce it, and who shall receive the goods and services that are created.

- What does it mean to have limited resources and relatively unlimited wants?
- Is scarcity the central problem from which all other economic problems flow? Why?
- Why does scarcity result in decisions and choices?
- How do personal economic choices affect the national economy?
- What are the basic issues involved in deciding what to produce, how to produce, and for whom?
- How does one's own values system help to determine what the economy will produce and consume?
- Why do available resources help an economy determine what to produce and how to produce it?
- What is the proper mix of private enterprise and government intervention?

Economic Systems and Resource Allocation   All economic systems have markets that are controlled either by individuals as they make personal decisions about what to buy or by government. That is, in the individual or free market, prices are set by the supply and demand of the goods or services in question. In the government or controlled market, prices are set by the state.

Economic systems are concerned with goods and services and how efficiently and effectively these are produced and distributed. Since every society faces limited resources and unlimited wants, the system helps to determine what goods and services will be produced with what resources using what organizational arrangement. Typical questions asked include the following:

- How does the private enterprise system work? What is the role of free choice by individuals in our society?
- How does supply and demand in the marketplace help set prices?

Economic Stability and Growth   Economies are inclined to move up and down, that is, move between boom and bust. The people, through government, try to develop policies that will better control these business cycles. This is done through taxes (fiscal policy) and by controlling the supply of money (monetary policy). The government also regulates parts of the economy to protect human health and to foster competition.

- What are the major functions of money?
- What are the roles and effects of the Federal Reserve System?

- What are inflation and recession, stagnation and depression, in economic, political, and social terms?
- What are some of the limitations of monetary policy?
- What is fiscal policy?
- How does government intervention and regulation affect free trade?

Measurement Concepts   Since there are a great deal of data to collect and study, economists must use numbers and mathematical formulas. They then communicate ideas about the economy so that individuals and the government can make better policies.

- What measurement tools do economists use for visual presentations of economics data?
- How do data displayed in numeric form help us to understand economic trends and conditions?

Evaluating Economic Actions and Policies   Economic policies must always be evaluated. There are always trade-offs to be made and people must be able to judge the economic actions of individuals, families, and governments.

- What is an economic goal?
- How do economic goals function in the political process?
- What is the relationship between economic freedom and an orderly government?
- Why do economic choices usually imply a trade-off among desirable goals?
- Why are concepts of equity, justice, opportunity, and perceived security all a part of economic decision making?
- What is the role and function of the individual consumer?

Geography

"Geography" comes from a Greek word meaning *description or study of the earth*. Geographers strive to understand the spatial arrangements of items on the earth. In addition, they study the causes and consequences of such arrangements. More important, modern geography is the study of *people* and their relationships to the earth. Thus, geography provides us with a spatial link between people and the earth, and all items on the earth in their varied locations and interactions. Geographers study the interconnections among physical features of the land, biological characteristics of the area, and human societies that reside there.

Geographers use many research tools. They are, in some cases, similar to other social and physical science methods, but geographers have special expertise in using maps to portray and study a variety of locations. Reading, interpreting, and making maps are skills integral to geographic education. Geographers must also use a variety of data sources such as the census, field work, questionnaires, aerial photography, and remotely sensed images (*Guidelines for Geographic Education: Elementary and Secondary Schools,* Joint Committee on Geographic Education, 1984, p. 2).

Basic Concepts and Questions from Geography

The National Council for Geographic Education (NCGE) and the Association of American Geographers (AAG) have also identified five fundamental themes in geography that all social studies programs should incorporate. They are location, place, human/environmental interactions, movement, and regions.

Location: Position on the Earth's Surface

- How can absolute and relative location describe the positions of people and places on the earth's surface?

Absolute Location: We can identify locations as precise points on the earth's surface by using an arbitrary, mathematical grid system of latitude and longitude.

Relative Location: We can identify the location of one point on the globe in relationship to another. For example, Mexico is south of the United States and north of Guatemala.

Place: Physical and Human Characteristics

- How do we give meaning and character to all places on the earth and distinguish them from other places?

People perceive characteristics of places according to their experiences or points of view. For example, we can describe the Central American isthmus as a tropical, mountainous region connecting North and South America; a region beset with political and social turmoil; an active volcanic region; a source of tropical agriculture products; a blend of Hispanic and Indian cultures; a collection of small, independent nations; examples of third-world development in the Western Hemisphere; or a source of difficulties in American foreign policy. Taken together, the physical and human characteristics of places help us understand the interactions between people and their environments.

Human/Environmental Interactions: Relationship with Places

- What factors give places on earth advantages and disadvantages for human settlement?

People continue to modify or adapt to natural settings in ways that reveal their cultural values, economic and political circumstances, and technological abilities.

Movement: Humans Interacting on the Earth

- How and why do humans interact with each other over the earth?

Spatial interaction can be as simple as a student's morning bus trip from home to school or as complex as assembling wood from Oregon, natural rubber from Malaysia, graphite from Mexico, tin from Bolivia, and paint produced in factories around the United States to manufacture pencils in Pennsylvania.

Regions: How They Form and Change

- Why is the *region* the basic unit of geographic study?

Geographers have developed regions as tools to study the human and physical environment. Geographers can delimit regions for specific purposes. Geographers in Texas defined the "I-35 corridor" as a region of population growth and economic development lying between Austin and San Antonio.

Regions perform a multitude of functions in geographic education. They define both convenient and manageable units upon which to build our knowledge of the world. They provide a context for studying current events. We may view regions as an intermediate step between our knowledge of local places and our knowledge of the entire planet. Eventually they help us to see the earth as an integrated system of places that we can comprehend as a planetary ecosystem (*Guidelines for Geographic Education: Elementary and Secondary Schools,* 1984, pp. 3–8).

History

History is a recorded narrative describing change and continuity over time through cause-and-effect relationships based upon available evidence and the author's frame of reference. Historians attempt to find out not only what happened, but also why it happened. History is the most studied and, perhaps, the least understood of the social studies subjects. During the last 100 years, it has also changed enormously in two fundamental ways. First of all, historians have changed their basic methods to include more behavioral science concepts and techniques, from psychohistory to historical demography. Also they are employing more quantification methods from the use of statistical analysis to new theoretical concepts drawn from economics and political science. Second, its content base in the United States has expanded to go beyond Western Civilization to include Africa, Asia, and Latin America. At the same time, historical content has become more specialized. Historians address such areas as women in history, the history of medicine, history of the common people, histories of minority groups, and labor history. Over the last half century, this special focus of many historians has come to be known as social history. We can find elements of social history in almost all history textbooks and in such publications as the College Board's *Academic Preparation in Social Studies* (Banks, 1986). Historians have tried to maintain their classical art of narrative explanation while experimenting with the more analytic prose of the social sciences.

Basic Concepts and Questions from History

With this background in mind, a closer look reveals that the discipline of history is structured upon such important concepts as evidence, frame of reference, record, cause-and-effect relationships, chronology, narrative, continuity, and change. Some powerful questions considered by historians include the following:

- How can a topic, issue, theme, or event best be conceptualized?
- What defines a historical period?
- What constitutes primary and secondary evidence?
- How do historians handle cause-and-effect relationships in a narrative explanation? Is the logic valid? Why? Why not?
- What biases or points of view seem to move the narrative?
- How well does the author place the story in time and space frameworks?
- How well does the historian explain complexities of relationships?
- Is the story compelling enough to invite the reader's attention?

Philosophy

The word "philosophy" in Western cultures is derived from ancient Greece and means *the pursuit of wisdom.* It was a general concept that stood for the pursuit of mental excellence. Of course, the two individuals who stand out in this early period are Plato and Socrates. In fact, Plato's *Dialogues* and the Socratic method are synonymous with philosophy.

In Western intellectual history, philosophy was the primary discipline. Early scholars recognized no division of knowledge. It is from philosophy that the other disciplines emerge.

Basic Concepts and Questions from Philosophy

The wisdom that philosophers pursue is what ties us to our cultural heritage and allows us to build the moral framework that gives meaning to human life. That framework consists of cultural concepts such as *justice, love, courage,* and *beauty.* Furthermore, wisdom helps deal with conditions that are dangerous to the human spirit such as arrogance, certainty, and loneliness. Philosophers probe these areas of human dilemmas and desires to help us gain meaning for the activities of our lives.

Meaning cuts through to the moral bone of society, baring the collective nerve and exposing the following questions: Who rules? Why? What rules should we follow? Why should we obey them? Will obeying rules lead me to the good life? These are the types of questions philosophers raise and try to answer. Other questions of common concern within the field include the following:

- What is virtue?
- Can virtue be taught?
- What is the nature of good and evil?
- What is the difference between knowledge of human nature and knowledge of the world?
- Is bad conduct mostly the consequence of ignorance?

- Given our history, how can we express hope for the future of human societies?
- Does ordinary law-abiding behavior come in part from a belief in the existence of divine law?
- When may the individual justly heed a "higher" law than that of the state?
- What is the difference between the good person and the good citizen?
- What price should individuals be prepared to pay for their ethical commitments?

Political Science

Like economics, political science is a policy science. It is the study of how societies allocate their power, resources, and values through their governmental systems. Governments are created to fulfill the human desire for order and stability. Political scientists also study the different ways in which people have organized their political systems and the value positions behind these systems. Each society determines its own interests and then creates the rules to meet them. Governments apply these rules in widely different ways from regulating speed on our highways to redistributing society's wealth or from making war to issuing fishing licenses.

Political science also includes the study of the structure of local, state, national, and international governments, how they function, and how they raise and spend money. Political scientists also study the political behavior of people to see how and why they act the way they do within a political system, be that system a family, school, city, nation, or business.

Basic Concepts and Questions from Political Science

Political System   A political system is created by people to maintain some degree of order and stability. A political system tries to make public decisions to solve problems collectively that cannot be solved individually.

- How does a local political system allocate values?
- How does a global political system allocate values?

Power   Power is the ability to make authoritative decisions within a political system.

- Where does the authority to use power originate?

Influence   Influence is the ability to help determine decisions made by those in power.

- How do individuals and groups attempt to influence governmental decisions?

Legitimacy   Legitimacy or the right to rule within a democratic form of government comes from the people.

- How do "the authorities" of a political community gain the right to rule?

Law   Laws are the rules of conduct established by people to control the behavior for some set of public principles.

- How are laws related to the religion, customs, and ideology of a people? (History)

Psychology

Psychology is one of the sciences that, along with anthropology and sociology, addresses human behavior. From the Greek, "psychology" means *the study of the mind,* and in the present context deals with what individuals and groups think, feel, and do. Psychologists study the behavior of people to gain insight into one's self and others. They describe and explain human interests and actions. As with other sciences, psychology raises more questions than it answers, but the appealing aspect of psychological study is its self-analysis and human focus. All of us, in one way or another, are people watchers, and psychology gives us a system for understanding what we see and experience.

Psychology is also a land divided. It is relatively easy to identify the following four frameworks or "schools" within psychology: humanists, behavioralists, structuralists, and Freudians. These different schools tend to see the individual as a spiritual need-fulfiller, a complex machine, a thinker, and a biological need-fulfiller, respectively. These categories are not mutually exclusive and all psychologists agree on the need to link motives with behavior and the need to study the relationships between environment and inherited traits. Most important, psychologists all practice the scientific arts. That is, their methods include replication and the basic principles and techniques of descriptive and inferential statistics.

It is important to note several key areas of tension and research within the field. For example, there is the debate over the biological versus environmental basis of behavior. Some psychologists emphasize the inborn, innate causes of behavior, and others the external events that influence development. They state these issues in terms of nature versus nurture, nativism versus empiricism, and heredity versus environment. Second, there is the conflict between behavioralists and phenomenologists. Some psychologists stress a strict empirical analysis of behavior, while others emphasize internal subjective experience. Third, there are those who believe in universal laws of behavior while others stress individual uniqueness.

Basic Concepts and Questions from Psychology

Personality Personality is that distinctive pattern of thought, feelings, and actions that help define the individual. There are three major theories that address personality development: the conflict model, where personality is shaped by the tensions between the individual and the group or by antagonistic forces within the individual; the consistency model, where personality is shaped by the individual's attempt to maintain consistent feedback from the community or group; and the fulfillment model, where personality is shaped by one great force within the person.

- How can knowledge of personality theories help teachers?
- Can personality be changed?
- What is deviant behavior?
- How are people motivated?

Perception Every individual sees the world in a unique way. Perceptions of the world are based upon our families, our history, our geography, our personalities, our goals, our communities, and our culture. Perception and our ability to communicate with one another are closely related.

- Why do different people see the world differently?
- Can we communicate better if we understand another person's "world view"?
- How are perceptions and learning related?

Sociology

Sociology is the science of understanding society in a disciplined way. Several other disciplines also study human relationships. These include anthropology, history, psychology, economics, and political science. What makes sociology distinct from the other social sciences is its focus upon social relationships at the group or societal level and its attempts to discover patterns in human group behaviors. However, sociologists also study behavior at the individual level. They examine properties of the social group (norms, roles, and status) and the influences they exert upon the individual. Sociologists observe and describe societies and generate theories about why these societies function in that way. They study such social phenomena as crime, family structures, and alcohol and drug abuse; they also develop theories that political, business, and social leaders can use.

The scientific method of formulating and testing hypotheses and constructing theories to explain and predict human social behavior better is the core of sociological inquiry. Therefore, sociologists rely upon a variety of research methods including experiments, case studies, and analysis of available data. They use such sources as census reports, crime records, public opinion polls, historical information, and cross-cultural observations.

Two common research methods that sociologists use are survey research and field observation. They use field observations to test and build theories and they call this method participant observation. Using this method, the sociologist enters a group or institution and tries to view the world from the perspective of the people being studied.

Basic Concepts and Questions from Sociology

Socialization   Socialization is the process of learning the *roles,* rules, relationship patterns, and culture of a society. Within this process we learn about *social stratification, status,* and how *institutions* help meet basic needs within the structure of society.

- How can changes in technology change the nature of social institutions?
- How are people and social institutions protected as well as victimized by culture and cultural change?
- How do various institutions help people meet their basic physical, psychological, economic, political, and social needs?
- What role do norms, values, and rules play in the establishment and functioning of an institution?
- Why may a person play several roles in the course of a day?
- How do social values, norms, and rules influence gender roles and minority status?
- How is status granted within a culture or institution?
- How do individuals become members of a group?
- How does the dominant culture socialize immigrants?
- How does schooling socialize youth into the larger society while retaining the individual's cultural uniqueness?
- Why and how do hierarchical structures operate in society?

Social Scientists and the Social Sciences

Now that we have briefly discussed each of the social sciences we need to consider how social scientists gather and interpret information and data. Social scientists attempt to discover and explain behavior patterns in individuals and groups. These explanations usually take the form of theories and generalizations that can be transferred from one situation to another. This might sound as if the major task of the social scientist is gathering information and building knowledge into theory. However, social scholars from John Stuart Mill (1867) to John Madge (1965) have advanced the idea that doing science is its own reward, and knowledge is simply the residue of inquiry. For at its best, science, as an attempt to solve practical problems and acquire knowledge, is the by-product of the scientist's search. If social scientists create theories, they see these as interesting and tentative models that help define the boundaries of a particular field and its relationship to other disciplines. For example, an understanding of the theory of supply and demand can help simplify the real world of the marketplace. The theory helps solve such problems as how to stop the wild fluctuations of the international monetary system. As scientists address the problem, they advance a theory and make it more sophisticated, perhaps, which might lead to new theories of the market.

Social scientists seek consistency and truth. Therefore, they build hypotheses about how the world works by generalizing from previous observations. Social science requires skill in the collection, organization, and communication of data. It takes imagination, creativity, and plain old hard work. Above all, it takes a commitment to the standards of the community of scholars who work in the field.

One of the major differences between the natural and social sciences is the way in which objectivity is perceived. Certainly, the pursuit of "objective" truth is futile in all philosophy and science, but the pursuit of objective truth in the social sciences is even more futile. At best, objectivity in the social sciences is an agreed-upon subjectivity. In other words, knowledge is always limited by the scientist's or observer's incomplete perspective. However, when a group or community shares common standards, they will also tend to reach agreement on questions of fact. Karl Mannheim (1936) called this phenomenon the "sociology of knowledge."

Social science inquiry always faces problems and conflicts of fact, definition, and values. For example, consider the task of formulating public policy for solid waste:

> Issue: How to handle the tons of garbage being generated from a particular city
> Factual Problem: How much garbage is there?
> How is it presently disposed of?
> What are the environmental dangers this disposal poses? How long will it take to contaminate the ground water?

What alternative solutions for disposal exist?
How will changes in the way garbage is handled affect the local economy?
Definitional Problem: What is a safe level for the percolation of contaminants into the ground water?
When does something become a contaminant?
Value Issues: Should people change their lifestyles or habits so that they produce less waste?
Should businesses be required to use biodegradable packaging?
Should certain industries that produce toxic waste by-products be closed down?

Social scientists will use many different methods to address the problems stated above. The most common things that social scientists do to gather and interpret data include studying documents, observing behavior, interviewing people, sampling populations, conducting controlled experiments, using statistical analysis, establishing longitudinal or long-term studies, and writing personal narratives. Whenever social scientists confront a problem or want to build or test a generalization they will often use several of the methods cited above. These are also methods that teachers should use in social studies instruction.

As social scientists collect information they organize it according to pre-established hypotheses. They then present the information in many forms using numbers, pictures, charts, and words to report on the social phenomenon under study.

The relationship between the social sciences and social studies education is direct. That is, since the major goal of social studies is citizenship, the social sciences must be used to provide the reservoirs of knowledge and methods necessary for students to develop their policy-making abilities, their historical and geographic perspectives, and their understanding of self, others, and social institutions. These are all necessary conditions for enlightened citizenship, and unless social studies teachers are well grounded in one or more of these disciplines it will be difficult to teach toward this goal.

Take, for example, the role of the social sciences in the skills of policy making. There are four general abilities and dispositions needed to develop policies. These include the following: 1) *envisioning,* that is, the identification, development, and evaluation of the social theories, principles, or preferred states of being toward which an individual or society wants to move; 2) *assessing the present situation,* including historical trends, quantitative information, and qualitative impressions related to the issue at hand; 3) *constructing, evaluating,* and *implementing policies;* and 4) *evaluating* the preferred state (principles) so that mid-course corrections can be implemented. Thus, being a citizen of our republic means that the student/citizen is a clear thinker, possesses important social science knowledge, and has the inclination to become involved in civic affairs.

Social Studies and Other Content Areas

If one reflects awhile upon the goals and purposes of social studies education, it becomes clear that there is a need to expand beyond the scope of the social science disciplines. The social studies must embrace the arts and humanities as well as mathematics and science. Since we are trying to understand people and their institutions we must use all areas of disciplined study that allow us to gain a comprehensive view. Therefore, social studies teachers must expand beyond the social science disciplines to gain the perspectives that the arts, humanities, mathematics, and sciences offer.

It may well be that the arts, including music, can give us the most honest assessment of human achievements, past and present. Literature is the first cousin to history, and any attempt to understand human motives and behavior without giving careful attention to the humanities would be like trying to understand baseball by simply reading the rule book. Without observation or participation in the drama of baseball the rules in a book are one-dimensional. The humanities can provide drama, accuracy, and passion to social studies. They afford us a creative extension from ourselves to the others both past and present who share the earth with us. The humanities provide a sense of wholeness and connectedness that might otherwise be missing. Art, music, and literature are metaphorical in their presentation and therefore, the most important idea is that the humanities can help us see more clearly our social and individual values. For example, literature such as John Steinbeck's *The Grapes of Wrath,* Woody Guthrie's music, and photographs taken at the time can illuminate the human side of the 1930s and help us feel closer to these people. Those social studies teachers who use the humanities make their classes more exciting and more real.

Two other fields that are important to systematic social study today are mathematics and science. The social sciences are making more and more use of statistical analysis, computers, and other technologies. Numbers and their manipulation are necessary to social studies methodologies. Consider the national polls that assess the popularity of the president or the most popular television programs. Or think about the databases ranging from census information to commodity markets. In these and many, many other instances, mathematics is important to the study of society (Hartoonian, 1989).

Science, as a way of thinking, has already greatly influenced the methods of the social sciences. However, it is becoming clearer that contemporary social issues almost always have scientific or technological dimensions. These call for a sophisticated mix of social and scientific knowledge and skills. From issues of war and peace, to acid rain, to genetic engineering, we are seeing more evidence for combining the knowledge and methods of science with the social studies. This is the case simply because we can address more comprehensively the important issues that emerge when we bring these two areas of study together.

The core of the social studies remains the traditional disciplines of history, geography, anthropology, economics, philosophy, political science, psychology, and sociology. However, it is evident that social studies teachers will have to work more closely with teachers from other academic areas in order to provide students a more complete and realistic picture of their world. Most important, however, is the understanding by social studies teachers that *all* these areas of study provide methods, knowledge, and ways of viewing the world that can help meet the major goal of social studies—citizenship.

SUMMARY

In this chapter we considered the nature of knowledge and what knowledge is most worthwhile. The subject matter of the social studies disciplines is more complex and far richer than any explanatory model or general description of the subjects. This complexity is due in part to the structures and methods of the disciplines. However, the communities of scholars and students who work with these disciplines also contribute to this complexity. These groups use the disciplines to form public policy, to make better social and personal decisions and to articulate new structures in the several disciplines. The knowledge that is of most worth is knowledge that can be used to understand personal and social issues. This knowledge comes from books, media, lectures, discussions with colleagues, simulation activities, and personal experiences. But, we must always remember that knowledge is created and becomes real for us when we see some use and meaning for it.

The several disciplines of the social studies that you have just reviewed exhibit complexity and richness. However, for these academic subjects to be useful to you and your students, you must be able to go beyond the lists of concepts, questions, and descriptions of knowledge. Create your own patterns of knowledge. You must use the concepts, questions, and methodologies in serious life situations directed toward a greater understanding of personal and social issues.

If you expect to develop a high level of integrity as a social studies teacher, then you must be able to see relationships or patterns within the disciplines you are using and between your disciplines and other academic areas.

Discussion Questions

1. Many of our major cities are facing problems like crime, riots, poor health care, and inadequate education. How can content from the social sciences help you construct policies to solve these problems?
2. How are the concepts of social science and social studies related to one another?
3. Do you believe that there are any differences between social science knowledge and natural science knowledge? What are they?
4. Do you think that social studies is a single discipline, an integrated area of study, or a school curriculum area that includes several single and integrated disciplines? Explain your reasons.

Student Learning Activities

1. Conduct two sets of interviews: one with history and/or social science faculty at a college or university and a second with middle or high school teachers of social studies. Develop a set of four or five questions for the interviews that address such items as
   a. their definitions of knowledge in the social studies disciplines;
   b. their views on the major future trends in their areas of study;
   c. their perceptions on whether the discipline is becoming narrower or more expansive in its scope;
   d. their concern with what students know in the social studies discipline;
   e. their theories on the best ways for students to learn social knowledge; and
   f. their understanding of how social studies can help in their own lives.

   Take the information from the interviews and see if teachers and social scientists view knowledge in the same way. Why? Why not?
2. The social studies disciplines include the following:

Anthropology	Economics
Geography	History
Philosophy	Political Science
Psychology	Sociology

   Think about how the eight social studies disciplines are alike and different. Working in small groups, place the eight disciplines in two or more categories based upon common attributes of the subject area.

Explain why you placed each discipline in the category you did and label the category.
3. Develop an annotated bibliography of at least one book or article from each of the social studies disciplines. Pick books that address the general nature of the discipline as opposed to special topics within the discipline. By sharing your reading list with classmates you should generate a more comprehensive bibliography for your use as a teacher/scholar.
4. Choose a friend or colleague and present to her or him your definitions of at least two of the social studies disciplines. For example, consider the following questions.

What is history?
How do you learn history?
How should history be taught?

NOTES

The Nature of Social Knowledge

In this textbook we define various terms as follows:

Generalizations: A generalization is a statement that shows relationships among concepts. There are two types of generalizations, synthetic and analytical. Synthetic generalizations are conditional statements that usually state cause-and-effect relationships. For example, if prices of a commodity increase, we can expect the amount of that commodity purchased to decrease. An analytical generalization is definitional in that it helps define a general class of ideas, people, and things. For example, all places on the globe have absolute and relative location.

Concepts: A concept is a category or set in which items with similar attributes or characteristics can be placed. Unlike synthetic generalizations, concepts cannot be proved true or false. They are labels or names given to a set that help us to simplify or classify our environment. Thus, we use concepts to identify, categorize, and communicate whole sets of phenomena. For example, the label "cities" may include notions such as political region, houses, commercial districts, government, transportation, stores, and so on. Concepts we commonly use in social studies are culture, community, nation, scarcity, habitat, change, tradition, and place.

Fact: Facts are pieces of information that have been verified objectively. Concepts are the labels we give to groups of facts that satisfy particular conditions. Sometimes facts may also be used as concepts, such as house, human, or animal.

References

Banks, J. 1986. *Academic Preparation in Social Studies: Teaching for Transition from High School to College.* New York: College Entrance Examination Board.

Bragaw, D. H. and Hartoonian, H. M. 1988. "Social Studies: The Study of People in Society." In R. S. Brandt (Ed.), *Content of the Curriculum,* ASCD Yearbook. Alexandria, VA: Association for Supervision and Curriculum Development.

Collier, M. 1971. "The Forgotten Discipline: Anthropology." In I. Morrissett and W. W. Stevens, Jr. (Eds.), *Social Sciences in the Schools: A Search for Rationale.* New York: Holt, Rinehart and Winston.

Hartoonian, H. M. 1989. "Social Mathematics." In M. A. Laughlin, H. M. Hartoonian and N. M. Sanders (Eds.), *From Information to Decision Making: New Challenges for Effective Citizenship,* NCSS Bulletin No. 83. Washington, DC: National Council for the Social Studies.

Hunt, M. P. and Metcalf, L. E. 1955. *Teaching High School Social Studies.* New York: Harper & Brothers.

Joint Committee on Geographic Education. 1984. *Guidelines for Geographic Education: Elementary and Secondary Schools.* Washington, DC: Association of American Geographers and National Council for Geographic Education.

Mannheim, K. 1936. *Ideology and Utopia: An Introduction to the Sociology of Knowledge.* L. Wirth and E. Shils, (trans.). New York: Harcourt Brace.

Madge, J. 1965. *The Tools of Social Sciences: An Analytical Description of Social Science Techniques.* Garden City, NY: Anchor Books.

Mill, J. S. 1867. "On Liberty." In J. Bentham (Ed.), *The Utilitarians: An Introduction to the Principles of Morals and Legislation,* 1961. Garden City, NY: Doubleday.

Plato. ND. "Dialogues." In J. Edman (Ed.) and B. Jowett (Trans.), *The Works of Plato,* Vol. 2. New York: Tudor.

Additional Readings

American Association for the Advancement of Science. 1989. *Project 2061: Social and Behavioral Sciences.* Washington, DC: American Association for the Advancement of Science.

Boulding, K. E. 1985. *The World As a Total System.* Beverly Hills, CA: Sage.

Easton, D. 1971. *The Political System: An Inquiry into the State of Political Science.* 2nd ed. New York: Knopf.

Gilliard, J., Caldwell, J., Dalgaard, B. R., Highsmith, R. J., Reinke, R., and Watts, M. 1988. *Economics: What and When. Scope and Sequence Guidelines, K–12.* New York: Joint Council for Economic Education.

Giroux, H. 1984. "Public Philosophy and the Crisis in Education." *Harvard Educational Review,* Vol. 54, No. 2, May. 186–194.

Hunt, M. P. and Metcalf, L. E. 1968. *Teaching High School Social Studies: Problems in Reflective Thinking and Social Understanding* (2nd ed.). New York: Harper and Row.

Jenness. D. 1990. *Making Sense of Social Studies.* New York: Macmillan.

Kaplan, A. 1964. *The Conduct of Inquiry: Methodology for Behavioral Science.* San Francisco, CA: Chandler.

Kuhn, T. S. 1962. *The Structure of Scientific Revolutions.* Chicago: University of Chicago Press.

McNeill, L. M. 1981. "Negotiating Classroom Knowledge: Beyond Achievement and Socialization," *Journal of Curriculum Studies,* Vol. 13, No. 4., October–December. 313–328.

McNeill, L. M. 1986. *Contradictions of Control: School Structure and School Knowledge*. New York: Routledge and Kegan Paul.

National Commission on Social Studies in the Schools. 1989. *Charting a Course: Social Studies for the 21st Century*. Washington, DC: National Commission on Social Studies in the Schools.

Ravitch, D. 1983. *The Troubled Crusade: American Education 1945–1980*. New York: Basic Books.

Ricci, D. 1984. *The Tragedy of Political Science: Politics, Scholarship, and Democracy*. New Haven, CT: Yale University Press.

Sanders, N. M. 1966. *Classroom Questions: What Kinds?* New York: Harper and Row.

Saunders, P., Bach, G. L., Calderwood, J. D., and Hansen, W. L. 1984. *Master Curriculum Guide in Economics: A Framework for Teaching Economics Basic Concepts* (2nd ed). New York: Joint Council for Economic Education.

Smith, F. 1986. *Insult to Intelligence: The Bureaucratic Invasion of Our Classrooms*. New York: Arbor House.

Steinbeck, J. 1986. *Grapes of Wrath*. New York: Penguin Books.

Wronski, S. P. and Bragaw, D. H. (Eds.). 1986. *Social Studies and Social Sciences: A Fifty-Year Perspective*. Bulletin No. 78. Washington, DC: National Council for the Social Studies.

America is woven of many strands; I would recognize them and let it so remain. . . . Our fate is to become one, and yet many.

Ralph Ellison

CHAPTER 4

Characteristics and Organizational Patterns of Social Studies

FOCUS QUESTIONS

- What are some positive and negative perceptions of social studies?
- How are social studies programs organized?
- What is a typical curriculum pattern for K–12 social studies programs?
- How does social studies content seem to reflect a changing society?
- How can social studies content help form a bridge to other content areas?
- Why are curriculum and communication closely related ideas?

OVERVIEW

Every social studies teacher has a responsibility to understand the total K–12 social studies curriculum. We need to know something about the content presented to our students before they arrive in our classes and to have some notion of the learning experiences they will receive after they leave us. While the organization of social studies content into courses and instructional units is a fundamental responsibility of social studies educators, the design of any specific social studies scope and sequence is the result of educational and political decisions made at the national, state, local, and classroom levels. Without a clear understanding and involvement in this process you can not hope to be a true professional educator.

The fundamental purpose of curriculum is to ensure that students have an educationally justifiable series of courses and concepts. At the local level, teachers plan curriculum by discussing why, what, and how they teach, as well as how the curriculum impacts students. This is a dynamic activity that also enables teachers to grow in their own understanding of content and the learning process.

The Major Characteristics of Social Studies

Teachers in all curriculum areas must answer four fundamental questions when organizing their programs. What does society expect us to achieve? What knowledge is unique to our area? How do we deal with the developmental stages of our students? What are the ideal learning environments? The answers to these questions show what is unique about each curriculum area.

All social studies teachers have their own ideas about the unique characteristics of social studies. They base these ideas on their experiences in social studies classrooms and on the thinking of the larger educational community. At the present time we can observe several negative and positive perceptions that people have about social studies. No doubt you could add to these lists.

Negative Perceptions
- Social studies programs are boring.
- There are too many graduation requirements in the social studies sequence.
- The content of social studies has little to do with today's issues and today's students.
- Social studies teachers do not really stress democratic citizenship in their classroom practices.
- Textbooks tend to be outdated.

Positive Perceptions
- The content of social studies is inherently interesting.
- The learning activities available to social studies teachers can truly engage students.
- Social studies can provide a fertile ground for teaching thinking and other skills.
- Social studies can provide a rich content for teaching time and space perspectives.

- Social studies has the potential to deal successfully with students of all interests and abilities.
- Social studies can provide an organized way to study the persistent questions of our culture and the immediate issues of contemporary society.

Take a few minutes and construct your own list of perceptions of social studies. How can you use these to improve instruction? What assumptions are you making about the nature of knowledge, of society, and of students in your list of perceptions?

Organizing Social Studies Programs

The ideal social studies program should be organized around three interrelated components: (1) knowledge, (2) processes, skills, and abilities, and (3) ethics and values.

A Base for Social Studies

The forces of change in all aspects of living and working have created a new imperative for the schools in their task of educating students. This imperative is that students must become more *knowledgeable* about the conditions, problems, and realities surrounding them, and must, at the same time, become more skillful in applying knowledge and seeing connections between knowledge and the world. Satisfying this demand is complicated because

Figure 4.1 Organizational Structure of the Social Studies Program

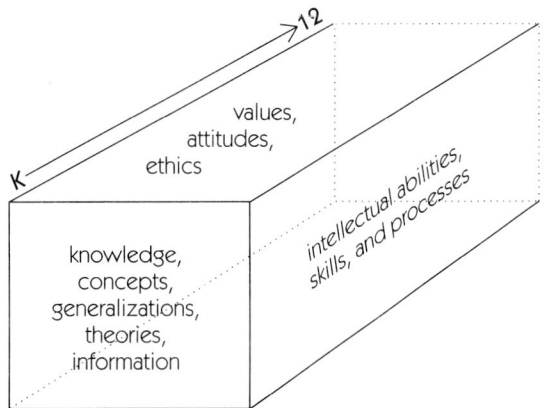

change occurs so rapidly that new knowledge confronts us even before we can understand the past. Besides the linear explosion of knowledge, combinations of new and old knowledge give the knowledge explosion a multidimensional characteristic that compounds the problem further. With each passing year, we can assume that a smaller proportion of knowledge will be learned. Social studies knowledge must be viewed not only as a product but also as a tool to be applied toward solving personal and social problems in a world of constantly accelerating rates of change.

In the time allocated for social studies in the schools, it is crucial that students acquire the most reliable, significant, and transferable units of knowledge and thought—concepts, generalizations, and theories—since these units transform, compress, and organize experience and provide a necessary part of the framework for thinking. Students must then master the most significant concepts, generalizations, and theories of social studies as well as develop reflective skills to learn more, to test what they learn, and to apply what they learn to the development of personal and public policies.

Social studies is concerned with (1) the concepts, generalizations, and theories of a discipline (namely, a conceptual framework) and (2) the methods and procedures utilized by scholars in developing or adding to the fundamentals. To achieve the fullest understanding of this knowledge teachers need to analyze cognitive processes, products, and teaching strategies. Although teachers should recognize the unique nature of each social science discipline, the reflective method is appropriate for all social inquiry and explanation.

Intellectual Abilities, Processes, and Skills

Skills deserve considerable attention throughout the social studies program. These skills include competence to locate and compile information, to present and interpret data, and to organize and evaluate source materials. Social studies teachers have a special responsibility for teaching students how to read materials directly related to the social studies, such as charts, maps, and graphs in newspapers and position statements offered by political officials. Social studies teachers should also teach the skills and methods that historians, geographers, and other social scientists use. Finally, it is necessary to incorporate higher levels of data-research skills such as identifying hypotheses, making warranted inferences, and reading critically. Students can practice all these skills when they engage in meaningful study of real issues and problems of people today and in the past.

Values, Attitudes, and Ethics

Social studies also must deal with the values, attitudes, and ethics that students and teachers bring to the learning situation as well as those studies in historical and present contexts. Social studies confronts complex questions rooted in conflicting attitudes and values. Therefore, it is neither desirable nor possible for social studies teachers to attempt to establish a "value-free" classroom; student behavior and instructional materials both are the products of value-laden judgments. Students must gain experience in discerning fact from opinion, objectivity from bias. They need to learn to identify their own value assumptions along with those of others. They also must learn to project and evaluate consequences of one value stance compared to another. More will be said about this in Chapter 6.

An Integrated Framework

In considering knowledge and the social studies program, the following questions are important:

1. Does the student have the opportunity to practice the craft of social study through involvement in the several levels of thinking such as interpreting and evaluating?
2. Does the student have the opportunity to study the several social studies disciplines and become aware of their uniqueness, subtleties, and interrelationships?
3. Does the student have the opportunity to use social studies knowledge in resolving issues?

From these questions we can generate the following goals:

1. The student has a basic understanding of the cultural heritage and historical significance of the local community, state, and country.
2. The student knows the historical development of the United States of America and recognizes the relationships between past and present conditions.
3. The student understands the fundamental principles of democratic government and the rights and responsibilities of citizens inherent therein.
4. The student knows the interrelationships that exist between our culture and others.
5. The student understands the many contributions made to the United States of America by other cultures and how he or she benefits from these contributions.
6. The student understands that there are persistent problems whenever there is interaction among people, groups, and nations.
7. The student demonstrates commitment to resolving social problems through knowledge and community service.
8. The student demonstrates an understanding of the ideas of others.

9. The student demonstrates an understanding of people from different cultures.
10. The student knows the significance of chronology and has an understanding of the perspectives of time, gender, and class.
11. The students knows how geography significantly influences cultural uniqueness.
12. The student understands the concept of culture in its various forms around the world.
13. The student knows that individual and group behaviors have social, psychological, economic, and political roots and consequences.
14. The student knows that while individual or group behavior is based on past experiences it also can be influenced by what the student thinks will happen in the future.

Students should meet these goals by the end of the twelfth grade.

The ideal social studies program, therefore, should strike a balance and integrate the components of knowledge, skills, and values. The above fourteen goals provide a basic integrative framework for the social studies program.

Curriculum Patterns

The social studies curriculum in any grade has direct implications for the curriculum in all other grades. It is necessary, therefore, that we view the curriculum as a whole.

Curriculum must have a structure that helps make decisions concerning daily schedules, learning activities, instructional resources, and even teacher education. There is no consensus as to which curriculum model is superior or most effective.

Teachers must understand the curriculum framework required in their school in order to build consistency into the experiences of learners. In the final analysis, what happens in the classroom constitutes the curriculum for a particular student. Thus, every social studies curriculum has a degree of freedom, compelling teachers to use their judgment. If teachers do not understand the underlying concepts and design of the curriculum, then they will be unable to plan daily learning activities that complement the curriculum and fulfill its goals.

Scope

Scope serves the important function of helping decide what to teach and what not to teach. Scope describes the themes, topics, and questions in the course content and defines the limits of the learning experiences that the program will include. If this were not so, teachers would be uncertain as to what units to select and how broadly they should deal with them.

Teachers use three general criteria to determine the social studies curriculum scope. They are the social science disciplines, society, and the individual learner.

The *disciplines-oriented* curriculum uses subject matter to establish the scope of the program. This approach relies on the theory that the best way for students to achieve educational objectives is through the mastery of the subject matter. That is, we learn history best by doing what historians do. The *society-oriented* curriculum uses issues and concerns of people as the major criteria for content selection. This approach is based on the belief that students attain educational objectives best by developing competence in solving problems of public policy and social issues. The *individual-oriented* curriculum is structured around the developmental stages of students and their interests. This approach is based on the belief that the best way to achieve educational objectives is to provide for the optimum development of the individual at each phase of his or her growth.

While the three approaches to organizing the social studies curriculum (disciplines-oriented, society-oriented, and individual-oriented) have certain common elements, they each carry different assumptions about (1) the purposes of schooling, (2) the priority of subject matter, (3) the definition of social studies, (4) the way students learn, (5) the roles teachers, students, and communities play, (6) the nature of human beings, and (7) the nature of society. All have their place in the social studies programs, and teachers will build lessons around all these approaches.

Perhaps the most important thing to remember is that major themes such as global perspective, tradition and change, citizenship, and place help define a program's scope. To some degree, any delineation of major themes is arbitrary. The themes, however, should be included at each grade level with increasing sophistication. Although different themes may be emphasized at various levels, they still are included at every grade and may be presented in any coherent order based on the maturity level and ability of the students.

The scope (or major themes and questions) of the social studies curriculum can be pictured as they expand across the total K–12 sequence and bring a sense of unity to the instructional program.

	K 1 2 3 4 5 6 7 8 9 10 11 12
	Citizenship ─────────────▶
	Global Perspectives ──────▶
Scope (Themes)	Place ─────────────────▶
	Change and Tradition ─────▶
	Etc. ──────────────────▶

Sequence

Sequence means that curriculum organization must provide for the continuous development of learning. In determining sequence, curriculum plans give some consideration to (1) maturity and experiences of the learner, (2) student interest, (3) prerequisite learning, and (4) difficulty level.

At the present time the most common K–12 sequence presents an expanding horizon content approach, starting with the immediate, familiar, and concrete environment in the primary grades and moving outward to the more distant and abstract in high school. This pattern will be discussed later in this chapter. A second sequence organization presents a spiral approach where certain concepts or themes are revisited as the program moves through the grade levels. This can be pictured as a spiral where a concept like culture is emphasized at grades K, 3, 6, 10, and 12.

The concept of culture is presented within the context of the developmental levels of the students and the content emphasis at each grade level. In other words, the concept of culture is taught in Kindergarten within the study of people and places around the world; communities such as Cairo are taught at grade 3; Mexico is taught at grade 6 within the study of world geography; Asia is taught at grade 10 within the study of world history; and families are taught at grade 12 within the study of sociology. Sometimes, however, a sequence will be organized in such a way that will suggest units on culture at several grade levels and let the teacher construct his or her own content base building on past learning and experiences in earlier grades.

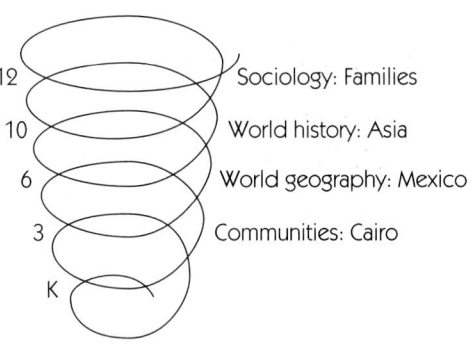

Theme of Culture

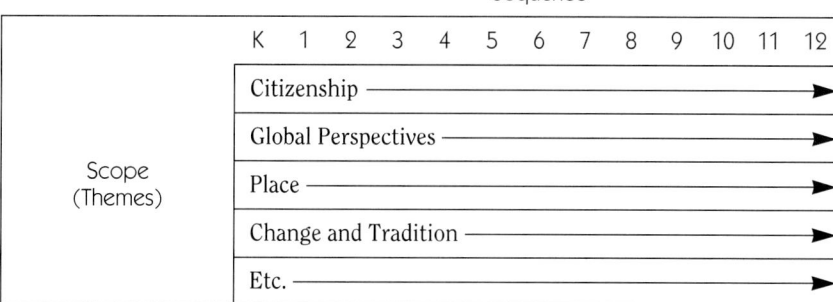

Interrelationships Among Time, Place, and Culture

Students need to study people at different *time* periods—past, present, and future. "Present time" dominates the curriculum from kindergarten through 12th grade, with "past time" being of next significance and "future time" being of least importance.

Place is another basis for scope and sequence. The usual order, based on theories about students' gradual expansion of awareness, is from the immediate to the remote. However, you should note that mass media has blurred the distinctions between immediate and remote environments. The important points to consider relative to "place" are that students have opportunities to study people who live in different places around the world, and they should understand the interrelationships between immediate and remote environments.

Culture as a factor in the determination of scope and sequence emphasizes a growing relationship between the student's culture and the cultures of others.

It is possible to interrelate time, place, and culture in interesting ways. Curriculum designers often take these factors and experiment with them to achieve the best possible balance for student study.

If, for example, the 10th and 11th grades offer courses in United States history and western civilization you may see a chart like the following:

		Time		
		Past	Present	Future
Place	Local	State History	City Government	State and Global Markets
	National	United States History	U.S. Economy	The U.S. in a Global Market
	World	Western and Non-Western History	Cultural Area Studies	Global Environmental Trends

This chart enables you to see the choices you have made about when and where you offer courses, and how these decisions allow you to study different peoples and cultures in time and space. What cultures are you addressing? Which areas of the world do you study? Which areas are left out? This information can create a picture of the balance of the middle and high school programs. For example, how many units deal with local issues of the past, present, and future? State? Nation? World? What are the relationships among the several places that the program includes? Is it possible to understand the present without knowing something about the past? The future? These are all questions that teachers must address if they expect their own instruction to be meaningful.

Scope and sequence is the systematic arrangement of curriculum that helps teachers determine what and how to teach. While the social studies program should be flexible, it is important to note also that every teacher in the district must be committed to the overall K–12 scope and sequence if the total program is to meet its goals. The program must be cumulative in nature, growing in complexity with each new unit of instruction.

Organizing Social Studies Content

As we have seen, the organization of social studies content usually addresses both academic and student-centered criteria that the educational community has established. Therefore, you will see that educators most often organize courses within discrete disciplines such as anthropology, economics, history, geography, philosophy, political science, psychology, and sociology. However, we can also organize content (courses or units) around two or more disciplines that focus on particular issues, themes, cultural groups, public policies, or personal concerns. Some of the course titles that we presently find in social studies include world history, world geography, area studies, United States history, anthropology, sociology, psychology, economics, law-related education, government, civics, philosophy, and contemporary issues.

As you survey the social, economic, and political diversity across the nation, you might assume that the scope and sequence of social studies programs would vary to that same degree. On the contrary, two studies in the earlier 1980s show strong similarities in middle and high school programs nationwide (Project SPAN Staff and Consultants, 1982, and Superka and Hawke, 1980).

Furthermore, since 1980 the sequential patterns of social studies programs within the several states has not changed a great deal (Council of State Social Studies Specialists, 1993, available from the National Council for the Social Studies). However, there are trends in the social studies curriculum of which you should be aware.

Trends Within the K–5 Program

Elementary schools are including more literature and whole-language teaching methods in the social studies programs. Teachers also are making more use of the local community as a learning site to develop observation, thinking, and communication skills. For example, 5th grade students may look at a local solid waste landfill in order to suggest the need for recycling in the community. They would need to study the geography, politics, and economics of the issue and prepare a policy statement for their local government to consider. Finally, there is increased emphasis upon geography and history as organizational frameworks for the social studies sequence in the elementary schools.

Trends Within the Middle School

Perhaps the most important trend in the middle school curriculum is the attention given to pre-adolescent developmental issues like rapid physical growth and peer influences on decision making. Middle schools are also placing greater emphasis on issues, problems, and themes (in-depth study) and giving less attention to content coverage. Continuing the K–5 trends of literature use and local community involvement, middle schools are also giving their students more opportunities to integrate social studies and other content areas to study real-life issues.

Finally, there seems to be a desire to emphasize both global issues and local problems. That is, making connections between the local landfill and global markets/international trade might suggest an issue that middle school students would study. They would bring to such study concepts and skills from several disciplines, and perhaps, develop a public policy statement they could share with local and national officials.

These trends continue to move very slowly. The typical middle school curriculum is still structured around elements of world geography and history as well as state and local history and civics.

Trends Within the High School

There are three significant trends in high school social studies curriculum: integration of world and United States history and geography; increased attention to citizenship as developing skills, attitudes, and knowledge to be better decision and policy makers; and greater emphasis on global, multicultural, and economic issues. These trends are already a part of the curriculum in many schools, and they probably will continue to influence curriculum for the next several years.

In addition, the use of technology seems to be increasing within the social studies curriculum.

Grade	Title of Course
Kindergarten	The Individual and the Group—Now and Long Ago
1	Home, School, and Communities in Time and Space
2	Communities—Local, State, and Nation
3	World Communities
4	State Studies
5	United States Studies—Geography and History
6	Cultural Regions in Time and Space
7	Global Regions—Connections in Time and Space
8	United States History and Citizenship
9	World Geography—Area Studies
10	World History
11	United States History (Some schools will offer a two-year sequence at the 10th and 11th grades in a United States/World History combination.)
12	Government, Economics, and Advanced Social Sciences

A Typical Sequence Pattern

While it is impossible to synthesize fifty or more scope and sequence patterns across the United States and in Canada, we can present a typical pattern. This pattern will be similar to the one you may encounter in your teaching assignment. For the most part these courses are year-long classes.

You might want to consider the above typical sequence in light of the following questions:

1. Given the time allocations in a typical school, what courses would you like to see offered to students in the 6–12 program?
2. How much time do you think should be spent on United States history, world history, geography, economics, and so forth?
3. Can you design a sequence that you feel is more relevant to students today? If so, try constructing such a design.

In an attempt to identify and endorse a scope and sequence to help teachers and others make sense of the social studies curriculum, the National Council for the Social Studies (NCSS) recommended three scope and sequence models. An NCSS Ad Hoc Committee on Scope and Sequence identified twenty-four characteristics that they used to judge several social studies scope and sequence proposals (*Social Education,* October 1989. pp. 375–376). The committee members indicated the following minimum requirements:

A social studies scope and sequence should:

1. State the purpose and rationale of the program;
2. Be internally consistent with its stated purposes and rationale;
3. Designate content at every grade level, K–12;
4. Recognize that learning is cumulative;
5. Reflect a balance of local, national, and global content;
6. Reflect a balance of past, present, and future content;
7. Provide for students' understanding of the structure and function of social, economic, and political institutions;
8. Emphasize concepts and generalizations from history and the social sciences;
9. Promote the integration of skills and knowledge;
10. Promote the integration of content across subject areas;
11. Promote the use of a variety of teaching methods and instructional materials;
12. Foster active learning and social interaction;
13. Reflect a clear commitment to democratic beliefs and values;
14. Reflect a global perspective;
15. Foster the knowledge and appreciation of cultural heritage;
16. Foster the knowledge and appreciation of diversity;
17. Foster the building of self-esteem;
18. Be consistent with current research pertaining to how children learn;
19. Be consistent with current scholarship in the disciplines;
20. Incorporate thinking skills and interpersonal skills at all levels;
21. Stress the identification, understanding, and solution of local, national, and global problems;
22. Provide many opportunities for students to learn and practice the basic skills of participation, from observation to advocacy;
23. Promote the transfer of knowledge and skills to life;
24. Have the potential to challenge and excite students.

Subsequently, the NCSS endorsed three scope and sequence models, finding that no single pattern is likely to be appropriate for students in all communities. These models are described in the October 1989 issue of *Social Education,* and we recommend that you should obtain a copy of these patterns for your personal files.

You should take some time to analyze the typical scope and sequence pattern discussed earlier and compare it to the NCSS proposals. What patterns do you see in these sequences? With what content would you have to be familiar if you were to teach in the middle school? In the high school? You might want to chart the amount of time devoted to the study of the United States, the study of the world, and the study of the several social science disciplines. Given that time allocation, what would you like to see offered to students within those categories? Why?

Influence of Newer Content Areas on Social Studies Curriculum Patterns

The organizational patterns of the social studies curriculum have a long history. We can trace our present 6–12 sequence at least back to the early part of this century (NEA Report, 1916). We also know that knowledge is rapidly expanding and new information is becoming available each day. Contemporary issues confront the social studies teacher with interesting and complex problems and opportunities. Because content and society are constantly changing, it is not surprising that new areas of study emerge that reflect these social dynamics of the contemporary world.

One way to think about emerging new content areas in social studies is through the metaphor of third-party politics in a democracy. Third parties usually come onto the political scene when the two major parties refuse to deal with or simply cannot accommodate the needs of a large and often vocal group of citizens. Knowing how difficult it is to achieve elected office, members of third parties will try to build their political planks into the platforms of one or both major parties. This is the way third parties assimilate their ideas into the mainstream of American politics. This process tends to satisfy third-party members and usually gives a lift to the major party, which alters its philosophy and/or practices to accommodate a broader base of constituents.

In much the same way, emerging new content is like a third-party plank trying to find a home within the established order of the social studies program. New content areas like global studies, law-related education, environmental education, peace studies, and private enterprise education show that students have needs that the standard program evidently does not address. Thus, these content areas, which are usually multidisciplinary, emerge most frequently as philosophical themes, units, or as skills within established courses. Sometimes, however, schools develop separate courses and implement them within the standard school program. Let us investigate three important emerging content areas within the social studies curriculum.

Global Studies

The increasing connections of human activities around the world has generated a need for a global outlook. Educators most often perceive global studies as a "perspective" that can provide a framework for a whole K–12 social studies program. This framework uses global consciousness as a context for inquiry. This might mean, for example, that teachers would present United States history from a broader world perspective. They would teach United States economic depressions of the 19th and 20th centuries as part of a global, interdependent economic system. Teachers would relate the wars in which we participated to global conditions over which we may have little control. In other words, global perspectives give our nation's history a broader context for study.

Global studies is a different and more inclusive way of viewing curriculum. It aims to prepare students for citizenship by developing a reasoned awareness of the dilemmas and promises of global interdependence. In one of the first statements on global education, Lee Anderson suggested the following capacities that global education should foster (in Collins and Zakoriya, 1982):

1. A capacity to perceive oneself and all other individuals as members of a single species of life who share a common biological status, a common way of adapting to their natural environment, a common history, a common set of biological and psychological needs, common existential concerns, and common social problems.
2. A capacity to perceive oneself, the groups to which one belongs, and the whole human species as a part of the earth's ecosystem.
3. A capacity to perceive oneself in the groups to which one belongs as participants in the transnational social order.
4. A capacity to perceive oneself, one's community, one's nation, and one's civilization as both culture borrowers and culture innovators who both draw from and contribute to a global bank of human culture that has been and continues to be fed by contributions from all people, from all geographical regions, and in all periods of history.
5. A capacity to perceive that the world's system and its component elements are objectives of perceptions, beliefs, attitudes, opinions, values, and assumptions on our part as well as on the part of others.

You might also want to read the statements on global studies that are available from most state education agencies.

As our economic, cultural, and political institutions become more involved with others around the world, we can assume that the social studies curriculum will give more attention to global studies.

Law-Related Education

The increased role of the law in the lives of the people and the concern over rising crime rates has stimulated interest in teaching young people about the law. Law-related education, as an emerging content area, is about thirty-five years old. Through national and state networks, law-related education has become one of the most accepted new areas in the social studies. The general goal of law-related education is to teach students about the foundation of our democratic society and their rights and responsibilities as citizens. Specifically, it teaches knowledge and skills pertaining to law, the legal process, and the legal system. The Law-Related Education Act of 1978 provided funding for schools and agencies to stress the fundamental values and principles that underlie our system of government.

It is possible to define law-related education as movement from characteristics that are harmful to responsible citizenship to characteristics that citizens need in a pluralistic and democratic society. Seen in these terms, the major focus of law-related education, then, is to move toward effective democratic citizenship. The following goals and achievements are central to law-related education:

In a successful law-related education program:

Students Moved Away From:	*Students Moved Toward:*
perceiving law as restrictive, punitive, immutable, and beyond the control and understanding of the people affected.	perceiving law as promotive, facilitative, comprehensible, and alterable.
perceiving people as powerless before the law and other socio-civic institutions.	perceiving people as having potential to control and contribute to the social order.
perceiving issues of right and wrong as incomprehensible to ordinary people.	perceiving right and wrong as issues all citizens can and should address.
perceiving social issues as simplistic.	perceiving the dilemmas inherent in social issues.
being impulsive decision makers and problem solvers who make unreflective commitments.	being reflective decision makers and problem solvers who make grounded commitments.
being inarticulate about commitments they make or positions they take.	being able to give reasoned explanations about commitments they make.
being unable to manage conflict in other than a coercive or destructive manner.	being socially responsible conflict managers.
being uncritically defiant of authority.	being critically responsive to legitimate authority.
being uncritically responsive to authority.	being responsibly opposed to illegitimate authority.
being ignorant about legal issues and the legal system.	being knowledgeable about the law, the legal system, and related areas.

being self-centered and indifferent to others.	being empathetic, socially responsible, and considerate of others.
being morally immature in responding to ethical problems.	being able to make mature judgments in dealing with ethical and moral problems.

SOURCE: Adapted from Turner, M. J. 1988. "An Evaluation of Law-Related Education: Implications for Teaching." In *Training Manual for Law in a Free Society*. Calabasas, CA: Center for Civic Education, p. 62.

The U.S. Department of Justice, Office of Juvenile Justice and Delinquency Prevention, has lent financial support to law-related education since 1978. Today, it funds a cooperative effort of national law-related education projects called the Law-Related Education National Training and Dissemination Program. (See the appendix at the end of this chapter for names and addresses of cooperating groups.)

In 1988, Mary Jane Turner of the Center for Civic Education reported that law-related education can help prevent or reduce delinquent behavior among juveniles. Her four-year study was an evaluation of law-related education programs undertaken by the Social Science Education Consortium of Boulder, Colorado, and the Center for Action Research (Turner, 1988). With this type of empirical support, as well as the quality of law-related education materials and teacher training conferences, it is clear that law-related education will continue to play a more central role in the social studies program.

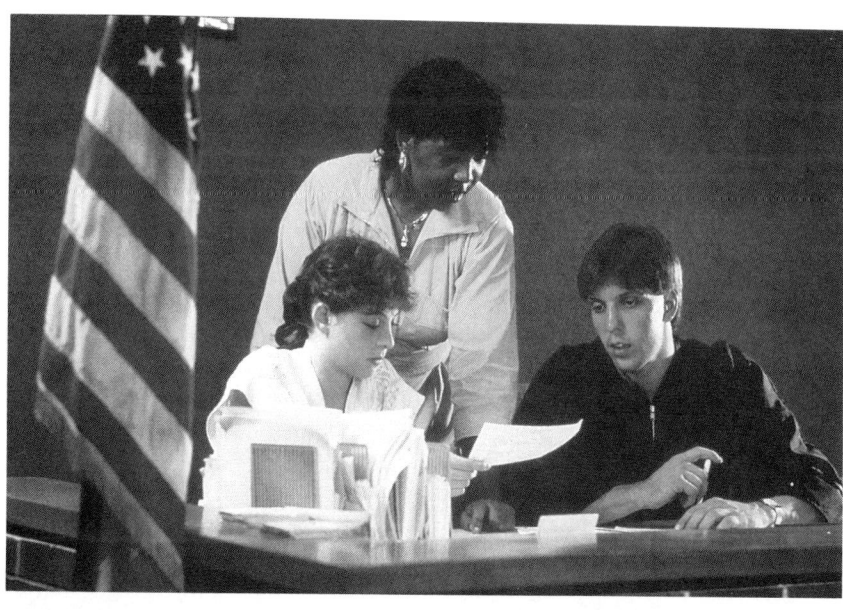

Environmental Education

The growing public concern over environmental deterioration has generated the environmental education programs. Environmental education is the most difficult area to define of the three new content areas we discuss here. This is because we can view environmental education as a science program or as "outdoor" education. The Environmental Education Act of 1970 (PL91-516) defined environmental education as the educational process dealing with our "relationship with the natural and man-made surroundings."

Environmental education subsequently has been defined as education aimed at producing citizens who are knowledgeable about the biophysical environment and its problems; as an interdisciplinary and integrated process concerned with resolving value conflicts between human beings and their environment; and, as person-environment relationship education (Engleson, 1987).

One of the best statements on environmental education comes from the Global Tomorrow Coalition (1985). The coalition outlines the following six areas of concern that present an agenda for environmental studies:

1. Growth—achieving balance among human populations, common material goods and services, and natural resources;
2. Business and economic progress—relationships among private enterprise, government, economic progress, and environment;
3. Environment—the importance of maintaining the global life support systems;

4. Development—relationships between the quality of life for present and future generations, the natural systems of each, and personal lifestyles of consumer choices;
5. Science and technology—cost and benefit concerns of modern applications of science and technology, especially long-delayed controls on toxic waste; and
6. National foresight—needed improvements in our ability to understand current national and global trends and to apply them in policy decisions (Global Tomorrow Coalition, 1985). Also see the *Global Ecology Handbook,* 1990, W. Coursen, editor.

These three examples of new content areas can provide some idea of the direction and speed of curriculum change in the social studies. Using the metaphor of third-party politics again, it is interesting to hypothesize on the new content areas that will appear in the social studies curriculum by the end of the century. What content would you like to be teaching in ten years? Why?

SUMMARY

We have presented several different ways to organize social studies content as well as provided a look at some new or emerging content areas. While there are variations in state curriculum designs, the overall contours of scope and sequence patterns across the United States are quite similar.

Knowing the general national and state patterns can be useful when you study the scope and sequence of the program in which you are teaching. It is not only your professional responsibility to know your local program, but you should be able to explain its rationale. Beyond this, it is always a good idea to contrast and compare your program with more "ideal" patterns that you find in the professional literature.

Above all, it is important to remember that curriculum is based on communication. This requires teachers to talk about what they teach, why they teach it, how they teach, and evaluate it. Teachers must also ask if what they are doing makes any difference in the lives of their students.

Discussion Questions

1. As a teacher, what are the advantages and disadvantages of participating in curriculum development?
2. What is meant by the statement "Curriculum is fundamentally a communication act"?

3. Do you believe that the social studies curricula with which you are familiar are too traditional or too modern? Defend your answer.
4. Since social studies is a bridge among disciplines it is often a place where administrators assign state-mandated content such as drug education and consumer education. How would you determine what content area legitimately belongs in the social studies sequence?
5. People have complained that the younger generation is out of touch with cultural heritage. This complaint goes back at least to ancient Egypt, where it has been found in hieroglyphic writing on tombs dating from 3000 B.C. Why do older generations tend to believe that younger generations do not care about their heritage? Is this true?

Student Learning Activities

1. Within a small group, brainstorm all the significant human needs you can. Group them under the categories of societal needs and individual needs. Then, rank them in order of priority—both within and across categories. Do your lists of needs suggest changes in the existing social studies curriculum?
2. Write down the dates 2000, 2010, 2020, then write underneath each date the most significant events, inventions, discoveries, or changes you think will occur by then. How should the social studies curriculum reflect these changes?
3. There is a great deal of curriculum similarity across the country. What would be the benefits and liabilities if these similarities became standardized by law or policy at the national level? At the state level? At the district level? At the school level?
4. Prepare a rationale statement for changing the curriculum so that it focuses more clearly upon the economic, political, social, and psychological lives of students. Try to keep in mind the following questions:
   a. What is the nature of the good life?
   b. How can the social studies program help move students toward the good life?
   c. What is the relationship between the good life and the healthy community?
5. In small groups of five to eight classmates, design the "ideal" scope and sequence for social studies grades 6–12. Your group should develop statements for the following:
   a. What information should you include for students to learn? Why? (Warning: Remember you will always have to leave certain information out simply because you include some other information.)
   b. What is the best way to sequence courses 6–12? (For example, should United States history come before world geography?) Defend your sequence using logical and developmental reasons.

c. What content would you include in the scope and sequence that is not in typical present-day social studies programs?

d. Have an experienced social studies teacher review your scope and sequence design. What concerns did this teacher raise?

APPENDIX

The following cooperating groups are part of the Law-Related Education National Training and Dissemination Program:

American Bar Association, Special Committee on Youth Education for Citizenship. 750 N. Lake Shore Drive. Chicago, IL 60611. 312/988-5725

Center for Civic Education/Law in a Free Society. 5146 Douglas Fir Road, Suite 1. Calabasas, CA 91302. 818/340-9320

Constitutional Rights Foundation. 601 S. Kingsley Drive. Los Angeles, CA 90005. 213/487-5590

Social Science Education Consortium, Inc. 3000 Mitchell Lane, Suite 240. Boulder, CO 80301-2272. 303/492-8154.

National Institute for Citizenship Education in the Law. 25 E. Street. N.W., Suite 40. Washington, DC 20001. 202/662-9620.

Phi Alpha Delta Public Service Center. 7315 Wisconsin Avenue, Suite 325E. Bethesda, MD 20814. 302/961-8985

References

Anderson, L. 1982. "Research on Teaching Issues in International Education: A Paper Prepared for the National Institute of Education." In H. T. Collins and S. B. Zakoriya (Eds.), *Getting Started in Global Education: A Primer for Principals and Teachers.* Arlington, VA: National Association of Elementary School Principals.

Council of State Social Studies Specialists. 1993. *National Survey: Social Studies Education K–12.* Des Moines: Iowa Department of Education.

Engleson, D. 1987. "The Emerging Concept of Environmental Education: Curriculum for the Twenty-First Century." *Forward.* Madison, WI: Wisconsin Association for Supervision and Curriculum Development.

Global Tomorrow Coalition. 1985. *Citizen's Guide to Global Issues.* Washington, DC: Global Tomorrow Coalition.

National Educational Association. 1916. *The Social Studies in Secondary Education: A Six Year Program Adopted Both to the 6-3-3 and 8-4 Plans of Organization:* Report of the Committee on Social Studies of the Commission on the Reorganization of Secondary Education of the N.E.A., A. W. Dunn, Secretary. Bulletin 28. Washington, DC: Government Printing Office.

National Council for the Social Studies. 1989. "In Search of a Scope and Sequence for Social Studies." *Social Education,* Vol. 53, No. 6, October. 375–403.

Project SPAN Staff and Consultants. 1982. *The Current State of the Social Studies: A Report of Project SPAN.* Boulder, CO: Social Science Education Consortium.

Report of the Ad Hoc Committee on Scope and Sequence. 1989. "Scope and Sequence Criteria." *Social Education,* Vol. 53, No. 6, October. 375–376.

Superka, D. P. and Hawke, S. 1980. "Social Roles: A Focus for Social Studies in the 1980s." *Social Education,* Vol. 44, No. 7, November–December. 577–586.

Turner, M. J. 1988. "An Evaluation of Law-Related Education: Implication for Teaching." In *Manual for Law in a Free Society.* Calabasas, CA: Center for Civic Education.

Additional Readings

Bruner, J. S. 1960. *The Process of Education.* Cambridge, MA: Harvard University Press.

Corsen, W. H. (Ed.). 1990. *The Global Ecology Handbook.* Boston: Beacon Press. (See especially Chapter 16.)

Dewey, J. 1915. *The School and Society.* Chicago: University of Chicago Press.

Dewey, J. 1916. *Democracy and Education. An Introduction to the Philosophy of Education.* New York: Macmillan.

Gleick, J. 1987. *Chaos: Making a New Science.* New York: Viking Press.

Goodlad, J. 1984. *A Place Called School: Prospects for the Future.* New York: McGraw-Hill.

Hartoonian, H. M. and Thompson, C. (Eds.). 1985. *Rethinking Social Studies Education.* Washington, DC: National Council for the Social Studies.

Hirsch, E. D. 1987. *Cultural Literacy: What Every American Needs to Know.* Boston: Houghton Mifflin.

Krug, E. A. 1969 and 1972. *The Shaping of the American High School.* Vol. 1: 1880–1920; and Vol. 2: 1920–1941. Madison: University of Wisconsin Press.

Lorenz, K. 1987. *The Waning of Humaneness.* Boston, MA: Little, Brown and Co.

National Council for the Social Studies. 1981. "Essentials of the Social Studies." *Social Education,* Vol. 45, No. 3, March. 162–164.

National Council for the Social Studies. 1986. "Scope and Sequence: Alternatives for Social Studies." *Social Education*, Vol. 50, No. 7, November/December. 484–542.

National Council for the Social Studies. 1990. *Social Studies Curriculum Planning Resources.* Dubuque, IA: Kendall/Hunt.

Rugg, H. O. 1926. "The School Curriculum, 1825–1890." In *The Foundations and Technique of Curriculum, Part 1: Curriculum-making Past and Present.* 26th Yearbook. National Society for the Study of Education. Bloomington, IL: Public School Publishing Co.

Taba, H. 1962. *Curriculum Development: Theory and Practice.* New York: Harcourt, Brace and World.

Tyler, R. W. 1949. *Basic Principles of Curriculum and Instruction.* Chicago: University of Chicago Press.

> It is better to know some of the questions than all of the answers.
>
> *James Thurber*

CHAPTER 5

Inquiry in Social Studies

FOCUS QUESTIONS

- How is social knowledge created, structured, and used?
- How can social studies disciplines help us understand human problems and human institutions?
- How do the conditions of people all over the globe determine the nature of social knowledge?
- What is the proper relationship between content and social inquiry skills?
- How does the setting or context of instruction shape the way in which students learn to engage in social inquiry?

OVERVIEW   It may well be that the human family is on the threshold of a new historical period or developmental stage. This stage will, as in times of rapid social change, suggest the need for new methods of thinking and inquiry. These new methods can enhance our understanding of social and ethical behavior as well as help create new concepts that can lead us into the future.

We are concerned in this chapter with the way social knowledge is created and used in real life and with simulated experiences. Within this context, two ideas are of great importance. First of all, we need to understand that inquiry is a way of creating social knowledge. And, second, we need to realize that inquiry is also a way of investigating personal and social issues. Both areas demand an understanding of the relationship between content and process; between reasoning skills and values; and between social inquiry and instructional context. These relationships are what we will study in this chapter.

The following questions can help you focus on the nature of inquiry and how knowledge is created, structured, and used:

- To what extent is there a universally accepted structure of knowledge for each of the social science disciplines? Or, is the structure specific to the thinking of various scholars?
- To what extent can social inquiry be an individual act?
- To what extent can the skills needed for social decision making be developed outside a social (two or more individuals) context?

How will your answers to these questions influence your social studies instruction?

Creating and Using Social Knowledge

Scholars use concepts, generalizations, and questions to explain the world. These are most often structured to conform to existing disciplines. As scholars explain the world or solve problems they often create new knowledge that is added to existing disciplines or expanded to new content areas such as psychohistory or bioethics.

One of the most important lessons that students can learn is that knowledge is something created by people as they try to explain something or solve problems. People develop public (or personal) policy when they take what is already known from common experiences or stored information and begin to ask questions about a new problem or issue. These types of activities are the processes that scholars and students also use to create knowledge. This knowledge comes from organizing information in different ways, establishing new generalizations, and inventing new concepts. Ideas such as "cold war," "Eurocentric," and "genetic engineering" are examples of new concepts. In the late 1970s when economists noted that inflation was more than 9 percent per year but the economy was not growing, they created the concept that is now part of the discipline of economics—"stagflation."

Students and teachers are members of a community of scholars actively engaged in carrying knowledge with them wherever they go, using it in many different ways, creating new knowledge, and even, on occasion, being victimized by incomplete or erroneous knowledge. Social studies educators generally agree that students should have "knowledge" of topics such as United States history, American government and politics, Western heritage, and non-Western cultures. Social studies educators also agree that their students should become proficient in critical thinking and problem solving. The selection and use of materials, the conduct of instruction, and the process of evaluation all will be influenced by the teachers' notions of what knowledge is, how it is learned, and how it is used.

The most abstract, transferable, and useful kinds of content are composed of concepts, generalizations, and theories. Specific facts and terminology are not useful by themselves but we need them to support these concepts, generalizations, and theories. This approach to content selection might seem quite abstract at first but it becomes meaningful as we relate it to what the student already knows, and as the student uses knowledge to explain reality. There is a basic relationship between how we classify knowledge (concepts, generalizations, and so on) and which teaching strategies we use in the classroom. For example, teachers may introduce the concept of **change** in elementary school and develop it further as the students mature. At the primary level teachers and students may discuss change as indicated by how many inches the students grow during the current school year. During the intermediate grades, students may learn about change by observing the growth of animals and plants. By the time the students reach middle school, they can study about changes in their local community; in high school they can study how an invention (such as the computer) has changed how information is transmitted to all of us.

However, teaching change as a concept alone can have only limited utility—that of concept development. To increase the students' knowledge of change, teachers also must deal with the concept at higher levels of sophistication. This usually means that teachers need to develop the concept within a context, story, or an issue. At the elementary school level students may study the changes that take place in a community over fifty years by observing and sequencing a set of pictures of the geographic area. At the secondary level teachers may address the concept of change by having students interview three generations of one or two families who have lived in the community and are aware of its changes. Students can then compile these reflections and write a local history of the area highlighting special events, trends, or turning points.

The principal kinds of knowledge we are dealing with are labeled concepts, generalizations, and theories. They make up a person's individual understanding, and each can be taught. Let us now look at the nature of concepts, generalizations, and theories and how they are taught.

Concepts

A concept is a categorization of things, events, or ideas; a convention; a carrier of meaning. Concepts are useful for many reasons. They aid in communication; they serve as tools for thinking; and in an era characterized by change and rapid growth in knowledge, concepts provide order and stability. The following explanations of attributes, classes, and symbols will be useful to describe concepts.

Attributes are distinguishable characteristics or properties of things, events, or ideas. A mountain, for example, has the features of being big and natural. A characteristic of a city is that it was constructed by people.

We perceive attributes with varying levels of awareness. Some attributes seem more important than others, while some that we commonly use might not be obvious. For example, when people try to explain the differences between Democrats and Republicans they readily mention attributes like liberalism and conservativism. Only after considerable effort do they state characteristics such as voting records, party platforms, and historical links.

Classes (classifications) are groupings of things, events, or ideas with the same or similar attributes. We can categorize people by attributes such as gender, occupation, kinship, age, and interests. Living things can be sorted as plants or animals, mammals or reptiles, birds or fish, domestic or wild. Oversimplifications, such as liberal or conservative politicians, and white, black, or yellow races abound in everyday conversation. People may characterize many classes as stereotypes—groupings with attributes based partly on fact but that are essentially false, and more emotional than substantive. We seem to classify practically everything according to attributes, and anything that defies ready classification often confuses, mystifies, or frightens us.

Each class can have a symbol that identifies the class and its members. The symbol is most often a term or group of words, but it could also be a gesture, number, picture, character, or mark. Whatever it is, the symbol serves as a convenient way to communicate about the class. We could label a classification composed of bird migration, river, wind, and mountain as "natural environment." We could label a group of human-produced things such as law, language, and religion as "culture." A name we might give to both groups together might be "human/environmental interactions." Within the culture category, we could name material things, like buildings, "artifacts" and non-material phenomena, like ceremonies, "non-material culture." The illustration on the following page shows examples of these interrelated classes and the symbols (words) that represent them.

Examples are things that have the distinguishing attributes of the category. A family is an example of a social system or open system because it has the attributes that distinguish a social system from a natural system, such as language, norms, laws, and socialization processes. **Non-examples** are things that do not have the key class attributes. Earth's water cycle is not a social system because it does not use language and it is a closed system.

■ ■ ■ ■ ■ ■ ■   Symbols in a Class System

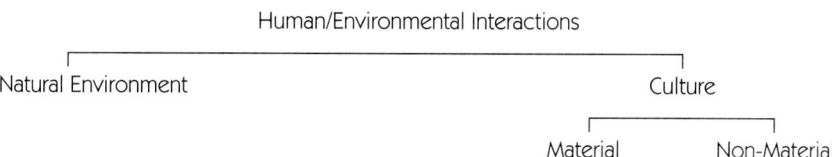

A **concept**, then, like "system," is the *label* a person gives to a class or grouping of ideas. A concept is a way of giving unity to diverse elements within a class. For example, the concept of culture organizes diverse attributes such as language, religious ceremonies, and cities into a unifying idea that we label "culture."

A student might read that a sociologist who was observing life in an urban society was studying culture. That student will develop a concept of culture quite different from one who hears a conversation linking culture with opera, Shakespeare, tuxedos, and champagne. Also, two students who study the same material may well associate different attributes. For example, if they are studying Inuits, one student might see that culture as superstitious and primitive while another student may associate the Inuit culture with terms like "religious" and "sophisticated environmental relationships."

Social studies teachers need to help students understand concepts by pointing out the relevant key attributes and by encouraging students to discuss them. If a student can define or explain culture in his or her own words, for example, there is evidence that the student has some understanding of the concept. Students also carry misconceptions about the world. In order to expose these misconceptions students should use their concepts in generalizations and test them for validity. Thus, the sophistication of the concepts that students develop should continue to increase and become more accurate. For example, you might ask your students, "What do the following terms have in common: store, bank, corporation, money, bond, and stock?" As a teacher you may want to add other related terms to this list. After the students have suggested similarities, you might ask them to group the following terms in some meaningful way:

bond	bank
stock	corporation
money	store

Then the students might be asked to label (name) the groupings. The label in effect becomes the concept.

A store of wealth	Economic institution
money	bank
stock	corporation
bond	store

After naming the groups you could have the students write a statement (generalization) about their analysis, such as "All corporations sell stocks and/or bonds to help finance their operations."

A more complex example related to social studies would be the following:

Let us say you are introducing a unit on the Inuit culture. You could start by posing this situation for the students to consider: "Suppose you are in a plane crash north of the Arctic Circle and you are the only person to survive the crash."

1. What questions would you need to ask yourself in order to survive?
2. What environmental and personal factors would you need to consider?"

As the students are suggesting answers to these questions you could be listing items that they mention on the chalkboard or overhead projector, such as climate, snow, ice, cold, wild animals, environment, tools, food, knowledge, hope, clothing, shelter, and so on.

Then you could ask the students to group these terms and label the groupings such as:

Nature	Culture
Climate	Tools
Snow	Knowledge
Ice	Hope
Animals	Clothing

This sort of introductory exercise could then lead to the question "How do the Inuit people who live in this region survive?"

The following chart is another example showing how a student may demonstrate greater understanding of concepts.

Content	Behavior	Example
The Concept of Culture as It Might Be Used in a Middle School or World Geography Class	*Kinds of Outward Behavior That Show Knowledge of the Concept of Culture*	*Examples Using the Concept of Culture*
The class studies the link between physical and cultural geography.	Given a new group of examples and non-examples of concepts, students will be able to identify examples and non-examples of the concept (classification).	Given a drawing or description of a community scene, students will be able to identify cultural and natural features.

Content	Behavior	Example
The class studies the issue of why there are different kinds of shelters in similar climates.	Given a new problem in which knowledge of the content is useful but not specified, students will use the concept to solve the problem (application).	Given pictures or descriptions of different shelters in the same natural environment and asked why different groups build different shelters, students will include the concept of culture in their explanations.
The class studies the relationship between physical and cultural elements in a new setting.	Students will be able to find or give examples of the concept not studied in class (synthesis).	If told to imagine a visit to a different land, students will be able to describe material and non-material cultural features they might find there.

Generalizations

A generalization is an attempt to derive a general principle from particulars. It is a statement that shows the relationship among concepts. A generalization involves whole classes of concepts rather than individual examples. In our previous exercise on the Inuits an example of a generalization would be "Knowledge of the environment is necessary to survival" or "The tools developed by the Inuits are unique to the complex relationship between the Inuit culture and the environmental demands of the region in which they live." Principles, hypotheses, and scientific laws are often generalizations as we define them here.

There are two types of generalizations: analytical and synthetic. Analytical generalizations state what a thing is. For example, bachelors are unmarried men. Or, an economic depression is the low point of the business cycle. Or, a republic is a state in which people exercise their power indirectly through their chosen representatives.

Synthetic generalizations bring together two or more concepts to form a more powerful statement. Often these statements show relationships among concepts in a way that suggests cause and effect relationships, or what are known as "conditional statements." Such a conditional statement might be *"If* the GDP falls for three quarters in a row, *then* chances are good that we will have a recession." Another example might be "Given an elastic demand curve, *if* the price of a commodity increases, *then* consumers will purchase less of the commodity. Or, *"If* a society is threatened by outside forces, *then* individuals will look beyond their personal differences and come together to meet the challenge." Synthetic generalizations can be the most powerful ideas used by social studies teachers and social scientists. From now on we will use the word "generalization" to mean "synthetic generalization."

The statement "Cultures change through innovation and diffusion" is an example of a generalization. It links the concepts of culture, change, diffusion, and innovation. Can you see cause and effect relationships in this new generalization?

A generalization is more compelling than a concept because it can be tested for truth and validity. Being somewhat arbitrary, concepts can be judged different or similar, but not true or correct. If people can agree on the meaning of concepts in a generalization, however, they can test the generalization by examining appropriate evidence and by reasoning.

Like concepts, generalizations can be represented by symbols and terms. Some generalizations have names or symbols. "Gresham's law," the "frontier thesis," and "the principle of diminishing returns" are some relatively well-known generalizations from economics and history. We could refer to the example that "Cultures change through innovation and diffusion" with a symbol like "the law of cultural change."

We can illustrate and test generalizations by examining cases that contain examples of the underlying concepts. A generalization can appear to be true, false, or only partially true. Replacing silver-bearing coins with non-silver-bearing coins, for example, is a positive or true case of Gresham's law (within a market, money that is more dear or valuable will be driven out by money that is less dear or valuable as people will tend to hoard the money of greater value). If the two kinds of coins both remained in circulation, this would be a negative case. The American colonists both created new inventions and borrowed cultural traits from the Native Americans, French, and Spanish. These changes in the British colonies between settlement and the American Revolution are positive examples of the generalization that cultures always change.

Generalizations, like concepts, are essentially internalized understandings. Students can show they understand a generalization by verbally explaining it, but they can demonstrate mastery better through observable behaviors such as the following.

Content	Behavior	Example
The generalization "All cultures change continually."	*Kinds of outward behavior that show knowledge of the generalization: "All cultures change continually."*	*Examples of using the generalization that "All cultures change continually."*
The class studies the impact of the immigration of Southern and Eastern Europeans on American cities in the late 19th and early 20th centuries.	Given examples of the concepts from which this generalization is formulated, students will be able to identify positive or negative relationships (classification).	Given descriptions of an old way of life and a new way of life in a community, students will be able to list instances of cultural change based on the descriptions.
The class studies the effects of U.S. policy in dealing with Native Americans.	Given a new problem in which knowledge of this generalization is useful but not specified, students will use the generalization to solve the problem (application).	If asked whether it is likely that a specified way of life (like that of the Hopi Indians) would not change for a century and why or why not, students will use the generalization in answering.
The class studies the trend data of manufacturing and international trade and develops an argument for what they predict will happen in the future.	Students will be able to create unique examples of this generalization (synthesis).	If asked to describe what the United States may be like twenty years from now, students will include in their descriptions a number of cultural innovations and/or diffusions.

Theories

A theory interrelates a number of concepts and generalizations in a grouping with an identity and meaning of its own. The component generalizations and concepts fit together in a pattern so that they add meaning to each other. Theory, as we define it here, is the most abstract knowledge, the furthest removed from specific facts. Theories find their greatest usefulness in **explanation**.

Figure 5.1 Theory of "Cultural Change." Cultures are dynamic, changing continuously through diffusion and innovation in response to new needs, problems, and opportunities; but cultures are also conservative, maintaining continuity with the cultural heritage. This establishes a tension that all cultures experience.

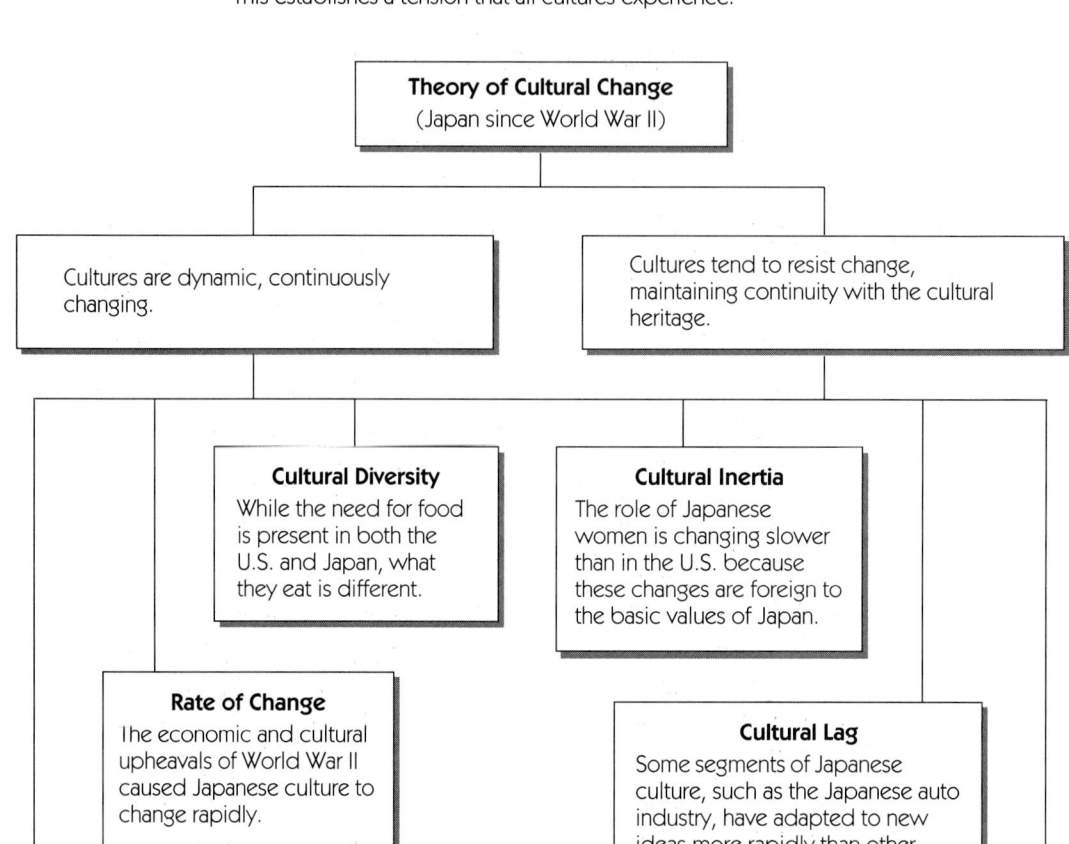

Theories include several kinds of commonly encountered abstractions. Darwin's evolution of species and Keynesian macroeconomics are well-known theories as we have defined them here. Systems, such as the political system; creeds, such as Christianity; myths, such as rugged individualism; and operational theories, such as the one for teaching knowledge we suggest in this text, may be considered theories. Each is a system comprised of interrelated concepts and generalizations.

Like the generalization, we can test the theory for truth and validity. We can determine, for example, whether predictions made according to the theory are realized, whether the theory is demonstrable, or whether it agrees with invariable law.

We can also name theories by symbols that are usually words. The theory in Figure 5.1 is labeled "Cultural Change." More familiar are the names of theories such as the atomic theory, theory of gravity, theory of relativity, economic determinism, laissez-faire capitalism, or existentialism.

In Figure 5.1 we have shown key concepts in the theory of cultural change in the boxes at the bottom with examples related to Japan since World War II. Generalizations appear above these concepts. The more specific ideas at the bottom support those above and the more abstract ideas at the top include or subsume the meanings of those below. We can identify the major concepts and generalizations in a theory by applying them to a specific situation.

Another way to diagram the theory of cultural change is with a concept web as represented in Figure 5.2.

Students could show their understanding of a theory by observable behaviors. Some are presented on the following page.

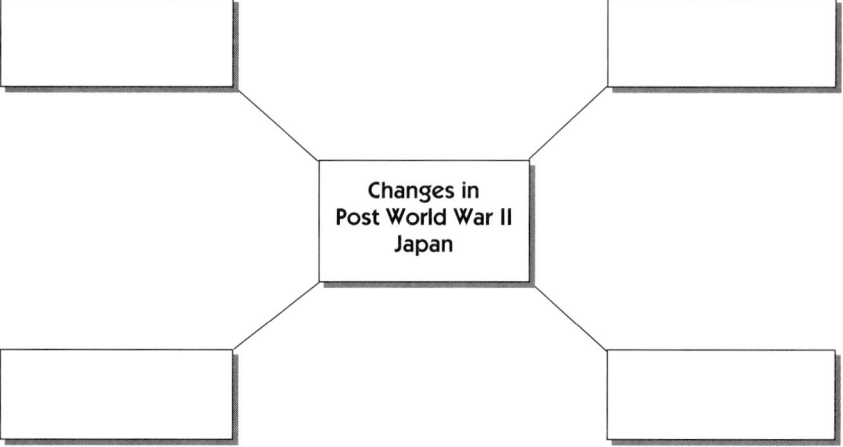

Figure 5.2 Cultural Change Concept Web. What factors caused cultural change in post–World War II Japan? Fill in those items that you believe to be important reasons for changes in Japanese culture. Now, relate those causes to the categories in Figure 5.1, such as innovation, cultural diversity, and so on

■■■■■■■■

Examples Using the Theory of Cultural Change	Kinds of Outward Behavior That Show Understanding of the Theory
In studying classical civilizations of Greece and Rome, students will be able to identify situations showing when cultural change has occurred and to point out examples of the generalizations and concepts that help explain the change.	Identifying major components of the theory in the fall of Greece and Rome (classification).
Predicting whether an economic development plan for a known situation (e.g., a city) will or will not work.	Developing a policy for the inner city of Los Angeles (application).
Writing a history of how an imaginary people developed their current way of life.	Explaining their understanding of historical change and creating unique situations involving the theory (synthesis).

Meaningful Knowledge

Theories and their component generalizations, concepts, and attributes form meaningful structures of knowledge. We can relate these kinds of knowledge in the social studies in a logical pattern. Concepts are related to generalizations, which in turn are related to theories.

Each kind of knowledge includes the simpler and related ideas to form its own unique meaning. Figure 5.3 illustrates this interrelationship of types of knowledge in a structure.

■■■■■■■■ **Figure 5.3** Interrelationship of Types of Knowledge. Examples of each kind of knowledge. Theory: circular flow of income

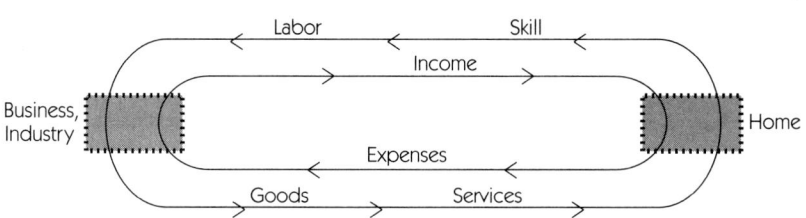

Generalizations:

1. What people spend on consumption and investment depends primarily on their income.

2. Changes in the level of total spending (private consumption and investment along with government spending) will cause changes in employment and real output.
3. Changes in the level of total spending will cause changes in the price level.

Concepts:
Price, money, production, GDP, employment, real output, inflation investment, spending, saving.

Figures 5.4, 5.5, and 5.6 illustrate how these elements of knowledge can be related to each other and to facts.

The chart in Figure 5.4 shows the relationship between the price of a good and the amount of that good people will purchase. When these schedules are brought together they form a generalization of supply and demand. Figure 5.5 illustrates the relationships among facts, concepts, and generalizations. The amount (of a good) supplied to the market will vary directly with the price. The demand will vary inversely with the price.

The diagram represented in Figure 5.6 is an admitted oversimplification. In any graphic presentation of knowledge one arbitrarily builds a structure.

Figure 5.4 Price Determination Theory in a Competitive Market: Generalizations

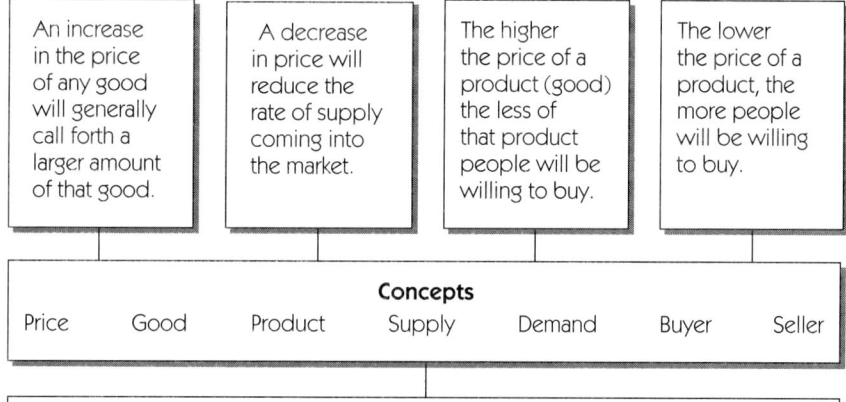

Figure 5.5 Price Determination Theory in a Competitive Market: Price Determination

1.40
1.30
1.20
1.10
1.00
Price
Supply Schedule
Demand Schedule
1
2
3
4
5
6
Quantity

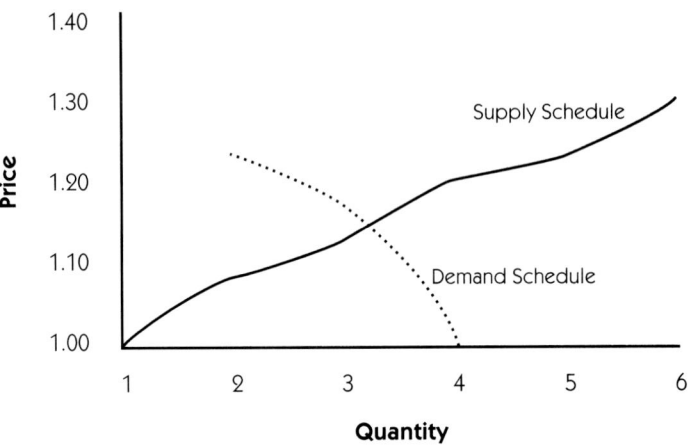

Figure 5.6 An Example of Interrelatedness of Knowledge

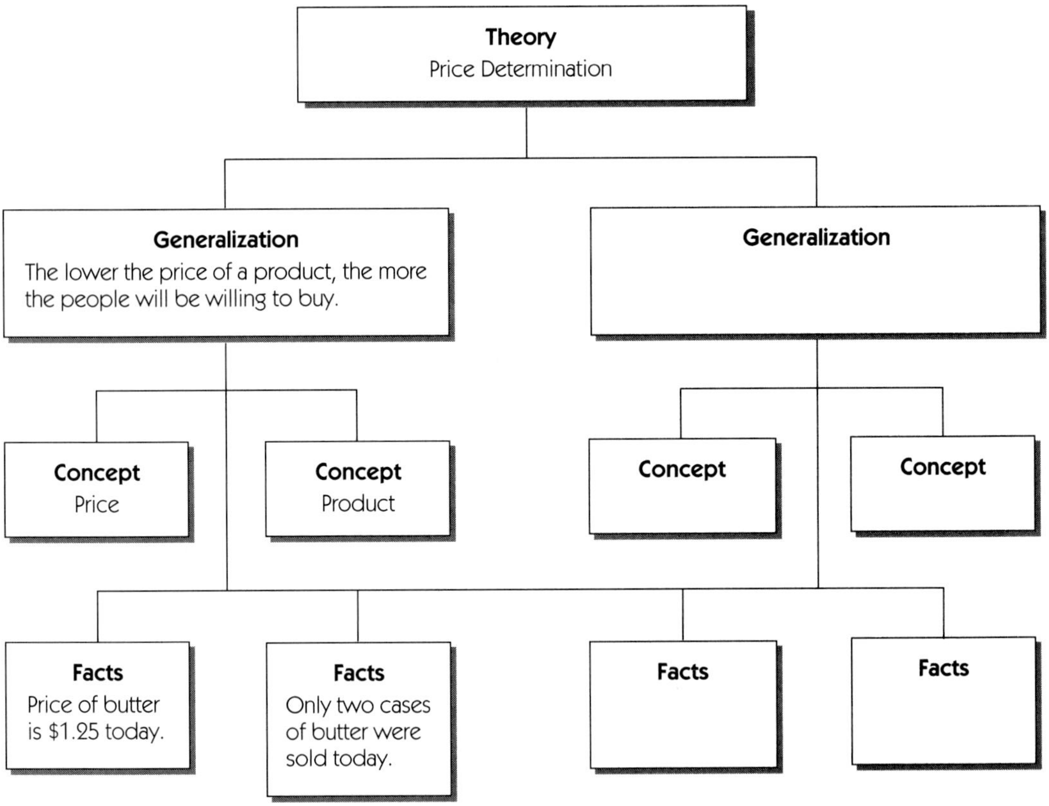

Theory
Price Determination
Generalization
The lower the price of a product, the more the people will be willing to buy.
Generalization
Concept
Price
Concept
Product
Concept
Concept
Facts
Price of butter is $1.25 today.
Facts
Only two cases of butter were sold today.
Facts
Facts

This structure is useful only if it serves to help show the interrelatedness among given elements. The important point is that teachers help students make sense of the information that is presented.

Structures of knowledge are dynamic and tentative in two ways. First, the individual student might alter a structure if a new experience causes him or her to change the generalization or its underlying concepts. Also, more specific knowledge in a structure may be forgotten as its meaning is subsumed in more general understanding. For example, in economic terms, the concept of *demand* means a want or need and an ability to purchase what is needed or wanted. Second, knowledge structures change and grow as cultures change and grow and as researchers argue about and change concepts, generalizations, and theories. Our knowledge of human behavior, for example, has grown and changed notably in the past few decades as anthropologists and psychologists developed new ideas.

Teachers should view concepts, generalizations, and theories as interrelated in order to teach structures of knowledge. Structure suggests a way to classify subject matter. It also provides some elements and relationships that teachers can use in instructional strategies. The overt behaviors related to each kind of knowledge suggest ways to develop and evaluate student mastery of the abstractions. The chart below illustrates the interrelated elements that teachers can use in teaching abstract knowledge.

■ ■ ■ ■ ■ ■ ■ Correlated Elements Useful in Planning Instruction and Evaluation of Kinds of Knowledge

Kind of Knowledge	Representative Communication	Behaviors That Demonstrate Knowledge
Theories	Diagram	Given some knowledge about a situation, students can predict additional events or aspects in the situation. Students can identify positive and negative cases. Students can find and create new examples or non-examples.
Generalizations	Verbalization	
Concepts	Simulation	
	Outline	
	Statement	
	Formula	
	Definition	
	Explanation	
	Classification	

The Universal Nature of Social Knowledge

Human conditions and human values determine the kinds of research people undertake. Common values such as survival, freedom, power, happiness, and justice influence social research. Since there is a great deal of interaction among people and global social systems, it is important to understand that events in any region in the world influence all other regions.

The social sciences and history are concerned with investigating and labeling the patterns of people's lives. All of us, for example, are interested in understanding the relationships that exist between ourselves and others, and between ourselves, social institutions, and natural systems. This suggests that we need to investigate the interrelationships of people and systems. However, we also need to ask how and why certain people and systems become isolated—from the single student in the classroom to the isolated community. How is the classroom a social system? How is the classroom related to other systems?

As we think about who we are and where and when we live, it becomes extremely important to understand both our ethnocentrism and our universal social consciousness. We need to ask, "Can we find ways to enjoy a more healthy existence with our fellow human beings and our global environment?" Our job as social studies teachers, then, is to help students understand that knowledge can be a powerful tool for citizens of the republic. Students need to arm themselves with this power if they expect to live a more healthy social existence.

Using Social Studies to Understand Human Problems and Institutions

The social studies disciplines help us see contemporary issues within a context of time (history) and place (geography). They give perspective to any event, problem, or trend we wish to study. The social studies disciplines also help us ask new questions about institutions and issues. For example, in analyzing the institution of school, we can place the study of education within a historical and geographic context. We can also ask questions about the political, economic, social, and legal makeup of the institution. For instance, in the study of education in America, we can examine such political aspects as the distribution of power in the school. We can analyze the relationship between student achievement and economic status. We can also look at social attributes such as the effects of classroom communication patterns on the achievement differences between boys and girls. In essence, the disciplines of the social studies suggest powerful concepts and questions for us to use as we study an institution like the school.

Consider the following concepts and questions.

> Political Science
> Concepts: Allocation of power, values, and resources
> Question: Did the introduction of classroom computers change the allocation of power between students and teachers?

Economics
Concept: Opportunity costs
Question: What resources in terms of books, teachers, and space must the school give up to purchase the computers?

History
Concept: Change
Question: How are schools today similar to and different from schools of the late 19th century? Has the introduction of classroom computers increased the rate of change?

The use of knowledge from the social studies disciplines is fundamental to good social studies instruction. Concepts such as need, institutions, culture, demand, or region, and the questions we can raise using these concepts, for example, "How does the institution of school help meet the needs of children in this community?" provide the basic materials for building lessons. Thus, it is extremely important for social studies teachers to use concepts and questions that reflect the latest thinking in the social studies disciplines. Teachers need to use the social studies disciplines as they develop instructional strategies. Social studies teachers should also use the methods of the social studies disciplines in their lessons. These methods include techniques of observation, interviewing, controlled experiments, and the use of primary and secondary documents. In all cases, these concepts, questions and attending methods should help students find meaning in their study of society.

Content and Social Inquiry (Reasoning) Skills

We can approach instruction in social studies in two different but *interrelated* ways. First, we can view social studies content as a story about continuity and change over time, an exciting narrative or analytical study about people, events, and issues. Second, we can understand content as a disciplined study or inquiry involving the creation, structuring, and use of knowledge. With this in mind, a closer look at the social studies disciplines reveals that they are built on such important concepts as narrative, change, continuity, chronology, cause and effect relationships, evidence, and frame of reference. In other words, we can define history and the social sciences as recorded narratives about the past or present. These stories describe change and continuity over time. They also seek to explain change and continuity through a series of cause-and-effect propositions based on evidence and shaped by the researcher's own frame of reference. Social researchers attempt to find out not only what happened but also why it happened, what trends they can suggest, how humans behave in certain social settings, and why they behave that way. Some of the most important questions that social scientists consider include the following:

- How can we best conceptualize a topic, issue, theme, or event?
- What defines a historical period? What defines a theme? What defines an issue?
- What constitutes primary and secondary evidence? How can we evaluate and use such evidence?
- How do we handle cause-and-effect relationships in a narrative or discourse?

Some questions social scientists consider in assessing the merits of explanations include the following:

- Is the logic of the explanation valid?
- What biases or points of view seem to drive the narrative?
- How well does the scholar place the story or study within the framework of time and location?
- How well does the scholar explain why events occurred?
- Does the evidence support the interpretations?

The dynamic use of these questions and the concepts they embrace are fundamental to the way in which social scientists conduct social inquiry. In social studies, as in other fields of inquiry, there are several interrelated components involved in the construction and use of knowledge. These components are comprehension or conceptualization, causality, validity of explanation, and creative extension. It is important that social studies teachers understand how social scientists conduct research so they can help their students ask questions about their own learning and question data generated by social scientists.

At the most basic level of study, students *conceptualize* the people, setting, story, or context of the inquiry with which they are concerned. Questions that ask what is going on, how have things changed, and how have they remained the same help establish the time and location context necessary to understanding the issue or topic under inquiry. Comprehension also includes the previous understanding and skills that students bring to the inquiry. (See Figure 5.7.)

The second level of study deals with *causality*. Once students comprehend the setting of the inquiry, they then must inquire how and why it acquired its characteristics. They should inquire into the cause-and-effect relationships and the logic they used in their own and others' explanations of social and historical developments. Specifically, students must seek an approach to the problem of change over time as well as recognize and explain major events, trends, or issues. (See Figure 5.8.)

At the third level, students inquire into the accuracy or *validity* of the explanations suggested at level two. Here they investigate bias, the nature of evidence, the methods of evaluation used to validate explanations, and how to deal with diverse and conflicting interpretations of data. (See Figure 5.9.)

Figure 5.7 Conceptualization

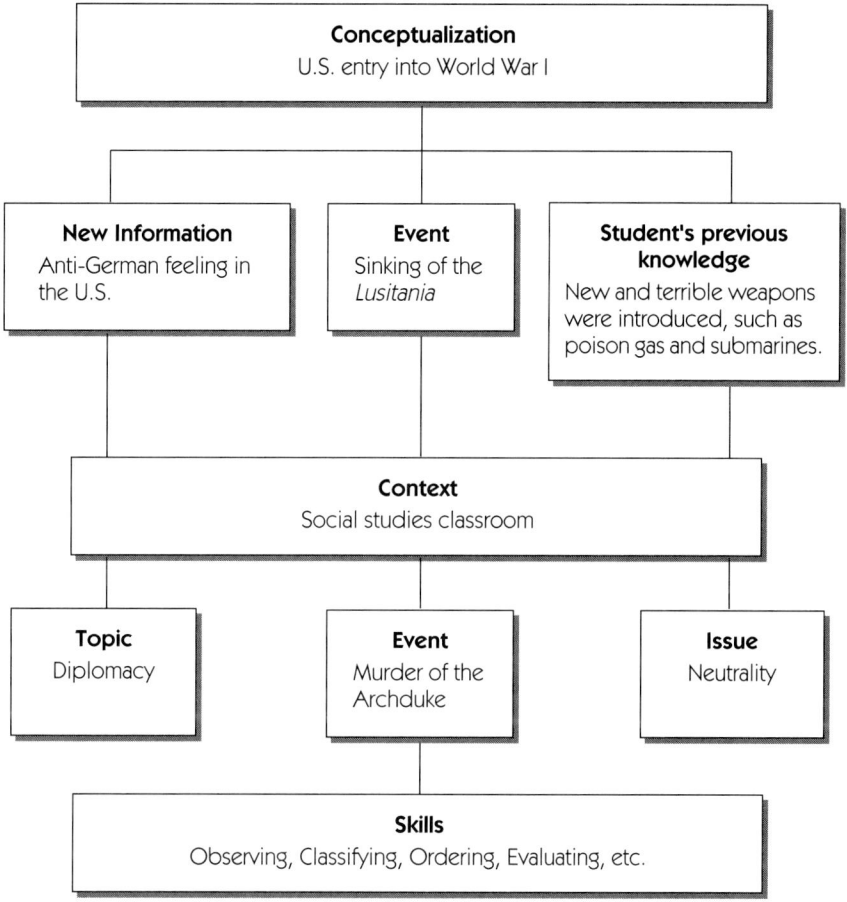

This chart shows that conceptualization depends upon the bringing together of new information, events, and the student's previous knowledge within a context that will focus upon issues, topics, and events requiring students to use skills such as observing, classifying, ordering, evaluating, etc.

Finally, the fourth level of study is concerned with *creative extensions,* that is, the student's inquiry into new settings and issues and the production of new knowledge. Creativity and independent study skills are paramount at this level as students seek to combine insight and experience with logic to gain new knowledge. Here students begin to develop their own interpretations by seeing the connection between different events and probing issues of causation and outcome. They also expand their use of knowledge by linking the past with the present. They explore the historical developments that help explain present similarities and differences among the world's peoples. In sum, this

■ ■ ■ ■ ■ ■ ■ **Figure 5.8** Causality

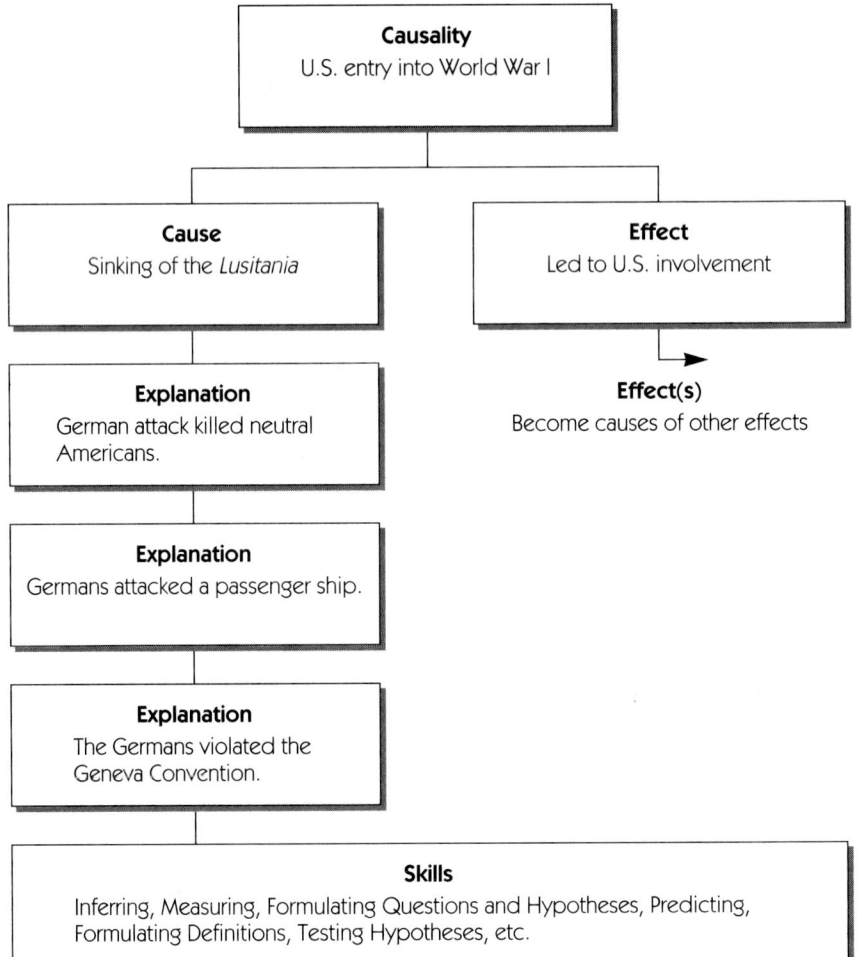

fourth level incorporates all other levels, thus creating dynamic inquiry and critical discourse. (See Figure 5.10.)

Let us now consider more closely the instructional questions and skills involved in each of the four components of the *conceptual model* just described. As we do so, we should note that the components and their related skills are not mutually exclusive. They should be understood as a total system where each element of the model is related to all other elements. For example, consider the four components and their related questions listed below as you design a unit on the Civil War.

Figure 5.9 Validity of Explanation

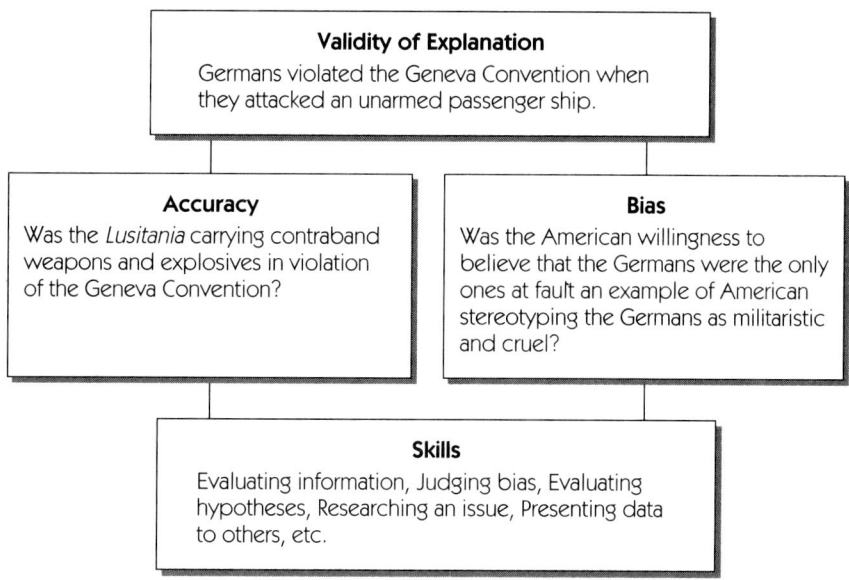

Figure 5.10 Creative Extensions

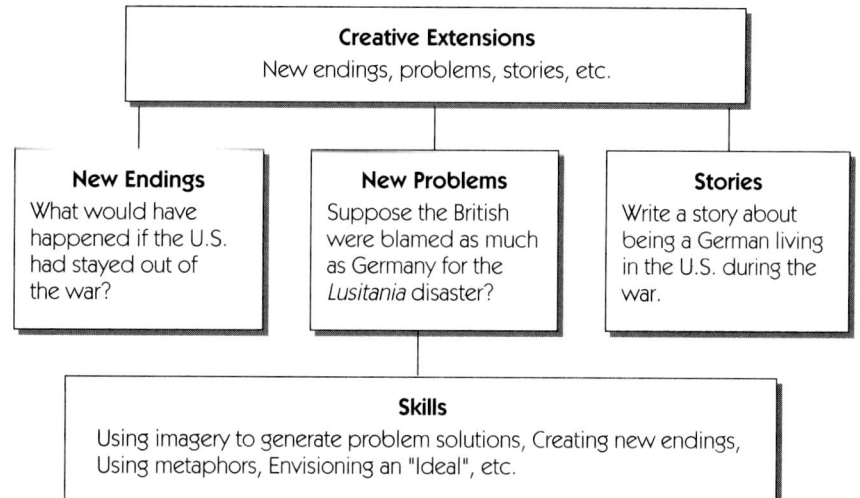

Conceptual Model

Comprehension/Conceptualization

- What is happening? Background information about the United States and Europe in the years preceding the war. An overview of the war itself.
- When and where is it happening? Timelines and maps.
- What are the issues and problems under study? Slavery, states rights, economic well-being.
- How can I describe what is going on in the setting(s) under study? Pictures, music, stories.
- What ideas can I bring to this study? List what comes to mind when you think of the Civil War.

The following is a sample of the skills involved in the process of comprehension/conceptualization:

- Identifying main ideas and supporting details
- Understanding information presented in a variety of forms
- Identifying similarities and differences
- Identifying issues and problems

Causality

- What cause-and-effect relationships can be discerned? Election of Lincoln and secession of the South.
- What is the logic of the arguments used to explain developments? Slavery versus anti-slavery argument. States-rights versus Union.
- How can I explain or interpret what has happened? Why did citizens of the South feel that their way of life was threatened by the abolitionists?

The following is a sample of the skills needed for understanding causality:

- Sequencing events or processes according to time, distance, quality, number, or function
- Formulating and testing hypotheses
- Drawing inferences

Validity of Explanation

- What is the best source of data? Letters, diaries, historical records, historical interpretations.
- What is the nature of the available evidence? Primary sources, secondary sources.

- How can we evaluate the evidence for accuracy and completeness? Compare two accounts of the same event.
- How can we recognize bias in the explanation? Emotional terms, unsubstantiated conclusions, stereotypes.

The following is a sample of the skills needed to assess validity of explanation:

- Judging the reliability of both primary and secondary sources
- Recognizing different points of view and detecting bias
- Evaluating hypotheses and generalizations
- Drawing conclusions (however tentative)

Creative Extension

- What new interpretations can we create to explain the historical events under study? What would have happened if Great Britain had helped the South?
- What knowledge (from other disciplines as well as the disciplines of social studies) do we need for the new explanation? What economic support could Great Britain have given the South and what difference would it have made?
- What different kinds of data presentations can we use in establishing a new explanation? Consider pictures, music, numerical presentations.
- What are some results of this event? How did these results influence the course of other events? Why was it 100 years before a Southerner was elected president of the United States?
- If the outcomes of this event were different, how might the results have changed? What would have happened had Lincoln not been assassinated?
- How through causation, continuity, contrast, generalization, or analogy do the events under study relate to the present? Civil rights, immigration, migration within the United States, states rights, multiculturalism.

The following is a sample of the skills necessary for creative extension:

- Generating new ideas and models
- Relating information in one area to larger historical or contemporary developments
- Comparing and contrasting information under study with related historical events and/or trends

Again, it should be noted that neither the four components of study (comprehension/conceptualization, causality, validity of explanation, and creative extension) nor their related skills are mutually exclusive. The components do, however, suggest activities in which students should be engaged if they are to understand social inquiry. The activities are, indeed, crucial to enable students to communicate not only about historical and contemporary social issues but also about the quality and accuracy of social inquiry itself.

Classrooms Conducive to Social Inquiry

The teacher must establish a conducive classroom setting and provide purposeful content in order to help students develop higher-order thinking skills. While the following example speaks to teaching history, it applies in any social studies class. What is critical to all areas of study is the ability to comprehend or conceptualize, deal with causality, explore validity or truth claims, and create extensions to new settings or disciplines within a learning environment that nurtures inquiry.

Let us consider a lesson about the Great Depression of the 1930s. This might be a lesson within a U.S. history course at the 10th or 11th grade. One of the first things that usually occurs in such a course is that level one conceptualization/comprehension teaching takes place. That is, the instructor wants students to know the setting, story, and context of the topic under study. What is going on here? How is this different from and/or similar to previously studied periods? In other words, the instructor wants students to conceptualize the theme, topic, or concept in terms of time, place, and circumstance.

From this point the teacher moves students to the second level—causality. Can we explain why the Depression occurred? What were the consequences of the Depression?

At level three the teacher and students investigate the truth or validity of the claims made by historians, economists, journalists, politicians, and family members as to why the Depression occurred as well as explanations for its aftermath. They evaluate the nature of the evidence for each, and they show the bias of each authority.

At the fourth level teachers encourage students to create their own questions, interpretations, stories, or explanations. They ask the students to apply or deal with potential extensions between the Great Depression and other fluctuations in the business cycle before and after the 1930s.

Teachers need to create an environment that encourages inquiry. Then, it should be clear that if teachers can motivate and instruct their students to move comfortably through these four levels, they will have a better chance to develop higher-order thinking abilities. This experience should also enhance students' reasoning and thinking abilities as they encounter new disciplines, topics, problems, or issues.

Activities that help students conceptualize, deal with causality, validate various claims, and pursue an independent and creative course of action should help them understand their behavior. For example, in the study of the

Civil War suggested earlier, students might start their inquiry with a "creative extension" activity like writing or developing a presentation about the course of American history if the South had won the Civil War. The teacher then would ask the students to address the validity of their stories by establishing and proving their cause-and-effect relationship claims. The students would present their stories as conceptualizations of 19th-century America that are supported with logic and data and that hold together as interesting and possible stories of our past. They then could compare their work with the more traditional stories of the 19th century. Some students might explore the role of women during the period, and how young people (ages 10–17) lived during this time. Here again, we might start with a creative extension of their stories about women and young people. The idea is to let the students request areas of study that interest them and that have potential for the deeper understanding of the topic.

Thus, within the classroom, students should have the opportunity to travel across all four categories of social inquiry. Activities within these areas will "force" students to do different things, ask different questions, and use different data and authorities. This does not suggest a sequence of activities, however. It does mean that the categories or levels of inquiry are interrelated, and while the order of presentation or involvement of students is arbitrary, teachers should use all levels and think of the scheme as a system or network. This requires a school setting where all members receive respect, where there is a conscious effort to develop standards of ethics (justice) and aesthetics (craft, quality, excellence), and where instruction is aimed at helping students see meaning in their personal lives.

We need to say a few words about the relationship between social inquiry and skills. What skills should be taught within each of the four categories (comprehension, causality, validity, and creative extension)? Are there skills that could help us teach conceptualizing, detecting cause-and-effect relationships, and discerning the validity of truth claims? The answer is yes *and* no. There certainly are skills, but social inquiry and higher-order thinking comes before, as well as after, "skill development." Methods of teaching that focus solely on skill development cause students to lose sight of the ultimate goal of encouraging social inquiry and higher-order thinking.

A metaphor might help us understand this idea better. Consider the sport of basketball. A basketball player, for example, learns many different skills—shooting, passing, dribbling, pivoting, and so forth. Coaches spend many hours "drilling" these, often separate, skills "into" their players. But basketball, like any complex human activity, is also a "mind game." The player has to reason through a series of decision options and make choices as accurately and as rapidly as possible. The player's ability is measured not so much in the execution of skills as in the ability to make appropriate decisions. The "game" player, as opposed to the "practice" player, is one who combines the ability to perform complex physical skills with an understanding of the subtleties of the game.

If we intend for our students to be better thinkers, then we must put them in daily interaction with people who are accustomed to thinking with exactness, refinement, and clarity, such as teachers, scientists, writers, or engineers. Also, we must encourage them to read the best authors, writers of reflective essays, and critics of social phenomena. By using the relationships that exist among social studies content, higher-order thinking, and context (setting), the student will have a basis for evaluating the quality of these interactions. That procedure will be the best guide for developing social inquiry.

SUMMARY

This chapter has given you the opportunity to study the elements of social inquiry and how people learn about the world. Your task as a social studies teacher is to reconstruct your "theories" of knowing and social inquiry to allow your students the opportunity to do likewise. It is in this process that students will try to understand their cultural heritage and solve personal and social issues. The students also can become better policy makers, better scholars, and better creators of knowledge.

With regard to social inquiry, there are three ideas teachers should remember. First of all, students create knowledge as they interact with texts, teachers, other students, and the learning environment. Second, a teacher must have some structure by which to organize information and knowledge. And, third, a teacher must understand the relationships among the various aspects of disciplined inquiry, that is, how higher-order thinking and the content of the social studies disciplines work together to help us solve problems and create new knowledge.

Discussion Questions

1. To what extent do you think that the definition of knowledge has changed over time? Defend your hypothesis.
2. It has been argued that individuals can enhance their thinking abilities best by being placed in social settings that allow them to solve real problems. This means applying in-depth knowledge, skills, and dispositions to the issue or problem at hand. This cannot be done through lecturing to students. Do you agree with these ideas? Why or why not?
3. Is it possible to develop higher-order thinking skills outside of a content area like history, economics, and the like? Why or why not?

4. Why do you think that it is important for a teacher to hold some notion or picture of knowledge structures in his or her mind before developing lessons for students?
5. How do people's preconceptions and biases or value systems influence the way in which they conduct social inquiry and the kinds of knowledge they accept as legitimate?

Student Learning Activities

1. Read a chapter from any middle or high school social studies textbook. Pick out the most powerful concepts, generalizations, and theories in the chapter. Next, compare and contrast your list with at least one other person in class. How do the authors emphasize specific concepts? Is there agreement about which concepts are emphasized?
2. Compile a list of issues that you believe are of importance to middle and high school students. Classify the issues into "personal" and "societal." You might want to check your list against a survey taken among middle school and high school students. In small groups suggest ways that students might investigate these issues.
3. Within a small group, select one historical event (American Revolution, the Great World Depression of the 1930s, etc.). Next, describe the following:
   a. How you would help students conceptualize this topic.
   b. How you would help students explain the reasons (causes) for the event.
   c. How you would help students sort out the integrity of the evidence presented (primary/secondary sources).
   d. How you would help students create their own story or description of the event.
4. Within a small group, construct a description of the kind of educational setting you believe to be most conducive to learning how to do social inquiry.

Additional Readings

Bastick, T. 1982. *Intuition: How We Think and Act*. Chichester, England: John Wiley.
Benne, K. D. and Tozar, S. (Eds.). 1987. *Society as Educator in an Age of Transition*. Eighty-sixth Yearbook of the National Society for the Study of Education. Part II. Chicago: University of Chicago Press.
Chance, P. 1985. *Thinking in the Classroom: A Survey of Programs*. New York: Teachers College Press, Columbia University.
Davidson, J. W. and Lytle, M. H. 1982. *After the Fact: The Art of Historical Detection*. New York: Alfred A. Knopf.

Dewey, J. 1910. *How We Think*. Boston: D. C. Heath

Geertz, C. 1983. *Local Knowledge: Further Essays in Interpretative Anthropology*. New York: Basic Books.

Goodlad, J. I. (Ed.). 1987. *The Ecology of School Renewal*. Eighty-sixth Yearbook of the National Society for the Study of Education. Part I. Chicago: University of Chicago Press.

Greene, M. 1988. *The Dialectic of Freedom*. New York: Teachers College Press, Columbia University.

Gross, R. E. and Chapin, J. R. 1973. *Teaching Social Studies Skills*. Boston: Little, Brown.

Hartoonian, H. M. 1980. "Reasoning as a Metaphor for Skill Development in the Social Studies Curriculum." *Theory and Research in Social Education,* Vol. VII, No. 4, (Winter). 59–78.

Hartoonian, H. M. 1980. "The First 'R'—Reasoning." *The Social Studies*, Vol. 71, No. 4 July–August. 156–162.

Kaplan, A. 1964. *The Conduct of Inquiry: Methodology for Behavioral Science*. San Francisco: Chandler.

Kurfman, D. G. (Ed.). 1977. *Developing Decision-Making Skills*. 47th Yearbook. Washington, DC: National Council for the Social Studies.

Madge, J. 1965. *The Tools of Social Science; An Analytical Description of Social Science Techniques*. Garden City, NY: Anchor Books.

Marzano, R. J., Brandt, R. S., Hughes, C. S., Jones, B. F., Presseisen, B. Z., Rankin, S. C., and Suhor, C. 1988. *Dimensions of Thinking: A Framework for Curriculum and Instruction*. Alexandria, VA: Association for Supervision and Curriculum Development.

McPeck, J. E. 1981. *Critical Thinking and Education*. New York: St. Martin's Press.

Newmann, F. M. (Ed.). 1988. *Higher Order Thinking in High School Social Studies: An Analysis of Classrooms, Teachers, Students, and Leadership*. (Report). Unpublished manuscript. Madison, WI: National Center on Effective Secondary Schools, University of Wisconsin.

Smith, F. 1975. *Comprehension and Learning: A Conceptual Framework for Teachers*. New York: Holt, Rinehart and Winston.

Toulmin, S. E. 1958. *The Uses of Argument*. Cambridge, England: Cambridge University Press.

Whitehead, A. N. 1933. *Adventures of Ideas*. New York: Macmillan.

> Whenever I have confronted that which was unfamiliar to me, I constantly sought neither to praise nor to condemn but only to understand.
>
> *Benedict Spinoza*

CHAPTER 6

Values Education

FOCUS QUESTIONS:

- Why is values education both cognitive and affective?
- How do history and the social sciences enhance our understanding of values?
- How can we teach values (education)?

OVERVIEW

A major goal of social studies instruction is the development of enlightened citizens (see Part I), which is, above all, the promotion of social responsibility (Lockwood and Harris, 1985). Therefore, it is important to understand how values and ethics education are treated in research and practice. While scholars agree on the importance of values and ethics in social studies instruction, there is less agreement on how we should define and teach this area of study. Of even more concern is the role of academic areas, such as history and economics, in teaching values. Can we teach history without teaching values? Without values, is economics only a poorly conceived mathematics program? If we say that academic areas and values are tied to one another, then whose values are we teaching? If we argue that values and academic areas are separate categories of knowledge, then what knowledge or information should we present to students? Should we teach philosophy? Religion? Literature? Given these kinds of questions, it is important for social studies teachers to develop a sound rationale for teaching values and becoming familiar with alternative instructional approaches. It is towards these goals that we now turn.

We start with the premise: *Teaching values is unavoidable.* Paraphrasing Emerson we might say, "I can't hear a word you are saying for what you are is speaking too loudly." A teacher's actions, dress, language, class activities, testing procedures, content selection, and general outlook on life all reflect and "teach" values to students. Yet, as educators, we seem to pay little attention to why, what, and how we teach values. All of us know people who would argue that values should be taught at home or in church or even in the community, but not in school. Others say values cannot be taught anyway, so we should not waste time with them.

Toward a Definition of Values

In trying to define values and values education, it is important to distinguish among several terms. Values is an inclusive concept encompassing both attitudes and beliefs. Attitudes are emotions or affective "leanings" toward people, places, events, and ideas. They are often unexamined. For example, an attitude toward jazz music may be positive or negative with no clear rationale for such a position. Beliefs, on the other hand, tend to be more cognitive in nature, suggesting preferences based upon evidence. The evidence need not be factual, only credible to those whom we respect, such as authorities, parents, peers, and teachers. For example, one may believe that jazz is wonderful music not necessarily from listening to jazz itself, but from a respect for an individual who likes jazz. If we value jazz, this means that we have an emotional leaning (attitude) toward it as well as a belief that jazz is a worthy musical form based upon its traditions, structures, and practitioners. Thus, values contain both beliefs and attitudes and are more deeply held than either. Values are also more resistant to change.

Values guide us by serving as the following:

1. A criterion necessary for moral decisions and actions, such as *honesty* in human relationships.
2. A description used to classify particular actions, attitudes, or beliefs, such as a beautiful performance, a just person, a worthy goal.
3. An intrinsic awareness, purpose, or meaning, such as a deep faith in God, an inner strength.

Oliver and Shaver (1966) defined values as objects or actions that we consider desirable. For example, if due process is a value, it simply means that to us the actions or procedures labeled "due process" are good and we should pursue them. Raths, Harmin, and Simon (1966) suggested that any assumption that we choose, prize, and repeat often enough becomes something we value. Hunt and Metcalf (1968) simply suggest that the term "value" should apply to only those things about which we make "judgments." All judgments are value judgments, they believe.

One of the most enduring arguments in the field of values education is whether values concepts and factual concepts are similar. This argument stems from the desire to stop forming rigid categories or distinctions between fact judgments and value judgments. It may be realistic, as Hunt and Metcalf (1968) argue, to see facts and values as opposite ends of the same continuum. In other words, at one end of the continuum we have statements that have clear and agreed upon meanings. At the value end of the continuum we have statements whose terms do not have clear and common meanings. For example, it is a fact that a person is six feet tall and a value that the person is beautiful.

The fact-value continuum can be a useful strategy in your teaching, but you must be clear and comfortable with the movement of concepts from one side to the other. For example, consider your decision to continue smoking. There is factual evidence that smoking is dangerous to your health. The evidence, however, consists of generalized statistics that do not necessarily apply to you personally. We also know that over the years, smoking has acquired negative social characteristics such as image, passive smoke, and cost. You personally may enjoy the taste; it helps you keep your weight down; smoking relaxes you; and the like. In making a decision about continuing to smoke, what reasons are most persuasive to you? Are the reasons you give more factual or more value-laden? How do you distinguish between value and factual claims? As you teach students to become better policy analyzers and decision makers, you may find the fact-values continuum useful. This approach allows you to see the interplay of facts and values with each affecting the other.

On the other side of the issue, there are those (Hartoonian, 1973; Wilson, Williams, and Sugarman, 1967) who suggest that values are conceptually different from facts and claim there is no fact-values continuum. Dealing with values means we must use a different language structure. For example, values must be approached through metaphor. Values like love, happiness, or justice, to these researchers, are beyond measurement, and, thus, different from facts that can be measured. "How do I love thee?" They would argue that because love is a value concept you cannot answer, "Let me *count* the number of things I bought thee." Thus, it is critical to consider how values and factual claims differ. In the smoking example, can we place the reasons for smoking on a continuum? What about the concept of love? Teachers should be clear about their own position on the relationship between facts and values.

Types of Values

Another way to think about values and values education is to consider the different types of values that appear in recent research literature. For example, values can be instrumental or terminal. Instrumental values are behaviors such as courage, rationality, or honesty that help achieve terminal values, such as wisdom, self-respect, or world peace. In other words, instrumental values are means and terminal values are ends. According to Rokeach (1973), a value is both a behavior pattern and a goal. Once a person internalizes a value, it becomes a standard for acting as well as evaluating the actions of others. This categorization of values is useful when considering the relationship and consistency between ends and means in any personal or public policy discussion. For example, the terminal value of winning among athletes is often at odds with the instrumental value of fair play.

Values can also be personal or social. Here again, the difference between personal and group values tends to overlap in that individual members share the values of the group. This classification of values can be useful when discussing issues such as gun control, environmental protection laws, abortion, and so forth. Do all people who favor environmental protection laws as an end accept the same means to achieve that end?

Values can be behavioral or substantive in nature. Behavioral or procedural values are much like those that Rokeach (1973) discussed in that they are necessary conditions to achieving other ends. They can, however, also be ends in themselves. For example, respect for other people is not only a desirable end-state for a citizen, but also a behavioral value necessary for a democratic classroom, legislature, or nation. Substantive values are generalizations usually based on observation or research, which individuals use to support their positions about politics, religion, history, and life in general. For instance, "The Church provides a useful function in the community," is an example of a substantive value.

■ ■ ■ ■ ■ ■ ■ **Types of Values**

Instrumental ———————————— Terminal
(Means)——————————————(Ends)

Personal ———————————————— Social
(Individual) ————————————————(Group)

Behavioral ———————————————— Substantive
(Action) ——————————————————(Reflection)

As you contemplate the several types of values you should remember that in social studies one of our major goals is to help students define values. Values are the criteria we use in making judgments about behavior, ideas, and events. The development of values in all of us is an ongoing process that helps us analyze, evaluate, and make consistent decisions.

What Is Values Education?

School is a moral enterprise (Childs, 1950; Burtt, 1965; Hartoonian, 1977; Gross and Dynneson, 1991) for it influences and controls human behavior and the general direction of social evolution. Therefore, differences and controversies among groups with different points of view will be inevitable. Many educators believe that they should remain neutral in this debate. However, from which issues would you like be excused?

- Should we have homogeneous grouping in our middle and high school social studies programs?
- Should the United States support nuclear research?
- Should we institute a negative income tax?

Would you categorize the above as "values" issues? If they are values issues, or if they suggest different value positions, should you discuss them in a social studies class? Teachers may be caught between two choices. On one side, they can try to remain neutral and just refuse to deal with values in any conscientious or systematic way. This position is based upon the notion of "value-free" science that some social scientists hold to be true. We believe that this position is untenable. On the other side teachers can help students explore historical and contemporary issues in ways that will illuminate value definitions, conflicts, and decisions.

A question that every teacher must ask is "*Why* should I teach values?" The position taken here is that teaching values is unavoidable. By definition, teaching is a value-laden craft. Thus, we should try to develop a definition as well as a historical context for values education.

Perhaps the best way to understand values education is to see it first within the historical context of the 20th century. As the tide of immigrants in the early part of this century arrived in the New World, as World War I altered previously held notions of personal and social responsibility, and as the Roaring 20s presented new threats to social stability, virtually every school in the United States became involved in developing the character of students through programs we might call values education (Hartshorne and May, 1928–1930). However, these researchers found, after evaluating the effectiveness of their programs, that the results were disappointing.

> . . .The mere urging of honest behavior by teachers or the discussion of values of honesty, no matter how much such general ideals may be emotionalized, has no necessary relation to conduct. . . . There seems to be evidence that such effects as may result are not generally good and are sometimes unwholesome. . . . The prevailing ways of inculcating ideals probably do little good and may do some harm. (Vol. I, p. 413)

Primarily because of the overpowering social upheavals of depression and war, values education subsided from the 1930s through the 1950s. However, in the 1960s it seemed to many that the core values of society were in trouble. Social problems including drug abuse, a more permissive attitude toward sexual conduct, increased suicide, the Vietnam War, and other trends and events led many to believe that the schools needed to deal with values. Add to this declining academic performance and the poor character models of people in leadership positions in sports, politics, and business, and citizens turned again to the schools. As in early years of the century, schools tried to respond to a real social need.

In 1966, two influential publications that changed the direction of values education were published: *Values and Teaching: Working with Values in the Classroom* (Raths, Harmin, and Simon, 1966) and "Moral Education in Schools: A Developmental View" (Kohlberg, 1966). The Raths, Harmin, and Simon approach was known as values clarification and the Kohlberg approach was called moral education. These two approaches would dominate values education for the next twenty years.

Values clarification, a program whose goal is to help students understand their own personal values, became more popular in the elementary and secondary schools. Moral education, which deals with stages of moral development in general, seemed to be more popular in colleges and universities. It is still difficult to determine the effectiveness or influence of these approaches in the classroom, but they dominated the educational research agenda for values education in the 1970s and 1980s. There were other approaches such as values analysis (Metcalf, 1971; Fraenkel, 1980), jurisprudential decision making (Oliver and Shaver, 1966), and values description (Hartoonian, 1977). However, researchers studied these approaches only infrequently and without any encouraging findings.

While you will have a chance to look at these approaches in more detail later on, you should note that even these two major programs of values clarification and moral education provide little assurance that students will develop a better character or make better moral decisions (Lockwood, 1978; Leming, 1987).

One of the researchers critical of Kohlberg's work is a Harvard University colleague, Carol Gilligan (1982), who argues that, based on different experiences, female moral development differs from that of males. Gilligan notes that Kohlberg overlooked these critical differences in much of his research, and she challenges many of his findings. Gilligan argues that perceptions of females concerning relationships, conceptions of self and morality, and experiences of conflict and choice differ from those of males. She also believes that females express these views in a "different voice." She argues that much of the baseline data used to measure moral development were based on responses of male subjects and their perspectives or experiences. She charges that Kohlberg did not consider experiences of females. Socialization processes and expectations seem to be a critical variable. Other researchers have found no differences in the stages of moral development attained by females and males. (See for example, Brabeck 1983; Gibbs, Arnold, and Burkhart 1984; and Walker, 1984.)

The arguments of Gilligan and others provide additional perspectives on moral development issues related to young people. Although Kohlberg focused his research in the United States, there is some evidence that moral development research conducted in other countries has produced similar results (Nisan and Kohlberg 1982; Snarey et al. 1985). We need further research to help us understand the thinking and reasoning processes young people use in responding to moral questions.

In addition to specific values education approaches, it is also important to consider the impact of textbooks as well as the school curriculum on students' attitudes and values. Certainly, one would think that social studies curricula and textbooks that focus on human values must have some influence on student values. The evidence for the influence of these curricula, textbooks, and practices on student values comes from three sources: research conducted on values clarification programs that use the traditional classroom as a control group; research on the influence of textbook bias on students; and the research on values education materials and student decision making. (Tibbetts, 1978; Guthrie, 1983). Again, the researchers found that the effects of the curricula, traditional classroom practices, and textbooks were extremely individual, personal, varied, and unpredictable.

What the above research findings suggest is that a number of variables affect students. These include the tone of the materials, the strategies of the teacher, and the attitudes and values that the student brings to the classroom. Grueneich (1982) found that children interpret stories based on their own unique life experiences rather than the explicit content of the story. She also found that children of different ages often form different interpretations (p. 41). The research of the 1960s, 1970s, and 1980s, like that of the 1920s, demonstrates that values-education approaches have little influence on student values and behavior. However, research over the past fifteen years would suggest three areas that seem to hold more promise for values education. These areas are: cooperative learning strategies, community study/social action programs, and establishing a just school setting (Leming, 1987).

Cooperative Learning

Cooperative learning strategies place students in small group learning situations. The achievement of the group assumes importance and students take responsibility not only for their own learning, but also for that of other group members. This type of learning environment results in positive social values and behaviors. Review of the extensive literature on this topic (Johnson, Maruyama, Johnson, Nelson, and Skon, 1981; Slavin, 1980) indicates that in addition to improving academic achievement students also develop positive social attitudes. They learn to get along better with people of different ethnic and racial backgrounds; they accept mainstreaming of students; and they show greater concern for the welfare of others. Cooperative learning strategies seem to hold great promise for social studies classroom organization.

Community Study/Social Action Programs

Community study/social action programs involve community service activities that students perform in their school or community. Activities range from helping the elderly to actively participating in social legislation aimed at changing some condition in the school or community. Because of the difficulty in doing research in these various settings and the personality differences of the students, the results of community study/social action programs are mixed (Jones, 1974; Newmann and Rutter, 1983).

Just School Programs

The just school programs are an extension of Kohlberg's work, substituting group or social norms for individual values. The just school approach has evolved within alternative school settings usually involving a very favorable faculty-to-student ratio. Within these settings students confront and discuss real problems related to social organization and often present solutions that the school then implements as social policy. In a sense, the group itself develops the rules for its own organizational life. Through a process of collective deliberation teachers and students propose rules, reach agreements, establish behavior standards, and finally, enforce and judge the rules. This approach does seem to alter student values and behaviors, basically because of the democratic setting and methods of decision making. This suggests that the classroom setting can contribute greatly in developing desirable behavior (Rutter, Maughan, Mortimore, Ouston, and Smith, 1979; Bliss, 1989; Hartoonian, 1992). In general, these latter approaches seem to work because there is *respect* for the student as an individual, real student *participation* in the life of the school or the community, and the *expectation* that the student will behave responsibly.

The goal of education is to help develop thoughtful citizens. A thoughtful citizen is one who understands his or her own values and those of society. Therefore, even if results on the effectiveness of some values education methods are mixed, we still need to explore and use established ways as well as find new methods of helping students understand the influence of values on their lives.

CHAPTER 6 Values Education 137

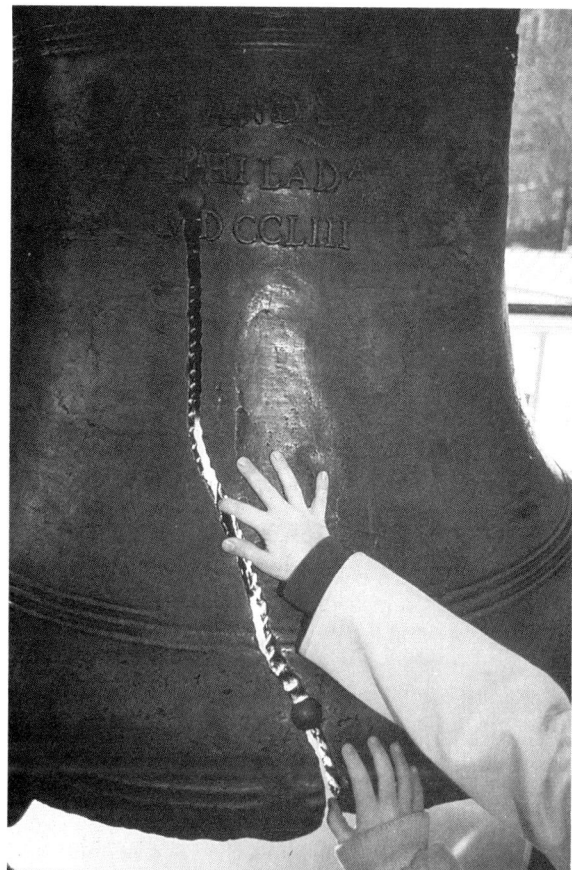

History and the Social Sciences

While some courses, like civics and contemporary issues, are interdisciplinary, most social studies courses are discrete classes in history or one of the social science disciplines. This means that the study of values, the impact of values education on the character of students, and the nature of the classroom setting are, for the most part, handled within history and social science classes. What is the relationship among history, the social sciences, and values?

History and Values

History may be defined as a way to identify the roots of present values by studying narratives from the past (Breisach, 1983). History is contemporary in the sense that we interpret it in the present. By linking the present with the past, history is always colored and illuminated by the worldview of the reader. History, because of its use of the narrative form of explanation, provides an excellent way of studying values. The stories of people, stories that we call history, can emphasize kings, wars, and the exploits of rich, white, middle- to upper-class men. Or, history can tell the stories about minorities, women, and the ordinary people. History can tell of progress or injustice, of common high purpose or oppression. The social studies teacher should understand that history operates at a number of different levels. Like any story or narrative there are values of the author, the reader, and the social settings. When we address these values we have a better chance of making history meaningful to our lives.

The narrative form of explanation can provide the link between history and the study of values. History is universal in that all people tell stories of their heritage. Because these stories are based on value structures they enable us to understand a particular worldview. History is basic to the concept of values because it portrays the human being as one who generates and uses values to explain the past. Thus, to understand history we must also understand the relationship between people and their value structures. For example, if a culture values individualism, courage, and conflict their history will emphasize those events, people, and ideas that help citizens develop those values. This might best be done through stories of war, heroines of business, the Western frontier, the Civil Rights movement, and grand events like space exploration. Immigrants to such a culture who have not developed this value structure will have some trouble understanding the significance of these stories.

The Social Sciences and Values

Values within the social sciences are not so much defined as they are charted. That is, how do values change and why? There is some agreement (Baier and Rescher, 1969) that individuals or groups may change their value positions through:

- Changes in information
  (research data on smoking and cancer)
- Political or ideological changes
  (exposure to advertising, propaganda, conditioning, indoctrination)
- Boredom or disillusionment
  (education for employment with few or no employment opportunities in the economy)
- Economic or technological changes
  (robots and job security)
- Demographic changes
  (the growing number of elderly in Western societies)

These are the kinds of issues social scientists might study that encourage students to explore their own value positions. Can you think of any other ways that values might be changed? Can you think of any values you hold today that are different from those held earlier in your life? Why did you change?

The social sciences are useful in helping us investigate core societal values such as the *survival* of the republic, the *welfare* of the people, the *justice* of economic policy, and the *advancement* of minorities. These values come to life when we use economic, political, and social information to study the kind of society we have, the standard of living of our citizens, and the costs and benefits of moving to a more desirable situation for all. As we study these core values within the context of the social sciences we use certain categories to show complementary and conflicting value claims. For example, the most commonly used categories for values study within the social sciences are self, group, society, nation, humankind, and the natural environment.

The social sciences are useful in studying the present situation among these categories as well as possible developments in the future. For example, how does the economic development of nations affect the global environment? To what extent can we consider the issue of human rights as a global issue when we identify citizens with a specific nation? What is the relationship between the well-being of the individual or family and the economic health of the nation?

Finally, the social sciences are useful in investigating why a certain group of values occupies a commanding position on the "value scale" of a particular society. In other words, people in every society have a set of values that they feel are important and from which they benefit. The social sciences can help us understand the reasons for such values and their relative importance.

Approaches to Values Education

There are many ways to classify values and values education including moral reasoning, value advocacy, value analysis, value description, and values clarification. Today we are giving more attention to creating a just classroom where attitudes, beliefs, and values can be taught. The following three things should be clear no matter how you eventually come to understand these approaches: First, these approaches are not mutually exclusive. Often it becomes difficult to tell where one approach ends and another begins. Second, they all have advocates inside, as well as outside, the profession. Third, it is difficult to determine the effectiveness of these approaches since changing attitudes or behaviors of students is a very complex process. However, it is important that you develop an appropriate rationale for the study of values. This will give you a framework for making decisions about values education. Let us look briefly at some of the major instructional approaches to values education. We will give special attention here to the value analysis approach because it uses narrative explanation. This is a fundamental methodology of history and the social sciences.

Value Advocacy

Value advocacy is perhaps the most universal and pervasive way in which we teach values. Every teacher, indeed, every person, advocates certain values. "All educational systems indoctrinate the oncoming generation with basic outlooks and values of the political order" (Key, 1961). Value advocacy embodies the idea of direct cultural transmission from adults to children.

All teachers, whether they admit it or not, are "advocates" in that they emphasize certain values or approaches over others. That is, they stress procedural or substantive values, instrumental or terminal values, values like justice or happiness, and so forth. So, in the final analysis, all approaches, either explicitly or implicitly, advocate values.

Value advocacy is the learning strategy that inspires, persuades, moralizes, and otherwise convinces students to adopt the "right" values. Thus, there is no need to develop decision-making skills because choices are already made for the student. Teachers in this approach are example setters, and they should present "right" values that the community has outlined.

Critics of the value advocacy approach charge that engaging students in this approach leads to disillusionment and other antisocial attitudes like bigotry, ethnocentrism, and cynicism. These attitudes occur when students have little opportunity to reflect upon the real/ideal dilemmas in life. For example, one of the beliefs of our republic is that all people are created equal. However, as students look around the real world they see that people are not treated as equal. How do principles like those that are stated in the major documents of our republic square with the facts of life in the United States? Critics of this approach express concern that teachers will expose students to only one side of this real/ideal dilemma. If we take this dilemma seriously, it means that we should advocate a commitment to basic societal values (Shaver, 1985) on the one hand, while at the same time help students reconcile the real with the ideal through reflective policy making (Bragaw and Hartoonian, 1988).

As Shaver (1985) states:

> It is reasonable and not in any way illogical to argue that we, and our students, should be committed to the basic values of our society and at the same time examine the meanings and applications of those values.

This would suggest that teachers can impart certain values to students, values that reflect the social theories and principles of a society. At the same time teachers can encourage students and insist that they engage in analysis and application of those values in their lives. Indeed, this is the central argument for teachers to go beyond value advocacy in their classroom and have students confront the real and the ideal in their lives.

Moral Reasoning

Moral reasoning uses moral dilemmas in history and contemporary settings to encourage students to make decisions. The central rationale of this approach is that students can enhance their moral reasoning abilities through properly led discussions of moral and ethical problems.

The moral reasoning approach is based on the research of Harvard psychologist Lawrence Kohlberg and his associates. This approach suggests a developmental process whereby students move up through various stages of moral reasoning. The students can achieve this upward progression through maturity and through intellectual practice with moral dilemmas.

The three developmental levels identified by Kohlberg are the pre-conventional, the conventional, and the post-conventional periods. Within each of these levels there are two stages. The resulting six stages constitute a taxonomy, meaning that one must move through a lower stage before achieving a higher stage.

At the pre-conventional level, people base moral judgments on the power of authority figures or the consequences of an individual's action. That is, "Will I be rewarded or punished for my behavior?" People base stage one behavior on the avoidance of punishment, the opportunity to earn rewards, or the psychological need to obey authority without question. At stage two of this level, people make decisions primarily to satisfy personal needs and to negotiate for mutually advantageous results.

At the conventional level, people base moral judgments on loyalty to others. In other words, loyalty to family, friends, school, church, and nation takes priority over simple personal needs and expectations. Individuals will work to maintain and justify the existence of the status quo. Therefore, at stage three people make decisions primarily to please or help others. They value good intentions and seek approval for proper behavior. In stage four of the conventional level individuals make decisions to maintain existing authority and social order. People place high value on doing one's duty to family, state, or group.

In the post-conventional level of moral judgment people value principles that go beyond the authority of the group. The individual seeks to do what is right in accordance with universal values and principles. He or she is concerned with high purpose, which transcends the individual and the group. Within this level, stage five decisions reflect the legal point of view. Therefore, right behavior is that which adheres to the rights and responsibilities upon which the society has agreed. Further, there is tolerance within this stage to change laws and rules. At stage six of the post-conventional level people make decisions using self-chosen ethical principles such as justice, equity, beauty, and human dignity. An individual's conscience guides moral reasoning in accordance with universal ethical values. In the late 1970s Kohlberg de-emphasized stage six since few people attain that level. As previously noted, however, Kohlberg's research was done exclusively with young men. Carol Gilligan's individual work (1982) and her work with colleagues (1990) suggest that when women are included in this type of study stage six behavior seems more attainable.

When we apply moral reasoning to the classroom, we ask students to confront moral dilemmas from either history or contemporary life. Through discussion, analysis, and logical reasoning students make and support judgments about what should happen in these dilemmas. It is important not only to arrive at "an answer," it is even more important to establish a rationale for that answer.

There are, of course, other reasons for using the moral reasoning approach such as developing self-esteem, improving attitudes toward school, and enhancing skills of rhetoric. According to Leming (1987) one of the best applications of this approach is the "Reasoning With Democratic Values" program as developed by Lockwood and Harris (1985). Using narratives and dilemmas from United States history such as the founders' belief in equality and their willingness to continue slavery. Students review facts, establish the historical setting, analyze ethical issues, and express reasons for arriving at certain decisions. While "Reasoning With Democratic Values" gives little direct attention to the Kohlberg stages of moral development, it does offer a well-conceived program for helping students improve their skills of ethical and moral reasoning.

Value Description

Value description focuses upon defining value concepts, developing generalizations, and building theories so we can better understand the role of values in personal and public decision making. Investigations focus on what is, not what ought to be.

We can describe this approach as "scientific." It is an attempt to describe reality based on observations. The most commonly used methodologies of this approach include survey research and observations of the habits of people (recreational, economic, sexual, educational, political, and so on). Again, the primary concern is with the state of reality as it appears rather than dealing with notions of what ought to be. Personal and societal values are identified, studied, defined, and normally applied to other concepts such as social class, race, levels of education, and so forth. The rationale here is that values provide descriptive power and information to explain the world as it presently exists. Within our mass media culture the value description approach is the one most commonly used. Consumer and political polls are, in essence, attempts to identify value positions of certain populations so that business and political leaders know what the people think and want. Social studies teachers and students should be aware of this approach with all its strengths and weaknesses.

Values Clarification

Values clarification is a decision-making process. In this approach students select solutions from a variety of alternatives. This process leads students to identify and clarify their personal values. The role of the teacher is crucial to the success of this approach since the teacher must help students clarify their values without violating the student's right to privacy.

Raths, Harmin, and Simon (1978) define values clarification as a process. It is a seven-step approach toward what the developers call *valuing*. These seven steps include:

1. Choosing freely—making choices without interference or pressure from others
2. Choosing from alternatives—making a choice after considering the costs and benefits of several alternatives
3. Considering consequences—picking an alternative after careful reflection of the consequences
4. Prizing your choice—believing that the choice is most worthy, important, or valuable
5. Affirming publicly—making public statements (rationales) about your choice
6. Acting consistently—behaving in a manner consistent with chosen values
7. Acting repeatedly—showing consistency in behavior and value relationships

Values clarification does not try to instill any set of particular values. However, it does advocate procedural values. Values clarification seeks to train students in a process of value preferences and application after careful reflection and choice making. The teacher's role in this approach is one of facilitator developing a climate of trust, selecting appropriate activities, withholding judgments, and asking important questions.

The questions most often asked in this approach resemble those used in client-centered therapy psychology (Hartoonian, 1977). For example:

- How do you feel about your choice?
- Can you say more than that?
- Is this what you mean?
- What alternatives do you have?

Values clarification uses many highly motivational activities to help students deal with value questions. The most common activity categories are forced choice activities, rank order activities, brainstorming, unfinished statements, checklists, and role playing (see *Values Clarification: A Handbook of*

Practical Strategies for Teachers and Students; Simon, Howe, and Kirschenbaum, 1972).

Values clarification also has its critics (Lockwood, 1977; Hartoonian, 1977). The criticism tends to fall within the following categories:

- Values clarification tends to promote ethical relativism, that is, the belief that one ethical position is as worthy as any other position.
- Values clarification has potential to invade the privacy of individuals.
- Values clarification can place the teacher in the role of therapist for which he or she probably has no training.
- Values clarification has little research support for the claims made in its rationale.

Values clarification has been, by far, the most popular values education approach through the 1970s and 1980s. It is also the most criticized. However, it does offer many motivational activities that can, under the right classroom conditions engage students in important discussions about their values and the values of society. Such activities might include rank-ordering difficult choices about who might live given a certain situation, or writing your own obituary, or deciding when it might be acceptable to steal something.

Classroom Setting

We have included classroom setting, or the just classroom, because of the recent attention educators have given to this concept. According to this idea the good school is a place where there is a sense of community (Bryk and Driscoll, 1988; Hartoonian, 1992). This place respects students and ideas, is safe, friendly, and has a high sense of aesthetic quality. That is, the school is a pleasing place to be. It is clean and has plants, flowers, and artwork that help students feel good about being there. Such schools report that teachers are more satisfied in their work and students show more prosocial behavior. As schools try to create safer environments for students, this approach will probably become more widely used.

Value Analysis

Value analysis emphasizes logic and reflective thinking. It encourages students to evaluate evidence rather than accept a preestablished judgment or value. Students who follow this approach should use rational thought to define, defend, and use their value positions.

Let us now look with some detail at one approach to value analysis. We will call this the "value profiles" approach. A value profile is a value position an investigator constructs using classification schemes. Value profiles of an individual may be consistent as that person moves from one situation to another, or they may change. The only claim here is that the investigator using this model of value analysis will be able to construct value profiles and in the process learn more about a value, a person, a group, or an event. In this example we will use *justice* as the value concept we are analyzing.

We will use three continua to build a value profile of an individual. These three continua are "self and other-person orientation," "situational and general value orientation," and "means and ends orientation." We will then study this profile in relationship to the concept of justice. That is, we will try to define those attributes of justice that are consistent with our intellectual and cultural heritage.

A major advantage of this approach is its usefulness in helping individuals discuss and understand value concepts like justice. We believe that we can best study the concept of justice by using analogy and discussing moral conflict.

> The first step in teaching virtue, then, is the Socratic step of creating dissatisfaction in the student about his [or her] present knowledge of the concept. This we do experimentally by exposing the student to moral conflict situations for which his [her] principles have no ready solution. Second, we expose him [her] to disagreement and argument about these situations with his [her] peers. (Kohlberg, 1970, p. 82)

This approach tries to help individuals come to a better "operational definition" of a moral principle like justice. This search for a universal definition of justice implies that there is a commonly held conception of the term. If we can arrive at a working definition of justice then we can conceive of a just society composed of just people. This would be an ideal society in the sense that it would offer a standard of perfection by which we could measure all existing societies. We might judge any proposed change or reform by its tendency to bring us nearer to, or further from, this ideal.

Justice, of course, is at the center of most philosophical questions with which Western writers deal. What is justice and how can it be realized? This is the main question, for example, in Plato's *Republic*. Through Socrates we view a number of attempts at definition: justice as honesty in word and deed; justice as helping friends and harming enemies; and justice as the interest of the stronger (*Republic of Plato*, 1945, p. 40).

Central to the argument of values education is the question of whether a person can discover a value like justice alone or only through the help of others. This question presents an unavoidable paradox. That paradox, simply stated, is that people forever remain separated from the philosophic knowledge of the good until someone leads them to its discovery. However, the person who leads this inquiry may superimpose certain preconceived social values. This is antithetical to the search for justice, because it outwardly directs into the mind rather than encourages the emergence of what is within.

The above discussion of the moral principle of justice and the paradox suggested by the search for justice should not suggest a "do nothing" attitude toward value analysis and moral education. On the contrary, it should only alert us again to the fact that the knowledge of the good begins with an understanding of the inherent limitations in our present analytical models. It should suggest that in the use of this approach *justice should be seen as a moral principle and not as a set of rules. This is the case because life is dynamic and complex while rules tend to be fixed and limited.* Thus, as students use the three value categories below, as they apply these categories to narratives for analysis, and as they discuss the concept of justice, they will constantly probe their awareness and build a more useful conception of justice.

As we begin to study the "value profile" approach to value analysis we will use a set of three continua upon which to find an individual's value position. The three continua ask us to consider the tensions between self and others; between situational and general values; and between goals and modes of conduct. It is important to first of all discuss individual facets to each continuum.

Does the behavior (including what the individual says) demonstrate a commitment to personal wants and avoidance of punishment? Or does the behavior demonstrate a commitment to universal principles and the establishment of mutual respect and trust?

Continuum I reflects the work of Kohlberg, who has analyzed moral behavior and has constructed a taxonomy of moral conduct (1966). In the Kohlberg schema, the individual first makes decisions to achieve personal wants and avoid punishment. He or she then seeks approval by conforming to norms and authority for their own sakes. As the individual matures, then he or she will seek self-accepted or autonomous principles and become concerned with establishing mutual trust and respect.

Kohlberg's analysis of moral development suggests that the teaching of values is a matter of helping individuals grow into increasingly advanced stages of personal decision making, enabling them to mediate their needs and those of others. Kohlberg sees a direct interrelationship between values education and personal development.

As a person makes decisions (lives from day to day) we can develop a picture of his or her reliance on self versus reliance on the group. This knowledge will help us understand that person's value profile and will also allow us to make better predictions of future behavior. Ultimately, when this continuum is used with the other two continua of this approach, we may have more clues

■ ■ ■ ■ ■ ■ ■ ■ **Continuum I**

Self-Orientation	Other Person (Mutual Respect and Trust) Orientation
Orientation Toward Obedience and Punishment	Orientation Toward Universal and Logical Principles or Conscience

about an individual's conception of the moral principle of justice. This process of studying a person will also ultimately help the investigator clarify his or her own concept of justice.

Continuum II represents analysis from another vantage point. It takes the notion of personal versus group value claims and views these from a situational versus a general position (relativism—universalism). The dichotomy suggested by Continuum II might be best stated in two questions. What should I do now? Why am I doing it? These questions are not mutually exclusive, for a moral principle is not only a rule of action but also a reason for action. The continuum also suggests a middle ground between allegiance to general rules or principles and some kind of individual, situational choice. It can be argued, of course, that any choice is based upon some moral system that the individual accepts.

Continuum II

Situational	General
(Honesty in a particular situation)	(Honesty)

Does the person's behavior demonstrate consistent adherence (at all times and in all places) to a particular set of rules? Or is the behavior situational?

It follows, however, that a person can opt for situational positions from time to time in his or her value choice. But, rationality, as the term is used here, means the willingness and the skill to weigh that value choice in the light of societal values. Let us look more closely at the tension between general and situational orientations and universalism versus relativism.

Chris and Leslie are discussing whether the Romans were morally justified in persecuting the Christians.

CHRIS: No, it was definitely wrong. People are entitled to worship as they please, as long as they do not interfere with others. Even though the Christians might have been causing some trouble, the Romans had no right to treat them so brutally and with such violence.

LESLIE: Well, you and I happen to believe in religious freedom, but it's obvious that the Romans didn't share this value. The Romans thought Christians a danger to their empire. Who are we to tell the Romans that they should respect Christianity? People in those days just believed in different values, so persecution was morally right from a Roman point of view.

CHRIS: I don't care who does the persecuting or when and where it happens. Persecuting a person for his or her religious belief is just wrong.

LESLIE: I don't think you have any right to tell other people what they should believe in. Each person or culture is entitled to hold whatever values they want.

Chris and Leslie appear to be deadlocked over whether they should generalize a commitment to a particular value (religious freedom) to a group (Romans) that evidently placed lower priority upon it. Do we have a moral right to apply our values universally to the actions of others? Instead, perhaps we should learn which values another group holds and then judge that group on its own terms—did it fulfill the values it holds as important? If we adopt the universalist approach, we sometimes feel a bit guilty for "imposing our values on others." Certain values in which we believe, such as individual freedom or toleration, tell us only to judge others by their own standards. Yet, if we adopt a completely relativist position, we do not allow ourselves to make any moral judgments except about our own actions. This could lead to such statements as "If the Nazis thought it was right to exterminate the Jews, then it was right for them; if my neighbor believes it is right to kill her child, then it is right for her. In neither case should I interfere, because that would be imposing my values on someone else."

Most people are neither extreme universalists nor extreme relativists. We can clarify discussion of moral issues if we challenge people to specify the extent of their commitment to either a universalist or relativist orientation. Without testing the philosophical framework underlying one's specific value choices, a discussion like the preceding could easily become deadlocked with Chris repeating, "Religious persecution is always wrong," and Leslie answering, "It may be wrong for us, but it was right for the Romans because they thought it was" (Adapted from Newmann and Oliver, 1970; 101–102.)

Continuum II helps students understand the ethical arguments that underlie value controversies. It helps students see that general rules simply confuse our thinking, preventing us from openly examining each situation on its merit. For example, as artificial kidneys and hearts are used to save people's lives, the money to purchase these become more scarce. A doctor who decides which patients shall have the devices is essentially deciding that some people will live and others die. Do we call the doctor a murderer? Do biblical commandments or principles of common law or state constitutions help us make this new moral choice? (Ibid., 103–104). What do you think?

> "However, . . . we could also argue that many situations do *not* differ in the most relevant or salient aspect of moral choice—both the American Revolution and Negro rebellion concern basic human rights and how best to attain them. Making explicit such commonalties among issues helps to clarify the issue over which people disagree. Comparing situations and testing whether principles of the past can be applied consistently does not necessarily make one a slave to accepting past principles. . . ." (Ibid., 103–104).

Continuum II, then, allows the student to evaluate a person's reasons for a value claim and place it on the scale between commitment to situational values and commitment to general values.

With Continuum III we expand further the value analysis approach by considering the complex notions of means and ends. Clearly, we have occasions in life when we must make decisions not only among conflicting goals, but also between goals and modes of conduct (or stating it differently, between instrumental and terminal values). There *may* be times when certain modes of conduct (cleanliness) are detrimental to certain goals (having a garden). Continuum III helps us to better understand the reasons for a person's decision to hold or accept a particular goal or behavior.

Continuum III

Goal	Modes of Personal Conduct
(Terminal Values)	(Instrumental Values)

Taken together, when we apply these three continua to a narrative, they can provide an analytical framework that can illuminate the student's value profiles.

We need to make three final points about this approach. First of all, we assume that the three continua do not apply equally in all narrative situations. For example, in any given narrative only one or perhaps two of the continua might apply. However, in those situations where we can use all three continua we will do it. Second, we reiterate that the main function of this model is to illuminate the "value position" of the person under investigation, and ultimately, the value position of the student.

Finally, there is this question: "What value profile (position on the three continua) is most consistent with the concept of justice as defined above?" We suggest the following diagram as an optimum value profile for the concept of justice.

I. Self-Orientation — Other-Person Orientation (Mutual Respect) ———————————✗—

II. Situational (Honesty in a particular situation) — General (Honesty) ———————————✗—

III. Goal (Terminal Values) — Modes of Personal Conduct (Instrumental Values) ——————✗——

The reason for the above placement rests on arguments presented previously. For example, the position on Continuum I toward other-people orientation calls attention to the principle of justice as a moral obligation to respect the right or claim of another person. The position on Continuum II toward the general or universalist orientation calls attention to the principle of justice as a rational commitment to general societal values. The location on Continuum III midway between terminal and instrumental values calls attention to the principle of justice as both a reason for action and a method of action. Justice implies a balance of the two notions of goal and method.

We present the following narrative to allow you to try out the value profile approach.

Sam Houston
by
John F. Kennedy

The first rays of dawn were streaking into the ill-lit Senate chamber of 1854 as one final speaker rose to seek recognition. Weary, haggard and unshaven Senators, slumped despondently in their chairs after the rigors of an all-night session, muttered "Vote, Vote" in the hopes of discouraging any further oratory on a bill already certain of passage. But Senator Sam Houston of Texas, the hero of San Jacinto, was not easily discouraged by overwhelming odds; and as his deep, musical voice carried the bold if unpolished words of a powerful message to his astonished colleagues, they shook off the dull stupor which had deadened their fatigued brains and sat upright and attentive.

The bill on which bitter and exhausting debate now closed was known as the Kansas-Nebraska Bill, the new "unity" device of the Democratic party and the latest concession to the South. It repealed the Missouri Compromise of 1820, and reopened the slavery extension issue thought settled in the Compromise of 1850, by permitting the residents of that vast territory from Iowa to the Rockies to decide the slavery question for themselves, on the assumption that the northern part of the territory would be free and the southern part slave. For Democrats and Southerners, this bill had become "must" legislation.

Sam Houston was a Democrat of long standing. And Sam Houston was a Southerner by birth, residence, loyalty and philosophy. But Sam Houston was also Sam Houston, one of the most independent, unique, popular, forceful and dramatic individuals ever to enter the Senate chamber. The first Senator from Texas, his name had long before been a household word as Commander in Chief of those straggling and undermanned Texas volunteers who routed the entire Mexican Army at San Jacinto, captured its general and established the independence of Texas. He has been acclaimed as the first President of the Independent Republic of Texas, a Member of her Congress, and President again before the admission of Texas into the Union as a state. He was no easy mark at the age of sixty-four, and neither sectional nor party ties were enough to seal his lips.

Sam Houston looked upon the Missouri Compromise, which he had supported in 1820 as youthful Congressman from Tennessee, as a solemn and sacred compact between North and South, in effect a part of the Constitution when Texas was admitted into the Union. Nor was he willing to discard the Compromise of

1850, which he had supported despite the enmity of Texas fire-eaters who called his vote, "the damnest outrage yet committed upon Texas." With rugged, homely but earnest eloquence, he begged his weary colleagues in an impromptu plea not to plunge the nation into new agitations over the slavery issue.

Sam Houston must have known the bill would pass, he must have known that not a single Southern Democrat would join him, he must have known that, as rumor of his position had spread the previous week, the Richmond *Enquirer* had spoken for his constituents in declaring, "Nothing can justify this treachery; nor can anything save the traitor from the deep damnation which such treason may merit." But, standing erect, his chin thrust forward, picturesque if not eccentric in his military cloak and panther-skin waistcoat (at times he appeared in a vast sombrero and Mexican blanket), Sam Houston, the "magnificent barbarian," made one of his rare speeches to a weary but attentive Senate:

"This is an eminently perilous measure; and do you expect me to remain here silent, or to shrink from the discharge of my duty in admonishing the South of what I conceive the results will be? I will speak in spite of all the intimidations, or threats, or discountenances that may be thrown upon me. Sir, the charge that I am going with Abolitionists or Free-Soilers affects me not. The discharge of conscious duty prompts me often to conform the united array of the very section of the country in which I reside, in which my associations are, in which my affections rest. . . . Sir, if this is a boon that is offered to propitiate the South, I, as a Southern man, repudiate it. I will have none of it. . . . Our children are either to live in after times in the enjoyment of peace, of harmony, and prosperity, or the alternative remains for them of anarchy, discord, and civil broil. We can avert the last. I trust we shall. . . . I adjure you to regard the contract once made to harmonize and preserve this Union. Maintain the Missouri Compromise! Stir not up agitation! Give us peace!"

"It was," Houston was later to remark, "the most unpopular vote I ever gave [but] the wisest and most patriotic." Certainly it was the most unpopular. When old Sam had first journeyed to the Senate, the baby-new state of Texas was primarily concerned with railroad, land, debt and boundary questions, without particularly strong Southern ties. But now, Texas with 150,000 valuable slaves and an overwhelmingly Democratic population consisting largely of citizens from other Southern states, identified its interests with those Houston had attacked; and with near unanimity, she cried for Houston's scalp as one who had "betrayed his state in the Senate," "joined the Abolitionists" and "deserted the South." By a vote of 73 to 3 the Legislature applauded Houston's colleague for supporting the Nebraska Bill, and condemned the stand of him who was once the most glorious hero the state had ever known. The Democratic State Convention denounced the great warrior as, "not in accordance with the sentiments of the Democracy of Texas." The Dallas *Herald* demanded that Houston resign the seat to which Texans had proudly sent him, instead of "retaining a position he has forfeited by misrepresenting them. . . . Let him heed for once the voice of an outraged, misrepresented, and betrayed constituency, so that Texas may for once have a united voice and present an undivided front in the Senate."

To make matters worse, this was not the first offense for Senator Sam Houston, merely—as described by the indignant Clarksville *Standard*—"the last feather that broke the camel's back." He had tangled with John Calhoun on the Oregon question, describing himself as a Southerner for whom "the Union was his guiding star," and who had "no fear that the North would seek to destroy the South notwithstanding the papers signed by old men and women and pretty girls." "The South has been beaten by the South—if united, she would have conquered!" cried an influential Dixie paper when Calhoun rebuked Houston and Benton for providing the winning margin for his opponents. But Sam Houston would only reply: "I know neither North nor South; I know only the Union."

He would have nothing to do, moreover, with Calhoun's "hands-off" slavery resolutions and "Southern Address," attacking that revered sage of the South for his "long-cherished and ill-concealed designs against the Union," and insisting to the Senate that he, Sam Houston, was "on this floor representative of the whole American people." But the Texas Legislature adopted Calhoun's resolutions, and cast a suspicious eye on the ambitious former President of Texas whose name was being mentioned, in the North as well as the South, for the White House in 1852 or 1856.

Finally, Houston had been the first prominent Senator to attack Calhoun's opposition to the Clay Compromise of 1850, quoting the Scripture to label those threatening secession as mere "raging waves of sea, foaming out their own shame..."

"Think you, sir, after the difficulties Texans have encountered to get into the Union, that you can whip them out of it? No, sir... we shed our blood to get into it.... We were among the last to come into the Union, and being in, we will be the last to get out... I call on the friends of the Union from every quarter to come forward like men, and to sacrifice their differences upon the common altar of their country's good, and to form a bulwark around the Constitution that cannot be shaken. It will require many efforts, sir, and they must expect to meet with prejudices that will assail them from every quarter. They must stand firm to the Union, regardless of all personal consequences."

Thus his lonely vote against the Kansas-Nebraska Bill, on that stormy dawn in 1854, was indeed the "last straw." It was loudly whispered about the Senate that this was the last term for the colorful General. Those illustrious Senators with whom he served, whose oratory could not attract the glory and romance which surrounded the name of Sam Houston, may have frowned upon his eccentric dress and his habit of whittling pine sticks on the Senate floor while muttering at the length of senatorial speeches. But they could not help but admire his stoical courage and rugged individualism, which has preface to a brief autobiographical sketch expressed more simply: "This book will lose me some friends. But if it lost me all and gained none, in God's name, as I am a free man, I would publish it...." (*Profiles in Courage.* John F. Kennedy, 1956; pp. 121–126)

Develop a value profile for Sam Houston based on the above narrative. Go back and apply the questions for each continuum to Houston. Where would you place Houston with regard to the following continua?

I. Self-Orientation Other-Person Orientation
 (Mutual Respect and Trust)

II. Situational General
 (Honesty in a Particular Situation) (Honesty)

III. Goal   Modes of Personal Conduct
    (Terminal Values)   (Instrumental Values)

Defend your value profile of Sam Houston in terms of your understanding of the concept of justice.

You can place other people, events, and groups on these continua, developing value profiles that can illuminate the concept of justice or any value concept. This is the essence of value analysis—illuminating value concepts in the lives of people.

SUMMARY

Values are pervasive in our lives, including our life in school. Thus, teaching values is unavoidable, but in many communities values education is also controversial.

We have considered several approaches to teaching and learning values and have asserted that these approaches are not mutually exclusive. Whichever approach you use, you will have to understand and defend the rationale, strategies, and desired outcomes of using the one you chose.

How do you think about values? Are they something to be inculcated into students? Are they social theories or political ideals rooted in our cultural heritage? Are they cultural universals to be understood by any "educated" person? Are they substantive or procedural notions? Can and should values be taught in school?

However you answer these questions you will have to understand that the teacher is ultimately responsible for the nature of values education in the classroom. Thus, he or she must have an informed rationale and method of teaching values. In the end, the teacher must defend the approaches used in the classroom. These rationales, goals, methods, and evaluation designs should be consistent with the total social studies program.

Discussion Questions

1. Do you agree with the argument that teachers cannot avoid teaching values? Why?

2. What is the relationship between values of personal preference and social values?
3. What are "family values"? How would you define family values using the three continua in this chapter?
4. Should students be free to choose values? Explain.
5. It has been noted that the culture or climate of classrooms is the most effective teacher of values in the school. To what extent should teachers pay attention to this assertion? What should teachers do about it?
6. What would you consider to be the most effective approach to values education? Why?

Student Learning Activities

1. Within small groups (five or fewer) research and study one values education approach and present a lesson to classmates emphasizing the major features of that approach. Structure the lesson (presentation) as follows:
   - Theoretical base and rationale for the approach
   - Major components or procedures of the approach
   - A lesson using the approach
   - Debrief and evaluate the approach
2. Some of the best real-world examples of value conflicts are in legal cases. The legal case method is a strategy with which all social studies teachers should be familiar. (See Law-Related Education Projects—American Bar Association: Division for Public Education.)

   The case study method provides opportunities to define, analyze, and act upon values within a societal context. Legal cases (historical or contemporary) also permit students to synthesize several values-education approaches by dealing with issues of facts, value conflicts, validity of arguments, congruency with social norms and constitutional law, and social implications of legal decisions. Thought-provoking questions include the following:
   - Should a city deny a parade permit to the Ku Klux Klan?
   - Should the people of the United States impose the death penalty as a punishment for serious crimes?
   - Should prayer be allowed in public schools?
   - Should abortion on demand be made illegal?

   Develop a simulation around a question like one of the above that can be played out in an appellate court. Use one or several judges and a team of "attorneys" for both sides of the issue. Consider the facts of the case, the value conflicts inherent in the case, the quality and validity of the arguments presented, definitional problems or conflicts, and consequences of the decisions.

3. Survey or observe your teachers and/or classmates to determine if they use any specific values-education approaches. How much importance do they place on values education? How do they define it? Is it integrated into other content lessons or taught separately? How are the results of values education evaluated?
4. Look at a literature selection used in a middle school or high school English class and identify the values that you believe are being discussed in that literature.
   a. How are the values defined?
   b. How are the values reflected in the lives of the major characters in the literature? (Note behavior, motivation, and consequences.)

References

Baier, K. and Rescher, N. (Eds.). 1969. *Values and the Future: The Impact of Technological Change on American Values.* New York: Free Press.

Bliss, T. 1989. "The Use of Groupwork in High School Social Studies." *Theory and Research in Social Education* Vol. XVII, No. 4, Fall. 303–315.

Brabeck, M. M. 1983. "Moral Judgment: Theory and Research on Differences Between Males and Females." *Developmental Review.* Vol. 3, No. 3, September. 274–291.

Bragaw, D. H. and Hartoonian, H. M. 1988. "Social Studies: The Study of People in Society." In R. Brandt, (Ed.) *Content of the Curriculum.* ASCD Yearbook. Alexandria, VA: Association for Supervision and Curriculum Development.

Breisach, E. 1983. *Historiography: Ancient, Medieval and Modern.* Chicago: University of Chicago Press.

Bryk, A. S. and Driscoll, M. E. 1988. *The High School as Community: Contextual Influences and Consequences for Students and Teachers.* Madison, WI: National Center on Effective Schools, University of Wisconsin. ERIC Document Reproduction Service ED302 539.

Burtt, E. A. 1965. *In Search of Philosophic Understanding.* New York: New American Library.

Childs, J. 1950. *Education and Morals: An Experimentalist Philosophy of Education.* New York: Appleton, Century and Crofts. (Reprinted 1971, New York: Arno Press and *The New York Times*).

Fraenkel, J. R. 1980. *Helping Students Think and Value: Strategies for Teaching the Social Studies* (2nd ed.). Englewood Cliffs, NJ: Prentice-Hall.

Gibbs, J. C., Arnold, K. D., and Burkhart, J. E. 1984. "Sex Differences in the Expression of Moral Judgment." *Child Development,* Vol. 55, No. 3, June. 1040–1043.

Gilligan, C., 1982, *In a Different Voice: Psychological Theory and Women's Development.* Cambridge, MA: Harvard University Press.

Gilligan, C., Lyons, N. P., and Hammer, T. J., (Eds.). 1990. *Making Connections: The Relational Worlds of Adolescent Girls at Emma Willard School.* Cambridge, MA: Harvard University Press.

Gross, R. E. and Dynneson, T. L., (Ed.), 1991. *Social Science Perspectives on Citizenship Education.* New York: Teachers College Press, Columbia University.

Grueneich, R. 1982. "Issues in the Developmental Study of How Children Use Intention and Consequences Information to Make Moral Evaluations." *Child Development*, Vol. 53, No. 1, February. 29–43.

Guthrie, J. T. 1983. "Research: Learning Values from Textbooks." *Reading Teacher*, Vol. 26, No. 6, March. 574–576.

Hartoonian, H. M. 1973, "A Disclosure Approach to Value Analysis in Social Studies Education: Rationale and Components." *Theory and Research in Social Education,* Vol. 1, No. 1, October. 1–25.

Hartoonian, H. M. 1977. "The Ethics of Our Profession: The Student and Schooling." *Theory and Research in Social Education,* Vol. 5, No. 2. August. 57–64.

Hartoonian, H. M. 1992. "The Geographic Imagination and School Report." In A. D. Hill (Ed.), *Interdependence in Geographic Education*. Boulder, CO: Center for Geographic Education, University of Colorado.

Hartshorne, H. and May, M. A. 1928–1930. *Studies in the Nature of Character:* Vol. 1, *Studies in Deceit*; Vol. 2, *Studies in Self Control*; Vol. 3, *Studies in the Organization of Character*. New York: Macmillan.

Hunt, M. P. and Metcalf, L. E. 1968. *Teaching High School Social Studies: Problems in Reflective Thinking and Social Understanding* (2nd ed). New York: Harper and Row.

Johnson, D. W., Maruyama, G., Johnson, R. T., Nelson, D., and Skon, L. 1981. "Effects of Cooperative, Competitive, and Individualistic Goal Structures on Achievement: A Meta-Analysis." *Psychological Bulletin*, Vol. 89, No. 1, January–May. 47–62.

Jones, R. S. 1974. "Changing Student Attitudes: The Impact of Community Participation." *Social Science Quarterly*, Vol. 55, No. 2, September. 439–450.

Kennedy, J. F. 1956. *Profiles in Courage.* New York: Harper and Row.

Key, V. O., Jr. 1961. *Public Opinion and American Democracy.* New York: Knopf.

Kohlberg, L. 1966. "Moral Education in Schools: A Developmental View." *School Review,* Vol. 74, No. 1, Spring. 1–30.

Kohlberg, L. 1970. "Education for Justice: A Modern Statement of the Platonic View." *Moral Education: Five Lectures.* Cambridge, MA: Harvard University Press.

Leming, J. S. 1987. *Values Clarification Research: A Study of the Etiology of a Weak Educational Research Program.* Unpublished Paper, Southern Illinois University, Carbondale.

Lockwood, A. L. 1977. "What's Wrong with Values Clarification?" *Social Education*, Vol. 41, No. 5, May. 399–401.

Lockwood, A. 1978. "The Effects of Values Clarification and Moral Development Curricula on School Age Subjects: A Critical Review of Recent Research." *Review of Educational Research*, Vol. 48, No. 3, Summer. 325–364.

Lockwood, A. L. and Harris, D. E. 1985. *Reasoning with Democratic Values: Ethical Problems in United States History.* 2 vols. New York: Teachers College Press, Columbia University.

Metcalf, L. E. (Ed.). 1971. *Values Education: Rationale, Strategies, and Procedures*. 41st Yearbook. Washington, DC: National Council for the Social Studies.

Newmann, F. M. and Oliver, D. W. 1970. *Clarifying Public Controversy: An Approach to Teaching Social Studies.* Boston: Little, Brown.

Newmann, F. M. and Rutter, R. 1983. "The Effects of High School Community Service Programs on Students' Social Development." NIE (Grant No. NIE G-81-

0009). Madison, WI, Wisconsin Center for Education Research. Published in *C.E.R. Newsletter,* Fall 1991.

Nisan, M. and Kohlberg, L. 1982. "Universality and Variation in Moral Judgment: A Longitudinal and Cross-sectional Study in Turkey." *Child Development,* Vol. 53, No. 4, August. 865–876.

Oliver, D. W. and Shaver, J. M. 1966. *Teaching Public Issues in the High School.* Boston: Houghton Mifflin.

Raths, L. E., Harmin, M., and Simon, S. B. 1966. *Values and Teaching: Working with Values in the Classroom.* Columbus, OH: Charles E. Merrill.

Raths, L. E., Harmin, M. and Simon, S. B. 1978. *Values in Teaching: Working with Values in the Classroom.* (2nd ed.). Columbus, OH: Charles E. Merrill.

Republic of Plato. 1945. New York: Oxford University Press. (Also available in other editions.)

Rokeach, M. 1973. *The Nature of Human Values.* New York: Free Press.

Rutter, M., Maughan, B., Mortimore, P., Ouston, J., and Smith, A. 1979. *Fifteen Thousand Hours: Secondary Schools and Their Effects on Children.* Cambridge, MA: Harvard University Press.

Shaver, J. P. 1985. "Commitment to Values and the Study of Social Problems in Citizenship Education." *Social Education,* Vol. 49, No. 3, March. 194–197.

Simon, S. B., Howe, L. W., and Kirschenbaum, H. 1972. *Values Clarification: A Handbook of Practical Strategies for Teachers and Students.* New York: Hart.

Slavin, R. E. 1980. "Cooperative Learning." *Review of Educational Research.* Vol. 50, No. 2, Summer. 315–342.

Snarey, J. R., Reimer, J., and Kohlberg, L. 1985. "Development of Social-Moral Reasoning among Kibbutz Adolescents: A Longitudinal Cross-cultural Study." *Developmental Psychology,* Vol. 21, No. 1, January. 3–17.

Tibbets, S. 1978. "Wanted: Data to Prove That Sexist Reading Material Has an Impact on the Reader." *Reading Teacher,* Vol. 32, No. 2, November. 165–169.

Walker, L. K. 1984. "Sex Differences in the Development of Moral Reasoning: A Critical Review." *Child Development,* Vol. 55, No. 3, June. 677–691.

Wilson, J., Williams, N., and Sugarman, B. 1967. *Introduction to Moral Education.* Baltimore: Penguin Books.

Additional Readings

Atkinson, B., (Ed.), 1950. *Walden and Other Writings of Henry David Thoreau.* New York: Modern Library. (Also available in other editions.)

Banks, J. A. and Banks, C. A. (Eds.). 1993. *Multicultural Education: Issues and Perspectives.* Boston: Allyn and Bacon.

Coombs, J. R. and Meux, M. 1971. "Teaching Strategies for Values Analysis." In L. E. Metcalf (Ed.), *Values Education: Rationale, Strategies, and Procedures.* 41st Yearbook. Washington, DC: National Council for the Social Studies.

Fraenkel, J. R. 1980. "Goals for Teaching Values and Value Analysis." *Journal of Research and Development in Education,* Vol. 13, No. 2, Winter. 93–102.

Fried, C. 1970. *An Anatomy of Values: Problems of Personal and Social Choice.* Cambridge, MA: Harvard University Press.

Gilligan, C., Ward, J. V., and Taylor, J. M. with Bardige, B. (Eds.). 1988. *Mapping the Moral Domain: A Contribution of Women's Thinking to Psychological Theory and Education.* Cambridge, MA: Harvard University Press.

Hare, A. P., Borgatta, E. F., and Bales, R. F. (Eds.). 1965. *Small Groups: Studies in Social Interaction.* New York: Knopf.

Kirschenbaum, H. 1977. "In Support of Values Clarification." *Social Education*, Vol. 41, No. 5, May. 398, 401–402.

Nelson, J. L. and Michaelis, J. U. 1980. *Secondary Social Studies: Instruction, Curriculum, Evaluation.* Englewood Cliffs, NJ: Prentice-Hall.

Newmann, F. and Rutter, R. 1985–1986. "A Profile of High School Community Service Programs." *Educational Leadership,* Vol. 43, No. 4, December/January. 65–71.

Noddings, N. 1984. *Caring: A Feminine Approach to Ethics and Moral Education.* Berkeley: University of California Press.

Rutter, R. and Newmann, R. 1989. "The Potential of Community Service to Enhance Civic Responsibility." *Social Education,* Vol. 53, No. 6, October. 371–374.

Thoreau, H. D. 1947. In C. Bode, (Ed.), *The Portable Thoreau.* New York: Viking Press.

■ ■ ■ ■ ■ ■ Any subject can be taught effectively in some intellectually honest form to any child at any stage of development.

Jerome Bruner

PART III

How Is Social Studies Instruction Implemented?

"How can social studies be taught?" is one of the four key questions that we address in this textbook. A simple response would be that social studies can be taught in many ways—but this response overlooks several fundamental issues related to instructional planning and implementation. It is imperative that teachers know their subject discipline in depth and have a background in learning theory. They must also be able to translate this knowledge into meaningful and practical classroom activities that promote student learning. Teachers also need to know themselves as persons, their students' needs and interests, and the community values and expectations. As a teacher you will be grappling with these issues daily. How you decide to respond to these challenges is an important responsibility.

Throughout this textbook questions are posed to stimulate your thinking and to encourage you to think of other questions concerning your teaching of social studies. Answers to important questions are not always easy; however, this section will help you begin to answer the "how" questions.

Already you have had several years of personal experience in schools. You have no doubt completed college course work in educational psychology, learning theory, and other behavioral sciences. You should reflect on what you studied about learning theory and apply this information specifically to social studies instruction. *Which* learning theorists seem to have had a major impact on social studies instruction? *How* might you apply some aspects of these theories in your classroom? *How* will you be able to take these ideas and make them work effectively for you?

Successful teachers engage in ongoing instructional planning. Curriculum plans should be viewed as flexible guides for instruction, as often the best-planned lessons may not be appropriate. In these cases both teacher and student flexibility and adjustment are essential. When planning it is useful to recall that student interests and goals may not match those of the teacher and that a variety of instructional strategies are needed to help students learn content, skills, and values. *Which* instructional strategies are you likely to employ in your teaching of social studies? *How* will you provide for active student learning?

As we have discussed, establishing a risk-free learning environment for students and teachers is an important characteristic in deciding how and what to teach. In creating a supportive learning environment you need to consider class organization, the selection and use of a variety of instructional resources, and the local community. A teacher should develop a repertoire of effective instructional strategies that extend beyond the textbook.

Social studies lends itself to promoting learning beyond the walls of the classroom and school. There is a rich variety of learning activities and opportunities that enable students to go beyond the textbook and use the community as a social science "laboratory." Alert social studies teachers will encourage young learners to become active participants in those school or community activities. These experiences extend social studies learning in practical and meaningful ways. *What* are some ways you might plan to use the community and its resources in your teaching?

Oftentimes students come into social studies classes lacking the communication and study skills to be successful learners. It is important for social studies teachers to take the time needed to help students become strategic learners in social studies. Students need to develop the reading, writing, communicating, and studying skills to be successful in social studies classes. Social studies teachers should also help students learn to pose questions and to respond to questions effectively.

FOCUS QUESTIONS

- How will you use your prior learning and personal experiences in formulating your own theory(ies) regarding social studies instruction?
- How will you select and use instructional strategies to help students learn the content, skills, and values called for in the lesson or unit?
- What does it mean to create and maintain a risk-free classroom learning environment?
- How will you help students develop the communication, thinking, and study skills to be successful in social studies?

FOCUS ACTIVITY

Teaching is not going to be easy, but there are many small and large rewards that result from thoughtful teaching. It will be helpful for you to jot down two or three "how" questions that come to mind as you begin this part of the textbook. After studying the "how" of instruction you should discuss your questions and possible responses with classmates and your social studies methods professor. To what extent is there a consensus concerning "how" social studies ought to be taught?

Project your teaching career several years into the future, say five to ten years from now. How would you like your students to describe their social studies program (the one you are teaching)? What goals will you need to accomplish for your students to learn and enjoy social studies? Share your vision of your career with classmates and discuss commonalties and differences in the visions.

The secret of education lies in respecting the pupils.
   Ralph Waldo Emerson

CHAPTER 7

Learning Theory, Social Studies Curriculum, and Instructional Practices

FOCUS QUESTIONS

- What responsibilities do students have for learning?
- What does teacher "folk wisdom" offer in promoting motivation and learning?
- To what extent have the findings of developmental and learning theorists influenced the shape of social studies curriculum and instructional practices?

OVERVIEW There are numerous theories regarding child development and learning. Knowing the characteristics of learners and learning theories is fundamental for effective teaching in any discipline. This chapter summarizes the major ideas of several theorists and researchers on the development of the learners and how they learn. Each of these theories offers numerous possibilities for organizing social studies instruction. Most teachers use some of the ideas from several theorists in developing social studies units and lessons.

Learners' Responsibilities

Learning has at least two interrelated definitions. First, learning refers to the information, skills, and values that people acquire through instruction or study. Second, learning refers to the modification of behavior based on prior experience or instruction. In both of these definitions change is a key ingredient of learning, and learning brings about change that may be either deliberate or unintentional. Change does not have to be conscious or planned, and learning and change regularly take place both inside and outside the classroom. It is also useful to view learning as extending beyond acquiring information and skills and to recognize that attitudes and emotions are also learned from various other sources (Hill, 1985). For example, the family, peers, media, and religious and other social institutions influence both learning itself and attitudes about learning.

According to Mayer (1987) there are at least four learning tasks that may take place at any one time in a classroom. For example, in social studies classes *response learning* might involve students' giving a correct response to recall questions such as "Who is the governor of our state?" or "When was the transcontinental railroad completed?" In *concept learning* students organize data into meaningful groups and categories to aid further learning. For instance, a social studies teacher asks the class to deal with the concept of "change" by having students list several causes for the decline of Rome. Then the teacher asks the class to group these causes into categories based on similarities. The teacher then may ask, "Why did you group these causes the way you did?" and "What might we label these causes?" *Rote verbal learning* asks students to respond verbally to specific directives such as "Recite the Preamble of the Constitution." *Prose learning* involves the learning of new information from written or spoken text. To facilitate prose learning the teacher might ask a student to summarize the information gleaned from the assigned readings or from viewing a video program or to report the highlights of a speech by a political candidate. The task of the teacher is to help students learn effectively in all four modes.

There are many factors outside the school setting, such as the home and community environment, intellectual ability of the student, family socioeconomic status, and personal goals, that influence learning. Teachers should not ignore these and other factors that are beyond the control of the school as they plan for instruction. Another important factor in student learning is personal motivation. Practices within the school as well as influences outside the school have an impact on student motivation. To promote student learning teachers need to plan a variety of learning activities that are appropriate to the curriculum content and to the ability, maturity, and interests of the students. Administrators and school boards should provide school environments that are conducive to learning and to secure the necessary resources to accomplish learning.

Ultimately, however, students are responsible for their own education and they are in control of what learning takes place. Learning is voluntary and cannot be forced. For example, the teacher may select the content with care, plan valuable learning activities, and use a variety of instructional materials to teach a quality lesson. However, if the student is not ready or motivated to learn, there is little the teacher can do to ensure that learning takes place. You as the teacher can utilize various motivation strategies, the best of which is to help students love learning and scholarship by modeling scholarship and the love of learning yourself. It is also important to understand that the student who does not want to learn does not have the same agenda as the teacher. For the moment at least, the student does not want or need the information being presented in the lesson. On the other hand, students who want to learn can generally do so by selecting challenging courses or seeking out teachers who are excited about the teaching and learning process. Students often decide to learn on their own if a topic is of particular interest to them and if the teacher is also excited about the topic.

Teacher "Folk Wisdom"

Over the years experienced teachers have suggested practices that serve them well. In general, these practices tend to be practical, reflect common sense, and are aimed at stimulating student learning. In addition, they reflect the culture of the school and community. During the 1950s and 1960s the development of student motivation techniques became a focus in teacher education. Motivation continues to be an important ingredient in the teaching/learning process and scholars now recognize it as being more complex than they had previously believed. For example, immediate rewards, such as recognition for accomplishments, may be a key motivational tool for some students. For others, a sense of personal accomplishment over a longer term may be a sufficient motivation to learn. Furthermore, peer pressure, societal expectations, and physical setting also contribute to the complexity of student motivation.

The following are some teacher practices that motivate student learning. These are based on teacher experiences and in some cases research findings.

- Use a variety of procedures and methods to stimulate learning.
- Try to relate each lesson to student concerns and interests.
- Praise students in public, but criticize in private.
- Learn the names of the students as quickly as possible and use them as much as possible. (This is also likely to help reduce discipline problems.)
- Monitor the success level of all students from those who have excessive failure to those to whom success comes easily.

- Be aware of individual differences and abilities. Make every effort to provide for them in planning learning activities and in making meaningful class and individual assignments. Take care to assign meaningful homework that is coordinated with classroom learning and does not become "busy work" or "trivial pursuit."
- Be enthusiastic about teaching and learning because it is contagious to many of the students.
- Allow students to be active partners in at least some aspects of classroom planning.
- Know something about the various social, political, economic, religious, and cultural values and traditions in the community, because schools reflect the local community.
- Be professional but friendly and caring; have a sense of humor.
- If possible and appropriate, be a "ham actor or actress" and use those talents, but be cautious as only a few teachers can use this technique successfully.
- From the beginning the teacher must establish and enforce consistently clear and reasonable rules of behavior that will create an acceptable atmosphere for learning. It is easier to ease rules rather than to "tighten" already established rules.
- Teachers need to develop their own style of teaching and discipline that matches their personality and talents.

Naturally, along with "positive" teacher behavior statements, there are some major "do nots." Some readers will not want to believe these statements now, but in time will probably come to see their value. Like any suggestions, there are always exceptions depending on the circumstances, settings, teacher personality and philosophy, and the particular group of students being taught.

- Do not try to be a "buddy" to the class as too much "buddyness" often results in a lack of respect for the teacher and may create discipline problems.
- Do not engage in excessive kidding or "put downs" because students generally do not have the same level of maturity as teachers and often do not understand limits in propriety. Often they do not recognize when the teacher is kidding.

It would be well for you to think about how you could use and avoid these practices in a social studies class and under what circumstances. What other similar teacher-experience statements do you recall hearing from your own experience, from classroom teachers, parents, and/or university professors? You should write these statements in your notebook as you consider learning theories and instructional practices.

How Have Research Findings Influenced Social Studies Instruction?

Hundreds and even thousands of books and articles have been written about the learning process. The work of numerous theorists and educators has been translated into classroom practices that have expanded greatly our knowledge of human learning. We have identified several major research theorists whose work can be grouped under the following labels: 1) learning theorists; 2) child development theorists; 3) mental discipline theorists; and 4) natural unfolding of human nature theorists. In the following pages we will discuss these theories and research findings that have had a major impact on social studies instruction and on education in general.

Developmental and Learning Theories

Theorists who study learning do not agree on the ways people learn. Behaviorists such as B. F. Skinner advocate structured learning that provides immediate feedback. Gestalt psychologists such as Jerome Bruner focus on the structure of the discipline, while David Ausubel encourages using advanced organizers to help students learn. Humanistic theorists such as Abraham Maslow and Carl Rogers believe it is important for human beings to explore their feelings. They also believe that self-expression of attitudes and values is integral to learning and well-being.

Behavioral Theory

Behavioral psychologists attempt to be "scientific" by utilizing and relying on objective observations of behavior as their major source of data. They seek to predict and control behaviors. They also believe there are fundamental continuities of behavior across animal species and that these animal behaviors can help explain human behavior. These theorists focus on observable events and study behavior as it interacts with the environment. The behaviorists study how stimuli affect behavior.

B. F. Skinner

One of the best-known theorists is B. F. Skinner. He wrote: "The methods of science have been enormously successful wherever they have been tried. Let us apply them to human affairs. If we can observe human behavior carefully from an objective point of view and come to understand it for what it is, we may be able to adopt a more sensible course of action" (1953, p. 5). He believed that once the specific conditions related to a particular behavior have been observed it is then possible to anticipate and predict a person's actions (behavioral changes) based on a repetition of those same conditions.

For Skinner the key to behavior control was reinforcement, or operant conditioning, as his theory is sometimes known. He argued that people initiate behavior on their own but will repeat certain actions if they receive rewards. For Skinner the environment was crucial. He believed that inherited characteristics, except by luck, do not influence behavior. Skinner argued it is necessary to analyze causes rigidly. If the behavior is desirable, then it is necessary to arrange conditions so as to reinforce the positive behavior. Behavior modification techniques have been developed to reinforce positive behaviors and at the same time discourage undesirable behaviors. Behaviorists deal with observable stimuli and observable behavior responses.

Skinner and other stimulus–response (S–R) theorists believe that teachers have an impact on their students, and they encourage teachers to influence student behaviors in consistent and positive ways. As recently as 1984, Skinner, writing in the *American Psychologist,* offered teachers the following guidelines for improving learning based on behavioral principles:

1. Teachers need to be specific about what is to be taught.
2. Teachers must teach basic skills first.
3. Teachers should provide students an opportunity to learn at their own pace.
4. Teachers should structure subject matter content. (pp. 947–954)

To apply these Skinnerian guidelines to social studies, teachers need to provide detailed guidelines about the lesson being taught. The objectives of the lesson must be very specific about what is to be learned, for example, skills to be developed and content to be learned. Since students have different learning styles and learn at different rates, teachers can use different techniques to accommodate their different abilities. Some teachers will develop study guides and worksheets with very clear directions and a series of questions to be answered. For example, all students must complete questions 1–10 on the study guide or worksheet, and those who work more rapidly complete additional questions from the study guide or worksheet or are given an alternative assignment for enrichment.

Educational Applications

Like Jean Piaget, who formulated many of his theories by observing his three children, Skinner also observed and questioned his daughter about learning. He examined her textbooks and assignments and analyzed student-teacher behaviors. He noticed the lessons were not well organized and became convinced that the principles of operant learning could be applied to education.

Skinner's study of learning and instruction led to the development of programmed instruction and teaching machines.

The basic mode of programmed instruction presents students with a set of instructional materials (stimuli). Students can then use these stimuli to teach themselves about a particular subject and then arrive at a predetermined conclusion. Upon completion of the task or lesson the student will receive immediate feedback. The student will get positive reinforcement for a correct response or encouragement to repeat the task if the initial response was incorrect. Skinner believed that immediate feedback was the key for successful learning. Programmed learning provided possibilities for immediate feedback. An important feature of successful programmed instruction is developing a lesson that progressively reduces the number of cues or prompts needed to elicit the correct answer.

Programmed approaches to learning have not lived up to expectations, partly because writing quality programs with short answers was tedious. Also the lessons were often developed for lower-ability students, and some teachers were uncomfortable with their role when using programmed instruction. Often low-ability students may benefit from programmed instruction because the lesson has a definite structure and allows students to repeat those parts that they may not readily understand the first time. Research findings about programmed instruction have been mixed, as is often the case. It has not been demonstrated that programmed instruction is more or less effective than other instructional procedures (Bangert-Drowns, Kulik, and Kulik, 1983–1984).

Coincidentally, the development of computers and teaching machines took place at approximately the same time. Some psychologists recognized the similarities of teaching machines and computers and began to develop computer-assisted instruction (CAI) programs. Today a fairly large number of computer programs are based on the S–R principle.

Suggestions for Using Behaviorist Theories in Social Studies Classrooms

While the use of behaviorist theories has declined, nevertheless it is useful to consider some examples of possible uses of S–R principles in social studies classrooms. Many of these are common sense behaviors and could be applied in classrooms in other discipline areas as well.

Illustrative Examples

- Describe the behaviors expected for students as they engage in a discussion regarding a current news story.

- After giving an assignment, review student answers immediately so the student has accurate information as he or she begins the next part of the lesson or unit.
- Ask students to provide feedback to each other so they can learn from each other through peer interaction.
- Even though a test was given some days previously, discuss the examination questions when returning the test so that students may review their answers and your comments on the test and learn from their own errors as well as from correct answers.
- When returning an assignment or when a student contributes to the class discussion, offer written or verbal praise as appropriate to the situation so the student receives deserved recognition, which will likely motivate the student to continue to learn.
- After completing a chapter in the textbook, give the students an immediate informal quiz to check for understanding and then have the students correct and discuss the quiz in class, which lets students know immediately areas they need to study for the chapter test.
- Offer a contract to students by reaching agreement upon what is to be learned (content), under what conditions (how), by what date (when), with the expected degree of success (result), and indicate the rewards for completing the contract.

Cautions Regarding Behaviorist Theories

A basic criticism of behaviorist theory revolves around the structured manipulation of the classroom environment. Critics also note the risk of establishing control of student behavior as a higher priority than student learning. Critics point out the ineffectiveness of S–R by noting that programmed instruction, which was popular in the 1950s, is no longer widely used in the schools (except for some computer applications). The primary reasons for this decline includes the cost of program development, ineffective programs, and poor implementation. The United States government sponsored several performance-contracting arrangements in the late 1960s and the early 1970s, but these failed to produce the desired learning outcomes.

Behavior modification programs also received their share of criticism for seeking what many believed would be excessive control that could have been self-destructive to those who were being shaped into submissive behaviors. In general, operant conditioning techniques in schools were less successful than had been anticipated.

Cognitive-Discovery (Gestalt-Field Psychology) Theory

While behaviorists generally agree upon a specific learning model, cognitive-discovery theorists believe that learning takes place when individuals grasp new relationships through insight. Basically, cognitive-discovery theorists hold that learning is a result of trying to make sense of the world around us.

They argue that people are processors of information, that people want to learn, and they do so by seeking additional information. Applying prior knowledge helps determine what we learn, remember, forget, and utilize in our daily lives (Peeck, van den Bosch, and Kreupeling 1982; Resnick 1981). Learning requires the use of mental abilities, beliefs, expectations, feelings, and learning contexts in order to think about specific situations.

Jerome Bruner

A leading spokesperson for Gestalt psychology is Jerome Bruner, who viewed intellectual growth as self-motivating. Gestaltists call attention to patterns and configurations and so emphasize the importance of relationships. Bruner's book *The Process of Education* (1960) stresses the importance of having students understand the structure of a discipline, such as history, economics, or geography, and has become something of a classic in education. He argues that when students have a grasp of the overall nature of the discipline, they are more likely to remember what they have learned and thus be more able to apply those principles in other settings because they have organized the information in meaningful ways. Knowing the structure of a discipline enables students to learn more complex knowledge because they have a basis for making connections and linking new information to existing knowledge and prior experiences.

Bruner describes three ways of knowing something:

Enactive involves learning by doing.
Iconic involves learning by using the senses and storing the images internally.
Symbolic involves learning by interacting with the environment through the use of language and other symbols and by internalizing the knowledge.

People learn to use these three modes of learning early in their lives, and as they mature they integrate these modes of learning and use them with greater sophistication throughout their lives. For example, let us suppose that students in a civics class are studying the environmental impact of pollutants from a local industrial plant. During the unit the class takes a field trip to the industrial plant for a tour and discussion of the plant's operation, its contribution to the local economy, and so forth. While they are at the plant the students ask questions of the plant personnel, observe how the plant disposes of waste that is believed to cause pollution, smell the product emitted into the environment, take pictures of the waste disposal process and the resulting smoke or sludge, and so forth. After analyzing their findings the students prepare a statement including several recommendations that is sent to the industrial plant manager and the environmental protection committee of the city council for study and action. The students also attend the city council meeting when the topic is discussed. One or two class members are asked to speak on behalf of the class concerning their study, statement, and recommendations. The city council members listen to the students and consider their recommendations in their policy deliberations. The students, therefore, have participated in the formulation of public policy.

In planning and implementing this instructional unit the teacher provided students with the opportunity to utilize Bruner's three modes of learning. Students had opportunities to learn by visiting the plant and to interact with the teacher, peers, and other adults. They also learned to use various instructional resources and were able to offer recommendations to the city council as active citizens in their community. Such a unit allows students to be active learners both in the classroom and in the community and is an attempt to provide meaningful learning experiences. This is a type of learning activity that is likely to remain with the students into their adult lives.

Bruner encourages teachers to use a discovery approach to teaching whereby students are confronted with problems and are asked to seek possible solutions through group interaction or by independent efforts. He argues that by providing opportunities for students to practice solving problems, students will gain confidence in their own learning abilities and will be able to apply these same procedural and processing skills into personal and social problem-solving efforts throughout their lives.

David Ausubel

According to David Ausubel, verbal learning occurs when the learner receives information through reading, listening, or by independent discovery. Ausubel argued that learning is facilitated when the learner has a structure or framework in which to relate new information.

To help students make sense of verbal information, Ausubel (1963) supported the use of advance organizers as an aid in learning and retaining those materials. For example, teachers could ask students to skim the chapter in advance of reading to gain a quick overview of the contents of the chapter. The teacher might also give the title of a film or video program and ask the students to hypothesize about the film's topic. Another example would be for the teacher to ask students to bring in examples of advertisements at the start of a unit on advertising in order to show different types of advertising techniques. Advance organizers act as mediating links at high levels of abstraction. Ausubel encourages teachers to present both verbal and visual materials before presenting detailed information. These materials should be both general and abstract so that students will have a structure or framework to use when learning the new detailed and specific information. It is important for students to have a conceptual framework (words and/or pictures) around which new information can be organized, connected, and interpreted. The use of advance organizers provides guidelines to help students grasp unfamiliar materials and transfer learning to new situations.

Educational Applications

Teachers who believe in this theory should present background information, pose thoughtful questions, and facilitate discussion so that students discover things for themselves rather than being told the answers. In this way the student generates knowledge from within rather than having information "poured in" by the teacher. This approach emphasizes thinking (cognition) and the ways in which relationships are formulated and discovered. In general, the cognitive-discovery theorists believe that as young people form their own concepts of the world, learning will be more meaningful and that these ideas are likely to be used and remembered longer than those learned by rote or presented by others. Ideas based on the work of Jerome Bruner and David Ausubel will be used as examples of theorists representing the cognitive-discovery approach to learning.

Suggestions for Using Developmental Learning Theories in Social Studies Classrooms

Some units of instruction that address an issue with no "right" or "wrong" answers lend themselves to the approaches of the cognitive-discovery theorists. The use of these and similar learning activities facilitate open inquiry and provide opportunities for students to become thoughtful problem solvers and decision makers.

Illustrative Examples

- Confront students with problems and help them seek solutions (however tentative) through group discussion or independent study. For example, today the former USSR is being reshaped. What are some possible directions the former USSR may take since several former republics have joined the Confederation of Independent States?
- Encourage students to ask a variety of broad and focus questions to gather the required information. For example, what events led up to the dissolution of the USSR?
- Pose questions that require students to apply, analyze, synthesize, and evaluate data; probe for further information (if appropriate). For example, what economic problems do the people of the former USSR face? How do these changes affect the daily life of the people in the

former USSR? Based on the information you have gathered from a variety of sources, what seems to be the direction of the former USSR? To what extent is there bias in the data you have collected?
- Encourage students to develop attitudes of inquiry and problem solving. For example, find a quotation from a prominent statesperson concerning the breakup of the USSR. What background information did the statesperson have when he/she made this statement?
- Emphasize contrasts as well as similarities. For example, how did revolutionary events of 1991 compare to those of the Russian Revolution of 1917?
- Stimulate informed guessing. For example, what do you see as the future of the CIS?
- Introduce a historical period through the use of visual images, documents, and sound. For example, use pictures and other media to show the overthrow of the tsar and the removal of former Soviet leader Mikhail Gorbachev from power.

Cautions Regarding Cognitive-Discovery Learning Theories

Just as there are critics of the behaviorist S–R learning theory there are also a number of criticisms of the cognitive-discovery approach to learning. At times learning by discovery may not be productive since genuine discovery is rare, time-consuming, and inefficient. With an emphasis on teacher and student accountability and testing, parents, legislators, and education critics fear that students will be unable to perform well on standardized tests and are uncomfortable with teachers being co-learners with their students. They want the teacher to teach; that is, lecture, have "correct" answers, and the like.

Teachers should be aware of these criticisms before relying heavily on a discovery approach to teaching. We encourage teachers to develop and use a variety of instructional procedures based upon different learning theories since there are many teaching and learning styles. At times the use of one theory may be more appropriate than at other times.

Humanistic Learning Theories

Humanistic learning stresses the importance of the whole child and is based on observable data as well as impressions and emotions. The humanists emphasize both affective and cognitive learning. They stress the importance of feelings, emotions, relationships, and personal fulfillment and argue that teachers should trust students and let them grow without undue interference. Two of the leading representatives of humanistic learning are Abraham Maslow and Carl Rogers. Their views are summarized in the following paragraphs.

Abraham Maslow

As an alternative to a behaviorist approach to learning Maslow (1968) assumes that if children are given a free choice they will select what is best for them because individuals determine and shape much of their own behavior. He urged parents and teachers to trust children, allow them to make choices, and let them grow without excessive interference by adults trying to shape their behavior. Rather, parents and teachers should encourage young people to make wise personal choices by providing for their physical safety, love, belonging, and esteem needs. This philosophy can be traced to the thinking of Jean Jacques Rousseau in his important book on education, *Emile,* which we encourage you to read.

Carl Rogers

In the early 1950s Carl Rogers (1951) developed a new approach to psychotherapy called client-centered (nondirective) therapy, which makes the client rather than the therapist the focus. Rather than teaching the client what was wrong, Rogers worked to establish a warm, caring, accepting, and positive climate. He soon learned that once clients became self-accepting, they were able to solve many of their problems without the aid of the therapist. As a result of successful experiences in these settings, Rogers (1980) proposed that classrooms become learner-centered so that students learn to educate themselves without undue reliance on the teacher.

Educational Applications

Maslow, Rogers, and other humanistic psychologists believe that students should not only acquire cognitive knowledge but also be encouraged to explore their feelings, communicate with others, and clarify their values and attitudes through various forms of self-expression. Teachers should create classroom environments that allow learners to develop skills in the affective domain. The concept of an open classroom is an example of a setting for humanistic learning. During the late 1960s and early 1970s many of the alternative schools were based on humanistic theories of teaching and learning. Today many of these same theories are observed in middle schools, high schools, and alternative schools. Humanistic psychologists believe individuals should develop their unique qualities to the maximum possible degree.

Suggestions for Using Humanistic Theories in Social Studies Classrooms

Humanistic education aims to help students improve their self-concept and increase their self-direction by encouraging creativity and curiosity. It also promotes the concept of learning how to learn. In a humanistic environment teachers encourage students to confront, communicate, accept, and understand their feelings. Humanists believe these are as important as learning facts, concepts, principles, and skills.

As you read the following illustrative examples of humanistic theories in social studies classrooms consider the following discussion scenario and think about your use of these theories.

> The local community has sufficient open land available to build a large shopping mall within the city boundaries. The mall, if built, would have some seventy-five taxpaying stores and businesses that would provide employment for several hundred workers and a nice tax base for the city, which would likely reduce local property taxes. On the other hand, as the environmentalists note, several hundred acres of valuable farmland would be taken from production and pollution would increase due to increased traffic and waste.

How would a discussion on this or other similar topics promote or hinder the use of humanistic theories?

Illustrative Examples

- Provide numerous opportunities for students to express their own ideas through small and large group discussions on topics that allow for the expression of divergent ideas and viewpoints.
- Allow opportunities for students to express their feelings and emotions so that students can learn about themselves and others.
- Provide a risk-free, nonthreatening environment of acceptance of students as individuals.
- Establish clear expectations and rules for classroom behavior. This helps students recognize that we as teachers expect them to live up to certain expectations because we care about them as individuals. This also shows students that they can expect to be treated in a fair manner by peers and teachers.
- Stress learning activities that lead to student success and the development of a positive concept about themselves and learning.
- Encourage students to take responsibility for their own learning. Do this by allowing them to pursue topics of special interest through different modes of learning such as individualized study or working in cooperative groups. This learning should take place in various settings such as the library, community, or elsewhere as appropriate to the assignment.
- Provide students with opportunities to express their values through a variety of decision-making activities.

Cautions Regarding Humanistic Learning Theories

Humanistic educators often bring criticism on themselves because they claim they teach students rather than subjects. By making such claims humanistic educators often give the impression that they have a monopoly on developing happy, well-adjusted, self-actualized persons.

This is an age of increased pressures for accountability in learning and a back-to-basics movement due in part to fewer resources allocated for education and low standardized test scores. In this atmosphere parents, school boards, and school administrators are not likely to be impressed if teachers say they want students to develop meaningful interpersonal relationships in order to be able to better express themselves. Today most adults expect teachers to teach subject matter content and basic skills. It is useful to keep in mind that many of the tests used currently to determine student achievement emphasize the ability to learn and recall specific facts and information.

Child Developmental Learning Theories

Developmental theorists are interested in the changes (physical, emotional, social, and cognitive) in human beings from conception to death. Many developmental changes are due to growth and maturation while other changes come through learning. Most psychologists would agree that maturation and interaction with the environment (nature and nurture) are both important. However, there is no general agreement on the degree of emphasis that they should place on either. Most theorists would probably agree that people develop at different rates, that development is orderly and involves a relatively logical progression, and that development is gradual. Jean Piaget and Lawrence Kohlberg, developmental theorists, have produced research that has important implications for social studies instruction.

Jean Piaget

The Swiss psychologist Jean Piaget has spent over fifty years studying the thinking of children. His research has produced a comprehensive theory of cognitive development in which he sought answers to the question "How does a person process knowledge?" Piaget (1932) concluded that cognitive development progresses through four clearly defined stages in the same fixed order with each stage having its own characteristics. The stages of cognitive development and their major characteristics appear in Table 7.1.

Through research Piaget has concluded that humans have an innate tendency to bring coherence and stability to their perception of the world. As learners assimilate experiences into their cognitive structure they modify or accommodate their previously held conceptions as they engage in new

Table 7.1 Piaget's Stages of Cognitive Development

Stages	Ages	Features/Characteristics
Sensorimotor Stage	Birth to 2	Develops awareness of body, sensory relationships, and objects
		Sensory experiences become coordinated
		Motor actions become coordinated
Preoperational Stage	2 to 7	Rapid development of language
		Egocentric speech and behavior predominate
		Centers on one feature or attribute and not able to shift focus
		Unable to conserve properties or objects
Concrete Stage	7 to 11	Infers relations among objects
		Performs decentering and reversible operations
		Increases in symbolic thinking and quantitative reasoning
		Able to classify and reclassify objects into superordinate and subordinate classes
		Becomes less egocentric and more socialized
Formal Operations Stage	12 to Adult	Develops logical and abstract thinking
		Able to formulate and test hypotheses, make predictions, define operations, and draw conclusions
		Able to analyze, synthesize, and evaluate abstract ideas

experiences. Each learner has a unique conception of the world because each person has had many different previous experiences. Piaget encourages teachers to assume that students have a built-in desire to learn so that they are able to make sense out of their experiences. He recommends that students interact with each other, with numerous situations, and/or with various objects. He would also argue that learning is its own reward.

While each of Piaget's four stages of development is important, we will focus on transitions from concrete to formal operations, which occur about the time students enter middle school or junior high. His theory holds that as people mature, they develop more powerful information-processing techniques. During these years students learn to deal logically with both hypothetical and real situations. They also learn to extend their thinking by using symbols as well as by using objects, and they learn to isolate relevant variables and possible combinations of variables. Finally, they learn to think in terms of probabilities and proportions. The application of each of these skills is important in daily life.

Educational Applications

Those who teach at the middle school level should keep in mind that these students will sometimes function at the level of formal operations and sometimes at the concrete level. Teachers should also be aware that students in different subject areas may not be thinking at a consistent operational level. In class discussions, it is important that teachers give students opportunities to explain, clarify, or extend their thoughts. When students are able to formulate consistent generalizations they are then capable of using formal thinking processes. For example, at the middle school level a teacher may provide a packet of cards with pictures of artifacts from a particular culture, such as Mayan culture. The teacher asks a student (or students in groups) to categorize the pictures based on a classification devised by the student. After this has been accomplished, the teacher will ask the student (or groups of students) to reclassify the pictures and explain their new grouping. With practice these experiences in classifying and reclassifying the artifacts will help students as they move into more formal operations. A wise teacher will be cognizant of these ongoing changes in the thinking processes of the students.

As they are developing formal thought and intellectual skills, students at the secondary level may experience role confusion. They may become preoccupied with abstract and formal matters concerning self and may become introspective. While adolescents are often egocentric the views of others become all-important. Often adolescents are willing to do things that are contrary to their earlier training and their own best interests due to peer pressure, which exerts a powerful influence for this age group.

Suggestions for Using Piaget's Theories in Social Studies Classrooms

The following teaching suggestions incorporate the basic principles of Piaget's theories at the middle school or high school levels.

Illustrative Examples

- Teach students to explain their thinking processes by asking them *how* they arrived at a solution to a problem, topic, or issue. For example, ask students what thinking processes and evidence they used to arrive at a particular decision or perspective.

- Keep in mind that some students are more interested in possibilities than reality. For example, if class discussions become unrealistically theoretical, or if students express contempt of adults for failing to solve pressing problems, it may be useful for the teacher to remind students of the complexity of the issue. The teacher may also need to present additional materials showing alternative views related to the issue.
- Remember that peer pressure and the reactions of peers are extremely influential to students at these levels. Many times students test their ideas to clarify their own thinking.
- Teach students how to be more systematic and logical in solving problems. For example, a sequence of activities could be required before arriving at a solution, however tentative.

Lawrence Kohlberg

Like Piaget, Lawrence Kohlberg became interested in moral development and the way people at different ages responded to rules. As a graduate student at the University of Chicago during the 1950s, Kohlberg developed an interest in stages of moral development. As a result of his subsequent research, Kohlberg (1963) developed a description of six stages of moral reasoning based on responses to a moral dilemma story. Before going further, we caution you to recognize that in subsequent years, Kohlberg modified some of these original descriptions of the stages of moral development (1978). Depending upon when they were published, Kohlberg's writings may have varied descriptions of these stages.

Table 7.2 reflects the sequence of moral development stages as expressed by Kohlberg. (See Chapter 6 on Values Education.)

After proposing his theory, Kohlberg engaged in extensive research to support his hypotheses that moral development stages are fixed, sequential, and universal. The research conclusions are mixed. Some research substantiates Kohlberg's work while some research raises questions concerning his approach and conclusions. For example, Carol Gilligan (1982) was critical of Kohlberg's work because his research in moral development studied male students and ignored the psychological developments of females; subsequently Kohlberg developed a rather complex scoring system in an effort to measure moral reasoning abilities. Again the research findings are mixed as to what extent the level of moral reasoning relates to moral behavior.

Educational Applications

Most of the work in moral education has involved examining moral issues focusing on the decision-making process. The most widely used moral dilemma is the story of Heinz who must decide whether or not to steal an

Table 7.2 Stages of Moral Development*

Level I: Pre-conventional Morality

Stage 1: *Obedience/Punishment* stresses that physical consequences determine whether a particular action is good or bad. Students should follow established classroom rules or be punished (physical consequences) by the teachers.

Stage 2: *Instrumental Relativism* suggests that obeying laws should be based on an exchange of favors or rewards (reciprocity). Students should help one another because one day they may need a favor.

Level II: Conventional Morality

Stage 3: *Interpersonal Concordance* involves taking the right action to impress others who are important to us. Students work hard on an individual or class project to impress visitors at the social studies fair.

Stage 4: *Law and Order* actions reflect the need to have rules to maintain social order and so fixed rules must be observed. Students respect authority and obey rules because they are expected to do so.

Level III: Post-conventional Morality

Stage 5: *Social Contract* reasoning recognizes that rights of individuals must be protected and that rules involve mutual agreements. Students follow existing rules because they are socially useful and have resulted from a social contract while at the same time individual rights are protected.

Stage 6: *Universal Ethical Principles* involves making moral decisions based on self-selected ethical principles. Students consistently make decisions on the basis of conscience, comprehensive ethical principles such as the Golden Rule, and a respect for the dignity of the individual.*

*It should be noted that in 1978 Kohlberg indicated he had concluded that Stage 6 was a theoretical idea and not usually encountered in real life.

expensive but new drug in order to save the life of his wife. After confronting the student with the dilemma, the teacher asks the student to decide what Heinz should do and then explain the reasons for the choice. Kohlberg used the explanation of the student to determine the level of moral reasoning. The response was categorized in one of the six stages of moral development to determine the level of moral reasoning.

Teachers who use moral dilemmas in the classroom often ask students various questions that probe or extend their reasoning. In many such activities, however, teachers merely accept student responses at face value and offer little, if any, guidance concerning the thinking-reasoning process. On the other hand, when properly used, moral reasoning can be of great help to students who grapple with social issues.

Suggestions for Using Kohlberg's Theories in Social Studies Classrooms

It is useful to remember that students at different levels of maturity will respond to moral conflicts in different ways. Teachers who keep this in mind should be able to pose more effective questions, which in turn may lead to more sophisticated levels of reasoning. Teachers can often help students become more aware of moral issues by using real or hypothetical examples from the daily experiences of young people rather than contrived stories.

Illustrative Examples

- Create a supportive classroom environment that will enhance open discussion.
- Ask students "why" questions that will encourage them to explain why they responded in a specific way.
- Address moral issues by identifying moral conflicts involved within the context of learning.
- Encourage students to examine issues from the perspective of different people involved. Sometimes role playing is useful.
- Allow students to work through the moral issues among themselves rather than having the teacher be the "authority" with the "answer."

"Do you promise to fool all of the people some of the time and some of the people all of the time, but never to fool all of the people all of the time?"

Cautions Regarding Moral Development Education

We caution you that, prior to using any of the learning activities involving moral education or values studies in the classroom, it would be wise to check with the principal. In many communities parents have insisted that schools *not* include any of these activities in the school program. These parents believe they have the responsibility for providing moral instruction to their children and do not want the schools interfering. In some instances school boards have specific policies prohibiting teachers from providing any type of moral-values education within the scope of the school curriculum.

How Are Students Motivated?

Motivation is integral for student learning and educational achievement. A challenge that teachers face every day is how to motivate students while at the same time recognizing their differences in age, maturity, abilities, interests, and attitudes. How teachers motivate students depends upon the social and psychological climate of the school, teacher values, student capabilities, and lifestyles. We believe, however, that the best way to motivate students is to have a motivated teacher who loves his or her craft.

Fundamentally, teachers are asking three questions about motivation: 1) What causes a student to begin to take some action? 2) Why does a student want to achieve a particular goal? and 3) Why does a student decide to persist to reach the goal? Most psychologists would agree that all students are motivated at least to some degree, even those who decide not to participate in learning. Teachers may consider students matching this latter description as being unmotivated. In truth, this may mean that a student is not motivated to complete the tasks the teacher has planned for the class and has other ideas of her or his own.

Teachers may want to ask themselves at least two additional questions suggested by Wlodkowski (1981): 1) What can I do to promote a positive student attitude regarding this lesson or activity? and 2) How will this lesson or activity meet the needs of my students both as individuals and as members of a group?

The following guidelines may be helpful to teachers as they consider classroom motivation:

- Establish a learning-oriented environment by tapping student interests, by arousing curiosity, by whetting students' appetites for knowledge, and by reducing student anxiety.
- Communicate to students positive expectations that they can learn.
- Understand and utilize the psychological and growth needs of students based on their level of maturity and desire for acceptance.

- Plan interesting lessons and use a variety of instructional materials and procedures to stimulate an enthusiasm for learning.
- Assist students to establish and attain reasonable goals that offer challenges and still allow for success. Any unpleasant consequences of student involvement should be minimized.
- Provide for specific, immediate, and frequent feedback on student assignments and tests; use grades and tests judiciously.
- Provide for praise and rewards for meeting agreed-upon objectives.
- Allow students to assume greater responsibility for their own learning, which includes opportunities for students to originate their learning activities in social studies.

How Do Teacher Expectations Influence Motivation?

Teacher expectations affect students in at least two ways: 1) the self-fulfilling prophecy and 2) the sustaining expectations effect. In 1968 Rosenthal and Jacobson presented data that reported the existence of a self-fulfilling prophecy in the classroom. The researchers administered a test of intelligence to a group of first- through sixth-grade students at the beginning of the school year. After the test was administered the teachers of some of the students were told that the test predicted substantial intellectual gains during the coming year. The students identified as "potential achievers" in reality performed no better or no worse than the "average" children. At the end of the school year, a second intelligence test was administered. The result of the second test indicated that the students who had been identified as "potential achievers" did, in fact, show significant gains in intelligence. These gains were attributed to the higher expectations teacher had for these children. This result has been labeled the "Pygmalion effect," which comes from the Greek myth of the sculptor, Pygmalion, who expected a statue he was working on to come to life. (George Bernard Shaw's story of the same title is the basis of the musical *My Fair Lady,* in which a Cockney flower girl, Eliza Doolittle, is transformed into a refined, aristocratic lady.) The original research and methodology were criticized and could not be replicated. However, other related research indicates that teacher expectations can and do influence student performance (Cornbleth, Davis, and Button 1974; Marshall and Weinstein, 1986; Leder, 1987).

Self-fulfilling prophecy is a false expectation that becomes true simply because someone expects it to be true. This means that a teacher's inaccurate belief about a student's behavior or ability may cause that student to perform in ways that match teacher expectations. For example, if a teacher expects a student to do well on an assignment or in class, frequently the student is a high achiever. This also holds true in the reverse if the teacher holds negative expectations concerning student achievement or behavior.

The sustaining expectation effect causes difficulty when students do in fact show greater achievement, but teachers fail to recognize this improvement or fail to change their expectations. Students are affected when teachers treat them according to expectations, and over time students tend to behave in ways to match teacher expectations. For example, average-ability students in low-ability groups may come to believe they are "dumb" and respond according to teacher expectations; for example, they fail to turn in homework assignments; they answer oral questions with few words; they rarely, if ever, raise their hands to respond in class; and they, perhaps, become discipline problems. Or, consider the student who has been placed in a low-ability class and who works hard, improves study skills, seeks to participate in class, and so on, but who is not moved to a higher level class but instead retained in the low-ability class because the teacher refuses to recognize his or her improvement. In either case the student is not being challenged and self-concept remains low. Student achievement, aspiration, motivation, and self-concept may also be affected by teacher expectations. Students often view themselves by the way teachers respond (or fail to respond) to them in the classroom.

There are at least eleven possible sources for forming teacher expectations, which include the following:

- IQ test scores
- Gender, when teachers anticipate greater behavior problems from males than females
- Family names
- Medical or psychological data from the permanent record files
- Ethnic background
- Language background
- Knowledge of older siblings
- Physical characteristics
- Previous achievement
- Socioeconomic status
- Actual behaviors

Can you think of other characteristics that are likely to influence teacher expectations regarding student performance?

Teacher expectations may well influence group processes, instructional procedures, the types of questions posed, the amount of positive encouragement given, the wait time between questions and student responses, the quality and quantity of responses, and the type of student-teacher interactions. Lower teacher expectations are often followed by decreased student motivation and aspiration. Teachers face the challenge of responding to students as individuals and as a class. Teachers need to be fair to all their students in helping them achieve their maximum potential. Treatment of students based on stereotyping is inappropriate. Belittling the talents of any student deprives the individual of an opportunity to meet his or her potential and becoming a contributing member of society.

What Can Parents, Administrators, and Others Do to Motivate Students?

There are no easy solutions to helping parents, administrators, and others motivate students. Many of the same practices suggested for teachers are applicable to others outside the classroom. Parental expectations, availability, and interest in school work may influence student motivation and interest. Wise parents will not set unduly high expectations for their children without being aware of their abilities, talents, interests, and goals. Ideally parents and students ought to be able to talk together to establish reasonable expectations concerning motivation and achievement. Being available and willing to listen and communicate are important in motivating students.

Administrators have the responsibility to create environments that facilitate student learning and motivation. They should encourage their faculties to follow the principles of classroom motivation. Administrators should also encourage regular parent-student-teacher communication.

Closely related to motivation is the notion of self-concept, which plays an important role in success or lack of success. The following section addresses self-concept related to school.

What Is Self-concept?

Defining self-concept is no easy task as the research literature reveals numerous definitions of this term. Within the literature "self-esteem" is sometimes used interchangeably with "self-concept." We will define self-concept as the perception we have of ourselves (strengths, weaknesses, abilities) and our actions, ideas, feelings, attitudes, and values. The development of self-concept begins at home and is influenced by peer interaction. Self-esteem is defined as a "sense of satisfaction and confidence in oneself" (McCown and Roop, 1992). We believe that self-concept is a function of achievement or the ability to do quality work.

Our own self-concept and how others perceive us are influenced by others and vary from one situation to another during the different phases of our lives. For example, there is self-concept related to cognitive academic achievement as well as self-concept related to the social, emotional, and physical aspects of our being. There is evidence that parental self-concept influences the development of self-concept in young people and that early parental care establishes the pattern for future development of self-concept. Young people already have well-established patterns of self-concept by the time they reach our middle and secondary schools. Parents, teachers, and significant others influence the self-concept of students. Often these self-concepts are difficult to alter, especially if they are negative.

For teachers the important questions are "How does self-concept influence student behavior in school?" and "How do school experiences influence self-concept?" In general, research cited by Woolfolk (1993) reports that students with a higher self-concept are likely to have more positive attitudes toward school and are likely to be more successful. There is no overall agreement on the effect of schooling on self-concept and vice versa. However, there is evidence that self-concept declines as students enter higher grade levels. It is also likely that successful school experiences may increase self-concept. For teachers this implies, among other things, accepting students for their efforts as well as their accomplishments, even when rejecting a particular behavior; establishing a risk-free classroom environment; providing realistic opportunities for student success; making a conscious effort to interact with all students; encouraging students to praise other classmates; and conveying personal interest and concern for student interests and needs.

At times it is useful or necessary for teachers to work with parents and others who also are concerned with a student's self-concept development. The parents and others may have valuable background information concerning the student about which teachers know little. For example, in the Behavior Rating Profile (Brown and Hammil, 1983) parents, teachers, and students rate student behaviors. The perceptions of each are compared in an effort to assist the student. A question teachers may want to ask themselves is "To what extent do I, the teacher, enhance parental expectations and evaluations of their children?"

There are several standardized tests which, if used correctly, may help teachers in diagnosing student self-concept. One such test is the Piers-Harris Children's Self-Concept Scale (Piers and Harris, 1984), a checklist used by students in group settings in grades 4 through 12. While this test was designed as a research tool, it may be used as a screening device by schools to identify students who may have possible self-concept needs and problems. Another such measurement tool is the Coopersmith Self-Esteem Inventories (1981). This test identifies students with possible needs in the area of self-concept. Both tests are best used as informal measurement devices and both encourage the development of local norms (McLoughlin and Lewis, 1986).

A student's self-concept is often linked to achievement, behavior, and classroom discipline. In general, a positive self-concept is related to positive classroom behavior while a negative or weak self-concept is often related to a lack of discipline and poor classroom behavior. Classroom discipline is a concern of both veteran and novice teachers.

What Are Some Guidelines Concerning Classroom Discipline?

The word "discipline" as we like to think of it derives from the word disciple. Teacher candidates and experienced teachers all have some concerns about classroom management, but if you are a *teacher* you will have disciples (students willing to learn) and few discipline problems (disruptive behaviors). Without going into a long discussion we want to reinforce the concept of discipline-disciple with some well-established practices that you should consider using in your classes. It is important to remember that even if the teacher is well prepared, there are some conditions and circumstances that lead to disruptive behaviors that are beyond the control of the teacher, including personal or family concerns, use of drugs and other dangerous substances, peer pressure, and self-concept. In these circumstances, sensitive teachers need to work closely with school social workers and guidance counselors.

It is useful for teachers to analyze their own techniques of group management. Jacob S. Kounin in his classic work, *Discipline and Group Management in the Classroom* (1970) noted that the following classroom management techniques appear to be successful:

1. Teachers who know what is going on in the classroom generally have fewer discipline problems. Often this means stopping disruptive behavior before it gains momentum. Kounin described this technique as "withitness."
2. Teachers should learn to handle overlapping activities smoothly so as to cope with two or more concurrent situations in the classroom without losing awareness of the problems.
3. Teachers should try to ensure smoothness and momentum in learning by eliminating or greatly reducing interruptions in the learning process. It is also important to be aware of student restlessness and inattentiveness and make the appropriate adjustments to facilitate learning.
4. Teachers should make every effort to keep the whole class involved and alert in learning even when working with individual students. For example, when asking questions, call on students in an unpredictable order so that other students are more likely to remain interested and less likely to engage in mischief or become bored. Or, if the class is dealing with complex materials, the teacher should call on several students in an unpredictable order, asking each to respond to one section.
5. Teachers should introduce a variety of instructional procedures and learning activities to the class, but also allow sufficient time for the more mature students to analyze complex ideas without interruption. The amount of time allowed for an activity is a judgment call on the part of the teacher.
6. Teachers need to be aware of the "ripple effect" when criticizing or correcting student behavior. The comments should focus on the undesirable behavior and not the personality of the student. It is important to specify the expected constructive behavior so that students will be reminded of teacher and class expectations.

In addition to Kounin, several other researchers (for example, see Doyle 1986; Emmer et al. 1989) have described several basic characteristics of well-managed classrooms not only for social studies but also for other disciplines as well. These may be summarized as follows:

1. Teachers have planned in advance how to handle classroom routines such as attendance, announcements, and dealing with media equipment. This means that teachers are familiar with school policies on these details. It is equally important that teachers demonstrate professional competency by being well prepared every day for each lesson.
2. Students know what behaviors are expected of them from the first day of class. Class rules are discussed and, when appropriate, students have helped to formulate such behavior rules.
3. Students are busy completing their assignments with little wasted time or confusion when a positive, businesslike, and supportive classroom environment has been established.
4. Teachers give clear and focused directions, establish a no-nonsense classroom tone, hold students accountable to complete the assignments, and give frequent feedback for positive reinforcement or constructive improvement. Teachers need to be consistent in their behaviors and expectations.
5. Teachers lead whole-class activities during the first part of the semester to help students become comfortable and successful in the classroom. For example, all of the students participate in a role-playing activity or simulation.
6. Teachers establish fair discipline policies that recognize the dignity of the students and which create an atmosphere conducive to learning. Teacher often encourage students to assist in formulating these policies. For example, students can suggest topics to discuss or suggest learning strategies that vary the type of and pace of instruction.

SUMMARY

How one views learning and developmental theory influences decisions about curriculum content and instructional procedures. Obviously each of these theories of teaching have supporters and critics just as they have positive and negative features. Most teachers will probably adopt an eclectic approach to teaching. Sometimes instruction may be more behavioristic; at times discovery lessons may be more appropriate; while at other times teachers may use humanistic education approaches to meet the planned objectives for a particular lesson. No one single approach is necessarily "best." Within district or school policies and practices, you are encouraged to try out a variety of strategies that build upon your interests and strengths. New strategies can be added throughout your career.

This chapter discussed various findings of theorists who have influenced the shape of social studies education. We included several instructional activities that exemplified these theories as well as criticisms and/or cautions concerning some of them. This chapter reinforced the important principle that teachers must consider the individual and group characteristics of their students when planning for instruction. Teachers need to be aware of new research findings concerning the teaching and learning process throughout their careers. They must also continue to learn more about the social science disciplines and other related curriculum content areas.

Discussion Questions

1. Why is it necessary to consider student attitudes, needs, interests, and prior experiences when planning social studies lessons and activities?
2. Reflect on your own learning. How do you learn? What learning processes did you use the last time you learned new knowledge, a concept, or skill? How do students learn? To what extent can students learn without thinking, without knowledge, and without the processing of information?
3. Including value-oriented and moral education topics in social studies programs is considered by some as being outside the responsibility of the school. To what extent is it possible or desirable to have a value-free curriculum or instructional program? Why might you include or exclude values and moral issues in your teaching of social studies?
4. The following are three scenarios that (with variations) may well happen in any social studies classroom. Read each scenario and decide how you might respond based on your developing teaching philosophy and your knowledge of learning theory. Assuming your first response was not helpful or effective, what are some other steps you might take in each case?

   Scenario I For this lesson, your world geography students are working quietly in small cooperative learning groups of four or five as they have done in the past. As you walk around the room to monitor progress and respond to questions you hear Leslie say loudly to members of the group, "I don't want to tell the others about agriculture in Russia. I want to do the report on the trans-Siberian railway—it's more interesting! Kim, just because you are the group leader, you can't tell me what to do." As you move toward the group, how will you respond and what actions are you likely to take?

Scenario 2 Your sixth period United States history class has been "the bright spot" in your day. The students are intelligent; they complete their assignments; they participate in class discussions and other learning activities; and they are willing to extend themselves beyond minimum requirements. However, recently you notice a change in the class. Assignments are now late or incomplete, during discussions no one volunteers to participate, the students complain about the tests, and "little accidents" such as books falling on the floor, pencils breaking, and so on, become more frequent. Something has obviously happened to change your sixth period students. What will you do to respond to the changes going on in this class?

Scenario 3 Kelly is in a 9th grade social studies class for less mature students. Kelly's academic record is poor. For example, Kelly reads two to three years below grade level and at least one grade level below that of other class members. Kelly regularly misbehaves in class by not bringing the necessary learning materials to class, not completing homework, disrupting other classmates, and so on. A previous teacher has called Kelly "the problem student—the worst kid in class." What steps are you likely to take to help Kelly get back on track? What might you say to Kelly so that Kelly knows you care and that learning is important?

Student Learning Activities

1. Consider a social studies instructional unit on a topic that is likely to be taught at both the middle school and senior high levels, such as the American Revolution, citizenship responsibilities, community issues, or another topic of your choice. How would the content, skills, and instructional procedures differ at each grade? To what extent do the characteristics of learners at these grade levels influence your curriculum and instructional decisions? To what extent is there a potential problem for overlap of learning if the same or similar content, skills, and instructional procedures are used at both grade levels? To what extent should the same or similar topics be taught at more than one grade level to reinforce the learning of that content? If repetition is considered to be undesirable, how might the potential of overlap be resolved?
2. To gain insight into thinking, researchers have designed various experiments to determine the level of thinking of young people at different ages and in different disciplines. Use the following experiment or one of your own choice to analyze the formal thought processes of young people in middle or high school.

Procedure: Ask middle or high school students to respond to the following statement.

At present there are several million people in our country who are functionally illiterate (unable to read or write at a satisfactory level). Assume you have the money and authority to establish programs to reduce or eliminate illiteracy. What ideas do you have to resolve this problem?

Objective: To gain insight into the ability of the student to engage in hypothesizing, to focus on possibilities or realities, and to deal in abstract ideas.

If more than one teacher candidate engages in this activity with several students, the results of these interviews should be shared with the class. What are some conclusions about thinking which you might express as a result of this activity?

References

Ausubel, D. P. 1963. *The Psychology of Meaningful Verbal Learning.* New York: Grune and Stratton.

Bangert-Drowns, R. L., Kulik, J. A., and Kulik, C. C. 1983–1984. "Synthesis of Research on the Effects of Coaching for Aptitude and Admission Tests." *Educational Leadership,* Vol. 41, No. 4, December 1983/January 1984. 80–82.

Brown, L. L. and Hammill, D. D. 1983. *Behavior Rating Profile.* Austin, TX: ED-PRO.

Bruner, J. 1960. *The Process of Education.* Cambridge, MA: Harvard University Press.

Coopersmith, S. 1981. *Coopersmith Self-Esteem Inventories.* Palo Alto, CA: Consulting Psychologists Press.

Cornbleth, C., Davis, O. L. Jr., and Button, C. 1974. "Expectations of Pupil Achievement and Teacher-Pupil Interaction." *Social Education,* Vol. 38, No. 1, January. 54–58.

Doyle, W. 1986. "Classroom Organization and Management." In M. Wittrock, (Ed.), *Handbook of Research on Teaching* (3rd ed.). New York: Macmillan.

Emmer, E. T., Evertson, C. M., Sanford, J. P., Clements, B. S., and Worsham, M. E. 1989. *Classroom Management for Secondary Teachers* (2nd ed.). Englewood Cliffs, NJ: Prentice-Hall.

Gilligan, C. 1982. *In a Different Voice: Psychological Theory and Women's Development.* Cambridge, MA: Harvard University Press.

Hill, W. F. 1985. *Principles of Learning: A Handbook of Applications* (4th ed.) Sherman Oaks, CA: Alfred Publishers.

Kohlberg, L. 1963. "The Development of Children's Orientations Toward a Moral Order: Sequence in the Development of Moral Thought." *Vita Humana,* Vol. 6. 11–33.

Kohlberg, L. 1978. "Revisions in the Theory and Practice of Moral Development." *Moral Development: New Directions for Child Development.* Vol. 1, No. 2. 83–88.

Kounin, J. 1970. *Discipline and Group Management in the Classroom.* New York: Holt, Rinehart and Winston.

Leder, G. C. 1987. "Student Achievement: A Factor in Classroom Dynamics?" *Exceptional Child.* Vol. 34, No. 2, July. 133–141.

Marshall, H. H. and Weinstein, R. S. 1986. "Classroom Context of Student Perceived Differential Teacher Treatment." *Journal of Educational Psychology.* Vol. 78, No. 6, December. 441–453.

Maslow, A. H. 1968. *Toward a Psychology of Being* (2nd ed.). Princeton, NJ: Van Nostrand.

Mayer, R. E. 1987. *Educational Psychology: A Cognitive Approach.* New York: Harper.

McCown, R. R. and Roop, P. G. 1992. *Educational Psychology and Classroom Practice: A Partnership.* Boston: Allyn and Bacon.

McLoughlin, J. A. and Lewis, R. B. 1986. *Assessing Special Students: Strategies and Procedures* (2nd ed.) Columbus, OH: Merrill.

Peeck, J., van den Bosch, S. B., and Kreupeling, W. J. 1982. "Effect of Mobilizing Prior Knowledge on Learning from Text." *Journal of Educational Psychology.* Vol. 74, No. 5, October. 771–777.

Piaget, J. 1932. *The Moral Judgment of the Child.* M. Gabain (Trans.) 1969. New York: Free Press.

Piers, E. V. and Harris, D. B. 1984. *The Piers-Harris Children's Self-Concept Scale.* Los Angeles: Western Psychological Services.

Resnick, L. B. 1981. "Instructional Psychology." *Annual Review of Psychology.* Vol. 32. 659–704.

Rogers, C. R. 1951. *Client-centered Therapy: Its Current Practice, Implications, and Theory.* Boston: Houghton Mifflin.

Rogers, C. R. 1980. *A Way of Being.* Boston: Houghton Mifflin.

Rosenthal, R. and Jacobson, L. 1968. *Pygmalion in the Classroom: Teacher Expectation and Pupil's Intellectual Development.* New York: Holt, Rinehart and Winston.

Rousseau, J. J. 1965. "Emile." In W. Boyd (Ed.), *The Emile of Jean Jacques Rousseau.* New York: Teachers College Press, Columbia University.

Skinner, B. F. 1953. *Science and Human Behavior.* New York: Macmillan.

Skinner, B. F. 1984. "The Shame of American Education." *American Psychologist*, Vol. 39, No. 9, September. 947–954.

Wlodkowski, R. J. 1978. *Motivation and Teaching: A Practice Guide.* Washington, DC: National Education Association.

Woolfolk, A. E. 1993. *Educational Psychology* (5th ed.). Boston: Allyn and Bacon.

Additional Readings

Ames, R. and Ames, C., (Eds.). 1989. *Research on Motivation in Education.* Vol. 3: Goals and Cognitions. New York: Academic Press, Inc.

Bauer, A. M. and Sapona, R. H. 1990. *Managing Classrooms to Facilitate Learning.* Englewood Cliffs, NJ: Prentice-Hall.

Biehler, R. F. and Snowman, J. 1989. *Psychology Applied to Teaching* (5th ed.). Boston: Houghton Mifflin.

Brabeck, M. 1983. "Moral Judgment: Theory and Research on Differences Between Males and Females." *Developmental Review*, Vol. 3. No. 3, September. 274–291.

Charles, C. M. 1992. *Building Classroom Discipline: From Models to Practice* (4th ed.). New York: Longman.

Cooper, H. M. and Good, T. L. 1983. *Pygmalion Grows Up: Studies in the Expectation Communication Process*. New York: Longman.

Coopersmith, S. and Bilberts, R. 1981. *Behavioral Academic Self-Esteem, A Rating Scale*. Palo Alto, CA: Consulting Psychologists Press.

Gage, N. and Berliner, D. 1991. *Educational Psychology* (5th ed.). Boston: Houghton Mifflin.

Gibbs, J. C., Arnold, K. D., and Burkhart, J. E. 1984. "Sex Differences in the Expression of Moral Judgment." *Child Development,* Vol. 55, No. 3, June. 1040–1043.

Jones, V. F. and Jones, L. S. 1990. *Comprehensive Classroom Management: Motivating and Managing Students* (3rd ed.). Boston: Allyn and Bacon.

Levine, C., Kohlberg, L., and Hewer, A. 1985. "The Current Formulation of Kohlberg's Theory and a Response to Critics." *Human Development*, Vol. 28, No. 2, March–April. 94–100.

Maslow, A. H. 1976. *The Farther Reaches of Human Nature*. New York: Viking Press.

Nisan, M. and Kohlberg, L. 1982. "Universality and Variation in Moral Judgment: A Longitudinal and Cross-sectional Study in Turkey." *Child Development*, Vol. 53, No. 4, August. 865–876.

Piaget, J. 1952. *The Origins of Intelligence in Children*. M. Cook (Trans.). New York: International Universities Press.

Shaftel, F. R. and Shaftel, G. 1982. *Role Playing for Social Values* (2nd ed.). Englewood Cliffs, NJ: Prentice-Hall.

Silvernail, D. L. 1985. *Developing Positive Student Self-Concept* (2nd ed.). Washington, DC: National Education Association.

Skinner, B. F. 1968. *The Technology of Teaching*. New York: Appleton-Century-Crofts.

Slavin, R. E. 1991. *Educational Psychology. Theory into Practice* (3rd ed.). Englewood Cliffs, NJ: Prentice-Hall.

Snarey, J. R., Reimer, J., and Kohlberg, L. 1985. "Development of Social-Moral Reasoning Among Kibbutz Adolescents: A Longitudinal Cross-cultural Study." *Developmental Psychology,* Vol. 21, No. 1, January. 3–17.

Stipek, D. J. 1988. *Motivation to Learn: From Theory to Practice*. Englewood Cliffs, NJ: Prentice-Hall.

Stolz, S. B., Wienckowski, L. A., and Brown, B. S. 1975. "Behavior Modification: A Perspective on Critical Issues." *American Psychologist,* Vol. 30, No. 11, November. 1027–1048.

Walker, L. J. 1984. "Sex Differences in the Development of Moral Reasoning: A Critical Review." *Child Development*, Vol. 55, No. 3, June. 677–691.

Wiles, J. and Bondi, J. 1993. *The Essential Middle School*. (2nd ed.) New York: Macmillan.

> Knowledge is the only instrument of production that is not subject to diminishing returns.
>
> *J. M. Clark*

CHAPTER 8

Characteristics of Successful Curriculum and Instructional Plans

FOCUS QUESTIONS

- What responsibilities do social studies teachers have in planning for curriculum and instruction?
- What processes are involved in planning the overall curriculum, the unit, and the daily lesson? How are these three planning levels interrelated?
- What social studies content issues need to be addressed in planning quality social studies programs?
- What are some ways to organize social studies programs and social studies content?
- What are some ongoing challenges facing social studies teachers in planning for instruction?
- How do community values, expectations, and reforms influence the nature of schooling and the structure of social studies programs?

OVERVIEW

Deciding what content to include or exclude in social studies courses has never been an easy task. Today this responsibility is even more challenging. The Information Age brings with it far-reaching changes in society, generating new knowledge that has important consequences for teachers and students as well as for our community, nation, and the world at large. We live, work, and play in an interdependent world.

Effective planning for social studies requires that teachers take responsibility for many important decisions concerning the curriculum content and its organization. In addition, teachers need to make decisions concerning instructional strategies, the learning environment, and the evaluation of student learning and program effectiveness. This chapter will present several ways to assist you in *planning* for effective social studies instruction. Later chapters will offer additional suggestions concerning social studies instructional procedures and describe ways of measuring student learning in greater detail.

Planning for Curriculum and Instruction

Quality social studies programs may be organized in various ways. Most often states or local school boards have recommended or mandated specific requirements such as United States history during the middle and secondary school years. Frequently state education officials have developed scope and sequence models for grades K–12. Other sources of scope and sequence models include the National Council for the Social Studies (NCSS), which has adopted three scope and sequence models, and textbook publishers, who frequently offer similar curriculum suggestions. There are other possibilities for organizing the social studies program since there is no universal agreement that one scope and sequence model is the one best model.

The important notion to keep in mind is that no matter how social studies programs are organized these programs should provide for reasonable balance of content; be arranged logically and coherently; enable students to develop knowledge, skills, and values; and meet the diverse needs of students, teachers, and the community. The questions that we will address include the following: "How can social studies programs be organized to teach students to become effective citizens?" and "How will social studies programs prepare students for the 21st century?"

Curriculum Planning—An Overview

Planning is an important part of a teacher's ongoing professional responsibility. Most likely, the planning process will move from the general to the specific, and from the yearly curriculum plan to the unit plan and finally to the daily lesson plan. Just as the unit plan is a focused portion of the yearly curriculum plan, the daily lesson plan is a more detailed portion of the unit plan. Most often the daily lesson plan will identify the content, concepts, values, and skills to be learned and evaluated, as well as describe the instructional procedures and resources to be used. For example, if the 8th grade curriculum focuses on citizenship throughout the year, one of the units may emphasize students becoming active *participants* in a local government issue such as whether or not to build a new middle school and, if so, in what location in the school district. The daily lesson would then develop this by requiring students to gather information about the issue, interpret and judge the data, and then recommend action to the school board. Their recommendations could be in the form of letters to the editor, presentations to the parent–teacher organization, and testimony before the school board.

In developing plans some teachers may first choose the instructional materials they wish to use and then develop a curriculum unit around these materials. At other times, teachers may decide to develop their own curriculum and select or create their own instructional materials. Also, as part of the planning process, we encourage teachers to discuss their individual planning efforts with colleagues so that gaps and needless overlaps in the total social studies program can be avoided or at least greatly reduced. We further encourage social studies teachers to discuss their plans with colleagues in other curriculum areas, including English, science, mathematics, art, and music, and, when feasible, work together to develop and use an integrated unit or overall integrated curriculum. Such a curriculum allows teachers from various disciplines to work together and develop instructional activities that cross discipline lines. For example, if an instructional unit is on the theme of "transportation" such activities might include reading about transportation through stories and diaries; listening to music with transportation themes; viewing artists' perspectives; working mathematical problems comparing times, speeds, and distances of particular modes of transportation; and examining scientific principles related to engines. Such units of instruction would enable students to link information from the perspectives of several disciplines.

Before effective instruction can be planned it is useful to have some type of overall curriculum guideline to follow. An analogy can be made between a curriculum plan and a football playbook. The latter includes numerous plays that can be used at various times throughout the game depending upon the specific situation. These plays are called not necessarily in the order they appear in the playbook, but are determined on the basis of the specific game situation. The key is for the coaches to select the right play at the right time. And so it is with curriculum. The curriculum plan, like the playbook, allows for some choice in making decisions as we organize our instructional program to meet state and local district guidelines.

Curriculum planning has at least four major functions: 1) it allows teachers to organize their courses to ensure that students learn the agreed-upon content, concepts, values, and skills for effective citizenship; 2) it enables teachers of social studies in several grade levels and in several social science disciplines to discuss with one another the value of social studies within the total school program; 3) it enables teachers to communicate these perspectives to the local community; and 4) it provides opportunities for teachers to gain new knowledge and to broaden their perspectives.

Curriculum provides an overall sense of direction to teachers. They then must decide the rationale and content, identify objectives, select materials, determine teaching strategies, and evaluate student learning. Certainly there are many facets to social studies planning, and we will divide planning into three parts: long-range curriculum planning, unit planning, and daily lesson planning.

Long-Range Planning

Most states have already prepared curriculum guidelines, planning guides, or frameworks which recommend or mandate certain requirements for schools under their jurisdiction. Such requirements may be very specific about course content, the amount of time for each instructional unit, the number of minutes of social studies instruction per day or week, the specific instructional materials to be used or not used, student achievement tests, and the like. Where such requirements are in place, often there are mandates that schools monitor their teachers to ensure compliance.

Some states recognize local school district autonomy for curriculum-oriented decisions. States that have few mandates or requirements rely on the policies and guidelines developed by each local school district and, by implication, the state to ensure quality education for the students of the particular district. This often means there is a wide diversity of teaching and learning expectations among school districts within a given state. In any case, there are likely to be state guidelines available to help social studies teachers in local districts plan the overall social studies curriculum.

Long-term curriculum planning is often a responsibility assigned to a group of teachers. However, in smaller districts or schools this responsibility may be assigned to a single teacher. At times, representatives from several nearby districts may plan curriculum together for implementation in their respective districts. This practice encourages teachers from several districts to work cooperatively and to communicate important ideas about teaching, learning, and curriculum. In districts that include elementary, middle schools, and senior high schools the school or district curriculum committee will ideally include teachers at each level who have a strong interest in social studies. The committee may also include administrators, community members, and in some instances, students. For purposes of this chapter, we assume that curriculum planning is done in a group setting for a single district and that the teachers and committee members already know one another.

Leadership for the curriculum planning group may be assigned to a social studies department chairperson, the school or district curriculum supervisor, or may emerge from within the group. The leader will be expected to establish a work plan of action; assign specific tasks; communicate with members of the committee, administration, and school board; coordinate the work of the committee; handle administrative details; and so forth.

The leader should make every effort to have a wide variety of reference resources available for use by members of the committee. These resources may include curriculum guides from other districts and states, professional journals and books, catalogs of instructional resources, sample textbooks, and so forth. The leader should take care to ensure that a pleasant and comfortable physical working environment exists. Depending on local district policies, those who work on curriculum development usually are rewarded with additional compensation or other benefits and opportunities. Often curriculum development takes place during the summer or on days especially set aside for this purpose.

As the group begins its work, the committee ought to develop a rationale or mission statement expressing the importance of social studies for the students in their district. In other words, *why* teach social studies? Chapter 1 of this textbook identified the central role of citizenship in social studies and suggested several themes that should be emphasized throughout social studies programs. Committee members could review those areas of suggested emphases and decide which are most appropriate. They should discuss the purpose of social studies for their particular district until they achieve an overall consensus among the curriculum committee members. This statement should be compatible with and complement the existing philosophy and goals statements of the district.

The next step is to identify several fairly broad goals for the overall social studies program. The committee may want to identify several long-range curriculum goals that all students should be able to attain either while they are enrolled in school or during their adult years. Statements such as these are often included in overall goal statements:

- Students will learn about our nation's heritage and its place in the community of nations.
- Students will value our democratic way of life and will be productive citizens.
- Students will acquire knowledge and skills necessary to make informed choices and policies as citizens, producers, and consumers.
- Students will appreciate cultural diversity and recognize the contributions of many cultures.

After agreeing on several broad overall goal statements, it will be useful for the committee to decide what specific courses will be offered and at what grade level. Ideally in grades 6–12 students should have opportunities for social studies instruction each year. The course work should include courses that study 1) life in the United States; 2) life in other cultures in various settings and time periods; and 3) at least one course in one or more other social science disciplines, such as anthropology, economics, geography, philosophy, political science, sociology, or psychology. It is most likely that studies of the United States and other cultures will be arranged by using history and/or geography as the organizing discipline in teaching the content of those courses.

Curriculum planning committees need to ensure that students have opportunities to complete courses in each of these three areas. At times the committee may find it necessary to delete courses that are no longer needed. At other times they may need to add new courses or revise existing ones to meet the changing needs of students and the community. An overall consideration in deciding which courses to teach is to encourage students to take one or more courses from each grouping. Students ought to have experiences in examining humankind in various settings, time periods, and cultures from the perspective of different social science disciplines.

Unit Planning

After deciding the overall social studies course offerings for a particular district, teachers must decide which course or courses are to be offered at a particular grade level (required or elective), for which students, and for what length of time (for example, year, semester, quarter, or other time period). The next decision will be the content, concepts, values, and skills the students are to learn in this particular course. "What do I, the teacher, want my students to take away with them from this course? How will this course impact their lives?" Within the time frame of the course, it is necessary to determine the units of instruction and decide approximately how much time to give to each unit. Teachers will need to give attention to the sequencing of learning experiences. Will they be presented in chronological sequence; as selected themes or problem-focused topics; as area or case studies; or in some conceptual order? Most likely instructional units will include combinations and aspects of these arrangements. The development of a draft outline of the major topics or key concepts to be included may be helpful at this point. Consideration ought to be given to the unit objectives, instructional procedures, instructional resources (textbooks and supplementary materials such as videos, computer programs and databases, and so forth), and student evaluation.

CHAPTER 8 Characteristics of Successful Curriculum and Instructional Plans

A sample unit outline that could be included in a one-semester economics course is presented as a guideline for consideration. As you examine the unit outline, think about how you would develop such an outline. You will need to consider the following:

Course	The school board has decided the particular course that will be taught at the school.
Grade Level	The district has decided which students by grade level (and in some cases by ability) are entitled to enroll in the particular course.
Time	The length of class periods per day has been determined previously by school board action.
Text	The text and various supplemental instructional materials have been approved by the school board. If new materials are to be purchased, district purchasing guidelines are to be followed.
Unit	Following state or district curriculum guidelines, considering the abilities of students and instructional resources available, the focus of the unit is determined and the time to be spent on a particular unit is decided.
Objectives	Objectives identify what it is the student is to learn in the particular unit. The objectives are to be written so that learning can be measured by having the student demonstrate how learning has taken place. The objectives and student evaluation of learning are closely linked.
Content	The content includes the information presented by the teacher; through readings; viewing media; using computer programs; by engaging in discussions with a variety of people, including teachers, classmates, and others; and by being an active participant in class.
Concepts	Concepts are identified on the basis of the content selected and provide a framework for learning.
Skills	Skills, like the content and concepts to be learned, are identified on the basis of the specific skills needed for the unit. They build on skills learned previously.
Resources	Most likely, teachers will use the textbook as a key resource. The teacher's guide may well include several recommended resources which may be available in the school or district media resource center. The media specialist is a most valuable partner in the development of curriculum, especially with his or her awareness of new materials available for acquisition through purchase or loan. Oftentimes a nearby university has many resource materials available for check out. Over time teachers will build their own materials resource file.

Student Evaluation Ideally, as the unit is being planned, teachers should give serious thought to evaluating student learning. There are a variety of evaluation processes available depending on the unit objectives and school policies. For example, are objective tests appropriate? Will essay questions be included? Will student reports and/or presentations be appropriate? Will an authentic performance assessment be effective? These questions ought to be answered in the initial planning process.

As beginning teachers plan their initial units of study it is good to seek ideas and comments from more experienced colleagues who have had opportunities to develop their own units of instruction. The precise learning activities are included in the daily lesson plan. The unit outline is a guideline to be used in developing the daily lesson plan.

■■■■■■■ Illustrative Unit Outline (High School)

Course:	Economics
Grade Level:	Junior/Senior
Length:	One semester
Time:	50 minutes per day
Text:	(*Title* and author)
Unit I:	Why Study Economics? (3 weeks)

Objectives	Content	Concepts
Students will:		
▪ explain why the study of economics is important in their lives.	What is economics?	Needs and Wants
		Scarcity
▪ discuss the basic economic choices each nation must make.	How are economic systems organized?	Opportunity Costs
		Trade-offs
▪ describe the major characteristics of an economic system.	What are the principal types of economic systems?	Productive Economic Systems
		Traditional Economies
▪ differentiate the characteristics of capitalism, socialism, and communism as economic systems.	What are some characteristics of the United States economy?	Market Economies
		Command Economies
	What fundamental questions must be decided by every economic system?	Mixed Economies
		Productive Resources

- identify the basic characteristics of the United States economic system.

- analyze the growth of the United States economy.

- suggest possible changes in the United States economy.

- show how opportunity costs influence economic decision making.

What are the economic goals of the United States?

How can economic analysis lead to social justice?

What are some key differences among alternative economic systems?

How are national economies linked to global economies?

Producers

Consumers

Capitalism

Socialism

Communism

Profits

Free Enterprise

Standard of Living

Skills	Resources	Student Evaluation
Decision making	Textbook pages _____	How will student learning be evaluated?
Interpreting economic charts, graphs, and tables	List titles of resources available locally	How will the teacher know how effectively the unit objectives have been met?
Predicting	Supplemental materials (print and nonprint)	Will teacher-prepared tests be used?
Analyzing data	Media: films, videos, filmstrips, records, laser discs	Will author-prepared tests be used?
	Computer programs, modem, FAX	Are there alternative ways to measure learning?
	Games and simulations	
	Possible guest speakers	

A similar unit outline is suggested for middle school social studies.

■ ■ ■ ■ ■ ■ ■ ■   Illustrative Unit Outline Middle School

Course:	Civics
Grade Level:	7th/8th Grade
Length:	Full Year

Time: 42 minutes per day

Text: (*Title* and Author)

Unit V: Citizens Make Decisions to Influence Policy (3 Weeks)

Objectives	Content	Concepts
Students will:		
▪ identify a problem, develop criteria to be used in decision making, and consider alternative possibilities.	What are some of the problems we face today? What are some ways we might seek to solve these problems?	Problem Solving Decision-making Consensus Building Public Opinion
▪ practice decision-making skills using a decision-making grid.*	How might we use a decision-making grid to help us make decisions?	Alternative Perspectives
▪ explain the reasons for making a particular decision.	How can we evaluate our decisions?	Criteria Beliefs Values
▪ apply the decision-making process to a "real" situation in the local community.	How can we share our decisions and recommendations with policy makers?	Taking Action
▪ formulate a policy to be shared with decision makers (policy makers/city officials). ▪ recognize that public opinion varies among community members.	How can we apply what we have learned about the decision-making process related to our "real" local problem of whether or not to build a new arena/convention center in town? (Note: Any other issue could be substituted.)	

Skills	Resources	Student Evaluation
Gathering data from many sources	Textbook pages ___ (List titles of resources available locally.)	In a cooperative group setting complete a decision-making grid and give reasons for the decision recommended.
Integrating a variety of data	Supplemental materials (print and nonprint)	Write a letter to a decision maker urging a particular course of action.

*A sample decision-making grid is included as Appendix A at the end of this chapter.

Analyzing conflicting data and perspectives	Media: films, videos, filmstrips, records, laser discs	Role play a decision-making town-hall-type of meeting in which the decision-making process is used to resolve an issue.
Listening	Computer programs, modem, FAX	
Communicating	Games and simulations	
Interviewing	Possible guest speakers	

Daily Lesson Planning

The preceding pages have painted a somewhat detailed description for curriculum planning. Daily lesson plans require you to use many of the same skills and processes. For example, if you are going to teach a lesson about recent immigrants to the United States, you may start to plan your lesson by focusing on the content you want the student to learn, or you could begin by thinking about the concepts (ideas or categories of ideas based on associations) that will

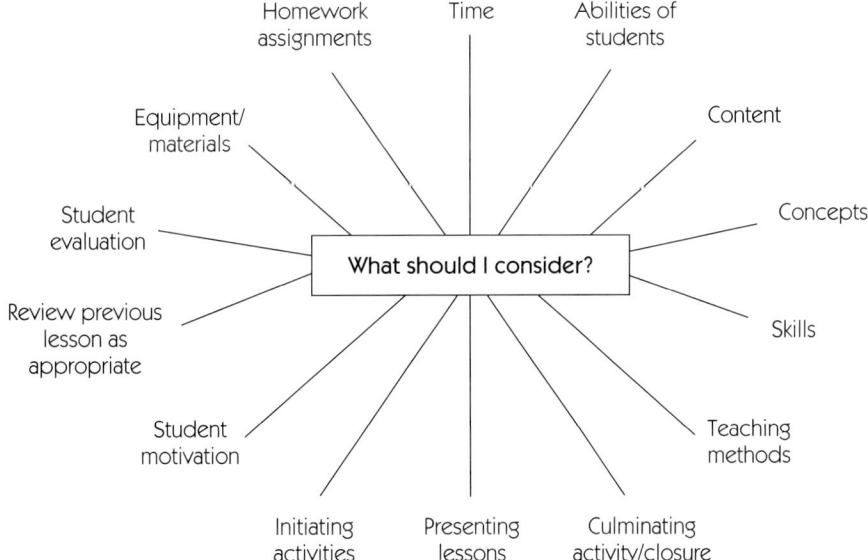

Figure 8.1 Social Studies Instructional Planning Time

be emphasized, or you could first identify the skills you want to stress during this lesson. Depending on where you initiate your planning, you will need to consider at a minimum, the content, concepts, skills, values, instructional procedures, resources to be used, and an evaluation of student learning. Planning is not necessarily a linear process but can begin at any place that is most effective for you.

The unit plan enables the teacher to develop the daily lesson. There is no single best lesson plan format for all teachers. Individual teachers need to make intelligent choices concerning lesson plan format based on the course, teaching methods, student interest and/or ability, and district or school requirements. Many districts require that teachers submit lesson plans for the coming week before leaving school on Friday. From time to time administrators, curriculum directors, or department chairpersons may review lesson plans with individual teachers. In some districts they are used in the teacher evaluation process. Lesson plans may be given to substitute teachers should the regular teacher be absent from class.

Some General Considerations When Planning

As you think about your daily lesson planning you should reflect on these and similar questions. Your thoughtful responses will help you to think through the planning process and help you to plan effective learning activities for your students.

1. To what extent will this lesson be of value for my students?
2. To what extent is this lesson realistic (content, concepts, values, and skills) given my students' interests, abilities, and expectations within the time, space, and instructional resources available to me?
3. To what extent does the plan recognize different learning styles and rates?
4. To what extent does this lesson provide opportunities for students to extend their learning experiences outside the classroom?
5. To what extent will the lesson involve the students in active learning rather than passive acceptance?
6. To what extent does this lesson relate to previous learning and how will it apply to future learning?
7. To what extent have my students been involved in the planning of this lesson or have I considered their previous comments and suggestions in formulating this plan?
8. To what extent have I considered community reaction to the topic of this lesson?
9. To what extent have I made provisions for evaluating student learning experiences?

After you have planned your daily lesson ask yourself these questions: "If I were a student in this class would I like the lesson and enjoy learning?" and "What would I learn from this lesson?"

The lesson plan format on the following pages is quite detailed to encourage you to think about the daily lesson from its beginning to its conclusion. It is unlikely that you will be required to write down all these components in your daily lesson plan, but you need to think through each aspect of the plan. It is useful to remember that making a lesson plan and implementing that lesson plan are not the same. Teachers are encouraged to make the plan sufficiently flexible to allow for unexpected situations, such as inoperable media equipment; fire drills, or other school activities and interruptions; and lack of student interest. On the other hand, students may become excited about one part of the lesson, and the teacher (and class) decide to linger on the lesson or activity longer than planned. As teachers gain experience in planning lessons, they will find the planning process seems less complex and time consuming.

It is useful to have a *title* for the lesson that describes the overall content. Middle and high school students often like to include the title in their notes for further reference. Most likely the class *time* will be for a single class period, which in most middle and high schools will range from 40 to 58 minutes. Of course there may be variations and at times a single lesson plan may be used for several periods of instruction. For example, if students are engaging in a United Nations debate a single lesson plan might cover all the class periods used for the debate.

The *grade level* should be included so that someone else examining the lesson plan is able to determine the grade level for which the lesson has been planned. For example, if economics is offered as an elective to junior or senior students or offered as a required course for 9th-grade students, the objectives, content, instructional strategies, and resources may differ considerably. Teachers will instruct a class of 9th-grade students in a somewhat different manner from a class of juniors and seniors. The time of day when the class is to be taught may also influence the content and instructional procedures selected. For example, if the class is just prior to lunch students may be hungry or if the class is the last one of the day, the students may be thinking about after-school events, activities, or jobs and family responsibilities that will soon take place.

Teachers need to decide why they are teaching a particular lesson, and therefore we recommend that teachers write down the *rationale* for teaching that specific lesson. In thinking about the rationale it is useful to reflect on these questions: "Why is this lesson important?" and "What important social studies content, concepts, skills, and attitudes will the students learn?"

Writing lesson *objectives* is an important aspect of planning. The objectives in the daily lesson plan identify *what* the student is to learn and *how* the learning is to be expressed. While there are ways to write objectives (some with greater detail than others) we recommend that objectives be written as follows.

Students will (this indicates that students in the class will be able to accomplish several behaviors or activities):

identify...
write...
translate...
interpret...
analyze...
judge...

These action words indicate the expected behaviors. For example, *identify* three issues in the last United States presidential election; *write* an essay explaining the importance of one of these issues; *translate* numeric data into a graphic format; *interpret* the data on the graph for someone else; *analyze* the editorial from the local press regarding one of the issues in the election; and *judge* the impact of one of the issues on your own life.

In this format the appropriate instruction, such as examining a chart or viewing a video that enables students to achieve each objective, is assumed. For most lessons, two or three objectives probably will be sufficient. It is not wise to try to teach too many important objectives in a single lesson. In order to teach the illustrative economics lesson we suggest the following objectives as possible examples.

Students will:

- identify the factors of production
- describe how land, labor, capital, and entrepreneurship have influenced the development of the United States economy
- compare United States productivity of 150 years ago with today.

Most likely the next step is to decide which *concepts* and *related concepts* are to be taught in the lesson. For the most part, teachers may decide to concentrate on two or three concepts and a similar number of related concepts for each lesson. For example, if you are teaching a unit on Latin American culture, you might in a single class period compare child-rearing practices in Latin America with those in the United States to examine the concepts of family structure, family traditions, and role expectations. Related concepts could include considerations of family values and the role of religion. These latter concepts may require extension into several lessons. Of course there are times when it is perfectly appropriate to teach additional concepts or focus on a single concept depending on the content of the lesson. The concepts and related concepts should be listed on the lesson plan for easy reference during the teaching of the lesson.

Each lesson will include the teaching or utilization of one or more *skills* related to social studies learning. You should identify the skills on the lesson plan. Using the concepts previously identified, skills to be taught in the lesson may include comparing and contrasting information about family life, discussion skills, and analyzing and interpreting data based on a video shown in class. These skills will be extended into subsequent learning activities. Teachers should introduce, teach, and utilize skills within the content of social science disciplines rather than teaching skills in isolation from each other and from a specific content. Most likely it will be necessary for the teacher to help the students make the needed linkages and application of skills to content not only in social studies but also with other curriculum content areas as well. For this reason, among others, we strongly encourage social studies teachers to talk with teachers of other disciplines and develop an integrated and coherent instructional program among disciplines within the school.

Students should learn to apply content, concepts, values, and skills learned in curriculum areas such as language arts, science, and mathematics to the social studies program and vice versa. For example, as students study about Latin America, the social studies teacher may ask the students to read a story or poem about Latin America, or the teacher may introduce the class to music from Latin America, or, when considering the continent, study the destruction of the rain forest and its impact on life in Brazil. Latin American demographic data also could be used to reinforce statistical concepts in social studies classrooms. Integrated learning helps the development of well-informed citizens.

Selecting Instructional Procedures

In selecting the *content* to be taught the teacher needs to identify the appropriate procedures and prepare teacher notes for use during the lesson. It is also necessary to identify the specific *management instructional procedures* to be used during the lesson. The approximate amount of time needed for each part of the lesson should also be included in the planning process.

For most lessons there are a variety of instructional procedures that could be utilized and the teacher must decide which best meet the objectives and fit the content and skills to be taught. Teachers should not only plan what they will do, but they should also anticipate what the students are to do and how the students are likely to respond. If the teacher reflects on both the teacher's role and possible student responses, the lesson will probably proceed more smoothly.

One way to plan for a lesson is to write down exactly what the teacher is to do and in a parallel column the anticipated student responses and behaviors. This part of the lesson plan may look like the following illustrative example.

Instructional Procedures

On the other hand the instructional procedures could be reversed and may look like the following illustrative example:

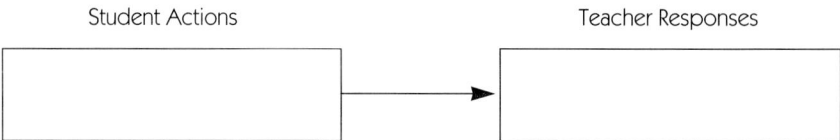

In planning the instructional procedures, you should take care to include initiating activities, developmental activities, and concluding activities for each lesson. Often the initiating activities are intended to motivate students and to focus their attention on the topic. The developmental activities should help students to extend their knowledge and learn the important aspects of the lesson. The concluding or culminating activities are to bring closure and point to the next lesson. Your selection of learning activities should be varied so as to avoid monotony, should promote active learning, should recognize student interest and maturity levels, and should allow for different learning styles, and so forth. Depending on school settings, some of the activities suggested could be used in more than one category; some may extend beyond the classroom and into the community; and some may require more than one day.

Examples of initiating activities that pique student interest and focus attention on a given lesson may include the following:

- Brainstorming what they know.
- Reading excerpts from a current newspaper article related to the topic being considered.
- Taking a field trip to a nearby site to stimulate curiosity.
- Examining an artifact or picture and forming hypotheses.
- Using media (computers, laser discs, or video).
- Inviting a guest speaker to introduce the topic being considered.
- Asking students to select concepts that they believe are important or that they would like to learn more about in greater depth.

- Asking students to write down questions they would like to have answered about the topic being studied.
- Creating a collage or bulletin board on the topic being studied.

The developmental activities help students to obtain new knowledge; develop additional skills; and form ideas, values, and attitudes concerning the topic. The following are some examples of developmental activities:

- Using a computer program.
- Reading from primary or secondary source materials.
- Analyzing economic tables, charts, and graphs to formulate generalizations.
- Interviewing local business leaders or government officials.
- Gathering data from a variety of sources.
- Creating a map of a region.
- Researching information for a report.

Concluding activities give students an opportunity to apply the knowledge and skills they have been learning. Such activities might include the following:

- Simulating a labor-management negotiation.
- Role playing a city council meeting discussing an issue currently before the city council.
- Debating a current local or national issue.
- Writing letters to public officials or the local press expressing their point of view on a given issue or topic.
- Preparing and presenting an individual or group project, such as a panel discussion, video program, or skit.
- Taking a unit test or quiz.

Instructional Choices

In deciding which instructional practices to use for a particular lesson you should give attention to the various learning styles of the students and your own teaching styles and strengths as a teacher. Some students benefit from direct instruction, while other students learn more effectively with indirect instruction. Some students may be better audio learners, while others may be more visual learners. Some students may learn more effectively in group settings, while others learn more effectively with individualized instruction. The following paragraphs discuss several commonly used instructional procedures. As appropriate to the setting, each may be an effective way of teaching social studies. Of course, there are numerous other instructional procedures that may be used in teaching social studies. Some of these ways are listed later in this chapter (see p. 218). The list is illustrative and is not intended to suggest these are the only ways to teach social studies. Effective teachers may combine several of these instructional procedures into quality lessons. It is usually a good idea to have several learning activities within a single class period.

Lectures

Most often middle school and high school teachers tend to teach as they remember being taught. They often recall the interesting lectures of a favorite professor or perhaps they recall a lecture from their middle school or high school social studies teacher. The lecture was exciting, delivered effectively and filled with interesting and useful content. However, more often than not lectures are boring to students, thereby allowing them to be passive learners unless the teacher poses thought-provoking questions and the students respond to them. In considering whether or not to use a lecture in your classes, you will need to remember that many students may not be highly motivated or interested in school. For younger or less mature students the lecture should be shorter. This means it will be necessary to have additional learning activities planned for each class session.

Teachers need to vary the instructional procedures within a class period, from day to day, and between instructional units. A well-organized and effectively delivered lecture is certainly appropriate to provide overview information, present large amounts of information within a short period of time, present information not readily available from existing instructional resources, and so forth. A lecture is inappropriate, however, when motivating students in the use of inquiry skills such as observation, organizing and grouping, or reaching tentative conclusions. While an explanation of these skills is important, a key ingredient is to provide students with many opportunities to practice these skills.

Class Discussions

Social studies teachers often plan for class discussions as one of their instructional procedures. While discussion skills are addressed in greater detail in Chapter 11, a few words about these important skills are included here. According to Dillon (1984) there has been limited research on discussions in classrooms. He reports that

> We do not know much about questioning and discussion. We have a volume of research on questioning—but not on discussion. We have a body of research on discussion—but not in classrooms. What we have is bits and pieces; the rest of the picture is blank. . . . The literature contains few studies but plenty of opinions and

free advice in essay articles, methods texts, and manuals. The greater part of knowledge is not contained in the literature at all but is privately held by skilled teachers as intuitive, implicit, knowledge-in-action.

Social studies teachers should not automatically assume that students have learned "how to discuss" or that they have developed the needed discussion skills. In may be necessary for teachers to review or teach these skills (listening, speaking, and responding) for use in social studies classes. Most likely teachers will need to teach negotiation and consensus-building skills as well.

In addition, to facilitate discussion social studies teachers need to be aware of the physical arrangement of the classroom as well as the intellectual and emotional environment. The arrangement of desks in a circle or semicircle may facilitate discussion, while desks in rows may hinder productive discussions. In planning for class discussions it is useful to reflect on questions such as the following: To what extent are the students encouraged to express ideas, offer opinions, or make suggestions without ridicule or "put downs"? Has a "risk-free" classroom environment been established? Are all or most students willing to participate? If not, is the teacher able to include everyone in the discussion? Does the discussion generate student-to-student interaction, or student-to-teacher or teacher-to-student interaction?

The amount of time allotted for discussion should allow students the opportunity to explore the topic in some depth. Teachers will at times need to extend the discussion beyond the anticipated time, while on other occasions they may decide to shorten the discussion depending upon how the discussion is going.

There are times when class discussions may not be appropriate. For example, when it is important for the teacher to impart a specific body of information that may not otherwise be readily available, a lecture may be more efficient. A discussion always will be less productive if both the teacher and student have not prepared adequately or have insufficient information.

Questions

The selection of questions to be used for class discussions usually comes from two sources. One source of questions comes from the social studies disciplines themselves. They are usually suggested in the student textbook, the teacher's guide, or similar questions that have been somewhat reworded by the teacher. The other source of class discussion questions comes from teachers and students as they develop "original" questions concerning the topic being studied.

Most questions used by classroom teachers can be grouped in two general categories: narrow and broad questions. For the most part narrow questions ask students to recall specific information, to show their memory of the subject matter, and possibly to apply their existing knowledge in new situations. Often it is the intent of narrow questions to have students reach a consensus on an answer. Extensive use of narrow questions may not allow students to have a useful class discussion, but rather such questions may lead to interrogation by the teacher and recitation by the students. Examples of narrow questions sometimes used in social studies classes include the following:

- How high is Mt. Fuji?
- What are the three major exports of Australia?
- Who is the current political leader in Canada?
- What are the factors of production?
- What is an oligopoly?

On the other hand, well-formulated broad questions usually are open-ended and value-oriented. They require students to use the skills of analysis, synthesis, and evaluation in reaching conclusions, however tentative. The use of broad questions for discussions provides for multiple responses from students, encourages divergent thinking, and allows for a consideration of alternative perspectives and viewpoints. Oftentimes teachers are unable to anticipate the many possible student responses.

Open-ended questions can involve students in formulating hypotheses, predicting subsequent actions, and making inferences from data presented. Value-oriented questions require that students make judgments about an issue, topic, or concern. The following are examples of broad questions for possible use in social studies classes:

- What are some ways new technologies may shape life in the 21st century?
- What actions might our state government take to encourage economic development within our state?
- What do you think are some ways we can work to achieve world peace?
- What do you think are some steps we can take to reduce prejudice in our society?

There is another type of question called a "focus question," which provides students with a sense of direction or focus for responding to questions at different levels. At the same time a focus question allows for a diversity of responses. Examples of focus questions are the following:

- What are some reasons why European nations were interested in exploring the New World?
- What might it be like to live in Central Europe as a teenager at this time in history?

- What suggestions would you give the leaders of two countries in order to end the military conflict between these nations?

We have used a series of focus questions at the beginning of each chapter of this textbook to help you concentrate on important topics addressed in this textbook. Depending on the objectives of the lesson, narrow, broad, or focus questions can be used to initiate the lesson. Questions may be used to review the previous day's lesson, review homework assignments, or serve as a catalyst for the day's lesson. When to use each type of question depends on the course content, daily objectives, student interest and abilities, and teacher skill in formulating and using quotations.

Just as preparing the questions is important to class discussion, the sequencing of questions is also important. In some cases it may be useful to begin with one or two narrow questions and extend the discussion through the use of broad questions. In other instances a more productive class discussion may be accomplished by beginning with one or more broad questions or through the use of focus questions. Of course the teacher needs to be ready to encourage or require that students clarify or extend their responses and support their statements with pertinent data. At times teachers may decide to allow the discussion to move in a direction other than what was planned initially if it seems appropriate and worthwhile to do so. Teachers ought to be ready to allow for a diversity of responses, to encourage questions from members of the class, and so forth. If disagreements arise, it may be necessary to help the participants understand the opposing viewpoints. During class discussions the teacher may serve as a facilitator who keeps the discussion going, encourages participation, and keeps order. On the other hand, the teacher might choose to be a discussion leader who is an active discussant or not.

Teachers need to be aware of the effective use of "wait time." Research completed by Mary Budd Rowe (1974, 1978) indicates that teachers often wait one second between the time they ask a question and call upon a student for a response. This pace allows the student little time to process the question and then formulate an answer and contribute to the discussion. She suggests that by lengthening this time to five seconds the quality of student responses and spontaneous teacher questions are likely to improve. Kenneth Tobin (1987), in reviewing fifty research studies on wait time in all fields over a twenty-five-year time period, argues that wait time is critical if teachers want to develop student thinking skills. He concludes that sufficient wait time provides for 1) lengthier and more detailed or complex responses, 2) increased student participation in discussion, 3) additional peer interaction, and 4) generally higher test scores on both teacher-made and standardized tests. Allowing sufficient wait time is particularly useful when asking broad questions, which require students to offer somewhat more detailed and elaborate responses.

Additional Instructional Procedures

There are many instructional procedures from which middle school and high school social studies teachers may select. Some procedures may be more appropriate for advanced students, others for less mature students; some for upper grade level students, others for lower grade level students; and some for a single social science discipline, others for use in integrated social science disciplines. Most likely teachers will at some time or other use most of these strategies. Teachers should try out many of these instructional practices to develop a repertoire of teaching possibilities that can be used to meet student needs. The teaching and learning activities listed here are illustrative examples and may be used in a variety of ways.

- Panel discussions, debates, and oral reports on the topics under discussion
- Mock elections of state or national leaders
- Mock legislative sessions, such as city council, Congress, or United Nations
- Simulations and games
- Computer programs
- Guest speakers
- Community studies, surveys, and questionnaires
- Field trips (local and more distant)
- Demonstrations
- Models
- Dramatizations and skits
- Role playing
- Library, laboratory research, or independent study
- Contests sponsored by outside organizations; for example, American Legion, Geography Bee, etc.
- Media, including films, video, filmstrips, slides, film loops, TV, and interactive video
- Small- and large-group activities (cooperative learning)
- Individualized learning
- Shadow experiences where a student follows the mayor, the principal, or some other person for a day
- Visual materials, such as bulletin boards or collages
- Displays and collections
- Periodicals
- Symbolic graphic materials, such as posters, graphs, cartoons, and time lines

Both long-term and short-term planning are clearly important components in the teaching and learning process. It is more than completing a particular lesson plan form to be turned in on Friday or filling in the infamous 2×3 yellow square box in a lesson plan book. Effective lesson planning and implementation helps students to learn and teachers to teach by reducing classroom management and discipline problems. We encourage you to allow sufficient time for the planning process, which will become less time consuming with practice and experience.

Using Media

Media in social studies classes often can help students to learn content, concepts, and skills and to formulate values and attitudes. Media may be used for initiating, developing, or concluding a lesson. Careful selection of media for classroom instruction is an important part of the planning process and should not be taken lightly. For effective use of media teachers need to preview materials and formulate student "pre-viewing" and "after-viewing" questions or activities. Using media without relating it to the lesson at hand is not recommended, because media tends to be neutral and leads to passivity. Teachers need to provide specific instructions to students when using media. For example, teachers may direct student attention to specific questions, scenes, or events and stop the program for a discussion before continuing.

Most social studies teachers plan to use films, filmstrips, laser discs, and video programs with some frequency in their classes. Guidelines for selecting non-print media are included in Appendix B (Chapter 10) in this textbook. In deciding to use media a major consideration should be to assist students in learning more effectively by reinforcing the content. Media of all types should not be used merely to fill in time or as a substitute for teacher preparation.

Selecting Instructional Materials

Teaching aids not found in your classroom should be listed on the lesson plan and scheduled ahead of time. If a single student textbook is used for the course, only the specific pages included in the plan for that particular day need to be listed. If several instructional resources are to be included in the lesson, a standard bibliographical form should be used that includes author, title, publisher, and date of publication. Media references should include the source of such material and the appropriate reference citations to facilitate ordering them from the school or district media center. This information will be useful for future reference identification. Such information may be needed when revising or extending the lesson for future use.

To avoid having a boring classroom and to keep the classroom dynamic and current more than one textbook is essential. Unfortunately, teachers often rely on the use of a single social studies textbook for information. This is not sufficient, since new information is created on a daily basis. Textbooks can provide basic information but need to be supplemented with a variety of instructional materials from many sources representing a variety of perspectives.

Most teachers agree that a single textbook is no longer sufficient in today's rapidly changing world, however, the single textbook is still used in most social studies classrooms over 90 percent of the time. Given this situation it is important to select quality textbooks, keeping in mind that textbooks must be used for at least five years, and the information contained in them becomes obsolete very quickly. In selecting a textbook (most likely serving as a member of a textbook selection committee) you will want to consider these questions:

- What is the copyright date?
- Who are the authors and what are their qualifications?
- Has the material been pilot tested in schools?
- Does the content "fit" the district's curriculum?
- Are important concepts and appropriate skills included?
- What kinds of questions and learning activities are included?
- What is the readability level of the textbook?
- Does the textbook portray women, girls, ethnic minorities, and the disabled in positive ways, and are they integrated into the text materials and not just "add ons"?
- How are the chapters organized?
- Are atlases, glossaries, indexes, pictures, charts, maps, and graphs included? Are they appropriate to the content?
- What supplemental materials are there? Teacher's guide? Student workbooks? Test questions? Visuals, such as transparencies, slides, and posters? Computer programs and video discs?
- What comments do some of my students make about these materials? (Whenever possible students should have an opportunity to examine the materials and offer their ideas and reactions.)
- Are the physical characteristics of the book satisfactory? Binding? Use of color? Size of print? Number of pages? Margin size?
- What is the cost of the book? Cost of supplementals?
- Will the publisher provide a staff development program if the book is selected? (This is different from a "sales presentation.")

Because students in a single classroom have a range of reading skills, it is important for the teacher to provide for these differences. For example, it is important that teachers provide an overview of new material as it is presented; construct an advanced organizer to help students organize, remember, and link prior learning to the new information to be learned; point out new vocabulary; ask students to examine the visuals (maps, charts, graphs, pictures) in the chapter; prepare outlines to be completed; and so forth. Students should be encouraged to skim the chapter so as to develop a notion as to the content material included in the chapter or unit. (For further information see Chapter 11.) Your course content area reading will offer specific suggestions that you will find helpful as you work with students who have poor reading skills.

Student Evaluation

On a regular basis teachers need to find out how well their students are learning, how well the course objectives are being met, and the effectiveness of the specific lesson to help plan for the following day. If for some reason the students had difficulty with some aspect of the lesson or if a specific objective was not met, the teacher needs to decide how to "reteach" the lesson. Teachers need to plan for a sampling of student learning for each lesson. This may be done by using a "thumbs up" if the student knows the answer to a question or a "thumbs down" if the student is unsure of the answer or does not know the answer. Or you may ask students to jot down one or two important things they learned in the lesson. A quick review of these responses will provide the teacher with a sense of what students have or have not learned. Of course, there are other ways to sample student learning. At the middle school and high school level, teachers often wait to evaluate students on a more formal basis at the end of the chapter or unit. You should include regular ongoing formal and informal evaluation of student learning in your planning. More information about measuring student learning is provided in Chapter 12.

Assignments

Assigning homework is a topic of considerable discussion and disagreement among educators. You need to think about this important issue so that assignments you require of students make sense and are related to previous and future learning.

Assignments have many purposes. For example, an assignment may require students to review previously learned information in preparation for new instruction, or an assignment may be enrichment by extending learning beyond the textbook. For assignments to have meaning to students it is important that students "know" what is expected of them and why the assignment is given.

One position concerning homework is that students on a regular basis should be given a reasonable amount of work to be completed outside of class in preparation for learning the following day. This argument is advanced by many as they examine the low level of student achievement in the United States compared to foreign students. Advocates of this argument point out that students from Japan and other nations, who rank higher than United States students on academic achievement tests, have not only a longer school day and school year, but also are assigned and expected to complete several hours of rigorous homework after regular school hours, which extends student learning (Cetron and Gayle, 1991).

Another position is that assigning work to be completed outside of class is difficult because many secondary students have after-school jobs or activities, come from home environments that are not conducive to learning, or are not motivated to complete school assignments. In these situations teachers often decide to assign work that can be completed during class time and turned in for possible grading at the end of the class period. In this way, some or all of the work is likely to be completed while the teacher is available to offer assistance.

When making assignments it is important to keep in mind that whether the work is to be completed in class or outside of class it must be meaningful and viewed as valuable as a learning opportunity by both students and teachers. Teachers should avoid busy-work assignments. Students are often bored by repetitious assignments or frustrated by assignments that are too difficult because the teacher has failed to focus them clearly. It is also necessary for students to receive early feedback for each assignment and to know how the assignments will be evaluated and used to determine student grades.

Alternative Activities

Even with the best-planned lesson, sometimes there is additional class time that should not be wasted, or it becomes evident the planned lesson ought to be set aside for revision, for use on another day, or just plain not used whatever the reason. For these and other reasons (such as to better meet the needs of special students, both talented and gifted as well as special education; to accommodate those who quickly finish an assignment; or for those who may need additional time to practice), teachers should have one or more alternative learning activities to insert within the unit when needed. The alternative learning activities may be developed to extend the lesson, to help students learn the content using a different strategy, or to reinforce learning. Alternative activities should be used to promote ongoing learning rather than wasting classroom time. For example, if students are studying the United States Civil War, an alternative activity could include a series of short readings using primary sources about life in the Union and/or Confederate armies. Students would then work together in small groups to examine the assumptions or point of view of the writer. For a more general approach for virtually any topic teachers could collect a series of political cartoons for the period or topic under discussion, make transparencies of the cartoons, and prepare a series of focus questions related to the cartoons under discussion.

As you gain teaching experience, you will develop a variety of such alternative learning activities. Again, these activities should not be busy work or time fillers, but should truly enhance student learning in social studies.

CHAPTER 8 Characteristics of Successful Curriculum and Instructional Plans   223

Comments, Observations, Reflections, and References

At the end of the day it is useful that teachers take time to reflect on the teaching and learning activities of the day. It is valuable for the teacher to make notes concerning the effectiveness of the lesson and note any problems that may have developed. Notes concerning individual progress or difficulties encountered by students may be included as well. Handouts and other instructional materials used in presenting the lesson should be attached to the lesson plan either for use the next time the lesson is taught, or for possible revision, especially if difficulties were evident. These notes may be useful for future planning or for reporting student progress to students, parents, and/or school counselors. Teachers often place their detailed lesson plans, the related learning materials, and teacher notes in a looseleaf notebook. This allows for easy deletion of materials no longer needed and addition of new information and learning materials.

Readers should study the following daily lesson plan format carefully and then consider the sample daily lesson plan presented later in this chapter. The one-day lesson plan is based on a curriculum unit for economics. It should be a useful reference when teaching a particular lesson.

■■■■■■■ Daily Lesson Plan Format

Title:	Name of lesson.
Time Required:	Time or number of class periods needed to complete the activity.
Recommended Grade Level:	Grade and/or ability level of students for whom the lesson is intended; time of year when presented.
Rationale:	A brief statement explaining the significance of the lesson. The statement may focus on what students should know or be able to do. Or, it may focus on the importance of the instructional approach being taken (such as use of games or simulation for motivational purposes or to have students apply certain skills, knowledge, etc.).
Instructional Objectives:	For each objective specify the particular knowledge, skills, or attitude the student is expected to learn and demonstrate.
Major Concepts:	List the concepts around which the lesson is mainly organized.
Related Concepts:	List other concepts that are subsumed in the lesson.
Learning Skills:	List the skills students are to develop in this lesson.
Materials or Resources Needed:	List the materials needed for the lesson (for example, books, games, media, computer programs, etc.).
Content:	Outline the content of the lesson being presented.
Instructional Procedures:	A description of the teaching-learning process to be used for student attainment of the objectives. This is to include both teacher procedures and actions and student responses and actions. How will the lesson be organized to facilitate student learning? How does the teacher begin the lesson? How much time is expected for each part of the lesson? How does the lesson relate to previous learning or expected and future learning? What will the teacher do? What are the students to do? How will the lesson conclude?
Student Evaluation:	A description of strategies, testing instruments, or other materials to be used for measuring student learning; evaluation activities and/or the test questions should be included. How will the teacher know if the objectives were achieved or if the lesson (or some part of the lesson) needs to be retaught?
Assignment:	What type of assignment will be given? Can all or part of the assignment be completed in class? Does the assignment extend beyond the text and promote student learning? Is the assignment to be completed by each student or does the assignment allow for cooperative learning? When is the assignment to be submitted?

Alternate Activity:	At times many of our initial lesson plans may not be appropriate for a variety of reasons. Therefore, it is helpful to have an alternative available. What is your alternative activity for this lesson or unit? How will you work with special needs students, those who finish the assignment early, or those who need more concrete instruction?
Comments, Observations, Reflections, And Reference Notes:	After class it is helpful to reflect on the day's lesson. What aspects of the lesson went well? Which aspects did not go so well? Were the objectives of the lesson achieved? What did the class and individual students learn today? Where should the lesson begin for the following class? Are there other ways to teach or reteach this lesson or some part of it?

(Attach your notes, handouts, or other materials as appropriate.)

■ ■ ■ ■ ■ ■ ■   Sample Daily Lesson Plan

Title:	What is Economics?
Time:	1 class period (approximately 55 minutes)
Rationale:	Individuals, businesses, and governments make choices each day in order to satisfy their needs and wants. Economics is the study of how choices are made to meet unlimited wants with limited resources. Students must understand the range of economic choices citizens and nations face on a regular basis so they recognize the implications of personal and national economic policies. This is the initial lesson to help students begin to consider the importance of economics for daily living.
Instructional Objectives:	Students will: • define economics • explain the importance of studying economics • identify one recent economic choice made by each of the following: an individual, a business, and a government or nation • recognize that the study of economics is value-laden
Major Concepts:	Economics Economic systems Consumers/Producers Scarcity/Choice Goods/Services

Related Concepts:	Government policies
	Opportunity cost
	Factors of production
Learning Skills:	Conceptualizing
	Classifying
	Gathering information
	Communicating
Materials:	Textbook (Chapter 1)
	Handout 1A: "Economic Headlines"
	Film: *Very Basic Economics* (1986). Illustrates basic economic concepts through dramatic vignettes. Producer: Aim; 20 minutes
Content:	I. Why study economics?
	A. Role of individuals (consumers and producers)
	B. Role of business
	C. Role of governments and nations
	II. What is economics?
	A. How are scarce resources allocated?
	B. What are the factors of production?
	C. Who makes economic decisions?
	III. Is economics a science?
	A. Economic systems
	B. Economic models

Management/Instructional Procedures

Teacher Behaviors	Student Responses
1. Management details, such as take roll, read bulletin, make announcements, etc.	1. Work on task if assigned, review homework, sit quietly, etc.
2. Indicate lesson objectives for the day	2. Listen and ask questions, if needed
3. Present students with Student Handout 1A "Economic Headlines" (or use an overhead transparency with the same information). Ask students to examine the handout and determine what the headlines indicate about economic issues and concerns. What information about economics can we glean from the headlines?	3. Examine the data and offer ideas about their possible meanings.

CHAPTER 8 Characteristics of Successful Curriculum and Instructional Plans 227

■■■■■■■ Economic Headlines Handout 1A

4. Write student responses to the questions on the chalkboard.

5. Ask students, "Why is the study of economics important?"

6. Extend discussion to include the role of individuals, businesses, and governments in economic decision making. (Use chalkboard or transparency as needed.)

7. Ask students to define economics.

4. Offer ideas as to meanings of the headlines.

5. Begin to offer answers to the question.

6. Listen, take notes, ask questions.

7. Offer their own definitions.

8. Extend discussion of definition to include resource allocation, how the factors of production influence economic decision making and the opportunity costs involved.	8. Indicate how economic decision making influences their lives and how they make economic decisions on a daily basis.
9. Present overview of economic systems and economic models.	9. Take notes, learn how economic models are used, develop a basic understanding of characteristics of economic systems.
10. Based on this information and discussion show a film and suggest what they should notice as they view the film.	10. View film and note definitions and examples included in the film which relate to the three basic questions. What is economics? Why study economics? How do economic decisions affect us?
11. Quickly review highlights of film and respond to student questions.	11. Offer insights into tentative answers to the above questions, pose other questions.
12. Bring closure to lesson by asking students to write a one-sentence generalization or paragraph summary about economic ideas that will be used for discussion at the beginning of class on the following day.	12. Write the sentence generalization or paragraph summary about economic ideas based on their prior knowledge of economics or what they have learned today.

Student Evaluation: Conduct informal evaluation by noting those who participated in posing or responding to questions; sample student learning by posing several questions for which they respond "thumbs up" if the statement is true or "thumbs down" if the statement is not correct. Examples of true/false statements that might be used could include 1) Economics concerns itself with the study of the production, distribution, and consumption of goods and services; 2) Economic growth is always desirable; 3) Opportunity cost is the next best good or service one must give up in order to get a particular item.

Assignment: Bring to class the following day a current newspaper or magazine article related to economics to share with the class. Alternative: Watch one of the network news programs and report on economic news contained in the newscast. Focus: How do economic events influence our daily lives and what are some likely consequences?

Alternative Activity:	If this film or a similar title is not available, and a computer is available, use the computer program "Economics: What, How, and For Whom" Diskette No. 1 What is Economics? Focus Media (1983). This computer program covers similar content information as the film.
Comments:	Would expect class to go well as there are several activities and modes of learning; may have to adjust content depending on quality of discussion; will complete this part in greater detail after class with ideas for revision; will note special problems, etc.

Social Studies and the World of Work

Business leaders have continued to express concern that a large number of young people are ill prepared to make a successful transition from our secondary schools to the world of work. They note that nearly two-thirds of young people enter full-time employment either prior to or immediately after completing high school. In addition, there has been concern that developments in business and industry are outdistancing the ability of the schools to prepare people for the world of work. The mismatch of skills between high school graduates and employment demands of business and industry are increasing rapidly. The market value of a high school diploma is declining. The high unemployment rate of young workers, especially for high school dropouts, is alarming. There is convincing evidence that a high school diploma is no guarantee of literacy.

Career preparation programs have been established to help students make the transition from school to work. Such approaches include career exploration such as a program in Cambridge, Massachusetts, known as Cityworks in which 9th graders build a city and explore jobs available in their city. Another initiative is Tech Prep, which involves high school and community college programs in specific occupations. Tech Prep programs operate in several states in various formats, but they often use applied and integrated academic curricula in social studies, mathematics, science, and communications. To meet employers' concerns more and more programs are being developed to help young people build linkages between school-based and work-based learning through youth apprenticeships, school-based enterprises, and youth service. Such programs can highlight the interconnectedness between social studies and society and allow for real-world learning experiences to be built upon standard classroom learning.

Although we disagree with the practice, many high schools often have arranged their curriculum so that students are tracked according to their interests and/or abilities, test scores, or teacher recommendation. However, other factors such as socioeconomic status, ethnic or racial backgrounds, language proficiency, learning styles, and gender may influence how students are assigned to a particular track. Often it is difficult for students to move from one track to another.

Most often there are three tracks: college preparatory, general, and vocational, although the exact names of the tracks may vary from school to school. For students electing or being counseled into the vocational or lower level track program, it is important they have opportunities to take challenging and interesting courses in the liberal arts areas (including social studies). These are courses that will help them to participate effectively in society as enlightened citizens. For vocationally oriented students who decide to continue their education by taking post-secondary vocational-technical courses, they too should be encouraged to continue with additional general education liberal arts courses. Business and industry leaders indicate they are interested in hiring well-rounded individuals who will be productive workers. Oftentimes the specific skills needed for a particular job will be provided by the employer as on-the-job training. We would argue that all students are entitled to a quality education that allows them to learn and equips them for the world after completing their secondary education.

A statewide study in Wisconsin in the mid-1980s addressing the transition of secondary students from school to the world of work reported employers' attitudes and perceptions concerning the quality and qualifications of young workers. Based on this study employers expect high schools to provide graduates with programs that "lead to competencies and job preparation skills for the world of work" (Oinonen, 1984).

Employers expect high schools to

1. prepare students for future, nontraditional employment;
2. use minimum competency tests for the basic skills;
3. improve and emphasize more:
    a. the basic skills of writing, spelling, grammar, mathematics, and reading (including interpretation of blueprints and instructions);
    b. effective speech, listening, and oral communication skills;
    c. economics of business and knowledge of business operations;
    d. technology or applied science;
    e. applied computer literacy;
    f. flexibility and adaptability in learning new skills for personal and career development;
    g. human relations, interpersonal and negotiation skills, and decision-making abilities;
    h. job application and interview skills;
    i. general positive attitudes toward work;
    j. knowledge of career ladders and career planning; and
    k. specific occupational and job entry skills (Oinonen, p. 31).

The same skills have been documented in other studies. *Workplace Basics* indicates employers want employees who have "learned how to learn"; employees who can engage in problem solving and creative thinking; and employees who have a sense of teamwork and organizational leadership (Carnevale, Gaines, and Meltzer, 1990). The Department of Labor Secretary's Commission on Achieving Necessary Skills (SCANS) (1992) echoes a similar message as do various other similar reports and publications.

In reality, many of these expectations focus on skills and reflect values that are needed to be effective citizens. Several of these employer expectations have specific implications for social studies programs.

Certainly most would agree that the entire school program is responsible for developing basic communication skills, a willingness to learn new skills, and an overall positive attitude toward work. The expectations for which social studies may have a more direct responsibility include the emphasis on knowledge of the economics of business and business operations and an emphasis on human relations and decision-making abilities. The latter abilities are also skills of good citizenship. We want to develop citizens who are effective in meeting the responsibilities that go with being adults and living in a democratic society.

There is also another dimension concerning social studies and the world of work. With the United States becoming more involved with the international community through economic, political, and cultural exchanges, teachers must provide students with opportunities to learn about other cultures in some depth. For example, as international trade activities grow between the United States and the People's Republic of China, this country will need to have persons well versed in Chinese language and culture representing the United States in such discussions and negotiations. Similar needs could be expressed concerning United States relations with other nations of the world.

Social studies teachers need to help students make the connections between the world of work and social studies course content. In an interdependent world, accurate and current social studies knowledge will become more and more valuable in our daily lives.

Social Studies for Community Service (Volunteerism)

The notion of community service can be traced to ancient history when individuals served the community for the benefit of many. The idea of service is inherent in our democratic way of life. As one examines history there are many individuals who served their local, national, or international communities at some personal sacrifice or cost. Today many individuals in all walks of life continue to engage in public service or volunteer activities throughout their lifetimes.

Ernest Boyer (1985) in one of the early national reports on education has strongly encouraged schools to require some type of community service activity as a prerequisite for high school graduation. Even prior to Boyer's recommendations, schools in several parts of the country already offered opportunities for student community service either for credit toward graduation or simply as a volunteer activity. Several Pennsylvania schools have reported an increase of school attendance for participants, including at-risk students, who are engaged in community service programs (Kazis, 1993). Maryland has a community service component as a graduation requirement. Such service programs enable students to take responsibility, learn skills, and contribute to community development and personal well-being.

One idea behind these opportunities was the notion of service, involvement, and returning something of oneself to the community. Such activities might include tutoring less able students; assisting in senior citizens centers; working in public or private agencies such as hospitals or youth organizations; serving internships; and the like. Most students found these experiences valuable because they were giving of themselves, serving others, and learning about new aspects of living. Schools often recognized the importance of student community service through awards and recognition programs, as well as by scholarship opportunities.

While community service activities can be organized in many places throughout the school curriculum, there are numerous opportunities for service from a social studies perspective. For example, students might become actively involved in a political campaign, participate in city or county council meetings, gather information about a local issue, write letters to the editor of the local newspaper, solicit community members' opinions through surveys or questionnaires, or volunteer at a local service agency such as the Red Cross, Girls and Boys Clubs, a museum, or library. In most communities service agencies are eager to have volunteer services of young people to assist with various aspects of their programs. Young people enjoy sharing their interests, abilities, and talents with others. They receive a sense of satisfaction and recognize the varying needs of other human beings.

There is another potential for community service that is available at every middle and high school. Schools as social institutions offer numerous opportunities for students to serve as class, club, or student council officers, to plan and participate in school events, to join a student service club, and so on. Those who care most about others are those who are most willing to serve others. They volunteer (or are elected) to serve because they care and have something to share with others.

Voluntary community service activities during the middle and high school years offer excellent preparation for continuing service to others during their adult years. Service to others helps to build community and is but one characteristic of being an active citizen. John Dewey once wrote, "A society is a number of people held together because they are working along common lines, in a common spirit, and with reference to common aims" (Archambault, 1964, p. 300).

SUMMARY

Quality social studies programs require effective planning for curriculum content, instructional procedures, and student evaluation. These important tasks require that educators communicate among themselves to provide students with social studies programs and courses that will prepare them for effective living in the 21st century. Decisions concerning curriculum and instruction ought not be made in a vacuum but must be made within the context of education in our society. Educators must give attention to the knowledge, skills, attitudes, and values that are included and excluded in social studies programs. These are not easy decisions.

This chapter addressed important characteristics of curriculum planning. Curriculum planning and implementation involves examining mandates or recommendations; recognizing the existence of new knowledge in the fields of education and social science disciplines; and selecting appropriate instructional strategies and materials. Evaluating student learning is an important aspect of planning. Teachers who plan effectively are likely to provide students with worthwhile learning experiences. Examples of long-range curriculum planning, unit planning, and daily lesson planning are included. Teachers must recognize the importance of both pre-planning and spontaneous planning. Social studies should address the concerns and values of society, the profession, and our students.

Planning for effective social studies programs is a career-long challenge for social studies educators. Quality planning for curriculum and instruction is fundamental for successful social studies programs.

Discussion Questions

1. How does the choice and use of questions help or hinder social studies teaching and learning?
2. What criteria should be used to select content, concepts, values, and skills that are to be emphasized throughout the middle and secondary social studies program?
3. What are some ways teachers can help students link newly acquired information with prior knowledge?
4. What are the advantages and disadvantages of the various ways to organize the instructional units that were identified in the text? What are some other ways in which you might organize an instructional unit?
5. If you were assigned to a school that had no social studies curriculum guide or one that is obsolete and incomplete how would you plan social studies program for your class?

Student Learning Activities

1. Secure a curriculum planning document from your state and one from a local district. How are these documents similar? How are they different? Examine a current social studies textbook and see how it "fits" these curriculum documents. To what extent are curriculum-planning materials likely to be helpful to new and experienced social studies teachers in planning curriculum for instruction?
2. Talk with an experienced social studies teacher at the middle school level and an experienced social studies teacher at the high school level about how they make decisions on what to teach (content), how to present a lesson (instructional procedures), how to select instructional materials, and how to evaluate student learning. Are there differences in the planning process? If so, what might account for these differences?
3. Choose a topic that you might teach in a social studies class. Identify and review two or three print and two or three nonprint instructional resources that you may decide to use to teach this unit or lesson. Write a brief annotation (with bibliographic information) for each resource you have identified and share your resource reference list with other members of the class. Such an annotated list will be a useful starting place if you should decide to teach a similar unit.
4. If a national or state social studies curriculum leader were invited to address your social studies methods class, what curriculum-related questions would you want to ask this person? Write down three or four such questions. These could also be used as a basis for a class discussion with your methods instructor and other classmates.
5. Select one of the following social science disciplines: economics, geography, or sociology, and discuss several specific ways social studies teachers can help students examine questions, problems, or issues from the perspective of this discipline. To what extent are there similarities among these disciplines? To what extent are there differences among these disciplines?
6. Select one or two of the illustrative learning activities listed in the "Additional Instructional Procedures" portion of this chapter and prepare a brief statement or lesson on how to use the learning activity at both the middle school and high school levels.
7. As you plan your own unit of instruction, keep a journal about the formal and informal planning involved in preparing such a unit of instruction.

APPENDIX A

Decision-Making Grid

Decision-making is a part of everyday life. Oftentimes important decisions are made with little or no thought. To enable learners to make quality decisions,

CHAPTER 8 Characteristics of Successful Curriculum and Instructional Plans   235

the use of of a decision-making grid is sometimes helpful. The following five steps are useful in making decisions.

1. Define the problem or issue.
2. Identify alternative possibilities.
3. Determine criteria to be used in making a decision.
4. Evaluate alternative choices in light of goals.
5. Examine the data and make a decision.

The following economic and political problem is offered for your consideration and discussion.

The local community has several areas of empty land available for development in the next twelve to eighteen months. The planning commission has three major proposals for land use on its agenda. The alternative plans are 1) to develop the area into a park with a playground, nature trails, and a zoo; 2) to allow the land to be zoned for commercial development which includes the building of a large regional shopping center; and 3) to allow the land to be subdivided into residential housing for low-income persons.

Considering each alternative and criteria, use a + or − sign to indicate your values and the recommendation you will present to the planning commission at its next meeting. You will need to be prepared to support your recommendations. In examining the issue of land use, what is important to you? You may add other criteria and consider other alternatives in reaching your decision. What is your decision?

Decision-Making Grid

Problem: Land use in a local community.

	\multicolumn{7}{c}{Criteria}							
Alternatives	Provide opportunities for recreation	Extend tax base for local economy	Create long-term employment for many	Useful all year	Promote tourism of the region	Increase traffic congestion	Etc.
Park facilities							
Shopping center							
Residential housing							
Other? (write in)							

Decision/recommendations:

References

Archambault, R. D. (Ed.). 1964. *John Dewey on Education: Selected Writings*. New York: Modern Library.

Boyer, E. L. 1985. *High School: A Report on Secondary Education in America*. New York: Harper and Row.

Carnevale, A. P., Gaines, L. J., and Meltzer, A. S. 1990. *Workplace Basics: The Essential Skills Employers Want*. San Francisco: Jossey-Bass.

Cetron, M. and Gayle, M. 1991. *Educational Renaissance: Our Schools at the Turn of the Twenty-First Century*. New York: St. Martins.

Dillon, J. T. 1984. "Research on Questioning and Discussion." *Educational Leadership*, Vol. 42, No. 3, November. 50–56.

Kazis, R. 1993. *Improving the Transition from School to Work in the United States*. Washington, DC: American Youth Policy Forum and Cambridge, MA: Jobs for the Future.

Oinonen, C. M. 1984. *Business and Education Survey: Employer and Employee Perceptions of School to Work Preparation*. Bulletin 4372. Madison: Wisconsin Department of Public Instruction.

Rowe, M. B. 1974. "Pausing Phenomena: Influence on the Quality of Instruction." *Journal of Psycholinguistic Research*, Vol. 3, No. 3. 203–224.

Rowe, M. B. 1978. "Wait, Wait, Wait. . ." *School Science and Mathematics*. Vol. 78, No. 3, March. 207–216.

Tobin, K. 1987. "The Role of Wait Time in Higher Cognitive Learning." *Review of Educational Research*, Vol. 57, No. 1, Spring. 69–95.

United States Department of Labor. 1992. *Learning a Living: A Blueprint for High Performance. A SCANS Report for America 2000*. Executive Summary. Washington, DC: The Secretary's Commission on Achieving Necessary Skills.

Additional Readings

Bloom, B. S., Englehart, M. D., Furst, E. J., Hill, W. N., and Krathwohl, D. R. 1956. *Taxonomy of Educational Objectives: The Classification of Educational Goals. Handbook I: The Cognitive Domain*. New York: David McKay.

Dillon, J. T. 1986. "Student Questions and Individual Learning." *Educational Theory*, Vol. 36, No. 4, Fall. 333–341.

Dillon, J. T. 1988. *Questioning and Teaching: A Manual of Practice*. New York: Teachers College Press, Columbia University.

Dillon, J. T. 1991. "Questioning the Use of Questions." *Journal of Educational Psychology*, Vol. 83, No. 1, March. 163–164.

Fraser, B. J. 1981. "Deterioration in High School Students' Attitudes Toward Social Studies." *Social Studies*, Vol. 72, No. 2, March–April. 65–68.

Freiberg, H. J. and Driscoll, A. 1992. *Universal Teaching Strategies*. Boston: Allyn and Bacon.

Gronlund, N. E. 1991. *How to Write and Use Instructional Objectives* (4th ed.). New York: Macmillan.

Krathwohl, D. R., Bloom, B. S., and Masia, B. B. 1964. *Taxonomy of Educational Objectives: The Classification of Educational Goals. Handbook II: The Affective Domain*. New York: David McKay.

Louisell, R. D. and Descamps, J. 1991. *Developing a Teaching Style*. New York: HarperCollins.

Oakes, J. 1985. *Keeping Track: How Schools Structure Inequality.* New Haven, CT: Yale University Press.

Pasch, M., Sparks-Langer, G., Garner, T. G., Starko, A. J., and Moody, C. D. 1991. *Teaching as Decision Making: Instructional Practices for the Successful Teacher.* New York: Longman.

Sanders, N. M. 1966. *Classroom Questions: What Kinds?* New York: Harper and Row.

Schug, M. C., Todd, R. A., and Beery, R. 1984. "Why Kids Don't Like Social Studies." *Social Education,* Vol. 48, No. 5, May. 382–387.

Taba, H. 1962. *Curriculum Development: Theory and Practice.* New York: Harcourt Brace and World.

Tobin, K. 1986. "Effects of Teacher Wait Time on Discourse Characteristics in Mathematics and Language Arts Classes." *American Educational Research Journal,* Vol. 23, No. 2, Summer. 191–200.

Weitzman, D. 1975. *The Brown Paper School Presents My Backyard History Book.* Boston: Little, Brown.

> We are handicapped by . . . policies based on old myths rather than current realities.
>
> *James William Fulbright*

CHAPTER 9

Effective Learning Environments for Students

FOCUS QUESTIONS

- How does the classroom environment in social studies promote or hinder student learning?
- How can academic freedom for teachers and students be protected?
- How can social studies teachers meet the needs of students from various diverse backgrounds?

OVERVIEW Successful social studies teachers are concerned with the learning environment. This includes the physical environment of the classroom, such as the arrangement of desks and other furniture, bulletin boards, shelves, and plants. The learning environment also includes the intellectual, aesthetic, ethical, and emotional climate of the entire school. Teachers need to plan instructional procedures that meet the needs and interests of their students. Teachers should recognize the unique characteristics of each student; select and utilize appropriate instructional materials; and be sensitive to community values and expectations. These decisions are sometimes difficult, but they are important components in planning for instruction and in establishing a conducive learning environment. In addition, teachers must be sensitive to their own professional needs.

Organizing Students and Classrooms for Effective Learning

A long-standing educational argument concerns the grouping of students in classes. The fundamental question is, "Should students be grouped on a homogeneous or heterogeneous basis in social studies classes?" The answer varies and convincing arguments and counterarguments have been offered for each position.

Homogeneous grouping refers to the assignment of students of similar abilities to the same classes. For example, a school may have a XX level of courses for gifted and talented students, X level courses for high ability students, Y level courses for students of average ability, and Z level courses for lower ability students. Of course the names and designations of these instructional groups may vary but the effect is the same. Students are assigned to classes based on test scores, goals, grades, teacher recommendations, and the like. However, at times other factors such as gender, ethnicity, family background, or socioeconomic status have been used in subtle or not so subtle ways in the grouping process. In some schools, once students have been assigned to classes in a particular track, school personnel are often reluctant to reassign students to classes at another instructional level. Therefore, students placed at a particular instructional level are often assigned to courses at this level throughout their school years. Assignment to a low track group may be likened to a lifetime prison sentence with parole unlikely.

Arguments offered in favor of this position suggest that it is easier to teach young people of similar abilities. Instructional materials can be based on their reading levels, and learning activities, assignments, and tests can be tailored to meet their needs. If students are assigned to classes on the basis of ability, often teachers prefer to teach courses for the above average or gifted students. Many times teachers are not eager to teach lower ability students and may communicate this attitude to students in various ways. Also teachers often have reduced expectations for student achievement in lower ability classes and may assign less rigorous work and call on students less frequently, smile less often, and seat them away from the teacher's desk, to the side or back of the classroom. Oftentimes lower ability students may not have access to the same information that is available to students in higher ability classes due to slower paced instruction and fewer instructional choices. Furthermore, low ability students may have access to less variety of current instructional resources and practices. For example, teachers may rely on more drill and practice activities, presuming such activities are appropriate to increase learning. Oftentimes teachers may not give these students the benefit of the doubt when answers on tests or assignments are borderline.

Heterogeneous grouping is another way to divide students for instruction. Simply put, heterogeneous grouping means assigning students of varying abilities to social studies classes. This means that classes will have students with a fairly wide range of abilities. Some will argue this practice is particularly appropriate for social studies since we must live and work with people with various backgrounds and abilities. Therefore, social studies classes ought to function in a manner somewhat like the reality of society. The argument favoring this arrangement of assigning students to classes suggests that students can and will learn from each other and assumes that an instructional unit can be learned equally well by all or most students. The challenge for teachers in heterogeneous classes is to meet the needs of individual students and to help them develop their intellectual abilities to their maximum capabilities. This may mean creating differentiated assignments and providing opportunities for both enrichment and remediation in the same class. Enrichment activities could include silent reading for which the student may or may not be asked to respond, mentor programs, field trips, and summer programs. Or the teacher and a group of students could engage in an instructional *conversation* (Tharp and Gallimore, 1988). In an instructional conversation the teacher uses questions with various levels of complexity based on student experiences and a "text," which could be a document, project, or media to help students to understand the issue by talking about its meaning and how it relates to their experiences. The conversation can originate from a media presentation created by one or more students for later showing to the class. Remedial instruction may include the use of alternative instructional materials, programmed instruction, games, or tutorial assistance.

Grouping within Social Studies Classroom

Social studies teachers do not always teach to the entire class. Periodically teachers regroup students in a variety of ways depending on the instructional objectives. Group membership may change from activity to activity.

Beatrice Ward (1987) suggests there are at least three types of instructional groups used by teachers: learning cycle groups, cooperative groups, and long-term ability groups. Each grouping arrangement may be used to meet different objectives.

Learning Cycle Groups

Learning cycle groups allow students with similar learning needs to work together for a short time period while a particular unit or topic is being studied. This may be called in-class ability grouping. For example, for a unit on

19th-century European imperialism, have students read the Kipling poem *White Man's Burden* and examine attitudes and behaviors or prejudice and stereotypes from the perspective of the British. A small group of the students could locate European colonial possessions in Asia, Africa, and Latin America and mark them on a map for use by the entire class. Another small group of students could seek information about the response of the colonized people to British colonization. When the instructional unit has been completed, the groups are disbanded. As other units are taught other short-term learning groups (perhaps involving other students) are established for a specific task.

Cooperative Learning Groups

While cooperative learning techniques vary, they have at least one similarity. They provide an alternative to "frontal teaching" whereby the teacher presents the lesson to the whole class simultaneously or assigns seatwork to individual students (Newmann and Thompson, 1987, p. 1). Cooperative learning activities enable students with different abilities and interests to work together in small groups and to learn from one another. Cooperative learning motivates students to learn and provides opportunities for students to get extra help. For example, higher ability students can do their best when they do not have to hide their abilities and talents. The effects of failure are moderated as lower ability students can be a part of a successful cooperative group. This will result in improved student achievement. For cooperative learning to be effective two conditions must be achieved: 1) the cooperative learning groups must have a meaningful group goal and all must work to achieve that goal, and 2) group success must result from the individual learning of all members of the group (Slavin, 1991).

Advocates of cooperative learning have recognized it as one way to improve social relationships among various groups of students, such as racial and ethnic groups, low and high achievers, disabled and nondisabled students, and to increase problem solving and communication skills. Cooperative learning activities may be more compatible with the cultural values and norms of some ethnic groups (Kagan, 1986). For example, some Native American and Mexican-American students are uncomfortable in competitive learning environments as cooperation is preferred within their social context (Kagan, Zahn, Widaman, Schwarzwald, and Tyrrell, 1985). Competition has not been a part of their cultural experiences.

For example, a small group of students might investigate a topic with each student completing one aspect of the study. The completion of the project requires cooperation and the final product is the result of the group's efforts. If a group is assigned the study of Australia, one could research its history; another could research its agricultural products. Others could examine its geographic features, its industry, and its demographic composition. After individual students gather their specific information, they share their findings

CHAPTER 9 Effective Learning Environments for Students   243

with the cooperative learning group, which in turn presents their information to classmates. Usually students are evaluated on the basis of the group effort and may be evaluated individually as well. Membership in cooperative groups usually changes from assignment to assignment.

In cooperative learning, teachers organize students into teams of four or five students with varying characteristics. Together they learn the required information and skills. Sometimes the goal of the team is to help improve each other's performance. At other times teams participate in academic games using a tournament format. Individuals as well as teams may score.

The jigsaw is another learning arrangement in which each student learns one unique aspect of the lesson and is then required to teach it to other team members. Sometimes a group completes a single assignment sheet and submits it for evaluation. Finally, there are small group investigations in which each group in the class is responsible for taking on and completing a different project or task. Research studies on cooperative learning suggest generally positive effects on student achievement in many subjects and grade levels (Newmann and Thompson, 1987; Slavin, 1991).

Augustine, Gruber, and Hanson (1989–90) report that cooperative learning promotes higher achievement, develops social skills, and places responsibility for learning on the student. Spencer Kagan indicates that several research studies conclude that cooperative learning leads to a more pro-social orientation among students (1989–90).

Cooperative learning and peer teaching are used more in middle schools than in secondary schools. While Newmann and Thompson (1987) report no systematic data on why high school teachers (grades 10–12) are less willing to use cooperative learning, they suggest several possibilities:

- Students at these grades are less responsive to the kind of rewards offered to students in lower grades.
- Students may prefer to receive information from teachers rather than from peers.
- Students may value individual achievement over cooperation as competition for grades increase.
- Teachers believe they need to cover more content.
- Teachers are likely to spend less time each day with individuals or groups of students compared to the amount of time available for teacher–student contact in the earlier grades.
- Teachers may view cooperative learning as inefficient especially if this method requires additional training (staff development) for the teachers who already believe they have more than enough responsibilities.

As businesses move toward greater quality control, they expect that workers will be working in teams and groups to solve problems and make decisions concerning job or product performance. As cooperation skills are demanded by business, it is likely that teachers, including middle and high school social studies teachers, will develop additional learning experiences involving the principles of cooperative learning. For example, the students are given a copy of their local government budget and are asked to reduce the overall budget by 20 percent from among the various categories. Students could be grouped to represent the town population; for example, large-business owners, small-business owners, home owners, environmentalists, senior citizens, and taxpayers, are asked to work together to present arguments to government officials supporting their position. Such group activities provide opportunities for students to work together and gather information in order to solve a problem. These skills are then likely to be carried into the workplace.

Additional research on cooperative learning is needed to examine results in both the cognitive and affective domains as there are a number of important questions that need to be addressed. For example, will certain students dominate? Do students learn as much as possible in cooperative groups? Does personality make a difference? Is motivation for learning improved? In some instances it may be useful to replicate some of the earlier studies. For cooperative learning to receive greater attention at the upper secondary level, it is likely that both teachers and students will need to receive instruction on how to use cooperative learning effectively. They will also need opportunities to practice the relevant skills. Teachers will also need to be reoriented to use new instructional strategies and become more knowledgeable about various learning styles and be willing to try out new ideas. It appears that cooperative learning is likely to be an instructional method used in the foreseeable future.

Long-Term Ability Groups

Long-term ability groups are often assigned on the basis of academic ability and usually do not change unless the academic performance of the student changes. Such groups may work together over the space of a semester or school year. Sometimes special instruction may be provided through "pull out" activities in which students are excused from their regular classes to engage in some special activity either for enrichment or remediation. For example, students of high ability might be "pulled" from regular classes once a week to participate in an "honors seminar" involving the reading and discussion of advanced texts such as *The Federalist Papers*; or students could be involved in an "intern" program working with a community social agency; or students could take a university course for credit. For students of lesser abilities, cross-age tutoring projects could be established. If middle school and high school students are required to teach a lesson (concept or skill) to younger students, the older students are likely to work hard to learn the lesson so as to be able to teach the younger students. It should be noted that while students may be placed in a group needing remediation in social studies, those same students may be assigned to a different level group in another subject area, such as mathematics or English.

Why Group?

Other suggestions that schools offer for grouping students include the following:

- To assure that all students are challenged to learn
- To increase student enjoyment in learning
- To teach students how to work with others
- To facilitate social interaction among students
- To motivate students to continue to learn
- To improve student self-concept, self-efficacy, and attitudes toward school
- To teach students how to learn in a variety of ways

As with any task, teachers need to decide if the lesson is suited for group learning and determine the group size and its composition. Groups may be formed on the basis of interests, abilities, tasks to be accomplished, personal preference, and so forth. It may be necessary to provide practice opportunities for students to learn the needed group communication and processing skills. Students may first be asked to write down ideas, share their ideas within the group, and then share the group's ideas with the whole class. In this way students have notes to refer to and practice sharing ideas in a smaller group before expressing them to the larger group. In addition, the teacher will have to consider his or her role in facilitating learning, providing direction, offering feedback, making suggestions, and monitoring student progress. One of the keys to any successful small-group learning activity is careful preparation by both the teacher and students.

Gifted and Talented Students

Within the past several years school districts and individual teachers have recognized the need to provide additional opportunities for students who are gifted and talented. Academically gifted and talented students come from all racial and ethnic groups and represent all socioeconomic backgrounds. They have different learning styles, interests, and motivations. It is important to note there is no single definition of "gifted" or "talented" and that states have different definitions and criteria for identifying these students.

Some people use the terms gifted and talented interchangeably. Some define giftedness as being an intellectual or academic ability. Some define talentedness as ability in one or more areas such as leadership, athletics, the visual and performing arts, and so forth. Other individuals consider giftedness as a higher level of ability except perhaps in athletics, where athletic talent is often recognized by economic rewards and status (Maker, 1987). We recommend that you find the definition and criteria used to identify gifted and talented students in the state where you expect to teach.

There is no one best program type to meet the needs of students who are gifted and talented. However, effective programs must respond to the unique needs and characteristics of these students and provide an environment that facilitates learning. Teaching methods, instructional materials, and content ought to be adapted to characteristics, skills, and needs of these students.

The content for gifted students should focus on the development of more complex and abstract ideas, concepts, and generalizations drawn from the several social science disciplines. These students should have more extensive opportunities to use the various research methodologies of the social science disciplines. Learning processes should emphasize the creation of knowledge through the use of reasoned inquiry rather than merely acquiring facts. Active learning opportunities and interactions are important components for extending learning of all students but particularly gifted students.

Teachers should encourage gifted students to extend beyond the textbook with problem-solving projects that challenge them to seek solutions by synthesizing or transforming existing information. Both of these efforts should be judged by professionals in the field. Media centers that serve these students must have access to a wide variety of print and nonprint resources that reflect a diversity of perspectives and viewpoints. Finally, the learning environment must be open and risk-free, and it must encourage new ideas and challenge students to extend these abilities. In this environment the teacher's role becomes that of facilitator of learning rather than an imparter of information. Not all teachers are comfortable and effective in this type of instructional setting and may prefer not to teach gifted and talented classes.

Some secondary schools offer advanced placement (AP) elective courses for students who are bright, motivated, and want to earn college credit while still in high school. Usually advanced placement courses are taught at the high school by an experienced high school teacher with an advanced degree in that discipline. Most often these courses use college-level textbooks, require additional outside readings (often from primary sources), encourage in-depth class discussions, and require written essays and research papers. Also, they require students to pass the national advanced placement examination in order to earn college credit.

This AP examination includes both objective and essay questions and is graded by specially trained social studies teachers and university professors. Many colleges and universities award credits that apply toward general education and/or degree requirements based on these examinations. At present advanced placement tests in social studies are offered in the following areas: United States and European history, American and comparative government, and economics. Currently there is some discussion about adding other social studies courses such as psychology to the AP program.

At times, districts may decide that it is not feasible to offer AP courses. They may decide to release individual students or groups of students to take college-level courses at a nearby college. If enough students are interested and it is convenient to do so, the high school may ask the local college to offer a college-level course at the high school for its students. The students may be taught by a qualified high school teacher, usually one with an advanced degree in the discipline, or by a college faculty member. The credits earned are regular college credits and usually may be transferred to other higher education institutions. Students enrolled in AP or other types of advanced study courses may have to pay additional fees and purchase additional instructional materials.

Other programs for bright social studies students include academic competitions sponsored by various colleges. Examples of these are the Olympics of the Mind and Academic Decathlon. National organizations also offer college scholarship opportunities through various social studies fairs, essay-writing contests, or test-taking competitions. It will be useful for you to find out what opportunities are available to middle and high school students. The social studies coordinator at the state education agency should have information about these various scholarship opportunities.

Special Needs Students

Meeting Student Needs*

Schools should enable students with varying abilities, interests, and backgrounds to develop to their maximum potential. Special needs students are categorized by type of impairment or disability—physical, mental, emotional, sensory, and neurological; or they may be gifted and talented students. Another group of students who require our attention are "at-risk" students who have been identified as being likely to drop out of school. Each of these groups of students will be discussed in the following sections.

Special needs students are those who differ from average students, and for them to develop to their maximum potential schools must modify standard school practices. Over the years society has come to recognize the right of all citizens to a free public education. Because some states have been less than responsive to these needs, federal legislation was required.

In 1977 the United States Congress passed the Education for All Handicapped Children Act (PL 94-142), which required states to provide special education services for disabled students at public expense. The law itself is complex. It requires that an appropriate education be provided in conformity with an individualized education program, which includes receiving adequate classroom instruction. Use of the term "least restrictive environment" allows students to be removed from special classrooms and be placed in classrooms with nondisabled students so that their lives are as normal as possible. The presumption is that all kinds of students should learn together and that "integration is better than segregation" (Ferguson, Ferguson, and Bogdan, 1987). Students should not be placed in special classes if they can be adequately served in a regular classroom. As teachers make curriculum decisions they need to consider at least the following:

- Course content
  Can the student read the materials?
  Has the student the prerequisite skills?

- Instructional activity
  Is the instructional strategy appropriate?
  Is the student engaged in active learning?

---

* Most states require teacher candidates to have course work or instruction on special needs students prior to certification. It will be useful to review information from this course prior to your student teaching. This will help you to meet the special needs of these students more effectively and efficiently in social studies classes.

- Student behavior
   What kinds of behaviors does the student exhibit?
   Can the student remain on task? (Hoover, 1990)

When modifying the curriculum, special attention must be given to textbooks and other written materials. Cheney (1989) suggests the following adapting strategies:

1. Change the learning task from one requiring reading and written responses to one that requires listening and allows for oral responses by using a tutor or cassette recorder.
2. Use group projects or allow oral reports.
3. Allow students to complete smaller amounts of material within a specific time frame.
4. Have students underline or circle responses rather than writing them.
5. Fasten materials to the desk to assist with coordination problems.
6. Provide for extra drill and practice activities (including the use of computer programs) for students who require additional time to learn the material.
7. Use visuals to present information.
8. Incorporate rhyming, rhythm, music, or movement into lessons as appropriate.
9. Keep distractions to a minimum.

Student expectations, instruction goals, record keeping, and student behavior patterns all pose dilemmas for classroom teachers. It is good teaching to be aware of each student's learning style and developmental needs. For the most part special needs students are more similar to than different from typical students; both groups of students have strengths as well as weaknesses.

Of course, the regular classroom social studies teacher should work closely with special services personnel. These teachers should also work with parents to help the special needs students to learn and develop to their maximum abilities. A positive environment will focus on the students' abilities and potential rather than on their limitations. Teachers may also find it necessary to teach nondisabled students about disabled students. Such instruction encourages the development of positive peer relationships.

In October, 1990, Public Law 94-142 was amended and became PL 101-476 "Individuals with Disabilities Education Act" (IDEA). This law is extensive and has been extended to include autistic children and children with traumatic brain injury and provides for "rehabilitation counseling" and "social work services."

Community social services agencies may provide resources for student and/or teacher use. The following organizations may also be of assistance to teachers.

American Foundation for the Blind. 15 West 16th St. New York, NY 10011

American Printing House for the Blind. 1839 Frankfurt Ave. Louisville, KY 40206

Captioned Films for the Deaf. Special Office for Materials Distribution. Indiana University. Audiovisual Center. Bloomington, IN 47401

"At-Risk" Students

Within recent years educators have recognized another group of special category students. These students have been identified as potential school dropouts and are described as being "at risk." Teachers believe these students will not have the necessary skills to succeed in our rapidly changing society. Based on what is known about these students, their backgrounds, and changes in society, there is every indication that the number of "at-risk" students will continue to increase. While precise definitions vary (Mann, 1986; Vito and Connell, 1988), there is a strong likelihood that "at-risk" students often have one or more of the following characteristics:

- They come from single-parent homes.
- They are from lower socioeconomic backgrounds.
- They are members of racial and ethnic minority groups.
- They may be below grade level in terms of academic achievement.
- They have lost their ability to cope with school work.
- They have a low self-esteem and self-concept based on low achievement.
- They have been "turned off" by school as a social institution within the community.
- They have experienced discipline problems (most likely truancy) at school which have resulted in suspension.
- They are alienated from society.
- They have high rates of drug and alcohol abuse and high criminal activity rates.
- They are not long-term, goal-oriented students but instead prefer immediate gratification: Males seek paid jobs, females leave to have children or to get married.
- They live in high growth states and are often enrolled in large-size school districts.
- They live in unstable school districts.
- They have low academic skills (but not necessarily low intelligence).
- They may be physically or mentally challenged.
- They have poorly educated, sometimes illiterate, parents who are likely to be school dropouts.

- They have less involvement in curricular or extracurricular activities.
- They speak English as a second language.

(Adapted from Druian and Butler, 1987; Wehlage, 1983; Kellogg, 1988.)

In analyzing successful programs for marginal students there is evidence to indicate that teachers do make a difference. Schools are urged to provide opportunities for success to counteract the negative messages that "at-risk" students receive from society on a regular basis. Teachers are encouraged to develop challenging experiential learning approaches. There is some evidence (Levin, 1986) that peer teaching, cooperative learning, and the use of computers are approaches that seem to work rather well for "at-risk" students. It appears that several characteristics of effective teaching in general have particular application for "at-risk" students. In teaching "at-risk" students the teacher should 1) emphasize learning by providing structure and support; 2) establish high expectations and attainable goals for all to maximize opportunities for success; 3) provide high quality instruction using active teaching rather than relying on print materials; 4) monitor student progress by providing frequent student feedback; and 5) enforce rules equitably.

Students from Various Ethnic and Cultural Backgrounds

Even though the United States has been a multicultural nation since its founding, recently a greater interest in multiculturalism has arisen. This interest in part is a result of an ever-increasing enrollment of students whose backgrounds reflect ethnic and cultural differences. For example, it has been projected that by the year 2000, approximately 40 million persons in this country will have a non-English-speaking language background. In some areas of our country, such as California and New York, students from various non-European ethnic and cultural backgrounds already constitute the majority of students. Care must be taken to ensure that these students receive quality education in preparation for adult citizenship responsibilities and their future roles in society as effective producers and consumers.

Teachers in all content areas need to be aware of differences in students' cognitive skills, cognitive styles, linguistic characteristics, and nonverbal communication behaviors. It is also important for teachers to be sensitive to differences in the school culture and those of the home and community. Many behavior expectations for both teachers and students in United States schools are often a source of confusion and tension for students and their parents from other cultures, thereby creating a "cultural conflict." For example, promptness in coming to school is an important characteristic of United States schools; in other cultures the concept of time is less important. Or consider another possible value conflict in that some groups prefer to learn cooperatively rather than competitively, and competition is viewed as distasteful. For some students, immediate gratification is of greater importance than preparation for some future goal, such as preparing for college or a job, or being successful when taking a standardized test. Also, individual members of any group are likely to be as diverse as they are similar. Teachers need to be careful not to categorize and stereotype students based on their backgrounds or on the teacher's predetermined biases and prejudices. Teachers who are successful consciously reject a deficit model, which focuses on what students *cannot* accomplish but instead build on the strengths and needs of students.

Given the nature of social studies content and the overall goals of most social studies programs, it is particularly important for social studies teachers to recognize cultural diversity, learn about their students' cultures, and then organize effective lessons that help students develop a sense of pride and achievement. They must help the young people in their classes appreciate cultural pluralism as a source of cultural enrichment. At the same time, teachers must help students understand they also have a common culture as citizens of the United States.

The skills associated with cultural sensitivity are developed over time. Social studies teachers want to 1) help students learn how and where to obtain accurate information about various cultural groups; 2) provide first-hand positive learning experiences with people from several cultural groups; 3) have students examine an event, issue, or historic time period from the perspective of another cultural group; and 4) allow for role-playing activities, which enable students to "walk in the shoes of another" to develop an empathy for others. Teachers should develop creative learning activities and select instructional resources that build on the strengths of the class. Both students and teachers bring to class numerous valuable experiences based on their backgrounds and cultural experiences.

Protecting Academic Freedom

An important part of the learning environment is the freedom that allows teachers and students to discuss a variety of issues and topics from several perspectives. Within the United States academic freedom is an integral part of our educational program.

Academic freedom is basic to our democratic society and has several definitions, which in part depend on the maturity level of the students. For example, academic freedom is likely to be viewed differently at the collegiate level than in the elementary, middle, and secondary schools. Some topics may be highly controversial in some communities but not in others. If in doubt about the appropriateness of a topic for study it is useful to first check with the department chairperson or school principal. Topics that are often considered to be controversial include issues in moral education, ethical issues, values analysis, activities that teach about a particular ideology or belief (for example, Marxism or socialism), and family education.

In 1975 the National Council for the Social Studies (NCSS) adopted a statement concerning teacher and student academic freedom in social studies. The NCSS statement notes that the professional obligation of the teacher is to "maintain a spirit of free inquiry, open-mindedness, and impartiality" and support students' freedom to learn. Teachers must be active in supporting and maintaining their own academic freedom and at the same time ensure students' rights to study a range of issues from various perspectives.

Social studies is an area where teachers are likely to discuss controversial issues. These controversial issues must have educational value; be significant, appropriate to the curriculum, and appropriate for student maturity; and take into consideration community standards and values. A well-planned discussion of a controversial issue may be one of the most exciting aspects of teaching social studies. Yet to have a productive discussion, careful teacher and student preparation is necessary. It is important to remember that quality discussions do not just happen; teachers carefully plan for these discussions and prepare their students for them.

For example, if the class is going to discuss controversial issues such as nuclear war, the death penalty, or the location of a new airport, the teacher may want to consider the following:

- Is this topic appropriate for the maturity level of the students?
- Are there sufficient resources and references in the school or local library or through interlibrary loan that reflect multiple perspectives on the topic?
- Is this topic related to the curriculum?
- Is it possible to have an informed discussion on this topic? What will my students contribute to and learn from this discussion?
- Is it likely that the students will be able to discuss this topic at home with parents or with other significant adults?
- Am I, the teacher, able to guide students in a professional and impartial manner?
- As the teacher, am I able to respond professionally to community pressure not to teach about this topic or to give greater weight to positions not my own? Am I likely to have appropriate administrative support?

Teaching Controversial Issues

Controversial topics may come spontaneously from a current event, from an issue facing the local community, or may be based on student input in planning for the class. In teaching about a controversial issue, a values continuum such as the following may be used to clarify the issues and reflect a range of attitudes.

■ ■ ■ ■ ■ ■ ■ ■ Topic: Should public transit employees have the right to strike?

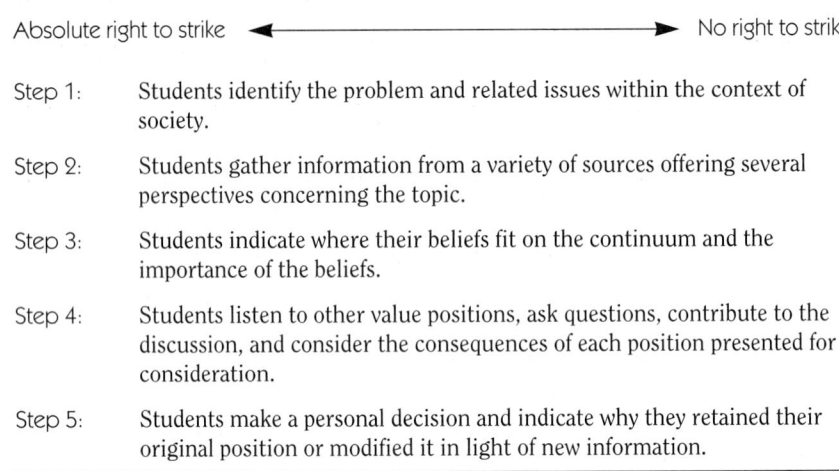

Step 1: Students identify the problem and related issues within the context of society.

Step 2: Students gather information from a variety of sources offering several perspectives concerning the topic.

Step 3: Students indicate where their beliefs fit on the continuum and the importance of the beliefs.

Step 4: Students listen to other value positions, ask questions, contribute to the discussion, and consider the consequences of each position presented for consideration.

Step 5: Students make a personal decision and indicate why they retained their original position or modified it in light of new information.

Another way to teach controversial issues is to use a debate format whereby one group of students argues the affirmative side of the issue while another group argues the negative side. In this format, however, it may be difficult for other alternative perspectives to be expressed.

If, however, undue pressure by a complainant or administrator is brought on the teacher for teaching about a controversial issue there are several actions that may be taken. For example, following the district procedures, the teachers may request a hearing before the school board. Before any hearing it is wise to keep a record of meetings with the complainant and administration and the substance of those discussions and review these notes before the hearings. Of course a record of the hearing should be kept as well. In some instances, it may be a good idea to have another teacher be present at the meeting as an interested observer.

In addition, the teacher may request assistance from groups such as the state and/or local professional educational organizations, NCSS and the state social studies council, and the American Civil Liberties Union. Their responses to such challenges will no doubt vary, but they are likely to offer assistance and support in the controversy. These groups are interested in protecting academic freedom for both teachers and students.

Community Expectations and Values

Teachers need to be sensitive to community values and expectations. This seems to be especially important in smaller communities where teachers are well known and their behaviors observed by the local townspeople. Oftentimes communities expect teachers to live in the district (although this expectation may not be written into policy). They are expected to support the local merchants by buying locally and by participating in community events. If this is the case, then the local merchants and town leaders are much more likely to support the schools because they view the teachers as integral participants in the local community by contributing to its well being.

Being sensitive to community values does not preclude teachers from speaking out or taking an active part in local issues. Nor does it mean that teachers do not have a life and interests outside of school and the local community. If a teacher is uncomfortable in a particular community it may be wise to consider seeking a teaching position in another community that has different values and expectations. Perhaps the teacher should move to a larger district where individual teachers may be less visible in the community.

SUMMARY

Social studies teachers face many challenges and must make decisions how to meet these challenges most effectively. The classroom and school environments shape teacher, student, and parent expectations concerning the teaching and learning of social studies.

Many topics in social studies lend themselves to controversy and may raise concerns within the community. Therefore, it is necessary for social studies teachers to be sensitive to community values and expectations, but at the same time be prepared to respond to controversy. Most schools and districts have policies and guidelines that support both teacher and student academic freedom. They have statements concerning academic freedom and the teaching of controversial issues.

Discussion Questions

1. What are some characteristics of a positive teaching and learning environment for social studies classes? How will you develop this environment in your classroom?
2. Assume you are assigned to teach two United States history classes during your first year of teaching. One class has students who are bright, inquisitive, and above average in ability. The other class has less mature students who are not particularly interested in school and believe that history has little or no relevance in their lives. How would

you proceed to teach each class? What are your expectations for each? What content, concepts, and skills would you teach to each class? What instructional strategies will you use? How will you challenge students in each class to reach their potential? How will student self-concept and self-esteem be addressed? In discussing these questions, you should try to be as specific as possible in your responses.
3. We provided several examples of topics considered by some to be controversial. What topics do you think are likely to be controversial in the coming decade? To what extent should these topics be discussed by middle school and high school students? If they are suitable for discussion, what approaches would you take?

Student Learning Activities

1. Examine several recent court cases involving academic freedom and/or censorship. What do each of these cases have in common? How are the issues distinct? What was the decision in each case and what impact did the decision have on teacher and student academic freedom? (Contact the American Bar Association or your state Bar for information on court cases.)
2. Contact several local school districts and state professional educational organizations to secure copies of their policies and/or guidelines related to academic freedom. Compare these statements and write one of your own that supports your beliefs about academic freedom and censorship.
3. Think about the many teachers who have instructed you throughout your school years beginning with kindergarten and extending through this academic year. Identify five to eight characteristics that made you remember them. Share these characteristics with your classmates. To what extent are there similarities? How will you want to be remembered by your students many years after they have left your classroom?

References

Augustine, D. K., Gruber, K. D., and Hanson, L. R. 1989–1990. "Cooperation Works!" *Educational Leadership.* Vol. 47, No. 4, December 1989/January 1990, 4–7. (Note: This entire issue is devoted to cooperative learning.)

Cheney, C. D. 1989. "The Systematic Adaptation of Instructional Materials and Techniques for Problem Learners." *Academic Therapy*, Vol. 25, No. 1, September. 25–30.

Druian, G. and Butler, J. A. 1987. *Effective Schooling Practices and At-Risk Youth: What the Research Shows.* (School Improvement Research Series Topical Synthesis #1). Portland, OR: Northwest Regional Educational Laboratory.

Ferguson, D. L., Ferguson, P. M., and Bogdan, R. C. 1987. "If Mainstreaming Is the Answer, What Is the Question?" In V. Richardson-Koehler (Ed.). *Educator's Handbook: A Research Perspective.* White Plains, NY: Longman. 394–419.

Hoover, J. D. 1990. "Curriculum Adaptation: A Five Step Process for Classroom Implementation." *Academic Therapy.* Vol. 25, No. 4, March. 407–416.

Kagan, S. 1986. "Cooperative Learning and Sociocultural Factors in Schooling." In *Beyond Language: Social and Cultural Factors in Schooling Language Minority Students.* Developed by the Bilingual Education Office, California State Department of Education. Los Angeles: Evaluation, Dissemination, and Assessment Center. California State University at Los Angeles.

Kagan, S. 1989–1990. "The Structural Approach to Cooperative Learning." *Educational Leadership.* Vol. 47, No. 4, December 1989/January 1990. 12–15.

Kagan, S., Zahn, G. L., Widaman, K. F., Schwarzwald, J., and Tyrrell, G. 1985. "Classroom Structural Bias: Impact of Cooperative and Competitive Classroom Structure on Cooperative and Competitive Individuals and Groups." In R. E. Slavin, S. Sharan, S. Kagan, R. Hertz-Lagarowitz, C. Webb, and R. Schmuck (Eds). *Learning to Cooperate, Cooperating to Learn.* New York: Plenum.

Kellogg, J. 1988. "Forces of Change." *Phi Delta Kappan.* Vol. 70, No. 3, November. 199–204.

Levin, H. M. 1986. *Educational Reform for Disadvantaged Students: An Emerging Crisis.* Washington DC: National Education Association.

Mann, D. 1986. "Dropout Prevention—Getting Serious about Programs that Work." *NASSP Bulletin.* Vol. 70, No. 489, April. 66–73.

Maker, C. J. 1987. "Gifted and Talented." In V. Richardson-Koehler (Ed.), *Education Handbook: A Research Perspective.* White Plains, NY: Longman.

National Council for the Social Studies. 1975. *Position Statement on the Freedom to Teach and the Freedom to Learn.* Washington, DC: National Council for the Social Studies. (Copies are available from NCSS.)

Newmann, F. M. and Thompson, J. A. 1987. *Effects of Cooperative Learning on Achievement in Secondary Schools: A Summary of Research.* Madison, WI: University of Wisconsin, National Center on Effective Secondary Schools.

Slavin, R. E. (1991). *Educational Psychology* (3rd ed.). Englewood Cliffs, NJ: Prentice-Hall.

Tharp, R. G. and Gallimore, R. G. 1988. *Rousing Minds to Life: Teaching, Learning, and Schooling in Social Context.* New York: Cambridge University Press.

Vito, R. and Connell, J. 1988. "A Longitudinal Study of At-Risk High School Students: A Theory Based Description and Intervention." In P. Eggen and D. Kauchak (Eds). *Educational Psychology Classroom Connections.* New York: Merrill.

Ward, B. A. 1987. *Instructional Grouping in the Classroom.* (School Improvement Research Series Close-Up #2). Portland, OR: Northwest Regional Educational Laboratory.

Wehlage, G. G. 1983. *Effective Programs for the Marginal High School Student.* Fastback 197. Bloomington, IN: Phi Delta Kappa. (See also ERIC Reproduction Document Service ED 235 132.)

Wehlage, G. G. and Rutter, R. A. 1986. "Dropping Out: How Much Do Schools Contribute to the Problem?" *Teachers College Record,* Vol. 87, No. 3, Spring. 374–392

Additional Readings

Anderson, L. N. and Pellicer, L. 1990. "Synthesis of Research on Compensatory and Remedial Education." *Educational Leadership,* Vol. 48, No. 1, September. 10–16.

Aronson, E., Blaney, N., Stephan, C., Sikes, J., and Snapp, M. 1978. *The Jigsaw Classroom,* Beverly Hills, CA: Sage.

Clifford, M. 1990. "Students Need Challenge, Not Easy Success." *Educational Leadership.* Vol. 48, No. 1, September. 22–26.

Curtis, C. K. 1991. "Social Studies for Students At-Risk and with Disabilities." In J. P. Shaver (Ed.), *Handbook of Research for Social Studies Teaching and Learning.* New York: Macmillan.

Delisle, J. R. 1991. "Gifted Students and Social Studies." In J. P. Shaver (Ed.), *Handbook of Research for Social Studies Teaching and Learning.* New York: Macmillan.

Gage, N. L. and Berliner, D. C. 1992. *Educational Psychology* (5th ed.). Boston: Houghton Mifflin.

Gay, G. 1991. "Culturally Diverse Students and Social Studies." In J. P. Shaver (Ed.), *Handbook of Research for Social Studies Teaching and Learning.* New York: Macmillan.

Good, T. L. and Brophy, J. E. 1986. "School Effects." In M. Wittrock (Ed.), *Handbook on Research on Teaching* (3rd ed.), New York: Macmillan.

Good, T. L. and Brophy, J. E. 1991. *Looking in Classrooms* (5th ed.). New York: HarperCollins.

Henson, K. T. 1993. *Methods and Strategies for Teaching in Secondary and Middle Schools* (2nd ed.). New York: Longman.

Oliver, D. and Shaver, J. P. 1967. *Teaching Public Issues in the High School.* Boston: Houghton Mifflin.

Slavin, R. E. 1990. *Cooperative Learning: Theory, Research and Practice.* Englewood Cliffs, NJ: Prentice-Hall.

> There never were in the world two opinions alike, no more than two hairs or two grains; the most universal quality is diversity.
>
> *Michel de Montaigne*

CHAPTER 10

Promoting Active Social Studies Learning

FOCUS QUESTIONS

- How do learning activities engage students in learning content and concepts, in developing skills, and in forming values in the social studies?
- Why is the selection of instructional materials and resources so important for social studies teachers?
- How can cocurricular activities extend social studies learning to other settings?

OVERVIEW Social studies programs provide students with valuable perspectives of subject matter content and methodologies drawn from social science disciplines—anthropology, economics, geography, history, philosophy, political science, psychology, and sociology. Social studies also includes content from the humanities, sciences, mathematics, and religious studies. Social studies programs may be presented in single discipline courses, such as world geography or economics, and in "fusion" courses, which combine the perspectives of several social science or related disciplines. Examples of these fusion courses include problems of democracy, environmental studies, ethnic studies, and science, technology, and society. Planning relevant learning activities for students is a major responsibility and requires thoughtful reflection by the teacher. This chapter provides several examples of learning activities that focus on individual disciplines and fusion courses.

Another important responsibility of the teacher is selecting instructional materials and resources. We will address several issues related to instructional resources: their selection and use. We will also discuss several examples of cocurricular activities related to social studies. We urge you to become active teachers in the classroom and regularly participate in cocurricular activities.

During the past several years hundreds of national and state reports have been written about reforming education. Several of these reports urge that local schools and businesses establish partnerships for their mutual benefit. We include some examples of these possibilities in this chapter.

Learning Activities That Motivate Students

Social studies provides a wealth of information and numerous opportunities for students to develop the thinking skills they need as informed and active citizens. For example, the study of history and philosophy enables students to learn about ideas, people, and events in the past; their impact on humankind; and their related consequences. Geographic information helps citizens make useful decisions about our physical and cultural environments. Information used to make economic and civic policies influences our lives on a daily basis. The behavioral sciences help us understand and respond to the varying human needs of those around us.

Throughout this textbook we have indicated that knowledge, values, and skills are important aspects of planning, and teachers need to pay attention to each interlocking component. We suggest several illustrative learning activities that teachers could use or modify for students at various grade levels. (See Figures 10.1 through 10.12.) As teachers develop meaningful learning activities they should include opportunities for students to develop skills in each of the categories that we described in greater detail in Chapter 5. Teachers may decide to emphasize only one of the skills categories in some lessons but they should give attention to all the skills sometime during the course. These illustrative learning activities extend beyond the use of a textbook and help students become active learners. We encourage teachers to plan a variety of learning activities that extend beyond the classroom.

The illustrative learning activities are organized around the topic questions, which allow students to respond to a broad question for which there may be no single correct answer. The intent is to require students to grapple intellectually with such questions and to realize there are likely to be several acceptable responses. The content selected for any learning activity may be based on student interest, school district curriculum requirements, or a current topic or issue of importance, such as a natural catastrophe in some part of the world or an event or concern related to the local community such as where to locate a new landfill.

Concepts and skills are selected to help students learn the content under study, extend their knowledge by linking previous learning in social studies and other content areas, and prepare for future learning. Students are expected to "apply" what they have learned in one activity to another setting as a means for assessing their learning.

In using such a planning model you can start at whatever point makes sense. Sometimes, the content to be learned will be the starting place for planning and at other times the learning activity may be selected based on specific skills to be developed. An important consideration to keep in mind is that planning is not a linear process. As mentioned previously, teachers will need to consider how they will bring closure to a particular lesson. Some lessons may take more than a single class period and so consideration must be given to homework assignments and resources available to students.

Using anthropology for illustrative purposes, we want to "walk" you through one of the sample learning activities and suggest linkages of content, concepts, and skills with each learning activity.

For example, if a goal of the lesson is to teach about the concept of culture the teacher may decide to use artifacts representing a particular culture such as the Aztec. After allowing the students to examine the artifacts (hands-on if possible or by visual observation), the teacher should ask the students to conceptualize the culture. Having done this, the teacher should ask the student to infer other possible values of importance to the culture. Next, the teacher could ask the students to explain why these values existed and to suggest their implications for this culture. The students consider causality by examining how the culture acquired its particular characteristics. Finally, students should extend their thinking and knowledge by utilizing their prior knowledge and relating these interpretations to the new topic of values and cultures.

Anthropology

One of the key organizing concepts in anthropology is culture. Culture focuses on the patterns, themes, and experiences that people hold in common even though they may live in diverse settings. (See Fig. 10.1.)

Economics

Economics is the study of how scarce resources are distributed to satisfy unlimited wants. The study of economics is often divided into two parts: macroeconomics and microeconomics. Macroeconomics concerns the economy as a whole and examines unemployment, inflation and deflation, and fiscal and monetary policy, for example. Microeconomics concerns the economic behaviors of individuals, households, businesses, and markets. Therefore, prices of goods and services, supply and demand, and the role of the government are part of microeconomics. The suggested learning activity relates to the economy of a third-world nation. (See Fig. 10.2 and Economics Scenario.)

Geography

The Joint Committee on Geographic Education (1984) identified five interrelated themes as essential elements in studying geography. These are location (site), place (particular area), relationships within places (human-environmental relationships), movement (relationships between places or spatial interaction), and regions (how they form and change). The geography learning activity that follows helps students study the physical and human characteristics of their own community. (See Fig. 10.3.)

History

History is the social studies subject most frequently taught in the schools. Throughout their school years virtually all students are required to study United States history for at least two or three years, world history for one or two years. Many schools also require a year of state and/or local history. Until recently, history usually focused on political, military, and economic events and provided a male perspective of events and people. Today, history courses often give attention to social history whereby students study the "common person" and the historical contributions of women and minority groups. The illustrative learning activity ties together aspects of social, political, and military history. It encourages students to use oral history techniques and to consider the importance of both primary and secondary materials as sources of information. (See Fig. 10.4.)

Philosophy

Philosophy in its broadest sense means the pursuit of wisdom. Philosophy is pluralistic and interdisciplinary. It deals with difficulties and paradoxes. The methods of philosophy include analysis and reasoning as well as description and interpretation. Its content deals with the major concepts and concerns of life. Concepts include justice, power, self, happiness, truth, beauty, and the notion of life itself. Philosophy is also concerned with issues of right and wrong, and it helps us learn to live with uncertainty. (See Fig. 10.5)

Political Science

Political science provides students with an overview of government structure, organization, and policies. Students studying political science also address such topics as power, its roots, applications, and consequences; and with leadership, its characteristics and responsibilities. They should have opportunities to study our government and its Constitution and to explore in-depth topics such as federalism, political processes, social legislation, and citizenship rights and responsibilities. In addition, political science courses should give some time to the study of governments in other countries and the role of international organizations and agencies. (See Fig. 10.6 and Political Science card series.)

Psychology

Psychology courses at the secondary level help students to understand themselves and others. In most schools psychology courses are electives for upper-level students. (See Fig. 10.7.)

Sociology

Sociologists study the behaviors and interactions of humans in groups and institutions. The content of sociology is usually of interest to students but in many schools sociology has been crowded from the curriculum. Usually this is due to increasing state requirements in other social science disciplines, most often in history, political science, geography, and economics. (See Fig. 10.8.)

Environmental Studies

The world community faces a number of environmental issues such as pollution, nuclear testing, energy costs, toxic waste, and population growth. Students need to have experiences confronting environmental issues and have opportunities to seek solutions (however tentative). The study of environmental issues need not be an "add-on" unit. Teachers can readily infuse the concepts and skills from these studies into existing programs (See Fig. 10.9.)

Global Education

Since World War II advocacy groups have argued for the inclusion of global perspectives into the school curriculum. They argued that young learners should recognize the interdependence of people and nations in a rapidly changing world. Today it is essential that we recognize that events taking place halfway around the world have an impact on all of us as we live during the last decade of the 20th century. Technology, utilizing satellite linkages, brings these events into our homes on a daily basis.

With the notion of a shrinking world before us, it is imperative that young learners have many opportunities to study about the people, places, and events in a global context. Business and political leaders remind us of our need to remain competitive in the world marketplace. In times of international natural disasters—for example, earthquakes and floods—many people and nations join together to assist the victims of such disasters. Global education with its roots in social studies content is an important way to help students gain perspectives and appreciations of others in a variety of world settings. (See Fig. 10.10.)

Law-Related Education

Law-related education (LRE) became a part of social studies programs in the 1960s as a result of the civil rights movement. Young learners wanted to acquire a better understanding of the law, including knowing their rights and responsibilities as citizens. As a result of this developing interest in the law there have been a variety of projects that focus study on the United States Constitution and Bill of Rights. Other programs have been developed that include content drawn from consumer law, street law, justice studies, and other similar areas.

Most law-related education courses include opportunities for students to visit and observe courts in session, to have classroom visits from law enforcement and judicial officials, and to participate in the national mock trial competitions. Many LRE lessons are interdisciplinary by nature and encourage students to grapple intellectually with a range of law-related topics such as local legal issues, including neighborhood disputes involving noise ordinances, landlord-tenant disputes, property and zoning disputes, and the like.

The expectation of those advocating LRE programs is that young learners will develop a knowledge base and respect for the law, which in turn will help them be more active in defending their rights and the rights of others. It is likely that such people will be more effective in making personal and social policy decisions. Several organizations (addresses below) such as the American Bar Association (and affiliated state bar associations), Center for Civic Education, Constitutional Rights Foundation, and the National Institute for Citizen Education on the Law (NICEL) all have educational materials to help teachers incorporate LRE content in social studies programs.* (See Fig. 10.11.)

Multicultural Education

During the past 30 years educators and the publishers of instructional materials have sought to correct distortions and inequities in textbook presentations

---

*American Bar Association (concerning immigrants and refugees), 750 N. Lake Drive, Chicago, IL 60611; Center for Civic Education, 5146 Douglas Fir Road, Calabasas, CA 91302; Constitutional Rights Foundation, 601 Kingsley Drive, Los Angeles, CA 90005; National Institute for Citizen Education in the Law (NICEL), 24 E Street, NW, Washington, DC 20001.

concerning the contributions and experiences of cultural, racial, and ethnic groups and those of women. While there have been significant improvements in these materials, equity and accuracy have not yet been achieved. Debate regarding the inclusion of multicultural education and its content continues today.

There is no general agreement on what content should be included or excluded in such programs. Yet many people believe that it is imperative that young people recognize cultural pluralism as important to our understanding the past and preparing for the future since the majority of the world's population are non-European and people of color. Some scholars argue that the curriculum needs to extend beyond that of "Western" civilization to include the perspectives and viewpoints of people of different traditions and cultures. Others would argue that ignoring the contributions of minority groups and women is not acceptable as past inequities of presentation must be addressed even though teachers and instructional materials either implicitly or explicitly present content primarily from the majority perspective. (See Fig. 10.12.)

The following illustrative learning activities, representing each of the social science disciplines discussed in this chapter, are provided on pages 266 through 282. They can be expanded into instructional units or modified to meet the needs of students and program objectives. Creative teachers can use these and other ideas as springboards in the development of additional learning activities:

10.1	Anthropology
10.2	Economics
	Economics Scenario
10.3	Geography
10.4	History
10.5	Philosophy
10.6	Political Science
	Political Science card series
10.7	Psychology
10.8	Sociology
10.9	Environmental Studies
10.10	Global Education
10.11	Law-Related Education
10.12	Multicultural Education

Figure 10.1 Anthropology

Topic Question
How Can Artifacts Help Us Learn about Various Cultures?

Content
Over time cultures change due to invention, diffusion, adaptation, and so on. Most culture groups have left behind physical objects (artifacts) that help us better understand characteristics of the culture.

Concepts
Culture
Values
Diffusion
Adaptation
Invention
Change

Illustrative Activity
Bring in several artifacts (or pictures of artifacts) from another culture for students to examine. Have the students generate a variety of questions they might ask about the culture based on these artifacts. Then ask students to consider questions such as the following: What is the artifact? What might its purpose have been? What do these artifacts reveal about the values of the culture? What might be some characteristics of this culture? How is this culture similar to or different from other cultures we have studied? How do you think this culture has changed over the years?

Skills Category
Conceptualization/Comprehension

Causality
Evaluation/Validity of explanation
Creative extension

Applications
Observing phenomena.
Comparing/contrasting.
Making inferences concerning the culture. Testing hypotheses.
Formulating conclusions (however tentative).
Developing a time capsule/discovery box of artifacts representing your own culture and community to be opened in 50 years. What should be included as indicative of our culture and community?

Figure 10.2 Economics

Topic Question
What is the Future of Povertania's Economy? *

Content
Developing nations in the Third World often have difficulty establishing a sound economic system. Some countries decide to establish a market economy while other countries establish a command economy. Sometimes distinctions between these two economies are not readily apparent.

Concepts
Developing country
Market economy
Command economy
Colonization
Role of government
Global economy

Illustrative Activity
Provide the students with copies of Economics Scenario: Povertania, and instruct the students to read it. Then ask the students, either individually or in small groups, to determine what advice economic experts representing market economies might offer to the government of Povertania. Then students should identify the advice economic experts from nations with command economies might suggest to Povertania. What are the priorities of each group of economic advisers? For the short and long run which recommendations are officials of Povertania most likely to accept and why? Then ask the students to return as economic advisors to Povertania ten years later. What are the possible results each group of advisors might find? What is the likely economic condition of Povertania?

Skills Category
Conceptualization/Comprehension

Causality

Evaluation/Validity of explanation

Creative extension

Applications
Comparing perspectives. Gathering additional information about the experiences of developing countries.

Inferring the political, economic, and social conditions of the country.

Recognizing differences of perspectives.

A new planet in the solar system has been discovered. It has an atmosphere similar to Earth and there is every indication the new planet can support life. You are among the first settlers who come from several nations to take up residence on this new planet. Therefore, you will be responsible for establishing an economic, political, and social system. What type of economic system would you recommend and why? What basic economic decisions do you need to make? What do you foresee as strengths of the system established? What are likely to be some problem areas? What might the planet look like in fifty years?

---

*Adapted from Laughlin, M. A. and Beining, T. J. (1987). "Participating in the Global Economy." In *The Senior Economist*, Vol. 3, No. l, Fall 1987. 13–14. © 1987, National Council on Economic Education, New York, N.Y. Used with permission.

Economics Scenario: Povertania

Povertania is a country that has been colonized by one of the European nations beginning in the late 19th century until its independence nearly four decades ago. When the European powers departed from Povertania, the colonizers left behind an abundance of partially developed natural resources, an expanding population, and a people with a low standard of living.

Existing production in Povertania is carried on by a small number of business people who sell their products to a small number of wealthy families within the country. The majority of the people, however, do not participate in the existing economy of Povertania. Government leaders want to improve economic conditions for their people and they believe that increasing trade can stimulate economic growth.

You and a panel of economic experts representing market-oriented nations (United States, Canada, and Western Europe) have been invited to spend time in Povertania. Your purpose is to advise the government concerning economic development and growth possibilities. Your first task is to write a list of actions for the government to take to make progress toward meeting their economic goals. What priorities do you and the panel members recommend?

Your second task is to list what actions a group of economic advisers from a command or modified command economy country such as Cuba might recommend. How might you explain the differences in the recommended actions?

CHAPTER 10 Promoting Active Social Studies Learning

Figure 10.3 Geography

Topic Question
What Can Local Maps Tell Us about our Community?

Content
Studying why cities and towns are located where they are and have the particular features they have.

Concepts
Maps
Natural features
Human-made areas
Settlement patterns
Location
Region

Illustrative Activity
Secure both a historic and a current map of your town or city (or sketch one if necessary). Then identify the human-made areas on the map, such as central and area business districts, residential areas (neighborhoods), recreational areas, suburbs, agricultural lands, major highways, and railroads. Next, point out the natural geographic features, such as rivers, lakes, hills, valleys. Ask students to hypothesize why human-made features are where they are and how they have changed over time. How does our community compare with nearby communities of similar size and with communities in other areas of our nation or around the world? Share your findings and ideas with the class.

Skills Category
Conceptualization/Comprehension
Causality

Evaluation/Validity of explanation
Creative extension

Applications
Examining why a town or city is located where it is. Determining human and physical characteristics of a city or town.

Describing how the location and characteristics of geographic features influence the location of human-made features.

Recognizing how human-made and geographic features shaped our community.

Write an article about a current issue facing your community, for example, attracting and locating new business or industry into the community, pollution in nearby waterways, etc., from the perspective of a geographer.

PART 3 Implementing Social Studies Instruction

■■■■■■■■ **Figure 10.4** History

Topic Question
How Can the Study of History Become Personal?

Content
United States' lengthy involvement in Vietnam and domestic reactions to the war.

Concepts
War
Draft resisters
Patriotism
Aggression
Pacifism
Limited war
Civil disobedience
National security

Illustrative Activity
Direct students to prepare several guiding questions to ask people about their experiences, attitudes, and feelings concerning the war in Vietnam. Students should then interview such people as family members, neighbors, veterans' groups, conscientious objectors, draft resisters, those who received deferments, and government leaders. The students should share these responses with the class and compare them with newspaper accounts, media newscasts, Congressional testimony, and other references from this time period. Students may consider questions such as these: How is the information provided by each of these persons similar? How do the accounts differ? What was the role of the media in portraying the Vietnam experience at the time and most recently? To what extent did the media shape beliefs, attitudes, and behaviors concerning the war? Over the years, to what extent have attitudes concerning the Vietnam experience changed? To what extent is it likely the national wounds from Vietnam will heal? Is it likely there could be another Vietnam for the United States? Which aspects of the war seemed to be most painful? If you had been of draft age during this time period, how do you think you would have responded?

Skills Category	Applications
Conceptualization/ Comprehension	Gathering information from a variety of primary and secondary sources. Surveying various groups concerning attitudes toward the war.
Causality	Comparing/contrasting information/perspectives concerning the war.
Evaluation/Validity of explanation	Determining the logic of reasons given. Explaining what happened. Making inferences. Judging the accuracy of primary and secondary source materials. Recognizing different frames of reference. Determining bias.
Creative extension	Asking students to compare the United States involvement in Vietnam with involvement in Kuwait or Somalia. How did the U.S. become involved in each conflict? What, if anything, was accomplished? How did the outcomes of each military action influence behaviors and attitudes of people on the homefront?

Figure 10.5 Philosophy

Topic Question
How Can Education Help a Person Become Better?

Content
In the classical view, the aristocracy rules because through education it has the greatest potential for virtue, and therefore, the clearest title to participate in government.

Concepts
Virtue
Aristocracy
Classical education
Government
Citizenship

Illustrative Activity
Ask students to read the following statement and reflect on questions such as: What is citizenship? What is civic virtue? How can young people learn to incorporate civic virtue into their lives? How can you participate in the civic life of your community and contribute to its well-being?

The founding fathers addressed the question of securing life, liberty, and happiness in two ways. First of all, they developed a system of checks and balances to place one person's ambition against another's. Second, they addressed securing individual rights through education. In fact, the founders were extremely uneasy about the feebleness of civic education in the new republic. Some historians have even argued that the founders who supported the Bill of Rights viewed it not only as a condition for ratification, but as a way for future generations to educate themselves into civic responsibilities (virtue). Together, then, the dual concepts of education and checks on ambition were to serve the republic in the development of civic consciousness (virtue). Citizens would develop the ability to criticize themselves and correct their own behaviors. This would lead to an enlightened sense of nationalism. These ideas of civic well-being function, of course, only when individuals can feel some self-worth as contributors to their families and communities. The premise upon which our republic is built, then, is the belief that virtue, law, and education work together as a total system. Individuals will be virtuous if they are educated so they might construct good laws within a setting of civility and a conception of the public good.

Skills Category
Conceptualization/
Comprehension
Causality
Validity of explanation
Creative extension

Applications
Identifying issues.

Formulating questions and testing hypotheses.
Checking accuracy of premises and logic.
Develop two arguments about the relationship between education and becoming a better person. In one statement, argue that education helps a person become better. In the second statement argue that while there may be a correlation between virtue and education, it cannot be proven that education causes a person to become better.

Figure 10.6 Political Science

Topic Question
Who is Qualified to be President?

Content
Electing a president is an important citizenship responsibility. There are three legal requirements candidates must meet; and they must possess personal characteristics and qualities that the electorate deems to be important. This lesson considers the necessary and desired qualifications for a person to be elected president.

Concepts
Presidency
Constitutional qualifications
Desirable qualifications
Decision making
Personal/family background
Electorate

Illustrative Activity
Provide students with data cards that contain biographical information on twelve potential presidential candidates. (Student data card information follows this lesson. The identification of these persons is included in Appendix A.) The students should work in pairs or small groups. Ask them to decide which of the ten persons, based on the available information, has the best qualifications to be president of the United States. They should rank the candidates from the most qualified (No. 1) to the least qualified (No. 12) and be able to defend their choices. In preparing students for this lesson it may be necessary to review the constitutional requirements for president. It also might be helpful to consider what additional qualifications and background experiences are desirable for presidential candidates. Ask students to consider and discuss additional information they would use to support or reject a candidate for president. To what extent are their views influenced by their parents, peers, community, and media? [Note: "Age as of this date" refers to the point of time in each individual's career the activities listed on the data card had been accomplished. For those who were elected president the "age as of this date" is the date just prior to their election to office.] This lesson has been adapted from M. Hobin (1974), "Clarifying What Is Important." in A. O. Kownslar (editor), *Teaching American History: The Quest for Relevancy* by the National Council for the Social Studies (Used with permission).

Skills Category

Conceptualization/ Comprehension

Causality

Evaluation/Validity of explanation

Creative extension

Applications

Identifying similarities/differences in information provided. Offering additional information for consideration.

Analyzing available data. Interpreting information. Predicting events. Participating in group discussion.

Recognizing differences of perspectives. Deciding who is qualified to be President.

Identifying desirable qualifications for candidates seeking election as student body president or to the student council or for other positions of leadership. Determining if student body elections are based primarily on merit and achievement or on popularity or personality and why. Are there ways to make the elections meaningful?

(Data card information follows; also identification of persons is to be included in Appendix A at the end of this chapter.)

Political Science: Who Is Qualified to Be President?

Card 1

Colleges Attended: Harvard University, Columbia University

Religion: Protestant

Career (Major Occupations):   Farmer, lawyer, state senator, assistant secretary of Navy, governor, vice-presidential candidate

Married: 27 years

Age as of this Date: 50   Children: 6

SOURCE: *The National Cyclopaedia of American Biography*. XXXVII, University Microfilms, 1967. 103.

Card 2

College Attended: None

Religion: Protestant

Career (Major Occupations):   Investor, druggist, bookseller, brigadier general in U. S. Army

Married: 1st spouse: 5 years until spouse's death; 2nd spouse: 1 year

Age as of this Date: 38   Children: 3 by first marriage

SOURCE: *Dictionary of American Biography*. Charles Scribner's Sons, 1928. 362–367.

Card 3

Colleges Attended: Morehouse College, A.B. and L.H.D., Croze Theological Seminary, B.D., University of Pennsylvania, Boston University, Ph.D., D.D., Harvard University, L.L.D., Central State College, Morgan State College

Religion: Protestant

Career (Major Occupations):   Protestant minister, teacher of philosophy at Harvard, president of a civil rights organization, 1 of 10 outstanding men for the year according to *Time* magazine, Nobel Prize winner, noted public speaker

Married: 15 years

Age as of this Date: 37   Children: 4

SOURCES: *Current Biography Yearbook 1965*. H. W. Wilson Co., 1966. 220–223; *Current Biography Yearbook 1968*. H. W. Wilson Co., 1969. 457.

Political Science: Who Is Qualified to Be President?

Card 4

College Attended: None

Religion: No specific denomination

Career (Major Occupations):   Land speculator and farmer, lawyer, U. S. representative, U. S. senator, U. S. judge, commander of U. S. armed forces

Married: 38 years

Age as of this Date: 62   Children: none

SOURCE: *Dictionary of American Biography, IX.* Charles Scribner's Sons, 1932. 526–31.

Card 5

College Attended: Columbia University

Religion: No specific denomination

Career (Major Occupations):   Writer, served as lieutenant colonel in Army, lawyer, member of a congress, member of a constitutional convention, secretary of the treasury

Married: 24 years

Age as of this Date: 47   Children: 8

SOURCE: *Dictionary of American Biography, VIII.* Charles Scribner's Sons, 1932. 171–179.

Card 6

College Attended: None (private secondary school in England)

Religion: Protestant

Career (Major Occupations):   Teacher, journalist, member of a labor union (trade union league), U.S. delegate to the United Nations, chairperson of the United Nations Commission on Human Rights, endorsed by a president for the Nobel Peace Prize, noted public speaker

Married: 27 years

Age as of this Date: 65   Children: 6

SOURCE: *Current Biography: Who's News and Why, 1949.* H. W. Wilson Co., 1950. 528–532.

Political Science: Who Is Qualified to Be President?

Card 7

College Attended: University of Alabama

Religion: Protestant

Career (Major Occupations): Lawyer, state assistant attorney general, state legislator, U. S. judge, state governor, party candidate for presidency, served in U. S. Air Force, noted public speaker

Married: 1st spouse: 26 years until spouse's death; 2nd spouse: 3 years

Age as of this Date: 55   Children: 4 by first marriage

SOURCES: *Who's Who in America*, II, Marquis Who's Who, Inc., 1972. 3300; *Current Biography Yearbook 1963*, H. W. Wilson Co., 1964. 454–456.

Card 8

College Attended: None

Religion: No specific denomination

Career (Major Occupations): Postmaster, lawyer, U. S. representative, store owner, state congressperson, served as captain in U.S. Army, noted public speaker

Married: 19 years

Age as of this Date: 51   Children: 4

SOURCE: *Dictionary of American Biography*, XI, Charles Scribner's Sons, 1933. 242–249.

Card 9

College Attended: North Carolina Agricultural and Technical State University, Chicago Theological Seminary

Religion: Protestant

Career (Major Occupations): Minister, political and civil rights activist, president of a citizen's advocacy group, political leader, candidate for party's presidential nomination, noted public speaker

Married: 24 years

Age as of this Date: 47   Children: 3

SOURCE: *Colliers Encyclopedia*, 13, Macmillan, 1987. 424–425.

Political Science: Who Is Qualified to Be President?

Card 10

College Attended: Marymount Manhattan College, Fordham University Law School

Religion: Catholic

Career (Major Occupations):   Teacher, lawyer, assistant district attorney, U. S. representative, member of party steering and policy committee, chairperson of party national platform committee, party vice-presidential nominee

Married: 24 years

Age as of this Date: 49   Children: 3

SOURCE: *Collier's Encyclopedia*, 9, Macmillan, 1987. 669–670.

Card 11

College Attended: No college education

Religion: Catholic

Career (Major Occupations):   Agriculture, labor organizer and leader, spokesperson for the poor and oppressed, military veteran, political activist

Age as of this Date: 49   Children: 6

SOURCES: *The World Book Encyclopedia* Vol. 3. Chicago: World Book, Inc., 1991. *Colliers Encyclopedia* Vol. 6. New York: Macmillan Educational Company, 1991.

Card 12

College Attended: No college education

Religion: Unknown

Career: Guide, interpreter, trailblazer

Age as of this Date: 29   Children: 2

SOURCE: *The Encyclopedia Americana: International Division* Vol. 24. Danbury, CT: Grolier, Inc., 1990. New York: Macmillan Educational Company, 1991.

■ ■ ■ ■ ■ ■ ■ ■ Figure 10.7 Psychology

Topic Question
How Do Attitudes Influence Behavior?

Content
Attitudes have their roots from many sources (family, friends, and society) and influence social behavior in positive or negative ways.

Concepts
Attitude
Belief
Emotion
Action
Behavior
Prejudice
Identification

Illustrative Activity
Ask the students to bring in several advertisements from newspapers or periodicals, or summarize a radio or TV commercial and place the summaries on the bulletin board. Have students identify the ways the advertisements appeal to the public and shape public attitudes. Ask students to categorize the strategies used by advertisers to persuade the public to buy or use the product or service. Students may then answer questions such as the following: Which strategies are used most often? To what extent are the advertisements successful? What messages do the advertisers want the reader/viewer to have? What audience is the focus of the advertisement? To what extent do the advertisements appeal to cognitive processes or emotional responses?

Skills Category
Conceptualization/
Comprehension
Causality
Evaluation/Validity
of explanation
Creative extension

Applications
Identifying issues. Identifying similarities and concerns. Categorizing information.

Formulating hypotheses. Making inferences.

Detecting inaccurate or incomplete information. Recognizing bias.

Pick out several groups (some real and some fictitious) and survey people in the community (or other students) concerning their attitudes about the groups. Try to determine how much awareness or information those interviewed have about the groups. Speculate on how their attitudes were formed. To what extent is there evidence of stereotyping, prejudice, halo effect, etc.?

■ ■ ■ ■ ■ ■ ■ ■ **Figure 10.8 Sociology**

Topic Question
What are Some Changing Roles of Women?

Content
Studying the changing roles of women in the United States and in other countries.

Concepts
Roles
Expectations
Norms
Minorities
Social change
Socialization

Illustrative Activity
Have students bring in pictures of women from the United States and other countries during different time periods and engaging in various tasks. (The teacher might also bring in pictures.) Post the pictures on the bulletin board. After the students have examined the pictures, ask them to write brief responses to these and similar questions: What positions and roles does each of the women seem to have? What are some values of society that are apparent in the photographs? How are roles assigned to females and males in each society? Over the years, how have women's roles and expectations changed? How do individuals interpret their roles? What are some projected roles for women and men in the 21st century? After the students have written their responses, the teacher should promote a class discussion of those questions. The teacher could ask the first question and make a list of the various student responses. Then the teacher could proceed to the second question and again list student responses. This could continue until all students have exhausted their responses and have defended them. By the end of the discussion (which could extend beyond a single class period) the students should have a deeper understanding of the role of women in various times and places in history.

Skills Category
Conceptualization/
Comprehension

Causality

Evaluation/
Validity of explanation

Creative extension

Applications
Organizing information comprehension based on observing pictures.

Formulating questions/hypotheses. Inferring roles of women in various cultures and time periods.

Responding to questions. Evaluating hypotheses. Expressing conclusions.

Writing an essay based on the changing roles of women and men from the perspective of a feminist or as one who believes in traditional roles for women and men. Then critique your essay from the perspective of the other person.

CHAPTER 10 Promoting Active Social Studies Learning   279

■ ■ ■ ■ ■ ■ ■ ■ Figure 10.9 Environmental Studies

Topic Question
What are Sources of Natural Resources? *

Content
Investigate the natural resources needed to make a product manufactured in your community.

Concepts
Natural resources
Raw materials
Manufacturing
Marketplace
Environment
Ecosystem
Policy issues

Illustrative Activity
Select a product, such as bicycles, paper products, shoes, or pens that is manufactured in your city or state. Contact the manufacturer and investigate what materials and processes are used in manufacturing the product. It is possible that this information is available through interviews or written materials prepared by the company. Consider questions such as the following: What is the source of the raw materials? What happens to the environment when the raw materials are extracted or harvested? To what extent are pollutants produced? To what extent is the ecosystem disturbed? If necessary, where were the raw materials refined? How are the resources transported? Are there by-products? If so, what are they and what is their use? What impact does the manufacturing process have on the environment? How does the manufacturer ensure that the environment is protected? To what extent, if any, should the manufacturer be subject to rigorous governmental/environmental controls? What controls, if any, should be imposed and at what costs and to whom? What jobs are provided by this employer? What does the company contribute to the community? In addition to contacting the manufacturer students should research information about the company that has appeared in the local press. They should also contact any environmental protection agencies for official government reports concerning the manufacturer. To what extent are these reports and perspectives similar? Dissimilar?

Skills Category	Applications
Conceptualization/ Comprehension	Determining the issues and problems. Gathering information.
Causality	Establishing cause-effect relationships.
Evaluation/ Validity of explanation	Examining and judging information. Formulating conclusions. Deciding if the product is essential for survival, necessary to maintain the present lifestyle, or a luxury?
Creative extension	Visit a landfill and consider the questions such as these: Why is trash collected? What did people do with trash before plastic bags, aluminum cans, or trash removal services existed? How does the quantity of trash in the United States compare to other countries? How is trash disposed of in other countries? How do manufacturers dispose of trash compared to individuals and families? What are the costs of trash disposal? How will trash be disposed of in the year 2000?

* Adapted from the Wisconsin Department of Natural Resources *Recycling Study Guide*, Madison, WI, 1988, p. 11.

Figure 10.10 Global Education

Topic Question
How can Information about Recent Immigrants Help Us to Understand Conflicting Values and Traditions?

Content
Except for native populations, the United States has been a nation of immigrants and remains so today.

Concepts
Immigrant
Immigration
Refugee
Values
Conflict
Cultural diversity
American Dream
Opportunity
Freedom

Illustrative Activity
In the 1970s and 1980s the so-called "boat people," primarily from Asia and Cuba, arrived in the United States, and for the most part were allowed to resettle in this country. In the 1990s boat loads of people from Haiti have attempted to enter the country and remain in the United States as have millions of other refugees who arrived in earlier years. Yet the policy of the United States has been to transport a large number of the Haitian refugees back to their homeland. Ask students to consider reasons why there has been a shift of United States policy on the question of refugee status for the Haitians. Also, have student reflect on the consequences of these policies and actions for those directly involved, for the nation as a whole, and on the image of the United States abroad and at home, which is being portrayed as discriminatory and selective. What is your position on this important issue?

Skills Category	Applications
Conceptualization/ Comprehension	Identifying issues involved with respect to current immigration policies.
Causality	Tracing United States immigration policies in a historic context from the beginning of the 20th century. Explaining why these policies changed with respect to the different groups. Discussing the short term and long term implications of these changing policies. Reviewing newspaper and media accounts of the circumstances in various nations that generated immigration to the United States.
Evaluation/ Validity of explanation	Examining the statements of various individuals and groups who are pro- and anti-immigration in terms of refugee settlement. Reading presidential and/or Congressional leaders' statements concerning their reasons whether or not to allow immigrant people to remain in the United States and become citizens upon meeting citizenship requirements.
Creative extension	Assume you have been invited to testify at a Congressional hearing related to possible changes in our current immigration policy. Prepare a statement either for or against the current United States position concerning immigration and refugees. In your statement explain your reasons for your views. How do your personal, moral, and ethical values influence your perspectives on this issue?

CHAPTER 10 Promoting Active Social Studies Learning

■ ■ ■ ■ ■ ■ ■ **Figure 10.11 Law-Related Education**

Topic Question
How Do Laws and Rules Influence our Daily Lives?

Content
Each day our behaviors are governed by the laws and rules that we are expected to follow.

Concepts
Law
Rule
Attitude
Behavior

Illustrative Activity
Ask students to write a description of everything they did since they awakened in the morning until the beginning of this class. After they have written the description of their actions, ask the students to indicate the specific rules and laws that influenced their actions thus far during the day. Afterwards have students share the descriptions with classmates in small groups and add other laws or rules they may have encountered thus far during the day. Then have the students discuss why they believe these laws and rules were enacted. To what extent should any laws or rules be changed?

Skills Category	Applications
Conceptualization/ Comprehension	Recalling their actions/behaviors from the time they awakened this morning until the present. Sequencing these behavior/actions in chronological order. Comparing laws and rules.
Causality	Determining why these laws/rules were enacted. Examining the consequences of these laws/rules on their own behaviors.
Evaluation/Validity of explanation	Speculating on possible results if these laws/rules were not in existence. Exploring possible revisions in existing laws/rules and the likely impact of such changes on their own lives.
Creative extension	Assume you are to be one of fifteen settlers in a new space station that will be placed in orbit by a rocket launch in the coming days. It is expected that you will be on the space station a minimum of one year. What kind of laws/rules are necessary for the space station settlers to put into place so there can be some semblance of law and order for the community occupying the space station? How will these decisions be made?

Figure 10.12 Multicultural Education

Topic Question
How Do Conflicting Values Create Tensions between Various Social, Ethnic, Cultural, and Other Minority Groups Including Women?

Content
Over the years Native Americans, the original inhabitants of North America, were forced to sign various treaties with the United States government. Most of these treaties were intended to subdue the Native Americans and give the United States government control of their lives. One ongoing controversy is the issue of fishing rights for Native American populations, which has not been resolved and is reported in the media on a regular basis.

Concepts
Tribal sovereignty
Treaty rights
Traditions
Values
Racism
Assimilation
Subjection
Justice
Fairness

Illustrative Activity
Over the years Native Americans and non-Indian populations have been embroiled in conflicts over fishing rights. For example, Native Americans in the Pacific Northwest, Wisconsin, and elsewhere have been involved in conflicts over fishing rights, including spear fishing, the right to fish "out of season," quantities of fish allowed, access to fishing areas, etc. Some of these conflicts involved not only rhetoric but violence as well. Ask students to find historic and recent examples of values in conflict over fishing and treaty rights, land use, etc., and examine the roots of the conflict. How were the conflicts resolved and with what degree of satisfaction to the parties involved? If the conflict has not been resolved, what are some possible solutions to the conflict? To what extent are your solutions likely to be accepted by those involved?

Skills Category	Applications
Conceptualization/ Comprehension	Identifying issues involved in the controversy. Posing research questions. Researching for information on fishing rights controversies.
Causality	Identifying values and perspectives of individuals and groups involved in the issue. Considering alternative perspectives to the issue.
Evaluation/Validity of explanation	Checking for accuracy of arguments presented by various groups. Recognizing bias. Examining accounts of the conflict from multiple perspectives. Considering the effect of the controversy on the participants and the larger community.
Creative extension	Popular novels and movies often address multicultural issues. Read a novel such as Amy Tan's *The Joy Luck Club* or *The Kitchen God's Wife*, Maya Angelou's *I Know Why the Caged Bird Sings,* or Mario Puzo's *The Fortunate Pilgrim* or view a movie such as "Dances With Wolves" or "Schindler's List" and identify the value conflicts addressed in these and other similar books or films. What issues were involved? What solutions were suggested? How might you address these and similar problems based on your experiences? Or, write your own story involving a cultural conflict over values and include a possible solution to the issue addressed in your story.

Selecting Instructional Materials

It is important to have a variety of learning activities and instructional materials. The identification and selection of quality instructional materials are important responsibilities as they greatly influence the teaching and learning processes.

Publishers of textbooks and learning materials attempt to be responsive to the marketplace and many would agree that the quality of published materials is significantly better than fifty years ago. There are critics who charge that authors and publishers are providing less challenging and less interesting instructional materials by "dumbing down" the content. Other critics argue that publishers have omitted important information and have ignored alternative perspectives. In the coming years it will be a good idea for you to keep a sharp eye on emerging changes within the textbook industry. For example, it is now technologically possible for publishers to provide textbooks tailor-made for individual school districts. If a district decides to create a course specifically tailored for its students for which there is no single textbook available, the district may decide to create its own textbook by using a variety of materials with appropriate publisher permissions. When deciding the feasibility of compiling its own textbook, districts need to consider the educational and economic costs and benefits of such a decision.

Most libraries and media centers have copies of *Textbooks in Print* (R. R. Bowker) and other general catalogues, which include a listing of current textbooks on the market. Publishers also advertise new textbooks and other materials in professional journals such as *Social Education, Journal of Geography*, and *The Social Studies*. Larger publishers often send catalogues or announcements of newly published materials to librarians, administrators, curriculum specialists, department chairpersons, and/or individual teachers. In areas where there are statewide or regional social studies conferences, publishers often display samples of their latest instructional materials. Teachers attending these conferences may examine the materials and request that sample copies of materials be sent to their school if they are members of the instructional materials selection committee. For the most part publishers are willing to send sample copies if they believe their materials might be selected for use in the local district. Teachers are cautioned not to abuse the opportunity to obtain sample materials by requesting those that are unlikely to get serious consideration or are too costly for purchase.

Historically social studies teachers (as well as those who teach in other content areas) have relied heavily on textbooks for information. This reliance on textbooks is reasonable given that textbooks are written by knowledgeable authors, are adopted by the district, and because access to newer information is not always readily available. Many social studies teachers have tended to teach as they were taught, hence a heavy reliance on textbooks.

Over the years the quality of textbooks has improved in terms of content currency, readability, use of photographs and other graphics, inclusion of women and minorities, and so forth. Yet no single textbook can provide for meaningful learning to all students. As a teacher you are encouraged to go beyond the textbook and incorporate the use of media, technology, and community resources into your lessons. The use of such resources, along with a knowledgeable and enthusiastic teacher, can help make learning a joy. What should be more exciting than learning about people and their activities over time in various settings?

On the other hand, textbooks can provide students with baseline information from which you the teacher can develop interesting learning activities. It is important that students learn how to use a textbook to glean information: specifically, how to use the table of contents, glossary, gazetteer, and index, and how to skim for key ideas and scan for specific information. In addition, students need to have ample opportunities to practice reading and interpreting photographs, maps, charts, and graphs. All in all the textbook should be viewed as one reference tool in the teaching and learning process.

Selecting appropriate instructional materials is an important responsibility for all teachers. Social studies teachers face special challenges in selecting instructional materials in that many social studies topics are value-laden and controversial by nature, and the materials often present a particular ideology or viewpoint.

Teachers are urged not to rely solely on publisher advertisements as publishers are in business to sell instructional materials and to make a profit. We strongly recommend that all new materials be evaluated by personal review, reading outside reviews, and/or field testing the materials before purchase to determine whether they are appropriate for the students and teachers of the school. Student opinion concerning textbooks is often helpful in determining the value and usefulness of the materials from a learner's perspective. Since textbooks and other instructional materials are expensive and most likely to be used unaltered for several years, it is important to select the best current materials available on the market. Sometimes teachers hear about new materials by word of mouth; this method of review has both pluses and minuses. On the positive side, teachers may have the opportunity to ask a different set of questions of a colleague using the materials than they would ask of a publisher's representative. On the negative side, sometimes teachers do not like to admit that their decision to select a particular instructional resource was a mistake.

At present, twenty-two states have state textbook adoption and instructional materials selection policies for choosing elementary, middle school, and/or high school textbooks or other instructional materials. For example, a state may select one textbook title for use by all students enrolled in United States history courses in that state. Other states may identify three to five textbook titles from which local districts may choose for use in that district. Still other states have no formal state guidelines and rely on local districts to select instructional materials which meet the needs of their students. Some districts or individual teachers may decide to develop their own instructional materials. In some districts these materials must be approved in advance by the local school board. Sometimes this responsibility may be delegated to the district administration.

Assuming that teachers have a voice in selecting instructional materials, we strongly encourage teachers to become active participants in the process and not leave this responsibility to others. Often a textbook/materials selection committee is established to review existing materials and preview new materials that have been requested from various textbook publishers. These new materials are judged against preestablished criteria. (See Appendix B for an example of a textbook/materials selection checklist.) The committee then forwards its recommendations to the administration for school board approval.

Responding to Challenges to Particular Instructional Materials

Periodically and with increasing frequency community members are questioning and challenging the use of certain instructional materials used in the local schools. Such materials are usually challenged on the basis of using language offensive to the challenger, dealing with controversial topics, or presenting ideologies contrary to the challenger's personal beliefs. Sometimes the works of individual authors are also questioned. Most districts take these challenges seriously and attempt to come to an agreement or mutual understanding acceptable to all involved.

For the most part districts have school board policies and procedures for responding to such challenges. These policies most likely include the criteria for selecting instructional materials such as recognition of the socioeconomic background, maturity, and intellectual levels of the students. Also these criteria often encourage diversity of views and interests, which will enable young people to develop knowledge and skills to make intelligent decisions in their daily lives.

Most often school districts have adopted a standard form to be completed by those challenging the use of particular instructional materials. These forms typically start by asking for information about the complainant (name, address, telephone, occupation) and bibliographic information (title, author, publisher, date, pages, frames). Then questions are included that enable district teachers and administrators to respond to specific points of concern rather than broad, emotion-laden charges, such as obscene language, racism, secular humanism, and the like. The following are examples of questions that could be asked:

- Have you read (viewed) the materials in their entirety?
- What is your specific objection to the material(s)? (Cite specific pages, passages, graphics, etc.)
- What is the author's main idea?

- Why do you think this material has been selected for inclusion in the curriculum or in the library?
- How is this material likely to be viewed by those using it?
- Are there students at other grade levels or in different courses who could use the material(s)?
- What reviews, if any, have you read related to this material?
- What actions and responses would you like the district to take concerning the material(s)?

Many times completing such a form will require a person to think through his or her complaint. If the parties involved are not able to reach an agreement following established procedures, then court cases may be initiated concerning the appropriateness and use of the challenged materials. Such actions are costly and time consuming for all involved. Court decisions concerning the further use of challenged materials are rather mixed. Some court decisions recognize the responsibility of school officials to select appropriate instructional materials while other courts have ruled in favor of community values. It will be useful to become aware of censorship issues related to teaching social studies.

Going Beyond the Textbook

Research indicates that approximately 90 percent of social studies instruction is directly from the textbook. This is unfortunate for at least two reasons: 1) the textbook offers limited information, most often from a single perspective, and 2) there are a variety of teaching and learning activities that extend beyond the textbook. Securing additional instructional materials will involve some costs such as teacher creativity, energy, and time; may require the purchase of supplies and/or materials; and may include the need to secure finances for field trips, and the like.

For example, teachers may set up model deliberative bodies, such as legislatures, United Nations, school boards, and other similar groups to discuss or debate selected current topics. To prepare adequately for their roles, the students will need to extend themselves beyond the textbook. Or, students may volunteer to work for a political party or group in a forthcoming election; engage in computer simulations; edit newspapers reflecting a particular historic time period or culture; create political cartoons or illustrations; develop media presentations; and so forth. The kinds of learning activities that can be developed by creative and imaginative teachers are unlimited. Such lessons have great benefits for both students and teachers. We strongly encourage teachers to create lessons that challenge students, extend beyond the school into the community, and require the use of several sources for information.

CHAPTER 10 Promoting Active Social Studies Learning   287

If teachers use media (videos, recordings, and music), they should take care to ensure that these learning tools fit the lesson and that they include meaningful pre-viewing and post-viewing learning activities in the planning. Otherwise the use of media may not reach its full educational potential. Since viewing is often a neutral rather than active process, students tend to disengage during this type of presentation. Many districts have media centers that have catalogs, instructional materials, and a variety of media resources. We encourage you to become familiar with these valuable resources and work closely with media specialists.

The use of daily newspapers and weekly news publications offers social studies classes additional possibilities to extend beyond the textbook. Ideally teachers will integrate current events topics into the existing program on a regular basis rather than relegating them to the first five or ten minutes of the class period or reserved for Friday after the weekly quiz. If social studies teachers teach primarily from the textbook and use the same type of learning activities on a regular basis, is it any wonder that students usually indicate that social studies is one of their least favorite classes? We encourage teachers to develop the notion that events in the present are rooted in history and do have meaning for today. Abstract concepts can be better understood by students if they can relate them to events of today. For example, when studying the concept of Native American treaty rights, students could examine the fishing rights controversies of today and consider Andrew Jackson's attitude toward the Cherokees. Quality social studies programs require solid content, a variety of teaching and learning activities, and an enthusiastic teacher.

Community Resources

Communities of all sizes have a variety of resources that are valuable in teaching social studies. It is useful to view the community as a social science laboratory to study important phenomena, events, and people that have an impact on the students' daily lives. Since the community is ever-changing, students can study these changes over time as they happen. The students can also consider the previous conditions leading to change and the subsequent results of change. Utilizing community resources in social studies enables students to develop a variety of skills, concepts, and attitudes. Students can also gain perspectives on their own lives by examining political, economic, and social institutions in their own community. There are many community resources to use.

One of the most valuable resources any community has to offer is its residents. Many community members would welcome an invitation to speak with students about a range of topics or issues. For example, local government officials or business leaders are often eager to talk with students. Parents and other family members can share their personal experiences and cultural heritage. Speakers from social agencies can discuss current issues with students; for example, substance and alcohol abuse, juvenile justice and crime, and changing family patterns.

Guidelines for Using Outside Speakers

Periodically social studies teachers will want to invite outside speakers to address their classes. If the speakers and students are prepared, this practice is useful for several reasons.

- It allows students to hear other perspectives about a topic.
- Students have the chance to learn from someone other than the teacher.
- It brings community persons to the school.
- Guest presenters often have a wealth of useful and interesting information to share with students.
- Students have the opportunity to develop and use a range of communication skills, including listening, posing questions, taking notes, considering other viewpoints, and writing thank you letters to the speaker.

Most school districts have policies and procedures concerning the use of outside speakers. They may include notifying the appropriate school administrators and parents as to the speaker and the topic to be presented in class. Notifying parents well in advance of the scheduled presentation gives them time to contact the teacher and the opportunity to request that their daughter or son not hear the speaker. If this is the case, then the teacher will need to plan an alternative learning activity for those students and not penalize the students for this parental decision.

Sometimes speakers are selected to present a particular viewpoint, such as the philosophy of a particular political party. In this case it is recommended that representatives from other political parties be invited to present their perspectives. For the most part students should be able to listen to and discuss a variety of views, but at the same time they should have the opportunity for a balance of perspectives.

If a speaker is likely to present a controversial message then it is sometimes useful to record the presentation with the speakers' permission. Then a record of the presentation will be available if challenged or for use with other sections of the course if the presenter can speak only to one class. At times it may be advisable to invite an administrator to attend the presentation if controversy over the content is likely.

When discussing many social studies topics, particularly controversial issues, students will ask teachers, "What do you think?" How to respond to this question is not always easy. Most teachers want students to develop independent thinking skills based on research evidence and may decide not to offer students their personal opinions, which might unduly influence student thinking during class discussions. Students often tend to give greater weight to their teacher's opinion than others because the teacher is an authority figure, assigns grades, writes recommendations for college admission, scholarships, jobs, and so forth.

On the other hand, if a teacher offers a personal opinion, we recommend the teacher clearly indicate that the opinion is but one view of the topic under discussion. The teacher should also explain the thinking processes that led him or her to that opinion. It is also useful to let the students know the opinion is subject to modification as new information comes to light. If the teacher alters her or his opinion we recommend that the teacher share the reasons for changing that opinion. It is important that the teacher model the behaviors expected of students.

Thoughtful social studies teachers may use field trips to local museums or businesses; interview local citizens or visitors to the community; develop service-oriented projects with community organizations such as senior citizen groups; engage in community surveys to determine, for example, the availability of cultural events, housing conditions, or government services; write a local history using oral history techniques complete with photographs and sketches; use oral history techniques to interview local people about their experiences in the Great Depression, Vietnam War, Civil Rights movements, and the like; or participate in an internship program with a community, governmental, business, or service organization.

Information students gather from such activities will need to be organized in logical ways to have meaning and relevance to their lives. For example, students can keep a diary of their experiences and at the completion of the activity reflect on the meaning of the experiences to them personally. Before engaging in these activities teachers must work with students to show them how to record the data they gather, interpret the data, and report their findings to the class. For example, if students (in groups or as individuals) are looking at changing architectural patterns in their city over time, they could take pictures of houses and buildings (churches, schools, museums, libraries) from various time periods and examine their ages, usages, types of architecture, or locations, recording their data on a form that the student had previously constructed.

Students may want to attach photographs or sketches of the buildings examined. In their reports (oral or written), students should indicate how they obtained their information and conclusions about the importance or impact these buildings have had on the community. It is important to have both pre-planning and follow-up activities to give meaning to any learning experience.

Just as students learn citizenship and decision-making skills in the community, they can also learn similar skills through a variety of school-related cocurricular activities. The cocurricular activities described in the following pages are cited as illustrative examples.

■ ■ ■ ■ ■ ■ ■ Buildings in Our City

Type of Data	Building No. 1	Building No. 2	Building No. 3	Etc.
Name of Building (if it has one)				
Type of Building				
Location				
When Built (approximate time period)				
Architectural Style				
Historical Significance				
Use of Building 50 Years Ago				
Use of Building Today				
Etc.				

Cocurricular Activities Related to Social Studies Content

Schools provide a variety of cocurricular activities for students ranging from honor associations such as the National Honor Society, to service organizations such as the Junior Red Cross, to special-interest clubs such as stamp collecting. Social studies content lends itself to a number of cocurricular activities. In some schools these programs may be included within specific social studies courses while in other schools these activities take place during in-school activity periods or outside the regular school day. The activities we describe below illustrate possible social studies-oriented cocurricular programs. Some programs function primarily during the school year, while others are mainly summer activities. Both types have a place in the curriculum and provide valuable learning and social opportunities for students. Many students report they have gained much personal enjoyment and self-satisfaction through such participation.

School Year Programs

Model United Nations High school Model United Nations (MUN) activities have been in existence for nearly fifty years. MUN participants represent the foreign policy of the country that has been assigned to them. For example, if a school has been asked to represent Austria, then students will seek to find out as much as possible about Austria as a nation, its history, its foreign and domestic policies, its economic system, and so forth. Those organizing the MUN conference select several topics for discussion that reflect issues recently discussed in the United Nations. In the past topics such as the Middle East, the law of the seas, peaceful uses of outer space, resettlement of refugees, and environmental issues have been on the agenda of many MUN conferences. Most often these meetings simulate the deliberations of the United Nations General Assembly and Security Council, although more elaborate MUN conferences may include topics assigned to the Economic and Social Council or other related United Nations agencies.

For many years the University of California at Berkeley has hosted several hundred high school students primarily from northern and central California for a two-and-a-half- to three-day conference. Georgetown University (School of Foreign Service) in Washington, D.C., hosts an invitational MUN with students coming from schools throughout the United States and some foreign countries. Other states also have various MUN activities that are often hosted by a university and held on campus. Some high schools also have less elaborate (and less costly) conferences for students coming from nearby schools. At these meetings schools may decide to send several delegations with each representing a different nation.

Students who participate in such activities learn not only about the United Nations and the nation they represent, but also about research and communication. In addition they learn social skills needed to interact with students from other schools, including the need to compromise and views from other perspectives; and they gain experiences staying in hotels, meeting new people, traveling to other cities in their home states or to Washington. For information about MUN you should contact the social studies specialist at the state education agency or the local or state world affairs council. The UNA-USA, 485 Fifth Avenue, Second Floor, New York, NY 10017, may have information about some MUN conferences.

Close-Up Activities The Close-Up Foundation sponsors a week-long conference in Washington for students and teachers to grapple with policy issues facing our country. Participants also have the opportunity to meet with and question decision makers who participate in the political process in our nation's capital. They also have opportunities to interact with students from other states and gain new perspectives about the issues being considered.

The Foundation also sponsors meetings that bring high school students together on a statewide basis for one or two days to discuss a wide variety of political, economic, and social policy issues that have important consequences for the state and nation. Recent topics for discussion included school prayer, aid to various nations, abortion rights, foreign trade imbalances, military spending, and environmental protection issues. These programs enable students to gain a practical knowledge of public policy issues that affect their lives and learn how individual and collective efforts influence public policy.

In some states, the state social studies council helps to promote and sponsor Close-Up groups in that state. In Wisconsin, for example, more than 300 students meet the day before the annual state social studies conference, which provides an excellent opportunity for social studies teachers and others to witness students actively involved in citizenship participation. Many of the student-proposed solutions are creative and deserve serious consideration.

The offices of the Close-Up Foundation are located at 49 Canal Center Plaza, Alexandria, VA 22314.

Mock Trial Competitions Law-related education (LRE) programs have received greater attention in recent years. For instance, mock trial competitions have been praised since many schools across the United States have participated in these programs. For the most part schools select five to seven students who are given a legal case to study. They are to prepare both defense and prosecution arguments based on the facts of the case and their knowledge of the legal system and the Constitution. The judges for the competition are lawyers, judges, and legal scholars.

Competitions are provided at the local, regional, and state levels. Winners of the state competitions advance to the national level, where they compete against other state-winning teams. Participants (advisors and parents as well) become actively involved in the process and find the experience to be intellectually stimulating. The opportunity to interact with peers with similar interests and backgrounds is a benefit from mock trial competitions and other similar social studies cocurricular activities.

This competition is sponsored by the American Bar Association. For information you should contact your local or state bar association office.

Stock Market Game The Stock Market Game, developed by the Securities Industry Association in cooperation with the National Council on Economic Education, provides students with an opportunity to learn basic economic concepts and principles related to the securities industry. Students, in teams or as individuals, who participate in the game are given $100,000 to invest in stocks over an eight- to ten-week period during either the fall or the spring semester. While playing the game students learn valuable skills and information about the marketplace, business, capital, securities, investments, and savings. Over this time, the students research and analyze the market, buy and sell stocks, study supply and demand, examine resource allocation, and make decisions concerning their investments. At the end of the game, winning teams receive recognition awards and are honored at a banquet with representatives from local stock broker companies and economic educators in attendance.

At present, middle and high school students in more than forty states participate in this learning activity each semester. Teacher staff development opportunities are offered to help teachers prepare for this game. For additional information concerning the Stock Market Game, contact the state council on economic education or the center for economic education on your campus. The address of the National Council for Economic Education is 1140 Avenue of the Americas, New York, NY 10036. The NCEE has a catalog of publications related to economic education available to teachers.

National Geography Bee For students in grades 4–8, the National Geographic Society conducts an annual Geography Bee. The competition is open to all schools that register. In January the students are given an objective test of their knowledge of geography. The 100 students in each state who scored highest on the written test then meet at a central location in each state during March or April for several rounds of oral questions. The state winner then goes to Washington, D.C., (along with his or her teacher) to be a contestant in the National Geography Bee. The national winner and runners up are awarded scholarships and other prizes. In recent years the national finals have been televised. The National Geographic Society, 17th and M Streets, N. W., Washington, D.C. 20036, can provide the name and address of the state coordinator for the statewide Geography Bee. NGS also has a catalog of its publications available for helping young people learn geography.

Summer Programs

High school programs in the summer are becoming more readily available for interested students. For example, in several states the business community, in cooperation with local chambers of commerce and schools, organizes a week-long program for students interested in the world of business. The Business World programs usually include one or two students per school who meet on a college campus for a week to learn more about fundamentals of the business world. For the most part the speakers are business leaders who offer perspectives on business. Sometimes representatives of other groups such as government and labor are also invited speakers. While attending Business World, students organize a business, create and sell a product or service, engage in marketing, and so forth. Students interact with a variety of people such as business leaders, students from other schools, teachers, and professors. They have an opportunity to apply economic concepts and principles in their simulated business ventures.

Parallel to the student activities, most Business World programs have sessions designed for teachers, who are invited to accompany their students. The teacher-oriented sessions provide current information about economic issues and the business climate in their state and nation, as well as resources for use in their classes the following academic year. Most often chambers of commerce pay the expenses of both students and teachers at the Business World conference.

Recently the National Endowment for the Humanities has established a number of summer programs for high school students on topics related to history and the humanities. Participants are selected on the basis of application and through nomination. Various groups such as American Field Service and Youth For Understanding offer international living and travel experiences for high school students. Teachers who have students interested in such programs can usually secure information from guidance counselors or administrators, or by contacting the sponsoring organization directly. Information is often published in professional journals and newspapers such as *Social Education* or *Education Week*.

SUMMARY

Social studies teachers face many challenges in promoting active learning and must make decisions how to best meet these challenges. An organizational model for effective learning activities has been suggested that addresses topic questions, content, concepts, skills, and applications. Selecting quality materials is an important responsibility in preparing for instruction. The classroom and school environments shape teacher, student, and parent expectations concerning the teaching and learning of social studies.

CHAPTER 10 Promoting Active Social Studies Learning

Since many topics in social studies lend themselves to controversy and may raise concerns within the community, social studies teachers must be sensitive to community values and expectations, but at the same time be prepared to respond to controversy. Many schools and districts have policies and guidelines that support teacher and student academic freedom. They also have statements concerning challenged instructional materials and the use of outside speakers.

Cocurricular activities are an integral part of the school experience of students, which enable them to learn new skills, develop interests, and share their talents. Community-based service opportunities are numerous and help young learners develop citizenship skills.

Discussion Questions

1. Reexamine the illustrative learning activities described in this chapter and discuss their effectiveness in stimulating active student learning. What activities might you create to promote active learning?
2. How can you make the local community a "social science laboratory"? How might the local community respond to these initiatives? What arrangements, in advance, must you make for activities that may take students away from the school building and require more than a single class period?
3. How can cocurricular activities enhance learning opportunities beyond the social studies classroom?

Student Learning Activities

1. If you are in a state that has a statewide textbook adoption policy, contact the state education agency to secure a copy of the criteria to be used in selecting or rejecting textbooks. Do these criteria apply to supplemental materials, software, and media? What information is provided to textbook publishers who wish to submit instructional materials for review and consideration? How are decisions concerning textbook selection actually made? Who is involved in the process?
2. Contact several experienced middle school or high school social studies teachers and ask them what they deem most important when selecting textbooks and other instructional materials? Are there other criteria you would consider when selecting instructional materials? If so, what are they? If not, why are the ones suggested sufficient?
3. Examine a state or district curriculum guide for some ideas about the content, concepts, and skills to be taught in social studies at grades 6–12. Using the guide select a topic of particular interest to you. Next

refer to the model suggested in the chapter and develop an illustrative learning activity. Share your learning activity with classmates and seek their opinions about the potential value of the activity for students.

4. Contact the director of student activities in a nearby school and find out what cocurricular activities are available that have some linkages to the social studies curriculum. What differences, if any, are there in cocurricular activities in middle schools and in high schools?

APPENDIX A

Data Cards for Presidency Activity

Card 1

Data about **Franklin D. Roosevelt,** as of **1945.** The American people elected Roosevelt president four times. Because of his New Deal programs designed to combat the severe financial depression of the 1930s and his leadership during World War II, many historians have classified him as one of the most effective chief executives ever to hold the office. Some of Roosevelt's critics, however, argue that he misused the power of the presidency by exerting extensive political pressure on Congress in order to secure passage of the New Deal legislation. He served as president from 1933 until his death in 1945. An attack of polio in the early 1920s left Roosevelt's legs partially paralyzed for the remainder of his life.

Card 2

Data about **Benedict Arnold**, as of **1801**. Before he joined the British in their attempt to defeat the rebels during the American Revolution, Arnold had served George Washington with distinction during military campaigns from 1776 to 1779. Distressed with financial worries and a feeling of not receiving adequate recognition from the Continental Congress for his services, he abandoned the American cause and became one of the most well-known traitors in American history.

Card 3

Data about **Martin Luther King, Jr.**, as of **1968.** Before he was assassinated in 1968, the Reverend Martin Luther King, Jr., had become one of the most active champions of the nonviolent civil rights movement. Beginning with his successful boycott of segregated city buses in Birmingham, Alabama, King rose to become leader of the Southern Christian Leadership Conference—one of the most effective organizations to lobby for federal civil rights legislation during the 1960s.

Card 4

Data about **Andrew Jackson**, as of **1829**. According to most historians of American life, Jackson was one of our most forceful chief executives. As president, Jackson asserted the supremacy of the federal government when South Carolina attempted to nullify federal tariff laws. His opposition to any form of monopoly was evident in his veto of legislation to recharter the powerful and half-public Bank of the United States.

Card 5

Data about **Alexander Hamilton**, as of **1804**. Until his death in a duel with Aaron Burr, he had served his country as an advisor to George Washington. His arguments for adoption of the federal Constitution were instrumental in its final approval. His financial genius helped to establish the young United States on a firm financial footing during its early years.

Card 6

Data about **Eleanor Roosevelt**, as of **1949**. Eleanor Roosevelt, wife of Franklin D. Roosevelt, became one of our country's most active champions of the poor, minority groups, women's labor unions, and civil rights. As Franklin Roosevelt's wife, she constantly served as an unofficial advisor for many of his New Deal domestic policies. After her husband's death in 1945, Mrs. Roosevelt was appointed a United States delegate to the United Nations.

Card 7

Data about **George C. Wallace**, as of **1974**. Until an attempt on his life crippled him in 1972, George Wallace had been an active and outspoken proponent of the cause of states' rights. This was especially evident when he began his first term as governor of Alabama, ran as a presidential candidate for the American Party in 1968, and campaigned as a Democratic candidate for the presidency in 1972. Since the attempt on his life, Wallace has been paralyzed from the waist down.

Card 8

Data about **Abraham Lincoln**, as of **1865**. With the exception of George Washington and Franklin D. Roosevelt, probably no other president ever entered office facing such immense problems as did Abraham Lincoln. Historians of

Lincoln's life generally agree that he did as much as any chief executive could have to lead the Union to victory in the Civil War and attempt to heal the wounds of that conflict for both the North and the South. On numerous occasions before and during his presidency, Lincoln suffered periods of severe mental depression. His untimely assassination occurred in 1865.

Card 9

Data for **Jesse Jackson,** as of **1988**. Jackson established himself as the preeminent black politician in the United States in the 1980s. He founded People United to Serve Humanity (PUSH), an organization to gain economic power for African-Americans, and persuaded large corporations that relied on African-American consumers to hire and promote more African-Americans. He sought to inspire a "rainbow coalition" to achieve political and economic goals. During the 1988 presidential primaries Jackson received nearly 7 million votes, carried the Democratic vote in several major cities, and won the Democratic primary in several states.

Card 10

Data for **Geraldine Anne Ferraro,** as of **1984.** Geraldine A. Ferraro was the first woman to win the nomination for vice-president from a major political party. She was one of two women who graduated in her Fordham Law School class. She was elected to the United States House of Representatives from a conservative ethnic district in Queens (New York), was a latecomer to the feminist movement, and became a major sponsor for legislation concerning economic equity for women. Heavy lobbying by Speaker of the House Thomas P. "Tip" O'Neill persuaded Walter Mondale to select Ferraro as the Democratic Party's vice-presidential candidate in 1984.

Card 11

Data about **César E. Chávez,** as of **1976.** César Chávez was born on a farm near Yuma, Arizona. At the age of 10 he became a migrant worker in Arizona and California when his parents lost their farm. He organized grape pickers in 1962 and his union merged with another union to form the United Farm Workers Organizing Committee (1966). He led a nationwide boycott of California table grapes and later a nationwide boycott of lettuce produced by nonunion growers. Personally committed to nonviolence, he told his followers, "The truest act of courage . . . is to sacrifice ourselves for others in a totally nonviolent struggle for justice."

Card 12

Data about **Sacajawea (Sacagawa)** as of **1812**. There is confusion about the precise date of her birth (probably in Idaho) and death (1784–1884?). Only woman to accompany the Lewis and Clark Expedition (1804–1805) as guide. Interpreter and trader, she taught men on expedition how to find edible roots and medicinal herbs. She made buckskins and moccasins. There are more monuments to her than any other American woman. She had been previously held captive in North Dakota. Her presence probably spared the expedition from hostilities with other Indian tribes as she would not have been with a war party.

APPENDIX B

Sample Textbook/Instructional Materials Evaluation Form

Title: _____

Author(s): _____

Publisher: _____

Date of Publication:_____ Edition: _____ Cost: _____

Types of Supplemental Materials to Accompany Textbook:

1. Teacher's guide	yes _____	no _____
2. Student workbook	yes _____	no _____
3. Student texts	yes _____	no _____
4. Visuals	yes _____	no _____
5. Computer programs	yes _____	no _____
6. Teacher staff development available	yes _____	no _____
Do the authors appear to be qualified?	yes _____	no _____
Was the material field-tested by teachers in classroom settings?	yes _____	no _____

Content	Low				High

To what extent

1. is the textbook's approach compatible with district or teacher philosophy?	1	2	3	4	5
2. do the instructional objectives fit district and school curriculum?	1	2	3	4	5
3. do the suggested scope and sequence match district needs?	1	2	3	4	5
4. are important social studies content, concepts, and skills included?	1	2	3	4	5
5. are the important social concepts and content presented in sufficient detail to assure a depth of understanding?	1	2	3	4	5
6. are materials current, accurate, and free from bias?	1	2	3	4	5
7. do materials include the contributions of minorities including women, racial, ethnic, and religious groups, older persons, and special needs persons?	1	2	3	4	5
8. do materials omit important content and concepts?	1	2	3	4	5
9. do materials reflect a point of time?	1	2	3	4	5

Comments:

Instructional Characteristics	Low				High

To what extent

1. is the material interesting to students?	1	2	3	4	5

2. is the material well written? 1 2 3 4 5

3. are materials suitable for the intellectual and maturity level of the students? 1 2 3 4 5

4. do end of section and chapter activities include questions that require several levels of thinking? 1 2 3 4 5

5. do student test questions adequately reflect the emphasis of the chapter and my objectives? 1 2 3 4 5

6. do materials allow for a variety of teaching and learning styles? 1 2 3 4 5

7. do materials encourage active learning? 1 2 3 4 5

8. is content relevant and suitable for the grade level? 1 2 3 4 5

9. are chapter and assignment lengths suitable for the grade level? 1 2 3 4 5

10. are materials comprehensible to the students? 1 2 3 4 5

11. are students likely to have the prerequisite skills and prior knowledge to use the materials effectively? 1 2 3 4 5

12. do graphics enhance the content? 1 2 3 4 5

13. do materials include maps, glossaries, and other social indicator data? 1 2 3 4 5

14. is the length of the book appropriate for the content and grade level? 1 2 3 4 5

Comments:

Physical Characteristics	Low				High

To what extent

1. are materials visually appealing (color, spacing, placement of graphics, etc.)?   1   2   3   4   5

2. are materials considered to be durable and lasting (binding, spine, etc.)?   1   2   3   4   5

3. do media materials have quality sound coordination with visuals?   1   2   3   4   5

4. are materials easy to store when not in use?   1   2   3   4   5

5. is special training needed to use the materials?   1   2   3   4   5

6. are materials printed on quality paper?   1   2   3   4   5

7. is the overall appearance of the material attractive and appropriate for the content and grade level?   1   2   3   4   5

Comments:

Overall Impressions:

Strengths:

Weaknesses:

Recommendation:

Name of evaluator _____

Date of evaluation _____

References

Hobin, M. 1974. "Clarifying What Is Important." In A. O. Kownslar (Ed.), *Teaching American History: The Quest for Relevancy.* 44th Yearbook. Washington, DC: National Council for the Social Studies.

Laughlin, M. A. and Beining, T. J. 1987. "Participating in the Global Economy." *The Senior Economist,* Vol. 3, No. 1, Fall. 13–14.

Textbooks in Print. 1993–94. New York: R. R. Bowker. (Note: This is an annual publication.)

Wisconsin Department of Natural Resources. 1988. *Recycling Study Guide.* Madison: Wisconsin Department of Natural Resources. 11.

Additional Readings

Allen, R. F. 1993. "Special Section on the Close Up Foundation." *The Social Studies,* Vol. 84, No. 5, September/October. 188–223.

Banks, J. A. 1991. *Teaching Strategies for Ethnic Studies* (5th ed.). Boston: Allyn and Bacon.

Center for Civic Education. 1991. *Civitas: A Framework for Civic Education.* Calabasas, CA: Center for Civic Education.

Downey, M. T. (Ed.). 1985. *History in the Schools.* Bulletin No. 74. Washington, DC: National Council for the Social Studies.

Fazio, B. 1992. "Students as Historians—Writing Their School's History." *The Social Studies,* Vol. 83, No. 2, March/April. 64–67.

Gall, M. D. 1981. *Handbook for Evaluating and Selecting Curriculum Materials.* Boston: Allyn and Bacon.

Joint Committee on Geographic Education. 1984. *Guidelines for Geographic Education: Elementary and Secondary Schools.* Washington, DC: American Association of Geographers and National Council for Geographic Education.

Levine, M. and Trachtman, R. (Eds). 1988. *American Business and the Public School: Case Studies of Corporate Involvement in Public Education.* New York: Teachers College Press.

Morton, J. S., Buckles, S. G., Miller, S. L., Nelson, D. M., and Prehn, E. C. 1985. *Master Curriculum Guide in Economics: Teaching Strategies: High School Economics Course.* New York: Joint Council on Economic Education.

Natoli, S. J. (Ed.). 1988. *Strengthening Geography in the Social Studies.* Bulletin No. 81. Washington, DC: National Council for the Social Studies.

Nelson, J. L. and Michaelis, J. U. 1980. *Secondary Social Studies: Instruction, Curriculum, Evaluation.* Englewood Cliffs, NJ: Prentice-Hall.

Starr, J. M. 1989. "Teaching the Vietnam War: Looking behind the Controversies." *International Journal of Social Education,* Vol. 4, No. 1, Spring. 86–93.

Wisconsin Department of Public Instruction. 1985. *A Guide to Curriculum Planning in Environmental Education.* Madison: Department of Public Instruction.

Wisconsin Department of Public Instruction. 1986. *A Guide to Curriculum Planning in Social Studies.* Madison: Department of Public Instruction.

Wisconsin Department of Public Instruction. 1993. *A Guide to Curriculum Planning in Global Studies.* Madison: Department of Public Instruction.

One must not always think so much about what one should do, but, rather what one should be. Our works do not ennoble us; but we must ennoble our work.

      Meister Eckhart

CHAPTER 11

Helping Students Become Strategic Learners*

> **FOCUS QUESTIONS**
>
> - What can social studies teachers do to help students learn and think more effectively?
> - Why is it important for social studies teachers to ask questions?
> - How can questions be used to improve and assess learning?
> - What learning strategies can students be expected to apply independently during social studies?
> - What guidelines should teachers follow when teaching learning strategies to students?

---

*This chapter was written by Kathryn A. Koch, president of Celebrate Kids, based in Fort Worth, Texas.

OVERVIEW

Social studies teachers need to help students become more effective learners and thinkers. Therefore, teachers need strategies to guide students in learning to observe, read, listen, study, and write. Guidelines teachers can follow to increase student learning and thinking are presented in this chapter. Suggestions are also made to teach students where they can find information, and what they can think about, think for, and think with.

Teachers and students ask many questions during social studies classes. With the right timing and type of questions and with appropriate responses to correct and incorrect answers, teachers can help clarify and extend student thinking. Students will more successfully and independently learn social studies content when they are taught strategies to increase their study skills.

Definitions of Intelligence, Thinking, Reading, Listening, and Studying

A theory of multiple intelligences has been proposed by Gardner (1983). He believes that a person can be gifted in any one of these seven largely unrelated types of intelligence: linguistic, logical/mathematical, visual/spatial, musical, bodily-kinesthetic, knowledge of self, and understanding of others.

Sternberg's (1985) model of intelligence has three components. Individuals can have strengths in one, two, or all three. One component is analytical intelligence and consists of the mental processes the individual uses. The second component involves coping with new experiences, labeled as creativity in some of Sternberg's work. He believes intelligent behavior in this component is marked by two characteristics: the ability to deal effectively with novel situations and the ability to become efficient and automatic in thinking and problem solving. Practical intelligence is the third component. This includes personal development, social development, work habits, and the importance of choosing an appropriate environment for the task, adapting to that environment, or reshaping it if necessary.

Intelligence also has three components as defined by Perkins (1986). These are the neurological efficiency of the brain, the learning strategies a person uses, and the person's knowledge base. As in the other models, a person can have strengths in one, two, or all three components. And, because these vary with topics being discussed, intelligence varies.

Thinking skills, clearly related to intelligence as defined above, are the cognitive operations students use. Marzano et al. (1988) have identified thinking skills as focusing, information gathering, remembering, organizing, analyzing, generating, integrating, and evaluating. Many would use these categories when selecting learning strategies (namely, study skills) for students to learn and use. There is very little difference between thinking skills and learning skills.

Much of the information necessary for learning and thinking comes from reading and listening. A popular and accurate view of reading is referred to as strategic reading. This can be extended to include listening and studying and can be defined in terms of what the learners do. Strategic readers, listeners, and studiers *analyze* their tasks and *plan* to be successful by thinking about the purposes, setting the best goals, and choosing the best learning strategies. They *monitor* and *direct* their own comprehension and retention. In other words, they think *while* they read, listen, and study and change their goals and strategies, as necessary, so they will be able to understand, remember, and use the information. Strategic learners are in control because they combine cognitive skill with motivational will.

A strategic reader might think in these ways when silently reading the following sentences about Indian resistance to the English settlers building more colonies in New England.

Text Portion	Student's Thinking
"The growing hatred led in 1675 to King Philip's War.	I wonder who King Philip is.
	I sure hope it tells me.
Metacomet, a proud Wampanoag chief whom the Puritans called King Philip,	O.K. King Philip is a chief whose real name is Metacomet.
	I don't know exactly how to pronounce that but I won't have to read it aloud, so as long as I recognize it when Mr. Hansen uses it, I'm all right. Maybe I should ask how to pronounce the tribe he's in charge of, though. I bet it's either Wam/pa/no/ag or Wam/pa/noag.
made an alliance with the Narragansetts and other Indian tribes" (Todd and Curti 1986, p. 38).	Now what are Narragansetts? Oh! They must be an Indian tribe because it says "other tribes." I'd better read to find out more about that alliance since yesterday Mr. Hansen had us talk about that other one.

Studying and reading are different processes. When studying, learners seek to comprehend *and* remember the material. "Studying is purposeful and deliberate in a way that normal reading is not" (Vaughan and Estes, 1986, p. 254).

It is helpful to categorize study skills by their purposes. Students who learn to apply a number of study skills will have "learned to learn" from their social studies instruction. In other words, they will be strategic learners.

Toward More Effective Learning

The quality of students' learning is very dependent on the expectations and activities of teachers. Those teachers who follow the advice in this section will positively influence the amount, type, and caliber of students' learning.

First, teachers need to "think aloud" about everyday concerns and social studies issues and events. Teachers should often model thinking by solving problems and making decisions verbally instead of thinking mysteriously in their heads, because students should see and hear *how* teachers think. Students need to understand that thinking requires effort and the willingness to keep trying when the first idea is not right. They need to believe that using effort does not indicate less capacity for thinking.

A second guideline is to expect all students to think. It is important for teachers to believe that a student will be able to respond eventually with a quality idea. Students can manipulate teachers into believing they are not capable and, if teachers treat them that way, they may actually become less able. During discussions and on assignments, teachers should ask questions that students believe they can answer. If students believe that most questions are extremely difficult they may develop an "I won't bother thinking" attitude. Teachers also need to avoid statements such as "This is a difficult question but who thinks they might know . . ." Many students will believe the question is not directed toward them and they may not even try to think of an answer.

A third guideline, which we will expand in the next major section, is to give students time to think. They need time to react to new information, recall relevant information from their memories, process the information so they can understand and retain it, and think critically and creatively about it. Students who are not given enough time to go through these stages will soon react with "Why bother starting to think? She won't give me enough time to do well anyway."

Fourth, it is important to involve as many students as possible during class activities. Classes that are dominated by a few vocal students are likely to have only a few active thinkers. Teachers can stop after a portion of a lesson and have all students write down something they have learned or a relevant question to ask another student. (It would be wise to tell them in advance of the lesson that they will be asked to do this.) Another approach is for the teacher to give the students thirty seconds to think of something they have learned. Then the teacher will give the students a minute or two to share their information with a person sitting close by. The teacher can ask for a few volunteers to share their ideas or those of the other students with the class. Although, at first, these methods may not be easy for teachers or students to use, they are worth trying because students will actively process the information, and thus be more involved.

Involvement during discussions is especially important. For a variety of reasons, middle and high school students may not want to raise their hands to volunteer even if they know an answer. Therefore, hand raising can frequently be eliminated. Instead, teachers should decide on whom to call and allow students to pass if they would prefer. After a risk-free environment is established, few students pass and when they do it is usually for legitimate reasons. Consider how thinking by the following students during a class discussion is interfering with their ability and/or willingness to think about the answer to the teacher's question.

> *Katie's thinking*: "I think I know an answer to that question. I don't believe it. I guess it would be safe to volunteer. But wait. Carmen always knows everything and she doesn't have her hand up. If she doesn't know I can't know. I must be wrong. I better not volunteer."
>
> *Carmen's thinking*: "I know that answer. I always get called on, though. I'm sick of giving these kids all the answers. I wish they'd think for themselves. I'm not raising my hand again today."
>
> *Dave's thinking*: "I haven't volunteered in awhile. I'll wait until some of these guys raise their hands. Then I'll raise mine. It will be safe. Mrs. Toft won't call on me anyway. She knows I'll be wrong and that makes her nervous. But at least she'll maybe think I'm trying."
>
> *Steve's thinking*: "I've got an idea. I can answer this one. I hope she calls on me this time. Come on, my hand's up. Are you blind, teacher? Call on me for once. She won't. She's waiting for one of her pets to call on, I bet. Why do I bother?"
>
> *Helen's thinking*: "I'm not going to raise my hand so I don't need to think. And if Mrs. Toft calls on me I'll just tell her I didn't have my hand up. She shouldn't call on me. That wouldn't be fair."
>
> *Betsy's thinking*: "I wish she'd move on already. This is so boring. Wait for four hands. Call on someone. Ask a new question. Wait for four hands. Call on someone. BORING! There's got to be a better way!"

As these examples demonstrate, the use of hand raising may *decrease* honest student involvement and retard quality processing of relevant information. Thinking may increase when hand raising is not used and teachers decide on whom to call, sometimes randomly, and at other times with a plan (Richardson-Koehler, 1987). Students will soon learn they have an equally good chance of being chosen to give an answer or ask a question. When teachers call on students in conjunction with a planned wait time they will find that student attention, confidence, class unity, and learning increase.

It may be effective to go down a row of students, use the diagonal, or call on every third student. The teacher can use the grade book to call on every fourth or fifth student alphabetically and to record who has had an opportunity to participate. A die can be rolled to determine which row will answer a question or that every fourth person will respond. One day, teachers can call on those who are wearing tennis shoes, sweaters, or something green. After carefully explaining their expectations, teachers can call on one student, who then chooses the next student to respond. Also, changing the desk arrangement occasionally from rows to a horseshoe shape and/or to groupings of four to six desks can positively influence involvement. The greater the variety of systems and arrangements, the greater the potential payoff.

Involvement will increase even further when teachers do not comment after each student response. For example, when every third student participates, teachers do not need to comment unless their responses are wrong or confusing. Using fewer teacher judgments, increasing student-to-student interaction, and asking questions that students know are worthwhile will increase the likelihood that a valuable discussion and not an interrogation will take place.

How Can Teachers Teach for Effective Learning and Thinking?

Teachers can increase students' learning and thinking (whether they are reading or listening) by teaching them what they can think about, think for, and think with and where they can find information (Chuska, 1986). It is possible for teachers to explain directly these four ideas and, when they use a number of them in different combinations, they require students to process information at several levels. Students will be able to think and make inferences about things that are explicitly discussed. Teachers can tell students what type of thinking to use in advance of the learning activity. This will enable students to improve their comprehension and retention; be more willing and able to contribute to class discussions; and increase their abilities to determine independently what is most important. Explanations of the four decisions teachers and students can make to increase learning and thinking follow.

First, teachers need to decide what is most important to *think about*. Students benefit from being told in advance of a lesson or assignment what to emphasize in their study. This is especially true early in the course when they are unfamiliar with the textbook and with the teacher's expectations and teaching style. Student thought, comprehension, retention, self-confidence, and participation may all improve when teachers help them to see what "really counts."

These *categories to think about* are relevant in social studies:

Person	Object	Problem	Opinion
People	Quantity	Solution	Examples
Place	Event	Idea	Purpose
Time	Situation	Fact	Source of Information

Table 11.1

*Students can **think for** different reasons using these and other "essay exam verbs":*

agree	defend	give cause and effect	outline	solve
analyze	define		predict	speculate
apply	demonstrate	give an example	prove	state
assess	describe	hypothesize	propose	summarize
capsulize	diagram	identify	react	support
classify	disagree	illustrate	relate	synthesize
comment	discuss	infer	reorganize	theorize
compare	distinguish	interpret	respond	trace
complete	evaluate	judge	restate	transfer
contrast	explain	justify	review	use
create	formulate	list	sequence	
criticize		name	show	

It is also beneficial to direct students to think about *comprehension subskills* such as main idea, detail, sequence, comparison/contrast, cause and effect, and important vocabulary.

The second decision involves what students should ***think for***. One way for teachers to guide students' thinking is to use traditional "essay exam verbs." These verbs (see Table 11.1) should not be reserved for written exams but should have prominence in all aspects of effective social studies teaching.

When preparing a lesson teachers should decide why they want their students to learn the information. For example, is it so they can apply, describe, evaluate, outline, relate, or support the information? Teachers should then share their goals (the verbs) with students at the start of the lesson. Then when teachers use these verbs to stimulate discussion the students will be more prepared. The teaching and learning are more likely to be matched.

The same preparations will benefit the students' reading comprehension and retention. It is not very helpful to say "think about it as you read," "think harder," or "think again." When giving a reading assignment or beginning a lesson, teachers can tell students to read or listen with certain thinking verbs in mind. For example, perhaps the information to be read from the economics textbook lends itself to a discussion and follow-up writing assignment using the following questions:

1. How could you *prove* the supply and demand principle holds true today?
2. *Support* why it is important for today's businessperson to be aware of the supply and demand principle. Can you *identify* others who need to understand it? (Include your reasons.)
3. Choose three important main ideas or details from the assignment. How would you *summarize* and *explain* them to someone who has not read the assignment?

If teachers have decided on these questions in advance, they can tell their students to "think when reading so you can prove the validity of the supply and demand principle; support why today's business leaders should be aware of the supply and demand principle; identify specific groups of people who need this information; summarize the highlights of the assignment; and explain the major points of the lesson to someone who has not read the assignment." This will be even more effective if teachers define and model the use of these verbs for their students.

The third decision involves what students can *think with*. In social studies classes, it would be important to think with new information, prior knowledge, facts, ideas, opinions, emotions, observations, and experiences. For a particular lesson, however, students' opinions might be the most important. If a teacher explains this in advance, students will be better prepared to react to the content at a personal level. Perhaps the teacher knows when assigning the next part of a chapter that she or he will ask the students to compare the facts presented by the authors to observations students have made in their community. Telling them this in advance will allow them to think with these facts and observations while reading. It is quite probable that the students will be more motivated to read and more confident during discussions.

The fourth decision involves the effective use of *different sources* of relevant information. In addition to the textbook there are library books, magazines, newspapers, pictures, demonstrations, lectures, media presentations, personal experiences, television programs, electronic databases, and people. It would be interesting to discover which of these sources students believe they are "allowed" to use. Students will benefit the most if they understand why each source is valuable and if one is more valuable at one time than another. For example, perhaps while studying prejudice in today's society, teachers could have one group of students study the popular press, while others view selected television programs or interview people of different ages and ethnic backgrounds. The types and reliability of information available from each source could then be analyzed.

The *think about*, *think for*, and *think with* information and the sources of information can be organized in several ways. Teachers will need to plan so they will include the relevant areas and use a variety of information sources. For example, when teaching a unit on political parties, the following chart might be an effective way to organize information.

Topic	Think About	Think For	Think With	Sources
Democratic and Republican Parties	People Time Events Main Ideas	Compare Evaluate Infer	New Information Prior Knowledge Emotions Observations	Popular Media Textbooks Library Books Campaign Literature People
Multi-Party Systems	Situation Opinion Details	Agree Disagree Explain Predict	New Information Prior Knowledge Emotions Observations	Popular Media Textbooks Library Books Campaign Literature People

Teachers can help students become more capable and confident learners when they expect students to think and when they create an environment that supports involvement. With the use of questions, and additional tools teachers can stimulate strategic thinking and learning.

Asking Questions

When used appropriately, questions can clarify and expand thinking. The value of teaching through questioning is not a new discovery.

> In the skillful use of the question more than in anything else lies the fine art of teaching; for in such use we have the guide to clear and vivid ideas, the quick spur to imagination, the stimulus to thought, the incentive to action. (DeGarmo, 1911, p. 226)

We present the purposes of questions, types of questions, and recommendations for the effective use of questions with middle and high school social studies students in this section.

Why Ask Questions?

Answers to oral and written questions provide feedback about the quality of teaching and learning. Effective teachers realize that incomplete or incorrect answers may reveal that the text or the lesson was unclear or perhaps the students were using inappropriate learning strategies. These might be why students were unsuccessful in the lesson rather than simply "not paying attention" or "obviously not reading carefully." Teachers should use questions and answers to determine student misconceptions about the content and the need to reteach the lesson.

In the same way, students should realize that their answers to oral and written questions provide feedback about the quality of their comprehension and retention. These answers can signal the need to relearn the information and/or choose a new learning strategy for the activity.

Questions should motivate students and keep them on task. Teachers also use questions to set purposes for learning and to stimulate students to practice skills associated with the content. Furthermore, questions can clarify connections between topics and cause students to activate relevant and important prior knowledge. And, questions help focus students' attention on the important information and stimulate active learning.

Questions cause students to think in certain ways. If a social studies teacher asks many cause-and-effect questions, students are likely to increase their understanding of causality. If a social studies teacher values the event, problem, or solutions he or she should ask questions about these. This is one way to suggest their importance to students. After many experiences, students will begin thinking about these before the teacher asks the questions. This will increase their confidence and abilities to answer questions. Therefore, teachers who do not want students to concentrate on every detail when reading and listening should not ask questions about them.

Discussion questions that are very different from those the teacher used on written assignments can be difficult for all students, but especially the less-skilled readers. For example, teachers who assign the "chapter check-ups," which typically have many detailed questions, and then ask main idea and prediction questions during class may have students who can do well on the written assignment or the class discussion but not both. This is because different types of reading and thinking are required. Teachers should tell students before the assignment or activity what to think about, for, and with. This will increase thinking, participating, and confidence while decreasing frustration (Clegg, 1987; Dillon, 1984; Gall, 1984).

In addition to teachers asking questions for these valuable reasons, students should be encouraged to ask questions of each other and of their teachers to facilitate meaningful discussions and to have their needs met (Alvermann, Dillon, and O'Brien, 1987). This is beneficial during whole class activities and when students are working in small groups. Curiosity is extremely important. Therefore, although students need to be on task, teachers should usually respond positively to students' questions, even if they seem a bit "off track."

Types of Questions

Questions should be asked *before* instructional activities. These questions act as advance organizers and can set purposes, indicate the most appropriate types of thinking, cause students to activate relevant prior knowledge, and motivate students by increasing their curiosity. Questions asked *during* instructional activities should increase students' understanding of the most important content and inform them about the quality of their comprehension. They also provide teachers with helpful information about the comprehensibility of the lesson. Questions asked at the *completion* of activities can help students increase their comprehension and retention and refine their ideas and opinions. These completion questions should connect new information with prior knowledge and help students to apply the information in appropriate ways (Cunningham, 1987; Gall and Rhody, 1987; Klein, 1988; Montague, 1987).

Teachers should use both planned and spontaneous questions. Effective and efficient teachers plan several questions to ask before, during, and after activities but also ask questions they had not considered in advance. This planned flexibility indicates that teachers are actively listening to students during discussions. This practice will increase teacher credibility.

Students benefit when teachers balance their use of convergent and divergent questions and memory and thinking questions. (Convergent questions have a limited number of correct answers and divergent questions have many correct answers.) Teachers should carefully match these questions to the purposes for the activities. They should also ask a variety of questions and ones that concern the most important content. When application of knowledge is the goal, students must go beyond rote memorization. As stated by Montague (1987), "If a teacher wants students to be able to use knowledge in any meaningful way, then the teacher must provide opportunities to use knowledge in the ways intended through teacher questions" (pp. 88–89).

Teachers can ask questions that frame important things to think about. Once teachers decide which categories they will stress (for example, people, events, problems), they can frame them by regularly asking students questions from these categories (Chuska, 1986). This prepares students for discussions, assignments, and tests. Their independent thinking skills will also increase because they will learn how to think about these categories. For example, several *event* questions include the following: When did it occur? Where did it occur? What reactions did it cause? Who was affected? Could it happen again? *Places* could be framed by the following questions: Where is it? What did it look like? Would you like to find yourself in this place? Why? What would you change about it?

Guidelines for Questioning Students

Teachers can share their reasons for asking questions with their students. Once students understand that teachers do not ask the questions just to assess their comprehension and attention, but to help students improve their own understanding and assess the quality of teaching, their class participation and comprehension of the topic may increase (Raphael and Gavelek, 1984).

Effective teachers use three wait times when questioning students. First, they often ask the question and then wait two to three seconds before calling on anyone. This increases the number of students actively attempting to answer the question. The second wait time of three to five seconds occurs after students are called on. This time allows the students to collect their thoughts. The third wait time is also three to five seconds long and occurs after students appear to be finished. Teachers wait in case students want to elaborate or further explain their answers (Rowe, 1986; Wilen, 1987). When all three wait times are used, the following benefits will result:

- longer student responses
- inferences will automatically be supported by evidence
- greater variety of responses on divergent questions
- more student questions
- fewer failures to respond
- fewer disciplinary problems
- greater student-to-student interaction and cooperation
- more students participating voluntarily
- increases in students' confidence
- improved achievement on written measures
- greater variety of teachers' questions
- greater variety of teachers' responses to answers
- better understanding and following of students' reasoning
- more conversation and less interrogation
- increased expectations for all students

Students and teachers benefit when a high percentage of questions are answered correctly. After a student answers a question correctly then teachers should ask another question or offer brief praise without losing the momentum. When a student is correct but hesitant it is important to tell the student that he or she is correct and ask for "process feedback." The student then explains to the entire class what thinking he or she used in answering the question.

Teachers should respond to incorrect or incomplete answers with corrective feedback, not criticism. The motivation and achievement of high-ability students are affected positively by justified mild criticism and correction that indicate they could have done better (Gall and Rhody, 1987; Montague, 1987).

When answers are incorrect or incomplete or students are unwilling to answer at all, teachers should try to determine the reasons. The first breakdown in the questioning process may be that the question is unfair. For example, if teachers ask students to read so they can compare and describe geographic locations, then they may not be able to answer "What ethnic group lives in this region?" If teachers believe the reason for few volunteers or wrong answers is the unfairness of the question, then reteaching is not in order.

A second breakdown in the questioning process can be in students' inability to understand the question. For example, the teacher may use unfamiliar vocabulary, or one question might have several parts that confuse the students. Because it might be seen as criticism of the teacher, students may not ask to have a question clarified. Therefore, teachers should analyze the situation to determine if the question is the problem. If it is, defining terms or rephrasing it may be all that is necessary.

The inability to remember the question is a third possible breakdown. Teachers have been known to listen to a long answer and say, "Thank you, Jenny. Paul, what do you think?" Since it has been several minutes since the question was asked, perhaps he honestly cannot remember the question. However, he may have learned through experiences that to ask, "Would you please repeat the question?" might get a "Weren't you listening?" response from his teacher. Therefore he may decide it is safer to say, "I don't know." Again, repeating the question when students are hesitant may be all that is necessary.

A fourth common breakdown in the questioning process is students' inability to identify and/or retrieve an answer. When teachers believe this is the problem, they can restate the question in a new way, ask another student to respond, or reteach the content. If the original question was divergent, students' confidence and abilities can be increased by slicing it to narrow its focus. For example, "Why is Washington, D.C., our nation's capital?" could be sliced to "What is one possible reason Washington, D.C., is our nation's capital?" The first implies that the teacher has a correct answer in mind and expects students to know it all while the second implies that any plausible explanation will be accepted. Many students will prefer answering the sliced question.

When answers are incomplete or students seem insecure in their responses, teachers might consider using a *probing* question such as "Why would you think that is so?" Teachers can use *extending* questions to have the students say more about the topic. For example, the teacher may ask, "Why is Washington, D.C., located between northern and southern states?" Teachers can use *clarifying* questions to have students restate their answers more clearly by asking students to expand their ideas. Such a clarifying question might ask, "Using other words, could you expand your ideas about the location of Washington, D.C.?" Teachers use *justifying* questions to have students give reasons or evidence for their response. In asking a student to justify an answer, the teacher could ask, "What did the North have to gain by having the capital moved from New York to Washington, D.C.?"

The fifth breakdown causing students to be unable to respond at all is that they are often uncomfortable being judged and uncomfortable with the judging method. They might also believe it is impossible to satisfy the teacher. For example, some middle and high school students will gladly answer questions that have one right answer. This is because they have a strong desire to know if they are right or to prove to others that they are. Others will not answer these questions because wrong answers are obvious and potentially embarrassing. The same is true for open-ended questions that have many right answers. Some students will respond to these and others will not. It is quite possible that after telling the students there was no one right answer a teacher might respond, "No that's not quite what I had in mind. Anyone else?" This "guess what is in the teacher's head" game is unfair, can cause students to distrust the teacher, and then not respond when they hear the same promise. If the class environment encourages risk taking the teachers could react to "I don't know" or "I'm not sure" responses with questions such as "What do you think I am asking?" or "What is making the question hard?"

Teachers who follow the recommendations presented thus far will find their students thinking and answering strategically. However, the suggestions relate to teacher-directed activities. This next section provides advice that more directly relates to students. Learning strategies that will allow students to succeed in and enjoy social studies classes are completely detailed. They are the main tools of strategic learners.

Learning Strategies

Because the range of reading abilities in typical high social studies classes can be ten years (Singer and Donlan, 1988), students will be more successful when taught strategies they can use when reading and studying. For example, an 11th-grade world history class could have students who read at the 5th-grade level and others who can read and comprehend college level texts with ease. In the middle school, it would not be unusual to find students who are still reading at a 2nd- or 3rd-grade level in the same classes with students with high school reading levels.

When one considers that social studies textbooks also have a range of difficulty, it is obvious that each teacher will have some students who have difficulty reading and comprehending the textbook and others who do not (Stetson and Williams, 1992). For example, Kinder, Bursuck, and Epstein (1992) analyzed the readability of ten American history textbooks published since 1985. They analyzed the readability level, quality of text organization, clarity of pronoun references, location and types of questions included, and vocabulary density. The readability varied from the 9th- to the 15th-grade level, with the mean being 10.9. There was also wide variability in the clarity of pronoun references and the number and types of questions included.

Reading levels are not the only reasons students differ in their abilities to read and comprehend social studies textbooks. Interests, past successes and failures, attention spans, emotional maturity, peer relationships, and other things all affect students' success and attitudes. Therefore, teachers should expect a range of ability in reading library books and popular press, understanding lessons, and completing activities and assignments. For these reasons, the teacher should teach learning strategies.

Students who have learned strategies will be independent and strategic readers, listeners, and studiers. This is because they have the skill and will to analyze their tasks and develop plans to be successful. They also monitor and direct their own understanding and retention. Although students will have developed some of these "skills and wills" in the elementary grades, they will need guidance in applying them. They will also need instruction in learning new strategies necessary for their current social studies class, and teachers should not assume that someone else has taught them. If students are taught learning strategies, they will become self-directed learners.

What Learning Skills and Strategies Should Social Studies Students Be Able To Use?

Skilled students are able to use learning strategies to increase their *motivation*; *manage* their time, materials, and environment; *locate, record, comprehend, remember,* and *use* information; and *regulate* their learning. Strategies from these eight categories work together and reinforce each other. Teachers should teach strategies that are appropriate for their goals and to enable their students to meet the demands of their curriculum, textbooks, and assignments. This section presents strategies students can use for each of the eight categories.

Motivate Motivated students understand that their successes and failures are contingent upon their own efforts. These students realize that the need to use effort to succeed does not indicate they are less skilled; only that they care about their learning. They use focused effort and they know they are responsible for their successes.

Students with positive attitudes about themselves, their teachers, social studies content, and assignments are more motivated than those with negative attitudes. Therefore, students should use "positive self-talk" to manage their own moods. They can create positive self-statements especially when preparing for tasks that are competitive, difficult, or were negative in the past. (Obviously, teachers' attitudes toward teaching, the content, and the students are important.)

Setting realistic learning goals increases students' confidence, competence, involvement, interest, and feelings of responsibility for their own behavior (Stipek, 1988; Winograd and Paris, 1988–1989). General goals without deadlines are not effective because students and teachers cannot recognize when the goals have been accomplished. Students will need assistance in learning how to set their own realistic and specific learning and attention goals. The following acronym can be used when teaching students to set their own learning and attention goals. SMART goals are *specific, measurable, attainable, relevant,* and *timed* (for instance, by Friday, within the next two weeks). Self-motivated students look for improvements as they evaluate themselves in light of their goals and compare their present performance to their past, rather than to others. Because they give themselves feedback, they are not totally dependent on a teacher's evaluation.

Manage Efficient, effective learners are able to manage their materials and time and adjust their learning environment both at school and at home. Students manage their materials by keeping necessary supplies and appropriate reference materials organized and readily accessible. These students also use a "homework drop spot" so they remember to take their homework to school with them.

Skilled, strategic learners are able to evaluate the strengths and weaknesses of study times and locations and then make the most appropriate decisions. For example, they learn to compare the quality of using the desk in their bedroom to the kitchen table and to the time before dinner when the house may be quiet to after dinner when there is more activity.

Students can manage their time when they focus their attention by reducing anxiety and fatigue. They also should select a suitable environment, preview their assignment, establish goals for their studying, and reward themselves at regular intervals.

Strategic studiers are able to manage their time when they are working on long-range assignments. They are able to identify and then schedule the project's steps so they complete the assignment on time. For example, students could complete a report by organizing specific steps. They could set target times, select a topic, formulate and select questions, gather and record data, and then prepare a rough and final draft.

Students use their time wisely when they choose the most appropriate learning strategies. Students should consider their goals and the difficulty of the assignment when deciding whether to read more slowly than normal and make notes. They should decide if they need to look up the meanings of unknown words and write a summary when they complete a reading assignment. For example, if details are important students would know to read more carefully than if they only needed to know one main idea and a supportive example.

Locate If students are to analyze and complete a task successfully they must recognize when new information is needed and know where to find it. Strategic students are able to use libraries and media centers efficiently. They can locate and select relevant books, periodicals, documents, reference books, and databases. These students are also familiar with community resources such as newspapers and organizations that provide relevant information. They also know they can get valuable information from people.

Once they have located a print information source, students should be able to use features like the table of contents, index, and glossary to locate what they need. Strategic students are able to use textbook headings to help them locate information. They understand that to find which cities are the largest they would look under "Populations of Cities" and not "Populations of Continents."

Scanning, an important location skill, is the ability to rapidly cover large quantities of print in order to find one item, such as a date or name. This is especially useful when trying to find a detail in material read previously.

Locating information from maps, charts, graphs, and tables is an important skill in social studies. Strategic students know why these graphics are used and they know to read the titles, headings, and legends to determine what is being displayed.

Record Strategic, independent social studies students are familiar with several ways to take notes when listening and reading. Notes are most helpful when information is important and/or difficult. Organization and complexity of the content should determine the method used. Taking notes can increase concentration and enhance students' comprehension and retention. No matter what system they use, strategic students use their own words and record the information in organized ways. These students record important main ideas, details, examples, relationships, and vocabulary. Also, so students can study from notes most effectively, they write on only one side of the paper. This allows them to examine an entire topic without needing to shuffle papers.

Students may benefit from an open-ended note-taking system. For example, students could complete the following sentences while listening or reading:

Three important main ideas I understand are:
Three relevant details or examples are:
These things surprised me:
I would like to discuss:
I don't understand:
I already knew:

Strategic students know to take organized notes. They may use a traditional outline approach, skip lines between topics, or use index cards with one main idea per card. Some may use one of the categorization or organizational strategies that we will present later in this chapter. Determining how the information is organized and then using that organization in the recording system has many benefits. Students who use organizational patterns can locate important information, integrate and synthesize information, and link new information to prior knowledge. They can also restructure prior knowledge and represent information visually. Finally, they are able to impose organization on unorganized information, write organized answers, and better retain the information. There are a number of methods for taking notes. The methods we suggest here are designed to increase active processing of information. Also, although they are presented here in the "record" section, note that they relate to other categories as well. They can increase students' motivation, comprehension, and retention and make those ideas easier to use. Thus, they are very valuable.

Concept Map A concept map presents important and related words in a diagram that reflects the concept's structure. Recognizing and then recording information with the organization used by the author or teacher facilitates comprehension, recall, and summarizing abilities. Common patterns used in social studies include description, sequence, definition, examples, comparison/contrast, problem/solution, and cause-and-effect. The concept map strategy is often referred to as a semantic map (Heimlich and Pittelman, 1986), web (Moore, Readence, and Rickelman, 1989), or graphic organizer (Tierney, Readence, and Dishner, 1985). The following examples and Figures 11.1–11.5 use a five-step strategy.

1. Choose the concept and write its main idea (phrase or word) at the top or in the center of the diagram. Survey the reading assignment and read any introduction, summary, and headings to determine how the material is structured. If students use a concept map during lectures, teachers should encourage them to listen for organizational clues in the lecturer's introduction. Otherwise, notes can be rewritten after the lecture when the organization becomes clear.
2. Identify main ideas and details and list important and related words in categories following the organization so relationships among words are clear.
3. Label categories, as appropriate.
   Note: The order of steps 2 and 3 can be reversed. At times, the categories will be known in advance so the labels would be in place prior to the listing of words.
4. Analyze and discuss the map. Add words and categories, if necessary. Verify and expand understanding.
5. Review the map to stimulate retention.

These five steps are illustrated in the following examples of concept maps.

K-Q-L-Q-F (What we Know, Questions We Have, What We Learned, Questions We Still Have, File It) With this strategy, students list information and questions in four columns or on four separate sheets of paper and then integrate what they know in a summary, concept map, or some other activity (adapted from Ogle, 1986; Carr and Ogle, 1987). First, individually or in groups, students record their prior knowledge or what they think they know in the *K* column. This will encourage them to use, evaluate, and then to integrate their prior knowledge with their new knowledge, which is critical for comprehension. Second, students record questions they are interested in having answered in the first *Q* column. This can increase interest and comprehension because purposes for reading or listening are made clear. Third, students

Figure 11.1 Concept Map: Inventions

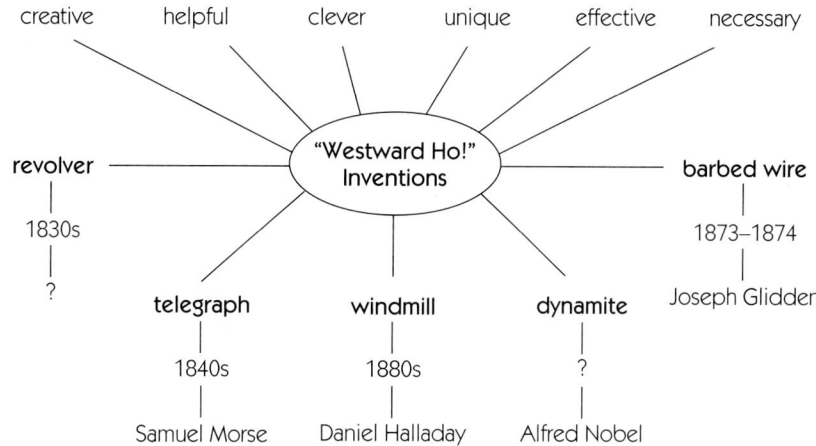

NOTE: The question marks signal areas for further research and understanding.

Figure 11.2 Concept Map: Categories of People

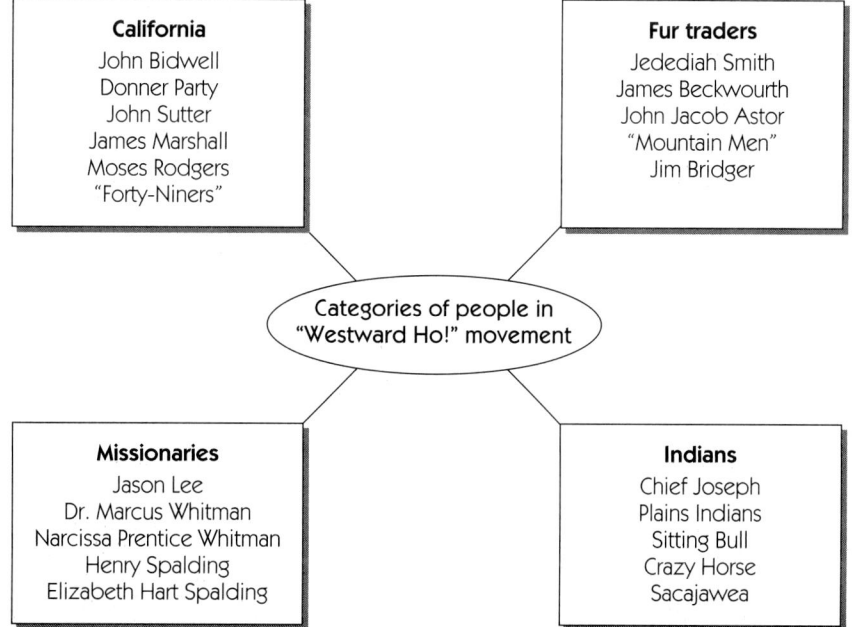

■■■■■■■■ **Figure 11.3** Concept Map: Problem/Solution Organization

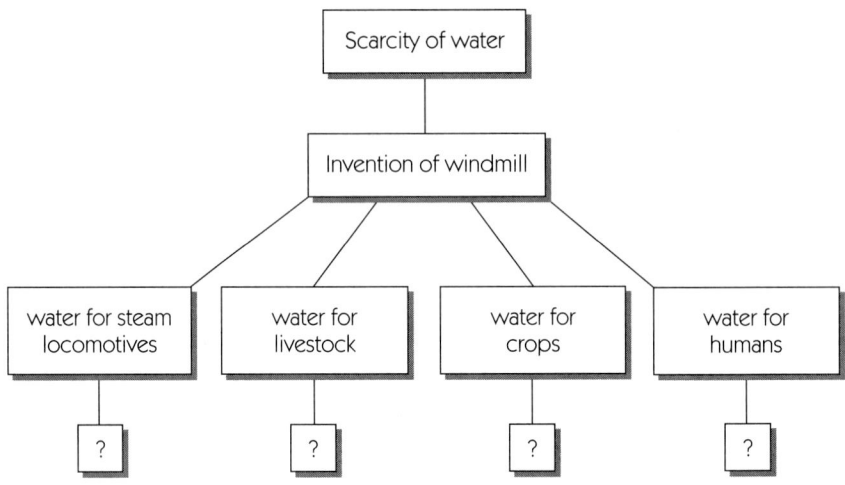

■■■■■■■■ **Figure 11.4** Concept Map: Comparison/Contrast Organization

Invention	Reason(s) Invented	Results	Inventor	Date
Revolver	need for repeating handgun	increased use of handguns	?	1830s
Telegraph	people moving West, anything else?	safer railroads, anything else?	Morse	1840s
Windmill	needed more water for railroads, livestock, crops, and people	people could go West and stay because cattle and crops lived	Halladay	1860s
Dynamite	deep gold and silver	easier mining, anything else?	Nobel	?
Barbed Wire	protect crops from cattle	ended the open range	Glidden	1873–1874

Figure 11.5   Concept Map: Cause-and-Effect Organization

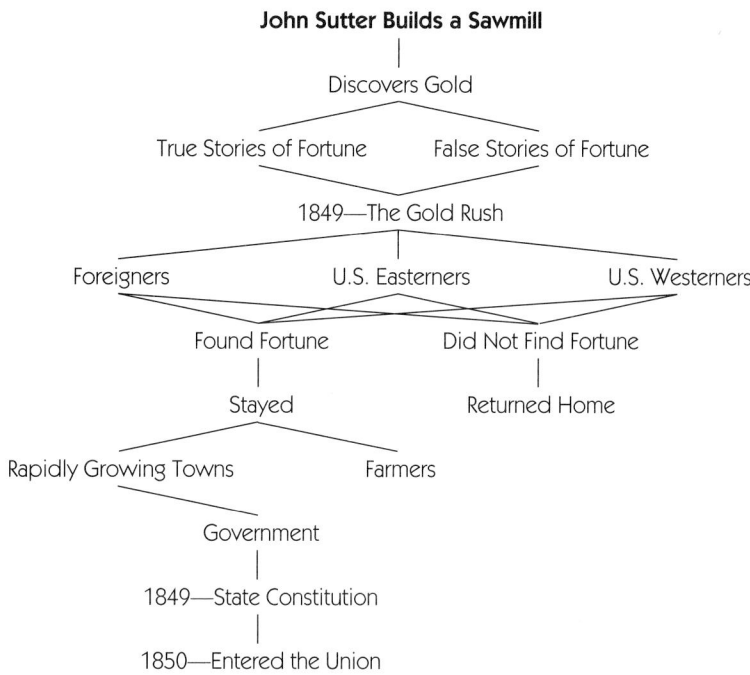

record new information in the *L* column to reinforce the content. Fourth, students go back to the *Q* column and mark questions that have not been answered that they are still curious about and list additional questions there or in a new *Q* column. Then, or after additional learning opportunities to have their questions answered, students select which information they believe they should "file" in their long-term memories. This encourages them to "throw away" prior knowledge that they now know is false and evaluate the other information in light of their goals and the teacher's purposes and expectations. Although this "file" step could simply be a discussion or students could analyze their columns without doing additional writing, some type of written activity is most beneficial. It makes the process of selecting what they retain more concrete. An example follows.

K–Q–L–Q–F Example (before the L, Q, and F steps are completed)

Important People in the "Westward Ho!" movement (See Figure 11.2)

What I **K**now
Missionaries explored the West.
Forty-niners were people who went west to mine for gold.
Fur traders were some of the first people to go west.
Inventors like Daniel Halladay and Joseph Glidden affected the "Westward Ho!" movement.

Questions I Have
Were there any women missionaries?
In what ways did several presidents influence the "Westward Ho!" movement?
Who were some of the fur traders?
How old were some of the important people?

What I **L**earned

Oh Rats (O-Overview, H-Headings, R-Read, A-Answer, TS-Test/Study) "Oh Rats" is a system for making notes while reading (Berrent, 1984; Irwin and Baker, 1989). This system is valuable because it makes studying the notes easier, which is an important step in any note-making strategy. "Oh Rats" requires five steps.

1. O-Overview: Students look over the reading assignment and carefully read relevant parts. These include the introduction, summary, chapter questions, and headings to set purposes and expectations for the reading.
2. H-Headings: Students fold their paper lengthwise so there are about three inches on the left side. On that side, they write down the first heading and ask themselves questions about that specific topic. Initially, they may want to write these below the heading. At least they should ask "what," "where," "when," "who," "why," and "how" questions.
3. R-Read: Students read the section with the heading in mind. They should think about and remember details that are relevant, essential, and specific to the heading.
4. A-Answer: Students list answers to questions from step *2* and other significant ideas on the right side of the paper. They continue the Heading-Read-Answer steps until they complete the assignment.
5. TS-Test/Study: Students reread notes and make any appropriate changes. Then they cover the answers to look only at the headings. Asking the questions about these main ideas and reciting the answers without looking at the notes facilitates long-term memory. They can check their answers by examining the notes, as necessary.

As described, "Oh Rats" is useful when reading something with main idea headings. Once students have learned this strategy well, they can apply the steps individually, if necessary, in other situations. For example, when listening, they can record main ideas on the left side of the paper, details on the right side, and do the test/study steps after the class. Because it is not always possible to recognize main ideas immediately, students could take notes in a list or outline format. Then, when the main ideas and details are clear, they can recopy their notes into this format.

Graphs and Tables Numerical data can often be recorded and summarized best in one of several graphs or tables. Picture graphs use illustrations to express quantities, bar graphs compare quantities using horizontal or vertical bars, pie graphs show how parts are related to the whole, line graphs show changes over time, and tables list facts in an organized way. When recording information on one of these, students should follow these steps:

1. Decide what content should be displayed.
2. Choose the graph or table with the most appropriate purpose and means of summarizing the content.
3. Clearly and completely label the legend that shows what each picture represents, the bars, parts of the pie graph, axes, and column and row headings.
4. Choose an accurate, descriptive title.
5. Complete the graph or table with the relevant data.
6. Analyze the graph or table and make any necessary changes to increase accuracy and clarity.
7. Review the graph or table to stimulate retention.

Comprehend Students who wish to comprehend a lecture or reading assignment effectively should review related material to activate prior knowledge and increase motivation. This could include skimming sections of a previous reading assignment and looking over notes from a previous class. They would also skim the new reading assignment and read the introduction, objectives, questions, and summary, as well as any assignment requirements prior to the learning activity.

Students who have good comprehension formulate questions or hypotheses and *predict* content based on textbook headings or main ideas stated by the teacher. They predict answers to textbook, teacher, and personal questions while reading or listening. These students recognize and use organizational patterns to determine what is important. They read or listen for important information. Students use purposes and past experiences with the content, textbook, teacher, assignments, and tests when deciding what is most important. For example, important information can include main ideas, details and relationships among ideas, examples, vocabulary, events, dates, problems, and solutions. Determining what is important depends on purposes for the reading or listening and how and why the information will be used in the future.

Integration of new knowledge with prior knowledge is important. Effective comprehenders organize information in their long-term memories much like information in a file drawer should be organized. Related information is "filed" together and tabs on the folders clearly identify the contents. This allows students to find prior knowledge easily, revise it if necessary, file new knowledge with it, and then use it all for new learning. Strategic comprehenders relate information to their own lives and create mental images. They also draw conclusions, make inferences, and understand the difference between facts and opinions.

Geographic maps are an important tool for organizing information in social studies. Comprehenders are aware of different types of maps and they know that the map title introduces the purpose of the map and its features. The legend explains data and the distance scale tells how far apart things are or how big something is. The grid system of horizontal and vertical lines (latitude and longitude) helps locate features on maps, and the cardinal directions indicate north, south, east, and west.

Summarizing information improves retention and comprehension because it allows the student to monitor completeness and clarity. Also it enables the learner to clarify distinctions between main and supporting ideas. The ability to summarize also leads to more coherent and complete essay exam answers. Summaries are easier to review and study than original text. The two key types of thinking required for summary writing are selection (judging what to include or reject) and reduction (condensing ideas). Strategic students understand that quality summaries must include all key ideas and must not introduce new or personal ideas. The summary includes the author's point of view and the summarizer's own words (Anderson and Hidi, 1988–1989).

Strategic students study important vocabulary words to comprehend and retain them. They can write definitions and then organize them for future study. They are able to use words in sentences that will help them remember the meanings and think of examples and non-examples of the words. They relate the words to their own lives, picture the words in their minds, and compare and contrast the meanings to words they know. Finally, effective students use the new words often and discuss their meanings with peers (Nagy, 1988).

Remember Skilled social studies students use learning strategies that help them remember information while listening or reading.

Students should understand and use these five principles of memory.

1. Decide to remember. For information to get to long-term memory, students must intend to remember it. This principle can be demonstrated by asking students to draw the front of a one dollar bill or fill in the letters and numbers on the phone without looking at them. Although they are very familiar with both, the tasks are difficult because they have never decided to remember the details. The same can happen with social studies information. A decision to remember is a necessary prerequisite of retention.
2. Understand before trying to remember. Understanding makes both learning and remembering easier and is a necessary condition for long-term memory. To demonstrate this principle, teachers can have students study a list of nonsense words for a brief time and then test recall. Results can be compared between recall of real words in random order and the same words in a sentence. The sentence should be easier, and students will probably recall it later in both the class period and

the week, although they forget the other two lists. For example, try these three lists. Which one is easiest to remember?

A. grest	jopted	wote	slavum	infiggy
B. care	you	this	trying	means
C. trying	this	means	you	care

3. Organize the information before and while trying to remember. Students who use methods such as organizational patterns, concept maps, and the recording of main ideas with their supporting details will retain information longer because it is organized. (This is why the sentence in the previous example is easiest to recall.) Students who work to organize new information linked with the old information will also improve their retention.
4. Allow time to remember. Without enough time, short-term memory can be overloaded, which causes items to be forgotten and not transferred from short-term to long-term memory. Also, items in long-term memory will be quickly forgotten because there was not enough time for them to become permanently fixed.
5. Use information that needs to be remembered. Information that is used often (namely, retrieved from and then returned to memory) will be retained longer and recalled easier. Frequent review perfects and confirms knowledge, makes recall easier, increases retention, and allows students to refine their personal reactions to the content. To prepare for class discussions and study for tests, strategic students regularly review homework, reading assignments, old tests, and study guides to predict what questions will be asked and to practice writing answers.

Students can improve their retention when they study the notes they have recorded, rewrite them with a more appropriate system, reread them, and test their memory and understanding as with the "Oh Rats" system. Strategic students know that taking notes is not enough. The notes must be studied.

Social studies teachers should encourage students to study with flash cards to increase their retention. It is possible to make matches such as vocabulary words with definitions and causes with effects. It is also possible to sequence events or categorize information. Furthermore, it is easy to separate out the information that they know from what they need to study further.

Retention also improves when students use self-recitation and review and when they study in groups. Answering questions orally is good practice. This is especially true when students use their own words and defend their answers to each other.

Use "Ideas and information received by students (through reading, listening, and library research) remain, as far as anyone can tell, dormant and largely meaningless in the mind *until used*" (Devine, 1987, p. 277). Strategies in this important area will assist students when using information to answer questions, complete assignments, take tests, write reports, and deliver oral reports.

Answering Process   Strategic students know how to answer questions during discussions and on written assignments and tests. They use these six steps (adapted from Gall, 1984; Raphael, 1986).

1. Understand the question. Students listen to or read the question to decide what type of answer is wanted. For example, by thinking about the question words, students can determine if the answer will be a date, cause, event, person, or opinion.
2. Look for and choose the answer. Students realize answers can be found in their memories, notes, handouts, textbooks, and/or supplementary materials. They decide on the likely sources, "search" for possible answers, and then select the most appropriate one.
3. Practice the answer. Confidence and competence can increase when students mentally recite an answer before responding. While doing this during discussions and on assignments and tests, students should confirm that their answer matches the question and will be accurate, complete, and clear to the listener or reader.
4. Write, say, or listen to the answer. After the mental rehearsal, students either answer the question or listen to someone else respond to it if they are participating in a class discussion.
5. Evaluate your answer. During a class discussion, students should evaluate the quality of their answer in light of the teacher's feedback. For example, if one student's answer is evaluated for its completeness and accuracy, every student with the same response should recognize that the feedback is also directed toward them. When writing, students should evaluate their answers for accuracy, completeness, organization, and clarity. Their penmanship must be legible.
6. Revise and store the answer, as appropriate. If the feedback or self-evaluation indicates the answer is not correct, it should be revised so that students receive and retain the correct information. Based on the importance of the question, students also decide if the answer should be stored in their long-term memory.

Strategic students approach each assignment and test with a positive attitude, compete with their earlier grades, and look for improvements. They are ready with necessary materials and they listen carefully to any instructions and advice, understand and follow the written directions, and plan their time.

Students need to read the questions carefully to understand them and they should learn to answer the easiest questions first. This will increase their confidence, and they will often remember answers to difficult questions by answering the easier ones first. When writing answers, major points should be obvious, students should pretend they are writing to an uninformed reader, and they should write legibly. This will help them proofread and teachers will not have to guess at what was written.

Strategic students learn from their incorrect answers. For example, they ask why the answer is wrong, why they got it wrong, and what they should do differently next time.

Written and oral reports are common assignments for middle and high school social studies students. Many of the recommendations in this chapter will help students write and deliver these reports. In addition, skilled and strategic report writers and presenters recognize the value of sharing their information with others and they prepare with their audiences (readers or listeners) in mind. They select an appropriate and manageable topic, recognize and state the purpose of the report, and select questions they most want to answer.

Students should gather information from appropriate sources, record the information with the most appropriate methods, and understand the information well enough to report it to others. Students decide on the main points, supporting details, examples, and opinions.

Students should select an appropriate language style (informal or formal) to use in their reports. They should proofread the written reports for accuracy, completeness, organization, clarity, vocabulary, grammar, spelling, punctuation, and neatness. Strategic students rewrite the report or practice the oral presentation, as necessary. They also seek and accept suggestions from readers and listeners.

Regulate Middle school and high school social studies students need to regulate their learning. Referred to as metacognition, strategies from this category are used by students to *monitor* and *direct* learning. This includes maintaining positive attitudes and committing to appropriate goals. Students regulate their learning by attending to the task and selecting appropriate strategies. They also use these strategies effectively and evaluate the quality of their comprehension, retention, and task performance (Weinstein, 1987; Winograd and Paris, 1988–1989).

Students who regulate their learning are able to recognize when they are having learning problems, identify the reasons and apply appropriate fix up strategies. Students can monitor the quality of their learning by attempting to summarize or paraphrase the information they are hearing or reading.

Students can also monitor and direct the quality of their learning and their ability to use what they have learned by pausing regularly to ask themselves questions. Using questions "leads the student to an active monitoring of the learning activity and to the engagement of strategic action" (Baker and Brown, 1984, p. 372). For example, the following questions may be useful:

- Have I learned what I wanted to learn?
- What else do I need or want to learn?
- Why is this information important?
- Do I understand?

- Will I remember this?
- Will I be able to use this?
- Will I be able to answer the teacher's questions?
- What might be an example of this?
- What strategies should I use to record, comprehend, and retain this?
- Have I recorded enough information?
- Why am I confused? Is it because of me, the textbook, or the lesson?
- How can I fix this problem so that I will understand, pay attention, record more effectively, or remember this?

Students who regulate their learning realize problems can be caused by difficulties in one or more of the strategy categories (motivate; manage; locate, record, comprehend, remember, and use information; and regulate). Strategic students know to apply fix-up strategies when solving their problems. For example, students can direct their learning by changing their goals to better reflect the reality of the task. They can use more effort on the difficult parts of the assignment, continue their studying in a more appropriate location, or locate additional information from a variety of resources.

Learning can also be directed by reading the questions more carefully on the next test, taking notes to increase attention, and previewing the reading assignment before the next class to be better prepared. Students may need to organize ideas before studying them, remember to activate prior knowledge, and predict the meanings of unknown words while reading or listening.

When confused, students can reread, often orally, to increase attention. It often helps to read past the confusing part because helpful information may follow. When necessary, students should ask someone for assistance.

Directing their own learning will be easier for students if they complete strategy analysis sheets and then review them on a regular basis. The following statements, designed for test-taking strategies, can be adapted for any number of strategies.

1. Now that the test is over, I think I did well/did OK/really blew it (circle one) because . . .
2. If I had one question to ask the teacher about the test, it would be . . .
3. I feel that I was well prepared/not prepared (circle one) to take this test. Therefore . . .
4. One thing I did well when taking this test was . . .
5. The easiest thing about this test was . . .
6. The hardest thing about this test was . . .
7. The next time I study for a test, I will . . .
8. The next time I take a test, I will . . .

The use of learning logs can also increase students' abilities to regulate their learning. In the log, students concentrate on cognitive and affective components of learning by writing about their reactions to academic activities and the quality of their performances. This allows them to recognize strengths to maintain and weaknesses to change.

Teaching and using the most relevant strategies will make a major, positive impact on students' attitudes and abilities. Strategies empower them to be strategic and independent *if* the strategies are taught well. This guidance is provided in the next section.

Teaching Guidelines

The suggestions that follow will be useful for increasing students' willingness and abilities to think. The students will also be able to apply strategies independently from the five categories (Duffy, Roehler, and Herrmann, 1988; Jones et al., 1987; Porter and Brophy, 1988; Weinstein, 1987).

These suggestions are incorporated into a teaching model, EMAQF, which consists of *explanation, modeling, assignments, questions,* and *feedback* (adapted from Irwin, 1991). Teachers who implement ideas from each of these five components and make certain that the ideas relate are more likely to have independent, strategic, and successful learners than those who do not.

Explanation First, teachers need to make thinking and learning strategies comprehensible for students.

Teachers should teach so students understand *what* the strategy is, *how* to use it effectively, *when* and *where* it would be useful, and *why* it facilitates learning. As with any effective teaching, the strategies should be reviewed and retaught as necessary.

Students need to believe that they can easily learn the strategies and that consistent use of the most appropriate strategies will improve their overall performance and grades. To increase the likelihood that students will discern this relationship, the first strategies that teachers should present are those that will have an obvious positive result. The first strategies the students learn should increase their understanding, retention, participation, and other outcomes that are valued by the teachers and/or students. Students benefit when teachers discuss the relationships between strategy selection, strategy use, and these outcomes with them.

In addition to direct instruction, teachers can share much of the information about strategies with students (and parents) on a course outline. Besides listing expectations for behavior, teachers can describe features of the textbook. They can also explain how classes will be run (for example, the use of lectures and group work) and give details of assignments and tests. This shows students what type of thinking will be beneficial and what learning strategies the teacher expects them to use. It is only fair to clearly delineate the course requirements and the means by which students can be successful.

It is also beneficial to use visual aids during and after the explanation stage. These can include posters, bookmarks, and brochures that students keep with course materials to remind them of the *what, how, when, where,* and *why* information. For example, students and teachers may remember to use the answering process if the steps are listed on a poster or designed as a bookmark by the students. Visual aids can increase teaching and learning effectiveness.

Modeling What has been explained needs to be modeled. Teachers can utilize concrete examples to talk aloud about their thinking and the reasoning they use to apply learning strategies.

Students' motivation and understanding will increase when they hear their teachers talking about how they think and what strategies they use in their own work. For example, teachers can share research findings from a graduate class and explain why they chose the content, how they conducted their study, and with what results.

Modeling also takes place when teachers identify the strategies they are using while teaching. This allows teachers to model for their students the reasoning and flexible thinking that is required to use the strategies successfully. For example, teachers can use concept maps, organizational patterns, and K-Q-L-Q-F when introducing the content from a chapter, recording ideas during a discussion, and facilitating a review. They could comment on their reasoning, and that of the students, so that students would completely understand the *what, how, when, where,* and *why* of knowledge. It is then more likely that these students will be able to use the strategies independently.

Assignments Teachers should use familiar and motivational content when introducing new learning strategies. Initial instruction using content that students see as difficult, irrelevant, or boring can cause negative first impressions about learning strategies. For example, rather than using textbook content when teaching students how to collect and record data, teachers could direct students to conduct a survey to determine students' favorite musical groups or what they would buy with $1,000. Their prior knowledge of the topics will also help them understand, study, and use the information. Once students are successful, they may be more willing to use the same strategies with course content.

What is explained and modeled needs to be used by students. So, it is beneficial to provide students with many opportunities to practice and use strategies on a variety of meaningful assignments. Otherwise, students may use strategies only in the context of the original instruction. Students who frequently use strategies are more likely to internalize the reasoning processes and, therefore, find the tasks easier and more enjoyable. This will lead to additional success because students can concentrate on the content instead of the mechanics of the strategies.

Inappropriate assignments can undermine both the quality of instruction in learning strategies and the atmosphere that encourages students' thinking. Social studies teachers who want students to think and use learning strategies must design assignments that require students to think.

Assignments can accomplish a variety of purposes. They can be designed to introduce, teach, or practice learning strategies; determine and activate students' prior knowledge; introduce, teach, or review content; check students' understanding or recall; facilitate learning, comprehension, and retention; motivate students; and assess the clarity and completeness of instruction.

Once teachers know what they need to accomplish, they can design an appropriate assignment. It may be possible to choose or adapt an assignment from the student's textbook or teacher's guide. However, these should not be assigned unless they serve a necessary purpose. For example, when "chapter check-up" exercises are assigned, students may read chapters to answer only those questions. If it is important for students to relate the chapter's information to prior learning and if this assignment does not require that, then assigning the "chapter check-up" is inappropriate.

Variety is important. Students' interest may decrease when they recognize the predictability of always completing the same type of assignment, especially if it seems unrelated to the teacher's evaluation methods. Teachers should use a variety of writing assignments. Writing before, during, and after class activities and assignments can increase motivation. Writing can also activate prior knowledge and integrate it with new knowledge. It can focus students' attention on important information, regulate learning, and improve learning because there is a permanent record of thoughts (Moore, Readence, and Rickelman, 1989; Nelms, 1987).

Students can write personal, interpretive, critical, and creative responses to their reading assignments and class activities. Nelms (1987) has suggested different purposes for social studies writing assignments. Writing assignments can serve to inventory knowledge by having students list and organize prior and new knowledge. Teachers can also assign writing to initiate learning by having students write questions, goals, and hypotheses. To consolidate learning, students react to ideas and make use of what they have read and heard. Writing to personalize learning involves both cognitive and affective purposes. With this type of writing, students are required to draw directly on their own experiences, attitudes, and values to deal with new concepts. Writing can also serve to clarify thinking because the writers can examine and refine this permanent record of their thoughts.

Moore, Readence, and Rickelman (1989) make further distinctions among writing assignments. They recommend the use of directed writing that specifies the exact nature of the assignment and free writing that allows students to choose their own task or format. For example, after teaching about the United Nations, teachers who assign directed writing projects might tell students to write letters. These letters could be from a delegate from France who is writing home during the first year of the United Nations and again ten years later. Teachers who assign free writing could ask students—by choosing to write diary entries, letters home, interviews, or a comparison/contrast fact sheet—to demonstrate their understanding of how different countries changed their attitudes toward the United Nations.

We also recommend conventional and enriched writing tasks. Conventional tasks are traditional school writing assignments that bear little relation to the writing done outside of school. These could include essay examinations, themes, research reports, and critiques. Enriched writing tasks have practical significance and use forms and audiences that occur outside of school. For example, after studying the role of debates in presidential elections, students could write affirmative or negative policy statements. They could write editorials or letters to newspaper editors from the perspective of the candidates, the parties, or the voters. Other discourse forms that would serve as enriched writing assignments include diaries, biographical sketches, summaries, poems, dialogues, telegrams, fact sheets, historical "you are there" scenes, interviews (actual and imaginary), speeches, plays and dramas, and songs and ballads.

Most social studies teachers will regularly assign homework. Teachers can design reading and writing assignments to prepare students for the next day's activities or to extend class learning activities. This homework could also require students to review and practice important content and/or strategies. As stated by Curwin and Mendler (1989), "Students have a right to be given homework that will enhance their learning, and teachers have a responsibility to give it to them" (p. 174).

Homework activities work best when they are explained so students know *how* to complete the assignments independently. Homework assignments that students understand and can do foster positive home-school relationships, improved student attitudes, increased motivation, and heightened abilities. Students are apt to be more successful when parents do not need to teach their children how to complete the assignments.

Homework should stress the most important content and learning strategies, be interesting, and be integrated into class activities. It should be challenging so students feel a sense of accomplishment when they are finished. High success rates are also desirable because they foster learning, motivation, effort, and cooperation.

Teachers should consider individual differences. Teachers can use students' abilities and interests to assign different topics, formats, and assignment lengths. Social studies teachers should remember that they are not the only ones assigning homework and therefore, assignments should be an appropriate length and intensity.

Teachers can ask students and parents to evaluate the relevance, difficulty, and length of typical assignments. This may be the only way teachers learn how long students spend on assignments. Ideally, teachers assign homework with enough time left in class for students to ask questions and begin the assignment. Also, homework can be assigned two or more days prior to the due date. This allows students a choice of when to do the assignments. It is also wise to respect students' schedules and not assign homework every day. The emphasis should be on the quality of homework rather than the quantity.

Homework should be important enough that teachers implement consequences for late, incomplete, or never-completed assignments. Teachers should correct and return homework quickly. It may be appropriate to assign some homework that can be self-corrected or corrected by peers. Teachers should not use homework to punish behavior or performance since students may come to resent these teachers and learning in general.

Teachers should discuss with the students the purpose for the assignment. When students understand why they have been asked to complete an assignment their attitudes and performance will improve. This information will also help students design their own assignments when given the opportunity (Canter, 1988; Curwin and Mendler, 1989; Devine, 1987; and Montague, 1987).

Questions As explained earlier in this chapter, questions can serve several purposes. One important role for questions is to determine if teachers need to review or reteach various learning strategies or content. And, to continue the EMAQF model, questions would concern what has been explained, modeled, and used on assignments.

Poor student response may be due to confusion with content, strategies, or both. For example, notes could be incomplete because students did not understand the topic well enough to select all the important information or because they did not pay attention to the lesson. Following answers to questions such as "Who was an important person involved in the event?" with "How did you decide she was important?" helps teachers and students determine if a strategy has been learned and used correctly. Teachers need to determine what caused the problem or wrong answer and, therefore, what to review and reteach—the content or the strategy.

Teachers need to ask questions to monitor *and* evaluate students. Monitoring involves observing students during the learning process to direct them by asking appropriate questions. This is one way students are able to monitor their thinking. Evaluation involves judgment and is often reserved for the finished assignments. While evaluating students' work, teachers can ask themselves key questions that will help them determine why students do or do not understand the content and/or the learning strategies. Teachers can use and adapt many of the questions listed within the *regulate* section of this chapter for this purpose.

While monitoring and evaluating, teachers should remember what they included during the earlier sections of the EMAQF model. This will help teachers decide how to react to strengths and weaknesses. It is also important for teachers to examine their motives for monitoring and evaluating. Students benefit when teachers have a positive outlook and look for improvements.

Teachers can ask these questions when monitoring and evaluating student thinking:

- How accurate is the student?
- How easily did the student arrive at the answers?
- Is the student using the most appropriate learning strategies?
- Is the student aware of the difficulty of the assignment?
- Is the student aware of the purpose for the assignment?
- What are the student's attitudes toward the content, strategies, and assignment?
- What are some probable causes for the learning difficulties?
- How can I use a student's strengths to remediate weaknesses?
- How effectively did I present the content and strategies?
- How effectively did I select and explain the assignment?

Feedback Students benefit from specific feedback about their thinking, their choices of learning strategies, and the accuracy and ease with which they use these strategies.

Students deserve to know what and why they did well so they can repeat the behaviors that led to success. Students who struggle also need to know specifically what to change in order to become successful.

Effective feedback is specific, helpful, private, and thoughtful. Teachers should use praise when students are successful (especially on difficult tasks) and constructive criticism when students struggle (especially on easy tasks). It is also important to attribute success or failure to things students control such as intrinsic motivation, effort, or selection of appropriate strategies. Teachers need to use feedback to affect the future, not just judge the past (Brophy, 1987; Stipek, 1988).

One of the principal goals of strategy training is to alter students' beliefs about themselves by teaching them that their failures can be attributed to the lack of effective strategies rather than to the lack of ability or to laziness (Jones et al., 1987).

Sample teacher feedback directed to strategy choice and use includes the following:

- "Your answers are right. I think it helped that you _____."
- "You did better locating the information because you _____."
- "I think you made your mistake because _____. Next time, try _____."
- "Your decision about where and when to study was smart because _____."
- "You are forgetting how to do it right because you have not used the 'Oh Rats' system enough yet. It will get easier. Let's use it again today."

SUMMARY

Strategic students who have the skill and the will to succeed will learn and retain social studies content most easily. These students should have social studies teachers who model their own thinking, expect students to think, give them time to think, and involve them during class activities. These teachers also tell their students about different sources of relevant information, what they might think about, and why they should think.

We also addressed the topic of questioning in this chapter. We included purposes for asking questions and different types of questions to ask. We also explained possible breakdown points in the questioning process.

We presented many specific learning skills and strategies from eight categories. Teaching those that are most appropriate increases students' motivation and their abilities to manage their time, materials, and environment. Using these strategies students will learn how to locate, record, comprehend, remember, and use information and regulate their learning.

This chapter also explained a teaching model to help students be independent, strategic, and successful. The five components are explanation, modeling, assignments, questions, and feedback.

Discussion Questions

1. How might you adjust your teaching if students are not participating and/or not doing well on your assignments?
2. If you could only implement two ideas discussed in this chapter, which two would you choose and why?
3. If you decide to devote class time to teaching learning strategies, how might you deal with an administrator who does not understand why you are doing this and seems concerned that you may not finish the textbook?

Student Learning Activities

1. Ask middle school and high school students their opinions of class participation and hand raising. With this input, design a system for student participation in social studies classes.
2. Try recording notes from the content of one of your college-level courses using at least one of the recommended strategies. Critique the method(s).
3. Examine at least one middle school or high school social studies textbook in light of the learning strategies suggested. Which strategy would be most beneficial to the students using this textbook? Share your choice with classmates and be prepared to support your choice.

References

Anderson, V. and Hidi, S. 1988–1989. "Teaching Students to Summarize." *Educational Leadership*, Vol. 46, No. 4, December 1988/January 1989. 26–28.

Alvermann, D. E., Dillon, D. R., and O'Brien, D. G. 1987. *Using Discussion to Promote Reading Comprehension*. Newark, DE: International Reading Association.

Baker, L., and Brown, A. L. 1984. "Metacognitive Skills and Reading." In P. D. Pearson, R. Barr, and M. L. Kamil (Eds.), *Handbook of Reading Research*. Vol. 1. New York: Longman.

Berrent, H. I. 1984. "OH RATS: A Note-Taking Technique." *Journal of Reading*, Vol. 27, No. 6, March. 548–550.

Brophy, J. 1987. "On Motivating Students." In D. C. Berliner and B. V. Rosenshine (Eds.), *Talks To Teachers*. New York: Random House.

Canter, L. 1988. *Homework Without Tears for Teachers*. Santa Monica, CA: Lee Canter and Associates.

Carr, E. and Ogle, D. 1987. "K–W–L Plus: A Strategy for Comprehension and Summarization." *Journal of Reading*, Vol. 30, No. 7, April. 626–631.

Chuska, K. R. 1986. *Teaching the Process of Thinking, K–12*. Bloomington, IN: Phi Delta Kappa Educational Foundation.

Clegg, A. A., Jr. 1987. "Why Questions?" In W. W. Wilen (Ed.), *Questions, Questioning Techniques, and Effective Teaching*. Washington, DC: National Education Association.

Cunningham, R. T. 1987. "What Kind of Question Is That?" In W. W. Wilen (Ed.), *Questions, Questioning Techniques, and Effective Teaching*. Washington, DC: National Education Association.

Curwin, R. L. and Mendler, A. N. 1989. *Discipline with Dignity*. Alexandria, VA: Association for Supervision and Curriculum Development.

DeGarmo, C. 1911. *Interest and Education: The Doctrine of Interest and Its Concrete Application*. New York: Macmillan.

Devine, T. G. 1987. *Teaching Study Skills: A Guide for Teachers* (2nd ed.). Boston: Allyn and Bacon.

Dillon, J. T. 1984. "Research on Questioning and Discussion." *Educational Leadership*, Vol. 42, No. 3, November. 50–56.

Duffy, G. G., Roehler, L. R., and Herrmann, B. A. 1988. "Modeling Mental Processes Helps Poor Readers Become Strategic Readers." *The Reading Teacher*, Vol. 41, No. 8, April. 762–767.

Gall, M. 1984. "Synthesis of Research on Teachers' Questioning." *Educational Leadership*, Vol. 42, No. 3, November. 40–47.

Gall, M. D. and Rhody, T. 1987. "Review of Research on Questioning Techniques." In W. W. Wilen (Ed.), *Questions, Questioning Techniques, and Effective Teaching*. Washington, DC: National Education Association.

Gardner, H. 1983. *Frames of Mind: The Theory of Multiple Intelligences*. New York: Basic Books.

Heimlich, J. E. and Pittelman, S. D. 1986. *Semantic Mapping: Classroom Applications*. Newark, DE: International Reading Association.

Irwin, J. W. 1991. *Teaching Reading Comprehension Processes*. Englewood Cliffs, NJ: Prentice-Hall.

Irwin, J. W. and Baker, I. 1989. *Promoting Active Reading Comprehension Strategies: A Resource Book for Teachers*. Englewood Cliffs, NJ: Prentice-Hall.

Jones, B. F., Palincsar, A. S., Ogle, D. S., and Carr, E. G. (Eds.) 1987. *Strategic Teaching and Learning: Cognitive Instruction in the Content Areas*. Alexandria, VA: Association for Supervision and Curriculum Development and Elmhurst, IL: North Central Regional Educational Laboratory.

Kinder, D. B., Bursuck, B., and Epstein, M. 1992. "An Evaluation of History Textbooks." *The Journal of Special Education*, Vol. 25, No. 4, Winter. 472–491.

Klein, M. L. 1988. *Teaching Reading Comprehension and Vocabulary: A Guide for Teachers*. Englewood Cliffs, NJ: Prentice-Hall.

Marzano, R. J., Brandt, R. S., Hughes, C. S., Jones, B. F., Presseisen, B. Z., Rankin, S. C., and Suhor, C. 1988. *Dimensions of Thinking: A Framework for Curriculum and Instruction*. Alexandria, VA: Association for Supervision and Curriculum Development.

Montague, E. J. 1987. *Fundamentals of Secondary Classroom Instruction*. Columbus, OH: Merrill.

Moore, D. W., Readence, J. E., and Rickelman, R. J. 1989. *Prereading Activities for Content Area Reading and Learning* (2nd ed.). Newark, DE: International Reading Association.

Nagy, W. E. 1988. *Teaching Vocabulary to Improve Reading Comprehension*. Newark, DE: International Reading Association.

Nelms, B. F. 1987. "Response and Responsibility: Reading, Writing, and Social Studies." *The Elementary School Journal*, Vol. 87, No. 5, May. 571–589.

Ogle, D. M. 1986. "K–W–L: A Teaching Model That Develops Active Reading of Expository Text." *The Reading Teacher*, Vol. 39, No. 6, February. 564–570.

Perkins, D. N. 1986. "Thinking Frames." *Educational Leadership*, Vol. 43, No. 8, May. 4–10.

Porter, A. C. and Brophy, J. 1988. "Synthesis of Research on Good Teaching: Insights from the Work of the Institute for Research on Teaching." *Educational Leadership*, Vol. 45, No. 8, May. 74–85.

Raphael, T. E. 1986. "Teaching Question-Answer Relationships, Revisited." *The Reading Teacher*, Vol. 39, No. 6, February. 516–522.

Raphael, T. E. and Gavelek, J. R. 1984. "Question-Related Activities and Their Relationship to Reading Comprehension: Some Instructional Implications." In G. G. Duffy, L. R. Roehler, and J. Mason (Eds.), *Comprehension Instruction: Perspectives and Suggestions*. New York: Longman.

Richardson-Koehler, V. (Ed.). 1987. *Educators' Handbook: A Research Perspective*. New York: Longman.

Rowe, M. B. 1986. "Wait Time: Slowing Down May Be a Way of Speeding Up!" *Journal of Teacher Education*, Vol. 37, No. 1, January/February. 43–50.

Singer, H. and Donlan, D. 1988. *Reading and Learning from Text* (2nd ed.). Hillsdale, NJ: Lawrence Erlbaum.

Sternberg, R. J. 1985. *Beyond IQ: A Triarchic Theory of Human Intelligence*. New York: Cambridge University Press.

Stetson, E. G. and Williams, R. P. 1992. "Learning from Social Studies Textbooks: Why Some Students Succeed and Others Fail." *Journal of Reading*. Vol. 36, No. 1, September. 22–30.

Stipek, D. J. 1988. *Motivation to Learn: From Theory to Practice*. Englewood Cliffs, NJ: Prentice-Hall.

Tierney, R. J., Readence, J. E., and Dishner, E. K. 1985. *Reading Strategies and Practices: A Compendium* (2nd ed.). Boston: Allyn and Bacon.

Todd, L. P. and Curti, M. 1986. *Triumph of the American Nation*. Orlando, FL: Harcourt Brace Jovanovich.

Vaughan, J. L. and Estes, T. H. 1986. *Reading and Reasoning Beyond the Primary Grades*. Boston: Allyn and Bacon.

Weinstein, C. E. 1987. "Fostering Learning Autonomy Through the Use of Learning Strategies." *Journal of Reading*, Vol. 30, No. 7, April. 590–595.

Wilen, W. W. 1987. "Effective Questions and Questioning: A Classroom Application." In W. W. Wilen (Ed.), *Questions, Questioning Techniques, and Effective Teaching*. Washington, DC: National Education Association.

Winograd, P. and Paris, S. G. 1988–1989. "A Cognitive and Motivational Agenda for Reading Instruction." *Educational Leadership*, Vol. 46, No. 4, December 1988/January 1989. 30–36.

Additional Reading

Cullinan, B. E. (Ed.). 1993. *Fact and Fiction: Literature Across the Curriculum*. Newark, DE: International Reading Association.

Doyle, M. A. E. and Barber, B. S. 1990. *Homework as a Learning Experience*. (What Research Says to the Teacher Series). (3rd ed.). Washington, DC: National Education Association.

Harker, W. J. (Ed.). 1985. *Classroom Strategies for Secondary Reading* (2nd ed.). Newark, DE: International Reading Association.

Lazear, D. G. 1992. *Teaching for Multiple Intelligences*. Bloomington, IN: Phi Delta Kappa Educational Foundation.

Marzano, R. J. 1992. *A Different Kind of Classroom: Teaching with Dimensions of Learning*. Alexandria, VA: Association for Supervision and Curriculum Development.

Muth, K. D. (Ed.) 1989. *Children's Comprehension of Text: Research into Practice*. Newark, DE: International Reading Association.

Wassermann, S. 1992. *Asking the Right Question: The Essence of Teaching*. Fastback 343. Bloomington, IN: Phi Delta Kappa Educational Foundation.

Wlodkowski, R. J. and Jaynes, J. H. 1990. *Eager To Learn: Helping Children Become Motivated and Love Learning*. San Francisco: Jossey-Bass.

> ■ ■ ■ ■ ■ ■   When elephants fight it is the grass that suffers.
> *Kikuyu proverb*

PART IV

How Are Students and Programs Evaluated?

THERE HAS BEEN an increasing interest in measuring student learning and teacher effectiveness during the past decade. National standardized tests, such as the National Assessment of Educational Progress (NAEP), as well as state and local evaluation efforts, have caused more people to ask questions about education. They include such questions as "How well are our students learning?" "How do our students compare to other students?" "Is our social studies program effective?" "How effective are our teachers?" Responses to these and similar questions are not always easy as there are variables, both within and outside the school, that require thoughtful study and response.

Teachers often measure student progress by classroom learning activities, by various teacher-made and standardized tests, and by evaluating student performance. It is common to think that students are learning if test scores are "above average." This, however, may be misleading and give a false picture of student progress and learning. We caution you that student progress and evaluation are controversial subjects that are likely to be around for the foreseeable future.

Just as there is an interest in student progress, there is interest in knowing the effectiveness of specific social studies programs. In some cases, before a new social studies program has been disseminated widely, there have been both formative and summative evaluation studies. These data provide an indication of likely results. Local curriculum ought to be evaluated by asking how well the outcomes match the objectives.

Finally, teachers are being challenged to demonstrate their effectiveness and content knowledge by passing state-mandated tests. In some areas teachers must prepare portfolios of work, which may include sample units, lesson plans, test questions given to students, examples of student work, and videotapes demonstrating actual classroom teaching. There are no well-defined or agreed-upon criteria for judging teaching effectiveness. The issue is complex and one that will continue to be in the forefront as educators and decision makers grapple with the problem of educational effectiveness.

As you begin your teaching career, you should identify questions you have concerning evaluation issues. What questions are most important to you at present and what questions are likely to be ongoing? How will you respond to questions that ask you about student learning, curriculum expectations, and your own effectiveness as a social studies teacher?

As you read this part of the textbook you should reflect upon possible answers to these questions.

FOCUS QUESTIONS

- Why is the trend toward measuring student learning most often accomplished at the knowledge level?

- Why have the attitudes of students, educators, parents, business leaders, government officials, and others toward evaluation changed over the years?

- To what extent are national or state standardized tests a measure of student learning?

- What are some ways students may demonstrate the skills and knowledge they have learned in practical settings or applied practices?

FOCUS ACTIVITY

Over your school years you have been evaluated numerous times. Most likely several evaluation techniques were used by your teachers at different grade levels and/or in various content areas. You should ask three to five classmates (outside of teacher education) the following questions by asking them to complete the questionnaire on evaluation techniques.

Survey of Evaluation Techniques

1. What types of evaluation techniques do you remember your teachers in junior high or middle school and high school using to evaluate your learning?

2. To what extent were different classes or courses (mathematics, science, art, music, physical education, etc.) evaluated differently? Please give some examples.

3. How did your teachers use the information from *your* evaluations to help *you* improve *your* performance (learning) in the classroom?

4. How have evaluation techniques changed in your post-secondary education experience?

5. To what extent do you believe the evaluations of your classroom performance reflected your learning and understanding of the content, concepts, and skills being taught?

6. What changes would you like to see in the way you are evaluated?

Based on your survey of findings, prepare a set of recommendations concerning how students in your teacher education program should be evaluated.

Using a similar questionnaire ask both middle school and high school students what they like and dislike about the way they are evaluated. To what extent are the responses similar/different? What conclusions might you make concerning the evaluation of student learning? How are these findings likely to influence the ways you evaluated student learning? Speculate on where the assessment/evaluation movement is likely to be ten years from now.

> Where I was born and where and how I have lived is unimportant. It is what I have done with where I have been that should be of interest.
>
> *Georgia O'Keeffe*

CHAPTER 12

Evaluation in Social Studies

FOCUS QUESTIONS

- What role does evaluation play in social studies classes and programs?
- What relationships exist among program objectives, learning activities, and student evaluation?
- Why has the accountability movement had such important consequences for students, schools, and communities?
- What roles do teachers, students, administrators, parents, and communities have in program evaluation?
- What are some ways to assess student learning in social studies that extend beyond pencil and paper tests and standardized tests?
- How might alternative assessment practices be used to enhance student learning in the social studies?
- What criteria can be used to evaluate the quality of social studies programs?

OVERVIEW   On a regular basis the media reports how well or poorly students are doing in social studies courses such as history, geography, and economics. It also publishes the results and trends of data from the latest Scholastic Aptitude Test (SAT) and American College Test (ACT). The media also regularly compares current scores with previous National Assessment of Educational Progress (NAEP) scores. Reporters of these news accounts often confuse the meanings of the terms *test, measurement, evaluation,* and *assessment* and use them interchangeably or incorrectly, which can be confusing and misleading. Therefore, it is important for education to define the terminology and agree on the definition (Popham, 1993).

In this chapter, a *test* is defined as a series of questions, each of which has a correct answer. The term *measurement* is evaluation reported in quantitative terms; it tells us how much or how many. It is fairly broad because educators and others can measure attributes or characteristics through the use of rankings, rating scales, and observations (for instance, "How does this student compare with others?") Measurement allows us to compare performance and characteristics among individuals by placing number values on those behaviors or traits. Measurement allows teachers to compare a student's performance on a particular task with the performance of other students (such as "How did the student perform on the last social studies test?"). Sometimes teachers may use qualitative measures such as student preferences, information from parents, previous experiences, and intuition in making value decisions concerning students.

Evaluation is comprehensive and includes information needed to make judgments required for educational decision-making (Dembo, 1988). Evaluation places a value on the data and provides an indication of worth, for example, how much of an attribute the student has. *Assessment* is the process of collecting, organizing, and interpreting data. Assessment is sometimes used synonymously with evaluation, but at other times assessment refers to the diagnosis of an individual's problems or abilities (Mehrens and Lehmann, 1987). Measurement and assessment are often interchangeable and determine rank or status; evaluation is one-dimensional and determines success or failure, worth or value. Each of these tools has a role in making educational decisions concerning lesson plans, grouping, individual learning, diagnosing pupil readiness for the next learning task, determining student progress, and grading to assess the effectiveness of instruction. Evaluation, properly used, is a tool for the improvement of instruction.

Goals of Evaluation

The three major components of teaching are planning, instructing, and evaluating. Evaluating seeks to answer two important questions: "How do we know we have met our objectives?" and "How do we know that we are making a difference?" Yet of the three components of teaching, evaluation often receives least attention. Teachers perceive evaluation as difficult. It becomes a burden when writing and grading tests, completing report cards, and sacrificing class instructional time to administer various district, state, or national standardized tests. Less experienced teachers will probably find evaluation to be the most difficult component of teaching.

Teachers also need to determine regularly and systematically the quality of the social studies curriculum and their instructional strategies. Teachers must see student evaluation and program evaluation as equal parts of any assessment plan.

Before starting a discussion of evaluation, it is important to understand three truisms. These will help you construct a coherent rationale by showing the relationships between students and program quality.

Truism No. 1
- Students tend to learn what they are taught.

This truism should seem obvious. However, many schools administer national standardized tests, which have little relationship with the content of the local district curriculum or the type of student being taught. For example, if the students are not required to take a world geography course and the test has several such questions, most likely the students will not perform well on that portion of the test. It is important to know the correlation between items on any standardized test and the curriculum content being taught. The important questions to ask are, "Does this test have questions that reflect the content of the curriculum being taught to our students?" If not, "Should we change our curriculum or change the type of test to be administered, and why?"

Truism No. 2
- Student achievement on a norm-referenced test may have more to do with the social and economic status of students and their attitudes toward scholarship than the curriculum or the teacher's ability to teach.

Student achievement or lack of achievement may have little to do with teacher effectiveness. At least two social institutions outside education are key variables: the family and the community. If both these institutions demonstrate strong support for education, student achievement in that school will be higher. The current accountability movement implies that if students are not successful, then the teacher has not been successful. This is true to a degree, but it is important for teachers to be able to assess student learning correctly and evaluate their own teaching as a function of that learning.

Truism No. 3
- Students learn most effectively in classroom and community environments that support reflective inquiry and accept the tentativeness of information. These settings also encourage students and teachers to grapple intellectually with the world of ideas as well as direct experiences.

It is imperative that teachers promote learning that extends well beyond the memorization of facts and information to the construction and growth of knowledge. It is important that issues and policies examined for study have meaning for students and the community. Unfortunately, all too often evaluation as practiced in many social studies classrooms does not extend much beyond the recall of memorized facts.

Types of Evaluation

Assessment devices are useful in gathering information concerning the achievement of objectives; for example, to what extent has change taken place? Those used most often in social studies are 1) formal and informal observations, checklists, and rating scales (see the following examples of these measurement tools); 2) oral or written questionnaires; 3) analyses of students' work samples; and 4) tests that provide information about content, skills, perspectives, and thinking processes. A developing trend to evaluate student learning is through the use of a portfolio, which is defined by Paulson and colleagues (1991) as:

> . . . a purposeful collection of student work that exhibit[s] the students' efforts, progress, and achievements in one or more areas. The collection must include student participation in selecting contents, criteria for selection, criteria for judging merit, and evidence of student self-reflection.

Formal and Informal Observations, Checklists, and Rating Scales

Informal observations during teaching help teachers gather a great deal of information related to student performance. Most likely teachers will observe not only academic accomplishments but also will notice the social, emotional, and physical development of students as well. Data gathered needs to be recorded accurately, systematically, objectively, and unobtrusively. Checklists include a listing of behaviors the observer is looking for, while rating scales are used to judge the frequency of a behavior or quality of performance.

■■■■■■■ Checklist   Yes   No

Is the student on task?   _____   _____

Did the student participate in the discussion?   _____   _____

Has the student turned in the assignment?   _____   _____

Is the student able to work in a cooperative
learning group?   _____   _____

Rating scales use numbers to rate a list of attributes, which can range from satisfactory to unsatisfactory or from always to never. One such sample is provided.

■■■■■■■ Rating Scale

Directions: Place an X under the number that most nearly reflects the student's behavior.

	1	2	3	4
The student:	Always	Usually	Seldom	Never

1. is prompt.

2. takes responsibility for his or her behavior.

3. is willing to be an active learner.

4. demonstrates leadership skills.

Within an evaluation program there is a place for both subjective and objective assessments. Subjective evaluation usually concerns attitudes, interests, values, appreciations, and patterns of behavior. It also includes making judgments. These judgments are often based on rating scales, student or teacher-kept checklists, individual pupil-teacher conferences, class discussions, logs, diaries, anecdotal records, pupil questionnaires, work samples, committee reports, homework, peer evaluation, pupil self-evaluation, sociometric instruments, and other nonquantitative information. Knowledge, skills, and understanding can be measured objectively. At times teachers use unobtrusive measures to help assess student learning. These techniques include student participation in cocurricular activities, involvement in voluntary community service, or use of reference materials.

Pearl Oliner (1976) has suggested that there are overt as well as covert reasons for evaluations:

> What we say we are doing when we attempt to evaluate are the overt functions. There are however, covert functions as well—ones that are not publicly stated,

that are frequently unrecognized and unintended, and that would probably be largely unacceptable to teachers, parents, and students. For example, an overt function of assigned grades is to help students assess their progress. A covert function, however, is to assign students to occupational roles and social class, for grades are of crucial importance in determining who goes on to vocational or professional studies. And while many people may accept the first function as a legitimate one, they may find the second highly objectionable.

The following chart prepared by Oliner illustrates several overt and covert functions of student evaluation.

Overt and Covert Functions of Educational Evaluation

Overt	Covert
To enable pupils and parents to judge performance (grading)	To punish and reward To assign occupational roles and social class
To group students for more efficient learning	To track students To facilitate administrative procedures To ease the burden of preparation for teachers
To retain or promote students in order to facilitate learning	To punish and reward To avoid the necessity of individualizing instruction To maintain standardized means of dealing with individuals
To motivate achievement	To control student behavior To ensure conformity
To diagnose learning disabilities	To label students To legitimate a negative self-image To justify to others student failure
To modify course objectives in accordance with student needs	To placate discontent To keep standards low and easily attainable
To modify instructional strategies, techniques, and resources	To innovate for innovation's sake To achieve recognition, special funds, and jobs To conform to current fads

SOURCE: Oliner, Pearl M. (1976). *Teaching Elementary Social Studies: A Rational and Humanistic Approach.* New York: Harcourt Brace Jovanovich. (Reprinted by permission)

Why Evaluate Student Learning in Social Studies?

The answer teachers most frequently give to the question "Why evaluate student learning in the social studies?" is likely to be "Because I am required to assign grades." This view is rather limited. Teachers need to consider evaluation when selecting content and concepts, identifying objectives, determining skills, deciding teaching and learning strategies, making needed adjustments, and making decisions about students. There are four important assumptions concerning the evaluation of student learning that guide the social studies instructional program.

- The first assumption is that student evaluation measures student learning and competence.
- The second assumption is that the majority of students will demonstrate increased knowledge and skills if teachers have used appropriate instructional procedures and materials. Remember, in large classes it is often difficult to adapt instruction for individual differences. There are often great variations in students' background, prior knowledge, level of interest, personal motivation, or reading and communication skills.
- The third assumption is that the use of both quantitative and qualitative data from several sources adds meaning to the evaluation of student learning.
- The fourth assumption is that student evaluation should be based on both general course learning and on projects that reflect individual student interest and knowledge (Hartoonian and Laughlin, 1989).

In general, there are four types of evaluation: placement, diagnostic, formative, and summative. Each interrelated type of evaluation is valuable for social studies teachers to use in making educational decisions.

Placement evaluation is used for placing students in the proper course or section before beginning the instructional sequence. To make these judgments teachers may use aptitude tests, pretests covering the specific course objectives and content, observations, and self-checks. Basically, teachers use placement evaluation to find out if the student has the requisite knowledge and skills and has learned the content that they have taught. Teachers also find placement evaluation useful in determining if student interests, aptitudes, attitudes, and abilities fit with a particular teaching style or method of instruction. These informal assessment tests are often teacher-made and are administered, graded or scored, and interpreted by the teacher.

Placement tests indicate the content or skills a student can recall. These test results should become the starting points for instructional planning. In some instances one or more students will need remedial instruction so as not to fall behind even further in the instructional sequence. On the other hand, teachers will need to plan enrichment instruction for those students who are able to work ahead of many of their classmates. Middle school teachers who meet regularly as a team are likely to use this method of evaluation for student achievement and placement. At this level it is often easier to shift students from group to group than in high schools due to class schedules and other constraints.

Diagnostic evaluation provides teachers with information about prerequisite skills and prior knowledge students already have about a particular topic. This information provides a baseline for instructional planning. It should be self-evident that if the class already knows a great deal about the topic, then teaching this material, content, or skill may be nonproductive. Likewise, if the students do not have sufficient prior knowledge and background experience, then teaching the particular topic may be self-defeating.

A diagnostic test may be a standardized test to determine how the scores of a particular class compare with the scores of other typical students at that same level (a norm group). This predetermined norm or standard has been determined by administering the test to a representative sample of students. Other standardized tests may measure students' learning skills. The standard references for information about standardized tests are *The Eleventh Mental Measurements Yearbook* (Kramer and Conoley, 1992), *Tests in Print III* (Mitchell, 1983) and *Test Critiques* (Gale Research, 1993). We encourage you to consult these references, which are available in most college libraries, to determine which test most closely meets the teacher and district objectives.

A second type of diagnostic test is a pretest. Teachers who want to pretest their students will write questions to reflect the goals and objectives of the particular unit of study. The test usually includes several types of objective questions that attempt to determine what a student knows about the topic prior to its introduction; for example, what does the student already know about the 1920s? Teachers may then use the results of the pretest in planning the learning activities for the unit. Often teachers administer the same test or a different form of the test at the completion of the unit as a posttest to determine student growth and change during the unit. For the most part, grades students earn on diagnostic tests are not used to determine unit or course grades.

The National Council on Economic Education has prepared norm-referenced standardized diagnostic tests to measure student learning in economics. At present the *Test of Economic Literacy* for students in grades 11 and 12 (Soper and Walstad, 1986) assesses student knowledge of basic economic concepts necessary for effective citizenship in our roles as consumers, producers, and voters. The test has a fairly detailed test manual and provides two equivalent test forms. Both forms measure the same economic concepts and content using different but similar questions. The questions are based on five levels of questions adapted from Bloom's *Taxonomy of Educational Objectives* (1956).

The levels of questions utilized are knowledge, comprehension, application, analysis, and evaluation. The test was designed primarily to help high school teachers evaluate and improve the quality of teaching economics at the secondary level. There is also a *Test of Economic Knowledge* (Soper and Walstad, 1987) for grades 7–9. Both tests are based on the content categories outlined in *A Framework For Teaching the Basic Concepts* (Saunders, 1991). The accompanying test manual details the test-norming process.

The National Council of Geographic Education also has developed a test that measures student learning in geography. This test can help teachers identify areas where students need additional instruction in geographic content and skills. It is not necessary for teachers to use all the items in a standardized pretest, only those that are appropriate to the unit objectives.

Formative evaluation occurs before or during instruction and answers the question "How is the student doing?" Information gleaned from formative evaluation enables teachers to know the effectiveness of their instruction, to appraise student progress, to make mid-unit curricular changes, to decide if it is necessary to reteach any parts of the unit, to determine the impact of instructional innovations, and to formulate educational plans. Formative evaluation information may be obtained either through more formal testing or through informal means. For example, is the use of a computer program effective in demonstrating how a business cycle influences economic decisions? Or is an inquiry lesson to teach the concept of supply and demand effective? Your evaluation of a lesson or program guides your decision to continue, revise, or abandon it. Homework assignments and periodic quizzes also help the teacher to determine the effectiveness of a lesson or assignment and to identify students who may need additional instruction or may need to move ahead at a faster pace. The basic concept in formative evaluation is to determine if particular learning activities or materials work the way they were intended.

Summative evaluation provides a summary of accomplishment level and occurs at the end of a unit of instruction. Its primary purpose is to answer the question "What does the student know at the end of this unit?" Although summative evaluation can take on a variety of forms (reports, projects, performances, presentations, and so forth) most often it is a test. These tests measure the products of instruction but offer no information concerning the processes used by students to answer the test questions. Student success on the test usually becomes a major factor in determining the student's grade. It reveals the success of the teaching and learning process.

The distinction between formative and summative evaluation is based on how the measurement data are used. Formative evaluation helps in planning for instruction by seeking to determine how well a student is progressing during instruction, while summative evaluation assesses final achievement. Teachers should view evaluation as regular and ongoing and as an important component of the teaching and learning process (Slavin, 1991).

Scores from tests have no meaning until the score of a student or class is compared to a reference point. Three types of reference tests used by teachers are norm-referenced, criterion-referenced, and self-referenced.

Norm-referenced tests are used to evaluate student learning over relatively large segments of the course content and are used in summative evaluation. Norm-referenced tests seek to answer such broad questions as "How much does this student know about economics?" or "How well is this student able to gather, analyze, and interpret information from a variety of sources compared to other students of similar age and with similar course work?" These tests make it possible to compare one student's score with other students' scores (referred to as a norm group). Then teachers can determine if a particular student's score is below average, around the average, or above the average for the comparison groups. Norm-referenced tests are useful in measuring overall student achievement and may be appropriate when only a small number of the top students can be admitted to a specific program (Woolfolk, 1993).

Assigning grades based on a curve is an example of norm-referenced evaluation. In this grading method teachers give the highest grade to the student with the highest score. Similarly, the student with the lowest score receives the lowest grade. In effect, this practice neutralizes the shortcomings of the teacher and allows only a certain number of students to earn an A grade and requires some students to receive a grade of F. Grading on a curve may well discourage students who received grades lower than expected from working to their ability on the next assignment. It is also difficult for students to know their precise standing in the class in terms of the grade they earned until the end of the grading period when a grading curve can be determined. We discourage grading on a curve because students' abilities, aptitudes, and skills are not distributed on a normal curve.

Some standardized tests are norm-referenced, and they provide grade-equivalent or percentile scores. Teachers and administrators may use them to find out how well their students compare to students of a similar age or grade level on a district wide, statewide, or nationwide basis. In fields such as science and mathematics, United States students have been tested to determine how they compare to students in other nations. Students from other countries often score better than students from the United States. Both the SAT and ACT are norm-referenced tests that provide students with information about their levels of achievement. Colleges also use them for admission purposes and to predict academic success. Other examples of norm-referenced tests with social studies components include the following:

Iowa Tests of Educational Development (social studies subtest) Chicago: Science Research Associates

Sequential Tests of Education Progress Series III (includes social studies) Monterey, CA: CTB/McGraw-Hill

SRA Achievement Series (includes social studies skills and tests for higher level cognitive processes) Chicago: Science Research Associates

Descriptions of these and other tests that may be appropriate for use by social studies teachers are available in *Tests in Print III* (Mitchell, 1983).

Norm-referencing is criticized in the educational literature primarily because teachers misuse the information in making educational decisions. These tests do not inform teachers whether or not students are able to move on to more difficult materials; are not particularly useful in measuring objectives in the affective and psychomotor domains; and tend to encourage competition and a comparison of scores (Hopkins and Antes, 1985). Norm-referencing is useful and appropriate for ranking students, citing achievement in terms of percentile scores, selecting students for programs that have quota requirements, and to decide how much or little a student has learned in comparison to others. Norm-referenced tests also measure a small number of course objectives, hide the quality of the course, and override individual and educational considerations (Clift and Imrie, 1981).

Criterion-referenced tests measure individual student achievement against a predetermined standard of performance based on an absolute standard or criterion of quality. They are useful for diagnosing student difficulties, measuring what has been learned, estimating student abilities, determining competencies, and encouraging cooperation rather than competition. Criterion-referenced tests encourage the use of questions that provide right or wrong answers rather than promoting problem solving. In selecting answers on criterion-referenced tests, the student is required to select from among predetermined answers offered as possible choices.

The criterion is usually determined by a teacher's experience, intuition, and values, and on records of past student performance. If the teacher establishes a low criterion the result may be unduly high grades and limited grade spread. If the criterion is too high, then a large number of students receive low grades. Those who perform well are judged proficient and those who fail are deemed deficient. Establishing the appropriate standards for criterion-referenced tests is not always easy. These tests allow teachers to set reasonable standards that serve as targets for student achievement. Criterion-referenced tests are being used with greater frequency because they fit local instruction, indicate what students have learned, and provide information needed to individualize instruction. The test scores indicate when reteaching may be needed.

Self-referenced tests allow teachers to measure students against the students' own self-performance, such as in a change of attitude or ability to complete a particular task. A dilemma that teachers face when using self-referenced tests is in deciding grades. Should a student who completes a less challenging learning activity at a lower standard of expectation receive the same or higher grade than a student who has completed a more difficult activity? In answering this question it is important for you to understand district and school policies concerning grading, and your policy must be consistent. In general, measurement specialists agree that grades should reflect achievement, with effort and behavior kept separate. Grading in relation to aptitude takes into account individual differences among students. Some teachers may want to use continuous progress grading based on individualized instructional programs. Such grades may reflect the skills mastered with no indication of how well the student is progressing in relation to classmates.

When selecting or constructing a test, educators need to consider two characteristics: *validity* and *reliability*. Simply put, validity is truthfulness: Does the test measure what it says it measures? For example, if the unit objective is to teach the role of government in our daily lives, the teacher determines the validity of the evaluation by how effectively it measures this objective.

Reliability refers to the extent to which the test produces consistent results. For example, if on several occasions students are evaluated with a reliable test, they should score similar results each time. Reliability and validity are closely related. It is important to realize that a test that is a valid measure of an objective must be reliable and that a test can be reliable without being valid. There are a number of excellent textbooks that can provide more detailed information concerning evaluation and its implication for learning. We encourage you to consult these references for greater understanding of this important aspect of teaching.

Issues in Testing

The Accountability Movement

The decade of the 1960s was an exciting time for schools and education because comparatively large sums of money were spent on education. The 1960s offered incentives for curriculum innovation, expanded educational opportunities, reduced restrictive rules, and encouraged people to dream beyond their immediate surroundings. These years were all too short to achieve the future-oriented, visionary goals held by many during this decade. At the same time, and often overlooked, was a move toward accountability. The basic question being asked by legislators and others was "If we are spending more money on education, what are we getting for our money?"

The basic idea of accountability is that someone is held responsible for meeting the agreed-upon goals and objectives. With the relatively large sums of money being spent on education, legislatures, foundations, and other funding agencies wanted to know if the money was being well spent, if the funded programs were serving the targeted population, and if program goals and objectives were being achieved.

The effects of accountability requirements are still with us today. For example, the National Commission on Excellence in Education (1983) and most of the several hundred subsequent national and state reports regarding the quality of education in the United States called for greater accountability by both teachers and students. By the late 1980s over three-fourths of the states had developed their own statewide accountability programs. Many school districts are reporting achievement in terms of the district meeting its stated objectives.

With more and more states and districts stressing teacher and student accountability it is likely that testing will remain an ongoing issue in the coming months and years. For example, the 1992 Gallup Poll indicated that nearly three-fourths of those polled favor the use of standardized tests to measure the academic achievement of students (Elam, Rose, and Gallup, 1992). Participants in the same poll one year later in 1993 placed an emphasis on using tests to identify areas in which students require additional help and on identifying areas where teachers need to improve their teaching skills. The public has a long history of support for national testing (Elam, Rose, and Gallup, 1993). In this discussion it is important to keep in mind at least two questions: "What is the quality of the test itself?" and "How is the test being utilized?" Over the years there are numerous examples of test abuse and misuse. For example, some states have been charged with inappropriate use of the National Teacher Examination in an attempt to remove less able teachers from classrooms. In another example, some districts have inappropriately used intelligence tests to classify a large number of minority students for placement in special education classes.

Minimum Competency Testing

The national report *A Nation at Risk* (National Commission on Excellence in Education, 1983) indicated that approximately 23 million adults in the United States were functionally illiterate. There are some estimates that as many as 60 percent of 17-year-olds are semi-literate (Mehrens and Lehmann, 1987). This means that they are functioning academically at the 8th-grade level. One result of the report was that states mandate the development and use of minimum competency testing to ensure both student and teacher accountability. These test scores are used to evaluate the state's educational programs and to compare the performance of schools, districts, and teachers. Some schools may use the test results to establish remedial programs so that students are able to pass the tests when they are retaken. In several states students were required to pass such tests as a condition for high school graduation or to participate in cocurricular activities. Many state legislators and others believed that close monitoring of established standards would encourage teachers and students to spend more time on the "basics" since academic-engaged time seems to be associated with learning (Lerner, 1981). Others disagreed by noting that teachers would have less freedom in deciding what and how to teach and expressed concern that testing would control the curriculum. They also noted that minimum competency testing focuses on minimums, not maximums. It was also noted that such tests might discriminate against minority students and those from impoverished backgrounds.

Bias in Testing

Minority group students and students from lower socioeconomic backgrounds usually score lower than middle-class students on most standardized tests (Burton and Jones, 1982), although the gap is lessening. This raises a number of questions concerning ethnic and gender test bias. Critics argued that these tests favored middle-class students who are likely to be more familiar with testing procedures and the content of the test. There have been attempts to develop culture-fair tests using nonverbal items so as to minimize language variation, but to date these attempts have not been very successful (Anastasi, 1988; Mehrens and Lehmann, 1987).

Experts, parents, and educators are more and more concerned about the effects of testing on minority students. Educators who use standardized test results for minority students need to be aware of test bias and cultural impacts, which are likely to affect student performance (National Commission on Testing and Public Policy, 1990). At times test anxiety may cause a student to perform below his or her abilities. To help all students overcome test anxiety teachers should teach test-taking skills, and, if possible, provide more time for test taking. Teachers should also simplify test-taking procedures and mechanics. In making decisions about students, educators are urged to go beyond standardized test scores and consider class participation and out-of-school performance, such as volunteer service in the community, cocurricular activities, jobs, and the like.

Curriculum-Based Assessment

A criticism of existing achievement and intelligence tests is that the results provide the teachers with information that may not be especially useful in planning for instruction. Often there is little match of what is taught in the classroom and what is tested using standardized achievement tests. Proponents of a curriculum-based assessment (CBA) argue that testing should be based on the curriculum, that test items refer to specific objectives, and that student performance indicates which objectives have or have not been mastered (Shapiro and Derr, 1990). While most often used at the elementary level, CBA assessments indicate what students know based on the curriculum and the rate students are acquiring new information (Travers, Elliott, and Kratochwill, 1993). CBA advocates also believe that remedial instruction and appropriate interventions should be provided to enable students to achieve the objectives (Deno, 1985). For example, a modified test covering the same content may be used, the test could be oral rather than written, or the student may be given a longer time to complete the task at hand. This approach is often used in special education and does provide opportunities to maximize instructional time. However, with larger classes and multiple teaching assignments it is difficult for teachers to meet the individual needs of all the students. Yet CBA is attractive to teachers and school psychologists (Rosenfield and Shinn, 1989).

We encourage you to reflect on these and other topics related to testing and evaluating both individual and group achievement and performance. Testing and accountability are here to stay and are likely to receive even greater attention in the years ahead.

Measuring Student Learning—Illustrative Examples

Once students enter school they are subjected to grading. Most often grading criteria are established by individual teachers within the framework of the district's grading philosophy. The use of grades is one way teachers and schools have to communicate useful and necessary information regarding student achievement to students, parents, other educators, and various interested parties concerned about student performance. Most middle school and high school teachers rely on pencil and paper tests to assign grades. Grades are also highly emotional. They communicate the relative values of a student's work in a particular class. For a student who does well grades are a positive reinforcer and self-satisfaction is high. For students who do not perform well or up to their own expectations or the expectations of others, however, low grades may be devastating and hinder the development or retention of positive self-esteem. If earning high grades is overemphasized, learning for knowledge or the joy of learning ceases to be a desirable goal as learning becomes interwoven with the competition for high grades.

As reported in Kindswitter, Wilen, and Ishler (1988), grades serve four purposes: 1) administrative, to determine promotion or retention, honors, transfers, class standing, and recommendations for admission to college or employment; 2) guidance, for advice on course selection and career choices; 3) informative, by communicating the results of evaluation to the appropriate people; and 4) disciplinary (though not recommended) and motivational, by providing knowledge of achievement as an incentive to students. Grades may have a negative impact on students and teachers in that they may also be subjective; be unreliable; bring about unfair competition among individuals or groups of students; preoccupy the time of students, parents, and teachers; fail to recognize individual differences; encourage low-level teaching of trivial information to be given back on tests; and support dependency.

Grades have different effects on students. Teachers, however, can develop a thoughtful and sensitive student evaluation plan by using a developmental approach to determining grades and by minimizing potential negative effects of grades. In general, it is wise to base grades on several criteria, including oral reports, creative projects, and active class participation, or the use of both essay and objective test questions (of various types) on a test.

Teachers may want to consider other methods for evaluating student learning, such as the following:

1. A *contract system,* which describes the type, quality, and quantity of work to be completed by a student in order to earn a particular grade. It appears to be more suitable for use with small classes and for independent study. Written contracts listing expectations are recommended so as to avoid misunderstanding of the criteria used to grade the assignment.
2. A *developmental or mastery learning approach,* which requires teachers to divide the course into several specific measurable objectives that most students can learn if given sufficient time and correct instruction. The grade is determined by the proficiency level of the units completed. Students who do not achieve minimum mastery are then given the time and opportunity to relearn the unit and then take a different version of the unit test. The development approach may be effective for individualized learning but may be difficult to implement for entire classes if a large number of students requires remedial instruction. Such remedial help is usually given by the classroom teacher who then assigns other, often "busy," work to the faster learners, before going on to the next instructional level or unit. At other times the remedial instruction is provided outside the framework of regular class time, such as during lunch, before or after school, or on weekends. Teachers may also use alternative textbooks, workbooks, and programmed instruction to provide remedial assistance. Development learning usually means that students have an 80 or 90 percent correct response and assumes that everything in an instructional unit must be learned equally well by all students.

    Developmental learning critics argue that such learning provides a "Robin Hood effect," that is, helping slower learners at the expense of more able learners. Beyond basic skills and hierarchial subjects a development learning approach may be hard to defend. There is also a concern that less content will be covered, which is an important predictor of achievement.
3. *Grading based on improvement or effort* has been a long-standing dilemma in judging student achievement. Some teachers develop an individual learning expectation score based on previous work, and they judge current work in relation to the students' own abilities. The focus

is on improvement in learning rather than on comparisons with other students. If a teacher uses such an evaluation system it is useful to keep in mind that the brightest and best students will improve the least because they already have some degree of competence for the content or skill being taught.
4. *Group grading* for group assignments or projects that are completed by using cooperative learning activities merits consideration. Group grading may help to reduce evaluation pressures on individual students by assigning group rather than individual grades for the learning activity. A balance and mix of individual and group grades seem appropriate in determining grades. Of course there are several inherent problems with group grading, such as some students may not contribute to the group effort, an individual student may dominate the group, some students may develop unrealistic expectations about their own abilities, and students (and their parents) are accustomed to students earning individual grades.

Each teacher needs to develop his or her own grading system that is fair, consistent, and compatible with the grading philosophy of the department and school. Whatever grading system is used, it needs to be conveyed to students, their parents, guidance counselors, school administrators, and the community so that all have a common understanding of what a particular grade means. Issues that need to be considered in determining student grades include student achievement, attitude, citizenship efforts, participation, extra credit, attendance, and the weight each has in determining the grade. Are the grades cumulative for a semester? What percents or point accumulations constitute an A, B, C, D, or F grade in this particular class? In general, an A grade reflects superior and outstanding accomplishment; B grades reflect above average, high quality work; C grades indicate a competent or average performance; D grades inform the student and others of low achievement and minimum passing; and F grades are interpreted as a failure or nonaccomplishment. What scales and symbols are to be used to communicate grades? Are pass/fail grades possible? To what extent will grades be adjusted for accelerated or less able students? Are grades criterion-referenced, which assesses a student's mastery of skills regardless of how well other students performed on the same test, or norm-referenced, which focus on comparing student scores with each other? This latter practice may result in grading on a curve. For the most part, criterion-referenced tests are closely aligned to the curriculum content and course objectives. Should grades earned in more difficult classes be given greater weight? Developing answers to these questions will help you develop a grading philosophy of your own.

It is important for students to receive constructive teacher feedback concerning accomplishments and lack of success. A valuable approach is to tell students *why* the response is correct so as to reinforce learning and increase motivation and *why* the response is not accurate so that students are less likely to make similar mistakes in the future. Both oral and written comments can be offered to help students improve their performance if the comments are personalized and if they offer constructive criticism. Respect is an important part of feedback to students.

Guidelines for Writing Questions to Measure Student Learning

All tests, teacher-made or standardized, should be constructed carefully, emphasize important content, concepts, and skills, and measure student learning based on the unit objectives. Test questions should not become trivial pursuit-type questions that emphasize rote learning and memorization of detail. As teachers prepare tests they should ask themselves, "What is it that I am testing?" and "How can I find out how well the students have learned?" The test should be viewed by both teachers and students as an integral part of the instructional unit. Ideally questions should be prepared as the unit is planned and not the night prior to the test, although the latter is likely to happen.

Textbook publishers generally prepare chapter and unit test questions to accompany their textbooks. Some of these questions are excellent, however many factual recall questions are included. Often questions included in textbooks and in author-publisher prepared tests are low-level questions requiring recall of separate pieces of information rather than asking for critical thinking and problem solving. Furthermore, publisher-prepared questions are not written specifically to meet the particular unit objectives, focus, or the needs of the students in your class. Teachers may decide to use some publisher-prepared questions along with several of their own. In constructing a test, you should include both objective and essay-type questions periodically.

Here are several general guidelines we suggest to help you write test questions:

- Test questions should be directly related to unit objectives and not be more difficult or easier than the objective itself.
- Test questions should include the content from the entire unit of instruction.
- Test questions should be written at the appropriate level of difficulty in terms of reading, content, concepts, skills, or processes involved.
- Each question should be clear and unambiguous, accurate, and written with the correct spelling and sentence structure.
- Questions should not be copied directly from textbooks as this tends to foster memorization.
- The test should be of proper length to allow students to complete it without the added undue pressure of time.

- Clear and precise directions should be written for each section of the test so that students may respond appropriately.
- The point value for each question or test section should be included so that students will know how much time to spend on each part.
- Items of the same type (multiple choice, binary choice, matching, fill-in or short answer, and essay) should be grouped together to facilitate student response.
- Within each type of question, the order of questions should be arranged in some logical or sequential order.
- The chapters included on the test and the title of the test should be indicated on the heading of the test, for instance, "Chapter 15—The Age of Napoleon."
- The test should include a place for students to write in their names, the section or period, and the date the test was taken.

Specific guidelines for the most common objective and essay-type questions are discussed in the next several pages. Illustrative examples of questions of each type are also included. Quality objective test questions are a real challenge and may take a relatively long time to construct, but are easier to correct either by the teacher or by electronic scanning if that format is used. It is suggested that teachers begin with multiple-choice questions and change to other types of objective test questions if the content or learning makes this desirable.

Multiple-Choice Questions

Many teachers assume that multiple-choice questions are used primarily for asking students to respond to questions that require a lower level of thinking. Multiple-choice items can test higher level objectives if students are asked to apply a concept or principle to new material or to analyze statements or assumptions. These latter questions, however, may be more difficult to prepare (Carter, 1984).

Multiple-choice questions consist of an incomplete sentence or question (stem) followed by three or four plausible options. One of the responses is predetermined as the correct answer. The other incorrect but closely related responses are the distractors. The stem should include as much of the wording as possible so that long phrases do not need to be repeated in each alternative answer. The answer choices should be approximately the same length so that unduly long or short responses do not influence the test-taker to choose or reject a particular option.

You should try to avoid negatively stated items, alternative answers that overlap, and clues that indicate clearly the correct answer or make it possible to eliminate incorrect answers. You should vary the position of the correct responses in a random manner to avoid establishing a pattern. The use of "all of the above" or "none of the above" as possible responses should be done sparingly as these possible responses may give away the correct answer. The following illustrative multiple-choice questions provide a format for preparing questions of this type.

■■■■■■■ Illustrative Examples: Multiple-Choice Questions

Directions: In the space provided write in the letter of the correct answer. (2 points)

_____ 1. Look at the map on page ___ of the atlas and identify which country borders Switzerland.

* A. Austria
  B. Belgium
  C. Spain
  D. Denmark

This question asks students to use a reference tool (atlas), examine a particular map, and respond to the question, which has one correct answer.

■■■■■■■ *Directions: Use the answer sheet provided and mark the correct answer by filling in the bubble. (2 points)*

1. What seems to be the purpose of the commission that wrote *A Nation at Risk*?

  A. to recognize the achievements of the United States educational system
* B. to bring about educational reform in this country
  C. to recommend that the Department of Education no longer have Cabinet status
  D. to encourage the use of school vouchers to allow for freedom of educational choice

This question asks students to identify the reason why *A Nation At Risk* was written. The distractors are of similar length and format.

Matching Items

Matching items are a modification of multiple-choice questions and are used to evaluate students' ability to make associations: persons and events; cause and effect; words and definitions; concepts and examples; and problems and solutions. It is wise to keep the number of items to be matched small (five to eight), provide at least one extra response to reduce the likelihood of guessing, and require that some responses be used more than once to minimize guessing. Grouping of items should be similar, such as people in one set of questions, places in another, and definitions in another. Dissimilar items should not be mixed. The items in one column should be arranged in some logical order, for example, chronological, alphabetical, or geographical. Homogeneous materials should be in both columns. So that students do not have to turn pages to match the items in a group, it is wise to keep the columns on the same page of the test. Most matching item questions are low-level recall-association type questions and are best used to test factual material. In the example below, students are asked to recall and identify particular people.

Illustrative Examples: Matching Items

Directions: Match the names of the people in Column A to the appropriate description of each in Column B. No description should be used more than once. (3 points each.)

Column A	Column B
_____ 1. Yassar Arafat	a. Israeli prime minister
_____ 2. Golda Meir	b. Secretary General of the United Nations
_____ 3. Richard Nixon	c. Military head of NATO defense forces
_____ 4. Anwar Sadat	d. President of the United States
_____ 5. Kurt Waldheim	e. Chief and leader of the Palestine Liberation Organization
	f. President of an Arab nation
	g. Representative to the United Nations

Directions: Match the following responsibilities of government with the branch of government responsible for this function. Write the correct letters in the space provided. The responses may be used more than once. (3 points each.)

Responsibility	Branch of Government
_____ 1. Decides on legal questions brought before the body	a. Executive
	b. Judicial
_____ 2. Has primary responsibility to ensure national security	c. Legislative
_____ 3. Has primary responsibility for protecting and caring for the environment	
_____ 4. Has control of the budget	
_____ 5. Has treaty-making responsibilities	
_____ 6. Brings impeachment charges	
_____ 7. Ratifies treaties	

A poorly constructed set of matching items might be the following:

Directions: Match the items in Column A with the items in Column B. (3 points each)

Column A	Column B
1. International organization founded in 1945 to ensure world peace	A. Security Council
	B. New York City
2. U.S. President at the end of World War II	C. Harry S Truman
3. The year North Korea invaded South Korea	D. October 24, 1945
4. The U.N. body that has veto power by its permanent members	E. World Peace Association
5. The headquarters city of the U.N.	F. 1950
6. The date the U.N. charter came into operation	G. UNICEF
	H. United Nations
7. The U.N. agency that provides care of young people	I. San Francisco

These matching items are poor because they are badly organized, and because the names, dates, and places in Column B are mixed.

The following questions are examples of "higher"-level questions which ask students to use synthesizing and evaluating skills to answer the question.

Synthesis: Select the sequence of actions in making a decision. (3 points.)
Sam and Mary Ann have inherited $200,000 from a wealthy relative. They must decide what to do with their inheritance, which was unexpected. Given what you know about the decision-making process, what sequence should they use in making a decision about their inheritance?

1. Identify criteria
2. State the problem
3. Evaluate the decision
4. Identify alternatives
5. Make a decision

_____	A. 1,2,4,5,3	_____	C. 1,4,2,5,3
* _____	B. 2,4,1,5,3	_____	D. 5,2,1,4,3

Evaluation: Evaluate the following statements. (3 points.)
Using information you have learned about the world economy, rank the following items in terms of their impact on the world's economic future.

1. Population growth
2. Long-term international conflict
3. Reestablishment of trade barriers among the nations of the world

* _____	A. 1,2,3	_____	D. 2,3,1
_____	B. 1,3,2	_____	E. 3,1,2
_____	C. 2,1,3	_____	F. 3,2,1

Binary Choice–Alternative Response Items

Questions that provide only two possible responses should be used only when two choices are plausible. Students may respond by marking True–False; T–F; right–wrong; yes–no; agree–disagree; and so forth. If this type of question is used, it is wise to include an equal number of true and false items and arrange them in random order. Words such as *all, always, never, none,* and other specific determiners usually mean the statement will be false, while the use of terms such as *generally*, *may*, or *should* usually indicate the statement is true. Each item should be completely true or false with the key element placed in the main part of the question or statement. The use of double negatives in a sentence should be avoided because this type of statement is confusing to the reader. A major drawback in using such questions is that students have a 50 percent chance of guessing the correct response. When using binary choice–alternative response questions, sometimes it is useful to ask students to rewrite false statements to make them true.

Illustrative Examples: Binary Choice–Alternative Response Items

Directions: In the space provided indicate whether the following statements are fact statements or opinion statements. Use "F" for fact; use "O" for opinion. (1 point each.)

_____ 1. Franklin D. Roosevelt called December 7, 1941 "a day of infamy."

_____ 2. The tax reform legislation of the late 1980s benefited virtually all taxpayers in the United States.

_____ 3. Settling disputes through arbitration is more effective than settling disputes by mediation.

_____ 4. Reverend Jesse Jackson is the best public speaker in the United States.

Directions: Mark an "X" by the geographic features and cultural characteristics of Ecuador. (2 points each.)

Ecuador

_____ 1. is a mountainous country.

_____ 2. is located in Central America.

_____ 3. includes a large indigenous population.

_____ 4. is the second largest country in Latin America.

_____ 5. is a Pacific Rim nation.

_____ 6. is located on the equator.

_____ 7. is a land-locked nation.

_____ 8. exports large quantities of tin and copper.

_____ 9. is considered a third-world country.

_____ 10. was part of Spain's New World empire.

Short-Answer Completion Questions

These questions require students to supply the correct or best answer by completing sentences, providing examples, defining terms, offering analogies, extending main ideas, and so forth. Completion questions require students to fill in the blanks, while short-answer items require a more detailed response to the question. Completion items are difficult to construct so that only one response is correct. Most often questions in this format are lower-level recall questions. Such questions should be used sparingly (Gronlund, 1988).

In writing short-answer completion questions it is important to avoid ambiguity and make certain that only one term (or a synonym) is an appropriate response, otherwise deciding correct or incorrect responses may be difficult. In writing such questions only key words should be omitted, but not so many words as to obscure the meaning of the question or statement. The size of the blanks should be uniform throughout the test and care needs to be taken to avoid using *a* or *an* before a blank, which could provide a clue to the correct answer.

Illustrative Examples: Short-Answer Completion Questions

Directions: Write your responses in the space provided. (5 points each.)

1. Write one example of British colonial policy in Africa in the 19th century.

   _____

2. Write one example of how employers exploited their employees in the United States during the 19th century.

   _____

Essay Questions

Some learning objectives are best measured through essay questions, which require students to create responses on their own. There are several important considerations in writing, using, and grading essay examinations.

For some teachers essay questions are easier and quicker to construct. However, grading the answers is often more difficult and time consuming, which makes it difficult to provide early and effective feedback to students.

Essay questions allow students to demonstrate higher-level thinking skills, such as the ability to organize ideas, apply knowledge, analyze and synthesize information, evaluate proposals, make inferences, interpret facts with insight and imagination, formulate hypotheses, make predictions, and offer opinions based on information through writing. Essay tests may also cover less material than objective tests because responding to essay questions requires more time. In most instances only two or three essay questions should be included on a single test administered during a single class period so that students will have sufficient time to read and understand the question, organize information, think about an answer, and write, edit, or revise parts of their responses.

There are two types of essay questions: 1) restricted response items, which establish limits for the response; and 2) extended response items, which allow for a fairly wide range of responses. Sometimes essay tests require that students respond to questions without the use of instructional materials and at other items students are to base their responses on materials such as photographs, maps, charts, graphs, documents, or artifacts that have been placed before them.

When writing essay questions it is better that precise terms such as *define, compare, defend a position, analyze,* or *evaluate* be used rather than the ambiguous term *discuss.* (Salvia and Ysseldyke, 1991). The following chart indicates the type of answer that is desired when terms such as the following are used in essay questions.

Table 12.2 Expected Essay-Type Responses

Term	Type of Answer Desired
Define, Describe, Identify, (Who, What, When, Which, and Where)	Gives meaning, offers essential characteristics
List	Enumerates
Discuss	Requires more than explanation, description or identification; assumes that implications and relationships among people, events, and issues will be included
Outline	Identifies key topics to present an argument
Develop	Takes an idea, topic, or issue and expands upon it
Summarize	Uses information or ideas from one or more sources and synthesizes the data into manageable size
Explain	Analyzes and makes clear a concept, event, or behavior that goes beyond a definition and describes why and how

Compare	Identifies and explains similarities
Contrast	Identifies and explains differences
Defend a position	Takes a position on an issue and supports the position taken with evidence and reasoning
Analyze	Takes a problem or issue and identifies the important issues and arguments
Evaluate	Gives value to something by enumerating and explaining the pros and cons of the alternative

Questions should be written clearly so that students will be able to demonstrate the required knowledge. It is useful to remember that examination anxiety may prevent an accurate evaluation of learning for some students and perhaps you will need to develop an alternative means of evaluation, such as an oral test.

It is recommended that a model answer and grading key be formulated as each question is written. Decisions need to be made concerning the scoring (value) of major points presented in the answer. As much as possible, papers should be read without identifying the writer so as to avoid the so-called halo effect. This may mean asking students to write their names on the back of the paper so that the grader does not know which student wrote the particular response. Sometimes knowing who wrote the answer may well influence the points given to the response. For example, if the student is of below average ability, a teacher may judge the response more critically while giving a "brighter" student the benefit of a doubt and more points.

When grading essay questions it is usually most efficient to grade one item at a time for each paper so that the same criteria can be applied at the same time. For example, read all of the answers for the first essay question before moving on to subsequent essay questions. And finally, to avoid the possibility of grading questions more severely or with greater leniency at the beginning or end, it is wise to shuffle the tests after the answers to each question have been read. It is also a good idea to spot-check the papers to be certain that the same criteria and standards were applied throughout the grading of each question so that those papers graded at the beginning or end do not receive either higher or lower grades than do papers with similar responses.

There is some evidence that a paper that is neat, has a polished style, uses correct spelling and grammar, and shows an impressive vocabulary in the middle of rather mediocre papers may receive a higher grade while a less polished paper in a group of excellent papers may receive a lower grade irrespective of the content. Such bias in grading (while unintended) may distort the grades assigned to students (Curzon, 1985).

Teachers seek to score essay responses as accurately and fairly as possible but need to recognize that they will be influenced by personal values, expectations, and attitudes. To ensure fairness in grading, at times it is valuable to ask a colleague familiar with your course, its objectives, and goals to grade your tests. In return you may offer to grade the tests from your colleague's classes. This practice can provide valuable insights and useful information concerning possible grading bias.

Illustrative Examples: Essay Questions

Directions: On a separate sheet of paper, write your answers to the following essay questions. The point value for each question is in the parenthesis following the question.

(Restricted Questions)

1. What steps did the United States take in its foreign policy to reduce the expansion and threat of communism from 1945–1955? To what extent was United States foreign policy behavior consistent in Europe and Asia? (10 points)
2. What efforts has the United States government made to ensure equality of opportunity for all since World War II? Consider civil rights legislation, court rulings, and executive orders that were intended to achieve equality for United States citizens. (20 points)

(Extended Questions)

1. The state legislature is considering a bill that would prohibit students (under 18) from having a drivers license unless they were enrolled in school and receiving passing grades in all of their classes. Write a statement for or against this proposed legislation and include evidence to support your position. (20 points)
2. Read the letters Abigail Adams wrote to John Adams while he was attending the Constitutional Convention. What advice does she offer her husband? Based on these letters, what can you infer about her interests and concerns? (10 points)

Poorly written essay questions fail to inform students how much detail is to be included in their responses. For example, if a student is asked on a test to "Discuss the situation in the Middle East," it is difficult to know what is expected in the answer. Is the student to discuss its history, geographic characteristics, economic development, or cultural achievements, role in international politics, social fabric? Such a question is too broad and allows a students to write about virtually any aspect of the "situation in the Middle East."

Other Considerations in Assigning Grades

As previously mentioned, at times it is very useful for teachers to consider using an oral examination and/or other means for evaluating student learning and assigning grades. It is also important that teachers instruct students on how to take a test and provide opportunities for students to practice this skill. Teachers should teach students test-taking skills by giving various practice examples in class. For example, if the test is to include interpreting numeric data in tabular form, the students should have many practice examples of interpreting such data. The teacher should provide feedback to students on the success or lack of success in these practice exercises. By practicing various types of test questions and receiving teacher feedback, students should be able to become successful test-takers. Secondary social studies teachers may believe test-taking skills have been taught in earlier grades or in other curriculum areas, but often this important skill development has been overlooked.

For students to do well on tests, teachers will want to tell students to consider the following:

1. Read the directions and follow them in answering the questions.
2. Know how much time is allowed for the test and decide how to allocate time allowed.
3. Skim the entire test quickly and look for the point value for each question or part of the test.
4. Answer the easiest questions first.
5. Underline key words on questions not answered quickly.
6. Eliminate incorrect responses and consider the plausible correct answers.
7. Review answers after completing the test.

For practice, teachers can use sample questions of their own creation or publisher-prepared questions that will not be used on the test. Students may be encouraged to practice test-taking skills in small groups and share their thinking processes as they respond to the practice questions.

For essay-type tests, the wise student will need to 1) know how much time is allocated and decide how to divide the time for each question based on point value assigned to the question; 2) read the question carefully; 3) outline or jot down ideas, key facts, or arguments that might be included in the response; 4) follow the directions in terms of what is being asked in the questions, for example, describe, evaluate, and analyze; 5) write clearly and legibly; and 6) proofread the answers for clarity, misspelling, incorrect grammar, and factual errors before turning the test into the teacher. Students should have ample opportunities to prepare practice essay answers for peer critique as well as for teacher comment.

The preceding paragraphs have addressed evaluation concerns in the cognitive domain. While affective change in students cannot be measured directly, it can be inferred from other behaviors. Teachers often use interest inventories, values questionnaires, attitudinal scales, and the like to gain an understanding of student attitudes, behaviors, and expectations. For example, in an informal conversation with the teacher, students may indicate that they now regularly watch the evening news because they have developed an interest in current events. Such a conversation would be some indication of a changed behavior for that student.

Ideally, tests, like homework and other assignments, should be reviewed and graded promptly and returned to students. Realistically, if a teacher has to grade papers from many large classes at the same time, this may not be possible. When returning tests to students it is a good teaching practice to review tests with students to clarify misunderstandings and misconceptions or to correct unintentional grading errors. Since some students are likely to be absent when a test is given, it is useful to decide and announce to the students in advance policies for making up tests (and other course work as well). This is especially important if the same test is to be taken by students who were absent when the test was given initially. If the tests have been returned to students, and the same test is to be used as the make-up test, some students are likely to share test information with one another. It is probable that several students will be absent on the day a test is given or a major assignment is due. If this is the case, it may be necessary to talk to students individually about the absence and make provisions for accepting late work.

Why Is the Development of a Test Bank of Questions Useful in Social Studies?

Writing quality test questions is not an easy task. All too often the preparation of test questions is left until the night before a test is scheduled. As a result the test may not adequately evaluate student learning because it was prepared hastily. Often this leads teachers to one of three possibilities: 1) relying primarily on author/publisher tests; 2) writing original questions that may be directly related to the unit objectives; and 3) using some combination of the above. The development and use of a test bank of questions by several teachers who teach the same course is one way to help teachers prepare better quality tests to more effectively evaluate student learning.

For example, suppose that all of the United States history teachers at the school or district level reviewed the tests they had given during the preceding year and extracted the "best" questions. These items would then be placed in a test item bank for use by all the teachers in the school or district. If there were "gaps" in questions, such as insufficient questions for a particular topic or time period, teachers could generate additional questions to fill the void.

The next step would be to field-test the questions to determine if the questions made sense to the test-taker. Test questions that were found to be deficient could be revised or discarded and other questions could be developed. By having a variety of questions on different levels of difficulty on each topic, teachers would have flexibility in choosing the questions that best matched their particular objectives. With the use of computers it is relatively easy to create a computerized test bank of questions to facilitate test construction.

Examples of computer programs useful in the preparation of tests include *Examwriter, QuickTests, Quiz Program, Test Factory,* and *Testmaster.* Some school districts have established test banks of questions from which teachers may locate and select appropriate questions, run a computer printout, and include questions from the test bank in developing their own tests. With the use of computers it is relatively easy to produce several forms of the same test for use by students in different sections of the same course. The computer can be programmed to select similar questions in terms of topic, degree of difficulty, and so forth.

As teachers use questions from the test bank, baseline data can be established that point to strengths and weaknesses in the course or program. This information is important for program evaluation and for local curriculum development and revision. If districts develop a series of comprehensive social studies tests to be administered to students at several grade levels, for example, in grades, 3, 6, 9, and 12, the tests should be cumulative. For example, several questions asked on the 9th-grade test should address the content, concepts, and skills that were taught in the overall K–9 social studies program and not be confined to the content, concepts, and skills that were taught in the 9th-grade social studies program.

Authentic Assessment

The term *authentic assessment* has no standard definition but is a central feature of school restructuring and is being proposed as a replacement for standardized testing and the traditional pencil-and-paper classroom tests. Archbald and Newmann (1988) have defined authentic assessment as "a valid assessment system that provides information about particular tasks on which students succeed or fail, but more important, it also presents tasks that are worthwhile, significant, and meaningful—in short, authentic." *Performance assessment* has been defined as "assessments in which the teacher observes and makes a judgment about a pupil's skill in carrying out an activity or producing a product" (Airasian, 1991).

Authentic assessment requires that assessment activities be similar to those used outside the classroom. For example, the student must produce something new rather than reproduce prior knowledge. Two such assessment activities are suggested. One activity might ask a student to attend a meeting of the local school board and to prepare a report (oral or written) on the major issues discussed at the meeting and to include his or her reflections on the issues discussed. Or another activity asks a student to analyze a proposed government program such as health care, crime reduction, or tax reform and to send his or her ideas and recommendations to members of the state's congressional delegation. It is intended to provide evidence that the student has accomplished the learning objectives; it provides evidence of performance or demonstration skills; and it emphasizes the use of knowledge and appreciation of skills in problem contexts (Stiggins, 1987). Performances and demonstrations can be videotaped to provide feedback to students and to allow others to evaluate the performance. Teachers in the areas of art, music, physical education, and vocational and technical education have used performance assessment to determine what students have learned and to determine how well specific objectives have been achieved.

Student Work Samples (Portfolios)

A relatively new and potentially valuable authentic assessment tool for social studies teachers is portfolio assessment. At present, models for portfolio review come primarily from writing and language arts classes where samples of classroom work are selected and placed in a portfolio (Gage and Berliner, 1991). Over time, the portfolio includes working drafts, papers rewritten for improvement, and other samples identified by the students to be included in the portfolio. The use of a portfolio allows students to reflect on their own learning and thus become self-evaluative. The content of that portfolio provides evidence of student learning (Paulson, Paulson, and Meyer, 1991).

In social studies, materials that could be added in the portfolio may include test results, projects, maps, reports, homework assignments, a bibliography of books the student has read, video- or audiotapes the student has seen or heard, creative efforts, a written autobiography, and so forth. Such materials can be a valuable tool for teacher-student discussion about student progress and, in some instances, may be shared with parents and others with student permission. Rather than assigning a letter grade, or in addition to a letter grade, the teacher may also include a written narrative about long-term student accomplishment. It is likely that portfolio assessment will become a fairly common assessment tool as it expands into various curriculum areas. The portfolio is an archive documentary of student performance. For teachers to interpret the results of these assessments, evaluation schemes need to be developed. Within the authentic assessment movement such evaluations are called profiles, which allow teachers and others to make reliable judgments about a student's level of proficiency. Developing such a profile evaluation and scoring scheme is the most challenging aspect of authentic assessment. Performance-based grading benchmarks become the standards by which student accomplishment is evaluated. Student self-assessment based on expected learning is an important component of authentic assessment.

This approach to assessment is demanding and places heavy emphasis on teacher judgment. Such a process requires a heavy investment in time and resources.

Evaluating Social Studies Programs

Program evaluation is a process in which teachers, administrators, parents, and the community establish a set of standards and collect and analyze data to answer the questions "How does the current social studies program match the desired goals for improvement?" and "What are the strengths and weaknesses of the several components of the social studies programs?" Educational goals, evaluation criteria, and current educational practices are constantly changing and thus program evaluation is not something fixed or static, but is flexible, dynamic, and complex.

Criteria for Evaluating Social Studies Programs

As schools use site-based management teams to make curriculum and instructional decisions concerning program effectiveness, it will be useful for you to be aware of some criteria that are often used to make judgments and decisions regarding program effectiveness. In constructing criteria for judging social studies programs it is important to establish a vision of desirable improvements to ensure quality programs. Without such a vision it will be difficult to make the needed program changes. The suggested questions that follow present an idea that may be ahead of existing practices.

- Is there an effective K–12 social studies curriculum committee with representatives from different grades, disciplines, and years of experience? In addition to teachers, are administrators, parents, community members, and students included on the committee? Does the committee have a reasonable budget to function effectively?
- Does the social studies program address the needs of the students and the community by including the study of history and other social science disciplines? Do all students have an opportunity for social studies instruction (enrichment and remedial) each year they are enrolled in school? Has a definite amount of time, for example, one class period per day for all students, been allocated to social studies? Are there opportunities for students to study about the culture and heritage of the United States, various global themes, and interrelationships among the several social science disciplines?
- Has the social studies curriculum committee worked to develop a district statement of philosophy, goals, and objectives? Does the program include meaningful social studies goals and objectives; a logical and coherent scope and sequence; an identification of key concepts and content, important skills, and attitudes; appropriate evaluation procedures to measure student learning and evaluate the curriculum; and an identification of appropriate print and nonprint references reflecting several perspectives for both teachers and students? Is there an opportunity for developing and teaching interdisciplinary units of instruction? Is social studies content integrated in other curriculum areas?
- Have student and faculty activities been reported in the media to increase community awareness concerning the accomplishments and needs of the social studies program? Is there a policy statement that

enables the community to understand and support the social studies program?
- Are social studies teachers able to develop and pilot new instructional programs, field-test new instructional materials, participate in active and applied research, and publish the results? To what extent are social studies teachers engaged in shaping the rationale for the changing nature of the social studies programs and instruction?
- Does the social studies program strike a balance between uniformity and flexibility?

In addition to evaluating the social studies curriculum it is important to evaluate instructional practices and resources. Key questions concerning instruction include the following:

- Have appropriate instructional activities been developed to help young people learn and use several levels of thinking and reasoning? Does the social studies program recognize and cultivate different kinds of intelligence, for instance, linguistic, artistic, mathematical, musical, spatial, and so forth? Does the social studies program recognize and respond to various learning-style preferences?
- Does social studies instruction demonstrate equality for all students?
- To what extent do students have access to a variety of reference materials in the classroom, in the media center, and in the community at large? Are the following instructional resources available in sufficient quantity and quality to serve the needs of students and teachers?
    Artifacts and models
    Audiocassettes, records, or tapes
    Computer software and modems
    Electronic databases
    Films (16 mm), filmstrips, and film loops
    Library and media center resources (both print and nonprint)
    Maps, charts, and globes
    Microfilm and microfiche readers
    Overhead projectors, screens, and transparencies
    Periodicals (current and with various perspectives)
    Projection panels
    Radios
    Record and cassette players and recorders
    Reference books (several varieties)
    Simulations and games
    Supplemental instructional materials (both print and nonprint)
    Textbooks (current and accurate)
    TVs, VCRs, and video disks or tapes
    Workbooks

Social studies programs are strong when the teachers are well qualified and continue to learn. Assessing professional development programs for social studies teachers is an integral part of the evaluation process. Issues such as the following need to be addressed:

- Are teachers active in their local, state, regional, and national professional organizations? Membership and active participation in such organizations allows social studies teachers to share concerns, glean ideas, and construct new knowledge through interactions with other social studies professionals.
- Does each school have a professional library that includes current literature on history, the social sciences, and education, and new research findings and practices in social studies education? Are there readily available prototype materials, curriculum guides, computer software, access to electronic databases, materials, and supplies to construct lessons or develop units of instruction, information on community resources, sample textbooks and related instructional materials, and so forth?
- Are staff development workshops and seminars planned to deal with such topics as curriculum revision, new instructional strategies, student assessment, materials evaluation and selection, newer technologies, new research findings, and the like?

Roles of Teachers, Students, Administrators, Parents, and the Community in Program Evaluation

The most important role for all involved in program evaluation is to seek and demand accurate information about the nature of the educational process. Since there is always more than one perception about the quality of any social system including education, the various people involved in that system should carry on a dialogue about the meaning and value of those experiences. This means that if we are interested in finding a common ground of accuracy and judgment, the social studies program should be observed and discussed from various viewpoints by people who are concerned with the quality of education in their community. These people include students, teachers, administrators, parents, and community members. What do different people see in the program? How valuable do they perceive the social studies program to be? What changes might be in order? Are there areas of agreement and disagreement among the various groups? To what extent is there a shared vision of improvement?

One approach that might be used to elicit the needed information is to provide several 5 × 7 color-coded index cards to those involved in the evaluation process and ask them to complete the following tasks: 1) on white cards ask the evaluators to write down strengths of the existing social studies program; 2) on separate green cards, ask the evaluators to write down weaknesses of the program; 3) on blue cards ask the evaluators to state why social studies education is important; and 4) on yellow cards, write down what they would change about the social studies program if given an opportunity to dream.

The evaluation leader is thus able to categorize the responses quickly and the group can readily "see" their statements. Areas of agreement and disagreement can be identified and examined easily. After discussing the statements, gaps and overlaps in the existing social studies program can be identified, new statements can be generated (if needed), priorities can be established, and plans made to initiate the needed changes or to confirm existing practices. The groups can then focus on those things they believe need to be accomplished and establish an implementation schedule to improve or maintain the quality of social studies education.

It is also useful to inform larger groups of citizens about the social studies program. Such information can be shared through the local newspaper, at presentations made to local service clubs, and by inviting community people into the school and encouraging them to interact with students and teachers. It is important to let people know about the quality of the social studies program and invite comments about it.

SUMMARY

This chapter introduced some of the complex issues involved in evaluating student learning. It included a discussion of four types of evaluation: placement, diagnostic, formative, and summative and suggested where each may be valuable for social studies teachers. In addition, some basic concepts related to norm-referenced, criterion-referenced, and self-evaluation were introduced.

Examples of several types of tests and test questions were provided. The need for accountability in education was discussed. Evaluating student learning is important for making curriculum decisions, communicating with parents and others, and informing students about their progress and achievement. The correct use of assessment data allows districts to inform the community about how well students are performing.

Program evaluation is a necessary complement to student evaluation. It is the way in which educational policies and decisions are made. As a teacher it is necessary to have accurate information concerning the conditions of the teaching environment and the relationship among the curriculum, instruction, and student achievement. Program evaluation is a cornerstone of the profession and in part helps determine student learning and teacher effectiveness.

Discussion Questions

1. In assigning grades to students, should the grade represent student achievement alone, or should it include student effort, work habits, and progress? What are the advantages and disadvantages of each method? What other alternatives can you suggest?
2. As a social studies teacher how would you deal with each of the following situations?
    a) A student has been found cheating on the semester final examination.
    b) A student has been mainstreamed into your classroom, performs to her maximum ability, but the quality of work is well below that of the student with the next lowest grade.
    c) A student who is the "star" of the basketball team has a chance for a college scholarship *if* the grade earned in your class is B or better. The work thus far averages to be a D+ or C–.
    d) A senior student is taking a social studies course required for graduation but is failing with two weeks remaining in the year.
    e) A student who works after school and on weekends to support family members who are on welfare does well on your tests and participates in class discussions, but has not turned in any homework assignments.
    f) If a student's writing ability is very weak would you allow him or her to take an oral test in lieu of a written test? Why or why not?
3. What is the relationship between evaluating student learning and evaluating social studies programs? Why do they complement one another?
4. Most often program evaluation is conducted by groups or teams of individuals, often representing different viewpoints and constituencies. What are some reasons for conducting program evaluation in this way?
5. What are some criteria that should be used in evaluating social studies programs?

Student Learning Activities

1. Since grading is an integral part of teaching, write your own philosophical approach to grading. What are your beliefs about evaluation? What factors will you consider to ensure that you develop a fair and useful grading system? Share your findings with your classmates in small-group settings and compare grading philosophies. On the basis of class discussion, was your original grading philosophy modified?
2. Review critically two or three chapters of a current social studies textbook. Afterwards examine critically the publisher-prepared tests for the same chapters and analyze the evaluation questions that have been included. To what extent do the questions match the stated objectives for the chapters? What is the level of the questions? What type of

questions are included? Are the questions written clearly and concisely? Can you answer the questions successfully? Try your skill at writing test questions by revising one of the chapter tests to fit your objectives.

3. Using this textbook, write two or three sample questions for each type of question discussed in the chapter (multiple choice, binary choice, matching, short answer/completion, and essay) that would be appropriate to measure student learning in this class. Trade your questions with a classmate, take each other's test, and critique the quality of the questions. What problems did you have in constructing the test? What problems might students have in taking the test? How could the questions be revised to measure your learning more adequately?

4. Examine several standardized tests that have a social studies focus or have sections related to social studies. What information does the test provide? How will this information be useful to you in planning? What other information is needed for you to make reasoned judgments about the teaching and learning process?

5. Simulate a five-member school evaluation team that has been formed to review the social studies program at a nearby middle school or high school. The team includes a social studies teacher from a nearby district, a student from a school several miles away, a middle school or high school principal, a local parent, and the owner of a large biotechnology plant located in the school district. The task of the group is to develop a social studies program evaluation plan. What will be evaluated? What criteria will be used? What data will be used in the evaluation process? What recommendations are likely to be made? How will the recommendations be disseminated?

6. Contact a representative from one of the regional accrediting associations or a state accrediting agency and find out what preparation is required before the program evaluation committee comes to the local school. How do the self-study documents help in program reviews and evaluations? How do the strengths and weaknesses identified by the program evaluation committee help local schools make curriculum, program, and instructional decisions? To what extent do accrediting associations or agencies make similar recommendations to the programs being reviewed?

7. Complete the following questionnaire to examine your beliefs about tests and evaluation in social studies. Develop a statement of your grading philosophy.

	Agree	Disagree	Uncertain
1. Objective tests measure a student's ability to recall information.			

	Agree	Disagree	Uncertain
2. Essay tests allow students to express their thinking processes.	_____	_____	_____
3. Tests prepared by textbook authors are often inconsistent with course goals and objectives.	_____	_____	_____
4. Taking time to teach test-taking skills is likely to increase test scores and reduce test anxiety.	_____	_____	_____

References

Airasian, P. W. 1993. *Classroom Assessment* (2nd ed.). New York: McGraw-Hill.

Anastasi, A. 1989. *Psychological Testing* (6th ed.). New York: Macmillan.

Archbald, D. A. and Newmann, F. M. 1988. *Beyond Standardized Testing: Assessing Authentic Academic Achievement in the Secondary School.* Reston, VA: National Association of Secondary School Principals.

Bloom, B. S., Englehart, M. D., Furst, E. J., Hill, W. N., and Krathwohl, D. R. 1956. *Taxonomy of Educational Objectives: The Classification of Educational Goals: Handbook I: The Cognitive Domain.* New York: David McKay.

Burton, N. W. and Jones, L. V. 1982. "Recent Trends in Achievement Levels of Black and White Youths." *Educational Researcher,* Vol. 11, No. 4, April. 11–14.

Carter, K. 1984. "Do Teachers Understand Principles for Writing Tests?" *Journal of Teacher Education,* Vol. 35, No. 6, November–December. 57–60.

Clift, J. C. and Imrie, B. W. 1981. *Assessing Students, Appraising Teaching.* London: Croom Helm and New York: John Wiley and Sons.

Curzon, L. B. 1985. *Teaching in Further Education: An Outline of Principles and Practice* (3rd ed.). London: Cassell.

Dembo, M. H. 1988. *Applying Educational Psychology in the Classroom.* (3rd ed.). New York: Longman.

Deno, S. L. 1985. "Curriculum-Based Measurement: The Emerging Alternative." *Exceptional Children,* Vol. 52, No. 3, November. 219–232.

Elam, S. M., Rose, L. C., and Gallup, A. M. 1992. "The 24th Annual Gallup/Phi Delta Kappa Poll of the Public's Attitudes Toward the Public Schools." *Phi Delta Kappan.* Vol. 74, No. 1, September. 41–53.

Elam, S. M., Rose, L. C., and Gallup, A. M. 1993. "The 25th Annual Phi Delta Kappa Poll of the Public's Attitudes Toward the Public Schools." *Phi Delta Kappan.* Vol. 75, No. 2, October. 137–152.

Gage, N. and Berliner, D. 1991. *Educational Psychology* (5th ed.). Boston: Houghton Mifflin.

Gale Research, Inc. 1993. *Test Critiques.* Vol. 10. Detroit, MI: Gale Research, Inc.

Gronlund, N. 1988. *How to Construct Achievement Tests* (4th ed.). Englewood Cliffs, NJ: Prentice-Hall.

Hartoonian, H. M. and Laughlin, M. A. 1989. "Designing a Social Studies Scope and Sequence for the 21st Century." *Social Education*, Vol. 53, No. 6, October. 388–398.

Hopkins, C. D. and Antes, R. L. 1985. *Classroom Measurement and Evaluation* (2nd ed.). Itasca, IL: F. E. Peacock.

Kindsvatter, R., Wilen, W., and Ishler, M. 1988. *The Dynamics of Effective Teaching*. New York: Longman.

Kramer, J. J. and Conoley, J. C. (Eds.). 1992. *Eleventh Mental Measurements Yearbook*. Lincoln, NE: Buros Institute of Mental Measurements, University of Nebraska Press.

Lerner, B. 1981. "The Minimum Competency Testing Movement: Social, Scientific, and Legal Implications." *American Psychologist,* Vol. 36, No. 10, October. 1057–1066.

Mehrens, W. A. and Lehmann, I. J. 1987. *Using Standardized Tests in Education* (4th ed.). New York: Longman.

Mitchell, J. V., Jr. (Ed.). 1983. *Tests in Print III: An Index to Tests, Test Reviews and the Literature on Specific Tests*. Lincoln, NE: Buros Institute of Mental Measurements, University of Nebraska.

National Commission on Excellence in Education. 1983. *A Nation at Risk: The Imperative for Educational Reform*. Washington, DC: National Commission on Excellence in Education.

National Commission on Testing and Public Policy. 1990. *From Gatekeeper to Gateway: Transforming Testing in America*. Chestnut Hill, MA: Boston College Press.

Oliner, P. M. 1976. *Teaching Elementary Social Studies: A Rational and Humanistic Approach*. New York: Harcourt Brace Jovanovich.

Paulson, F. L., Paulson, P. R., and Meyer, C.A. 1991. "What Makes a Portfolio a Portfolio?" *Educational Leadership*, Vol. 48, No. 5, February. 60–63.

Popham, W. J. 1993. *Educational Evaluation* (3rd ed.). Boston: Allyn and Bacon.

Rosenfield, S. and Shinn, M. R. (Eds.). 1989. "Mini-series on Curriculum-Based Assessment: A Comparison of Models." *School Psychology Review*. Vol. 18, No. 3, 299–316.

Salvia, J. and Ysseldyke, J. E. 1991. *Assessment* (5th ed.). Boston: Houghton Mifflin.

Saunders, P., Bach, G. L., Calderwood, J. D., and Hansen, W. L. 1984. *Master Curriculum Guide in Economics: A Framework for Teaching the Basic Concepts* (2nd ed.). New York: Joint Council for Economic Education.

Shapiro, E. S. and Derr, T. F. 1990. "Curriculum-Based Assessment." In T. B. Gutkin and C. R. Reynolds (Eds.), *The Handbook of School Psychology* (2nd ed.). New York: John Wiley and Sons.

Slavin, R. E. 1991. *Educational Psychology: Theory into Practice* (3rd ed.). Englewood Cliffs, NJ: Prentice-Hall.

Soper, J. C. and Walstad, W. 1986. *Test of Economic Literacy*. (2nd ed.). New York: Joint Council on Economic Education.

Soper, J. C. and Walstad, W. 1987. *Test of Economic Knowledge*. New York: Joint Council for Economic Education.

Stiggins, R. J. 1987. "NCME Instructional Module on Design and Development of Performance Assessments." *Educational Measurement: Issues and Practice*. Vol. 6, No. 3, Fall. 33–42.

Travers, J. F., Elliott, S. N., and Kratochwill, T. R. 1993. *Educational Psychology: Effective Teaching, Effective Learning.* Madison, WI: Brown and Benchmark.

Woolfolk, A. E. 1993. *Educational Psychology* (5th ed.). Boston: Allyn and Bacon.

Additional Readings

AERA-APA-NCME. 1985. *Standards for Evaluation and Psychological Testing.* Washington, DC: American Psychological Association.

Berlak, H., Newmann, F. M., Adams, E., Archbald, D. A., Burgess, T., Raven, J., and Romberg, T. A. 1992. *Toward a New Science of Educational Testing & Assessment.* Albany: State University of New York Press.

Brandt, R. 1992. "On Performance Assessment: A Conversation with Grant Wiggins." *Educational Leadership.* Vol. 49, No. 8, May. 35–37.

Feuer, M. J. and Fulton, K. 1993. "The Many Faces of Performance Assessment." *Phi Delta Kappan.* Vol. 74, No. 6, February. 478.

Haney, W. and Madaus, G. 1989. "Searching for Alternatives to Standardized Tests: Whys, Whats, and Withers." *Phi Delta Kappan.* Vol. 70, No. 9, May. 683–687.

Hanna, G. S. 1993. *Better Teaching Through Better Measurement.* Ft. Worth: Harcourt Brace Jovanovich.

Harris, K. H. and Longstreet, W. S. 1990. "Alternative Testing and the National Agenda for Control." *The Social Studies,* Vol. 81, No. 4, July/August. 148–152.

Herman, J. L., Aschbasher, P. R., and Winters, L. 1992. *A Practical Guide to Alternative Assessment.* Alexandria, VA: Association for Supervision and Curriculum Development.

Hopkins, C. D. and Antes, R. L. 1990. Classroom Measurement and Evaluation (3rd ed.). Itasca, IL: F. E. Peacock.

Lieberman, A. 1991. "Accountability as a Reform Strategy: A 'Kappan' Special Section." *Phi Delta Kappan.* Vol. 73, No. 3, November. 219–220.

Maeroff, G. I. 1991. "Assessing Alternative Assessment." *Phi Delta Kappan.* Vol. 73, No. 4, December. 272–281.

Marzano, R. J., Pickering, D., and McTighe, J. 1993. *Assessing Student Outcomes: Performance Assessment Using the Dimensions of Learning Model.* Alexandria, VA: Association for Supervision and Curriculum Development.

McLaughlin, M. W. and Phillips, D. C. (Eds.). 1991. *Evaluation and Education: At Quarter Century.* Ninetieth Yearbook of the National Society for the Study of Education. Part II. Chicago: University of Chicago Press.

Mitchell, R. 1992. *Testing for Learning: How New Approaches to Evaluation Can Improve American Schools.* New York: The Free Press.

Stanley, S. J. and Popham, W. J. 1988. *Teacher Evaluation: Six Prescriptions for Success*. Alexandria, VA: Association for Supervision and Curriculum Development.

Sweeney, J. E. 1992. "School Climate: The Key to Excellence." *NASSP Bulletin.* Vol. 76, No. 547, November. 69–73.

"Testing: Concepts, Policy, Practice, and Research." 1981. *American Psychologist.* Vol. 76, No. 10, October. (A special issue addressing issues related to testing.)

Walberg, H. J. and Haertel, G. D. (Eds.). (1990). *The International Encyclopedia of Educational Evaluation.* Oxford, England, and New York: Pergamon Press.

Worthen, B. R. 1993. "Critical Issues That Will Determine the Future of Alternative Assessment." *Phi Delta Kappan.* Vol. 74, No. 6, February. 444–448, 450–454.

■ ■ ■ ■ ■ ■   Do not seek to follow in the footsteps of the men of
old. Seek what they sought.
Matsuo Basho

PART V

What Challenges and Opportunities Lie Ahead?

THE WORLD HAS changed dramatically in the last few years. For example, the political and economic changes in Eastern Europe and the former Soviet Union were almost unthinkable only a decade ago. Advances and breakthroughs in technology, medicine, and other areas have been just as remarkable. Even greater changes are ahead for us as we move into the 21st century. What changes in students, schools, and society do you foresee in the coming years? What are the forces that are likely to shape the next century?

Information based on new research findings doubles approximately every twenty-four months or less. It should be obvious that information (and this textbook is no exception) presented to learners today will become obsolete very quickly. This information load, however, becomes more manageable as computer capacities increase. It is important that we as teachers help young people "learn to learn" so that they have the needed skills and are in a position to engage in lifelong learning. The educator's task today is to help students pay less attention to information per se and give greater attention to the training of their minds, so they can function effectively within subject fields and across disciplines. The use of computers within subject areas will help facilitate this task. This practice is at the heart of developing intellectual skills for the future. This is a new responsibility that rests upon you as you continue to learn about yourself and acquire additional information to generate new knowledge about the teaching and learning process.

Without a doubt, the shape of the 21st century will continue aspects of the 20th century but move forward into vistas not yet imagined. How can you prepare and help students be prepared for the future? And, how can you prepare for the changes in your own professional life?

Becoming a professional social studies teacher is not an easy task. It takes an intellectual curiosity, a love of service to others, a commitment to the profession, and an ability to grow personally and professionally. Some of the ways you can become a professional include the following:

1. maintaining a desire to learn in your content areas and in ways to help young people learn more effectively;
2. joining and becoming an active member in the National Council for the Social Studies, its state and local affiliates, and other professional organizations;
3. reading widely in your content areas, education, and other disciplines to remain current in your knowledge of the world and its ongoing rapid changes; and
4. seeking an understanding of interrelationships of events in the world both past and current.

By stretching intellectually and reflecting thoughtfully on new ideas, trends, and issues you are likely to recognize changes in students, schools, and society. This will position you to be a more effective, caring, and sensitive teacher. A major goal of many teachers is to help young people to experience the joy and accomplishment of learning by learning how to learn. What plans will you make to meet the ongoing challenges of teaching throughout your career?

FOCUS QUESTIONS

- How do you see the newer technologies influencing your professional life and those of your students?
- To what extent is the use of a computer likely to broaden the perspectives of your students?
- How will the computer and its use redefine our concept of the classroom?
- As you think about your responsibilities as teacher what steps will you take to continue to be an effective teacher?

PART 4 What Challenges and Opportunities Lie Ahead?

FOCUS ACTIVITY

Reflect on your earlier school years and consider the various learning technologies that were available to you as a learner. Write down at least ten or more of these technologies and indicate what you learned by using the particular technology. Be sure to include technologies from the primary and intermediate grades as well as those you used in junior high or middle school and high school.

Technology	Grade Level	Learning Activity	Used Currently	Comments
1.				
2.				
3.				
4.				
5.				
6.				
7.				
8.				
9.				
10.				

In general, what could you conclude as a learner about your use of technology over the years? How are your experiences with technology for learning likely to influence your use of technology as a teacher?

Share your conclusions and/or expectations related to your experiences with and expectations of technology with your classmates. To what extent are there commonalties of experiences?

Project a career path for yourself beginning with your student teaching experience until your retirement. What factors are likely to influence your career? When you conclude your career in education how would you like your students and colleagues to remember you?

> The wave of the future is coming and there is no fighting it.
>
> *Anne Morrow Lindbergh*

Chapter 13

The Information Age and Technology

FOCUS QUESTIONS

- How has the development of new technologies influenced the shape of society, schools, and the curriculum?
- What types of computer programs are available in social studies and how might they be used in the teaching and learning processes?
- What are some considerations when deciding to purchase or use computers and related software for classroom instruction?
- With the development of the newer technologies, how will you change your approach to teaching?
- What constitutes abuses of technology? What are some possible solutions to these abuses?

OVERVIEW   As we think of future scenarios various multidimensional images come to mind. One image will include the use of high technology, which could range from computers that extend learning possibilities, to satellite transmissions that link us instantaneously with the rest of the world, or to robots operated by computer-driven technology that may prove helpful for selected teaching and learning tasks. Whatever the technology currently in use, and new configurations yet to be developed for teaching and learning, the individual teacher will remain as an integral part of the educational process. Technologies can enhance and stimulate quality teaching but not replace overall teaching skills. Though teacher roles may change, technology cannot perform the overall job of a teacher as education moves forward toward the 21st century. Computers and other technologies should be viewed as tools that allow teachers to expand their own capabilities and allow students to have access to a variety of information from many sources. Teachers are able to interact with students, provide feedback, think, make ethical judgments, understand languages, and draw on personal prior knowledge and experiences.

Microcomputers have become an integral part of our everyday life. Already we rely on communications technology to send and receive electronic mail, transfer funds electronically, provide weather reports via satellites, aid in medical diagnosis, conduct and transact business via computer teleconferencing, organize personal information such as addresses and telephone numbers of friends, make airline and dinner reservations, engage in personal shopping, enjoy the challenge of electronic games, and so forth. The flow of information into our daily lives from many sources is important in making informal decisions concerning our personal choices. Creative persons often use the computer to design new solutions to ongoing and emerging problems. The use of technology helps society collectively to reduce isolation and ignorance, to increase productivity and effectiveness, and to enhance institutional capabilities to improve the human condition. Some have argued that computers have contributed or will contribute to "intellectual regeneration" (Ehman and Glenn, 1987). This suggests that computers and other newer technologies will help learners develop new skills that are required to adjust to constant change. As students manipulate existing ideas and information to solve problems, new solutions to problems are likely to be forthcoming. A knowledge of computer-related skills is rapidly becoming as necessary for all people as are communication skills. Computers make information accessible and allow students to organize and express their learning in various ways.

Influences of New Technologies

Most of the students who are currently enrolled in our schools will spend the majority of their lives living and working in the 21st century. Educational plans for these students are being formulated today. Most often these plans are made on the basis of our past experiences, both positive and negative, and on the basis of our vision and expectations of the future. For example, a review of earlier forecasts related to the possible uses of computers in education does not match current practices. Educational planners and decision makers need to consider trends such as the following, which are discussed on a regular basis in various media. These trends represent ideas from a range of writers.

- The job market will continue to change rapidly and large numbers of workers will need to be more highly educated (trained) than at present. Most likely workers will have several careers and will hold various jobs, many not yet created, in diverse fields during their lifetimes. Based on projected demographic information most of these new jobs will be in service and information-oriented businesses. The person entering the job market is expected to have basic computer skills and be willing to expand his or her already existing technological skills.
- Businesses will develop new partnership arrangements with schools. The schools will be training not only pre-adolescents and adolescents but also adult workers in need of new training or retraining. This suggests a possible restructuring of the school day and the school year to integrate adult learners in need of technical skills into the public school system.
- There will be a greater emphasis on general education content in areas such as social studies, science and technology, mathematics, and in communication skills such as writing, speaking, and listening. Human relations skills, thinking processes and skills, and citizenship competencies will need to be infused throughout the K–12 curriculum. It is expected the use of computers and other technologies will expand the learning environment.
- Minority populations will become the majority population in numerous large and middle-sized urban areas throughout the country. This is already true in several states. The primary language of these students will not be English. In some instances there are likely to be strong clashes of conflicting values among the various ethnic groups and between generations. Access to computers and other technologies will become imperative.
- Schools will need to adapt to population and demographic shifts; new national priorities; changing family patterns and lifestyles; and economic and social changes in the composition of the work force, especially those related to women and other minority groups. Female students need to have multiple experiences to learn about and use technology in school.
- Technology can allow teachers and students to create multicultural instructional materials that allow students to "see" each other in a positive way. Computer software designers (and others who create curriculum and materials) will need to think about issues from various perspectives and how such materials help to shape cultural perspectives.
- Political, economic, social, and military events throughout the world along with changing social and cultural values will change the way technology is viewed and used in society. The educational climate at the national or state level and in the local district may shift due to events

taking place within the global community that have an impact on the schools. For example, learning environments may well focus on higher-order thinking and problem-solving skills as students seek solutions to real-world problems.
- A shift from a mass-media emphasis to personal media use over which the individual has greater control is anticipated. At the same time, in some jobs, cooperation and group decision-making skills among workers will become more and more important. There is likely to be greater use of personal computers that are linked in a network to facilitate learning.
- New research findings and technological developments may enable us to remodel the structure of logic and knowledge as we know them today.
- The gap between the rapid increase of technological developments and the human ability to accept and adjust to these changes is likely to increase. Teachers are often willing to learn new skills in order to be more effective teachers.
- The ever-widening chasm between the wealthy and the impoverished, rural and urban areas, and majority and minority populations in the United States and around the world have important implications for education. In general the wealthier schools are investing more resources into technology, while the impoverished are not able to do so, thus increasing the existing technology gap. Using computers can have an equalizing effect for at-risk students and other learners in wealthier districts.

We encourage you to be aware of other emerging trends that are likely to shape not only education but society as well. Within the past two and a half decades the role of computers and computer technology has come to play an ever-expanding role in our daily lives. The knowledge explosion in the Information Age suggests an ever-increasing role for the computer and its related technologies. Yet, John Goodlad in *A Place Called School* (1984) reported that in most social studies classrooms a teacher was leading more than thirty students through the daily lesson with the teacher doing most of the talking (lecture or demonstration) while the students were being passive participants (working alone, using their textbooks, or completing worksheets) in the learning process. Active learning and a passion for learning were missing. Many social studies classrooms in the 1990s are as Goodlad described a decade earlier.

Computers in the Schools

Schools have access to many technologies, some as old as pencil and paper, and some as new as lasers and fiber optics, which influence teaching procedures and student learning. We make no attempt to discuss all possible educational technologies. Rather, we will describe computers as instructional

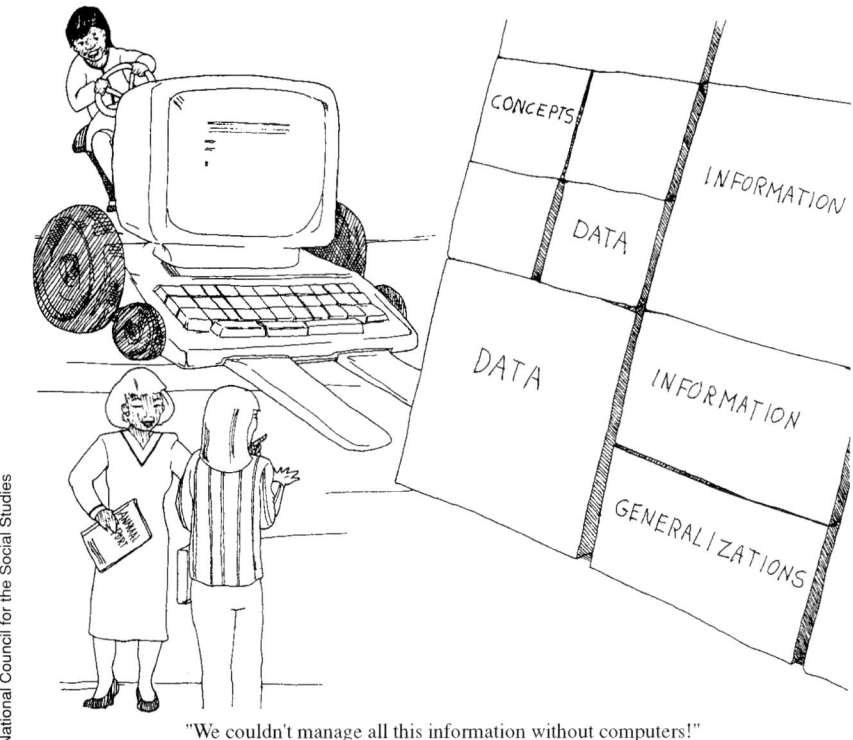

"We couldn't manage all this information without computers!"

tools—which allow students to learn by doing rather than being told what to do through lecture and assigned readings—and several technologies that seem to have significant impact on social studies instruction and learning.

The term "educational technology" has many definitions. Some product definitions give emphasis to materials and equipment. However, Tickton (1970) has suggested a process definition that is more relevant to teaching and learning. He writes that educational technology is a systematic way of designing, carrying out, and evaluating the total process of learning and teaching in terms of specific objectives, based on research in human learning and communication and employing a combination of human and nonhuman resources to bring about more effective instruction.

Among the important technological developments in the past quarter century have been advances in the silicon chip, which made it possible to develop and produce smaller, less expensive computers. Microcomputers made their entry into schools for instructional, organizational, and administrative purposes. These new technologies will, no doubt, influence the potentials and constraints of education. Virtually all teachers will need to become competent and confident in their use. The computer has the potential to be an authoritarian controlling device or it can draw teachers and learners together as they share in the teaching and learning process. Social studies teachers need to be alert to the numerous learning possibilities as well as the limitations of computers. Teachers will need to make decisions concerning computer usage based on a knowledge and understanding of teaching and learning principles and related educational issues. These uses of computers have educational, social, and economic implications for all levels of education.

Computers seem to be well established in the schools as more than two million computers are already there. Personal and individual computers can be linked to mainframe computers with powerful information systems or to videodisc or videotext systems. It is clear that computers have caught the interest and imagination of students, parents, and educators and have become the new technical and cultural frontier in education and are believed to be a new revolutionary force in education (Simonson and Thompson, 1994).

By now teachers and students usually have reasonable access to computers at school, and social studies teachers are likely to integrate computer learning opportunities into the social studies instructional program. It has become fairly clear that computers, unlike other educational innovations, such as programmed instruction, competency-based training, airborne television, single loop films, or learning packets, are no longer a fad but will, in fact, remain a regular part of the teaching and learning environment. As new computer-related tools are created it is likely there will be greater reliance on technology as an instructional tool.

Ellen and Michael Vasu (1987) have developed a three-level framework of computer literacy for educators. While their focus was on the social science disciplines in higher education, their framework is effective for middle and high school social studies programs as well. At the basic level (Level I) teachers should know the fundamentals of the computer systems—both hardware and software. Level II focuses on the instructional applications of computer technology in specific discipline content areas. The third level requires interaction between discipline knowledge and computer knowledge in the instructional design and development of instructional software. Most teachers will focus on Level II competencies. Teachers need not be computer programmers. The outline presented in Table 13.1 is adapted from the Vasus' Computer Literacy Framework for Educators.

Two years earlier Mary Montag-Torardi, after a nationwide survey of computing experts, defined computer literacy as "an understanding of computer characteristics, capabilities, and applications, as well as an ability to implement this knowledge in a skillful productive use of computer applications suitable to individual roles in society" (Montag-Torardi, 1985, p. 863). Later, Oviatt (1990) documented the above definition.

Montag-Torardi identified the knowledge, skills, and attitudes of a computer literate person. Her four categories are:

1. Computer systems—an appropriate and knowledgeable use of equipment and programs needed for computer applications.

2. Computer applications—the ability of a person to evaluate, select, and implement practical computer applications to do meaningful and efficient work.
3. Computer programming—the ability to direct the computer through the use of programming languages.
4. Computer attitudes—an individual's feelings about the use of computers in appropriate ways.

Table 13.1 Computer Literacy Levels for Educators

Skills/Competencies

Level I	
Basic knowledge	Understanding of basic computer jargon (such as disk drive, CPU, menu-driven, control keys, memory, save, retrieve, etc.)
	Ability to use basic application programs (for example, word processing, classroom-related software, etc.)
	Elementary understanding of basic hardware components
Level II	
Instructional applications	All of the above plus ability to select and match software with instructional objectives and individual needs of students
	Ability to evaluate classroom-related software in terms of effective instruction and instructional design principles
	Application skills in using classroom-related software, instructional management software, and test-scoring software
	Ability to match design of classroom-related software to individual instructional needs and abilities
Level III	
Instructional design and development	All of the above plus ability to design classroom-related software, incorporating effective instructional principles
	Ability to develop (program) instructional software

SOURCE: Adapted from Lillie, Hannum, and Stuck, *Computers and Effective Instruction: Using Computers and Software in the Classroom.* (1989). New York: Longman.

Additional competencies within these categories were refined and updated by Oviatt. These competencies are included in *Educational Computing Foundations* by Simonson and Thompson (1994; pp. 441–449).

Computers extend the intellectual capabilities of individuals by making learning an active process that requires students to think more precisely in making thoughtful decisions. Newer developments in computers and computer programs enable students to practice reasoning, write their own programs, analyze data, and conduct a dialogue with a computer. Computers are useful in performing repetitive tasks, remembering and manipulating large quantities of data, and making consistent unbiased decisions for which they have been programmed. It can be expected that with new advances in voice recognition and synthesization people will be able to talk to a computer and receive answers from it. Without a doubt computers are becoming more and more important in the educational process and, in many instances, have replaced books and other print media as teachers create learning materials by including information from multiple sources and from multiple perspectives. For example, in teaching about World War II teachers can gather resource materials and construct their own customized books (Bruder, 1993). Teachers could organize information from newspapers, diaries, press conferences, photos, and radio broadcasts in ways that meets the objectives of the lesson. Most existing textbooks include little first-hand information but, rather, present students with predigested material. Many libraries no longer have card catalogs as library collections have been computerized. Major reference books and indexes, such as *ERIC* and *Education Index*, are on CD-ROM and are updated regularly. Some states have recognized the use of laser disks as textbooks.

As teachers plan for instruction involving the use of the computer, they will need to keep in mind Piaget's theories of learning, which have implications for computer instruction by providing ever-expanding environmental learning opportunities (Williams and Williams, 1984). Students operating at Piaget's *concrete stage* of development can use the computer to solve various problems presented in concrete terms and with graphics. Learners at this developmental level can learn to manipulate sequences of events simultaneously. As students develop the ability to learn at the level of *formal operations,* they can use the computer as a tool to hypothesize and solve problems on an abstract level. A few students will be challenged to learn computer programming languages to investigate the realm of possibility and to explore and apply probability to social problems. Most teachers and students will function successfully by using new and existing software in the teaching and learning process.

How Can Computers Help Educators?

At present computers in education are most often used for helping students learn and as a management system for teachers for record keeping, filing, assessing reading levels of instructional materials, test construction, and so forth.

In general there are five educational applications for computers. The computer can 1) be used as a tool to perform various functions; 2) be used as a tutor; 3) become the learner through student programming; 4) be a subject for study; and 5) be used to manage classroom information.

The literature on computers in education includes many names such as "computer-assisted or computer-aided instruction (CAI)"; "computer-based instruction (CBI)"; or "computer-assisted or computer-aided learning (CAL)." For the most part these terms are interchangeable although some writers offer more precise definitions.

During the past quarter century as computers and computer usage became less costly and more readily available, various types of computer software programs were developed in most curriculum content areas. Initially, computer software programs in social studies seemed to lag behind other curriculum areas in terms of quality and quantity. Over the years, however, a greater variety and higher quality of social studies computer programs have been developed and are currently available in the market for use with computers manufactured by several companies.

As with any new technology there are problem areas. For example, while schools have purchased several million computers, there remains a shortage of computers for teacher and student use. Some social studies classrooms have only one computer available for class instruction or individual use. To remedy this condition teachers may decide to make use of a computer with a projection panel to demonstrate the content, concept, or skill being taught. Teachers often lack knowledge about using computers in their classes and are not necessarily convinced that incorporating computer activities in their social studies classes is beneficial for student learning. Those teachers willing to include computer learning activities frequently find that existing social studies software is not well integrated into the existing curriculum. At present it is difficult to determine the effectiveness of using computers to teach social studies due to the limited research studies directly related to social studies.

Computer Programs for Social Studies

Existing computer software may be divided into four areas: 1) stand-alone programs, which can be inserted into the curriculum at a specific point; 2) supplementary materials, which have been designed to accompany specific instructional materials; 3) utility programs, which enable the user to generate data and materials; and 4) integrated packages, which are used to teach content and skills and to record student achievement (Ehman and Glenn, 1987). Just as teachers use more than one approach in teaching, computers offer several possible approaches to learning.

Stand-Alone Computer Programs *

Stand-alone programs (drill and practice, simulations, games, tutorials, and databases) are designed to relate to general social studies content areas. Teachers using these programs must decide where to incorporate them into social studies. Stand-alone generic database programs hold great promise for use in social studies classes. A database is a collection of information on specific topics that are stored, updated, and managed in an electronic retrieval network. Today there are thousands of databases covering a range of topics, such as status of legislation, census data, bibliographic information, and so on.

Examples: *The Social Studies Tool Kits: Our Nation and Our World* and *Hello USA* and *Hello World* (Great Lakes Software, Tom Snyder Productions, Watertown, MA).

These two database programs enable students grades 5–12 to analyze data, correlate information, create weighted indexes, evaluate correlations, and formulate their own theories. These programs allow students to explore our changing world and nation graphically using more than 300 separate data files. The programs are updated annually.

Textbook and Supplementary Computer Programs

Within the past decade major textbook publishers began to supplement their existing printed textbook materials with computer programs related directly to specific chapters or units. These publishers sought to make the textbooks and related printed materials more appealing to the reader; to promote computer literacy for students (and indirectly, teachers); and to help teachers decide when and how they could incorporate computer programs into social studies instructional programs to promote student learning.

Example: *Visual Archive of American History* (Scott Foresman, Glenview, IL)

This database program comes with lesson plans, student worksheets, and a data entry form. Such programs help students to integrate the text with computer programs.

Utility Computer Programs

Utility programs are flexible and allow the user (teacher or student) to make materials such as posters, transparencies, certificates, worksheets, cards, signs, and the like. Word processing, spreadsheets, computer grade books, and

---

* The computer programs offered as examples may well fit under more than one program type. No endorsement of the programs' usefulness in all classrooms is intended. The examples cited are a starting place for teachers to begin when considering the use of computers in the social studies classroom.

so forth are included in this grouping and have become important teaching and learning tools. Most of these programs are relatively easy to use.

Word processing programs are designed to allow for efficient collecting, editing and revising, storing and saving, and printing of written materials. These programs allow users to enter the program, make changes (revising, inserting, replacing, moving, and deleting), save the text, and print a new version of it.

Spreadsheets allow users to organize and manipulate numeric data in sets of rows and columns called cells. These types of data can be entered in the cells: labels and values; labels identifying categories on the spreadsheet, such as student names; and values and numerical data, namely grades. A spreadsheet can accept mathematical formulas and automatically compute the numeric data. A sample of a spreadsheet using student grades may look like the following table presented below.

Examples of word processing and spreadsheet programs are *Microsoft Word* (Redmond, WA) and *Appleworks* (Claris Corp., Mountain View, CA). Examples of grade book programs include *MECC Grade Manager* (Minnesota Education Computing Consortium, St. Paul, MN), *Grade Book Deluxe* (Edusoft, Berkeley, CA), *Report Card* (Sensible Software, Troy, MI), and *Grade Busters* (Tom Snyder Productions, Watertown, MA).

These grade book programs allow teachers to compute final grades automatically, average test scores, and generate individual student progress reports. Many teachers find such programs to be time savers although some teachers prefer to use a spreadsheet program, which allows them to create a grade book that reflects their personal preferences, needs, and styles.

Table 13.2 Sample Spreadsheet with Student Grades

Elizabeth Keating—Sociology Grades

	Test 1	Test 2	Report	Homework	Project	Total	Percent
Possible Points	25	25	50	50	100	250	
Gould, P. S.	18	20	40	48	89	215	86%
Johnson, M. A.	20	19	42	38	91	210	84%
Korff, M. Y.	21	23	45	42	92	223	89%
Mijares, G. M.	25	24	48	50	98	245	98%
Peters, W. M.	24	21	50	49	93	237	94%
Sullivan, J. M.	23	20	39	40	88	210	84%
Young, N. L.	20	18	44	45	90	217	86%

Programs with desktop publishing tools allow students to create reports and newspapers using clip art and various sized fonts. *BannerMania* (available from Broderbund, San Rafael, CA) provides students with opportunities to create exciting banners for display and to enliven a classroom.

Integrated Computer Packages

As computers have improved and newer technologies have been introduced, developers are designing total learning packages. Most of these packages are designed to teach basic reading and writing skills. In the area of social studies, with the use of CD-ROM and laser disk technology, there are several programs currently available. To explain the complexities of the computers to young learners (and teachers), you may want to use the computer/CD-ROM program *How Computers Work: The Complex World of Computers Made Simple* (Time Warner Interactive, 1993, and available from the Zenger Media, 10200 Jefferson Boulevard, Culver City, CA 90232-0802). Besides providing a history of computing, the program explains how computers handle various functions, for example, input, processing, memory, output, programming, and applications. Various hands-on activities are included as are working samples of several software programs. New programs are being developed on a regular basis and we encourage you to stay current in this rapidly changing field.

These programs are part of an integrated software package that includes word processing, spreadsheet, page layout, graphics, and database applications. One advantage of an integrated software package is that it allows users to transfer data from one application to another and thus increase work efficiency when using several programs. Because these integrated programs have been so popular in the schools, several companies have developed printed products with ideas about how to use these programs.

It is important to remember that research concerning the use of computers in social studies classes is just beginning and these initial efforts often provide limited findings and conflicting results. Short- and long-range research is needed concerning the use and effectiveness of computers and the newer technologies and how teachers use computers for instruction and/or management. Research is also needed to determine student learning outcomes when using computer instruction and the impact of computers and other new technologies on the social studies curriculum. Just how computers and the new technologies shape and influence knowledge, attitudes, beliefs, and values are other areas that need further exploration. Thus far the computer provides teachers with one more teaching mode and offers students an additional tool for learning.

Instructional Techniques Used in Computer Programs

For the most part computer software programs may be categorized as using one of the following instructional techniques.

- *Drill and practice:* Drill-and-practice computer programs are probably the most common ones used in schools, are similar to pencil-and-paper worksheets or programmed instruction, and assume that instruction on the topic has already been given. These programs have a high degree of predictability and enable the learner to practice skills, to review previously studied lessons, and to master or relearn content. These direct instruction programs ask relatively simple questions of the learner, elicit responses, and provide immediate feedback (corrective or qualitative) and evaluation related to the learner's performance. The computer can perform consistently and with patience for an extended time period. Also, data related to student achievement can be quantified.

  An advantage of computer drill and practice learning over the pencil-and-paper worksheet is that the computer lesson provides feedback after each response so that a student does not engage in repeated practice using incorrect information or procedures. Most often drill-and-practice questions emphasize learning basic facts and recalling specific information. Many of the programs are boring and follow a predictable format similar to the earlier teaching machines. Questions included in these programs are usually low-level recall questions for which a single correct response is expected. For the most part, the student is a passive learner. Good teachers have long been aware that negative comments to students discourage student learning. Similarly, therefore, computer responses to student answers should be positive, nonthreatening, and encouraging so that the student will want to continue to learn. These programs are relatively easy to design and run on the simplest level. Approximately 75 percent of the available software is the drill-and-practice–type program although more programs requiring higher level skills are available on a regular basis.

  Examples: *All Star Drill* (Tom Snyder Productions, Watertown, MA); and *Cliffs Studyware for Economics* (available from Zenger Media).

  All Star Drill allows students in grades 10 and up to review materials using a baseball game format. Two social studies disks are available for play: *States and Capitals* and *World Geography.* Teachers can also add their own questions to the program. In *Cliffs Studyware for Economics,* students answer questions related to theories and vocabulary for thirty-one categories of economics at their own pace. The test mode format allows students to simulate classroom test-taking pressures and it offers hints to students to pinpoint weak spots and to improve scoring.

- *Tutorial:* A computer tutorial program is intended to teach new information, concepts, or skills to the learner or it may be used to reteach the same material as necessary. Tutorial programs are often used on a one-on-one basis. These programs may allow students to respond to questions using their "natural language," which in turn is interpreted by the computer. In general, these programs present information (text and/or pictures) in small steps; check for comprehension; monitor student performance, and, if needed, reteach the information to correct learners' earlier misunderstanding through practice and reinforcement; ask follow-up questions; and again evaluate the learner's performance. The cognitive objective for most tutorial programs is to help learners acquire and comprehend information. Tutorial programs that integrate videodisc images might help students apply previously acquired information by engaging the student in Socratic-type dialogues (Siegel and Davis, 1986).

Tutorial programs may be useful in smaller schools that otherwise might not be able to offer certain social studies curriculum content areas. As researchers discover more about how people learn concepts and the relationships of concepts, it is likely that the quality and quantity of tutorial programs will improve.

Examples: *Appian Way History Software: Data—100 Series.* (Appian Way available from Zenger Media; produced in England) and *European History Study Disks* and *Shakespeare On Disk* (available from Zenger Media; produced in England).

The Appian Way series enables students to become historians by examining primary and secondary source materials and documents. Both students and teachers can add documents and link them by subject and source to compare with related documents. Through interactive programs the European history disks present an overview of European history from Renaissance through post-World War II and includes tutorials and review questions.

- *Educational games:* The use of games as an instructional procedure is old. In general, games have rules, provide a challenge, are delimited in time and space, have a finite number of things that can happen, and end after a certain number of plays with winners and losers. Educational games also have instructional objectives and may be used to introduce or enhance a unit, to reinforce learning, or for post-instructional review. For example, learners may score points by competing against themselves, another person, against the computer, or a previous high score. By playing, learners have the opportunity to learn new content and concepts and to practice skills including decision-making. They also have an opportunity to apply previously learned concepts by creating new situations and manipulating the environment. Students often become actively involved with the content because of fancy graphics and fantasy situations that are highly motivational and encourage learning. Games may be used to maintain a rapid learning pace and may be useful in memorizing and retaining facts.

Examples: *Decisions, Decisions, American History Pack, Critical Issues Pack, Prejudice, The Environment,* and *On the Campaign Trail* (Tom Snyder Productions, Watertown, MA).

This series (ten separate titles) combines role playing, debate, decision making, and critical thinking, which places students in the midst of challenging real-life controversies based on historical and contemporary issues. The programs can be used in cooperative learning groups or by the whole class and are designed to support various teaching styles. Students learn to make social policies in structured, nonthreatening environments. Other examples include the Carmen Sandiego programs. Titles include *Where in the World Is Carmen Sandiego?*, *Where In the USA Is Carmen Sandiego?*, *Where in America's Past Is Carmen Sandiego?*, and *Where in Space Is Carmen Sandiego?* (Broderbund, San Rafael, CA; available from Zenger Media).

- *Simulations:* Social studies teachers have used simulations effectively for years. As computer technology has improved, for example, through graphics, rapid data processing, branching, and interactive capabilities, simulations are becoming an important form of computer instruction and can facilitate higher levels of thinking and the application of ideas to more complex problems other than those encountered within the computer simulation itself. They have the capability to incorporate complex realities more effectively than class lectures, discussions, and printed materials. Simulations often use graphics rather extensively.

Simulations are simplified models that allow learners to become part of a simulated reality in order to give them a better understanding of another time or setting. These programs usually concentrate on teaching interrelationships of several factors. Simulations allow students to "weigh" the interrelationships of information and instruct the computer to project these changes in the model.

Simulations provide a context for students to study historic events; social, political, military, and economic conflicts; and to project future scenarios based on their earlier decisions without fear of the consequences if they were to make the same decision in the real world. Simulations help students to understand and solve interdependent problems and offer insights into the past, present, and future. For example, economic simulations may vary inflation, unemployment, interest rates, prices, and so forth; history simulations might involve a military conflict; a geography simulation might vary atmospheric conditions to see how they might affect soil usage, water supplies, crop yields, and so forth; and an environmental simulation might ask students to examine political, social, economic, and environmental consequences of building a highway in a particular location. Students often develop a sense of control over outside events (and their own learning) and are then able to focus their attention on the ways different processes and knowledge variables affect the situation and to understand relationships among one or more of the ever-changing variables. Often simulations may include activities to help students relate simulation learning with experiences in their everyday lives and encourage students to experiment with computers in other classes.

Examples: *You're the Banker* (Federal Reserve Bank, Minneapolis, MN); *Ellis Island: The Immigrant Experience* (Educational Activities; available from Zenger Media); and *Decisions, Decisions: Prejudice* (Tom Snyder, Watertown, MA).

The first program places students in the role of a banker who makes decisions based on economic principles. It is excellent for teaching economic concepts related to money and banking. *The Immigrant Experience* asks students to take on the identities of teenage immigrants from Italy who make decisions, respond to unexpected events, and make their way in the United States. It includes a teacher's guide, background information, and follow-up activities.

Other simulation programs including *Oregon Trail* (MECC, St. Paul, MN) and *SimCity* (Maxis; available from Broderbund) place people in events, such as traveling to Oregon or in making decisions about how to govern a city.

- *Inquiry/problem solving:* Computers encourage students to explore important social studies concepts using a question–answer dialogue format to develop problems and seek solutions. In effect students are able to formulate and test hypotheses by using synthesis-level thinking skills. The students ask the computer a question and the computer responds to the question and offers comments. There are computer programs that require the students to use cooperative decision-making processes that promote the development of social participation skills. Problem-solving learning experiences help students gain greater confidence in the use of these skills and others as they practice decision-making and problem solving both as individuals and as members of a group.

Example: *Uncle Sam's Budget Balancer* (Banner Blue; available from Zenger Media).

This program allows students to explore various ideas that would reduce the federal deficit. Included is President Clinton's 1993 budget along with more than 300 options. It is likely that future budgets will also be available on disks. The goal is to eliminate the deficit in five years. Users may better understand the deficit by examining the costs in dollars per taxpayer or percent of GDP. The program can spark discussions about the consequences of various economic and political choices. (The program can be copied freely as long as it is not modified.)

- *Models:* The computer allows students to develop and create their own models and then test the model to determine its appropriateness for the learning task at hand. By using a model, students are able to develop rules to predict and test the model's operation. By using observation and prediction skills students are able to make assumptions and note the consequences of changing conditions, which provide students with experiences in solving problems by using higher-level thinking skills.

Example: *Earthquest Explores Ecology* (available from Zenger Media).

Maps, graphs, and 15 interactive challenges allow students to become eco-explorers in six biosphere simulations, trying to save the planet from ecological peril. Students consider cause-and-effect events and determine population rates while confronting ecological problems at home and abroad.

- *Graphics usage:* Computers are powerful instructional tools that enable teachers to present nontextual material in visual form. It has been said by many that a picture is worth a thousand words. There are computer programs that allow students to develop and construct two-dimensional color charts, maps, graphs, and diagrams in sequential order quickly and efficiently. This information allows students to make judgments based on existing data. These judgments may then be demonstrated graphically and in many cases correlations can be made between sets of data. For example, bar graphs enable learners to make comparisons of numbers in different categories; circle graphs also deal with numerical data but focus on proportions; line graphs indicate trends of continuous data and allow for extrapolation and prediction. Graphics enable the learner to examine large quantities of data in a compact format (Collis, 1988).

Graphics often help to explain a difficult abstract concept by allowing the student to "see" what is happening; to analyze and interpret data; and to present and communicate information to persons and groups who need the information. Pictorial data can be perceived quickly by the brain and should support and enhance the written part of the assigned lesson. Computer-generated graphics also complement teacher lectures and student work with visuals which provide additional ways to represent concepts, ideas, and information inasmuch as learners have different learning styles.

Teachers may be somewhat uncomfortable using graphics if they have not been taught how to interpret information that is presented graphically. The problem then becomes self-perpetuating if students do not know and are not instructed in how to interpret nontextual visual representations. One way to help students learn this skill and develop new aptitudes is to ask them to transform the information they have learned into visual form rather than always having them verbally describe or explain their understanding or application of a concept.

Example: *Time Out Graph* (Beagle Brothers, Inc., San Diego, CA). Graphic programs enable students to grasp relationships as they view data graphically and use data to make their own graphs. Data can be displayed as pie, bar, line, or other graphing formats.

Other useful graphics programs include *Timeliner* and *MAC Timeliner* (Tom Snyder Productions), which allow teachers and students to produce timelines so they can look for patterns, chart major events, and use the graphics in various desktop publishing documents.

- *Word processing and writing:* The computer aids students in their writing by allowing them more easily to try out words, phrases, sentences, and paragraphs to organize information for meaning. These may then be deleted, edited, corrected, and revised.

Students are able to focus their attention and energy on organization, composition, and clarity of expression without the drudgery of recopying or retyping their work. Word processing skills may well contribute to a shift from the product of learning to the process of learning. There is some evidence that suggests that writing skills improve as students use word processing as a tool in writing. Learners do not have to settle for acceptable work to complete the assignment but can work to achieve high quality work. Today there are various word processing and writing programs that include spelling and grammar checkers and that also note sentence length and complexity.

Examples: *Research Paper Writer* and *Group Grammar* (Tom Snyder Productions). These programs help students become better communicators of the written word. The *Research Paper Writer* takes students step by step through the writing process from deciding a topic focus to the final document. The program emphasizes research analysis, writing, and thinking skills. *Group Grammar* presents students with illustrated stories that allow students to study various parts of grammar, such as the parts of speech and punctuation. The program can be used by individual students, small groups of students, or by a class in a computer lab.

- *Diagnosis of errors:* The computer is becoming a useful tool that allows teachers to determine forgotten and/or incorrect student learning. This application would appear to be most appropriate for students who have been unable to learn the materials, suggesting an overall misunderstanding about the content, concept, or skill that needs to be corrected. After diagnosing systematic errors, teachers may then develop and incorporate additional remedial learning activities before the errors have been repeated and are embedded in the student's mind. Diagnostic capabilities could be incorporated into many types of computer programs such as drill and practice and tutorial. Much of the early work in using a computer for diagnostic purposes has been in the field of mathematics. It is likely that diagnostic capabilities can also be included in future social studies computer programs.

Evaluating Computer Software

As with other instructional materials (textbooks, supplemental materials, and media) computer software needs to receive careful evaluation to determine whether or not it is appropriate for use in social studies classes. A decade ago Williams and Williams estimated that about 5 to 6 percent of the more than 3,000 software programs available in 1984 were in the field of social studies at the elementary, middle, and high school levels. Komoski (1984) estimates that only about 5 percent of all educational software merits high recommendation. There has been little improvement in the ensuing years, although many ineffective programs have been discarded. There are, however, important differences between evaluating other print and nonprint media and computer software programs.

Just as there are some things that computers do very well, within the context of the classroom, there are things that computers cannot do as effectively as other learning resources. Before considering criteria for evaluating computer software, teachers need to respond to these and similar questions:

1. Do I have sufficient technical knowledge and skill to use the computer effectively in my class? Do I appreciate the teaching and learning potential and limitations of the computer?
2. What preparation will I need in order to be comfortable and competent in using the computer and related technologies?
3. How will my role(s) and mode of presentation be changed?
4. What efforts must I put forth to ensure access to the computer and needed programs?
5. How will the educational climate (organization, management, and discipline) of my classroom change and with what likely result(s)?
6. Will my use of the computer enhance student learning (knowledge, skills, attitudes, and values), motivation, and interest? Is the computer the most effective way to teach this lesson? Will the program save teacher time?

Bright (1987) has identified three general categories that are useful to evaluate computer software. The categories are computer instructional design, appropriate use of computer capabilities, and the technical quality of computer programs.

Instructional design includes evaluating the accuracy of the program content, the accuracy of presentation of information, and suitability of pedagogy used in the program. Teachers may want to consider these and similar questions when reviewing the instructional design of computer software programs.

- Are the objectives of the computer software clearly specified and appropriate for my curriculum content and for the range, maturity, and ability levels of my class or individual students? Do the author's objectives accurately reflect what the program really teaches? Are there hidden objectives in the program? Could the objectives of the lesson be achieved without the computer?
- Is the program oriented towards the individual learner, small groups of learners, or the class as a whole rather than toward the teacher? Who are the intended users of the program? Is instruction based on what the learner must be able to do? Does the program foster active student involvement? What is the role of the teacher? Is the program related to other classroom activities? Is the teaching method sound?
- Is the program designed to teach my students important social studies content and to help them learn concepts and generalizations? Is there a

match between content and objectives? Is the content of the program current and accurate? Is the content presented clearly and divided into reasonable chunks of information? Are there suggestions for using the program?
- Are women and minorities portrayed accurately? What knowledge, skills, and values are taught by these materials? Is the program as appealing to female as to male students? Is culture bias nonexistent?
- Is the program motivational and likely to maintain the interest of my students throughout the lesson? How much time is needed to teach, learn, and practice the content and/or skills included in the program? Are the main points reviewed and/or summarized throughout the program as well as at the end? Will the program provide a reasonable challenge to my students? Does the program accommodate a range of student proficiencies? Does the program provide for a high rate of student success?

In determining the appropriateness of using computer programs the teacher should investigate whether the capabilities and special features are used effectively. Teachers ought to consider some of the following important capability components:

- Is the power of the computer used effectively? Is the computer being used as an electronic page-turner? The use of the computer to present large amounts of information that could be presented in the printed mode (printing, photocopying, or dittoing) is not cost effective. The printed mode allows the learner to read at a pace appropriate for the task.
- What type of interactions are allowed between the learner and the program? For example, in indicating incorrect student responses, how does the computer respond? Are the error messages friendly and helpful? Does the program provide helpful directions to correct errors? Is the feedback specific in indicating why the response is incorrect? How is the program structured? Is there immediate feedback? Does the program meet the attention span of the learners? Does the program encourage the retention of information? Can the program be modified to meet individual learning needs? Does the program proceed at the right speed for the learner? Are there time limits for student responses? Do diagrams illustrate accurately the concept or content presented? Is the screen layout consistent, clear, and uncluttered? If sound effects are included, are they integral to the program?

High technological quality in computer software programs will help learners. Teachers need to ask questions similar to these:

- Is the program well written? Are the directions clear? Will students understand the language and vocabulary level used? Is the format of the program appropriate? Does the program include the use of graphics, color, and animation (visual processing)? Does the visual image on the screen draw attention to relevant content information? Is the lesson presented logically? Is the content and information correct? Did the program maintain student interest? Are there escapes? Can a program be saved for later use? Does the program maintain a continuous record of student achievement?
- Is the software protected from misuse by students? Is the program vulnerable to input error? Is it easy to correct errors? Reviewers are encouraged to assume the role of students (both successful and unsuccessful) to determine if the program may "bomb out" before instruction has been completed. If possible, prior to purchase, it is useful to observe students using the program.
- Is the program compatible with the equipment? Are the hardware requirements clearly indicated and in simple terms? How much memory is needed? What technical problems need to be corrected? What additional hardware or software would make the lesson more effective? Can the volume of sound be controlled or turned off?
- Are the documentation and support materials for learners and teachers sufficiently detailed, clear, and accurate? Are there instructions for running the program? How much knowledge of the computer is necessary? Can back-up copies be made legally and with relative ease? Are there provisions for "helps" from the producer or distributor? Can the program be previewed before purchase? Is there evidence the program has been field-tested in schools with students?
- How much time must the teacher spend with the program before the students can begin to use it? Is the teacher able to modify the program? Is the program versatile? Is the program flexible for use in various teaching and learning situations? Is record keeping (within the program or through printed materials) possible? Will this program allow for more challenging and rewarding teaching and learning experiences?

Evaluating computer software is time consuming and hard work, and it is difficult for a teacher alone to sort out the software useful for the classroom. As with other learning activities, it is important to keep in mind that what works for one teacher or class may not work for another. The teacher's personality, values, motivation, and experience have a bearing on the effectiveness of including educational computing in social studies programs.

Numerous guidelines to help teachers evaluate computer software are available from the National Council for the Social Studies (NCSS), state education agencies, educational computer centers, and computer publications. In addition, teachers may want to consult Resources in Computer Education (RICE)*, an electronic database with current information about computer software. *The Digest of Software Reviews**,* provides summaries of reviews of instructional computer software. In addition, the Alberta provincial department of education, Alberta Education, publishes a collection of reviews in *Computer Courseware Reviews*.*** Teachers should not rely entirely on catalogues for information about specific programs but instead establish files of computer reviews and information. It is often faster to review complete evaluation reports prepared by others than to conduct another evaluation.

Teachers may want to review such educational journals as *Classroom Computer Learning, The Computing Teacher, Electronic Learning, Teaching and Computers, Technology and Learning, Technological Horizons in Education,* and *Journal of Research on Computing in Education,* which provide information and regular reviews of new computer programs in social studies. Currently some of these journals are available to educators at no charge. *Social Education, Social Studies,* and *Journal of Geography* periodically review computer software programs and provide useful articles related to the use of computers in social studies. Other educational and technical journals also include information about programs and the emerging technologies. In general, written or verbal descriptions of programs are more helpful and objective than ratings based on numbers and stars. Checklists may be useful tools in evaluating computer software if the evaluation criteria are adequately defined and explained. These reviews are valuable for initial screening of programs before deciding whether or not testing would be useful. Where possible, however, teachers should try out the program prior to purchase.

Databases

Databased instruction is deeply rooted in several social science disciplines. Database programs incorporating social indicator information are becoming more readily available along with spreadsheets and graphing programs. Database programs may be open ended, allowing students to design their own database by selecting categories for managing data. These programs enable students to collect, file, access, and analyze their own data in more efficient ways and then to make inferences similar to those of social scientists about the meaning of the data. Social mathematics competencies and various related skills such as organizing information, formulating and testing hypotheses,

---

*RICE is available through the Bibliographic Retrieval Service, Lathem, NY.
**The *Digest of Software Reviews* is available from Education, 1341 Bulldog Lane, Suite C, Fresno, CA 93710.
***ature*Computer Courseware Reviews* are available from Computer Technology Project, Alberta Education, 121160 Jasper Avenue, Edmonton, Alberta, Canada, T5K 0L2.

analyzing relationships, examining trends, and drawing conclusions (however tentative) may be enhanced through the use of database programs. Students are able to become active participants in their own learning and learn to become consumers of social science information.

Another use of computers in social studies classes is as an electronic information service (EIS) to help students locate and secure information from a variety of sources. For example, assume a high school student has been assigned to write a term paper or to present a report on a broad topic such as land use in Latin America or on the efforts to bring about world peace. Often students are not highly motivated to complete such an assignment and even if they are, the range of current reference materials may be lacking or not readily available. This is where EIS can be helpful. By using computer-generated references, information from several databases can be located and gathered quickly since EIS will provide exact references for bibliographic resources, which saves time. To complete the assignment students are required to use the same searching skills as in "traditional" research methods and develop new telecommunication skills as well.

What is involved in using EIS? Basically EIS consists of millions of pieces of information on particular subjects that is stored in data banks. Within the data bank are databases, which are smaller collections of information on more specific topics. An analogy to the data bank is a large department store that has merchandise arranged by departments—clothing to garden equipment. Within the section for clothing are items for women, men, and children.

Equipment for EIS includes a computer with two disk drives, a printer (nice though not essential, but helpful to make a printed copy of the information), modem, cable connections (as necessary), and a telecommunications software program. With the equipment in place, the next step is to subscribe to an electronic information service. There are several such services but the ones most likely to be of use to social studies educators and their students are the following.

CompuServe (Columbus, Ohio) offers a variety of electronic news services and information databases. One of its databases is the nine million word, 20-volume *Groliers Academic American Encyclopedia* (AAED), which allows the user to search for information based on matches for one or two key words. It is anticipated that the *World Almanac* will soon be available in a similar format on a compact computer disk.

BRS/SEARCH SERVICE (Bibliographic Retrieval Services, Lathem, New York) is an information service that provides on-line searches of professional databases. *BRS Colleague Educator* is a special service for educators that accesses twelve databases including AAED, ERIC, and ABSTRAX, with detailed abstracts from widely read periodicals. BRS also provides on-line classroom instruction on information retrieval.

DIALOG (Palo Alto, California) enables users to search more than 200 databases for bibliographic references and abstracts. Two databases of interest to social studies teachers are *American History and Life,* which has information on United States and Canadian history, current affairs, politics and governments, and area studies; and *Magazine Index,* which includes references to more than 400 popular magazines.

Teachers working on developing curriculum or revising their instructional units and lesson plans will find using the resources identified in the Educational Resources Information Center (ERIC) database a valuable resource. The ERIC collection includes journal articles, documents, research studies, conference presentations, curriculum guides from several states and Canadian provinces, instructional units, and position papers. While providing typical bibliographic information, there are annotations (abstracts) related to each reference. Journal articles are available in libraries or from University Microfilms Incorporated (UMI, Ann Arbor, MI), while most of the documents are available from the ERIC Document Reproduction Service (EDRS, Arlington, VA). The documents are available in microfiche format and/or paper copy format. The cost of securing documents is relatively inexpensive. In addition, ERIC develops and disseminates its own publications program of books, digests, and resource packets (Risinger, 1989). If you are not already familiar with ERIC, you are urged to become knowledgeable about this valuable database and its usefulness to educators.

Hundreds of electronic bulletin boards are available at present. These enable educators to communicate with each other on a regular and ongoing basis concerning a range of topics extending from microcomputer technology to the needs of special learners.

These services are not free and costs and charges vary. Expenses include start-up costs, on-line connect time, individual database costs, telephone switching networks, and other miscellaneous costs. Teachers and students need to be familiar with the various steps involved in logging on to secure the desired information in order to keep expenses reasonable. Each of these data banks has specific procedures and its subscribers are provided with an instructional manual.

For the most part schools do not yet have sufficient financial resources to utilize this technology extensively. However, as satellite transmissions become less costly, accessing distant computer databases by students becomes more realistic. Teachers will have to decide whether or not these financial outputs for equipment and services, as well as teacher preparation, make sense for them to incorporate EIS in their social studies classes.

Additional Educational Technologies

Without a doubt other technologies will be used more extensively in the schools. Prospective teachers might consider some of the following technologies as examples for use in social studies classes.

Satellite Technology Satellite technology offers the opportunity to disperse information to several sites simultaneously. For example, students will be able to see, hear, and speak with people in other states and countries, which should facilitate learning about people and cultures in other settings. In addition, teachers can videotape broadcasts (within existing copyright laws) for future use in classes. Satellite technology will enable students to have firsthand knowledge of an important Congressional debate, a major policy speech before the United Nations, or other specific events from around the globe. The new technology will enable students in widely scattered areas to extend their horizons by being able to participate in international, national, and state learning activities while remaining at the local school site. Teachers may also use this technology for staff development programs. For example, often presentations by keynote speakers or special sessions at NCSS meetings are transmitted to the schools of teachers who are unable to attend the annual NCSS convention.

Interactive Learning Technologies Interactive video systems such as Instructional Television Fixed Service (ITFS) transmitted from low-power television, microwave, two-way cable, and fiber optics offers exciting possibilities for schools to share courses and teachers by allowing students to have access to courses not otherwise available at their school. For example, in a given school there may be an insufficient number of students to offer an Advanced Placement (AP) course. However, individuals or small groups of students could enroll in an AP course that would be offered via ITFS or fiber optics networks. In that way one teacher could instruct and interact with students at multiple sites. Many states or groups of school districts in a geographic region are creating networks of schools and universities through fiber optics connections. Instruction can be offered from one site and learners at other sites can see and talk with the instructor and transmit assignments and the like through the use of FAX machines. Modems allow students to download information from databases and to talk with people around the world. For example, students in River Falls, Wisconsin, can regularly contact peers in Moscow to learn of developments in Russia and the perspectives of Moscow students on common events.

Teleconference Phone An example of a newer technology for teaching social studies is the teleconference phone, which becomes an electronic bridge to enable students and teachers to communicate with a telephone guest. These guests are people who otherwise would be unable to address a particular class. For example, a person in the public eye is contacted either by telephone or letter and asked to talk with the class about a specific topic at the time the class regularly meets. The guest uses any telephone to call the students at the agreed-upon time. The students meet in a room with a regular telephone line for their teleconference phone that broadcasts the call over a loudspeaker so that all can hear and participate. For larger groups a portable amplifier is often used.

In general, students prepare for the telephone guest by developing a series of questions that they would like to have their guest address. Although the guest cannot be seen, there is a high energy and interest level among the students because they and the guest can interact. Visual references (maps, charts, or pictures) around the room help students see who is talking or see what is likely to be described by the guest. Of course, as the number of students participating grows, the less individual interaction there is likely to be with the guest.

Faculty can also benefit by using the teleconference phone for staff development opportunities. Consultants and other experts who may be costly or have limited time are invited to address faculty members about important issues in education and social studies. Such telephone conferences enable teachers to interact with leaders in the field and to have access to current information (Galvin, 1985).

The use of the teleconference phone enables students and teachers to learn directly from those in the news or from experts rather than relying solely on what is presented in the press or on television. Direct access to and interaction with many people is likely to have an important impact on learning and teaching. The use of this technology means that information is just a phone call away.

Telestudying Students often resist completing homework assignments they view as busywork, boring, or involving solitary study. They also complain of the time delays in receiving learning assistance and feedback. Certainly, that teachers cannot be available twenty-four hours each day. However, it is possible for a computer to be available with which the student can interact at any time of the day or night. Such efforts offer the potential to reinforce the learning covered in school; provide opportunities for direct and immediate feedback; and are available at times when it is convenient for students to study.

Videodisc Technology Videodiscs, similar to a long playing phonograph record, can store massive amounts of digital information (moving colored pictures and sound) that has been encoded by laser (optical videodisc). Videodisc players use another low-power laser to read the information on the disk that can be either graphic or textual and can be intermixed with audio and video information. The information recorded on the disk can be accessed very rapidly through the use of bar codes and a bar code reader, which enables the user to have control over the presentation and pacing of materials. A bar code is a series of vertical lines of different widths that represent information. The bar code reader is an electronic device that reads the bar code information, which enables the user of a laser disk to move to predetermined places on a disk almost instantaneously.

A single 12-inch laser videodisc can hold information approximately equivalent to a full encyclopedia, 675 slide trays, or up to thirty minutes of full motion audio and video. Videodiscs may be viewed as a sophisticated textbook that can be divided into topics or chapters to enable the student to review information presented earlier. For example, National Geographic programs have built-in computer interfaces and utilize bar code readers to find the desired text or images.

Videodisc interfacing will allow for a more rapid transfer of data and bring about a greater storage capacity. This will allow students to manipulate printed text and still and moving pictures with high quality sound while the computer records responses, provides feedback, and stores a record of student performance. This makes it possible for students to become active participants in their educational experiences. When considering possible uses of the videodisc and other new technologies we assume that virtually all these educational experiences will include a visual component. Visual learning allows the students to develop visual memories and to view the world from various perspectives and settings. As teachers, we need to ask how student learning experiences might be changed through the use of interactive visual technology.

Much of the present technology allows only the "reading" of information. This capability allows us to develop electronic books or portable information bases that can be used with microcomputers. By the early 1990s IBM introduced the program *Columbus*, which allows the user to both read and write on the disk. Other new programs have the same capacity. Interactive video should be an exciting enhancement to our existing knowledge about computer technology. Of interest to social studies teachers will be ABC Interactive programs *In the Holy Land*, related to the Israeli/Palestinian problems in the Middle East, and *The Campaign for the White House* (both available from Optical Data Corporation, Warren, NJ), which chronicles the 1988 presidential race between George Bush and Michael Dukakis.

Robots Although the concept of the robot can be traced in myth and history to the Greeks, the term was first used by the Czech dramatist Karel Capek in his satirical play, *R.U.R.*, in 1921. Robots in the Capek play were humanoid and were engineered and operated to be more efficient than people. Today robots are computerized machines that are able to function in ways similar to humans.

Originally robots were developed to move heavy objects and to perform tasks that were dull, dirty, dangerous, or repetitious. However by 1986 four refinements—vision, hearing, speaking, and touch—were being studied carefully. By the 1980s robots were being used fairly extensively in some industries, such as automobile manufacturing for General Motors. At this writing the United States and Japan are the two nations using robots most extensively and their use is expected to increase in the coming decade. It may be premature to speculate about robots in our lives, but we can expect that robots will become more sophisticated, be assigned to a variety of tasks, and have an impact on our personal and professional lives.

The precise role of robots in schools is not yet known. As social studies teachers we need to help students learn about robots and their anticipated role(s) in our lives, consider related social policy issues, and make ethical judgments concerning their use in the electronic age. Joseph Deken writing in *Silico Sapiens: The Fundamentals and Future of Robots* (1986), tells us that we must recognize that the emergence of robotics is as important as the development of the transistor and that robots may be the next or last step in the fast moving computer revolution. Deken urges us not to abdicate our human prerogatives and responsibilities but to use our insights, values, and judgments in making important decisions concerning robots in our lives. Social studies teachers need to help students examine the future when the use of robots in education and their more extensive use in the marketplace are likely to have a great impact on their lives in terms of learning, jobs, and leisure.

Virtual Reality One of the newest developments for computers in schools is the field of virtual reality. Virtual reality is a computer-generated, interactive, multimedia environment in which the user becomes an active participant in a "virtually real world." The user becomes a part of the action on the screen and enjoys the sensation of actual participation. Most often the user wears a head-mounted display system with optical stereo liquid crystal display video goggles and headphones. The participant wears a data glove to interact with the environment by pointing, grasping, rearranging objects in the environment, and facilitating movement through the environment (Simonson and Thompson, 1994). Thus far most classrooms are unable to provide such instructional tools due to costs and limited software.

Without a doubt virtual reality has a role to play in classroom teaching and learning. Audio-visual media allows students to see the real world from their classrooms while virtual reality programs include the sensation of becoming one with the simulated environment (Henderson, 1991). These programs can be highly motivational as active participation is required.

Stuart and Thomas (1991) list several uses of virtual reality in classrooms. Virtual reality enables students to do the following:

- Explore places and objects to which students would not have access.
- Explore real things that could not be examined effectively without alterations of scale, size, and time.
- Create places and things with altered qualities.
- Interact and collaborate with people in remote locations who have similar interests.
- Create and manipulate abstract conceptual representations.
- Interact with virtual beings, such as historical figures who represent different philosophies and viewpoints participating in simulated negotiations.

Various uses of virtual reality are in the science, writing, and reading curriculums. For social studies Helsel (1992) suggests using virtual reality to duplicate experiences in other countries so students can participate in historical events and interact with simulated persons who had participated in the event.

One virtual reality program requires a computer, monitor, and software. This program is *Virtus Walk-Through* (Virtus Corporation, Cary, NC) in which the user constructs a model, sees it on the monitor as it appears in three dimensions and "walks through" the object. The program can be used to draw simulations of real or imaginary objects and allows the user to "walk around," trying out variations of the original plan (Pantelidis, 1993).

With further refinements this media is likely to expand as teachers integrate virtual reality systems and programs into their curriculum. The use of virtual reality can assist students to explore ideas, theories, build new models, and create new knowledge.

Hypermedia Hypermedia "combines methods of representation, such as video, graphics, animation, and text, and converts the information represented in the formats in a multitude of paths to create an environment that affords immediate, yet random, access to large amounts of information" (Simonson and Thompson, 1994). The hypermedia environment is interactive in that the user works with a computer and videodisc to explore a particular topic in the way the user decides. Teachers using hypermedia are able to adapt instructional materials to meet the learning styles of individual students (Marchionini, 1988). Students are then able to integrate new information with their existing information base. Simonson and Thompson (1994) offer several cautions concerning the use of hypermedia:

- There is a fear that hypermedia may be used as an alternate delivery system to support traditional didactic teaching rather than having students explore information or construct knowledge in their own way.
- Despite its potential, constructing lessons and applications is time consuming as teachers discover that creating quality programs is challenging. As new hypermedia software becomes available this task is likely to be simplified.
- The equipment needed to set up and connect a hypermedia system is costly and time consuming. Teachers may not have the interest, knowledge, or skill to operate such a system.
- Assessment of student learning will be a challenge since it is likely that students using hypermedia tools will learn different information. For the most part teachers are used to having students learn the same information and take the same test. To assess students' learning it is likely that students may need to create, demonstrate, and communicate what they have learned about a particular topic.

- Students who may be used to linear learning will need instruction in the use of hypermedia and opportunities to explore and become comfortable with the open-ended nature of the hypermedia environment.

At present there are two major hypermedia tools available. They are Apple's *HyperCard* (available only in Macintosh) and IBM's *LinkWay*. Using the vocabulary of *HyperCard*, *stacks* allow the users to explore the information in a stack in their own way by looking for particular text, graphic, audio, or video information about the topic. Hypertalk, the programming language that is part of the *HyperCard* system, allows users with little or no programming experience to create fairly sophisticated stacks of information easily.

Users access the information in stacks, which have *background* data that appear in *cards* or a collection of cards. Cards may include text or graphics that may be shared with other cards. *Fields* are areas on cards where the information is recorded. *Buttons* exist on cards and provide immediate access to other cards in the stack for additional information. The construction of buttons gives access to information or reference documents and indexes using the same word. The result is a variety of data that are linked in various ways. From these data, users then manipulate them in ways which are meaningful.

IBM's *LinkWay* is comparable to Apple's *HyperCard* and is a true hypermedia authoring system, although IBM refers to it as a color-system, well-documented multimedia package. The strength of *LinkWay Live!*, its most recent version (1992), is its ease of use. It also includes paint and text editing programs, a font editor, and has image captive capabilities. *LinkWay* lessons build on *pages* that are collected into *folders* (similar to *HyperCard*'s stacks). Each page includes *fields* used for text materials; *pictures* which display graphics; *buttons* which cause actions; *lists* which present the body of text, and *media* that control audio, video, or animation.

LinkWay is relatively easy to learn and some teachers may begin to use it at upper elementary grades where students design reports, projects, and presentations. Some educators believe the use of hypermedia may be a way for students to learn with computers rather than learning about them. The use of hyperdocuments may well create worthwhile contexts in which students can learn most effectively.

Ongoing Issues

While the newer technologies have been used to some degree in social studies classes, there are a number of important educational issues that are not yet resolved. For example, the selection of the appropriate technology for particular learning processes often is a difficult decision. Another concern is that while fairly sophisticated hardware has been developed, the development of pedagogically sound instructional materials (software) for a particular technology lags behind. Due to costs of developing software and the potential for limited sales, software publishers most often develop computer programs for home rather than school use. In order to bring about improvements in educational computer software it will be necessary for program developers and educators to talk to one another and work together.

The instructional design of educational programs (pacing, reinforcement, student development, and the like) and understanding of human learning processes are important keys in the effective utilization of the newer technologies. At present there is limited information concerning the interrelationships of learning from the newer educational technologies.

Other issues not to be ignored include the relatively large initial and recurring costs of the new technologies, rapid obsolescence of the hardware due to more advanced technologies, compatibility of equipment, management of the technologies, and the need for sound research on the new and emerging technologies and their effectiveness in social studies classes. There is a danger of overinvestment in computers and computer software, which may force their use for five years or longer to amortize costs. Teacher attitudes toward the use of technology and teacher preparation are likely to change as the role of the teacher expands from that of instructor, tutor, diagnostician, classroom manager, evaluator, disciplinarian, counselor, and so forth, to that of technician, selector of technology and programs, individualizer of instruction, scheduler, advisor, and other similar tasks.

Most educators would probably agree that computers and the newer technologies can promote student learning and to a certain degree require problem-solving abilities to figure out how to access, manipulate, and control the flow of information. These skills are often learned through experimentation and trial-and-error efforts, which result in the development of problem-solving strategies. Students are then empowered to control their learning needs as they gain in confidence and creativity.

What is not clear at this time is exactly how and to what degree computers and other technologies can assist learning. It is possible that an overuse of computers could stifle the creative imagination of some students while for other students the use of computers may open avenues for creative and original problem solving. Clearly additional research is needed as is the need to identify and define important questions to be asked of researchers (Clegg, 1991). Such questions might include the following:

- How and for whom is computer learning useful? Does what students learn with a computer transfer to other curriculum areas? What impact do computers have on our culture and sense of community?
- To what extent will the progressive use of computers and newer technologies increase learning potentials? Will teacher initiative in the teaching and learning process be hindered or enhanced?

- To what extent are interactive video systems effective in providing different approaches to learning, presenting different learning styles, and teaching content in various subject areas? Is there a gender difference concerning computer-related learning activities?
- What is the shape of the curriculum—more flexible or standardized? When are certain computer-related skills taught? To what extent should students rely on computers for calculations, spelling, grammar checking, and other similar tasks?
- To what extent will students who have access to computers at home have an advantage over those who do not? Does this suggest the cost of high technology will limit information to those who can afford to pay for it? Will students in poorer schools suffer a comparative disadvantage? Is there a geographic inequality in which students in some states have less access to computers?

At least three other issues will need to be considered. Some critics fear that because of the high costs of equipping a school with the new technologies, only a few schools in wealthier areas will develop instructional programs that utilize the newer technologies for teaching and learning. According to Shane (1987), about 80 percent of the teachers use computers for drill and practice rather than to develop higher-order thinking skills. This finding suggests the less able student is likely to have more opportunities to use computers than brighter students. Also there is some evidence that schools teach computer programming more often to white male students but use drill-and-practice exercises for ethnic minority and female students. David Moursund (1984) has recommended that districts allocate 2 percent of the budget for hardware, software (including selected support materials), staff development, and computer coordinators with some money set aside for contingency needs. Over time, districts following this or a similar policy should be able to secure the needed newer technological resources.

A fundamental question is "Who should have access to the limited computer resources available in most schools?" A related issue is whether or not to establish a computer laboratory or to place computers in sufficient quantity into classrooms so that computer learning activities can be integrated into regular classroom learning activities. Are all students encouraged and allowed access to the computers? How can a computer serve all?

At this time, there are initial research studies that indicate that female students have less access and instruction related to computer learning beginning in the elementary school (Chen, 1986; Swadener and Jarrett, 1986). If this trend continues, that means, among other things, that females will not be prepared for a number of careers and jobs that require technical knowledge and skills and will increase the existing inequities that are likely to become even more deeply ingrained in society. The lack of knowledge of the new technologies and their uses may threaten the educational and career opportunities that have been achieved by women and minorities thus far.

Research by Schubert (1986) indicates that females are interested in using computers to improve the quality of their work rather than studying about computers. Existing computer programs are often biased in content; see for example *Oregon Trail*. There are, however, two programs that seek to address this concern. *The Neuter Computer: Computers for Girls and Boys* includes more than fifty school-based, gender-neutral learning activities by the Computer Equity Training Project (Women's Action Alliance, NY) and *EQUALS in Computer Technology* (University of California, Berkeley). The Women's Action Alliance also publishes a newsletter, *Computer Equity News*, which promotes gender equity and includes specific ideas and strategies for dealing with computer equity problems. It is important that social studies teachers ensure equity of opportunity for both girls and boys in computer and other new technology learning. Eliminating these inequities requires a long-term commitment of both time and money. Attitudes and expectations concerning computer usage will need to be modified. Nelson and Watson (1990–1991) note that after two decades, gender differences still exist. "Males are encouraged from preschool years to engage in computer-based activities. Females typically are generally more ignored both at home and at school. Most of the software that is marketed and then purchased by families and schools is based on male-oriented themes" (p. 351). There is evidence that males use computers at home more frequently than females. It is not clear, however, if parents tend to favor males when buying computers or if males are more influential in persuading their parents to buy them computers.

Research statistics concerning gender differences in science and mathematics education suggest that girls working on computers with girls perform better than girls working with boys (Martin, 1991). Aman (1992) suggests that girls be engaged in informal activities using computers so they have opportunities to gain computer experiences and thus gain more positive attitudes toward computers.

To overcome the gender gap related to the use of technology, Canada and Brusca (1991) offer the following recommendations.

1. Adopt a proactive stance, recognize a gap exists, and take steps to overcome inequalities by creating teaching strategies and learning opportunities that facilitate female students' learning about and working with computers.
2. Structure the social and physical environment in the classroom to facilitate female students' learning opportunities by reducing competition for computer usage and by recognizing female learning and social styles such as peer tutoring, teamwork, and networking, which allow for the making of personal connections.
3. Promote the integration of computer work and programming skills across the curriculum as computer technology has applications for all curriculum areas and is not the domain of any academic discipline.

4. Programmers must eliminate stereotyping and stereotypic themes from computer software programs. For example, many electronic games have male-oriented themes that focus on sports, competition, and violence or destruction. At the same time some programs continue to portray females in passive roles that require rescue by males.

Clearly, the gender gap with respect to females and technology is multifaceted with no easy solutions. It is, however, critical that teachers and computer program developers be sensitive to female learning styles and interests, as well as their cognitive, social, and psychological development that is expressed in a "different voice" as "women's ways of knowing" (Gilligan, 1982; Belenky, Clinchy, Goldberger, and Tarule, 1986).

On the other hand, there are those who hold a very different view concerning the impact of technology. These critics argue that because the costs of

© Joel Gordon 1992

technology will be reduced, the public school system as we know it today will be weakened since a part of learning may be removed from the public schools and moved to homes and work sites and funded with private money if confidence in public schools continues to decline. These critics would argue that public education will become like a poverty-stricken ghetto without sufficient operational funds, as education moves from the public to the private sector. An equitable distribution of resources for technology is critical to ensure that income and gender gaps are overcome. These social and educational issues are likely to occupy the attention of politicians, educational leaders, and researchers in the foreseeable future.

Abuses of Technology

As society becomes more and more technologically oriented, schools have a responsibility to teach about ethical issues related to computer use. Computer crime is relatively new and not yet fully comprehensible. Basically computer crime includes activities in which a computer is used to commit a criminal act. These crimes may include but not be limited to the destruction of information by changing or erasing information available on a computer; stealing information from a computer database; stealing service, such as using a school computer for personal use if this is not allowed; physical destruction of computer files; altering data, such as changing grades; and software piracy, which involves the illegal copying of software (Weller, Repman, Rooze, and Parker, 1992). How will society deal with computer theft, vandalism, fraud, and pranks?

It is difficult to estimate the actual amount of software piracy, but one market research company found that approximately 50 percent of the software being used was copied illegally. Software piracy is a federal crime and punishable in civil and criminal courts by imprisonment and fines (Kinzer, Shorwood, and Bransford, 1986). As teachers we tell students not to copy each other's work, but if teachers pirate software, what kind of role models are they presenting to students?

Another related question is "Who has access to the information stored in databases?" It is necessary that districts balance the right of student individual privacy with the "need to know" by authorized teachers, counselors, and other educators. How is information shared or denied to segments of competing populations? For example, what information is "confidential" and what information is available to the public under the Freedom of Information Act?

The matching of unrelated computer records to create a new database is a widely debated topic. Matching involves using information in ways not originally intended (Kinzer, et al., 1986). For example, information reported to one government organization is shared with another agency; for example, driver's license and automobile registration records are shared with welfare or employment offices. Those who favor matching of computer data argue the use of computers is an efficient way to detect fraud and arrest criminals. On the other hand, opponents view matching of information as an invasion of personal privacy. It was estimated in 1984 that on the average the name of each United States citizen was entered in at least seventy federal, state, local, and private files and that on a daily basis information is shared among these files (Galloway, 1984). This is an important legal and ethical issue for educators to consider as student records and their own employment records could be used for matching purposes.

As the issue of computer crime becomes more and more critical it is important that teachers teach about computer ethics and discuss the implications of unethical uses of computers. Computers in and of themselves are neutral, neither ethical nor unethical. The way an individual chooses to use or abuse the computer becomes the ethical issue. Topics to discuss in teaching about computer ethics may include a discussion of privacy issues and computer criminal and noncriminal activities. The *Computing Teacher* (February 1987) has published a "Code of Ethical Conduct for Computer-Using Educators," which should be examined in some detail by social studies teachers who decide to use computer instructional programs. Schools have a duty to teach the topic of computer ethics and responsibilities.

Weller et al. (1992) have created a hypermedia program that enables students to participate in computer ethics decision making. The program, piloted on junior high school students, involves an examination of ethically difficult situations from the perspectives of the involved, making a decision, and experiencing the consequences of the decision. This type of program helps to make computer ethics decisions more relevant and personal to the students.

Computer Viruses

A computer virus is a programming code that has been designed to replicate itself and perform another task, such as erasing a computer screen. These viruses are becoming a major problem for those working with computers. The virus is buried within the computer's operating system and gives commands to copy itself on every program or disk stored on the hard drive of the infected computer. Whenever a new disk is used the virus goes along and when it is introduced into a clean computer the virus spreads to the new operating system. It is virtually impossible to keep viruses out of machines as they can be spread by newly purchased and sealed software, pirated software, and from unauthorized use.

Viruses can carry out specific instructions, replicate themselves, and alter software programs to include copies of themselves (Maxwell and Lamon, 1992). Viruses are invisible and can exist and operate without the user's knowledge. The virus operates like a time bomb waiting to explode. It can enter the system and then erupt and destroy the system. It is sufficiently powerful to shut down a mainframe computer and wipe out the contents on a hard drive. Computer networks facilitate the spread of viruses. Those who create such viruses do so deliberately to wreak or cause havoc with computer systems. Users need to rely on disinfectant programs to detect and remove viruses. One such program, *Disinfectant 2.9,* authored by John Norstad at Northwestern University, helps to detect and remove some Macintosh viruses. It can be used on either a hard or floppy disk. Like other computer programs, disinfectant programs must be updated as new viruses develop.

Future Uses of Computers in Social Studies

Lillie, Hannum, and Stuck (1989) present three general scenarios concerning the use of computers in education in the coming years. These are certainly appropriate to social studies just as they are to education in general.

> *Scenario I:* Computers will continue to be one of the many instructional tools used by teachers and students. They will be used mainly for word processing, to prepare young people for the world of work, for both drill-and-practice and tutorial instruction, and as a reward for good behavior or completing assignments on time. The integration of computers in the schools will remain very much like it is at present and schools are likely to continue to operate in traditional ways.
> *Scenario II:* Some schools will use computers as instructional tools to indicate they are current and knowledgeable about educational trends. Teachers will receive opportunities for staff development, but eventually computers will not be used in any significant way. It is most likely that computers will be used more for management purposes than for instruction.
> *Scenario III:* With the increasing availability of computers some experts predict that computer technology will change the basic process of education, with instructional changes taking place in order to maximize the capability of the new technologies and to personalize and individualize instruction (Toffler 1980; Bramble, Mason, and Berg 1985). These changes will be the result of 1) a public policy focus on accountability and evaluation; 2) advances in computer technology to store, process, and retrieve large amounts of data and the expansion of low-cost networking; 3) advances in computer software including voice input and output; and 4) the development of integrated learning systems that will enhance instruction by combining the most effective instructional practices with advances in computer and other newer technologies. (Lillie, Hannum, and Stuck, 1989; pp. 175–182)

Some teachers are likely to become more skilled at creating and writing their own programs, which should bring about improvement in computer programs. There is likely to be a sense of pride and accomplishment when using a computer program developed by oneself and then shared with students and colleagues. Such teacher-made programs can be developed to meet the particular needs of specific groups of students.

SUMMARY

Whether or not instructional technology is useful depends upon whether the new technology fills an educational need for both students and teachers. The newer technologies can be used effectively in small or large groups, by pairs or individuals, or in cooperative learning groups. These technologies allow for flexible instruction and take into account varied learning styles. Potential users of the newer technologies can use them to extend their thinking skills and reasoning abilities; to think in symbols; to use codes and languages to communicate with others; to develop new instructional paradigms; to understand their world; and contribute to the well-being of that world and the people living there.

It is important that social studies teachers when deciding whether or not to use the new technologies do not lose sight of the underlying pedagogical principles and basic learning needs of students when considering any innovative approach to teaching. These technologies enable teachers to offer learning experiences that cannot be provided by other means. It would be wise to make full use of computers and the newer technology as young people often already have considerable experience with these before coming to social studies classes. To this end it may be necessary for teachers to develop new teaching systems to help students learn more effectively.

Discussion Questions

1. Think of your own experience with computers. What type of learning, skill development, and student performance may be expected after students use computer programs for learning?
2. To what extent do existing computer programs have the potential to help students develop thinking skills needed for today and the future? What fundamental changes, if any, must we make in the social studies curriculum to prepare students for the Information Age of today and for the 21st century? How can teachers be more effective social studies teachers in classrooms that have access to newer technologies?
3. Given the importance of the social and cultural context for learning, what are some likely influences of technology on learning in social studies?
4. How can social studies teachers use technological developments as tools to stimulate efforts to reinvigorate the social studies curriculum?
5. How will the new technologies force teachers to adjust their teaching style? To what extent will students need to develop new learning

strategies to receive maximum benefit from the use of computers and the newer technologies?
6. To what extent is teaching with computers different from or similar to other teaching aids, past or present? What advantages or disadvantages do computers have for whole-class or small-group teaching and learning and for individualized learning?
7. What steps would you take if you discovered one of your students was engaged in a computer crime, such as altering school records, making illegal copies of a popular computer software program, or copying another student's work from the computer and submitting it as his or her own work?

Student Learning Activities

1. Visit a nearby middle school or high school to investigate to what extent social studies teachers incorporate computer learning activities into their courses. Interview the teachers (and students if possible) to find out how the computers are used in social studies classes. What programs are used most frequently, what are the teacher and student attitudes concerning the use of computers, and who has access to the computers? Share the findings of the interviews with classmates.
2. Develop a lesson plan for one of your social studies classes that includes the use of a computer. Which program(s) did you select? Why? What content and skills are students likely to gain from using this program? How will student learning be evaluated?
3. Review at least three social studies computer programs for middle school and high school students representing different social science disciplines. One review should examine a drill-and-practice or tutorial program; another review should be for a simulation or game program; and the third review should examine a problem-solving or word-processing or writing program. As you examine the programs, consider the questions posed in the chapter concerning evaluating computer programs. Begin to develop a file of computer critiques by sharing your analyses with classmates.
4. If you are interested in computer programming, develop a computer program that could be used during the preclinical or student teaching experience. Demonstrate the program for your classmates and, if possible, try out the program in a nearby social studies class.
5. Arrange to visit a local school district office and a local business to find out how computer technology is used in each organization. What inferences could you make about the computer technology now in use? What are some future plans for incorporating the newer technologies into the organization? What are some implications of these findings for your teaching of social studies?

References

Aman, J. 1992. "Gender and Attitudes Toward Computers." In C. D. Martin and E. Murchie-Beyman (Eds.), *In Search of Gender Free Paradigms for Computer Science Education*. Eugene, OR: International Society for Technology in Education. ERIC Document Reproduction Service ED 349 941.

Belenky, M. F., Clinchy, B. M., Goldberger, N. R., and Tarule, J. M. 1986. *Women's Ways of Knowing: The Development of Self, Voice, and Mind*. New York: Basic Books.

Bright, G. W. 1987. *Microcomputer Applications in the Elementary Classroom: A Guide for Teachers*. Boston: Allyn and Bacon.

Bruder, I. 1993. "What's New in Textbooks?" *Electronic Learning,* Vol. 13, No. 1, September. 14.

Canada, K. and Brusca, F. 1991. "The Technological Gender Gap: Evidence and Recommendations for Educators and Computer-Based Instruction Designers." *Educational Technology Research and Development,* Vol. 39, No. 2, 43–51.

Chen, M. 1986. "Gender and Computers: The Beneficial Effects of Experience on Attitudes." *Journal of Educational Computing Research,* Vol. 2, No. 3. 265–282.

Clegg, A. A., Jr. 1991. "Games and Simulations in Social Studies Education" In J. P. Shaver (Ed.), *Handbook of Research on Teaching and Learning*. New York: Macmillan.

"Code of Ethical Conduct for Computer-Using Educators: An ICCE Policy Statement." 1987. *Computing Teacher,* Vol. 14, No. 5, February. 51–53.

Collis, B. 1988. *Computers, Curriculum, and Whole-Class Instruction: Issues and Ideas*. Belmont, CA: Wadsworth.

Deken, J. 1986. *Silico Sapiens: The Fundamentals and Future of Robots*. New York: Bantam New Age Books.

Ehman, L. H. and Glenn, A. D. 1987. *Computer-Based Education in the Social Studies*. Bloomington, IN: ERIC Clearinghouse for the Social Studies/Social Science Education. ERIC Document Reproduction Service ED 284 825.

Galloway, J. L. 1984. "How Your Privacy Is Being Stripped Away," *U.S. News and World Report,* Vol. 96, No. 17, April, 30. 46–48.

Galvin, J. M. 1985. "Teleconferencing Brings the World to the Classroom." *The Social Studies,* Vol. 76, No. 6, November/December. 236–237.

Gilligan, C. 1982. *In a Different Voice: Psychological Theory and Women's Development*. Cambridge, MA: Harvard University Press.

Goodlad, J. 1984. *A Place Called School: Prospects for the Future*. New York: McGraw-Hill.

Helsel, S. 1992. "Virtual Reality and Education." *Educational Technology,* Vol. 32, No. 5, May. 38–42.

Henderson, J. 1991. "Designing Realities: Interactive Media, Virtual Reality, and Cyberspace." In S. K. Helsel and J. P. Roth (Eds.). *Virtual Reality: Theory, Practice, and Promise*. Westport, CT: Meckler.

Kinzer, C. K., Shorwood, R. D., and Bransford, J. D. (Eds.). 1986. *Computer Strategies for Education: Foundations and Content-Area Applications*. Columbus, OH: Merrill.

Komoski, P. K. 1984 "Educational Computing: The Burden of Insuring Quality." *Phi Delta Kappan,* Vol. 66, No. 4, December. 244–248.

Lillie, D. L., Hannum, W. H., and Stuck, G. B. 1989. *Computers and Effective Instruction: Using Computers and Software in the Classroom*. New York: Longman.

Marchionini, G. 1988. "Hypermedia Learning: Freedom and Chaos." *Educational Technology,* Vol. 28, No. 11. November. 8–12.

Martin, R. 1991. "School Childrens' Attitudes Towards Computers as a Function of Gender: Course Subjects and Availability of Home Computers." *Journal of Computer Assisted Learning,* Vol. 7, No. 3, September. 187–194.

Maxwell, J. R. and Lamon, W. E. 1992. "Computer Viruses: Pathology and Detection." *The Computing Teacher.* Vol. 20, No. 1, August–September. 12, 14–15.

Moursund, D. 1984 "The Two Percent Solution—Funding for Use of Computers," *NASSP Bulletin,* Vol. 68, No. 472, May. 49–54.

Nelson, C. S. and Watson, J. A. 1990/1991. "The Computer Gender-Gap: Children's Attitudes, Performance, and Socialization." *The Journal of Educational Technology Systems,* Vol. 19, No. 4. 345–353.

Oviatt, L. 1990. *Development of a Standardized Test of Computer Literacy.* Unpublished master's thesis. Ames: Iowa State University.

Pantelidis, V. S. 1993. "Virtual Reality in the Classroom." *Educational Technology.* Vol. 33, No. 4, April. 23–27.

Risinger, C. F. 1989. "Locating and Using ERIC and Other Data-Collection Sources." In M. A. Laughlin, H. M. Hartoonian, and N. M. Sanders (Eds.). *From Information to Decision Making: New Challenges for Effective Citizenship.* Bulletin 83. Washington, DC: National Council for the Social Studies.

Schubert, J. G. 1986. "Gender Equity in Computer Learning." *Theory into Practice,* Vol. 25, No. 4, Autumn. 267–275.

Shane, H. G. 1987. *Teaching and Learning in a Microelectronic Age.* Bloomington, IN: Phi Delta Kappa Educational Foundation.

Siegel, M. A. and Davis, D. M. 1986. *Understanding Computer-based Education.* New York: Random House.

Simonson, M. R. and Thompson, A. 1994. *Educational Computing Foundations* (2nd ed.) New York: Macmillan.

Stuart, R. and Thomas, J. C. 1991. "The Implications of Education in Cyberspace." *Multimedia Review.* Vol. 2, No. 2, Summer. 17–27.

Swadener, M. and Jarrett, K. 1986. "Gender Differences in Middle Grade Students' Actual and Preferred Computer Use." *Educational Technology,* Vol. 26, No. 9, September. 42–47.

Tickton, S. G. (Ed.). 1970. *To Improve Learning: An Evaluation of Instructional Technology: A Report by the Commission on Instructional Technology.* New York: R. R. Bowker.

Torardi, M. M. 1985. The Development of a Computer Literacy Assessment Instrument. Paper presented at the annual convention of the Association for Educational Communication and Technology. Anaheim, CA. ERIC Reproduction Document Service ED 256 342.

Vasu, E. S. and Vasu, M. L. 1987. "Integrating Computers into Social Science Curricula: Computer Literacy and Beyond." *Social Science Microcomputer Review,* Vol. 3, No. 1, Spring 1985.

Weller, H., Repman, J., Rooze, G., and Parker, R. 1992. "Students and Computer Ethics: An Alternative to Preaching." *The Computing Teacher,* Vol. 20, No. 1, August–September. 20–22.

Williams, F. and Williams, V. 1984. *Microcomputers in Elementary Education: Perspectives on Implementation.* Belmont, CA: Wadsworth.

Additional Readings

Adams, D. M. and Fuchs, M. 1986. *Educational Computing: Issues, Trends and a Practical Guide.* Springfield, IL: Charles C. Thomas.

Bitter, G. G., Camuse, R. A., and Durbin, V. L. 1993. *Using a Microcomputer in the Classroom* (3rd ed.) Boston: Allyn and Bacon.

Blease, D. 1986. *Evaluating Educational Software.* London, England, and Dover, NH: Croom Helm.

Bramble, M., Mason, E. J., and Berg, P. 1985. *Computers in Schools.* New York: McGraw-Hill.

Braun, J. A., Jr. 1986. *Microcomputers and the Social Studies: A Reference Guide for the Middle and Secondary Grades.* New York: Garland.

Bruder, I. 1992. "Multicultural Education Responding to the Demographics of Change." *Electronic Learning,* Vol. 12, No. 2, October. 20–23, 26.

Cetron, M. J. with Sorians, B., and Gayle, M. 1985. *Schools of the Future: How American Business and Education Can Cooperate to Save Our Schools.* New York: McGraw-Hill.

Chen, L. C. 1990–1991. "Interactive Video Technology in Education: Past, Present and Future." *Journal of Educational Technology Systems,* Vol. 19, No. 1. 5–19.

Choido, J. J. and Flaim, M. L. 1993. "The Link Between Computer Simulations and Social Studies Learning: Debriefing." *The Social Studies,* Vol. 84, No. 3, May/June. 119–121.

Collins, C. and Mangieri, J. N. (Eds.). 1992. *Teaching Thinking: An Agenda for the Twenty-First Century.* Hillsdale, NJ: Erlbaum.

Deim, R. 1986. "Computers in a School Environment: Preliminary Report of the Social Consequences." *Theory and Research in Social Studies*, Vol. 14, No. 2, Spring. 163–170.

Eraut, M. (Ed.). 1989. *The International Encyclopedia of Educational Technology.* Oxford, England: Pergamon.

Geisert, P. G. and Futrell, K. 1990. *Teachers, Computers, and Curriculum: Microcomputers in the Classroom.* Boston: Allyn and Bacon.

Glenn, A. D. "Democracy and Technology." 1990. *The Social Studies,* Vol. 81, No. 5. September/October. 215–217.

Kearsley, G., Hunter, B. and Furlong, M. 1992. *We Teach with Technology: New Visions for Education.* Wilsonville, OR: Franklin, Beedle.

Kushan, B. 1991. "Creating the Global Classroom for the 21st Century." *Educational Technology,* Vol. 31, No. 4, April. 47–50.

Kushan, B. and Dawson, T. 1992. "The Global Classroom: Reaching Beyond the Walls of the School Building." *Technology and Learning,* Vol. 12, No. 4. January. 48–51.

Levin, T. and Gordon, T. 1989. "Effect of Gender and Computer Experience on Attitudes Towards Computers." *Journal of Educational Computing Research,* Vol. 5, No. 1. 69–88.

Maddux, C. D., Johnson, D. L., and Willis, J. W. 1992. *Educational Computing: Learning with Tomorrow's Technologies.* Boston: Allyn and Bacon.

McClintock, R. O. (Special ed.). 1988. "Marking the Second Frontier." In *Teachers College Record,* Vol. 89. No. 3, Spring. 345–351. (This entire issue focuses on computers and education.)

Merrill, P. F., Hammons, K., Tolman, M. N., Christensen, L., Vincent, B., and Reynolds, P. 1992. *Computers in Education* (2nd ed.). Boston: Allyn and Bacon.

Miller, S. K. 1987. *Selecting and Implementing Educational Software*. Boston: Allyn and Bacon.

Mitzel, H., E. 1981. "On the Importance of Theory in Applying Technology to Education." *Journal of Computer-Based Instruction,* Vol. 7, No. 4, May. 93–98.

Norton, P. 1992. "When Technology Meets the Subject-Matter Disciplines in Education—Part One: Exploring the Computer as Metaphor." *Educational Technology,* Vol. 32, No. 6, June. 38–46.

Norton, P. 1992. "When Technology Meets the Subject-Matter Disciplines in Education—Part Two: Understanding the Computer as Discourse." *Educational Technology,* Vol. 32, No. 7, July. 36–46.

Norton, P. 1992. "When Technology Meets the Subject-Matter Disciplines in Education—Part Three: Incorporating the Computer as Method." *Educational Technology,* Vol. 32, No. 8, August. 35–44.

Olson, B. and Krendl, K. A. 1990–1991. "At-Risk Students and Microcomputers: What Do We Know and How Do We Know It?" *Journal of Educational Technology Systems,* Vol. 19, No. 2. 165–175.

Papert, S. 1993. *The Children's Machine: Rethinking School in the Age of the Computer.* New York: Basic Books.

Perelman, L. J. 1992. *School's Out: A Radical New Formula for the Revitalization of America's Educational System.* New York: Avon.

Reingold, H. 1991. *Virtual Reality*. New York: Summit Books.

Roszak, T. 1994. *The Cult of Information: A Neo-Luddite Treatise of High Tech, Artificial Intelligence, and the True Art of Thinking.* Berkeley: University of California Press.

Salem, J. 1992. "Hypercard: The Two-Dimensional Manipulative." *Computing Teacher*. Vol. 19, No. 6, March. 47–49.

Squires, D. and McDougall, A. 1994. *Choosing and Using Educational Software: A Teachers' Guide.* London: The Falmer Press.

"Technology, Trends, and Gizmos*: A Timeline for the '90s . . . and Beyond." 1990. *Technology and Learning,* Vol. 11, No. 1, September. 92–98.

Toffler, A. 1980. *The Third Wave.* New York: Morrow.

Toffler, A. 1990. *Powershift: Knowledge, Wealth, and Violence at the Edge of the 21st Century.* New York. Bantam Books.

Vockell, E. L. and Schwartz, E. M. 1992. *The Computer in the Classroom* (2nd ed.). New York: Mitchell McGraw-Hill.

> We must dare to think about "unthinkable" things because when things become unthinkable, thinking stops and action becomes mindless.
>
> *James William Fulbright*

CHAPTER 14

Professional Social Studies Teachers

FOCUS QUESTIONS

- What are some appropriate professional growth activities for social studies teachers? Why is professional growth an ongoing concern of social studies teachers?

- What are teachers' responsibilities and opportunities in professional organizations?

- What career opportunities are there for social studies teachers within education and in fields outside of education?

- What are some causes of job-related stress for social studies teachers? How can teachers learn to manage these tensions? How might a personal time management plan be of value?

- What nonteaching responsibilities do social studies teachers have?

OVERVIEW At best, basic teacher preparation programs provide a minimum of entry-level skills and information for the beginning teacher. Teachers, like other professionals, need to remain current in their fields in order to provide accurate and up-to-date information to students, parents, and to the larger community; to consider and incorporate new research findings related to the teaching and learning processes; to remain enthusiastic learners themselves; and to reflect thoughtfully and critically on new information in order to create new knowledge. A basic assumption is that the professional teacher must pursue additional learning throughout her or his professional career, as we believe that the half-life of a baccalaureate degree is now about three years or less.

This chapter brings together many of the issues and concerns of teachers who, in reality, often express similar personal and professional concerns whether they are beginners or veteran teachers. Such concerns address staff development and professional growth opportunities, teacher ethics, non-teaching responsibilities, faculty morale, activities of professional organizations, career possibilities within education, and so forth. Individual teachers will respond to similar concerns in very different ways. When reading this chapter you should try to determine how you might respond and react to these and other related issues.

Opportunities for Professional Growth

Throughout their careers teachers will need to update their information and knowledge base to remain current, and so professional growth has an important role in a teacher's professional life. There are various ways for social studies teachers to grow both professionally and personally. Teachers are expected to be knowledgeable of social science disciplines and education content, skills related to the learning and teaching processes, characteristics of learners, and much more. Ongoing professional growth and learning is judged to be necessary for teachers at all stages of their professional careers. Professional development programs can renew existing strengths, develop new skills or knowledge, and enhance personal and professional competencies for self-improvement. The following ways illustrate professional growth opportunities that could be extended or modified to meet the needs and expectations of teachers, administrators, school boards, and the community.

One of the most common ways for teachers to participate in professional growth programs is to enroll in graduate courses in education, in one of the social science disciplines, or in a closely related discipline area at a nearby college to meet recertification requirements. Teachers often earn advanced degrees by planning a graduate program that meets college institutional requirements for a graduate degree, school district expectations, and the needs and interests of the teachers. Many colleges offer specially designed programs, courses, or workshops for teachers during the summer or academic year. Sometimes school districts offer teachers opportunities for retraining in another field to meet the changing or emerging needs of the district. Depending on the collective bargaining agreement school districts may pay or reimburse teachers' tuition costs and materials for graduate education. Earning additional credits leads to higher pay on the salary schedule.

Recently major colleges with funding from various educational foundations, educational organizations, and the federal government have developed special summer programs for social studies teachers. These programs usually last from three to six weeks, are intense, and focus on a particular topic or theme. Competition for acceptance and scholarships in these programs is often keen, but qualified teachers are encouraged to apply for these learning opportunities. Information about these programs is announced in social studies journals and other educational publications. Often school principals or department chairs receive announcements concerning these opportunities. It is wise to ask them to share this information as it becomes available with other interested social studies teachers. Attending such programs is rewarding in that participants have the opportunity to meet and interact with colleagues with similar interests from other districts and states, study a topic in depth, catch up with professional reading, gather new ideas, and in some instances, develop new materials for use with students during the coming academic year. Many times a modest stipend is offered to the participants.

School districts sometimes offer short courses, conferences, workshops, institutes, symposia, retreats, seminars, clinics, or other programs that offer continuing education units (CEUs) to teachers who complete them. For example, districts often bring in outside consultants for intensive workshops on a particular topic, such as reviewing and developing the social studies curriculum or how to use a new computer program. At other times local district personnel present such programs, which offer recognition for the presenters.

Other district-related professional growth opportunities could involve working with a student teacher or intern from a nearby college. At present several states and districts have structured induction programs designed to help beginning teachers make the transition from student teacher to professional teacher. Experienced classroom teachers are often asked to be mentors for the beginning teachers. Serving as a cooperating teacher or mentor is often recognition of one's skills as a teacher, and it enables the experienced teacher to serve the profession by sharing his or her experience and expertise with a novice teacher.

New ideas for teaching are often gleaned from colleagues by observing and visiting with teachers in one's own school or in other nearby school districts. At times districts will release a teacher for one or more days to visit other schools and/or to attend conferences and workshops sponsored by professional organizations, the state education agency, or other districts. Teachers return to their classes refreshed and with additional perspectives related to the teaching and learning process. Somewhat related is the opportunity to serve as a reviewer on a state or regional accreditation committee, which allows teachers the opportunity to interact with colleagues at the school being reviewed and with other members of the accrediting evaluation committee. New insights are gained and quality programs are confirmed through these opportunities.

Summer internship experiences with business or government agencies are sometimes available to teachers. Some businesses hire teachers for summer employment and give them the opportunity to work in several departments for a broad overall experience within the business. Other times the business might focus the teacher's expertise in only one department. Internships enable teachers to contribute to the business world, learn more about private enterprise, exchange perspectives about education with business leaders and workers, and earn some money. Arrangements for internships are usually established several months in advance.

Rather than working for business, some teachers may decide to engage in volunteer community service activities as a way of returning something to the community. Nonprofit organizations and civic groups often welcome teacher volunteers with skills and talents that can be utilized to help the organization better serve its clients.

Vacation months also provide time for teachers to travel and/or study abroad. A well-planned trip to another country can be a valuable learning experience in visiting historic sites, studying the people and culture, observing geographic features, or participating in cultural activities such as concerts, drama productions, and local folk festivals. Teachers can also bring back interesting artifacts and pictures for classroom use. North American colleges frequently offer summer courses abroad, which include opportunities for study and travel. Colleges abroad sometimes organize special summer courses for teachers from other countries. Home visits with families and tours of international businesses in other countries often can be arranged if sufficient time is allowed for preparation. Sometimes teachers are able to secure summer employment in another country, which also can be a valuable professional growth experience. Travel throughout the United States and Canada can also contribute to professional growth.

Closer to home, teachers may decide to engage in individually planned activities such as a structured reading program of significant books related to their field of interest and teaching responsibilities. Others may decide to learn to use a computer on their own or to develop (or revise) a computer program for use in their classes the following year. Such individual plans are often recognized as important components of staff development.

During the past several years the National Endowment for the Humanities (NEH) has had modest sums of money that it has made available to teachers for independent research related to some aspect of their teaching responsibilities. Districts may ask teachers to help solve some problems or meet some needs through research or working with nearby college faculty members. These opportunities for research are also viewed as another component of staff development.

Clearly, there are numerous opportunities available for the professional growth of teachers. Most local school districts have specific policies and guidelines concerning professional growth expectations and requirements. It is wise to check with the appropriate district administrator to be certain that individual plans for professional growth meet the district specifications.

Pre-Service Professional Growth Opportunities

Many college students have an interest in working with young people in a variety of ways. For example, teacher candidates often seek opportunities to work with various community agencies and nonprofit organizations for their own personal growth and to give something of themselves. Organized young peoples' programs at local Girls and Boys Clubs, scout troops, athletic teams, recreation programs, Big Sisters and Big Brothers, church-related groups, and the like offer valuable opportunities for prospective teachers to work with young people in settings outside of school. These experiences often help college students decide whether or not to choose a career in education.

Planning, organizing, implementing, and evaluating such activities provide valuable firsthand learning experiences and interactions with young people and adults. In instances where admission to teacher preparation programs is highly competitive, volunteer activities such as those described may provide an admission edge over a person without similar experiences. These early volunteer community service experiences are often helpful in securing the first teaching positions. Administrators are interested in hiring faculty who show they are committed to young people.

We recognize fully that college students are already busy meeting graduation and certification requirements; making personal, professional, and career decisions; and in some cases, maintaining a job and/or raising a family. We nonetheless strongly encourage prospective teachers to take advantage of the various social, cultural, and recreational activities of the college, participate in student government or other student organizations, such as the student organizations for prospective teachers, and to read widely both fiction and nonfiction works in books and periodicals. Such experiences are valuable preparation not only for teaching but for continuing personal and professional growth.

Staff Development Opportunities

School districts have always been interested in improving the quality of education and often provide one-time in-service programs featuring a speaker. Today such a practice is deemed inadequate as educators now recognize that staff development is ongoing. The decade of the 1980s brought a greater focus on staff development in light of the many national and state studies and reports concerning the quality of education. The 1990s continues an emphasis on regular staff development programs.

To have quality education in schools, school district officials are recognizing that staff development is a critical variable in any school improvement program. Districts, either voluntarily or under state mandate, are working on planning staff development programs. In some states recertification of school personnel is directly related to completing staff development programs. Some districts have a full-time or part-time person responsible for coordinating staff development programs.

In general, staff development programs for all teachers most likely include opportunities for performance improvement consistent with personal, district, school, and departmental goals. Other staff development programs may be related to career opportunities within the district, or for new teachers, an orientation to district organization, expectations, policies, and specific job responsibilities. Some districts also include programs related to the personal, mental, emotional, and physical well-being of the teacher. At given times or for certain individuals some of these programs may have a higher priority or be given a greater emphasis. As teachers reach different stages of their professional careers their needs for staff development will vary.

Prior to offering such programs, many districts conduct some type of faculty needs assessment to determine teacher priorities and interests concerning staff development programs. Districts often involve teachers in planning such programs through staff development advisory committees and similar groups. The delivery of staff development programs will vary depending upon the purpose(s) and nature of the program.

Often districts may plan staff development programs for the entire staff on topics such as suicide prevention, AIDS education, "at-risk" students, and similar topics. At other times staff development programs may be offered to a small and specific group of teachers on a topic such as the use of a new textbook or instructional program in geography. At times teachers may not appreciate staff development programs, but we encourage teachers to attend and participate in such sessions with the notion that most likely the program will present some useful new idea or information for later application.

Staff development in social studies might include such activities as curriculum planning; developing new or revising existing courses; developing test banks of questions for use in measuring student learning; preparing department accreditation reports; introducing new programs and/or technologies; reviewing and evaluating the selection of instructional materials; or improving thinking, writing, and reading skills in social studies.

For such programs to be effective there must be sound planning; administrators and school boards need to provide time for reflection, research, reading, exchanging ideas, and planning; and money must be allocated that should include costs for substitute teachers and/or summer pay for teachers, consultants, materials, and physical environments conducive to planning. During the staff development process attention needs to be given to new findings based on current research related to teaching and learning. For accountability purposes an evaluation component needs to be included in any staff development program.

Professional Expectations of Teachers

Teachers serve various publics and are viewed somewhat differently by each one. For example, administrators often expect teachers to teach the curriculum, motivate students to learn, maintain discipline, handle related administrative tasks, and so forth. The community expects teachers to teach students, become a part of the community and partake in community activities, and reinforce and uphold the values of the community. Students often view teachers either as friendly and helpful or as authority figures who seek to control some aspect of their lives. Colleagues may see each other either as competitors or as fellow teachers striving to accomplish the same goals—to help young people learn in order to be effective citizens in the adult world.

Teacher Ethics

Teachers are role models for students and are expected to be responsible citizens within the local community. They are judged by peers and colleagues on the basis of their ethical behavior. As such, teachers are expected to develop and maintain a sense of ethical behavior derived from society's moral values, professional standards, and by general principles in specific situations which raise ethical standards.

All teachers have a professional responsibility to assume an ethical perspective toward their teaching (Stark, Lowther, and Hagerty, 1986). This requires a:

> [c]ritical understanding of the moral basis of teaching and [a] working knowledge of the value principles and processes of inquiry involved in the ethical thinking, feeling, and acting. . . . Teachers need a firm grasp of the standards and some awareness of the informal judiciaries created within the profession and by local school boards to judge instances of noncompliance. (Strom, 1989, p. 268)

Teaching is intrinsically moral as it impacts others. Teachers use knowledge, skills, and values, and they exercise power, make curriculum decisions, and deliberate about values issues in education. A teacher's approach to teaching affects the behaviors of others. The development of ethical sensitivity to many ongoing educational issues presents numerous challenges to teachers as they seek to make a positive difference in the lives of their students.

Nonteaching Responsibilities

By now it should be obvious to teacher candidates that teachers have both teaching and nonteaching professional responsibilities. These latter responsibilities often include a variety of tasks such as extra duty assignments, which may be subject to teacher union–school board collective bargaining negotiations. The right for teachers to bargain collectively is based on the specific laws of the various states. These laws vary considerably in detail and scope from one state to another and teacher candidates are urged to become familiar with the laws of the states where they hope to teach.

The nonteaching tasks that may be subject to negotiation could include the following responsibilities, which allow teachers and students to work together in settings outside the classroom and sometimes allow teachers to earn additional pay for extra work.

Supervision Middle and high school teachers are often asked to supervise a variety of activities, which could include the loading and unloading of school buses, monitoring students in hallways and restrooms between classes, school assemblies and pep rallies, students on buses transporting students to athletic contests, and taking tickets at school events. School districts often assign supervision duties to teachers to ensure the safety of students and to have teachers become participants in a variety of nonteaching activities related to students and the school.

Advising One of the most common duties assigned to teachers is related to advising student clubs, organizations, and activities. Social studies teachers may be assigned to activities directly related to social studies, such as Model United Nations, mock trial competition, the history club, Close Up, academic competition, Citizen Bee, Geography Bee, and student council. They may also be assigned as a class advisor. Very often the class advisor begins with incoming freshmen and remains with the class until it graduates from high school some three or four years later. Of course, social studies teachers with coaching experience and the appropriate state licenses (if needed) may be asked to coach one of the school's girls or boys athletic teams or to coordinate the Pep Club or cheerleading squad.

Teachers in most curriculum areas are usually required to participate in the advisor-advisee program if such a program exists in the school. Often teachers with a specific interest in a student activity such as photography or stamp collecting may volunteer to organize an activity and work with students who have similar interests. These activities are an integral part of the school experiences for students, and advisors have an important role in these activities.

Attending school events Most schools encourage teachers to attend school events voluntarily to see students perform in musicals, athletic events, plays, and the like. Teachers usually enjoy these experiences as it allows teachers and students to know one another and interact outside the formal classroom. At these events, teachers may have the opportunity to meet the parents or guardians of their students in a more informal environment.

To ensure teacher participation at selected school events, school administrators often require that teachers attend traditional school-community activities such as back-to-school nights, open house during public school week, parent-teacher meetings, graduation, and other similar events. Depending on the size of the school and its activities, many schools require that teachers sign up for attending and/or supervising a certain number of events each year. If this is the case, individual teachers usually receive a reminder of their responsibilities for the particular event or activity. Failure to fulfill these responsibilities (without sufficient cause and/or notice) may force the administrator to place a letter of reprimand in the teacher's personnel file.

Department or team meetings   For the most part high schools are organized by disciplines into departments while middle schools are often organized by interdisciplinary teams. Larger high schools usually have a department head who may be elected by members of the department or appointed by the administration for a certain time period. The precise duties and responsibilities of the department chair may vary greatly. Most often departments meet once or twice a month to decide on curriculum, select instructional materials, work on scheduling, recommend students for specific classes or levels of classes, and provide information to the administration regarding the social studies program. Teachers are expected to attend department meetings and to contribute to the well-being of the social studies program and department.

Working with colleagues   Schools have a variety of professional persons who fill various teaching and nonteaching responsibilities. It is necessary and appropriate for teachers to work with other professionals such as colleagues in other disciplines, curriculum specialists, guidance personnel, librarians and media specialists, social workers, health-care specialists, business managers, and administrators. Cooperating with colleagues in each of the groups requires the development of communication and interpersonal skills and a willingness to work together for the benefit of the students.

The guidance counselor, for example, may be able to offer valuable insights concerning individual students and their hopes, aspirations, fears, and frustrations. Such information may be helpful to the teacher when planning for instruction. However, relationships between counselors and teachers may not always be positive due to differing perceptions and expectations concerning the role of the counselor. Many counselors believe their primary role is that of helping individual students. Teachers who work with students mainly in groups are concerned when individual students become disruptive. Often teachers expect the counselor to tell the disruptive student to behave in class and to provide a solution or alternative to the problem behavior so that the class may continue to function smoothly. These differing expectations may be a source of conflict between teachers and counselors and thus create a tension between professionals who both care about students but often in different ways.

School social workers, school psychologists, and health care specialists often provide valuable family and health-related information to teachers concerning student health problems such as allergies, chronic illnesses, and physical disabilities. Teachers in turn can offer information to these specialists concerning student performance, attitudes, and behaviors in class.

The stereotype of a librarian as a custodian of books should by now be dispelled. Librarians, now often called media specialists because of their expanding roles, provide valuable assistance to both faculty and students in such areas as community resources, computer software, and curriculum resources. Social studies teachers are strongly encouraged to work cooperatively with media specialists in selecting print and nonprint resources for the media center, in developing instructional units that require students to learn or extend library searching skills, and in helping students select appropriate resources for class or individual projects and/or course requirements.

Media specialists generally welcome suggestions from teachers and students for additions to the library and media center collections. Within their budgets and other constraints most media specialists are willing to secure instructional resource materials for teachers and students who regularly use the library effectively. The media specialist should be viewed as a valuable colleague in providing numerous supports for effective instruction. In planning an instructional unit involving the use of media resources, teachers should be certain the media center has the necessary resources available or is in a position to secure them. If students are to rely rather heavily on the local public library, it is recommended that teachers contact the library's personnel to know what resources may be available there or how they might be secured, perhaps through a database search and interlibrary loan. These media specialists appreciate knowing in advance of ways they might assist students in securing the needed information to complete a class assignment or project.

Today many districts have curriculum specialists who are responsible for curriculum leadership. Some districts select a single person with overall curriculum responsibilities, while larger districts may have curriculum specialists for each discipline. In addition to curriculum efforts, these specialists are often responsible for staff development and may well work with individuals or groups of teachers on a regular basis.

In addition to certified personnel, schools employ a large number of noncertified persons such as bus drivers, cafeteria and maintenance workers, clerical staff, grounds keepers, and other skilled personnel. These people are the ones who help to keep the schools functioning and provide valuable services to students, faculty, and parents. Often some students will talk with these people, who in turn may offer teachers insights into the behaviors or concerns of students. Together, all those who are employed at the school should work together for the benefit of the students.

Completing administrative reports On a regular basis teachers are asked to attend various meetings and to complete a multitude of forms. The meetings may range from attending regular faculty meetings to meeting with parents, participating in decisions regarding special needs students, completing individual educational plans, and attending professional meetings representing the school. Schools also require that teachers complete numerous forms. Some examples of these forms may involve taking student attendance each period, maintaining a grade book, filling out class size reports, ordering media, completing federal or state survey reports, and so forth. At times the paperwork is burdensome, but those who request and need the data appreciate the prompt response to their requests for information.

Professional Organizations

Most teachers belong to one or more professional organizations. In most states teachers are encouraged or required to join the local and state educational organizations affiliated with the National Education Association (NEA) or the American Federation of Teachers (AFT) as well as the national organization. In addition to these two comprehensive major educational organizations with membership drawn from various grade levels, disciplines, and areas of responsibilities, there are several professional organizations that *should* be of particular interest to social studies teachers.

The largest professional organization for social studies educators is the National Council for the Social Studies (NCSS). Membership includes elementary, middle school, and high school teachers and administrators, curriculum specialists, college and university faculty members, and others with an interest in social studies education or the social science disciplines.* NCSS offers its members a valuable publication program, which includes *Social Education, Social Studies and the Young Learner*, bulletins, "how-to-do-it" pamphlets, and newsletters. In addition, it organizes international, national, and regional conferences for social studies teachers in various cities throughout the United States, Canada, and Kenya. These conferences include presentations by nationally known speakers, numerous workshops and sessions (many conducted by classroom teachers who want to share their ideas, learning activities, and instructional materials with colleagues), displays of the latest print and nonprint social studies educational materials, and field trips to points of particular interest to social studies educators. The interaction with publishers and colleagues enables participants to preview and obtain new instructional materials, discuss issues with colleagues from other districts and states, exchange ideas, and talk with leaders in the field of social studies.

Most states have state social studies councils and other professional social studies organizations to serve the interests and needs of the social studies/social science teachers of the particular state. For the most part these groups have annual statewide conferences and workshops, publish a newsletter or

---

*The addresses of the professional organizations mentioned in this chapter and other organizations of interest to social studies teachers are included in Appendix on page 457.

journal, and may offer other programs such as state study tours. The social studies methods instructor should have information available concerning the state social studies council and its activities. If not, the social studies education specialist at the state education agency should have this information readily available. Incidentally, for university students who join the NCSS and/or state social studies council the cost of membership is greatly reduced to encourage students to become active members of their professional organizations early in their careers.

As professional educators, social studies teachers should become active participants in these organizations by making a presentation (sharing experiences and ideas) at the annual conference, volunteering to serve as a chairperson or facilitator at the annual meeting, offering to serve on a committee, sending in ideas to the newsletter or journal editor, or otherwise assisting with the activities of the council. Teachers who share their energy, talents, and time with colleagues find these experiences personally enriching and professionally worthwhile and rewarding. Many long-term personal and professional friendships begin by meeting colleagues at professional meetings. The authors strongly recommend active membership in the NCSS and state social studies councils.

Since social studies teachers have majored in an academic social science discipline, there are one or more national social science discipline organizations of which teacher candidates need to be aware. Some of these organizations hold special sessions and other programs designed for secondary teachers during their annual conferences. In some instances, they may have a publications program designed especially for the precollegiate teacher of that discipline.

History teachers may be interested in becoming members of the American Historical Association or the Organization of American Historians. These are the two major history organizations in the United States. There are, of course, history organizations that focus on the history of particular geographic areas or time periods. Most of these organizations also publish journals and may present national meetings for their members. In some areas, state and county historical societies are active in various projects of local interest, such as museum work, restoring historic buildings, conducting student tours of historic sites, and organizing local oral history projects. Many hold regular meetings and publish informative newsletters for their members. These historical societies welcome new members who have similar interests in history.

Social studies teachers with an interest in economics should become familiar with the programs, materials, and other publications of the National Council on Economic Education (NCEE). This nonprofit, nonpartisan organization, founded in 1949, has developed outstanding print and nonprint resources for teachers. The NCEE, through its network of affiliated state councils and centers for economic education, provides a variety of services for educators in the form of workshops, materials, resources, staff development programs, and the like. If a center for economic education is not located at the local university campus, write to the NCEE for the name and address of the nearest center for economic education and state council director, and request a copy of *Checklist,* an annotated listing of NCEE publications currently available. Economics teachers may be interested in joining the American Economics Association or one of the various regional, state, or specialized economics organizations. The Foundation for Teaching Economics provides media and curriculum resources for middle school teachers and students. Several states are in the process of organizing state associations for teachers of economics.

There are three major geographic associations that may interest geography teachers. The National Council for Geographic Education (NCGE) is organized for geography teachers and presents an annual conference for geography teachers and geographic educators at various sites throughout the United States, Canada, and the Caribbean. NCGE also publishes the *Journal of Geography,* various teacher and student instructional materials, and newsletters with some articles focusing on teaching geography at the middle and high school levels. The American Geographic Association is developing programs and publications to help young people learn more about the world so that they will become geographically literate. The National Geographic Society has developed state geography alliances in all fifty states that provide in-service opportunities for teachers, and the Society conducts a Geography Bee at the local, state, and national levels for students in grades 4 through 8. The national winner receives a substantial scholarship to help toward a college education.

The American Political Science Association is the professional organization for political scientists, and like other organizations conducts annual conferences and publishes a journal. Political science and government teachers also may be interested in becoming active in programs focusing on various citizenship education and law-related education programs such as those provided by the Constitutional Rights Foundations, the Center for Civic Education, and the American Bar Association.

Behavioral science teachers may decide to join the American Anthropological Association, American Psychological Association, or the American Sociological Association. Some of their publications and programs may be useful to secondary teachers. The members of these organizations are primarily college and university faculty, researchers, and graduate students majoring in these disciplines.

The department chairperson or major professor ought to have information regarding the membership details for these organizations. If they do not, contact these organizations directly. The library most likely has a reference guide containing the names and addresses of these and other professional organizations of interest. Some of the organizations may also have state-affiliated associations, and the national association should be able to provide details regarding these state groups.

We strongly encourage teacher candidates to be active, contributing members of social studies professional organizations. Interacting and working with a variety of colleagues on programs are richly rewarding professional experiences.

Getting Your First Teaching Job

On a regular basis the media reports a shortage of qualified teachers. This information is both accurate and misleading. It is true that in some academic disciplines and geographic regions of the country there are teacher shortages, but unfortunately this is not usually the case for social studies teachers. According to *The ASCUS Annual: A Job Search Handbook for Educators* (1994) the field of social studies has a greater supply of teachers than the current demand requires.

Will the surplus of social studies teachers continue? Most likely the answer is "Yes." It is, however, a difficult question to answer accurately as the situation may change due to several unpredictable actions. For example, it is uncertain how many persons who are prepared to teach secondary social studies will actually enter the teaching profession; nor is it certain how many previously prepared teachers will decide to enter or reenter the field if positions become available. Several states are considering early retirement legislation that would allow experienced teachers to retire at an earlier age with no loss of retirement or health-care benefits. Many of the eligible teachers likely would take advantage of this opportunity and retire early. If this becomes reality, job opportunities for new teachers should be available in most fields, including social studies. Geographic location and demographic changes will also influence job availability.

Changes in certification requirements in some states may allow persons not previously prepared for teaching to enter the profession through alternative certification programs. University towns, urban areas, and larger cities often have a surplus of social studies teachers compared to rural areas, which often face difficulties in attracting and retaining teachers. A teacher's mobility due to personal preferences, family circumstances, and so forth may well determine whether he or she will secure a teaching position in a desirable setting.

Most college and university career planning and placement offices invite representatives from various school districts to come to the campus and interview students on campus. However, before the interview there are some preliminary steps that need to be taken. Each candidate should prepare in writing a plan of action for securing a teaching position. Next, job applicants will need to write a resume and cover letter; compile a professional file (including letters of recommendation); secure copies of transcripts and credentials; and practice interviewing skills. This latter step is an important determinant in whether or not the job is offered.

It is wise to anticipate the types of questions that may be asked and to practice interviewing for a position. If possible, the practice interview should be taped for later critiquing. Most interviewers are interested in hiring teachers who genuinely like and have empathy for young people. The career planning and placement office, university student teaching supervisor, or education advisor will be able to assist teacher candidates in preparing these materials. Candidates should begin to assemble their professional files early during the last semester of the teacher preparation program so that as positions are announced, the teacher candidates will be ready to apply for positions for which they are qualified and interested.

The career planning and placement office also receives notification of many jobs throughout the state and nation. In some states the state education agency operates a teacher employment office at little or no cost to prospective teachers. Of course there are private organizations that have job listings and try to match teachers with available positions for a fee. If a private organization is used in the job search, check their placement rate record carefully and read any contracts thoroughly before signing. School district personnel offices may be contacted directly concerning teaching position vacancies. It is also wise to contact any friends who might be helpful in securing an interview.

After applying for a position and waiting a reasonable time, it is important to follow up the original letters of application and interviews with letters, telephone calls, or a personal visit regarding the status of the application. Keep in mind that sometimes districts will not know if there is a vacancy until a few days before school starts or even a few days after school opens, especially if there have been unanticipated population shifts or resignations during the summer months. At times there may be mid-year vacancies or part-time positions as well. Some persons may want to consider placing their names on the list for substitute teachers in one or more districts. When permanent positions become available, districts often give preference to those whose work they know through substitute teaching. Again, each district has its own policies and procedures, and it would be wise to check with the personnel office of the districts as to their hiring procedures. Expenses, such as letters, resumes, postage, telephone calls, travel, clothing, and so forth to secure a teaching position are the responsibility of the applicant.

Career Opportunities

In the past most people prepared themselves for careers in which they expected to remain for a number of years or until retirement. This is no longer necessarily so. Today many preparing for careers in education will decide not to teach, many will decide to teach for a relatively short period of time and withdraw from education, and many will teach for a few years before assuming other responsibilities in education.

For those who decide to remain in education, there are additional career possibilities within the field. For example, teachers often take additional courses to prepare themselves to become administrators. Often they begin by becoming vice principals and principals at middle schools or junior high schools, and then vice principal or principal at a high school. Some may decide their career path goal is to become a district superintendent. Most often superintendents begin this part of their career in a smaller district and move progressively to larger districts.

Other possibilities include additional course work, many times at the graduate level, to become certified in another subject discipline or in special areas such as bilingual education, special education (including gifted and talented), or in special services such as counselor, school social worker, school psychologist, school business manager, or curriculum supervisor. Sometimes course work for additional certification may fit within the requirements of graduate degree programs and when completed the teacher will have earned a graduate degree as well as additional certification and will then be in a position to apply for other positions in education.

Depending on the size and needs of the district, these specialized positions may involve part-time teaching and part-time service in the area of specialization. Inasmuch as these positions require additional certification and/or graduate degrees, the salaries are higher than those of classroom teachers and may require a longer contract year. Quality persons are needed in each of these areas.

Teaching positions are often available in nonpublic school settings. Approximately 80 percent of the private schools in the United States are church-affiliated. Teachers who teach in private schools often do so for religious motives and frequently work for lower salaries than their counterparts in public schools. Many who decide to teach in private schools do so because of fewer discipline problems, stricter discipline policies, stronger parental support and interest, and more time for available for instruction and homework. For some, private school teaching provides an attractive alternative to public school teaching.

Another source of job possibilities include the Department of Defense (DOD) schools. The DOD operates more than 300 schools in more than two dozen countries. These DOD schools enroll approximately 170,000 students and employ 7,500 educational personnel (Ryan and Cooper, 1992). There are other American schools, many operated privately, in other countries as well. To teach overseas, applicants usually need to have stateside certification and have completed at a minimum of one to three years of successful teaching within the United States. The university career planning and placement office should have information concerning teaching opportunities abroad.

There are a variety of nonclassroom careers in education outside of pre-elementary, elementary, middle, and secondary schools. For example, some teacher candidates may aspire to teach in community or technical colleges, or at public or private colleges and universities. Within these institutions of higher education there are various possibilities such as academic staff; faculty; department chair; administrative positions such as dean, chancellor, provost, or president; and specialized service areas such as admissions officer, registrar, career guidance counselor, health services provider, student services liaison, librarian, or research director. Many of these positions require a doctoral degree.

Governmental agencies at the county, regional, state, and federal levels have education or education-related positions such as curriculum supervisors, program specialists, teacher certification directors, pupil assessment and evaluation personnel, researchers, and various other possibilities. The federal government also assists education and has several regional research and development centers, regional laboratories, equity centers, and overseas schools. International organizations such as UNESCO and the World Bank also provide opportunities for education-related employment.

In some states the state historical society is a governmental agency but in other states it is a private organization. There may be education-related positions available that enable the person to work in various capacities with young people and/or adults. Museums and local historical sites may also employ educators to direct their programs. Unpaid volunteers often work with the professional staff.

Business and industry leaders are interested in hiring persons with experience in education. For example, newspapers and broadcast media often have educational reporters. Textbook publishers hire editors, writers, curriculum and computer software developers, and sales representatives.

At present a number of private consulting firms provide specialized services and expertise to schools, sometimes in the form of research services, staff development, and so forth. At the same time business, industry, labor unions, and agricultural cooperatives are responding to the professional and personal development needs of their own employees or members and often provide a variety of professional development opportunities and services. Many will have full time personnel employed in educational or training positions.

Recently there has been an expansion of firms providing educational services that may not be available in the K–12 settings. These services may include tutoring in reading and study skills, test preparation, student motivation, child-rearing practices, computer training, and so forth. We anticipate a continued growth in these areas due to the changing needs of society.

Professional organizations such as the National Council for the Social Studies, the National Council on Economic Education, the Association for Supervision and Curriculum Development, the National Education Association, the American Federation of Teachers, and other similar groups (including their state and local affiliates) employ a number of persons, many with a background in education. Some of these positions may include executive director, staff member, curriculum writer, field worker, researcher, and so forth. In addition, there are other educational organizations such as Phi Delta Kappa and Pi Lambda Theta that serve their members in various ways, including publications and conferences.

Career Possibilities Outside of Education

Many of the skills that perspective teachers developed in their teacher preparation are generic and can be applied in other settings. For example, teachers have engaged in long-range and immediate planning, made decisions, implemented these decisions, worked under the pressure of deadlines, diagnosed student learning and behaviors, tracked student progress, managed groups, used a variety of resources, developed interpersonal communication skills with students and adults, and worked independently and with colleagues.

These skills are valued by American business, industry, and government, and many firms hire full- or part-time people for a variety of positions. It may be useful to examine the latest *Occupational Outlook Handbook* to find out what positions are available in specific social science disciplines. It is also important to remember that many jobs that will be available in the 21st century have not yet been created and that other jobs will diminish in numbers or disappear altogether. It appears the greatest increase of jobs will be in the service sector of the economy.

Causes of Job-Related Stress for Teachers

In recent years the various national reform reports have judged harshly the quality of teaching in our nation's schools. Teachers have been portrayed negatively as ill-prepared, incompetent, and uncaring, and the quality of their work has suffered. Students are judged frequently as being unprepared for the world of work or post-secondary education. These reports generally assume that virtually all teachers fit this negative image. Positive perceptions of teachers and community support for teachers have diminished and teachers have often responded by assuming a defensive stand in light of these ongoing criticisms.

Teachers usually experience stress as a part of their professional lives each day. Individuals experience stress when the demands of the job are more than they can handle. Teaching is a stressful job for many reasons. For example, consider the following:

- Teachers are isolated from adult professionals for most of the day. They lack the time to share with other teachers.
- Teachers are harassed in classes and in the hallways by students whose misbehavior ranges from failing to pay attention to attacking physically or verbally. In some cases only one or two students create the problems,

"I may need a few more minutes before I'm ready to shape young minds into a Gestalt world view".

rather than there being a lack of discipline within the whole school. A lack of discipline is an emotionally draining aspect of teaching.
- Teachers fear they are giving much to others but are not able to grow sufficiently either personally or professionally. Teachers often believe that parents are unwilling to be involved in the schools.
- Teachers in high schools may encounter 150–175 or more unique students every day, each with separate interests, abilities, problems, personalities, and so forth. Feeling the stress of numbers is complicated even further if there is a high student turnover.
- Teachers are not often consulted or involved in creating policies although they will have to implement these policies. Teachers are demoralized when they realize how little respect they are given when decision makers fail to regard teachers as professionals.
- School routines such as bells, paperwork, reports, deadlines, and interruptions are negative aspects of the job.
- Preparation time is often taken up by reacting to crises or telephone calls to parents.
- Upon their return students who have been absent require additional attention to secure assignments, get individual make-up work, take separate tests that must be evaluated, all of which requires additional teacher effort.

- Teachers are expected to provide additional assistance to special needs students, meet with parents, consult with supervisors, sponsor after-school activities, attend various school functions, and the like. These often become a burden and consume a teacher's time.
- Teachers often have inadequate supplies due to district cost control measures and are asked to do more with less. Often equipment is lacking, obsolete, broken down, or must be shared by several individual teachers or departments. Many teachers are assigned to schools with deteriorating physical facilities.
- Low pay, with any raises based primarily on years of service and additional credits earned; long hours in and out of the classroom; and a lack of recognition or appreciation by students, parents, administrators, and the community all contribute to stress. For many teachers, recognition, prestige, and higher status come only after leaving the classroom for an administrative or specialized position in a district.

These school-related stressful circumstances and whatever additional stressful circumstances are occurring in the teacher's personal life (such as death or illness of a family member, divorce, debts, difficulties with family members, unemployment of a spouse, and so forth) make stress a major health problem. Other professionals also experience job-related stress and as a result many companies are developing wellness programs intended to maintain or improve the health of their employees. Education has been slow to respond to these issues.

Beginning teachers face some special stressful times during the first year of teaching such as

1. getting started on the job, which means getting used to students, personnel, and routines at the school;
2. getting settled in a new community, making new friends, and establishing a personal life outside of school;
3. making and being responsible for one's own personal and professional decisions;
4. planning, implementing, and evaluating learning activities on a daily basis, while planning ahead to the next unit of instruction (each day means one or more "new" lessons);
5. developing and carrying out an effective discipline policy; and
6. participating in required school activities such as attending athletic contests, performances, open house, graduation, and the like.

Teachers and other professionals need to develop stress-coping strategies that fit individual needs and interests. These strategies can include attending cultural events, reading for enjoyment, watching TV, engaging in sporting activities, going shopping, prayer, meditation, walking in the woods or along the shoreline, talking with family and friends, engaging in arts and craft projects, keeping alert to changing methods, avoiding talking about school after hours, subscribing to professional journals, being flexible, and keeping a sense of humor. It is also important to maintain physical health by getting sufficient sleep and eating balanced meals.

As teachers we encourage our students to continue to learn and so teachers also need to continue their learning. This does not necessarily mean taking additional graduate courses or attending another professional meeting; rather, it means modifying one's lifestyle and engaging in activities that are meaningful. On a regular basis, teachers need to have personal time for themselves.

Several teachers have indicated they reduce their stress level in these ways:

- I talk with my spouse who is not a teacher.
- I like to swim and go bowling.
- I like to get all of my family members out of the house and "bake up a storm."
- I like to rent a video that will make me laugh, thereby reducing my tensions and helping me relax.

What stress reducers do you now use? Are there other stress reducers you may try out in the future?

SUMMARY

Earning initial certification and securing the first teaching position are exciting moments and important milestones. Beginning teachers have learned many basic teaching methods and have adequate knowledge of the field, yet there remains a need for continuous learning at both the personal and professional levels. The need for staff development has always been noted, but perhaps even more so today with new knowledge being created so rapidly. Staff development programs provide opportunities for teachers to learn new information.

Teaching is a challenging career offering endless choices both within the traditional K–12 educational setting and outside this setting. Career possibilities exist in public and private K–12 schools and districts, in higher education, in business and industry, in government service, and in professional organizations.

In recent years teacher stress has received increasing recognition through the media. Teachers will need to develop and utilize a variety of coping mechanisms in order to remain effective teachers. Much of the stress is due to circumstances outside the school. To reduce teacher stress, society may have to restructure and transform the shape of education. This will be a costly and difficult task.

Discussion Questions

1. What seem to be the major causes of teacher stress? What are some ways to reduce or eliminate the causes of stress? How can teachers be helped in coping with stress and in developing coping strategies?
2. What are some ways you as a social studies teacher would expect to contribute to the social studies community of scholars and to the larger community as well?
3. What are some characteristics of effective staff development programs for social studies teachers?
4. How can active participation in professional organizations help teachers remain current in social studies? Besides reading professional journals, what are other sources of new ideas for teaching social studies?

Student Learning Activities

1. Interview several teachers and other school personnel concerning job-related stress. Then interview several others in occupations considered to be stressful, such as a law enforcement officer, doctor, nurse, air traffic controller, firefighter, stockbroker, or professional athlete. What are causes of stress for each career? Are the stresses similar or different? How might these professionals cope with job-related stress? What suggestions would you have for beginning teachers concerning stress during their first years of teaching?
2. Prepare a tentative personal and professional growth plan for the first five years of your career in teaching. What are your goals and how will you seek to achieve them?
3. Interview several experienced teachers to find out which professional growth opportunities have been most helpful to them. In talking with the teachers, ask them about their roles and activities in both professional and community organizations. What experiences were deemed most helpful or valuable to them?
4. Arrange to become a member of the National Council for the Social Studies, the state, and/or local social studies organization and the national or state organization of your social science academic discipline major, such as the American Historical Association. If possible plan to attend a state social studies conference or other professional meeting. Share your experiences with your classmates.
5. Check with the college or university career planning office on the employment opportunities in teaching social studies and/or related fields. What job prospects are available now or are likely to be available when your student teaching has been completed? Is it likely that you will need to relocate to another region in the state or elsewhere? What

criteria will you use in deciding whether or not to accept or reject a teaching position?
6. Prepare a sample resume and teaching employment letter of application. Ask classmates, the methods professor, and/or the director of the career planning office to critique your efforts. Are the letter and resume effective? If possible, role play an interview (on video if convenient) and have the interview critiqued.

APPENDIX

List of professional social studies and social science organizations

National Council for the Social Studies
3501 Newark Street NW, Washington, DC 20016

American Historical Association
400 A Street SE, Washington, DC 20003

Organization of American Historians
112 N. Bryan Street, Bloomington, IN 47408

National Council on Economic Education
1140 Avenue of the Americas, New York, NY 10036

American Economic Association
2014 Broadway, Suite 305, Nashville, TN 37203-2418

Foundation for Teaching Economics
260 Russell Boulevard, Suite B, Davis, CA 95616

National Council for Geographic Education
Indiana University of Pennsylvania
16A Leonard Hall, Indiana, PA 15705

Association of American Geographers
1710 16th Street NW, Washington, DC 20009

National Geographic Society
17th & M Street NW, Washington, DC 20036

American Political Science Association
1527 New Hampshire Avenue NW, Washington, DC 20036

Constitutional Rights Foundation
601 Kingsley Drive, Los Angeles, CA 90005

Center for Civic Education
5146 Douglas Fir Road, Calabasas, CA 91302

American Bar Association
750 N. Lake Shore Drive, Chicago, IL 60611

American Anthropology Association
1703 New Hampshire Avenue NW, Washington, DC 20009

American Psychological Association
750 First Street NE, Washington, DC 20002-4242
American Sociological Association
1722 N Street NW, Washington, DC 20036

References

Association for School, College and University Staffing. 1994. *The ASCUS Annual: A Job Search Handbook for Educators*. Evanston, IL: Association for School, College and University Staffing.

Ryan, K. and Cooper, J. M. 1992. *Those Who Can, Teach* (6th ed.). Boston: Houghton Mifflin.

Stark, J. S., Lowther, M. A., and Hagerty, B. M. K. 1986. *Responsive Professional Education: Balancing Outcomes and Opportunities*.(ASHE-ERIC Higher Education Report No. 3). Washington, DC: Association for the Study of Higher Education.

Strom, S. M. 1989. "The Ethical Dimension of Teaching." In M. C. Reynolds (Ed.), *Knowledge Base for the Beginning Teacher*. Oxford, England: Pergamon.

United States Department of Labor. Bureau of Labor Statistics. 1992–1993. *Occupational Outlook Handbook*. Washington, DC: Bureau of Labor Statistics.

Additional Readings

Armstrong, C. 1993. "Do's and Don'ts for Beginning Teachers." *Principal,* Vol. 73, No. 1, September. 30–31.

Byrne, B. M. 1992. *Investigating Causal Links to Burnout for Elementary, Intermediate, and Secondary Teachers*. Presented at the annual meeting of the American Educational Research Association, San Francisco. ERIC Reproduction Document Service ED 344 886.

Chall, J. 1975. "Restoring Dignity and Self-Worth to the Teacher," *Phi Delta Kappan*, Vol. 57, No. 3, November. 170–174.

Descy, D. E. 1992. Instructional Media Utilization, Classroom Learning and Teacher Education." In *Mankato Statement: The Journal of the College of Education.* Spring. Also available from ERIC Document Reproduction Service ED 344 575.

Fennick, R. 1992. *Combating New Teacher Burnout: Providing Support Networks for Personal and Professional Growth*. Presented at the conference for College Composition and Communication, Cincinnati, OH. ERIC Document Reproduction Service ED 349 580.

Frase, L. E. *Maximizing People Power in Schools: Motivating and Managing Teachers and Staff. Successful Schools: Guidebooks to Effective Educational Leadership*. Vol. 5, Newbury Park, CA: Corwin. Also see ERIC Document Reproduction Service ED 351 806.

Grusko, R. and Kramer, J. 1993. *Becoming a Teacher: A Practical and Political School Survival Guide.* Bloomington, IN: ERIC Clearinghouse on Reading, English, and Communication. ERIC Document Reproduction Service ED 358 501.

Krasnow, M. H. 1993. *Waiting for Thursday: New Teachers Discover Teaching.* Paper presented at the meeting of the American Educational Research Association, Atlanta, GA: ERIC Document Reproduction Service ED 360 290.

Loucks, H. E. 1993. "Teacher Induction: A Success Story." *Principal,* Vol. 73, No. 1, September. 27–29.

McCammon, L. A. 1992. "The Story of Marty: A Case Study of Teacher Burnout." *Youth Theatre Journal,* Vol. 7, No. 2. 17–22.

Natale, J. A. 1993. "Why Teachers Leave." *Executive Educator,* Vol. 15, No. 7, July. 14–18.

Orlich, D. C. 1989. *Staff Development: Enhancing Human Potential.* Boston: Allyn and Bacon.

Prosise, R. and Heller, M. 1993. "Mentoring for Beginning Middle Level Teachers." *Schools in the Middle,* Vol. 2, No. 4, Summer. 20–22.

Reynolds, M. C. (Ed.). 1989. *Knowledge Base for the Beginning Teacher.* Oxford, England and New York: Pergamon.

Roe, B. D., Ross, E. P., and Burns, P. C. 1989. *Student Teaching and Field Experiences Handbook* (2nd ed.). Columbus, OH: Merrill.

Ruhl-Smith, C. and Smith, J. M. 1993. "Teacher Job Satisfaction in a Quality School: Implications for Educational Leaders." *Journal of School Leadership,* Vol. 3, No. 5, September. 534–548.

Tomlin, M. E. 1993. "The Evolution of a New Teacher." *Executive Educator,* Vol. 15, No. 2, March. 39–40.

United States Department of Labor. Bureau of Labor Statistics. 1992–1993. Outlook 1990–2005. Washington, DC: Bureau of Labor Statistics. (Note: Published every two years.)

Walsh, K. J. and Shay, M. J. 1993. "In Support of Interdisciplinary Teaming: The Climate Factor." *Middle School Journal,* Vol. 24, No. 4, March. 56–60.

Young, T. A. 1993. "Helping New Teachers: The Performance Enhancement Model." *Clearing-House,* Vol. 66, No. 3, January/February. 174–176.

> There can be hope only for a society which acts as one big family, and not as many separate ones.
>
> *Anwar al-Sadat*

Epilogue

How Might the 21st Century Shape Social Studies Education?

FOCUS QUESTIONS

- What might the world look like in the 21st century?
- What will schools look like in the 21st century?
- What new responsibilities will citizens face in the 21st century?
- How might social studies education change in the future?
- What role should social studies educators have or take in shaping the future of education?

OVERVIEW Probes into the future are always exciting and, at the same time, frightening. Yet human consciousness demands that we investigate this hidden area in order to understand who we are. In a real sense, our behavior and the health of our community are functions of what we think will happen to us tomorrow. It might even be argued that one of the main attributes of being human is the ability to develop a conception of the future. To deny a person a vision of the future is to deny hope and with it, perhaps, his or her virtue and humanity. Proverbs 29:18 puts it this way: "Where there is no vision, the people perish." In the original Semitic, of course, the text used the word "virtue" for "vision." Where there is no *virtue*, the people perish.

The "future" is a concept rooted in our imagination. Devoid of facts, it exists in our individual and collective minds as an area full of fear and excitement. It is filled with both dread and delight and makes the perfect seed bed for human hopes and dreams. The future is an imaginary region consisting of time and setting within which we can think about our personal behavior. Thus, we can use the concept of future as a way of self-reflection as well as a process for thinking about institutional, professional, and community changes.

Visions of the future, then, appear from our imaginations. They are images that come from us. In a real sense, we do not predict the future, we create it. So any attempt to study the future carries with it the need to study ourselves. What do we love? What are our needs? What have we built? What are we building today? The answers to questions like these may provide the most accurate images of the future. While it might be interesting to probe these, as well as other questions, the focus here will be on the questions of human needs, social roles, and the relationship between social studies education and a rapidly changing world.

What Might the World Look Like in the 21st Century?

Any view of the future and our ability to prepare for it will always depend on the interactions of our historical wisdom and the spatial settings in which we live. In a way the future is already with us. The demographic data for our nation and world suggest interesting pictures—pictures of growth, diversity, and dislocations. This interaction between the present and future defines our perceptions and our needs, and while gross needs are universal they are refined for various cultures by specific historical and geographical differences. For example, while all people must deal with the need for food and shelter, they respond to those needs according to a culture, time, and place and, thus, are specific to the particular worldviews of that culture. Therefore, we should understand that there are many different future worldviews that represent cultural and personal mindsets. Future worldviews of individuals in Malaysia are different from those in Michigan, yet both are caught up in the same global network. It is this tension and interaction between global and local worldviews that makes any picture of the future blurred. The relationship of local to global suggests a tension that can best be described as a tautness between unity and diversity. While the global culture of economic markets, mass media, and interdependent military systems is becoming more homogenized, local cultures are becoming more diverse and heterogeneous. It may be that this sense of global unity gives local groups the freedom to express their uniqueness. Because of this interplay between local and global cultures, projections as well as predilections of the 21st century become very difficult.

Probing and building the future is one of our most useful and interesting activities. Scenario building is one important method for thinking about the future. Human behavior is often a function of what we think will happen to us tomorrow. Construct your own "picture" of the future. Why are some of our pictures of the future positive? Why are some negative? What would have to change personally as well as socially in order to create a positive future?

The future might also be seen as an extension of past and present trends. In 1980, Alvin Toffler, writing in *The Third Wave*, suggested that Western society had evolved through two major economic revolutions and was now well into a third. The first major change occurred when people moved from being hunters and gatherers to being farmers. This agricultural revolution—raising domestic crops and animals—he called the first wave. With the advent of agriculture, people accumulated surplus food and could stay in one place long enough to build cities and increase their population. They could specialize in different occupations and crafts. All these changes put more pressure on the land and eventually required the need to find new ways to increase the production of food, other goods and services, and transportation. Toffler called this increased activity the second wave—the industrial age. This was a period dominated by the intensive use of labor, fossil fuel, and capital.

The third wave Toffler identifies as the information/electronic age. This is the economic/cultural stage in which we are now living. It does not mean that waves one and two have completely disappeared, only that their importance in the society has diminished. Note that Toffler's wave theory does not apply equally to all areas of the globe, as economic development is uneven across the world.

A significant difference exists between the first two waves, the agricultural age and the industrial age, and the third wave, the information age. This difference has to do with conceptions of labor, product, and process. The first and second ages were product revolutions while the information age is a process revolution. The notions of product and process differ in their conceptualization of economic capital. Information and knowledge have become the capital of today. Knowledge has always been related to power; now it has also become the very center of our economic system. Knowledge is not, of course, a physical and finite resource, but an abstract and infinite one. We must, however, develop ways to use or interject knowledge into our economic, political, and social systems in much the same way that fossil fuel was injected into the economies of the late 19th and 20th centuries. Just as our economy became energy-intensive with the industrial age, today it is becoming knowledge and information intensive, while at the same time, demanding less labor. The emergence of information as a major form of energy is finally becoming recognized. It is the first energy form, which metaphorically, stands outside the second law of thermodynamics. That is, it is not "running-down" nor is it generating heat and friction; it can also be stored with minimal loss almost indefinitely. Economically speaking, we are seeing a shift from products built with high temperatures, high pressures, and high energy to processes built with low entropy with little disorder to the earth's energy system. An illustration of this shift is the reduction of the size of computers because of the replacement of vacuum tubes by the microchip. What once took a three-story building to contain can now fit into the space the size of one's fingernail.

This emphasis upon low entropy, on information, and on process represents a break in the story of our cultural evolution. Building upon the base formed by agriculture and industry, we are beginning a new evolutionary period of the human species. That is, while the third wave is still quite young, beginning after World War II, we are already moving into a fourth wave that we might call the global, micro-biotechnological age. The global, micro-biotechnological age has as its base the powerful combination of the computer and the explosion of knowledge within a global context. This will allow the focused power of information to blast through new resource and development frontiers. This revolution seems to promise a whole store of "super-stuff." From microbes that can clean up oil spills in the ocean to artificial life and artificial intelligence, we are seeing the science laboratory and our own technologies alter our realities. We are also experiencing ethical dilemmas that our ancestors could not even imagine. This "fourth wave" is driven by knowledge as applied to natural and social phenomena and is alien to the more traditional notions of subject matter or discipline study.

As you think about and discuss future scenarios, you might want to read *Seven Tomorrows* by Hawken, Ogilvy, and Schwartz. Although published in 1982, it still presents a rational set of future possibilities for humankind. It deals with the power of choice in determining the future.

What Will Schools Look Like in the 21st Century?

One of the institutions that is being redefined today is the school. While the general or major goals of education have not changed—*creating* a learning society, *creating* individuals who love to learn, *creating* enlightened citizens—the means of achieving these goals are in question. There is also a growing feeling that, perhaps, these goals are no longer enough and we must pay greater attention to goals of employment, security, health, and human relationships. What is your feeling about these goals? What is your definition of education? *Your* answer to these questions will help shape the schools of the future, for you will have a role to play in this evolution.

Context

In 1983 the National Commission on Excellence in Education stated that we are "a nation at risk" because of the poor quality of our schools. This pessimistic but important report is consistent with other findings and statements from the early 1980s to the 1990s. There is a cry for educational reform, but it is not clear what these reforms will look like. It is within this context that you will work, because social studies teachers will, no doubt, lead in reviewing, explaining, and implementing ideas from national, state, and local reports and policies.

Purposes

Virtually all of the reports pay some attention to the basic purpose of citizenship education (within and outside of the social studies curriculum). The Carnegie Forum on Education and the Economy (1986) states, "The primary purpose of schooling is the development of students' understanding of their civic and social responsibilities." In a similar vein the National Commission on Excellence in Education's 1983 report declares, "Our concern goes well beyond matters such as industry in commerce. It also includes the intellectual, moral, and spiritual strengths of our people which knit together the very fabric of our society. For our country to function, citizens must be able to reach some common understandings on complex issues, often on short notice and on the basis of conflicting or incomplete evidence." These are typical of the kinds of statements found in the reports that address the overall purpose of education. It is curious, however, that these purpose statements have received little or no media attention. Perhaps, it is time for social studies educators to bring attention to these purpose statements.

Content

The reports suggest that social studies represent a category within the "new basics." Specific attention to content looks very traditional with emphasis upon United States and world history and citizenship (political and economic study), geography, and so forth. The Carnegie report specifically calls for a course in civics and a program of community service that shows consistency with stated citizenship education goals. Perhaps the best example of forward-looking content tied to the goal of citizenship is found in the National Social Studies Standards published by the National Council for the Social Studies (1994):

Standards, Thematic Strands, and the Social Studies Curriculum
    We recognize that our world is changing rapidly. Students in our schools today will be citizens of the 21st century. They are living in the midst of a

knowledge explosion unlike any humankind has ever experienced. Because schools and teachers cannot teach everything and because students cannot learn all that could be known, we have developed a set of standards to do two things. First, the standards serve as guides for making decisions about curricular scope and depth. Secondly, standards set forth statements about what all students should know and be able to do as a result of instruction. Thus, the standards are criteria for making decisions about why, what, and how to teach and learn. The social studies standards address what is unique and essential to the social studies program, and can help answer the following questions:

- What content themes, characteristics and perspectives are essential to the social studies curriculum?
- What intellectual, social, and other skills should social studies help to develop?
- What democratic civic ideals and practices should be fostered?
- What persistent public issues should be addressed?
- What characteristics are essential to effective social studies learning experiences?

With attention to the changing nature of knowledge, the importance of linking knowledge to intellectual and socio-civic skills, the common good, multiple perspectives, and persisting issues that require value choices, while fostering the conception of school as a learning place, social studies educators can better implement the content standards recommended here, as well as those standards developed in discrete social studies disciplines. The standards are organized in ten thematic curriculum strands:

- CULTURE (Anthropology, Philosophy, Religion)
- TIME, CONTINUITY, AND CHANGE (History)
- PEOPLE, PLACES, AND ENVIRONMENTS (Geography)
- INDIVIDUAL DEVELOPMENT AND IDENTITY (Psychology)
- INDIVIDUALS, GROUPS, AND INSTITUTIONS (Sociology)
- POWER, AUTHORITY, AND GOVERNANCE (Political Science)
- PRODUCTION, DISTRIBUTION, AND CONSUMPTION (Economics)
- SCIENCE, TECHNOLOGY, AND SOCIETY (integrated disciplines)
- GLOBAL CONNECTIONS (integrated disciplines)
- CIVIC IDEALS AND PRACTICES (integrated disciplines)

The strands are interrelated. That is, to understand culture students need to understand continuity and change over time, the relationship of people, places and environments, and civic ideals and practices. To understand time, continuity, and change students need to understand the relationship of people, place and environments, culture, groups, and institutions. The total set of standards thus presents and represents a holistic scope of content that a student should experience throughout every level of the school program. (NCSS, 1994)

Teaching Strategies

With regard to the issue of teaching strategies, few of the reports deal with questions of how to present content in ways that are challenging and exciting for all students. The one significant exception is the *Paideia Proposal,* by Mortimore Adler, (1982) which offers great detail relative to teacher/student behavior. Other exceptions are found in the new standards literature in the several social sciences as well as the NCSS standards. While some attention is given to the development of reasoning and critical thinking skills, most emphasis is placed upon mastering content in the main disciplines through increased course requirements and increased systematic testing of students. Thus, the significant teaching strategies implicit in the reports would suggest a didactic base. This is particularly troublesome for teachers of social studies who would like to try varied strategies, but will be rewarded for didactic methods.

What do you think schools will look like in ten years? How will the role of teachers change, if at all? Do you think schools will be much like they are today? Would you like to see them change? Why? Why not?

What New Responsibilities Will Citizens Face in the 21st Century?

Responsibility can best be defined as a response—ability, or the knowledge, skills, and values, to respond competently and ethically to conditions around us. As the world becomes more interdependent and complex, the role of citizen will become more demanding; and those of us who refuse to take up this expanded role will find ourselves at a great disadvantage. The great concern for many educators is whether we can encourage our students to prepare for civic responsibility with the same intensity with which they prepare for jobs. If we assume an increase in the rate and complexity of social change, then it becomes extremely important for students to embrace the expanded role of citizen. This is the case because economic and civic issues are tied together so that it becomes increasingly difficult to tell where one ends and the other begins. That is, the economic success or failure of a person is entwined with that person's ability to operate as an enlightened citizen. For example, as economic institutions become increasingly tied to global markets, nations and states will play a more important role in economic decisions. Political policies will become political/economic policies that affect the lives of all citizens. The North American Free Trade Agreement between the United States, Canada, and Mexico, for instance, will be experienced by almost every citizen in each nation and beyond.

The economic person will need to know how to influence political decisions that will benefit individual and nation as well. There are many reasons for this symbiotic relationship: (1) economic systems now include more cultural and political elements, that is, markets are always encased in culture; selling goods in China, for example, will demand more cultural and political knowledge; (2) science and technology are creating new problems as well as benefits for people, and these problems demand civic or public judgments, such as the use of machines to keep people alive; and (3) the increasing reality of a global economy presents a complex web of interdependence of people and ideas that call for new policies concerning the proper mix of private and public control over markets, such as in the use of the oceans and international limits on fishing.

How Might Social Studies Education Change in the Future?

The growing interrelationships between education for citizenship and education for employment will cause social studies education to become more important in the future. The most significant change will be in its new role as the core of the school curriculum, serving as an integrator of the several other content areas that make up general education. We must keep in mind that, for the most part, the future will be very much like the present. In fact, it is most appropriate to suggest that the best place to see or study the future is in our own past and present. If we want to know the future, we must, first of all, know our past and our present condition. There are, however, two important changes for us to consider in the social studies programs of the future. First of all, as local and global issues become more complex, and as the world becomes more interdependent, single discipline approaches to the study of these issues will be insufficient.

Second, because of the growth in information and knowledge it is becoming more and more important for educators and the general public to consider the questions "What knowledge is of most worth?" or "Whose knowledge is of most worth?" With these considerations in mind, we suggest seven criteria that social studies programs of the future should address. These criteria are based upon the NCSS national standards (1994) and all social studies teachers should study these standards as they can provide a unified or didactic picture of the social studies curriculum.

We will start by asking two questions: "What should students in social studies programs study?" and, "How will the social studies serve as the integrating discipline for general education?"

If social studies is to become the integrating discipline in schools of the future then you, as a social studies teacher, will have to assume leadership in developing and restructuring school programs. Your training should enable you, better than teachers of other disciplines, to understand the relationship between society and the institution of the school and to help integrate knowledge from other subject areas. This leadership, however, will be directly related to your ability to deal with the question "What should our students study?" We are suggesting seven criteria (in question form) that define a social studies curriculum framework that includes most, if not all, other subject areas.

1. *How do people experience life and try to bring meaning to their lives?*
   This question stresses the need to study how people in different times and places use a wide range of symbols—from language to art—to understand the world and their place in it. We need to understand the wide array of options that people use to express meaning in their lives. Teachers can help students see their experiences in a variety of ways and create a context in which to evaluate and extend their own ideas of meaning.

2. *How does human evolution change our conception of who we are?*
   This question brings out one of the many relationships that social studies can construct between the natural and social sciences and the humanities. Our species has witnessed three powerful evolutionary forces. The first we can call natural selection, when human beings basically interacted with nature and this selection was, indeed, natural. The weak did not survive, and in many cases, neither did the young nor old. But, with civilization, the evolutionary process was altered by culture, which is the second revolutionary force. People, sharing institutional memberships, provided for the weaker members of the group and the gene pool changed to accommodate more diversity. More often than not, we see ourselves as members of families, churches, schools, corporations, cities, states, and nations and not as "natural" human beings. We are culture-bound and this fact protects and limits us. Culture also placed us on a different evolutionary road from the one on which our early ancestors traveled.

   The third evolutionary path that now spreads before us is a biological-genetic road. We can now alter the genetic makeup of individuals to accentuate certain traits. Culture not only interacts with nature here, but the very definition of human being can be altered by what particular cultures find attractive. Given this possibility, we need to know, who are we? Who were we? What is expected of us? And, what are we capable of doing to ourselves? To the natural world? To the future?

3. *How have our cultural institutions shaped our worldview?*
   This question addresses the need to study institutional change and the role of institutions in defining our perceptions of the world. The interactions between culture and nature produce human needs that are

satisfied by institutions whose members share certain rules. Institutions undergo change with the advent of new ideas or external pressures. These institutional changes cause needs and culture to change as well. Understanding this dynamic of institutional and cultural change and how these changes affect our perception of the world is the focus of our study. Since people all over the world share membership in similar institutions this study can also serve as a way to help us understand our common humanity.

4. *How do people in different societies and in different times and places make economic choices and organize for the production and consumption of economic goods and services?*

   This question probes the fundamental activities of human beings. For example, we can examine different societies in different times and places by looking at consumer habits and the kinds of goods and services people produce. We can also consider the levels of technology in these societies and what their production and consumption tell us about their sense of justice, happiness, work, and the relationship between the type of economic market and the type of government needed to have such a market.

5. *How do human beings through their institutions, communities, and as individuals interact with the environment?*

   We have reached a point in history where we are capable of radically altering nature. Yet most citizens seem to know very little about the symbiotic relationship we share with the environment. Acid rain, deforestation, the greenhouse effect, the depletion of the ozone layer, the erosion of soil, polluted water and air, the use of dangerous chemicals, and nuclear waste are only some of the persistent problems confronting us. Resolving these issues will demand an evaluation of personal and social goals, a new commitment to all forms of life, a new effort to construct knowledge of how the natural world works, an illumination of our ethical principles and their relationship to our behavior, and reflective action on how we can make our communities better.

   Nature is also something to celebrate, to enjoy, and to use to help us find out who we are. Our relationship with nature is both physical and spiritual, and we express our attitudes with bulldozers as well as with art and music.

6. *How do we develop and express our values?*

   More than any other, this question may help us to anticipate the future by studying the values that have motivated and controlled people over time. Even though these values may change, they present our best indicators of future behavior. What spiritual habits do we all share? What obligations do we acknowledge? How do we express our beliefs?

7. *How do we understand our place in time and space?*

   While this question addresses the importance of chronology and spatial relationships, its main thrust is to show the importance of when and where we live in creating our conceptions of past, present, and future. Perhaps the most important idea here is that of "creating the future." As human beings we are constantly creating our personal and collective futures from our memories. Memories are constructed out of landscapes as well as time. This means that a person or community without a sense of history and geography is incapable of envisioning and building a future. Without an historical or geographical perspective a person or community will end up in a future created by someone else. We are, indeed, travelers through time and space and the importance of this fact cannot be lost, particularly by social studies teachers.

What Role Should Social Studies Teachers Play in Shaping the Future of Education?

Because of their knowledge of history, geography, social trends, and social systems, social studies teachers should be in the best position to help lead in the construction of new models of education for the future. The most important considerations with regard to restructuring education are what to keep; what to throw away; and what to build anew.

As a responsible social studies teacher you have a marvelous opportunity to assume a leadership role in reshaping education in your school. To this end you may want to become a reformer by assuming the following responsibilities.

You should become active in the National Council for the Social Studies and your state social studies and other professional organizations and become more knowledgeable about the issues under discussion, such as testing and assessment in the social studies. As you examine these issues, you will need to think about and decide how these issues will impact your life as a social studies teacher. You will want to discuss these issues with colleagues and decide how you will resolve these issues personally and professionally. Also be active in schoolwide or district programs and staff development opportunities in working to revise the social studies curriculum and improve instruction to make social studies learning exciting for kids.

It is important that you become and remain knowledgeable about what has been suggested about issues in the past so as not to reinvent the wheel. The wise social studies teacher knows what has been done in the past and builds on those experiences. Many issues facing us today have their roots in the past. For example, outcome-based education can trace its roots to the behavioral objectives movement in the mid-1960s. The educational pendulum moves back and forth every so many years.

On a regular basis social studies teachers need to pause and evaluate themselves in terms of their own personal and professional growth, their instructional approaches, and their future plans. As change takes place in society and in your personal lives you will need to make certain adjustments.

There is no such thing as a risk-free life and so risks as a part of change are inevitable. As change takes place it is important to keep in contact with colleagues and mentors so you can maintain a fresh outlook on your teaching of social studies. You are likely to have a competitive advantage over many teachers in other disciplines in being a leader in change because of your background in and orientation to the social studies.

Within this leadership role, you might consider the following activities:

1. Continue to keep up to date on the content of the field.
2. Become involved with your professional organizations and note the issues with which they are dealing. Ascertain how their goals fit with yours and discuss those goals with people who agree as well as with those who disagree with you.
3. Focus on one issue in education that concerns you and envision how to deal with it. Note how your professional organization can help you in this endeavor.
4. Research the issue so that you do not waste time reinventing the wheel. Learn what other people have already created.
5. Evaluate yourself. Have some idea of what you can and cannot do and allow yourself to grow in knowledge and action.
6. Work at change. Remember that there is no such thing as a risk-free life, but it does seem that with good work, success is more likely.
7. Celebrate your vision and work with colleagues so that you can maintain a fresh outlook on your profession. Note again that you have a comparative advantage over teachers of other disciplines in helping to construct the future.

SUMMARY

We have suggested here that while the future is devoid of facts and lives only in our personal and collective imaginations, each of us also plays some role in constructing the future. Given the nature of contemporary social change, it becomes important that social studies educators play a more significant role in this process of "creating the future." We have suggested seven questions and areas of study that the curriculum should address and have argued that these areas form a necessary structure of knowledge for citizens in the 21st century. We have also encouraged you to enter the debate on the nature of the future and have suggested specific activities through which you may assume a leadership role in constructing personal and social policies about the future.

EPILOGUE How Might the 21st Century Shape Social Studies Education? 477

Discussion Questions

1. What is your understanding of the notion that "we create the future"? If you agree with this idea, what responsibility does it place on you?
2. Look ahead to the year 2020 and envision yourself teaching in a large urban school. What types of assignments will you be giving your students? What will be the content focus of your lessons? What materials and equipment will you be using?
3. What social and technological trends from the past do you see continuing into the future?
4. Review the seven questions cited in this Epilogue and suggest how you might incorporate those questions into your major area of teaching responsibility (such as United States history, world geography, economics, government, and so on).
5. Prepare an argument for educational change. Base your rationale on such items as
   a. the nature of contemporary middle and high schools;
   b. the nature of social change;
   c. the knowledge explosion;
   d. why your ideas for change should be taken seriously; and
   e. what benefits would accrue to students and society because of your proposal.

   What do these items (a through e) have to do with your teaching of United States history, world history, economics, political science, and so forth?

Student Learning Activities

1. Interview a class of middle or high school students with reference to their perceptions of the future. First of all, ask them to write out answers to the following kinds of questions:

   What will your personal future look like in 20 years?
   What will you be doing?
   Where will you live?
   What will your lifestyle be?
   What will be the nature of your income?
   Will you have a family?

   The purpose of these questions is to ascertain a view of one's "personal" future. We have conducted similar surveys, which have shown that the majority of high school students see their personal futures as positive.

On the other hand, we have found quite the opposite, that is, a more pessimistic view of students' perceptions of the future health of the community, state, country, and globe. To pursue this comparison, ask the same students on a separate survey what community or social problems do they see that have the potential for disaster? What trends do they see in the world that seem positive?

After you have received narratives from individuals or from small groups of students on their personal and community futures, it would be instructive to discuss with them the congruence or lack of congruence that exists between these two views of the future.

2. Within small groups of three to five individuals, address the statements listed below. Try to come to a consensus on each statement, collectively agreeing or disagreeing on the validity of each statement. If there are words that group members disagree on with regard to the definition, these words can be defined in any way that the group suggests as long as all individuals within the group agree. Individuals and groups should be able to explain the reasoning for their choices.

Education and the Future

Agree–Disagree

_____ 1. The best way to prepare for the future is to know the past.

_____ 2. In a time of rapid social change, attention should be placed upon the synthesis or integration of knowledge as opposed to the separation of knowledge into specific disciplines.

_____ 3. Teaching integrated or interdisciplinary knowledge is less efficient than teaching knowledge that is separated by discipline categories.

_____ 4. A curriculum that places major emphasis upon basic skills provides the best foundation for future learning.

_____ 5. Middle school and high school programs should emphasize career education in their curriculum as a more sure way to prepare students for the future.

_____ 6. Your behavior is more a function of your view of the future than it is a function of past experiences.

_____ 7. The collective (or community) futuristic perceptions of a people shape the direction of education for the young.

3. Within small groups, construct a middle or high school of the future. Describe the course of study or curriculum, the kind of activities the students will do, where the instructional program will take place (inside and/or outside the school building), the relationship between the school and the larger community, and evaluation strategies both for the students and the program.

References

Adler, M. J. 1982. *The Paideia Proposal: An Educational Manifesto.* New York: Macmillan.

Carnegie Forum on Education and the Economy. 1986. *A Nation Prepared: Teachers for the 21st Century.* Washington, DC: Carnegie Forum on Education and the Economy.

Hawken, P., Ogilvy, J., and Schwartz, P. 1982. *Seven Tomorrows: Toward a Voluntary History.* New York: Bantam Books.

National Commission on Excellence in Education. 1983. *A Nation at Risk: The Imperative for Educational Reform.* Washington, DC: National Commission on Excellence in Education.

National Standards for Social Studies. 1994. *National Standards for Social Studies.* Washington, DC: National Council for the Social Studies.

Toffler, A. (1980). *The Third Wave.* New York: Bantam Books.

Additional Readings

Bennett, W. J. 1994. *The Index of Leading Cultural Indicators: Facts and Figures on the State of American Society.* New York: Simon & Schuster.

Bennett, W. J. 1993. *The Book of Virtues: A Treasury of Great Moral Stories.* New York: Simon & Schuster.

Bronowski, J. 1977. *A Sense of the Future: Essays in Natural Philosophy.* Cambridge, MA: MIT Press.

Gore, A. 1992. *Earth in the Balance: Ecology and the Human Spirit.* Boston: Houghton Mifflin.

Fukuyama, F. 1992. *The End of History and the Last Man.* New York: Macmillan.

Joseph, P. B. and Burnaford, G. E. (Eds.). 1994. *Images of Schoolteachers in Twentieth-Century America: Paragons, Polarities, Complexities.* New York: St. Martin's.

Kaplan, I. (Ed.). 1994. *Rebuilding the Schoolhouse: Views and Issues in Education.* Boston: Allyn and Bacon.

Leonard, G. B. 1968. *Education and Ecstasy.* New York: Delacorte.

Merchant, C. 1980. *The Death of Nature: Women, Ecology and the Scientific Revolution.* San Francisco: Harper and Row.

Odekirk, K. A. 1993. *The Community Learning Center.* Unpublished paper. Green Bay, WI: University of Wisconsin–Green Bay.

Sadker, M. and Sadker, D. 1994. *Failing at Fairness: How America's Schools Cheat Girls.* New York: Charles Scribner's Sons.

COPYRIGHT ACKNOWLEDGMENTS

Page 13, ©Mark Burnett/PhotoEdit; 26–28, ©National Council for the Social Studies. Used with permission. 30, ©1993 Mick Stevens and The Cartoon Bank, Inc.; 40, ©Mary Kate Denny/PhotoEdit; 45–46, ©National Council for the Social Studies. Used with permission. 52–53, From Bragaw, Donald and H. Michael Hartoonian, "Social Studies: The Study of People in Society," in Content of the Curriculum, 1988 ASCD Yearbook (pp. 11–15.) Ronald Brandt, ed. Alexandria, Va.: Association for Supervision and Curriculum Development. Copyright 1988 by ASCD. Used with permission of ASCD and of National Council for Geographic Education. 57, ©Robert Brenner/PhotoEdit; 63, ©1993 Peter Steiner and The Cartoon Bank, Inc.; 66, ©1993 Roz Chast and The Cartoon Bank, Inc.; 91, National Council for the Social Studies. Used with permission. 95, ©Richard Hutchings/PhotoEdit; 96, ©Mark Richards/PhotoEdit; 137, ©Jeff Greenberg/PhotoEdit; 150–153, chapter on Sam Houston from *Profiles in Courage* by John F. Kennedy. Copyright ©1955, 1956, 1961 by John F. Kennedy. Copyright renewed ©1983, 1984, 1989 by Jacqueline Kennedy Onassis. Foreword copyright ©1964 by Robert F. Kennedy. Copyright renewed. Reprinted by permission of HarperCollins Publishers, Inc.; 151, Library of Congress; 184, ©1993 Jack Ziegler and The Cartoon Bank, Inc.; 223, Frank Weiner; 243, ©Richard Hutchings/PhotoEdit; 267, Adapted from Laughlin, M.A. and Beining, T.J., 1987. "Participating in the Global Economy," in *The Senior Economist,* vol. 3, number 1, Fall 1987, pp. 13–14. Copyright ©1987, National Council on Economic Education, New York, N.Y. Used with permission. 287, Frank Weiner; 336, Tony Freeman/PhotoEdit; 353–354, Excerpt and chart from *Teaching Elementary Social Studies, A Rational and Humanistic Approach* by Pearl M. Oliner, copyright ©1976 by Harcourt Brace & Company, reprinted by permission of the publisher. 399, ©National Council for the Social Studies. Used with permission. 428, ©Joel Gordon 1992; 457, ©1993 Frank Cotham and The Cartoon Bank, Inc.

INDEX

AAED. *See Groliers Academic American Encyclopedia (AAED)*
ABC Interactive programs, 421
Ability groups, 241–242, 245
ABSTRAX, 417
Academic Decathlon, 247
Academic freedom, 252–255
Accountability movement, 360–361
ACT. *See* American College Test (ACT)
ADL. *See* Anti-Defamation League (ADL)
Adler, M., 471
Administrative reports, completed by teachers, 448–449
Administrators, 188, 383–384
Advance organizers, 174–175
Advanced Placement (AP) program, 247, 419
Advising, 446
Affective domain, testing in, 377–378
AFT. *See* American Federation of Teachers (AFT)
Agricultural age, 467
AHA. *See* American Historical Association (AHA)
Airasian, P. W., 379
Alberta Education, 416
All Star Drill, 407
Alternative activities, 222
Alvermann, D. E., 314
Aman, J., 427
American Anthropology Association, 451, 462
American Bar Association, 99, 264n, 451, 462
American Civil Liberties Union, 254
American College Test (ACT), 350, 358
American Economics Association, 451
American Federation of Teachers (AFT), 449, 455
American Field Service, 294
American Foundation for the Blind, 250
American Geographic Association, 451
American Historical Association (AHA), 9, 10, 450, 461
American History and Life, 418
American Political Science Association, 9, 451, 461
American Printing House for the Blind, 250
American Psychological Association, 451, 462
American Sociological Association, 451, 462
Analytical generalizations, 107
Anderson, L., 93
Anderson, V., 328
Answering process, 330–331. *See also* Questions for class discussion
Antes, R. L., 359
Anthropology, basic concepts and questions from, 58–59 connections with social studies, 58 definition of, 57–58 learning activities in, 261, 266 professional organization in, 451
Anti-Defamation League (ADL), 11
AP program. *See* Advanced placement (AP) program
Appian Way History Software, 408
Apple Computer Corp., 424
Appleworks, 405
Archambault, R. D., 232
Archbald, D. A., 379
Arnold, B., 296
Arnold, K. D., 135
Arts, social studies and, 72
ASCUS Annual: A Job Search Handbook for Educators, 452
Assessment. *See also* Evaluation of students; Testing, authentic assessment, 379–380 curriculum-based assessment, 362–363 definition of, 350 performance assessment, 379
Assignments, daily lesson planning and, 221–222 guidelines for teachers on, 334–337 homework assignments, 221–222, 320, 336–337 homework drop spot, 320 pros and cons on homework, 221–222 purposes of, 335 writing assignments, 335–336
Association for Supervision and Curriculum Development, 455
Association of American Geographers, 461
Associations, 449–452, 455–456, 461–462. *See also* specific organizations
"At-risk" students, 248, 250–251
Attitudes, 82–83
Attributes, 104

Audiovisual materials. *See* Media; Visual aids
Augustine, D. K., 244
Ausubel, D., 174–175
Authentic assessment, 379–380

Baier, K., 138
Baker, I., 326
Baker, L., 331
Bangert-Downs, R. L., 171
Banks, J., 64
BannerMania, 406
Barr, R. D., 8, 14
Barth, J. L., 8, 14
Basho, Matsuo, 391
Behavior modification programs, 172
Behavior Rating Profile, 189
Behavioral theory, cautions regarding, 172 definition of, 169 educational applications of, 170–171 Skinner and, 169–171 suggestions for use of, in classrooms, 171–172
Beining, T. J., 267
Belenky, M. F., 428
Bellah, R, N., 16
Berg, P., 431
Berliner, D., 380
Berrent, H. I., 326
Bias in testing, 362
Binary choice-alternative response test items, 371–373
Bliss, T., 136
Bloom, B. S., 12, 356
Bogdan, R. C., 248
Boyer, E., 232
Brabeck, M. M., 135
Bragaw, D. H., 11, 51, 140
Bramble, M., 431
Bransford, J. D., 429
Breisach, E., 137
Bright, G. W., 413
Brophy, J., 333, 339
Brown, A. L., 331
Brown, L., 19
Brown, L. L., 189
BRS Colleague Educator, 417
BRS/SEARCH SERVICE, 417
Bruder, I., 402
Bruner, J., 161, 173–174, 175
Brusca, F., 427–428
Bryk, A. S., 144

Bulletin boards, 418
Burkhart, J. E., 135
Bursuck, B., 318
Burtt, E. A., 133
Business World, 294
Butler, J. A., 251
Button, C., 186
Butts, R. F., 7–8

CAI. *See* Computer-assisted instruction (CAI)
CAL. *See* Computer-assisted learning (CAL)
Campaign for the White House, The, 421
Canada, K., 427–428
Canter, L., 337
Capek, K., 421
Captioned Films for the Deaf, 250
Career education, 229–231
Career opportunities, for teachers, 453–456
Carmen Sandiego programs, 409
Carnegie Forum on Education and Economy, 469
Carnevale, A. P., 231
Carr, E., 322
Carter, K., 367
Causality, 37, 118, 120, 122
CBA. *See* Curriculum-based assessment (CBA)
CBI. *See* Computer-based instruction (CBI)
CD-ROM, 402, 406
Center for Action Research, 95
Center for Civic Education, 95, 99, 264n, 451, 461
Center for Civic Education/Law in a Free Society, 95, 99
Cetron, M., 222
CEUs, 441
Challenges to instructional materials, responding to, 285–286
Change. *See also* Future trends; cultural change, 59, 109–112 in social studies education, 35 teaching about concept of, 103 in values, 138–139
Chávez, C. E., 298
Checklist, 451
Checklists, for evaluation, 352–354
Chen, M., 426
Cheney, C. D., 249
Child development theories, definition of, 179 educational applications of Piaget's theory, 181 Piaget and, 179–182 suggestions for using Piaget's theories in classrooms, 181–182
Childs, J., 133

Chuska, K. R., 310, 315
Citizenship education, civic action, 32–33 democratic beliefs, 29–31 exercise on, 2–3 as goal of education, 16 history of, 1–2, 6–9, 14–15 importance of, in NCSS statement, 29–33 as theme in social studies education, 33 in twenty-first century, 469–472
Citizenship Education Project, Columbia University, 11
Cityworks, 229
Civics, sample outline on, 205–207
Clarifying questions, 317
Class discussions, 214–215, 308–310. *See also* Questions for class discussion.
Classes, definition of, 104
Classroom Computer Learning, 416
Classrooms. *See also* Instruction; Learning; Learning activities; Learning environments; Students; Teachers; behavioral theory used in, 171–172 cognitive-discovery theory used in, 175–176 conducive to social inquiry, 124–126 discipline in, 189–191 grouping within, 240–246 humanistic theories used in, 177–178 Kohlberg's theory of moral development used in, 184 organizing of, for effective learning, 240–245 physical arrangement of, to facilitate discussion, 215 Piaget's theories used in, 181–182 values education and, 144
Clegg, A. A., Jr., 314, 425
Client-centered therapy, 177
Cliffs Studyware for Economics, 407
Clift, J. C., 359
Clinchy, B. M., 428
Clinton, B., 33
Close-Up activities, 292
Co-curricular activities, Business World, 294 Close-Up activities, 292 Geography Bee, 293 mock trial competitions, 292–293 Model United Nations (MUN), 291–292 Stock Market Game, 293 summer programs, 294
Cognitive development, Piaget's stages of, 179–181
Cognitive-discovery theory, Ausubel and, 174–175 Bruner and, 173–174 cautions regarding, 176 definition of, 172–173 educational applications of, 175 suggestions for using, in classrooms, 175–176
College Entrance Examination Board, 64
Collier, M., 58
Collins, H. T., 93
Columbia University. *See* Teachers College, Columbia University

Columbus, 421
Commission on the Reorganization of Secondary Education, 7, 9–10
Communication, as knowledge-related activity, 53, 54–55
Community, involvement of, in program evaluation, 383–384 resources in, 288–290 values and expectations of, 254–255 values education and, 136 volunteerism in, 231–232
Community service, 231–232, 442
Community study, in values education, 136
Competency testing. *See* Minimum competency testing
Competitions, academic, 247
Comprehension, as learning strategy, 327–328 questioning and, 311 in social inquiry, 118, 119, 122
CompuServ, 417
Computer-assisted instruction (CAI), 171, 403
Computer-assisted learning (CAL), 403
Computer-based instruction (CBI), 403
Computer Courseware Reviews, 416, 416n
Computer crime, 429–430
Computer Equity News, 427
Computer Equity Training Project, 427
Computer literacy, 400–402
Computer viruses, 430–431
Computers and computer programs, abuses of, 429–431 access to, 426 computer crime, 429–430 computer viruses, 430–431 databases, 416–418, 429–430 desktop publishing tools, 406 diagnosis of errors, 412 drill-and-practice programs, 407, 426 educational applications for, 403 educational games, 408–409 electronic information service (EIS), 417–418 ethical code on, 430 evaluation of software, 412–416 future uses of, 431 gender gap and, 426–428 grade book programs, 405 graphics programs, 411 inquiry/problem solving programs, 410 instructional techniques in, 406–412 integrated computer packages, 406 issues concerning, 424–429 models, 410 overuse and inappropriate use of, 425–426 problem areas concerning, 403 simulations, 409–410 software for social studies, 403–412 spreadsheets, 405 stand-alone programs, 404 for test preparation, 379 textbook and supplementary computer programs, 404 tutorial programs, 407–408 use of, in schools, 398–412 utility programs, 404–406 word processing programs, 405, 411–412

Computing Teacher, 430
Computing Teacher, The, 416
Concept learning, 166
Concept map, 322, 323–325
Concept webs, 111
Concepts, in anthropology, 58–59 attributes and, 104 change as, 103 classes and, 104 compared with generalizations, 108 definition of, 75, 104, 105 in economics, 60–61, 113 examples and, 104 examples of teaching of, 105–107 in geography, 62–64 in history, 64–65 and inquiry in social studies, 104–107 in philosophy, 65–66 in political science, 67 in psychology, 68 in sociology, 69 values concepts versus factual concepts, 131
Conceptualization, in social inquiry, 118, 119, 122
Concluding activities, 212, 213
Concrete stage, of cognitive development, 180–181, 402
Connell, J., 250
Conoley, J. C., 356
Constitutional Rights Foundation, 99, 264n, 451, 461
Content, 47, 117. *See also* specific disciplines
Continuing education units (CEUs), 441
Contract system, 364
Controversial issues, 252–255, 285–286, 289
Conventional morality, 141, 183
Convergent questions, 315
Conversation, instructional, 241
Cooper, J. M., 454
Cooperative learning groups, 135–136, 242–245
Coopersmith, S., 189
Coopersmith Self-Esteem Inventories, 189
Cornbleth, C., 186
Council of State Social Studies Specialists, 15, 88
Counselors, 447
Counts, G., 9
Course outline, 333
Coursen, W., 97
Criterion-referenced tests, 359
Cultural change, 59, 109–112
Cultural conflicts, 251–252
Cultural ecology, 59
Cultural groups. *See* Racial and ethnic groups
Cultural sensitivity, 252
Cultural universals, 58
Culture, as basic concept in anthropology, 58 in curriculum, 34, 87–88 definition of, 58 interrelationships among time, place, and, 87–88 sequence of, 86 teaching about concept of, 105–107

Cunningham, R. T., 315
Curriculum and curriculum planning, for career education, 229–231 coursework identified in, 202 decision-making grid for, 234–235 disciplines-oriented curriculum, 85 for environmental education, 96–97 functions of, 200 for global studies, 92–93 goals identified in, 201 for high school, 89–90 historical development of, 9, 15–16 individual-oriented curriculum, 85 influence of newer content areas on, 92–97 interrelationships among time, place, and culture, 87–88 for K-5 program, 89, 90 for law-related education, 93–95 leadership for, 201 long-range planning, 200–202 for middle school, 89, 90 mission statement in, 201 overview of, 198–200 scope and sequence patterns in, 84–87, 90–92 society-oriented curriculum, 85 for special needs students, 248–249 steps in, 201–202 themes in, 85 trends in, 88–92 unit planning, 202–207 for volunteerism, 231–232
Curriculum-based assessment (CBA), 362–363
Curriculum specialists, 448
Curti, M., 307
Curwin, R. L., 337
Curzon, L. B., 375

Daily lesson planning, alternative activities in, 222 assignments in, 221–222 class discussions in, 214–215 content for lesson, 210–211 evaluation of students in, 221 format of, 224–225 general considerations in, 208–211 grade level for lesson, 209 instructional materials selection and, 219–221 instructional procedures selected, 211–213, 218–219 learning styles of students and teaching styles of teacher, 213–214 lectures in, 214 media selection and, 219 model of factors in, 207 notes on following teaching, 223 objectives in, 209–210 questions for class discussion in, 215–217 questions regarding, 208 rationale for lesson, 209 sample economics lesson plan, 225–229 steps in, 209–211 time for lesson, 209 title for lesson, 209
Data gathering skills, 31
Databases, 404, 416–418, 429–430
Davis, D. M., 408
Davis, O. L., Jr., 186
Decision making, as knowledge-related activity, 53, 55–56 on moral issues, 182–185 in social studies education, 31

Decisions, Decisions, 408–409
DeGarmo, C., 313
Dekens, J., 422
Dembo, M. H., 350
Deno, S. L., 363
Department of Defense (DOD) schools, 454
Department or team meetings, 447
Derr, T. F., 362
Desktop publishing tools, 406
Developmental activities, 212, 213
Developmental learning approach, 364
Devine, T. G., 329, 337
Dewey, J., 9
Diagnostic computer programs, 412
Diagnostic evaluation, 356–357
DIALOG, 417–418
Digest of Software Reviews, 416, 416n
Dillon, D. R., 314
Dillon, J. T., 214–215, 314
Disabilities, students with, 248–250
Discipline, 189–191
Disciplines-oriented curriculum, 85
Discovery learning, 174–176
Discussions, 214–215, 308–310. *See also* Questions for class discussion
Dishner, E. K., 322
Disinfectant 2.9, 431
Divergent questions, 315
DOD schools, 454
Doyle, W., 191
Drill-and-practice computer programs, 407, 426
Driscoll, M. E., 144
Druian, G., 251
Duffy, G. G., 333
Dynneson, T. L., 133

Earthquest Explores Ecology, 410
Economics, basic concepts and questions from, 36–37, 60–61 daily lesson plan on, 225–229 definition of, 59 interrelationships of types of knowledge in, 112–115 learning activities in, 261–262, 267–268 macro-economics, 59 measurement concepts in, 61 micro-economics, 59 professional organizations in, 450–451 Stock Market Game, 293 tests in, 356–357 unit outline in, 204–205
Education. *See also* Social studies; citizenship and, 1–2, 6–9, 14–15, 469–471 goals of, 2, 6–8, 16, 136 purposes of, 469 in twenty-first century, 469–471

Education for All Handicapped Children Act (PL 94-142), 248
Education Index, 402
Education Week, 294
Educational games, 408–409
Educational Resources Information Center. *See* ERIC
Educational technology, 399. *See also* Computers and computer programs; Technologies
EIS. *See* Electronic information service (EIS)
Elam, S. M., 361
Electronic bulletin boards, 418
Electronic information service (EIS), 417–418
Electronic Learning, 416
Eleventh Mental Measurements Yearbook, 356
Elis Island: The Immigrant Experience, 409–410
Elliott, S. N., 362
EMAQF model, 333–339
Emerson, R. W., 130, 165
Emmer, E. T., 191
Employment, preparation for, 229–231
Employment opportunities, for teachers, 452–456
Enactive learning, 173–174
Engel, P., 18–19
Engle, S. H., 17–18
Environmental education, 96–97, 263, 279
Environmental Education Act of 1970, 96
Epstein, M., 318
EQUALS in Computer Technology, 427
ERIC, 402, 417, 418
Essay questions, 373–376, 377
Essentials of social studies, 25–37
Estes, T. H., 307
Ethics, on computer use, 430 NCSS Statement of Ethical Principles, 44 in social studies, 44, 82–83 of teachers, 445 universal ethical principles, as stage of moral development, 183
Ethnic groups. *See* Racial and ethnic groups
European History Study Disks, 408
Evaluation, of computer software, 412–416 definition of, 350 of instruction and instructional materials, 299–302, 382 program evaluation, 345–346, 380–384 roles of teachers, students, administrators, parents, and community in program evaluation, 383–384
Evaluation of students, accountability movement, 360–361 in affective domain, 377–378 authentic assessment, 379–380 bias in testing, 362 binary choice-alternative response items for, 371–373 contract system and, 364 criterion-referenced

tests, 359 curriculum-based assessment, 362–363 daily lesson planning and, 221 developmental or mastery learning approach and, 364 diagnostic evaluation, 356–357 essay questions for, 373–376, 377 exercise on, 346–348 formative evaluation, 357 goals of, 350–352 grading, 358, 363–366, 375–378 guidelines for writing test questions, 366–367 issues in testing, 360–363 matching items for tests, 369–371 minimum competency testing, 361–362 multiple choice questions for, 367–368 norm-referenced tests, 358–359 observations, checklists, and rating scales, 352–354 overt and covert functions of, 353–354 placement evaluation, 355–356 portfolios, 352, 380 questioning for, 338 rationale for, 355–360 reliability of tests and, 360 self-referenced tests, 359–360 student work samples, 352, 380 summative evaluation, 357–358 test bank of questions for, 378–379 types of, 352–360 validity of tests and, 360

Evaluation of teachers, 346, 383

Examples, definition of, 104

Examwriter, 379

Exercises, citizenship and social studies, 2–3 content of social studies education, 48 evaluation techniques, 346–348 "how" questions on teaching of social studies, 163 on learning technologies, 393 rationale statement, 40–42

Explanations, 118, 121–123, 333–334

Extending questions, 317

Facts. *See also* Information; Knowledge; definition of, 75 fact-value continuum, 131 role of, 52

Feedback, 338–339, 365–366. *See also* Grading

Female students, and computer use, 426–428

Ferguson, D. L., 248

Ferguson, P. M., 248

Ferraro, G. A., 298

Field observation, 69

Field trips, 289–290

Focus activities. *See* Exercises

Focus questions, 216–217

Formal operations stage, of cognitive development, 180–181, 402

Formative evaluation, 357

Foundation for Teaching Economics, 451, 461

Fraenkel, J. R., 134

Framework for Teaching the Basic Concepts, The (Saunders), 357

Freedom, in social studies education, 36

Freedom of Information Act, 429

Frontal teaching, 242

Fulbright, J. W., 439

Fusion courses, 259–260

Future trends. *See also* Computers and computer programs; Technologies; in citizens' responsibilities, 471–472 on computer uses in social studies, 431 and concept of future, 466 importance of, 465–466 schools in 21st century, 468–471 social studies education and, 475–476 societal trends, 396–398 and teachers' leadership role, 475–476 in technology, 395–396 world of 21st century, 466–468

Gage, N., 380

Gaines, L. J., 231

Gale Research, Inc., 356

Gall, M., 314, 315, 316, 330

Gallimore, R. G., 241

Galloway, J. L., 430

Gallup, A. M., 361

Galvin, J. M., 420

Games, computer, 408–409

Gardner, H., 306

Gavelek, J. R., 315

Gayle, M., 222

Gender gap, and computer use, 426–428

Generalizations, analytical generalizations, 107 compared with concepts, 108 definition of, 75, 107 in economics, 112–113 inquiry in social studies and, 107–112 synthetic generalizations, 107–108 testing of, 108

Geographic maps, 328

Geography, basic concepts and questions from, 62–64 definition of, 61 Geography Bee, 293 integration with history, 54 learning activities in, 262, 269 professional organizations in, 451 research tools of, 61–62 tests in, 357

Geography Bee, 293, 451

Gestalt-field theory. *See* Cognitive-discovery theory

Gibbs, J. C., 135

Gifted and talented students, 246–248

Gilligan, C., 134–135, 142, 182, 428

Global studies, capacities fostered by, 93 curriculum for, 92–93 learning activities in, 263–264, 280 in social studies education, 34–35

Global Tomorrow Coalition, 96–97

Goals. *See also* Objectives; of education, 2, 6–8, 16, 136 of evaluation, 350–352 of law-related education, 94–95 realistic learning goals for students, 319–320 SMART goals, 319–320 of social studies, 6–8, 14–15, 83–84, 201
Goldberger, N. R., 428
Goodlad, J., 398
Governmental agencies, teaching positions in, 455
Grade Book Deluxe, 405
Grade book programs, 405
Grade Busters, 405
Grading, 358, 363–366, 375–378, 405
Grading on a curve, 358
Graduate programs, for social studies teachers, 440–441, 454
Graphic organizer. *See* Concept map
Graphics computer programs, 411
Graphs, note taking from, 327
Groliers Academic American Encyclopedia (AAED), 417
Gross, R. E., 133
Group grading, 365
Group Grammar, 412
Grouping of students, cooperative learning groups, 242–245 heterogeneous grouping, 241 homogeneous grouping, 240–241 learning cycle groups, 241–242 long-term ability groups, 245 rationale for, 245–246
Gruber, K. D., 244
Grueneich, R., 135
Guidance counselors, 447
Guthrie, J. T., 135
Guthrie, W., 72

Hagerty, B. M. K., 445
Hamilton, A., 297
Hammill, D. D., 189
Hand raising, 308–309
Hannum, W. H., 401, 431
Hanson, L. R., 244
Harmin, M., 131, 134, 143
Harris, D. B., 189
Harris, D. E., 142
Hartoonian, H. M., 51, 131, 133, 134, 136, 140, 143, 144, 355
Hartshorne, H., 133
Hawke, S., 88
Hawken, P., 468
Health care specialists, 448

Heimlich, J. E., 322
Hello USA, 404
Hello World, 404
Helsel, S., 423
Hermmann, B. A>, 333
Heterogeneous grouping, 241
Hidi, S., 328
Higher education, teachers in, 454–455
Hill, W. F., 166
History, basic concepts and questions from, 64–65 definition of, 64 early teaching of, 8–9 essay on Sam Houston, 150–153 example of social inquiry in, 119–123, 125 integration with geography, 54 learning activities in, 262, 270 professional organizations in, 450 social history, 64 value profile for Sam Houston, 153–154 values and, 137–138
Hobin, M., 272
Homework assignments. *See* Assignments
Homogeneous grouping, 240–241
Honors seminar, 245
Hoover, J. D., 249
Hopkins, C. D., 359
Houston, S., essay on, 150–153 value profile for, 153–154
How Computers Work, 406
Howe, L. W., 144
Human rights, 35
Humanistic theories, cautions regarding, 179 definition of, 176 educational applications of, 177 Maslow and, 177 Rogers and, 177 suggestions for using, in classrooms, 177–178
Humanities, 72, 294
Humans, as basic concept in anthropology, 58 interactions between environment and, in geography, 62–63 social studies used to understand human problems and institutions, 116–11
Hunt, M. P., 52, 131
HyperCard, 424
Hypermedia, 423–424, 430
Hypotheses, in social sciences, 70, 71

IBM, 421, 424
Iconic learning, 173–174
IDEA. *See* Individuals with Disabilities Education Act (PL 101-476)
Imrie, B. W., 359
In the Holy Land, 421

490 Index

In-class ability grouping, 241–242
Individual-oriented curriculum, 85
Individuals with Disabilities Education Act (PL 101-476), 249
Industrial age, 467
Influence, 67
Information. *See also* Facts; Knowledge; connections between previously learned and new information, 52, 54 obsolescence of, 391 role of facts, 52 use of, 329–331
Information Age, 391–392, 395–396, 398, 467–468
Information sources, 312, 313, 320–321, 402.
See also Databases; Instructional materials
Information versus knowledge, 50
Initiating activities, 212–213
Inquiry in social studies, causality in, 118, 120, 122 classrooms conducive to, 124–126 comprehension/conceptualization in, 118, 119, 122 concepts and, 104–107 conceptual model of, 122–124 content and social inquiry skills, 117–121 creating and using social knowledge, 102–115 creative extensions in, 119–120, 121, 123 generalizations and, 107–112 meaningful knowledge and, 112–115 skills needed for, 125–126 social studies used to understand human problems and institutions, 116–11 universal nature of social knowledge, 115–116 validity of explanation in, 118, 121, 122–123
Inquiry/problem solving computer programs, 410
Institutions, as basic concept in sociology, 69 social studies used to understand human problems and institutions, 116–11
Instruction. *See also* Classrooms; Computers and computer programs; Values education; and headings beginning with Learning; alternative activities, 222 assignments and, 221–222, 320, 334–337 for "at-risk" students, 251 behavioral theory on, 169–172 child development theories on, 179–185 class discussions, 214–215, 308–310 classrooms conducive to social inquiry, 124–126 cognitive-discovery theory on, 172–176 computer-assisted instruction (CAI), 171 concluding activities in, 212, 213 daily lesson planning for, 207–229 developmental activities in, 212, 213 discipline and, 189–191 discovery approach to, 174 EMAQF model of, 333–339 evaluation of instructional practices, 382 explanation in, 333–334 feedback in, 338–339 future trends in, 471 guidelines for strategic learning, 308–339 "how" questions on teaching of social studies, 161–163 humanistic theories on, 176–179 initiating activities in, 212–213 Kohlberg's moral development theory on, 182–184 and learners' responsibilities for learning, 166–167 lectures, 214 modeling in, 334 motivation and, 167–168, 185–189 Piaget's child development theory on, 179–182 programmed instruction, 171, 172 questioning in, 215–217, 219, 313–318, 337–338 research findings on learning, 169–185 self-fulfilling prophecy and, 186 sustaining expectations effect and, 186–187 teacher "folk wisdom" on, 167–168 themes used in, 38–39 types of instructional procedures, 211–213, 218–219
Instructional materials. *See also* Computers and computer programs; Media community resources, 288–290 creativity in, 286–290 daily lesson planning and, 219–221 evaluation form for, 299–302 evaluation of, 299–302, 382 form for challenged materials, 285–286 newspapers and weekly news publications, 287 outside speakers, 288–290 responding to challenges to, 285–286 selection of, 219–221, 283–286, 299–302 textbooks, 219–220, 283–284, 286, 318, 333
Instructional planning, alternative activities in, 222 assignments in, 221–222 class discussions in, 214–215 daily lesson planning, 207–229 decision-making grid for, 234–235 evaluation of students in, 221 format of daily lesson plan, 224–225 general considerations in, 208–211 instructional materials selection and, 219–221 instructional procedures selected, 211–213, 218–219 learning styles of students and teaching styles of teacher, 213–214 lectures in, 214 media selection and, 219 model of factors in, 207 notes on following teaching, 223 questions for class discussion in, 215–217 sample economics lesson plan, 225–229
Instructional Television Fixed Service (ITFS), 419
Instrumental relativism, as stage of moral development, 183
Integrated computer packages, 406
Intellectual skills, 31. *See also* Thinking
Intelligence, definitions of, 306
Interactive learning technologies, 419
Interactive video, 421
Intern program, 245

Interpersonal concordance, as stage of moral development, 183
Interpersonal skills, 31–32
Iowa Tests of Educational Development, 358
Irwin, J. W., 326
Ishler, M., 363
ITFS. *See* Instructional Television Fixed Service (ITFS)

Jackson, A., 297
Jackson, J., 298
Jacobson, L., 186
Jarrett, K., 426
Jefferson, T., 6
Jigsaw, 243
Johnson, D. W., 136
Johnson, R. T., 136
Joint Committee on Geographic Education, 62, 262
Joint Council on Economic Education, 11
Jones, B. F., 333, 339
Jones, R. S., 136
Journal of Geography, 283, 416, 451
Journal of Research on Computing in Education, 416
Journals, 416. *See also* specific titles of journals
Just school programs, in values education, 136
Justice, in social studies education, 36 value profile of, 145–154
Justifying questions, 317

Kagan, S., 242, 244
Kazis, R., 232
Kellogg, J., 251
Kennedy, J. F., 150–153
Key, V. O., Jr., 140
Kinder, D. B., 318
Kindswitter, R., 363
King, M. L., Jr., 296
Kinzer, C.K., 429
Kirschenbaum, H., 144
Klein, M. L., 315
Knowledge, attributes of, 47 broad perspective versus narrow concentration, 50 and communication and negotiation with others, 53, 54–55 concepts and, 104–107 connections between previously learned and new information, 52, 54 as content, 47 content versus method, 50 creating and using social knowledge, 102–115 creation of, 53, 55 decision making and, 53, 55–56 generalizations and, 107–112 information base and, 52, 54 intellectual abilities, processes, and skills, 82 interrelationships of types of, 112–115 issues related to, 50 knowledge-related activities, 51–56 logic and, 53 meaningful knowledge, 112–115 as methodology, 47 policy decisions and, 55–56 role of facts in, 52 as shared experiences, 47 social knowledge in social studies education, 50–56 in social studies, 81–84 in social studies education, 29 sociology of knowledge, 70 time and space perspectives in, 54 universal nature of social knowledge, 115–116 versus information, 50
Koch, Kathryn A., 305
Kohlberg, L., 134, 135, 136, 141–142, 145, 146, 182–184
Komoski, P. K., 412
Kounin, J. S., 190
K-Q-L-Q-F strategy, 322, 325–326
Kramer, J. J., 356
Krathwohl, D. R., 12
Kratochwill, T. R., 362
Kreupeling, W. J., 173
Kulik, C. C., 171
Kulik, J. A., 171

Lamon, W. E., 430
Laser disk technology, 406
Laughlin, M. A., 267, 355
Law, as basic concept in political science, 67
Law and order, as stage of moral development, 183
Law-related education (LRE), curriculum for, 93–95 goals and achievements of, 94–95 learning activities in, 218, 264 mock trial competitions, 292–293
Law-Related Education Act of 1978, 94
Law-Related Education National Training and Dissemination Program, 95, 99
Learning. *See also* Strategic learning; and headings beginning with Instruction; assignments and, 221–222, 320, 334–337 concept learning, 166 definitions of, 166 enactive learning, 173–174 explanation and, 333–334 feedback and, 338–339 guidelines for teachers to enhance student learning, 308–310 iconic learning, 173–174 influences on, 166 involvement of students in, 308–310 learners' responsibilities for, 166–167 modeling and, 334 motivation in, 167–168 prose learning, 166 questioning and, 215–217, 219,

313–318, 337–338 research findings on, 169–185 response learning, 166 rote verbal learning, 166 strategic learning, 308–339 symbolic learning, 173–174 teacher "folk wisdom" on, 167–168 teaching for effective learning, 310–313

Learning activities, in anthropology, 261, 266 Business World, 294 Close-Up activities, 292 co-curricular activities, 291–294 community resources for, 288–290 creativity in, 286–290 in economics, 261–262, 267–268, 293, 294 in environmental studies, 263, 279 field trips, 289–290 in geography, 262, 269, 293 in global education, 263–264, 280, 291–292 in history, 262, 270 in law-related education, 218, 264 mock trial competitions, 292–293 Model United Nations, 291–292 motivational aspects in, 260–261 in multicultural education, 264–265, 282 in philosophy, 262, 271 in political science, 262–263, 272–276, 296–299 in psychology, 263, 277 in sociology, 263, 278 Stock Market Game, 293 student involvement in, 308–310 summer programs, 294

Learning cycle groups, 241–242

Learning environments. *See also* Classrooms; academic freedom and, 252–255 for "at-risk" students, 248, 250–251 definition of, 239–240 for ethnic and cultural groups, 251–252 for gifted and talented students, 246–248 organizing of, for effective learning, 240–245 for special needs students, 248–250

Learning logs, 332–333

Learning strategies. *See also* Computers and computer programs; answering process, 330–331 comprehension, 327–328 concept map, 322, 323–325 K-Q-L-Q-F strategy, 322, 325–326 learning logs, 332–333 locating information, 320–321 managing materials and time, 320 memory skills, 328–329 metacognition, 331–333 motivation, 319–320 note taking, 321–327 "Oh Rats" strategy, 326 reading levels and, 318 regulating learning, 331–333 test-taking strategies, 330–331, 332 using information, 329–331

Learning styles, 213–214

Learning theories, behavioral theory, 169–172 cognitive-discovery theory, 172–176 humanistic theories, 176–179 Kohlberg's moral development theory, 182–184 Piaget's child development theory, 179–182

Least restrictive environment, 248
Lectures, 214
Leder, G. C., 186
Legitimacy, as basic concept in political science, 67
Lehmann, I. J., 350, 361
Leming, J. S., 134, 135, 142
Lerner, B., 361
Lesson planning. *See* Daily lesson planning
Levin, H. M., 251
Lewis, R. B., 189
Librarians, 448
Library sources. *See* Information sources
Lillie, D. L., 401, 431
Lincoln, A., 297–298
LinkWay, 424
Literature, social studies and, 72
Lockwood, A. L., 134, 142, 144
Logic, knowledge and, 53
Long-range curriculum planning, 200–202
Long-term ability groups, 245
Lowther, M. A., 445
LRE. *See* Law-related education (LRE)

MAC Timeliner, 411
Macroeconomics, 59, 261
Madge, J., 70
Madison, J., 1, 16–17
Magazine Index, 418
Maker, C. J., 246
Mann, D., 250
Mann, H., 7
Mannheim, K., 70
Marshall, H. H., 186
Martin, R., 427
Maruyama, G., 136
Marzano, R. J., 306
Masia, B. B., 12
Maslow, A., 177
Mason, E. J., 431
Mastery learning approach, 364
Matching items, for tests, 369–371
Matching of computer data, 429–430
Materials. *See* Instructional materials; Media
Mathematics, 72, 427
Maughan, B., 136
Maxwell, J. R., 430
May, M. A., 133
Mayer, R. E., 166
McCown, R. R., 188

McLoughlin, J. A., 189
Measurement, definition of, 350. *See also* Evaluation of students; Testing
MECC Grade Manager, 405
Media. *See also* Computers and computer programs; Instructional materials; Visual aids; daily lesson planning for, 219 evaluation of, 299–302, 382 future trends concerning, 398 selection of, 219, 287
Media specialists, 448
Mehrens, W. A., 350, 361
Meltzer, A. S., 231
Memory skills, 328–329
Mendler, A. N., 337
Mental Measurements Yearbook, 356
Metacognition, 331–333
Metcalf, L. E., 52, 131, 134
Methods, as knowledge, 47
Mexican-Americans, 242
Meyer, C. A., 380
Microcomputers. *See* Computers
Micro-economics, 59
Microeconomics, 261–262
Microsoft Word, 405
Mill, J. S., 70
Minimum competency testing, 361–362
Minority students. *See* Racial and ethnic groups
Mitchell, J. V., Jr., 356
Mock trial competitions, 292–293
Model United Nations (MUN), 291–292
Modeling, 334
Models, 410
Montag-Torardi, M., 400
Montague, E. J., 315, 316, 337
Moore, D. W., 322, 335
Moral development; cautions regarding moral development education, 185 conventional level of, 141, 183 educational applications of Kohlberg's theory, 182–183 example of, 146–147 gender issues in, 134–135, 142, 182 Gilligan on, 134–135, 142 Kohlberg on, 134, 135, 141–142, 146, 182–184 post-conventional level of, 141–142, 183 pre-conventional level of, 141, 183 stages of, 183 suggestions for use of Kohlberg theory in classrooms, 184
Moral dilemmas, 182–185
Moral education, 134
Moral reasoning, 141–142
Mortimore, P., 136

Motivation, administrators and, 188 guidelines for teachers on, 185–186 learning strategies for, 319–320 parents and, 188 questions on, 185 self-concept and, 188–189 teacher expectations and, 186–187 in teaching/learning process, 167–168, 185–189
Motor Voter Bill, 33
Moursund, D., 426
Multicultural education, 264–265, 282
Multiple-choice questions, 367–368
MUN. *See* Model United Nations (MUN)
Murra, R., 8
Music, 72

NAEP. *See* National Assessment of Educational Progress (NAEP)
Nagy, W. E., 328
Nation at Risk, A, 361
National Assessment of Educational Progress (NAEP), 350, 354
National Commission on Excellence in Education, 361, 469
National Commission on Testing and Public Policy, 362
National Commission on the Social Studies, 11
National Conference on Christians and Jews (NCCJ), 11
National Council for Geographic Education (NCGE), 357, 451, 461
National Council for the Social Studies (NCSS), 10, 18, 26–28, 88, 90–91, 198, 253, 254, 415, 419, 449, 455, 461, 469–471, 472
National Council on Economic Education (NCEE), 11, 293, 356, 450–451, 455, 461
National Defense Education Act (NDEA), 12
National Education Association (NEA), 7–11, 15, 92, 449, 455
National Endowment for the Humanities (NEH), 294, 442
National Geographic Society (NGS), 293, 451, 461
National Institute for Citizenship Education in the Law (NICEL), 99, 264n
National Science Foundation (NSF), 12
Native Americans, 242
NCCJ. *See* National Conference on Christians and Jews (NCCJ)
NCEE. *See* National Council on Economic Education (NCEE)
NCGE. *See* National Council for Geographic Education (NCGE)

NCSS. *See* National Council for the Social Studies (NCSS)
NDEA. *See* National Defense Education Act (NDEA)
NEA. *See* National Education Association (NEA)
Needs, as basic concept in anthropology, 58
Negotiation, 53, 54–55
NEH. *See* National Endowment for the Humanities (NEH)
Nelms, B. F., 335
Nelson, C. S., 427
Nelson, D., 136
Neuter Computer, The, 427
New technology. *See* Computers and computer programs; Technologies
Newmann, F. M., 136, 148, 242, 244, 379
Newspapers and news publications, 287
NGS. *See* National Geographic Society (NGS)
NICEL. *See* National Institute for Citizen Education in the Law (NICEL)
Nisan, M., 135
Nondirective therapy, 177
Non-examples, 104
Nonprint media. *See* Media
Norm-referenced tests, 358–359
Norstad, J., 431
North Central Association's Foreign Relations Project, 11
Note taking, 321–327
NSF. *See* National Science Foundation (NSF)
Numerical data, recording, 327

Obedience/punishment, as stage of moral development, 183
Objectives. *See also* Goals; of computer software, 413 in daily lesson plans, 209–210, 224, 225 test questions and, 366 in unit plans, 203, 204–206
Objectivity, in social sciences, 70
O'Brien, D. G., 314
Observation, field observation in sociology, 69 for student evaluation, 352–354
Occupational Outlook Handbook, 456
Office of Juvenile Justice and Delinquency Prevention, 95
Ogilvy, J., 468
Ogle, D. M., 322
"Oh Rats" strategy, 326
Oinonen, C. M., 230
O'Keeffe, Georgia, 349

Oliner, P., 353–354
Oliver, D. W., 131, 134, 148
Olympics of the Mind, 247
Open-ended questions, 216
Operant conditioning. *See* Behavioral theory
Oregon Trail, 410, 427
Organization of American Historians, 450, 461
Organizations, 449–452, 455–456, 461–462. *See also* specific organizations
Ouston, J., 136
Outside speakers, 288–290
Oviatt, L., 400, 402

Paideia Proposal (Adler), 471
Pantelidis, V. S., 423
Parents, involvement of, in program evaluation, 383–384 student motivation and, 188 student self-concept and, 189
Paris, S. G., 319, 331
Parker, R., 429
Participation skills, 32
Paulson, F. L., 352, 380
Paulson, P. R., 380
Peeck, J., 173
Perception, as basic concept in psychology, 68
Performance assessment, 379
Pericles, 1–2
Perkins, D. N., 306
Personality, as basic concept in psychology, 68
Phi Alpha Delta Public Service Center, 99
Philosophy, 65–66, 262, 271
Piaget, J., 170, 179–182, 402
Piers, E. V., 189
Piers-Harris Children's Self-Concept Scale, 189
Pittelman, S. D., 322
PL 94-142, 248, 249
PL 101-476, 249
Place, in curriculum, 87–88
Place Called School, A (Goodlad), 398
Placement evaluation, 355–356
Planning for curriculum and instruction, community service (volunteerism), 231–232 daily lesson planning, 207–229 decision-making grid, 234–235 employment preparation, 229–231 functions of curriculum planning, 200 long-range planning, 200–202 overview of curriculum planning, 198–200 unit planning, 202–207
Plato, 65, 145

Policy making, 55–56, 70–71
Political science, basic concepts and questions from, 67 definition of, 66 learning activities in, 262–263, 272–276, 296–299 professional organizations in, 451
Popham, W. J., 350
Porter, A. C., 333
Portfolios, 352, 380
Positive self-talk, 319
Post-conventional morality, 141–142, 183
Power, as basic concept in political science, 67
Pre-conventional morality, 141, 183
Preoperational stage, of cognitive development, 180
Pre-service professional growth opportunities for teachers, 443
Presidency activity, data cards for, 272–276, 296–299
Pretests, 356
Probing questions, 317
Problem solving computer programs, 410
Professional development for teachers, 439–445
Professional organizations, 449–452, 455–456, 461–462. *See also* specific organizations
Program evaluation. *See* Evaluation of social studies programs
Programmed instruction, 171, 172
"Project Social Studies", 12
Project SPAN Staff and Consultants, 88
Prose learning, 166
Psychologists, 448
Psychology, 67–68, 263, 277, 451
Public policy. *See* Policy making
Pygmalion effect, 186

Questions for class discussion, answering process and, 330 331 breakdowns in, 316 318, 337 338 clarifying questions, 317 convergent questions, 315 divergent questions, 315 extending questions, 317 focus questions, 216–217 guidelines for, 315–318, 337–338 justifying questions, 317 media use and, 219 for monitoring and evaluating students, 338 narrow versus broad questions, 215–216 open-ended questions, 216 planned versus spontaneous questions, 315 probing questions, 317 rationale for, 313–314 sequencing of, 217 sources of, 215 timing of, 314–315 types of questions, 314–315 wait time and, 217, 316
Questions for tests, binary choice-alternative response items, 371–373 essay questions, 373–376 guidelines for writing, 366–367 matching items, 369–371 multiple-choice questions, 367–368 test bank of questions for, 378–379
QuickTests, 379
Quiz Program, 379

Racial and ethnic groups, computer use by, 426 cooperative learning and, 242 learning environments for, 251–252 test bias and, 362 trends pertaining to, 397
Raphael, T. E., 315, 330
Raths, L. E., 131, 134, 143
Rating scales, 352–354
Readence, J. E., 322, 335
Reading, strategic, 307
Reasoning. *See* Inquiry in social studies
Regions, as basic concept in geography, 63–64
Reliability, 360
Repman, J., 429
Report Card, 405
Rescher, N., 138
Research methods, in sociology, 69
Research Paper Writer, 412
Resnick, L. B., 173
Resources in Computer Education (RICE), 416, 416n
Response learning, 166
Rhody, T., 315, 316
RICE. *See* Resources in Computer Education (RICE)
Richardson-Koehler, V., 309
Rickelman, R. J., 322, 335
Robots, 421–422
Roehler, L. R., 333
Rogers, C. R., 177
Rokeach, M., 132
Roles, as basic concept in sociology, 69
Roop, P. G., 188
Roosevelt, E., 297
Roosevelt, F. D., 296
Rooze, G., 429
Rose, L. C., 361
Rosenfield, S., 363
Rosenthal, R., 186
Rote verbal learning, 166
Rousseau, J. J., 177
Rowe, M. B., 217, 316
Rugg, E., 9
Rugg, H., 9

Rumpf, A. H., 11
Ruskin, J., 47
Rutter, M., 136
Rutter, R., 136
Ryan, K., 454

Sacajawea, 299
Salvia, J., 374
SAT. *See* Scholastic Aptitude Test (SAT)
Satellite technology, 419
Saunders, P., 357
SCANS, 231
Scarcity and choice, in social studies education, 36–37
Scholarships for college, 247
Scholastic Aptitude Test (SAT), 350, 358
School events, teacher participation in, 446–447
Schubert, J. G., 427
Schwartz, P., 468
Schwarzwald, J., 242
Science, 70, 72–73, 427
Scientific method, 69
Scope, of curriculum, 84–85, 90–92
Seattle, Chief, 49
Self-concept, 188–189
Self-fulfilling prophecy, 186
Self-referenced tests, 359–360
Self-talk, 319
Semantic map. *See* Concept map
Sennett, R. A., 16
Sensorimotor stage, of cognitive development, 180
Sequence, of curriculum, 86–87, 90–92
Sequential Tests of Education Progress Series III, 358
Seven Tomorrows (Hawken et al.), 468
Shakespeare On Disk, 408
Shane, H. G., 426
Shapiro, E. S., 362
Shared experiences, as knowledge, 47
Shaver, J. M., 131, 134, 140
Shaw, B. G., 186
Shermis, S. S., 8, 14
Shinn, M. R., 363
Shorwood, R. D., 429
Siegel, M. A., 408
Silico Sapiens (Dekens), 422
SimCity, 410
Simon, S. B., 131, 134, 143, 144

Simonson, M. R., 400, 402, 422, 423
Simulations, 409–410
Skinner, B. F., 169–171
Skon, L., 136
Slavin, R. E., 136, 242, 244, 357
SMART goals, 319–320
Smith, A., 136
Snarey, J. R., 135
Social action programs, in values education, 136
Social contract, in social studies education, 36 as stage of moral development, 183
Social Education, 14, 91, 283, 294, 416, 449
Social history, 64
Social inquiry. *See* Inquiry in social studies
Social knowledge. *See* Knowledge
Social Science Education Consortium, Inc., 95, 99
Social sciences. *See also* Anthropology; Economics; Geography; History; Philosophy; Political science; Psychology; Sociology; hypotheses in, 70, 71 inquiry in, 70–71, 101–126 objectivity in, 70 policy making and, 71 professional organizations in, 450–451, 461–462 questions in, 117–118 social studies and, 11–12, 71, 259–260 theories in, 70 values and, 138–139
Social stratification, 69
Social Studies, 416
Social studies. *See also* Classrooms; Curriculum and curriculum planning; Instruction; Students; Teachers; Values education; and specific disciplines; attitudes in, 82–83 base for, 81–82 causality in, 37 characteristics of, 26–28, 80–81 civic action in, 32–33 culture in, 34 curriculum and instructional planning in, 198–235 curriculum patterns in, 9, 15–16, 84–97, 469–71 definitions of, 16–19 democratic beliefs in, 29–31 disciplines in, 56–69, 259–260, 470 early history of, 8–10 essentials of, 25–37 ethics in, 44, 82–83, 430, 445 freedom and justice in, 36 future trends and, 475–476 global perspectives in, 34–35 goals of, 6–8, 14–15, 83–84, 201 history of, 8–15 human rights in, 35 inquiry in, 101–126 integrated framework for, 83–84 intellectual abilities, processes, and skills in, 82 knowledge in, 29, 50–56, 81–84 knowledge-related activities in, 51–56 music and, 72 negative perceptions of, 80 new social studies in late 1960s and 1970s, 12–14 from 1916 to 1950, 10–11 organizational structure of, 81–84, 88–92 participation skills in,

32 positive perceptions of, 80–81 rationale for, 6–8, 14–15, 40–42, 201 scarcity and choice in, 36–37 and sciences and humanities, 72–73 scope and sequence patterns in, 90–92 social contract in, 36 social sciences and, 11–12, 71 spatial relationships in, 37 themes of, 33–39, 45, 85 thinking skills in, 31–32 tradition and change in, 35 traditions within, 14–15 in understanding human problems and institutions, 116–117 values in, 82–83

Social Studies and the Young Learner, 449
Social Studies, The, 283
Social Studies Tool Kits, The, 404
Social workers, 448
Socialization, as basic concept in sociology, 69
Society-oriented curriculum, 85
Sociology, basic concepts and questions from, 69 definition of, 68–69 learning activities in, 263, 278 professional organization in, 451 research methods in, 69 scientific method in, 69
Sociology of knowledge, 70
Socrates, 65, 145
Software. *See* Computers and computer programs
Software piracy, 429
Soper, J. C., 356, 357
Southern Regional Council, 11
Spatial relationships, in social studies education, 37
Speakers from community, 288–290
Spinoza, B., 129
Spreadsheets, 405
S-R theory. *See* Behavioral theory
SRA Achievement Series, 359
Staff development for teachers, 420, 439–440, 443–444. *See also* Professional development for teachers
Stand-alone computer programs, 404
Standardized tests. *See* Testing
Stark, J. S., 445
State historical societies, 455
State social studies councils, 449–450
Status, as basic concept in sociology, 69
Steinbeck, J., 72
Sternberg, R. J., 306
Stetson, E. G., 318
Stiggins, R. J., 379
Stimulus-response (S-R) theory. *See* Behavioral theory
Stipek, D. J., 319, 339

Stock Market Game, 293
Strategic learning, answering process and, 330–331 assignments and, 221–222, 320, 334–337 comprehension and, 327–328 comprehension subskills, 311 explanation and, 333–334 feedback and, 338–339 guidelines for teachers to enhance, 308–310 information sources and, 312, 313, 320–321 learning strategies for, 318–333 management of materials and time and, 320 memory skills and, 328–329 metacognition and, 331–333 modeling and, 334 motivation and, 319–320 note taking and, 321–327 questioning and, 215–217, 219, 313–318, 337–338 regulating learning and, 331–333 teaching for, 310–313 teaching guidelines for, 333–339 thinking about skills, 310–311, 313 thinking for skills, 311–312, 313 thinking with skills, 312, 313 using information and, 329–331
Strategic reading, 307
Stress for teachers, 456–459
Strom, S. M., 445
Stuart, R., 422
Stuck, G. B., 401, 431
Students. *See also* Classrooms; Evaluation of students; Instruction; Learning; academic freedom of, 252–255 "at-risk" students, 248, 250–251 discipline of, 189–191 female students and computer use, 426–428 gifted and talented students, 246–248 grouping of, 240–246 hand raising by, 308–309 involvement of, in class activities, 308–310 learning styles of, 213–214 minority students, 242, 251–252, 362, 426 motivation of, 167–168, 185–189, 319–320 self-concept of, 188–189 special needs students, 248–250
Study skills, 307
Sugarman, B., 131
Summarization, 328
Summative evaluation, 357–358
Summer programs, for social studies teachers, 441, 442 for students, 294
Superka, D. P., 88
Supervision, as teacher responsibility, 446
Survey research, in sociology, 69
Sustaining expectations effect, 186–187
Swadener, M., 426
Symbolic learning, 173–174
Synthetic generalizations, 107–108

Tables, note taking from, 327
Talented students. *See* Gifted and talented students
Tarule, J. M., 428
Taxonomy of Educational Objectives, 12, 356
Teachers. *See also* Classrooms; Instruction; academic freedom of, 252–255 administrative reports completed by, 448–449 advising as responsibility of, 446 career opportunities for, 453–456 career possibilities outside education, 456 classroom discipline and, 189–191 computer literacy of, 400–402 department or team meetings for, 447 ethics of, 445 evaluation of, 346, 383 expectations of, and student motivation, 186–187 "folk wisdom" of, on instruction, 167–168 getting first teaching job, 452–453 graduate courses for, 440–441, 454 in higher education, 454–455 involvement of, in program evaluation, 383–384 leadership role of, 475–476 nonteaching responsibilities of, 445–449 participation in school events by, 446–447 pre-service professional growth opportunities for, 443 in private schools, 454 professional development of, 392, 439–444 professional expectations of, 445–452 professional organizations for, 449–452, 461–462 self-fulfilling prophecy and, 186 sources of teacher expectations, 187 staff development for, 420, 443–444 stress from job-related causes, 456–459 and student self-concept, 188–189 summer programs for, 441, 442 supervision as responsibility of, 446 sustaining expectations effect and, 186–187 working with colleagues, 447–448
Teachers College, Citizenship Education Project, 11
Teaching. *See* Classrooms; Instruction; Learning
Teaching aids. *See* Instructional materials
Teaching and Computers, 416
Teaching machines, 171
Team meetings, 447
Tech Prep, 229
Technological Horizons in Education, 416
Technologies. *See also* Computers and computer programs, abuses of, 429–431 CD-ROM, 402, 406 educational technology, 399 gender gap and, 426–428 hypermedia, 423–424, 430 interactive learning technologies, 419 issues concerning, 424–429 laser disk technology, 406 robots, 421–422 satellite technology, 419 and societal trends, 396–398 teleconference phone, 419–420 telestudying, 420 trends in, 395–396 videodisc technology, 420–421 virtual reality, 422–423

Technology and Learning, 416
Teleconference phone, 419–420
Telestudying, 420
Test bank of questions, 378–379
Test Critiques, 356
Test Factory, 379
Test of Economic Knowledge, 357
Test of Economic Literacy, 356–357
Test-taking strategies, 330–331, 332, 377
Testing. *See also* Evaluation of students; accountability movement and, 360–361 in affective domain, 377–378 bias in, 362 binary choice-alternative response items for, 371–373 computers used in test preparation, 379 criterion-referenced tests, 359 curriculum-based assessment, 362–363 definition of test, 350 diagnostic tests, 356–357 essay questions for, 373–376, 377 grading and, 358, 375–378 guidelines for writing test questions, 366–367 issues in, 360–363 matching items for, 369–371 minimum competency testing, 361–362 multiple-choice questions for, 367–368 norm-referenced tests, 358–359 placement tests, 355–356 pretests, 356 reliability and, 360 self-referenced tests, 359–360 standardized tests, 345, 356–357, 358 test bank of questions for, 378–379 validity and, 360
Testmaster, 379
Tests in Print III, 356, 359
Textbook and supplementary computer programs, 404
Textbooks, 219–220, 283–284, 286, 299–302, 318, 333
Textbooks in Print, 283
Tharp, R. G., 241
Themes of social studies education, 33–39, 45, 85
Theories, 70, 109–112
Thinking. *See also* Learning; comprehension subskills, 311 definition of, 306 giving students times to think, 308 information sources and, 312, 313 in social studies education, 31–32 teacher's expectations about student thinking, 308 teacher's thinking aloud, 308 teaching for effective thinking, 310–339 thinking about skills, 310–311, 313 thinking for skills, 311–312, 313 thinking with skills, 312, 313
Thinking about skills, 310–311, 313
Thinking for skills, 311–312, 313
Thinking with skills, 312, 313
Third Wave (Toffler), 467
Thompson, A., 400, 402, 422, 423

Thompson, J. A., 242, 244
Thompson, J. C., 422
Thurber, J., 101
Tibbetts, S., 135
Tickton, S. G., 399
Tierney, R. J., 322
Time, in curriculum, 87–88
Time management, 320
Time Out Graph, 411
Timeliner, 411
Tobin, K., 217
Todd, L. P., 307
Toffler, A., 431, 467
Traditions, 14–15, 35
Travers, J. F., 362
Turner, M. J., 95
Tutorial computer programs, 407–408
Tyrrell, G., 242

Uncle Sam's Budget Balancer, 410
UNESCO, 455
Unit outlines, civics sample outline, 205–207 economics sample outline, 204–205 guidelines for, 203–204
Unit planning, 202–207
United Nations, Model, 291–292
U.S. Department of Education, 15
U.S. Department of Health, Education, and Welfare, 12
U.S. Department of Justice, Office of Juvenile Justice and Delinquency Prevention, 95
U.S. Department of Labor, 231
Universal ethical principles, as stage of moral development, 183
University Microfilms, 418
Utility computer programs, 404–406

Validity, of explanations, 118, 121, 122–123 test validity, 360
Value analysis, 134, 144–154
Value description, 142
Value profiles, 144–154
Values, behavioral versus substantive, 132 change in, 138–139 of community, and controversial issues, 254–255 core societal values, 139 definition of, 130–131 fact-value continuum, 131 history and, 137–138 instrumental versus terminal, 132, 149 personal versus social, 132, 147–148 social sciences and, 138–139 in social studies, 82–83 types of, 132–133

Values advocacy, 140
Values clarification, 134, 143–144
Values education, approaches to, 139–154 classroom setting in, 144 community study in, 136 cooperative learning in, 135–136 definition of, 130–131 description of, 133–136 historical context for, 133–134 history and, 137–138 just school programs in, 136 moral reasoning, 141–142 rationale for, 129–130 social action programs in, 136 social sciences and, 138–139 and types of values, 132–133 value analysis, 134, 144–154 value description, 142 value profiles, 144–154 values advocacy, 140 values clarification, 134, 143–144 variables in research on, 135
Valuing, 143
Van den Bosch, S. B., 173
Vasu, E., 400
Vasu, M., 400
Vaughan, J. L., 307
Videodisc technology, 420–421
Virtual reality, 422–423
Virtus Walk-Through, 423
Viruses, computer, 430–431
Visual aids, 334. *See also* Media
Visual Archive of American History, 404
Vito, R., 250
Vocabulary, 328
Vocational education, 229–231
Volunteerism, 231–232, 442
Voting registration, 33

Wait time, 217, 316
Walker, L. K., 135
Wallace, G. C., 297
Walstad, W., 356, 357
Ward, B., 241
Watson, J. A., 427
Wehlage, G. G., 251
Weinstein, C. E., 331, 333
Weinstein, R. S., 186
Weller, H., 429, 430
Wesley, E., 9
Widaman, K. F., 242
Wilen, W., 316, 363
Williams, F., 402
Williams, N., 131
Williams, R. P., 318
Williams, V., 402
Wilson, J., 131

Winograd, P., 319, 331
Wlodkowski, R. J., 185
Women's Action Alliance, 427
Woolfolk, A. E., 189, 358
Word processing programs, 405, 411–412
Work world. *See* Career education
Workplace Basics, 231
World Almanac, 417
World Bank, 455

Writing assignments, 335–336, 411–412
Wronski, S. P., 11

You're the Banker, 409–410
Youth For Understanding, 294
Ysseldyke, J. E., 374

Zahn, G. L., 242
Zakoriya, S. B., 93

STAFFORD LIBRARY
COLUMBIA COLLEGE
1001 ROGERS STREET
COLUMBIA, MO. 65216